Sacramento City Unified School District

THE ETHNIC

ALMANAC

by Stephanie Bernardo

Doubleday & Company, Inc.

Garden City, New York

1 9 8 1

For David, the fourth generation

Library of Congress Cataloging in Publication Data

Bernardo, Stephanie.
   The ethnic almanac.

   Bibliography: p.
   Includes index.
   1.   Minorities – United States – Miscellanea.
   2.   United States – Ethnic relations – Miscellanea.
   I.   Title.
   E184.A1B426   973'.04

Library of Congress Cataloging In Publication Data

ISBN: 0-385-14143-2 Trade
ISBN: 0-385-14144-0 Paperbound (Dolphin Books edition)
Library of Congress Catalog Card Number 78-14694

PREFACE

What do wedding rings, Democratic donkeys and Christmas trees have in common?
Was the birth control pill invented by a Catholic or a Jew?
Why do Arab-Americans titter when they buy Biz detergent?
How did an Irishman make pizza America's number-one snack food?
Who was the first Black American millionaire?
Which Italian-American made his fortune selling Chinese food and was honored as Minnesota's "Swede of the Year"?
How did a Russian-American make his fortune marketing "electric flowerpots"?
Which Lithuanian immigrant made maternity clothes fashionable?
Which ethnic group makes the most money? It you think it's the WASPs, you're in for a surprise.

The answers to these and other burning questions are scattered throughout *The Ethnic Almanac,* a fact book about America's ethnic groups from A to Z, including Armenians, Zuñi Indians, and everyone in between.

The Ethnic Almanac takes a look at the customs, culture and traditions various ethnic groups brought to America from the other side. It examines the contributions that immigrants and children of immigrants have made to our language, literature, business, art, science, technology, health and general welfare. Its purpose is to amuse, inform and entertain you with facts about your own heritage and that of your friends, neigbors and relatives. More than a reference book, *The Ethnic Almanac* contains information culled from thousands of books, encyclopedias, periodicals, newspapers and private sources, all of which adds up a vivid ethnic picture of American history.

If you've ever wondered about the ethnic origins of our superstitions, slang expressions and slur terms — you'll find them here. If you've ever felt a small twinge of pride when a member of your ethnic group hit a home run, discovered a cure for a disease, or won an Academy Award — you'll want to read about the history of "your people" in *The Ethnic Almanac:* when they emigrated here, what they've accomplished and how they've changed the course of American history.

Space limitations preclude a complete profile of every ethnic group in America. Hence, the top 36 (based on U.S. Census and immigration statistics) were chosen. The ten most populous are included in Chapter 2, while the rest will be found in Chapter 4.

No one creates a book alone, and many friends, relatives and acquaintances of every nationality contributed their ideas, time and suggestions for this volume. Some of the "ethnic helpers" who deserve credit include: Stephen Rizzo (Italian), Emily Nader Rizzo (Lebanese), June Martinez Madia (Puerto Rican), Carolyn Sobolewski Manthey (Polish), Carole Stranz Owen (Austrian), Tony Bernardo (Italian), Regina Sirutis Reddy (Lithuanian), Joy Malloy Colyandro (Irish), Melinda Arnold Nader (English), Mike Trandafirescu (Romanian), Nelly and Costa Tsonopoulos (Greek), Elfrieda Hueber (German), and, especially, Joseph Gonzalez (Dominican).

MANY THANKS TO . . .

Marilyn Alcott, D'Agostino's
AMF, Inc.
Paul Asciolla, Italian-American Foundation
Belgian Ministry of Foreign Affairs
Margaret Bicket, Prince Matchabelli
Carl Blumay, Occidental Petroleum
Harry Boesch, Kellogg's
Judy Bogardus, AMPEX
William Bostelmann Associates
Milton Bradley Co.
Esther Bromberg, Museum of the City of New York
R. Brune, Deere and Company
Anita Bryant
Ashley Burner, Burns International Security Systems
Roy Carlson, Wurlitzer
Elmo Celentani
Janet Christiaansen, Miller Brewing Company
Thomas Cockerill, Heublein
The Coleman Company, Inc.
Jerry Daly, Consolidated Foods
Ralph de Vine, Tootsie Roll
John Deats, Foote, Cone and Belding
Delta Air Lines
Harvey Dixon, National Park Service
E. I. Du Pont de Nemours
Frank Farnan, Black and Decker
F. D. Feiler, Friendly Ice Cream
Benjamin Fisher, Fisher Scientific
Gail Freckleton, Eastman Kodak
Helen Fremgen, Colgate-Palmolive
Ronald Froehlich, Maytag Company
Freuhauf Corporation
Diane Garrison, Tiffany and Co.
General Foods
Pat Gerber, Levi Strauss
B. F. Goodrich
Goodyear
Judy Gordon, Rowland Company
William Gowen, Bulova Watch
Thomas Gray, Brown-Forman Distillers
Vera Green, Pullman Inc.
Ron Greenberg, Ron Greenberg Productions

Gulf and Western Industries
Haggar Company
Betty Hale, Mobil Oil
Hanna-Barbera Productions
Dorothy Hays, Holiday Inns
Hershey Foods Corporation
Betty Hession, Marriott Corporation
Uta Hoffmann, German Information Center
Jacqueline Hook, Getty Oil
Nell Hopson, Uncle Ben's Foods
John Horty, Wyeth Laboratories
Evelyn Kanarek, Morton-Norwich
H. Keith, Neiman-Marcus
Korean Overseas Information Services
Kraft, Inc.
Thorn Kuhl, Warner-Lambert
Diane Laurel, Kurzweil Computer Products
Greg Lennes, International Harvester
Donald S. Leslie, Hammermill Paper
Crawford Lincoln, G. C. Merriam Co.
Lord & Taylor
Susan McGreevey, Wm. Underwood
Jane McGuinness, W. R. Grace
Frank McGuire, Wm. Hetherington and Company
Helen Magaw, Hoover
Ralph Major, Pitney Bowes
Victor Mangual, Goya Foods
Marion Mann, Avon
Joan Mebane, Philip Morris
Helen Morris, Union Carbide
Morris County Free Library, reference room staff
Motorola, Inc.
William K. Murphy, Murphy Door Bed Co.
New York Public Library, Mid-Manhattan Branch
Roger Nunley, Coca-Cola
Michael Ogiens, CBS Television
Col. Barney Oldfield, Litton Industries
Maurice O'Reilly, Borden Foods
Susan Ostrem, 3M
Ann Packard, Parker Brothers
De Anna Pakenham, Joseph Schlitz
Parker Pen Co.

Joseph Patterson, Westinghouse Electric Corp.
Charles Patteson, Hammacher, Schlemmer
Procter & Gamble
Jim Progar, Meridian Public Library
Jim Purks, the White House
Random House, Inc.
Edward Rankin, Cannon Mills
Kenneth Rapp, U.S. Military Academy
Dan Rather, CBS News
Orville Redenbacher
Claire Robert, Peter Paul
Edward Rollins, R. J. Reynolds
Ronzoni Macaroni Co.
Fay Rosen, Maidenform
Max Rosey, Nathan's
Thomas Ross, Oneida
Safeway Stores, Inc.
James Samberg, Bausch & Lomb
Henry Sandback, Del Monte
J. P. Saurer, Consulate General of Switzerland
Robert Seman, Phelps Dodge Corp.
E. A. Senior, S. B. Thomas, Inc.
Alexis Shantz, The Nestle Company
Cecil Shaw, Famous Amos Cookies
Carl Shryock, Diebold

J. Sirmans, CBS Entertainment
H. P. Smith, F. W. Woolworth
Ken Smith, National Baseball Hall of Fame
Marge Soroka, Planned Parenthood
H. H. Von Spreckelsen, Bethlehem Steel
Mark Stansbury, Holiday Inns
Bart Starr, Green Bay Packers
Steinway & Sons
E. Leigh Stevens, Castle & Cooke
Stokely-Van Camp
Robley Sundmacher, Olympia Brewing Company
Anita Terauds, American Latvian Association
Van Cleef & Arpels
Howard Van der Meulen, NBC
Lynn Weaver, Adolph Coors
Lu Ann West, Borden Foods
Chester A. Williams, Singer Company
A. J. Winograd, Pabst Brewing Company
Suzanne Wren, Bendix
Jean Zukerman, Public Relations Board

and to everyone else who supplied corporate literature, ideas, suggestions and tidbits of information.

CONTENTS

INTRODUCTION
A NATION OF HYPHENATED AMERICANS

We are Mexican-Americans, Irish-Americans, Black Americans, Jewish-Americans, WASPs and Americans whose origins have been obliterated through time and intermarriage. From the native Indians who migrated from Asia more than twenty thousand years ago, to the new arrivals who deplane from jumbo jets daily, we are a nation of foreigners—a country of immigrants joined together under one flag.

However diverse our backgrounds, we are all Americans under the skin—some of us may have been here a little longer or may be more privileged with wealth and social standing, but all of us have contributed to the definition "American" by giving our customs, culture and traditions to this new land.

The Wasp Ideal   In the eighteenth and ninteenth centuries, most newcomers to the colonies were obsessed with eliminating the "hyphens" from their names. The immigrants who came to our shores wanted to be Americans—not Polish-Americans, Italian-Americans or Spanish-Americans—but *real* Americans (whatever that might be). They wanted to belong, and to many settlers that meant leaving their "roots" behind and conforming to the norns established by America's power group—the WASPs.

The British colonists or WASPs (White Anglo-Saxon Protestants) were the American majority in 1790 when the first U.S. Census was conducted. They comprised almost 75 per cent of the population, and being "number one" they were able to establish English as the common language, make the laws, rule the churches and set the precedents for all who followed from the other side.

Ethnics on the Rise   During the nineteenth century, the colonial influence began to wane as new immigrants began arriving in America by the millions. More than 28 million immigrants descended upon our shores between 1820 and 1900—most of them Europeans seeking refuge from famine, war and poverty. Often, whole villages transported themselves across the sea to establish new homes in America, and unlike the earlier Germans, Jews and Italians who emigrated here in small numbers and were quickly absorbed into the mainstream of American life, the new immigrants did not immediately remold themselves to fit into WASP society; instead they created their own "ethnic" societies.

The 1840s witnessed the emergence of a new concept in America: that of the "ethnic group"—a group of Americans sharing a common ancestry, culture, language, nationality, race or religion which drew them closer together in the new world. Comforted by voices that spoke familiar dialects and by neighbors who celebrated the same holidays, the immigrants chose to seek out "their own kind" and cling together for moral support. Bound by their common interests and traditions, the "Little Italys," "Chinatowns" and "Kerry Patches" of New York, San Francisco and Boston provided a sense of continuity for

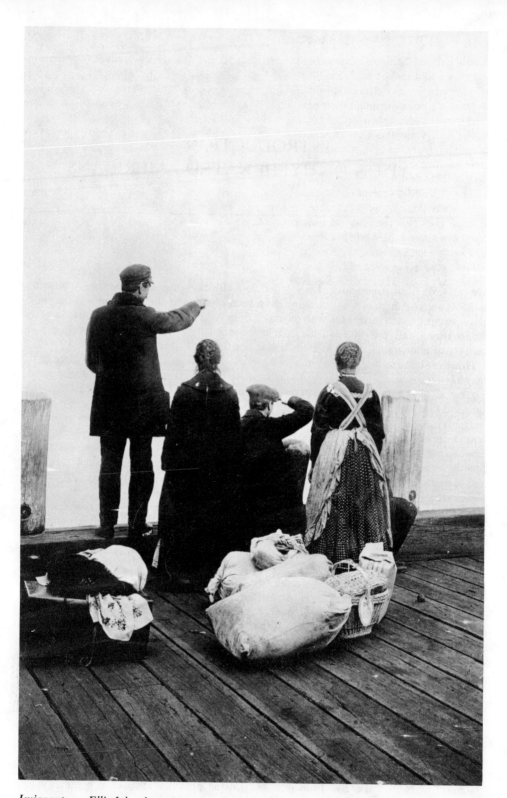

Imigrants on Ellis Island awaiting ferry to Manhattan in 1912. (Courtesy: American Museum of Immigration)

newly arrived Sicilians, Cantonese and Irishmen, and fostered a feeling that this new country could indeed be called "home."

The new immigrants established ethnic enclaves — "islands" within American cities, where they could maintain their national identity, enjoy ethnic foods, attend ethnic church services and speak their native language. It was not uncommon for immigrants to live and die in America without ever speaking a word of English. They didn't have to! There were ethnic butchers, bakers, priests and casket makers who attended to the needs of the local communities and enabled the new arrivals to live life in much the same manner as they had in the "old country."

The Second-Generation Rebels Safe in their ethnic neighborhoods, many first-generation Americans were able to preserve their individuality — but, much to their dismay, their children often turned their backs on the "old-world ways." The second generation considered their ethnic differences a source of embarrassment, a kind of social *faux pas*, somewhat like using the wrong fork when dining in a fancy restaurant. Members of the second generation were often self-conscious about their ethnicity and refused to speak the native language. They married outside their ethnic group, moved out of the ethnic neighborhoods and ate Wonder Bread with every meal in an effort to "Americanize" themselves. They believed in the "melting pot" theory of American culture and sought to dissolve their differences in it.

The Melting Pot Flops America was indeed supposed to be a "melting pot" — the place where all the cultures of the world would dissolve into a pureed vegetable soup. But, instead of dissolving into a puree, the various ingredients that were thrown into the pot remained whole. They did impart their own individual flavor to the stock, and they did manage to pick up some character from the sauce they floated in, but they still remained separate, islands unto themselves, changing only a bit, and uneasily, around the edges. Somewhat like immigrants who adopt Western clothing, but still wear turbans with their pin-striped business suits, many ethnic Americans were able to change only their public image and appearance — they could not change their private, innermost selves.

Ethnic Revival Luckily, a good deal of our nation's ethnic self-consciousness has disappeared over the past few decades. Today, many of the third and fourth generation are proud and curious about the heritage of their ancestors and are actively searching for their "roots." Ethnics have come of age in the 1970s, and instead of apologizing for their differences, Americans are celebrating their heritage. We've learned to be proud of our "hyphens" and have started to acknowledge that we can be Japanese-Americans, German-Americans and Russian-Americans — and still be loyal, faithful citizens. We have realized that it is our differences that made America great, by preventing cultural stagnation and providing a constant stream of fresh ingredients for the "un-melting" pot.

PART I

From the Other Side . . .
to the Promised Land

1 THE FIRST IMMIGRANTS

Although the American Indians weren't immigrants in the strictest sense of the word, they were the first people to enter the New World. Crossing a land bridge that existed twenty thousand years ago, the Indians came from Asia to Alaska and spread across two continents to inhabit almost every region of North and South America.

They were the first immigrants, the original Americans, but they eventually became foreigners in their own land. They were red men trapped in a white man's society, outnumbered and overpowered by the Europeans they had so generously welcomed to their shores.

BRIEF CHRONOLOGY OF THE AMERICAN INDIAN, A.C. (After Columbus)

1492 ♦ There were an estimated 900,000–1,500,000 Native Americans inhabiting the area that eventually became the United States. ("Civilization" started taking its toll soon after Columbus's discovery, and by 1880 there were a mere 250,000 American Indians left in the U.S.)

1616 ♦ Trappers, traders and settlers had started several permanent colonies in America, and had begun to introduce their European ways to the Indians. More deadly and destructive than the firearms and alcohol the Europeans brought with them were the diseases they introduced to populations of Indians who possessed no natural or built-up immunity. Many thousands of Indians died this year as a result of a smallpox epidemic that raged throughout New England, afflicting tribes living between Narragansett Bay and the Penobscot River. Later, the Indians would fall prey to malaria, typhus, cholera and tuberculosis.

1620 ♦ Had it not been for the generosity of the Indians, the Massachusetts Bay Colony established at Plymouth would surely have perished. The Algonquian chief, Squanto, showed the newcomers when and how to plant corn and how to fertilize their crops with dead fish. He also taught them how to construct suitable housing and how to make the most of the edible wild plants that abounded in the virgin forests of the Northeast.

1621 ♦ A peace treaty was signed between the Wampanoag Indians and the Pilgrims. The first Thanksgiving was also celebrated this year in tribute to the good harvest and "lasting" peace that reigned between the two groups.

1622 ♦ The Virginia settlement was not quite as "peaceful" as the one at Plymouth, Massachusetts. The first massacre at Jamestown took place this year and 347 settlers were slain. Retaliation and warfare continued between the two groups for twelve years.

1626 ♦ The best land deal, and the first land swindle in the history of America, took place when Peter Minuit bought Manhattan Island from the Canarsie Indians. Acting as agent for the Dutch West India Company, Minuit bought the island for $24 worth of beads and trinkets. (The value of the dollar at that time made the purchase price closer to several thousand dollars, but it was still a very low price to pay for such valuable real estate, even in the seventeenth century.) Unfortunately, the Canarsie Indians had no real claim to the land—they were natives of Brooklyn and, in effect, swindled Peter Minuit out of $24 worth of beads. At a later date, the Dutch were forced to make other payments to the true inhabitants, the Manhattan Indians.

1637 ◆ Connecticut settlers conducted a sneak attack on a Pequot village and burned it to the ground. More than six hundred Indians lost their lives in the blaze, and Cotton Mather, the Governor of Plymouth, later wrote: "It was a fearful sight to see them frying in the fire . . . But the victory seemed a sweet sacrifice and they [the colonists] gave praise thereof to God."

Known as the Pequot War (when the settlers won, it was a "war," when the Indians won, it was a "massacre"), this conflict was a turning point in Indian-immigrant relations, proving that the white man was determined to take the Indians' lands and was going to be hard to eliminate.

1653 ◆ Probably the first book ever printed in an Indian dialect was John Eliot's *Catechism in the Indian Language*. In 1661, Eliot finished translating the Bible into Algonquian after thirty years of labor. He used it to convert the "heathens" and by 1674 he had four congregations with a total of about two thousand Christian Indians.

1672 ◆ In order to make their deliveries through rain, sleet, hail and gloom of night, the colonial postal clerks in what is now New York State had to employ Indian couriers to shuttle mail between New York City and Albany during the winter months. The inexperienced white settlers found the winter weather too harsh for the "swift completion of their appointed rounds."

1723 ◆ The first permanent school for American Indians was built in Williamsburg, Virginia, through funds provided by English scientist Robert Boyle.

1725 ◆ The first recorded instance of scalping by white men took place. A party of ten bounty hunters led by Captain Lovewell took ten scalps and received a hundred pounds in payment for each grisly souvenir. Contrary to popular literature, scalping was not a universal practice among Indian tribes. Originally, scalps were taken only by the Cree and the Teton Dakota, but when the Europeans began paying other tribes for the scalps of their enemies, the practice spread.

1738 ◆ Smallpox continued to take its toll and spread to the Cherokee Indians of Georgia via white slave traders who frequented Charlestown, South Carolina. This dreaded disease decimated almost half their tribe.

1758 ◆ The first state reservation was established in Burlington County, New Jersey. Known as Brotherton, the reservation was home to almost two hundred Lenni Lenape (Delaware) Indians. Brotherton was put up for sale in 1802 when the Delawares accepted an invitation from the Indians of New Stockbridge, New York, to live with them on their land near Lake Oneida.

1789 ◆ Congressional policy stated: ". . . good faith shall always be observed towards the Indians; their lands and property shall never be taken from them without their consent."

1804 ◆ The Louisiana Territory Act served notice that the United States intended to move Indian populations to land west of the Mississippi River, with or without their consent.

1810 ◆ In the past seven years, white settlers north of the Ohio River had gained more than 30 million acres of Indian land. Alarmed by the rapid rate at which the Indians were losing ground, Tecumseh (1765–1813), a Shawnee chief, attempted to organize an Indian confederacy of tribes to unite the red men against their common enemy. He opposed further acquisitions of Indian territory by white settlers, stating: "These lands are ours. No one has a right to remove us, because we were the first owners."

1817 ◆ President James Monroe refuted Tecumseh's claim to the United States with his statement: "The earth was given to mankind . . . no tribe, or people have a right to withhold from the wants of others more than is necessary for their own support and comfort . . ."

1824 ◆ The Indian population of the

United States was estimated at 471,417 — less than half the number that existed in the continental United States when Columbus first discovered America.

To promote the general welfare of our remaining "first citizens," the Bureau of Indian Affairs was established this year.

1825 ◆ After being bribed by Georgia state officials, William MacIntosh of the Creek tribe signed a treaty agreeing to relinquish his tribe's claim to the 10 million acres of land they held in the state of Georgia. He acted without the consent of the entire Creek nation, a direct violation of Creek custom and law which carried the death penalty for transgressors. MacIntosh was executed by a fellow tribesman and the treaty was annulled.

1830 ◆ Stating that "the policy of the general Government toward the red man is not only liberal but generous," President Andrew Jackson signed the Indian Removal Act into law. Aimed at removing the powerful Choctaw, Chickasaw, Cherokee, Creek and Seminole nations (the "Five Civilized Tribes") from the Southeast, the bill led to forced migrations west of the Mississippi known as the "trail of tears."

1838 ◆ Within 10 years after Congress passed the Indian Removal Act, some 70,000 Indians would journey down the "trail of tears" to their new homes in Indian Territory. Ill prepared for their long winter's trek westward, many Indians died along the way.

Contrary to the Indians' description of their forced removal, President Martin Van Buren maintained this year that the Indians ". . . have emigrated without any apparent reluctance."

1864 ◆ The Civil War drained the energy and manpower of the U.S. and halted the push westward, but there was still little peace to be found in Indian Territory. On November 29, more than three hundred Cheyenne and Arapaho Indians were slaughtered at their camp at Sand Creek, Colorado.

1868 ◆ The 14th Amendment specifically denied the Indians the right to vote. A clause "excluding Indians not taxed" denied reservation dwellers the rights given (at least on paper) to most other American men.

1869 ◆ The first American Indian appointed as Commissioner of Indian Affairs was Brigadier General Ely Samuel Parker (Donehogawa), a Tonawanda Seneca chief who served from 1869 to 1871.

1871 ◆ Congress passed the Indian Appropriation Act and ruled that Indian tribes were no longer considered separate, independent governments. This freed the United States from the burden of negotiating treaties with the Indians, and made the native Americans national wards. This act merely served to echo a long-held government opinion that "It's cheaper to feed the Indians for a year than to fight them for a day."

1874 ◆ During the preceding two years, more than 3,700,000 buffalo had been killed on the plains. Only 150,000 were taken by Indians for use as food, clothing and leather. The rest were slain almost systematically as part of a plan designed to crush the Plains Indians' economy. As General Philip Sheridan saw it, the wholesale slaughter of the buffalo could only benefit white America: "Let them kill, skin, and sell until the buffalo is exterminated . . . it is the only way to bring lasting peace and allow civilization to advance."

(The killing continued until 1900, when all that remained of an estimated 60,000,000 animals were perhaps 30,000 buffalo scattered throughout the United States.)

1875 ◆ There was "gold in them thar hills," and white settlers began encroaching on Indian territory in the Black Hills of Dakota, hoping to strike it rich. The treaties which guaranteed the Indians their land "as long as the rivers shall run and the grass shall grow" were not upheld.

1876 ◆ Custer died early in the battle against the Sioux and Cheyenne Indians on the Little Big Horn River. The Seventh Cavalry suffered a crushing defeat: 266 white men were killed, while only 22 Sioux left this earth for the "happy hunting ground."

The only survivor in Custer's command was a horse named Comanche. When Comanche died, his remains were shipped to the Smithsonian Institution, where he is currently on display.

1877 ◆ Although the Indians won at Little

Big Horn, their victory only served to make the U.S. troops hunger for revenge. The Indian population was slowly dwindling while the number of white settlers was rapidly increasing, and in the long run, despite Custer's crushing defeat, the cavalry had time, money and manpower on its side.

The Nez Perce War ended in October when Chief Joseph surrendered to save the lives of his remaining eight hundred followers: "I am tired of fighting," he said. "It is cold and we have no blankets. The little children are freezing to death. My people, some of them, have run away to the hills, and have no blankets, no food; no one knows where they are — and perhaps freezing to death. I want to have time to look for my children and see how many of them I can find . . . Hear me, my chiefs! I am tired; my heart is sick and sad. From where the sun now stands I will fight no more forever."

1885 ♦ Surrender wasn't enough to save the Nez Perce Indians, and this year only 287 of their people were still alive. They were living as captives on reservations, many of them too young to remember their people's previous life of freedom.

This year, Sitting Bull (Tatanka Yotanka), the hero who led his tribesmen to victory over Custer at Little Big Horn, entered show business and toured with Buffalo Bill's Wild West Show.

1886 ♦ The Southwest tribes were defeated, and the capture of Geronimo in Arizona crushed the Apaches. Ironically, just as our "first Americans" were stripped of their homeland, the "old stock" American settlers were beginning to view the "new" immigrants as a threat to national peace and security, fearing that the large influx of peasant masses might deprive them of "their" land.

1887 ♦ The Dawes Severalty Act provided for Indian lands to be divided among individuals rather than remain under tribal ownership. Each family was "given" 160 acres of land, which was to be held in trust by the U.S. government for 25 years to prevent exploitation of the Indians by unscrupulous white men. This year, the Indians held almost 138 million acres of land, but by 1932 almost 90 million of those acres had found their way into white hands.

In 1895, Sitting Bull began a national tour with Buffalo Bill's Wild West Show. (Courtesy: New York Public Library)

1889 ♦ Sitting Bull gave up his career to try to prevent his people from selling their rights to the Great Sioux Reservation. But, despite his best efforts, the Sioux signed away their rights to 9 million acres for the government to use for railroad grants. When a newsman asked him how the Indians felt about giving up their land, Sitting Bull replied angrily, "There are no Indians left but me!"

1890 ♦ Having lost their land and their way of life, the Indians were destined to remain captives on their reservations forever. The only hope left for them to defeat the white man was through divine intercession. Only a "messiah" could save their people, and when a Nevada Paiute Indian, Wovoka, offered them hope through his "Ghost Dance" religion, the Indians clutched at it.

Indians everywhere began to dance

Not all American Indians lived on reservations. This Iroquois family was living at 511 Broome Street in New York City during the early 1890s. (Courtesy: Museum of the City of New York)

and practice nonviolence in the belief that, when spring came, all the dead Indians and game would return to life. A great flood would then drown all the white men, while the Indians found refuge in the mountains, and once again only Indians would inhabit America.

Unfortunately, their dancing alarmed white settlers, and government officials attempted to stop the Ghost Dancers by arresting their leaders. During the arrest of Sitting Bull a scuffle resulted and he was mortally wounded. Indian belief in Ghost Dancing was so strong that no one attempted to avenge Sitting Bull's death.

Two weeks later, at Wounded Knee Creek, 350 unarmed Sioux were slaughtered at their camp. They believed that their ceremonial costumes would magically protect them from the soldiers' bullets, and what had begun as a vision of peace ended in bloodshed. Ghost Dancing was over, and there were no more major Indian uprisings.

1900 ♦ Despite an 1868 treaty which prom-

ised a teacher for every 30 Indian children, illiteracy on the reservations approached 56%.

1907 ♦ Indian Territory and Oklahoma Territory were merged into the new state of Oklahoma.

1913 ♦ The U.S. Mint honored the "vanishing red man" and the vanishing buffalo with the Indian-head nickel, the first five-cent piece issued since the Liberty-head coin of 1883. The new nickel was designed by James Earl Fraser; thirteen Indian chiefs modeled for a composite portrait. The animal model? That was "Black Diamond," a resident of the New York Zoological Gardens.

1916 ♦ The first Indian Day was held on May 13 by the Society of American Indians, to honor their people and strive to improve their living conditions.

1924 ♦ An act of Congress made the American Indians citizens. "All non-citizen Indians born within the territorial limits of the United States be, and they are hereby declared to be, citizens of the United States." They were also required to pay federal and state taxes, but were excused from paying tax on their reservation land.

1929 ♦ Senator Charles Curtis of Kansas became the first Vice-President of the United States of American Indian ancestry. He served as VP under President Herbert Hoover from 1929 to 1933. His election as Senator was another "first" for American Indians, and he served in that position for more than twenty years.

1931 ♦ U.S. population was 122,775,046. Only 332,000 were American Indians.

1939 ♦ Kateri Tekakwitha was declared venerable by the Roman Catholic Church. She was the first American Indian to be honored with this preliminary step on the way to sainthood.

1940 ♦ American Indians registered for the military draft for the first time. Approximately twenty-five thousand Indians served their country during World War II, representing almost one-third of the able-bodied Indian males between the ages of eighteen and fifty.

1946 ♦ The Indian Claims Commission was established to settle disputes over lost land and broken treaties. (Since then 615 claims have been filed and $669.2 million has been awarded.)

1950 ♦ The Ute Indians were awarded $31,700,000 compensation for tribal lands taken in Colorado and Utah between 1891 and 1938.

1960 ♦ There were 509,000 Indians and 43,000 Alaskan natives living in the United States. Of these, 453,000 lived on federal Indian reservations in 23 states.

1968 ♦ The Indian Civil Rights Act was passed, requiring that Indian consent must be given before the state can assume jurisdiction on reservation lands.

1969 ♦ First modern Indian demonstration occurred as Native Americans seized Alcatraz Island.

1970 ♦ New Mexico's Blue Lake and the 48,000 acres of land surrounding it were returned to the Pueblo Indians.

1973 ♦ Marlon Brando rejected his Academy Award "Oscar" as Best Actor, protesting that the motion picture industry has done much to harm the identity of the American Indian.

1977 ♦ Charlie Hill, a member of the Iroquois nation from Wisconsin, made his TV debut on October 20 as a stand-up comedian specializing in "Indian jokes."

1978 ♦ Maine Senator William Hathaway announced a compromise settlement of $37 million to be awarded to members of the Passamaquoddy and Penobscot Indian tribes, who had demanded return of the northern two-thirds of Maine, where there are now 330,000 non-Indian landholders.

1980 ♦ On March 14 representatives of the Passamaquoddy and Penobscot tribes agreed in principle to abandon their claims to the northern two-thirds of the state of Maine in return for a $27 million Federal trust fund and a $54.5 million Federal land acquisition fund.

♦ Pople John Paul II declared Kateri Tekakwitha beatified and worthy of veneration, bringing the "LIly of the Mohawks" one step closer to Roman Catholic sainthood.

"FIRSTS" AND FACTS ABOUT AMERICAN INDIANS

FIRST HANGOVER Before the Dutch arrived in the New World, the Indians had never tasted alcoholic beverages. An early settler in New Netherland noted that the natives there "have nothing with which they can become intoxicated" and had no word in their language for "drunkenness." The first recorded incidence of tippling among the Indians occured in 1609, when Henry Hudson invited some natives aboard the *Halve Maen* and extended his hospitality by giving them "so much wine and Aqua Vitae, that they were all merrie . . ."

HOW, KIMOSABEE! When the Wampanoag Indians welcomed the Pilgrims to Plymouth Colony in March, 1621, the first words spoken by their delegate, Samoset, were not "How," "Ugh," or "Kimosabee." Samoset greeted the new arrivals with the words "Welcome, Englishmen!"— a phrase he had learned from English fishermen who frequently visited the coast of Maine.

LAST OF THE MOHICANS James Fenimore Cooper's novel was based on the life of Uncas, a famed Mohegan chief who died in 1683. Banned by the Pequot and Narragansett tribes for befriending the European colonists, Uncas sided with the English in the Pequot War in 1637. Memorials in his honor are erected at Norwich, Connecticut, and Cooperstown, N.Y.

IN THE EYE OF THE BEHOLDER The Flathead Indians of Western Montana were regarded as "unattractive" by the neighboring tribes of the Pacific Coast. All of the other Indians in the Northwest bound their infants to cradleboards during their first year of life, causing a permanent deformation of the skull. To them, a pointed head was a sign of beauty, and the "flatheads," with their normal-shaped craniums, were regarded as strange.

U.S. CONSTITUTION According to Stan Steiner, the principles embodied in the U.S. Constitution were modeled after the Five Iroquois Nations constitution drawn up by the Mohawk, Seneca, Onondaga, Oneida and Cayuga tribes around the year 1500. Their agreement guaranteed freedom for all individuals, and provided each tribe

Approximate locations of Indian tribes prior to the European colonization of America.

with equal representation at a grand council which decided on general policy for the Five Nations. Benjamin Franklin was aware of the Indian constitution, and advised sending delegates from the Albany Congress to study the Iroquois system.

WEST POINT APPOINTEE The first American Indian admitted to the U.S. Military Academy was David Moniac (1802–1836) of the Creek tribe. He graduated from the Military Academy in 1822 as a second lieutenant and rose to the rank of major. Ironically, he was killed in the Battle of Wahoo Swamp in 1836 while fighting against the Seminole Indians in Florida.

SON OF "WORM" Crazy Horse (1844–1877), the Oglala Sioux who fought with Sitting Bull in a vain attempt to stem the white man's invasion of the Black Hills in 1875, was originally called "His Horse Looking." (He was also known by the nickname "Curly.") But, after he had distinguished himself in battle, his father gave him his own name, "Crazy Horse," and took the name "Worm" for himself.

ROCK OF AGES Many Indians bitterly resented the missionaries who came to America to bring "religion" to them. In 1873, Chief Joseph of the Nez Perce tribe said that his people did not want the white man's schools because the missionaries who were in charge would build churches of

Chief Joseph of the Nez Perce tribe. (Courtesy: New York Public Library)

various denominations. "They will teach us to quarrel about God. We do not want to learn that. We may quarrel with men sometimes about things on this earth, but we never quarrel about God." Despite his best efforts, thousands of Indians converted to Protestantism and Catholicism. But, in an effort to retain some of the Indian flavor, many of the hymns were translated into Indian tongues. Instead of singing "Rock of Ages" at prayer meetings, the Mohawks would sing "Ni-io-ta-tia-ta-nons-tat."

VANISHING RED MAN This phrase became well known after the 1880 Census revealed that there were a mere 250,000 American Indians living in the United States, compared to the almost 1,000,000 Indians estimated to be living in North America when Columbus first arrived in the New World.

THE CLEVELAND SPIDERS That's what the Ohio baseball team was originally called before the name was changed to the Cleveland Indians in honor of Louis Sockolexis, a Maine Indian who was the first native American to play pro ball.

CHIEF HARRIET The first white woman to become an Indian chief was Harriet Converse. Given the name Ga-is-wa-noh, "the watcher," Harriet was made a chief of the Six Nations tribe in September 1891. She had previously been adopted as a member of the Seneca tribe in 1884, in recognition of her services to the residents of the Tonawanda Reservation.

IWO JIMA PIMA Ira Hayes, a Pima Indian serving in the United States Marine Corps, was one of the five men who raised the American flag at Mt. Suribachi on Iwo Jima during World War II. The photograph won a Pulitzer Prize in 1945, and skyrocketed Hayes into the public eye. "Everywhere we went," Hayes said in 1953 after spending the night in a Chicago drunk tank, "people shoved a drink in our hands and said we were heroes. We knew we hadn't done much, but you couldn't tell them that. And I guess I was sort of a freak, because I was an Indian . . . I kept getting hundreds of letters. And people driving through the reservation would come up to me and say: 'Are you the Indian that raised the flag at Iwo?' I got sick of hearing about the flag-raising. Sometimes I wished that guy had never made the picture."

Unable to cope with all the attention he received, and unable to return to a "normal" life on the Gila River Indian Reservation in Arizona, where he had lived until he enlisted in the Marines, Hayes found solace in drink. He dried tragically on January 25, 1955, at the age of thirty-two, from exposure and alcoholism.

MOHAWKS ON HIGH STEEL In the days before reinforced concrete and prefab construction, there was a great demand for riveters—the men who joined heavy steel beams together with red-hot metal bolts. The work was dangerous—hundreds of feet in the air, every step might be your last—but high salaries attracted a steady stream of men willing to risk their lives for a better standard of living.

Among these men the Mohawk Indians stood out for their grace and their ability to walk on high steel.

Members of the Caughnawaga Reservation in Quebec were first trained as high-steel workers in 1886 when the Dominion Bridge Company began constructing a cantilever bridge across the St. Lawrence River. The Mohawks were employed as common laborers, but every chance they had, the Indians would climb out onto the half-completed steel skeleton to see how work was progressing. The Mohawks seemed to have little fear of walking on narrow girders and beams, and their agility made an engineer assigned to the project wonder if they would be interested in riveting. He trained one riveting gang, and soon there were Mohawks working all over Canada constructing steel bridges and buildings. They later migrated to the United States and many settled in New York, where they worked on thousands of skyscrapers, including the Empire State Building and the United Nations.

In 1970 there were 15,477 American Indians employed as construction workers in the United States.

NAVAHO "CODE TALKERS" The Navaho language is so complex, and relies so much on proper expression of the few syllables that make up a single verb form, that the language is almost impossible to counterfeit or learn as an adult. For example: Depending upon your pronunciation, the Navaho word "ni'á" can mean either "A set of round objects extends off in a horizontal line" or "I bought it."

*wounded in
battle*

*killed
an enemy*

*slit throat
and scalped
enemy*

Say it with feathers: Large feather head-dresses were not worn by all Indians. A single feather worn by a Dakota (Sioux) Indian was enough to tell strangers at a glance about his deeds as a warrior.

Aware of the unique characteristics of this language, the U.S. Armed Forces decided to train Native Americans as radio operators during the Second World War, rather than invent codes that the enemy could easily steal or break.

Indians from many different tribes were trained by the Armed Forces, but the best known and the most numerous were the Navahos. In 1942 there were only 28 non-Navahos who could use the language correctly. Since most of these 28 were missionaries, and none happened to be German or Japanese, the Navaho language was a perfect communications weapon for combat troops in the Pacific islands.

Four hundred twenty Navahos were trained as code talkers. They invented new words to describe twentieth-century weapons, and played a significant role in the war effort by releasing troops from the time-consuming chore of enciphering and deciphering messages. U.S. troops were now able to make split-second changes in tactics with complete peace of mind, knowing that it was virtually impossible for the enemy to intercept their radio transmissions.

THIS LAND IS YOUR LAND In 1970, the Americans Indians owned 2.2% of the United States. Various tribes and individuals held about 50,000,000 acres of trust land, exclusive of the federal land used for Indian reservations.

RICH MAN, POOR MAN, INDIAN CHIEF The richest Indians in the United States are the Aguas Calientes of California. There are only about 172 of them, but they own over 31,000 acres of land in Palm Springs, the California resort known as the "miilionaire's sandbox."

This desert land was awarded to the Aguas Calientes in 1876–1877, and was placed in trust for them by the U.S. government. In 1960, the value of the tribal lands was about $12 million, and each member was worth an estimated $335,000. The lands are still held in trust, but they are leased out to builders in Palm Springs, where real estate prices have been zooming for years. With some property valued at more than $50,000 an acre, the Aguas Calientes are probably worth somewhere in the neighborhood of $1.5 billion, or about $9 million each.

By contrast, the poorest Indians in the United States are probably the Sisseton

Sioux of South Dakota, who had per capita assets of $19.12 in 1958.

♦ The first Indian-English dictionary was published in 1643 to help settlers in New England understand the language, customs and traditions of their Native American neighbors. Written by Roger Williams, it was entitled *A Key into the Language of America, or a Help to the Language of the Natives in New England.*

♦ The first Indian newspaper, *The Cherokee Phoenix,* was published weekly in English and Cherokee from 1828 to 1835 at New Echota, Georgia, the onetime capital of the Cherokee Nation. The paper was edited by Elias Boudinot, an Indian who took the name of the famous philanthropist who is often called the "Father of Thanksgiving."

♦ The first American Indian ballet, *Koshare,* was written by Louis W. Ballard (1931–   ), a Cherokee-Sioux from Oklahoma. *Koshare* was first performed in 1960 by the Harkness Ballet troupe, and had its premiere in major American cities during the ballet company's 1967 tour.

♦ Dr. Lionel de Montigny, a U.S. Assistant Surgeon General of Chippewa-Cree ancestry, is the first American Indian to reach such a high rank. In charge of Indian Community Development for the U.S. Public Health Service, Dr. de Montigny received his M.D. from the University of Wisconsin in 1961, but claims he took the easy way out: "Becoming a medicine man is much harder, and involves much more sacrifice than becoming a doctor." (Over the years the Indian Health Service has become much more responsive to the spiritual and physical needs of Indian patients. Today many hospitals routinely allow medicine men to work with M.D.'s to aid in a patient's recovery.)

♦ Leo Johnson of Fairfax, Oklahoma, was the first Indian to enter the Air Force Academy. Johnson completed his studies in 1962 and went on to distinguish himself as a captain and pilot, receiving several air medals and the Air Force Commendation Medal for his valor.

STATISTICALLY SPEAKING –
INDIANS IN THE UNITED STATES TODAY

PLACE OF BIRTH: In 1970 there were 769,572 American Indians and 34,378 Eskimos and Aleuts living in the United States. 14,488 were foreign-born, and another 6,632 were born while their mothers were visiting abroad or were at sea.

MOTHER TONGUE: There are approximately 250 different Indian languages spoken today, but only 242,967 Indians claimed one of these languages as their mother tongue. Only 1,699 spoke Aleut or Eskimo. The majority (383,764) spoke English as their first language.

RESERVATIONS: There are 267 reservations in the continental United States. The Bureau of Indian Affairs also maintains trusteeship over 51,372,762 acres of tribally owned land.

Over 480,000 Indians live on or near reservations. The five states with the highest Indian populations in 1977 were:

Arizona	140,156
Oklahoma	120,460
California	106,800
New Mexico	99,818
Alaska	70,166

Surprisingly, in 1970, there were more Indians living in New York State (28,355) than in Montana (27,130), Texas (17,957) or Wyoming (4,980).

TRIBES: There are 493 recognized Indian tribal groups in the United States.

INCOME: The average per capita income for reservation dwellers was estimated at $1,520 in 1975. Urban Indians had an average income of $2,108, while rural Indians only received $1,142.

The mean income for Indian families in 1970 was $6,857. Only 1% of 149,122 families had an income of $25,000 per year or more; 7% received more than $15,000; and 22% received more than $10,000 per annum.

Eight per cent of all Indians had an income of less than $1,000 annually, and 33.3% were below the poverty level.

EDUCATION:In 1977, approximately 18,700 Indian students were receiving college scholarship grants. The school dropout rate in the mid-1970s was 35%, an improvement over the 42% dropout rate of the late 1960s.

There were 256,559 Indians between the ages of 3 and 34 enrolled in school in 1970. Of those more than 25 years old (322,652): 12,195 had completed 4 or more years of college; 36,273 had some college education; 107,324 had finished high school; 182,408 had attended high school; and 24,906 had received no formal education.

OCCUPATION:There were 162,453 Indian male workers and 105,706 women workers in 1970. 10,754 men, or 6.6%, were employed as professional or technical workers. Surprisingly, the women were doing a little bit better, with 8,184, or 7.7%, of their work force employed as professionals — accountants, architects, doctors, lawyers, teachers, etc.

Most Indian males were employed as operatives (27,872) and craftsmen (25,725); most Indian women were employed as service workers (19,401) and clerical workers (18,524).

FIFTEEN LARGEST INDIAN TRIBES IN THE UNITED STATES

In 1970 the American Indian population stood at 792,730, up 51.4% from the 1960 Census. The reason for the large increase in the Indian population was a new census policy which allowed respondents of mixed ancestry to report the race with which they identify themselves. At the time 59% of all Indians (452,134) belonged to only 15 tribal groups (there are 493 officially recognized tribes in America).

1.	Navaho	96,743
2.	Cherokee	66,150
3.	Sioux (Dakota)	47,825
4.	Chippewa	41,946
5.	Pueblo	30,971
6.	Lumbee	27,520
7.	Choctaw, Houma	23,562
8.	Apache	22,993
9.	Iroquois	21,473
10.	Creek, Alabama, Coushatta	17,004
11.	Papago, Pima	16,690
12.	Shoshone, Northern and Southern Paiute, Chemehuevi	14,248
13.	Blackfeet	9,921
14.	Yuman	7,635
15.	Tlingit, Haida	7,453

EIGHTEEN FAMOUS AMERICANS WITH
INDIAN ANCESTORS

Like the rest of the "immigrants" who settled in America, many of the American Indians married outside their ethnic group and diluted their heritage in the mainstream of American life. They moved from the reservations and dissolved into the "melting pot."

1 DICK ALLEN (b. 1942)

During the 1972 baseball season, Richard Anthony Allen's 37 homers and 113 runs batted in earned him the Most Valuable Player award in the American League. One of nine children born into a poor farm family, Dick recollects that his mother, who is part Cherokee, "almost worked herself to death taking in washing to feed us" after she and her husband separated.

Despite impaired vision in his left eye, Dick was an excellent student and top athlete at Wampum High School in Pennsylvania. He turned down the more than 50 college scholarships offered him upon graduation and signed a $60,000 contract with the Philadelphia Phillies right out of school. He started his major league career in 1963 after only three years in the minor leagues.

2 JOHNNY BENCH (b. 1947)

In 1968, Bench, who is one-eighth Choctaw Indian, was the first catcher in history to be named Rookie of the Year. He stands six feet one inch tall; his throwing hand is so large that it can hold as many as seven baseballs at one time.

Bench's father was a semi-pro catcher who turned to truck driving to support his family; he taught Johnny all he knew about the game. He helped him practice, and taught him to throw for specific targets and to aim with accuracy from a distance of 250 feet. Bench made receiving an art, and in 1970 became the first catcher in fifteen years to receive the Most Valuable Player award.

3 ANITA BRYANT (b. 1940)

Lyndon Johnson once told his favorite singer, "Honey, I want you to sing . . . when

(Courtesy: Anita Bryant)

they lower me in the ground." True to her word, Anita Bryant sang the "Battle Hymn of the Republic" at his funeral in 1973.

Of French-Scottish-Dutch-English-Irish-and-Cherokee ancestry, Anita made her singing debut at the age of two with a rendition of "Jesus Loves Me." She sang in church choirs, in talent shows and on TV variety hours, and even had her own local TV spot while she was still in high school.

A second runner-up in the 1958 Miss America Pageant, Bryant earned her first gold record in 1959. Over the years she has had numerous best-selling records and albums in sacred, patriotic and show music categories. Recently she has embarked on a highly controversial campaign against civil rights for gay people in Dade County, Florida, and nationwide.

4 JOHNNY CASH (b. 1932)

Born in the backwoods of Arkansas, Johnny Cash emerged from a life of poverty to become a giant in the country music field. One-quarter Cherokee Indian, Cash began writing songs and singing on a local radio station at the age of twelve. His mother took in laundry to pay for his singing lessons, but it wasn't until his Air Force days that he was able to buy his first guitar.

His first hit record, "Cry, Cry, Cry" was recorded in 1955, and by 1958 he had sold over 6 million records, including "Folsom Prison Blues" and "I Walk the Line." Although he is noted for a large repertoire of prison songs and gives free concerts at penal institutions such as Folsom and San Quentin, Cash was only behind bars once. He spent a night in the El Paso jail for crossing the Mexican border with some Dexedrine tablets.

5 CHER (b. 1946)

Pop singer Cherilyn La Pierre's background includes, French, Turkish, Armenian and Cherokee Indian ancestors. Cher and her former husband, Sonny Bono, became rock stars in 1965 with their recording of "I Got You, Babe" which sold over three million copies and established them as a show-biz duo. Although they split personally and professionally in 1974, the couple returned to television and continued their act for a while after the divorce, but Cher now has established herself as a solo performer.

6 REDD FOXX (b. 1922)

In his autobiography, Malcolm X wrote, "Chicago Red was the funniest dishwasher on this earth." Malcolm X was speaking of Redd Foxx, the black comedian, whose maternal grandmother was a full-blooded Indian, and whose great-great-grandfather was African. Other mixed ancestors contributed to his light skin and his hair color, which earned him the nickname "Chicago Red."

Before his rise to the top, there were some hard times for John Elroy Sanford (Foxx's real name). Black performers were not in demand, and he had to work as a dishwasher, a busboy and a cart pusher in New York's garment district to support himself. He built his reputation playing small night spots and recording "party" records, and became famous for his "blue" material and jokes.

According to *Show Business Illustrated,* Foxx made "his first outing as a headliner in an ofay club" in 1962, when he opened at the Summit on Hollywood's Sunset Strip. He was soon commanding salaries of over $1,200 per week; by 1970, he was earning $1,000,000 a year playing Las Vegas clubs. In 1972, Foxx became a household word thanks to his hit television series, *Sanford and Son.*

7 JAMES GARNER (b. 1928)

A popular television and movie actor, James Bumgarner was born in Norman, Oklahoma, a descendent of early settlers of the Oklahoma Territory who intermarried with American Indians. He dropped the "Bum" from his name when he got his first nonspeaking part on Broadway as a judge in *The Caine Mutiny Court Martial* in 1954. He made the most of the situation, and claims to have swiped his acting style from Henry Fonda, the star of the play, whom he watched night after night during most of the 512 performances Garner sat through.

Garner's career was firmly established in 1957 when he played the leading role in the TV series *Maverick*. His latest series, *The Rockford Files,* has proved to be as successful as the first.

8 BILLIE JEAN KING (b. 1943)

Billie Jean started taking tennis lessons at the age of 11, when she realized there weren't too many opportunities for women in softball. She was also searching for a more "ladylike" sport, so she decided to trade in her bat for a racquet.

Of Irish, Scottish, English and Seminole Indian stock, Billie Jean gives her ancestors some credit for her tremendous strength on the tennis court: "My mother always tells me that the Indian blood gives me my stamina." Besides stamina, she also had determination: she walked the 3 1/2 miles to school each day, solely for the purpose of strengthening her legs.

Billie Jean King was the first female athlete to break the $100,000 barrier; in 1972 she became the first woman ever named "Athlete of the Year" by *Sports Illustrated* magazine; and in 1979 she became the first woman to win 20 Wimbledon titles.

9   LORETTA LYNN (b. 1932)

Music was her escape route from Butcher Hollow, Kentucky, a small coal-mining town, where Loretta Lynn was married at the age of 14 and bore four children in four years. The daughter of a coal miner who died of black lung disease, and the grand-daughter of a Cherokee Indian, Loretta recorded her first song in 1961. Her career took off in 1964 when she was voted Top Female Country Vocalist by *Record World, Billboard, Music Business* and *Cashbox,* and she's been riding high on the country music charts ever since.

10   "MOMS" MABLEY (1894–1975)

Born Loretta Mary Aiken, of mixed Black, Cherokee and Irish ancestry, Moms contended, "I wasn't raised to be black or white. God made us all equal . . . and died for us all."

Her great-grandmother had been a slave, but life was better for Moms, who rose to fame as a comedienne after a long, hard struggle. In 1974, a year before her death, she said: "TV's been good to people like me and Redd Foxx. We came up when it was tough. It's too bad it took so long, though. Now that we've got some money, we have to use it all for doctor bills."

11   ROBERT MITCHUM (b. 1917)

Of Irish, Norwegian and American Indian ancestry, Mitchum has built his screen reputation portraying soldiers, cowboys and adventurers in such classics as *West of the Pecos,* 1945; *Thirty Seconds Over Tokyo,* 1945; *One Minute to Zero,* 1952; and *Heaven Knows, Mister Allison,* 1957.

Where did he pick up his style for playing "tough" guys? Probably from real life: he once lived in the tough Hell's Kitchen section of New York; was part of a Georgia chain gang at the age of sixteen; and even earned his living as a professional boxer before he set his sights on Hollywood.

12   DOLLY PARTON (b. 1946)

A "cross-over" performer who has emerged as a rockabilly superstar in the past few years, Dolly Parton is of mixed Irish, Dutch and Cherokee ancestry. She was the fourth of twelve children born in a shack near Sevierville, Tennessee, in the foothills of the Great Smoky Mountains. Her family was so poor that Dolly dressed in rags and had to use flour and Mercurochrome instead of face powder and lipstick.

Today, she enjoys wearing outrageous sequined costumes, expensive makeup, and mile-high wigs. She's flashy, but feels her stage appearance is a "little joke" she can share with her audience.

13   DAN RATHER (b. 1931)

According to Dan, his heritage was pure Texas Baptist until his grandmother's father "took an Indian woman." Raised in Houston, Texas, Rather has been a CBS news correspondent since the late 1950s. He was singled out to bear the brunt of the Nixon administration's displeasure with the press and the broadcast media in the 70s, but he remained cool and composed through it all. Today Rather says: "If a truck runs over me tomorrow, what I would really love to have someone tell my kids is that their father wouldn't buckle—not under Lyndon Johnson, not under Richard Nixon." Dan Rather has been chosen to succeed the veteran anchorman of the CBS Evening News, Walter Cronkite.

(Courtesy: Dan Rather)

14 ROBERT RAUSCHENBERG (b. 1925)

Born in Port Arthur, Texas, Rauschenberg numbers among his ancestors a German immigrant grandfather from Berlin, and a full-blooded Cherokee Indian grandmother. Raunschenberg, often called the "father of junk sculpture," has been confusing gallery-goers for more than twenty-five years, ever since his first one-man show opened in New York in 1951.

His canvasses combine household objects with "urban debris" — paint, old tin cans and other junk. One of his best-known constructions is entitled "Momogram 1959." It consists of a stuffed angora goat with an automobile tire stuck in its middle.

Another of his famous works, entitled "Accident" (photo-mechanical reproductions of car accident photographs), won first prize at the International Exhibition of Prints held in Yugoslavia in 1963.

15 BURT REYNOLDS (b. 1936)

What ever made a nice young man pose nude for *Cosmopolitan*'s centerfold? Well, it was a "first" for a respectable women's magazine; it certainly couldn't hurt his "macho" image as an actor; and it was done so tastefully that even his Italian mother and his Cherokee grandmother would be hard pressed to find it "offensive."

Reynolds' career definitely improved after his stint as a male model. Prior to his 1972 "premier appearance," he claims his films from the early 1960s were "the kind they show in airplanes and prisons, because nobody [in the audience] can leave."

16 WILL ROGERS (1879–1936)

Humorist Will Rogers was billed as the "Cherokee Kid" when he worked in Texas Jack's Wild West Circus in South Africa, but when he returned to America in 1904 he earned himself a reputation as the "philosopher on horseback."

He was only one-eighth Cherokee, but he was proud of his Indian heritage. He once told an audience of "blue bloods" at Boston's Symphony Hall, "My own forefathers . . . didn't come over like yours on the Mayflower — they met the boat."

17 BART STARR (b. 1934)

Born Bartlett Starr in Montgmery, Alabama, Starr has some Cherokee Indians among his ancestors. As a quarterback for the Green Bay Packers, he led his team to victory in the first Superbowl, held in 1967.

(Courtesy: Bart Starr)

18 JESSAMYN WEST (b. 1902)

Her first book, *The Friendly Persuasion* (1945), was a collection of stories told to Jessamyn by her mother. The stories were about her ancestors (Irish, Scotch and Welsh Quakers) who settled in southern Indiana in the nineteenth century. The stories told to Jessamyn in childhood also included tales of her father's ancestors, one of whom was a Comanche Indian.

Jessamyn was encouraged to write while recovering from a lengthy bout with tuberculosis that almost claimed her life. One of her distant relatives is also a famous "writer" — former president Richard Nixon, who is descended from Frank Milhous, Jessamyn's great-uncle.

2 THE HUDDLED MASSES

BRIEF CHRONOLOGY OF AMERICAN IMMIGRATION

1562 ♦ A group of French Huguenots established a colony on Parris Island, near Beaufort, South Carolina, but abandoned it after two years.

1565 ♦ The first permanent European settlement in the United States was established at St. Augustine, Florida, by the Spanish, under the authority of Don Pedro Menendez de Aviles.

1607 ♦ The first permanent English settlement was founded at Jamestown, Virginia.

1614 ♦ The first major Dutch settlement was founded near Albany, New York.

1620 ♦ The Pilgrims arrived in America, after a 63-day voyage from England, and established a colony at Plymouth, Massachusetts.

1623 ♦ The Dutch settled the Hudson River Valley.

1629 ♦ Five shiploads of Puritans, totaling about 900, arrived in Massachusetts Bay.

1648 ♦ The treaty ending the Thirty Years War stipulated that only three religions would henceforth be tolerated in Germany—Catholic, Lutheran and Reformed. With religious intolerance as their motivating force, large numbers of German immigrants belonging to small religious sects, such as the German Baptist Brethren (Dunkers), began arriving in America.

1654 ♦ The first Jewish immigrants, from Brazil, settled in New Amsterdam when Pernambuco (now Recife) was recaptured from the Dutch by the Portuguese.

1790 ♦ When the first U.S. Census was conducted, the "ethnic mix" of America was as follows: 60% English, 9.5% Irish, 8.6% German, 8.1% Scottish, 3.1% Dutch, 2.3% French, 0.7% Swedish, 0.8% Spanish, 0.8% "unclassified."

1795 ♦ The Naturalization Act was passed. From now on a residence period of five years and a renunciation of foreign allegiances and titles of nobility would be prerequisites for citizenship.

1798 ♦ The Alien and Sedition Act was passed, granting the President power to deport any alien considered a danger to the nation, and to imprison anyone "who attempted to impede lawful processes of government, write or publish or utter any false and malicious statements about the President, Congress or the U.S. Government."

1810 ♦ The U.S. population was 7,239,881, including 1,211,364 slaves and 186,746 free Negroes.

1815 ♦ Mass immigrations to North America from Europe started this year.

1819 ♦ On March 2 the first immigration law requiring a numerical tally of immigrants was passed. For the first time, statistics on the number of new arrivals would be kept by the government.

♦ The "Passenger Act" put an end to the German "redemptioner" trade, whereby a large number of Scotch-Irish and German indentured servants were "sold" for fare and costs by sea captains when their ship docked in America.

1820 ♦ U.S. population was 9,638,453. This year alone, some 151,000 new immigrants arrived.

♦ In an attempt to quell heavy emigration, the government of Prussia made it a crime to urge anyone to emigrate. Later, even reading a letter or favorable article on the subject would become a criminal action.

1827 ♦ French-Americans organized the first Mardi Gras celebration in New Orleans.

1830 ♦ U.S. population was 12,866,020. During the next decade more than 573,000 immigrants would arrive in the United States.

1837 ♦ Scandinavian immigration began in earnest, spurred on by Ole Rynning's *True Account of America for the Information and Help of Peasant and Commoner.*

♦ Steerage passage for German immigrants leaving from the port of Bremen was $16.

1840 ♦ According to the sixth national census, there were 17,069,453 Americans. During the next decade 1,479,000 would arrive here from foreign shores.

♦ Samuel Cunard, a Canadian, established the first transatlantic steamship line. His first ship left Liverpool on July 4 and arrived in Boston on July 19.

1841 ♦ Five shipwrecked Japanese were rescued at sea by an American vessel. Four were put ashore at Honolulu, but the fifth, Manjiro Nakahma, sailed on to the mainland to become America's first Japanese immigrant.

1845 ♦ The United States annexed Texas after it declared independence from Mexico in 1836. This action led to the Mexican-American War in May, 1846.

1846–1848 *Phytophthora infestans* raged through the potato fields of Ireland, resulting in mass starvation and emigration from the Emerald Isle.

1848 ♦ The treaty of Guadalupe-Hidalgo ended the Mexican-American War. According to the terms of the treaty, the United States acquired Colorado, Arizona, New Mexico, Texas, California, and parts of Utah and Nevada in exchange for $15 million.

1851 ♦ 250,000 Irishmen and 20,000 Frenchmen arrived in America this year.

1854 ♦ German immigrants accounted for more than 50% of the 400,000 new arrivals who sought refuge in America this year.

1855 ♦ Castle Garden was opened as an immigrant receiving station in New York.

1860 ♦ New York became "the largest

Between 1855 and 1892 Castle Garden served as an immigrant clearing center. (Courtesy: German Information Center)

Irish city in the world," with some 203,760 Irish-born citizens out of a total population of 805,651.

1862 ♦ The Homestead Act granted willing settlers title to 160 acres of farm land, provided that the acreage be tilled for five years. By 1890, some 375,000 homesteaders had received 48 million acres of land. During the same period, the railroad companies acquired over 20 million acres.

1863 ♦ The Conscription Act, which allowed anyone to evade military service provided that he pay $300 or enlist a substitute for three years of service, set off four days of rioting in New York. The working-class Irish, to whom $300 was almost a year's wages, were outraged; they took out their anger on the Negroes, whom they believed were responsible for the war. Hundreds of blacks and whites were killed, the Colored Orphan Asylum was burned, and property damage amounted to several million dollars. (That's uninflated 1863 dollars!)

1864 ♦ To meet the labor crisis caused by the Civil War, Congress passed an Act to Encourage Immigration. It was repealed in 1868.

1870 ♦ The U.S. population totaled 38,558,371. During the coming decade, more than 3 million immigrants would call America their new home.

1880 ♦ The U.S. population stood at 50,155,783. Between 1880 and 1890 more than 5.2 million immigrants were to enter the United States.

1882 ♦ Congress approved the first act to restrict immigration on August 3. No paupers, convicts, and physically or mentally defective persons were permitted to enter, and a tax of 50 cents per person was imposed on all incoming immigrants.

1883 ♦ The Southern Immigration Association was formed to promote European immigration to the South. Without the slaves to till the land, there was a great need for cheap, foreign labor.

1886 ♦ The statue of Liberty Enlightening the World was dedicated on October 28 by President Grover Cleveland. She started lighting the way for new arrivals just at the time when nativism was growing in America and many Americans were considering ways to keep the "foreigners" out.

1890 ♦ Besides being "the greatest Irish city in the world," New York had as many Germans as Hamburg, and 2.5 times as many Jews as there were in Warsaw.

1892 ♦ Ellis Island replaced Castle Garden as the main port of entry for European immigrants. Some 20 million persons were detained here before the center was closed down in 1954. In its heyday, an average of 2,000 new arrivals were processed daily.

1893 ♦ Queen Liliuokalani of Hawaii was overthrown in a bloodless revolution led by American planters. The Republic of Hawaii was established, and Sanford B. Dole became the first president.

1894 ♦ Congress created the Bureau of Immigration.

1898 ♦ Hawaii was annexed by the United States as a Territory. Almost 60,000 Japanese residing in Hawaii at the time were then able to proceed to the mainland without passport restrictions.

1899 ♦ After the Spanish-American war, the Puerto Rican people were finally free from Spanish rule. However, self-government only lasted seven months before the island fell under the "protection" of the United States.

1900 ♦ The U.S. population was 75,994,575. During the past ten years more than 3,687,000 immigrants had arrived in the United States. But, during the next ten years more than 9 million persons from Southern and Eastern Europe would begin streaming into the country.

1910 ♦ The Mexican Revolution sent thousands of peasants to the U.S. border seeking employment.

1917 ♦ The Jones Act made Puerto Ricans U.S. citizens and also made them eligible for the draft.

1924 ♦ The Johnson-Reed Act established immigration quotas based on the ethnic population of the United States in 1890. These quotas were designed to severely restrict the flow of immigrants from Southern and Eastern Europe and nonwhite nations, in favor of the "old stock" nations of Northern Europe.

1930 ♦ U.S. Population was 123,203,000. During the past decade only 528,000 new immigrants had arrived in America, the lowest figure since the 1830s.

1933 ♦ According to a poll, the preferred

According to O. Henry, the "[Statue of Liberty] was made by a Dago and presented to the American people on behalf of the French government for the purpose of welcomin' Irish immigrants into the Dutch city of New York." (Courtesy: Theatre and Music Collection, Museum of the City of New York)

ethnic groups in America were: Canadians, English, Scots, Irish, French, Swedes, Germans, Spaniards.

1934 ♦ The Tydings-McDuffie Act limited Filipino immigration to the United States to 50 persons per year.

1940 ♦ The Alien Registration Act, also known as the Smith Act, called for the registration and fingerprinting of all aliens. This year some 5 million aliens were registered.

1942 ♦ The Bracero Program strongly encouraged Mexicans to come to America as farm and agricultural workers, due to the labor shortage created by World War II. The program was not terminated until 1964.

1948 ♦ The Displaced Persons Act signed

by President Truman opened America to some 205,000 Europeans who were displaced by the ravages of war.

1952 ♦ The McCarran-Walter Immigration and Naturalization Act was passed, extending token immigration quotas to Asian nations.

1965 ♦ The Cuban refugee airlift program began, six years after Fidel Castro assumed power in Cuba. For the next eight years, Cubans were admitted to the U.S. under special quotas.

♦ The immigration bill signed by President Johnson eliminated race, creed and nationality as a basis for admission to the United States. As soon as the old quota system was removed, immigration from non-European nations increased sharply.

1970 ♦ President Nixon amended the 1965 Immigration Act, and further liberalized admission to the United States.

1972 ♦ Congress passed the Ethnic Heritage Studies bill to encourage bilingual education and programs pertaining to ethnic culture.

1979 ♦ Congress appropriated more than $334 million in rescue and resettlement funds for Vietnamese "boat people."

1980 ♦ A new wave of Cuban refugees embarked for the U.S. on the so-called "Freedom Flotilla."

Most of us can trace our presence here to the turmoil or oppression of another time and another place. Our nation has been immeasurably enriched by this continuing process. (Former Secretary of State Cyrus Vance, 1979)

The Ethnic Top Ten

Who Came to America? Everyone! There probably isn't an island, atoll or republic that hasn't donated at least one citizen to the United States in the past two hundred years. Our nation is a conglomeration of the rest of the world and our citizens have been culled from the four corners of the earth.

No one knows for certain how many immigrants sought refuge in America prior to 1820, because no one was counting. There simply weren't any official records kept of new arrivals. But, since 1820, almost 50 million more newcomers have found their way to the "promised land."

Why did they choose America? There is an old Italian proverb that says it all: *"Chi sta bene non si muove"* — "He who is well off doesn't move."

And, true to that statement, almost everyone who came to our shores wanted to escape from religious persecution, political oppression or economic hardship. There were a few stalwarts who came here looking for adventure, viewing America as a gigantic unexplored camping ground, but for the most part the "poor, tired and hungry" who emigrated here had survival on their minds. The Irish came when the potato crops failed; the Italians came when the soil they farmed was depleted; the Jews came to escape religious persecution; and wars and revolutions brought us scores of exiles from Germany, Austria, Poland, Russia and Mexico.

They left their homelands for a second chance at life, and they chose America because the streets were reputedly "paved with gold." But, far from finding golden streets, what did await the majority of the unskilled, uneducated immigrants who ventured here at the turn of the century was *more* poverty, *new* diseases, *heartier* vermin and life in a five-story walk-up. There was discrimination lurking here, too, and each new group—the last to disembark on shore—became the "scapegoats of the hour," accused of taking jobs away from the "Americans" who had arrived weeks earlier on the same docks.

Fifty million immigrants can't be wrong! Despite the indignities, slurs and exploitation they often suffered at the hands of cruel labor bosses and swindlers, the immigrants kept pouring into America. They kept coming here because America *was* a land of opportunity, a place where they could hope to better their lot in life—if not for themselves, then at least for their children.

Immigrants Admitted: 1891-1970

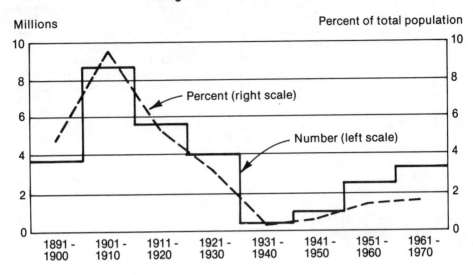

Immigrants Admitted From Major Contributing Countries: 1891-1975

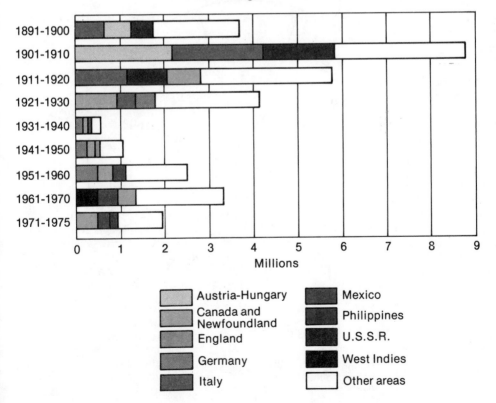

The immigrants "came, saw and conquered" America. They learned the language, the customs and survival techniques in this strange new land. Many of them prospered, and their children, in many cases, surpassed their parents in income, education and occupational status. Fifty million immigrants were right about America—it was a land of opportunity and a place they could call "home."

Top Ten Ethnic Groups Since immigration officials first started keeping track of the "huddled masses" who entered the United States, ten nations have led the rest of the world in contributing new citizens to our shores. Between 1820 and 1975, 38 million immigrants entered the United States from Germany, Italy, Great Britain, Ireland, the former Austro-Hungarian empire, Canada, Russia, Mexico, the West Indies and Sweden.

These nations, the "Immigrant's Top Ten," were responsible for over 80% of our newcomers, but immigration statistics alone are not enough to qualify for the "Ethnic Top Ten." Other factors have to be considered, such as differing birth rates, mortality, peak decades of immigration and bookkeeping errors. Bookkeeping errors? Of course! Many of the immigrants who entered the United States were classified according to the nation that controlled their homeland at the time. For example, according to immigration records, only 3,782 Lithuanians have ever entered the United States in the past 155 years. Yet, according to U.S. Census statistics, there were 76,001 Lithuanian-born Americans living in the United States in 1970. Where did all the Lithuanians come from? Excluding cloning as a possible answer, the only other logical source is Russia. When the Lithuanians entered the United States they were listed as citizens of Russia, thus inflating the statistics for that nation. Similar discrepancies occurred for the Austro-Hungarian empire;

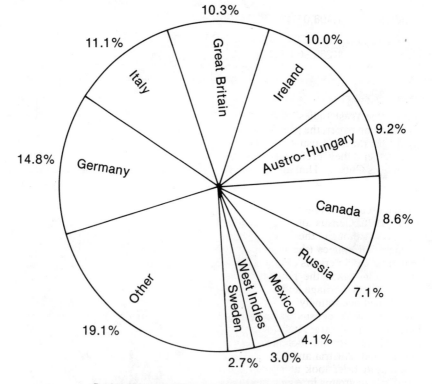

During the past 155 years, almost 81 percent of all newcomers to the United States emigrated from these ten nations.

The Immigrant's Top Ten — 1820-1975

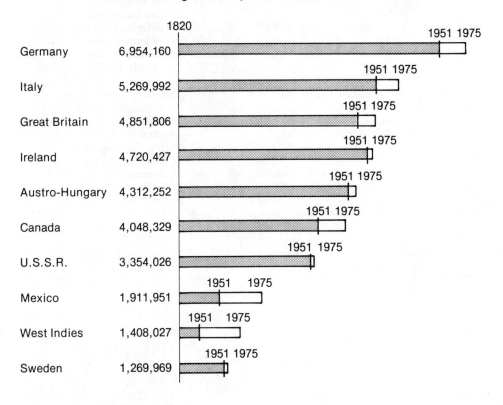

	1820	
Germany	6,954,160	1951 1975
Italy	5,269,992	1951 1975
Great Britain	4,851,806	1951 1975
Ireland	4,720,427	1951 1975
Austro-Hungary	4,312,252	1951 1975
Canada	4,048,329	1951 1975
U.S.S.R.	3,354,026	1951 1975
Mexico	1,911,951	1951 1975
West Indies	1,408,027	1951 1975
Sweden	1,269,969	1951 1975

and while "the West Indies" makes a nice, neat category on paper, the people from that part of the world don't usually lump themselves together—they prefer to be known individually as Cubans, Haitians or Dominicans.

A better estimate of the ten most populous ethnic groups in America today comes from the 1970 Census of Foreign-Stock Americans. Although the census omits third-generation ethnics (the grandchildren of immigrants) and persons of mixed ancestry, at least it "takes the people's word" about their ethnic heritage and allows them to be classified accordingly.

Based on 1970 census statistics, the "Ethnic Top Ten" are: Italy, Germany, Canada, Great Britain, Poland, Mexico, Russia, Ireland, Austria and Sweden.

Let's take a brief look at the ten most populous ethnic groups in America today — their history, accomplishments and progress in the "promised land."

THE "ETHNIC TOP TEN"
or
THE TEN MOST POPULOUS FOREIGN-STOCK* GROUPS IN AMERICA

Italian	4,240,779
German	3,622,035
Canadian	3,034,556
British	2,465,050
Polish	2,374,244
Mexican	2,339,151
Russian	1,943,195
Irish	1,450,220
Austrian	975,325
Swedish	806,138
Total:	23,250,695

*Includes foreign-born Americans, and native-born Americans with at least one foreign-born parent.

THE ITALIANS

America was discovered by an Italian, named for an Italian and explored by such Italian adventurers as Giovanni Verrazzano (the first European to sail into New York Harbor), John Cabot, the discoverer of Newfoundland (real name: Giovanni Caboto) and Enrico Tonti (the "Father of Arkansas"; he manned a seventeenth-century trading post on the Arkansas River).

An Italian (William Paca) signed the Declaration of Independence, and another, Philip Mazzei, collaborated with Thomas Jefferson on several essays about political freedom, giving Jefferson food for thought when he said: "all men are by nature equally free and independent." But despite their early arrival in the new world, and their auspicious beginnings, it wasn't until the late nineteenth century that Italians began to emigrate in sufficient numbers to have an impact on American society as an "ethnic" group.

In 1850 there were only about four thousand Italians living in America. By 1900 their ranks had swelled to almost half a million, and in the decade 1900–1910 more than 2 million Italians entered the United States. Most were unskilled, uneducated peasants from the South, but they were willing to work hard for low wages in order to survive in this new land. Why did so many southern Italians emigrate to the United States? In the words of one man, they came because they had to: "We plant and we reap, but never do we taste white bread . . . We cultivate the grape, but we drink no wine. We raise animals for food, but we eat no meat." A feudal land-lease system and heavy taxation left the peasants with nothing for themselves; when political upheaval, earthquakes, volcanic eruptions, and vineyard blight started to take their toll on the population, the Italians could stand no more. Each new catastrophe sent the Southerners streaming to America.

At one time Italians were at the bottom of the economic ladder and a public notice recruiting laborers for the Croton Reservoir in 1895 advertised the following pay scales:

COMMON LABOR	White	$1.30 – $1.50
	Colored	$1.25 – $1.40
	Italian	$1.15 – $1.25

These Sicilians were "westward bound," seeking their fortune in the gold fields of California. For the most part, however, the Italians settled in urban industrial areas where jobs were plentiful for unskilled laborers. (Courtesy: New York Public Library)

The "Hurdy-Gurdy" man played music while his monkey danced and passed around a tin cup for donations. (Courtesy: Museum of the City of New York)

Since then, Italians have entered all walks of life, rising from such stereotypic occupations as organ grinders, shoemakers and barbers to the professional world — as doctors, lawyers and executives of large corporations. They started many successful enterprises including banks (The Bank of America), wineries (Gallo, Italian-Swiss Colony), and even a nationally famous peanut business (Planters). They are our largest foreign-stock group today, with more than 4 million first- and second-generation citizens, and a total Italian-American population estimated to be as high as 23,000,000.

"Firsts" and Facts About the Italian Experience in America

Disappointed man Although there has been some controversy concerning his "discovery" in recent years, Christopher Columbus is still honored every October for his 1492 voyage to the New World. Even if he is eventually discredited, Columbus probably wouldn't care—he died a disappointed man who spent the remainder of his life trying to find a way *around* America, and he refused to accept credit for his discovery while he was alive.

Christopher Columbus. (Courtesy: New York Public Library)

Amerigo the Beautiful? It was Martin Waldseemuller, a German mapmaker, who first suggested naming the New World in honor of Amerigo Vespucci, the Italian who explored South America in 1502. In his 1507 Cosmographiae Introductio, which included maps of Vespucci's voyages, Waldseemuller wrote (referring only to South America): ". . . I see no reason why it should not be called Amerigo, after Americus, the discoverer, or indeed America . . ." Although Waldseemuller tried to credit Columbus with discovering the new world in later editions of his book, the name America stuck and soon both continents had acquired Italian surnames.

Italians in Colonial America There weren't too many Italians residing in New Amsterdam, so when the record keepers took a survey in 1639, they simply listed Peter Caesar Alberto as 'the Italian" of Kings County, and he is believed to be the first Italian ever to reside in Brooklyn, New York. Although Italians weren't politically strong in the 1700s, Onorio Razzolini became the first Italian to hold public office in America when he was appointed Armourer and Keeper of Stores in Maryland in 1736.

Opera The first Italian opera performed in America was *The Barber of Seville*, presented at the Park Theater in New York in 1825. It wasn't until 1832 that the first Italian opera troupe visited New York at the invitation of Lorenzo Da Ponte, the first professor of Italian appointed at Columbia College in 1825 and the librettist of some of Mozart's greatest operas.

He May Have Been First Antonio Meucci (1808–1889) was a hard-luck inventor who claimed to have invented the first "telephone." Meucci applied for a U.S. patent for his device almost five years before Alexander Graham Bell patented his telephone, but Meucci was never able to prove that his device actually worked. When his case came to court, all Meucci had left were his working plans. His wife had sold his invention as scrap metal for a mere $6.00, when Meucci was hospitalized after a ferryboat accident and she was in desperate need of some quick cash.

Keep Out the Riffraff Count Luigi Palma di Cesnola (1832–1904) was an Italian immigrant with a short memory. After he married into an aristocratic "American" family and became a trustee of the Metropolitan Museum of Art in 1878, the Count became an outspoken opponent of the "new immigration" and favored strong restrictions to keep the "huddled masses" from entering America.

Religion The first Catholic Church dedicated to the service of Italians in New York City was established in 1867, but it wasn't until 1968 that an Italian-American was appointed to head a diocese of New York. The first Italian-American bishop of Brooklyn was Francis Mugavero, the son of Sicilian immigrants.

Francesco at the Bat The first Italian to play major league baseball was Ping Bodie. He played for the Chicago White Sox from 1911 to 1919, but none of his fans guessed that he was Italian because he had changed his name from Francesco Pezzolo to Ping Bodie (???) on the advice of his manager. He later played for the New York Yankees with the "Great Bambino," Babe Ruth, who *wasn't* Italian despite his nickname.

Money Generoso Pope was the first Italian-American to become a millionaire. He started his career as a water boy on a road gang and went on to become the owner of a sand and gravel contracting company. He also distinguished himself as the pub-lisher of *Il Progresso*, New York's daily Italian language newspaper, and as a powerful Tammany Hall leader in the 1930s.

Italian-American All the Way The first opera written by an Italian-American, about Italian-Americans, and performed by Italian-Americans, was *The Saint of Bleecker Street*. Gian-Carlo Menotti's (1911–   ) Pulitzer Prize-winning opera had its premiere at the Broadway Theater in New York on December 27, 1954.

Politics When John Pastore became Governor of Rhode Island in 1945 it was a first for the Italian-American community. In 1950, Pastore became the first Italian-American in the U.S. Senate. He retired in 1977 after spending 42 years in public office and over two decades in the Senate.

Millionaire in the Making Leandro Rizzuto (1938–   ), the son of a Sicilian-born barber from Brooklyn, is the chief executive and controlling stockholder of Conair Corporation, the nation's largest manufacturer of blow dryers. Rizzuto founded a hair-roller manufacturing company in 1959 with his father's help and a bankroll of $200, and turned it into Conair, a $50-million corporation, in less than twenty years.

The Other Side

Country:	ITALY
Capital:	Rome
Official Name:	Republica Italiana (Italian Republic)
Official Language:	Italian
National Anthem:	"Inno Di Mameli" (Hymn of Mameli)
	Written in 1847 by Goffredo Mameli, with music by Michele Novaro, the hymn calls upon the citizens of Italy to unite and fight for independence. Adopted as national anthem in 1946.
National Flag:	Vertial bands of green, white, and red. Originally designed by Napoleon as the banner of the Italian Legion for the 1796 campaign, the flag was later adopted by Victor Emmanuel, who added his coat of arms to the center. When he became king of Italy in 1861 his flag became the national flag of Italy, but the Arms of the House of Savoy were removed from the tricolor after World War II.
Coat of Arms:	Since 1946, the coat of arms has been a star surrounded by a laurel wreath and an oak branch, with a cogwheel in the foreground. The star stands for unity, the laurel and oak represent republicanism, and the cogwheel symbolizes industry.
Major Religion:	Almost 95% of the population is Roman Catholic. Only Spain has a higher percentage of Catholic citizens.

ITALIAN IMMIGRATION TO THE UNITED STATES

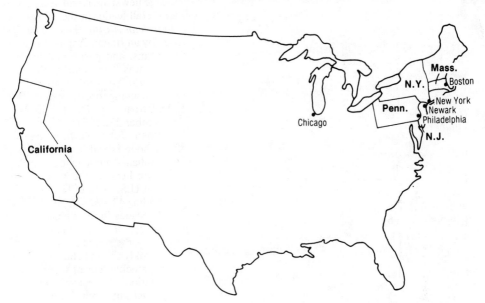

1821–1830	409	1901–1910	2,045,877	(Peak Decade)
1831–1840	2,253	1911–1920	1,109,524	
1841–1850	1,870	1921–1930	455,315	
1851–1860	9,231	1931–1940	68,028	
1861–1870	11,725	1941–1950	57,661	
1871–1880	55,759	1951–1960	185,491	
1881–1890	307,309	1961–1970	307,617	
1891–1900	651,893	1971–1975	93,506	

Total (1820–1975): 5,269,992

1970 Census

Foreign-born Italians	1,008,533
Native-born, 2nd generation	3,232,246
Total Foreign-stock Population	4,240,779
Estimated Italian-American Population	23 million

*Main Ethnic Epicenters**		*U.S. Cities** with Most Italians*	
New York	1,330,057	New York	1,004,771
New Jersey	551,889	Philadelphia	229,250
Pennsylvania	444,841	Chicago	197,175
California	340,675	Boston	192,349
Massachusetts	294,318	Newark	139,367

* States with largest foreign-stock populations—i.e., foreign born residents and their children.
** Standard Metropolitan Statistical Areas.

THE GERMANS

Since 1820, when immigration officials first began keeping tabs on those who entered America, almost 7 million Germans have made their home in the United States. That's over 15% of America's immigrants over the past 155 years, and by their sheer numbers alone the Germans were bound to have a great influence on the customs, culture and traditions of our country.

Even if your ancestors weren't German, if you've ever munched on a hot dog, attended a gymnastics class, had a few beers with the boys, traveled over (or bought) the Brooklyn Bridge, attended kindergarten, scribbled on a blackboard, enjoyed freedom of the press, or tracked a rocket on its way to the moon, then your life has been touched by the 7 million Germans who found their way to our shores.

The first great wave of German immigration began in 1683, and at the outbreak of the Revolutionary War in 1776 there were over 225,000 Germans living in North America — 10% of the total population. The Napoleonic wars and harsh economic conditions triggered the second wave of German immigration in 1825, and by the time the nineteenth century drew to a close an additional 5 million Germans had settled in the United States.

They came from a cross-section of the population: they were rich and poor; educated and ignorant; Protestant and Jewish; old, young and middle-aged. The Germans and their descendants became politicians, farmers, bridge builders, educators, musicians, artists and businessmen. They gave us wedding rings, Christmas trees, the Democratic donkey, the Katzenjammer Kids, Studebakers, Chryslers and Wurlitzers (Gee, Dad!). They made their mark on America's map with place names such as

"From the Old World to the New World." German immigrants crowd aboard a Hamburg steamer bound for New York in 1874. (Courtesy: German Information Center)

Frankfort, Indiana; Berlin, New Hampshire; Bismarck, North Dakota; and "New" cities galore: New Munich, Minnesota; New Braunfels, Texas; New Bremen, Ohio; and New Holstein, Wisconsin.

Some German immigrants themselves were immortalized as place names in America (Harpers Ferry, West Virginia, the site of John Brown's famous 1859 raid, was named for Robert Harper, a German immigrant), while others made a name for themselves among the top industrial corporations of America. Weyerhaeuser, Singer, Hammermill, Heublein, Bausch and Lomb are but a few of the German names that spell big business in American today.

German immigration to America peaked in the late nineteenth century, and many of our present German-American citizens have been native-born for two or three generations. As a result, many have lost the national identity of their ancestors as the language, customs and traditions fade through intermarriage and the erosion of time. In addition, anti-German feelings, generated during World Wars I and II, helped break down the ethnic ties among many German-Americans.

"Firsts" and Facts About the German Experience in America

The German "Mayflower" Nicknamed the "German *Mayflower*," the good ship *Concord* brought a group of Mennonites from the Rhineland to Germantown, Pennsylvania, in 1683. Led by Franz Daniel Pastorius (1651–1720), the "Father of German immigration to Pennsylvania," the group of German and Dutch immigrants fared well during their first year in America. The next year, however, Pastorius wrote to his parents and said, "send only Germans [to the New World] . . . the Hollanders, as sad experience has taught me, are not so easily satisfied which in this new land is a very necessary quality."

Blackboards Although they're no longer made of slate, and they usually come in green instead of black, almost every classroom in America has a "blackboard" on which teachers scrawl homework assignments. The man to thank for all those childhood memories of chalk and dust erasers is Christopher Dock, a German-American pedagogue from Skippack, Pennsylvania, who first introduced chalkboards as a classroom teaching aid in 1714.

Freedom of the Press Orphaned when his parents died en route from Germany to New York, John Peter Zenger (1697–1746) was forced to apprentice himself to a printer before he left the ill-fated ship that brought him to the New World in 1710. He learned his trade well and opened a printing shop in 1726. Later, with financial backing from his friends, Zenger was able to establish his own newspaper, the *New York Weekly Journal*, in 1733.

The Concord *brought early German settlers to Pennsylvania. (Courtesy: German Information Center)*

Charged with libel for criticizing the British governor, William Cosby, Zenger was fortunate to have engaged the services of a clever Philadelphia lawyer, Andrew Hamilton. Hamilton's defense was flawless and Zenger was acquitted after it was proved that he was guilty of no crime except printing the truth. The Zenger case was an important precedent for the establishment of freedom of the press in America as a basic Constitutional right.

Changing Times In 1764 some 600 German immigrants settled at Saxe-Gotha in South Carolina. They spoke German, observed German feast days and festivals, and served their favorite sausages and other eth-

Numb. II.

THE
New-York Weekly JOURNAL.

Containing the freſheſt Advices, Foreign, and Domeſtick.

MUNDAY November 12, 1733.

Mr. *Zenger.*

INcert the following in your next, and you'll oblige your Friend,
CATO.

Mira temporum felicitas ubi ſentiri qua velis, & qua ſentias dicere licit.
Tacit.

THE Liberty of the Preſs is a Subject of the greateſt Importance, and in which every Individual is as much concern'd as he is in any other Part of Liberty: Therefore it will not be improper to communicate to the Publick the Sentiments of a late excellent Writer upon this Point, ſuch is the Elegance and Perſpicuity of his Writings, ſuch the inimitable Force of his Reaſoning, that it will be difficult to ſay any Thing new that he has not ſaid, or not to ſay that much worſe which he has ſaid.

There are two Sorts of Monarchies, an abſolute and a limited one. In the firſt, the Liberty of the Preſs can never be maintained, it is inconſiſtent with it; for what abſolute Monarch would ſuffer any Subject to animadvert on his Actions, when it is in his Power to declare the Crime, and to nominate the Puniſhment? This would make it very dangerous to exerciſe ſuch a Liberty. Beſides the Object againſt which thoſe Pens muſt be directed, is

their Sovereign, the ſole ſupream Magiſtrate; for there being no Law in thoſe Monarchies, but the Will of the Prince, it makes it neceſſary for his Miniſters to conſult his Pleaſure, before any Thing can be undertaken: He is therefore properly chargeable with the Grievances of his Subjects, and what the Miniſter there acts being in Obedience to the Prince, he ought not to incur the Hatred of the People; for it would be hard to impute that to him for a Crime, which is the Fruit of his Allegiance, and for refuſing which he might incur the Penalties of Treaſon. Beſides, in an abſolute Monarchy, the Will of the Prince being the Law, a Liberty of the Preſs to complain of Grievances would be complaining againſt the Law, and the Conſtitution, to which they have ſubmitted, or have been obliged to ſubmit; and therefore, in one Senſe, may be ſaid to deſerve Puniſhment. So that under an abſolute Monarchy, I ſay, ſuch a Liberty is inconſiſtent with the Conſtitution, having no proper Subject in Politics, on which it might be exercis'd, and if exercis'd would incur a certain Penalty.

But in a limited Monarchy, as *England* is, our Laws are known, fixed, and eſtabliſhed. They are the ſtreight Rule and ſure Guide to direct the King, the Miniſters, and other his Subjects: And therefore an Offence againſt the Laws is ſuch an Offence againſt the Conſtitution as ought to receive a proper adequate Puniſhment; the ſevera. Conſtil.

The New York Weekly Journal *printed John Zenger's "libelous remarks," which were later deemed to be nothing but the truth. Zenger's trial helped to establish the principle of freedom of the press for all Americans. (Courtesy: German Information Center)* nic foods. By 1850 the town had lost all evidence of its German origin — save for the popularity of German sausages and special Christmas sweets. In thousands of towns all over America, this scenario would repeat itself over and over again until the only remnants of the German ancestry of many Americans could be found in a predilection for sauerkraut and wursts.

Westward Ho! Without the Conestoga wagon the West might not have been tamed, and without the chuck wagon many a cowboy would have been left howling at the moon for a square meal out on the range. Both wagons owe their existence to German settlers in America. The Conestoga was first manufactured by German immigrants to Pennsylvania, erroneously known as Pennsylvania Dutch. They designed these covered wagons with bowed bottoms to make the cargo sag toward the center and keep it from shifting during transit over rough terrain.

The chuck wagon was invented by Charles Goodnight (1836–1929), a cattleman whose great-grandfather had emigrated from Germany to Virginia. The first brothers to make commercial chuck wagons were Germans, too — Henry and Clement Studebaker.

The Studebakers started manufacturing chuck wagons in 1852 with a total capital investment of $68. Their fledgling business was spurred on by the Civil War, and by 1895 they were the world's largest manufacturers of transportation, artillery and ambulance wagons — all powered by horses. Still in existence today as Studebaker-Worthington, the company manufactured horseless carriages between 1902 and 1966.

Washington Crossing the Rhine? A famous painting depicts George Washington and his troops preparing for a sneak attack on the Hessians at Trenton, New Jersey. The artist was Emmanuel Gottlieb Leutze (1816–1868), a German who settled in Philadelphia in 1859. Although the painting is bold and realistic in style, it contains some historical errors; the flag depicted in the painting was not adopted until the year following the attack, 1777, and the river Leutze used as a model was not the Delaware, but the Rhine.

The painting has also been criticized as an excellent example of how *not* to cross a river: passengers are standing up and leaning over the sides; the boat is overcrowded; and upended bayonets pose a threat to the soldiers in Washington's command.

Unknown Timber King Friedrich Weyerhaeuser (1834–1911), the "Timber King," built his multimillion-dollar empire so quietly that he was not even listed in *Who's Who* until three years before his death. When asked what were the reasons for his outstanding business success, Weyerhaeuser replied, "The secret lay simply in my will to work. I never watched the clock and never stopped before I had finished what I was working on."

Friedrich Weyerhaeuser (1834–1911). (Courtesy: German Information Center)

Costly Bridge John Augustus Roebling (1806–1869), a civil engineer and wire-cable manufacturer from Muhlhausen, Germany, built the Brooklyn Bridge at great personal expense. Hailed as the "Eighth Wonder of the World" when it opened in 1883, the bridge cost Roebling his life, and made an invalid of his son Washington (1837–1926). The father died while making land surveys for the bridge; the son suffered from caisson disease (the bends) contracted while inspecting the bridge foundations.

Crime Fighter Thomas Nast (1840–1902) drew this self-caricature in response to reader demand for a little humor to enliven a tabloid full of crime and disaster. Known as the "Father of American political cartoonists," the German-born Nast helped smash the Tweed Ring with his clever cartoons. Nast also established the donkey and elephant as symbols of the Democratic and Republican parties, and created the modern image of Santa Claus flying through the sky with his reindeer.

Born in Landau, Nast was brought to New York as a child by his father, a trumpeter in a military band. Nast fought corruption, exploitation and prejudice with his pen, prompting President Lincoln to remark, "our cause has no better campaigner than Thomas Nast—his allegorical drawings never failed to rouse deep enthusiasm and they always came when we needed them most."

Thomas Nast (1840–1902). (Courtesy: German Information Center)

The Other Side

Country: **WEST GERMANY**

Capital: Bonn
Official Name: Bundesrepublik Deutschland (Federal Republic of Germany)
Official Language: German
National Anthem: "Das Deutschlandlied" (Song of Germany)
National Flag: Adopted in 1950; the horizontal bands of black, red and gold represent the German confederation and the Weimar Republic.
Coat of Arms: Eagle
Major Religions: Lutheran, Roman Catholic

Country   **EAST GERMANY**

Capital: East Berlin
Official Name: Deutsche Demokratische Republik (German Democratic Republic)
Official Language: German
National Anthem: "Auferstanden aus Ruinen" (Arisen from Ruins)
National Flag: Black, red and gold horizontal stripes. After the Communist regime assumed control, the coat of arms was added in 1959 to differentiate the East and West German flags.
Coat of Arms: Represents a cross section of society: a wreath of grain for the peasants, a hammer for the workers, and a compass for the intellectuals.
Major Religions: Protestant, Roman Catholic

GERMAN IMMIGRATION TO THE UNITED STATES

	1821–1830	6,761	1901–1910	341,498
	1831–1840	152,454	1911–1920	143,945
	1841–1850	434,626	1921–1930	412,202
	1851–1860	951,667	1931–1940	114,058
	1861–1870	787,468	1941–1950	226,578
	1871–1880	718,182	1951–1960	477,765
(Peak Decade)	1881–1890	1,452,970	1961–1970	227,866
	1891–1900	505,152	1971–1975	93,506

Total (1820–1975):   6,954,160

1970 Census

Foreign-born Germans	832,965
Native-born, 2nd generation	2,789,070
Total Foreign-stock Population	3,622,035
Estimated German-American Population	25.5 to 33 million

Main Ethnic Epicenters*		U.S. Cities** with Most Germans	
New York	516,216	New York	344,752
California	360,656	Chicago	224,587
Illinois	312,070	Philadelphia	99,536
Wisconsin	234,767	Milwaukee	89,783
New Jersey	219,178	Detroit	88,947

*States with largest foreign-stock populations—i.e., foreign-born residents and their children
**Standard Metropolitan Statistical Areas

THE CANADIANS

The history of Canada parallels that of the United States, since it, too, is a land of "foreigners." Out of a total 1976 population of almost 23 million, there were only 117,105 Indians and 15,900 Eskimos living in Canada—all the rest were "immigrants," and almost 11% of the population has entered Canada as recently as the end of World War II.

Most Canadians are of British (44.6%) or French (28.7%) descent. Major ethnic groups represented in the last Canadian census (1971) were: Germans (1,317,200), Italians (730,820), Ukrainians (580,660) and Dutch (425,945). In addition, there were 118,815 Chinese, 37,260 Japanese and 34,445 Blacks.

Although more than 4 million Canadians have found their way to the United States since 1820, it is not known how many were native-born Canadians and how many were merely "foreigners" who paused to rest in Canada on their way to the United States because immigration restrictions were more lenient for our northern neighbors.

The peak decade for Canadian immigration to the United States was the 1920s, when over 920,000 new arrivals crossed the

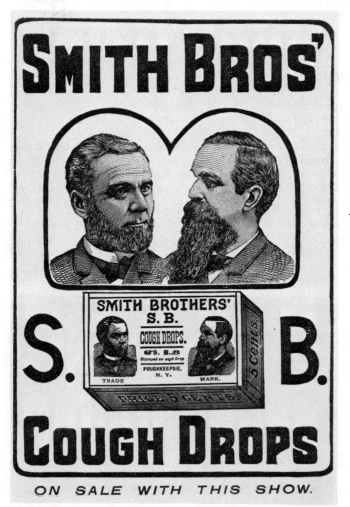

The Smith Brothers have been soothing America's sore throats for over 100 years. (Courtesy: New York Public Library)

border. Canadian immigration was still strong in the 1960s, when 413,000 new immigrants made their way to the states, but in recent years the flow has declined.

Some Canadians live and work in the United States most of their adult lives, but maintain close ties to their homeland by continually traveling back and forth across the border. So many of our Canadian-born hockey players, celebrities, and singers live here full-time that it is hard to remember that they aren't technically "Americans" since they haven't applied for citizenship.

The Canadians have *given* us economists (John Kenneth Galbraith), educators (John Coleman, President of Haverford College in 1974, who made news by working as a blue-collar laborer for two months), television producers (Reuven Frank, former president of NBC), and *lent* us sportsmen (Bobby Orr, hockey; Ferguson Jenkins, baseball; Ron Turcotte, jockey), musicians (Hank Snow, Joni Mitchell, Neil Young and Paul Anka) and entertainers (David Steinberg, Donald Sutherland, Ruby Keeler and Genevieve Bujold).

Canadians also contributed much to the American way of life – we recognize ice hockey as a Canadian invention, but what about basketball? It would be difficult to face a winter cold without the Smith Brothers to soothe our aching throats; and can you imagine detective movies without lie detectors to ferret out the truth? How could Americans face Sunday brunch without Canadian-style back bacon? Who in our culture is more "American" than Superman? Yet he, too, was an import, so to speak – the brainchild of a Toronto-born cartoonist, Joe Shuster.

"Firsts" and Facts About the Canadian Experience in America

Cajuns   The Cajuns trace their ancestry back hundreds of years to Nova Scotia and New Brunswick, where French Catholic settlers first established outposts in the New World. In 1775, they were run out of Canada by the English after the Britons obtained the Maritime Provinces from France. Drawn to southwestern Louisiana and its French cultural heritage, the Acadians settled in towns such as Lafayette, St. Martinville, and New Iberia, where they flourished and incorporated some Southern ways into their culture. Unlike many other Americans, the Cajuns (the name is a corrupted form of "Acadians") remained rather isolated and did not assimilate completely into the mainstream of American life.

One of America's most prominent athletes of Acadian ancestry is Ron Guidry, the "Ragin' Cajun" and star pitcher of the New York Yankees who led his team to a World Series victory in 1978.

Mother Lode   The richest silver vein in the world was the Comstock Lode, first discovered in 1856 by Ethan and Hosea Grosh. The unfortunate brothers died before they could record their claim, and it wasn't until 1859 that the mine was claimed by Canadian-born prospector Henry Tompkins Paige Comstock (1820–1870).

When "Old Pancake," as Comstock was known, filed his claim, he turned Virginia City, Nevada, into one of the Old West's most famous boom towns. Money flowed like water, and many fortunes were made – it has been estimated that one vein alone produced over $200 million worth of gold and silver ore. The only person who didn't profit from the Comstock Lode was Comstock himself, who sold it for a song.

Door to Door   The founder of the Fuller Brush Company, Alfred C. Fuller (1885–1973), was an immigrant from Nova Scotia who settled in the U.S. in 1903. He only had $375 in his pocket when he crossed the border, but two years later he was on his way to becoming a "household word" when he started manufacturing his famous brushes in the basement of his sister's home and selling them door-to-door for two bits apiece.

Sister Aimee   Aimee Semple McPherson (1890–1944), the Canadian-born preacher and onetime paramour of Milton Berle, came to the U.S. in 1917 with little more than a leaky tent and a reputation as a faith healer. Twelve years later 80 branches of her International Church of the Foursquare Gospel were flourishing in America. At the time of her death, there were more than 400 Foursquare churches scattered throughout North America.

Born Aimee Elizabeth Kennedy, she worked for the Salvation Army until the age of seventeen, when she was converted at a Pentecostal revival meeting. Her religious zeal was so intense that she even married the evangelist who converted her, Robert James Semple, and when he died of typhoid fever she took over his pulpit. Aimee ended her life by an overdose of sedatives, and her son continued her religious work. Today, there are more than 89,000 members of her church in the United States and Canada.

Canadian Truth Seeker One of the first polygraphs, or "lie detectors" used to catch fibbers was invented by John Augustus Larson (1892–1965), a Canadian-American psychiatrist.

Larson graduated from Boston University in 1914 and devised his first polygraph in 1921, a year after receiving his doctorate from the University of California. Through his studies, he observed that lying involves a conscious "effort" that truth-telling does not; the fear of being caught causes an involuntary flow of adrenalin to surge through the subject's body, resulting in slight physiological changes. Larson's machine, therefore, measured pulse rate, breathing rate, blood pressure and perspira-tion—all of which are increased when one tells a "little white lie."

The polygraph is not infallible, but it has proven useful in some instances, even though test results are not permitted in court as legal evidence.

No Quota for Canadians 187,000 immigrants came to Canada between 1861 and 1871, while during that same period almost 154,000 Canadians entered the United States. During the 1870s 353,000 newcomers found their way to Canada, and 383,000 Canadians crossed the border seeking new lives in America. When the Johnson-Reed Act of 1924 went into effect, total immigration to the United States from outside the Americas was limited to 150,000. No limits, however, were placed on the number of Canadians or of Central and South Americans permitted to enter each year, and a steady stream of the world's poor made their way to Canada in an attempt to enter the United States. Since the end of World War II, however, more and more immigrants have elected to stay in Canada. In 1975, Canada was still among the top ten sources of newcomers to the United States, although the numbers were declining. In that year, 11,215 immigrants crossed the border— less than half the number of Canadians (22,709) who emigrated to the United States in 1971.

The Other Side

Country:	CANADA
Capital:	Ottawa
Official Languages:	English and French
National Anthem:	"O Canada"
	(Finally adopted in 1980 after years of debate, "O Canada" remains controversial. French-speaking and English-speaking legislators have yet to agree on the lyrics of the anthem.)
National Symbol:	The maple leaf
National Motto:	Mari Usque ad Mare (From Sea to Sea)
National Flag:	Red maple leaf on white ground, between two vertical red borders. Dates to 1965, when the Red Ensign (which included the British Union Jack) was dropped to reduce French-English tensions in Canada.
National Holiday:	July 1, Dominion Day
Major Religions:	Roman Catholic, United Church of Canada, Anglican Church of Canada, Presbyterian

CANADIAN IMMIGRATION TO THE UNITED STATES
1821-1960

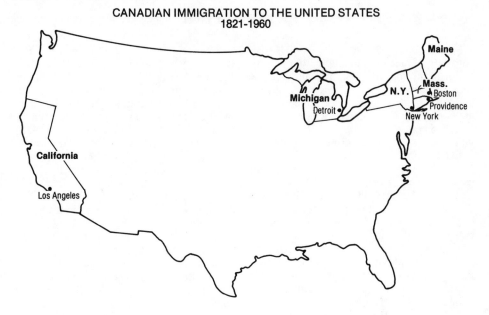

1821–1830	2,277	1901–1910	179,226	
1831–1840	13,624	1911–1920	742,185	
1841–1850	44,723	1921–1930	924,515	(Peak Decade)
1851–1860	59,309	1931–1940	108,527	
1861–1870	153,878	1941–1950	171,718	
1871–1880	383,640	1951–1960	377,952	
1881–1890	393,304	1961–1970	159,665	
1891–1900	3,311	1971–1975	79,621	
		Total (1820–1975):	4,048,329	

1970 Census

Foreign-born Canadians	812,421
Native-born, 2nd generation	2,222,135
Total Foreign-stock Population	3,034,556

*Main Ethnic Epicenters**		*U.S. Cities** with Most Canadians*	
Massachusetts	466,942	Detroit	220,983
California	439,862	Boston	215,409
Michigan	353,154	Los Angeles	174,729
New York	286,047	New York	92,473
Maine	136,801	Providence (R.I.)	73,066

*States with largest foreign-stock population—i.e., foreign-born residents and their children
**Standard Metropolitan Statistical Areas

THE BRITISH

Samuel Johnson once called the British colonists a "race of convicts [who] ought to be thankful for anything we allow them short of hanging." His statement was insulting, but, alas, somewhat true, since almost 40% of the Englishmen who came to America between 1607 and 1776 were convicted drunks, debtors or runaway servants.

In addition to our language, our legal system and many of our customs, the British gave America "blue laws," puritanical outlooks on life; the pillory, the stocks and dunking stools; and the right to be tried by a jury of our peers. But Americans never believed in "blind obedience" and, being rebellious by nature, we chose to drive on the opposite side of the road, refused to use the metric or Celsius scales, and took the music to their national anthem for "America," but changed the words.

Dressed in their best kilts, these Scottish brothers made a fetching picture on Ellis Island as they awaited admittance to the United States. (Courtesy: American Museum of Immigration)

Some of our states are named after British royalty and nobility (Delaware for Lord De La Warr; Virginia for the "Virgin Queen," Elizabeth; and New York for the Duke of York), but there are also thousands of cities, towns and streets that were named after "commoners" (Garfield, Ohio; Madison, Wisconsin), while other towns and places in America took their names from places in England—for example, Plymouth, Salem and New London.

The British chapter of American history did not end with the Revolutionary War—the British kept coming by land, by sea and eventually by air. Between 1820 and 1975 almost 5 million Britons came to America seeking fame, fortune and adventure. But, despite the large numbers, their ranks were not large enough to maintain the overwhelming lead they once enjoyed as our major ethnic group. When the first U.S. Census was conducted in 1790, the majority (77.7%) of the 2.75 million people living in America were of British birth or ancestry. By 1972, British-Americans were only 14% of the population as non-English-speaking immigrants "out-demographed" them in births and arrivals.

If you think the British-Americans are the most affluent group in America today, you're in for a surprise—they have been outdone by the Russians, who earn more and are better educated than any other ethnic group in America.

But don't feel sorry for the British: they are still one of our most prominent ethnic groups, with more than their share of rich men and immigrant success stories. British corporate heads, industrialists and innovators include Welshmen (William George Fargo of Wells Fargo Express, Benjamin Duke of Tobacco fame and banker J. Pierpont Morgan), Scotsmen (Alexander Graham Bell, Thomas Edison and Cyrus McCormick), and Englishmen (the Wright Brothers, John Underwood of typewriter fame and Marshall Field of merchandising, publishing and manufacturing). The English also gave us the Mayo Brothers and their clinics, Walt Whitman, Emily Dickinson, Edgar Allan Poe, Barbara Walters and many of our politicians, presidents, and statesmen.

"Firsts" and Facts About the British Experience in America

Eight-Day-Old Wonder The Youngest person of historical note has to be Virginia Dare, the first English child born in North America. Her parents, Ananias and Ellinor Dare, were members of Sir Walter Raleigh's short-lived colony at Roanoke Island, North Carolina.

Corporate Profit Makers Hungry to match the huge profits the Spanish and French had reaped from their colonies in the New World, a group of wealthy London merchants organized a stock-holding company which proposed to settle a colony in America for the purpose of producing goods for export to Europe. The London Company's charter was approved by King James I in 1606, and they quickly set about to find a group of unfortunate, poverty-stricken or religiously persecuted souls willing to risk the perilous voyage to the New World.

The Puritans, who had fled from England to Holland to escape persecution for their religious beliefs, were the answer to the London Company's dreams. Eventually 120 of them agreed to sail for America in 1606. Of these, only 104 survived the voyage; another 60 perished during the winter of 1607.

Later on, the London Company found the huge profits they were seeking in tobacco, and by 1620 they were offering "virgin English women" to colonists in exchange for 100 or 200 pounds of tobacco.

Never on Sunday Restrictive "blue laws" which prohibit certain activities on Sunday are still in effect in many states today, thanks to the Puritans. Luckily, local legislatures have eased up a bit since the New Haven Colony first printed the original laws in 1638 (bound with *blue* paper, hence the name), otherwise we wouldn't be able to shave, joy ride, kiss babies, hear organ music, cross rivers, read common prayers, make mince pies, dance, play cards, or play "on any instrument of music, except the drum, trumpet and jewsharp."

Some of the original laws stated that "no woman shall kiss her child on the Sabbath or fasting day . . . [and] no one shall travel, cook victuals, make beds, sweep house, cut hair or shave on the Sabbath day." Why, the Puritans even chained children's swings together on Sunday, and to ensure that all married persons lived together, the penalty for living apart was a prison term.

Famous Family One of the most creative families in America has to be the Wyeths. Descended from Nicholas Wyeth, an Englishman from Suffolk who emigrated to New England about 1640, there is an artistic branch of the family as well as a scientific one. The latter founded the great American drug company Wyeth Laboratories, while another branch contributed three generations of famous American artists—N. C. Wyeth, Andrew Wyeth, and his son, Jamie. N.C.'s great-great-grandfather, Noah Wyeth, became the most notorious member of the family by taking an active part at the great Boston Tea Party in 1773.

Poor Heating Makes Strange Bedfellows The Puritans put up a good front and pretended to be "holier than thou," but they couldn't have been completely heartless when it came to romance—after all, they did bring the custom of "bundling" with them to the New World. Back in the seventeenth and eighteenth centuries, not much was known about insulation or "R" values, and heating systems were rather inefficient. Besides, firewood was too precious to squander on roaring fires after dinner, so the only way to keep warm after the sun went down on a cold winter's night was by getting under a pile of blankets. If strangers stopped by or if a young man came to "court" his girl friend, it was perfectly permissible to hop into bed—fully clothed, of course!

Since the whole family slept in one room, many pairs of watchful eyes kept tabs on young couples. To be doubly safe, cautious families inserted special "bundling" boards between the pair to reduce the possibility of any hanky-panky. Despite their best efforts, Washington Irving noted in his *History of New York,* "Wherever the practice of bundling prevailed, there was an amazing number of sturdy brats born . . . [without] benefit of clergy . . ."

The practice began to disappear about 1785 when heating improved and reformers began to lobby for an end to the custom.

Sail Away The first floating theater in America was built by a British immigrant actor, William Chapman, in 1831. Chapman and his family floated from town to town along the Mississippi, stopping to perform for culture-starved Americans in the first half of the nineteenth century.

The Tune Is Familiar On July 4, 1831, a Baptist minister, Dr. S. F. Smith, introduced the song "America" to his congregation at the Park Street Church in Boston. He had composed the words himself, but he took the tune from an old German songbook, since he wasn't musically talented. Ironically, Smith lifted the same tune that the British had appropriated from the Germans for their national anthem, "God Save the King!"

Brand-name Sewing Thread Coats and Clark's thread mills are named after two families from Paisley, Scotland. George and William Clark established their mill in Newark, New Jersey, in 1860; it was later merged with the Coats family mill in Pawtucket, Rhode Island.

America's Favorite Mail Men The men behind all those Pitney Bowes postage meters and mailing machines were Arthur Hill Pitney (1871–1933), born in Quincy, Illinois, and Walter Harold Bowes (1882–1957), an English immigrant from Bradford, Yorkshire, who came to the United States seeking his fortune in 1893.

Mixed Ancestry Part of the reason for the decline in the percentage of British-Americans in the United States over the years is due to the great American habit of marrying outside one's own ethnic group. (Census officials list all persons of mixed ancestry under the category "Other.") One of Benjamin Franklin's modern-day descendants is Yukiko Irwin, a resident of New York City whose grandfather, a trader from Philadelphia, was the first American permitted to marry a native woman in Japan, in 1866.

When I emigrated to the United States, my English friends thought I was nuts. Why jettison a burgeoning career and start again in a country where I did not know a solitary soul? It wasn't as if I were a starving Sicilian or a refugee from Hitler's Germany. I had drawn a first-class ticket in the lottery of life, and here I was, embarking in steerage. "Why? Partly because I wanted adventure. Partly because I figured that the same effort would produce three times as much lucre in America as in little England. . . . And partly because my imagination had been fired by books I had read, starting with *Huckleberry Finn,* going on with Willa Cather, Edith Wharton, and Sinclair Lewis, and culminating in *John Brown's Body,* Stephen Vincent Benét's narrative poem about the Civil War.

DAVID OGILVY
Blood, Brains, and Beer
1978

The Other Side

Country:	GREAT BRITAIN

Capital:	London
Official Name:	United Kingdom of Great Britain and Northern Ireland
Official Language:	English
National Anthem:	"God Save the Queen" ("God Save the King," when one rules)
National Flag:	British Union Flag or Union Jack, adopted in 1801.
Regional Flags:	England, Scotland and Wales have their own unofficial flags: England's is St. George's Cross, used for more than seven hundred years — a red cross on a white field; the Welsh flag depicts a red dragon on a green and white field (the dragon has been a symbol of Wales for more than two thousand years); and Scotland flies St. Andrew's Cross — white on a blue field.
Major Religions:	Church of England, Church of Scotland, Presbyterian, Roman Catholic, and Methodist.

BRITISH IMMIGRATION TO THE UNITED STATES

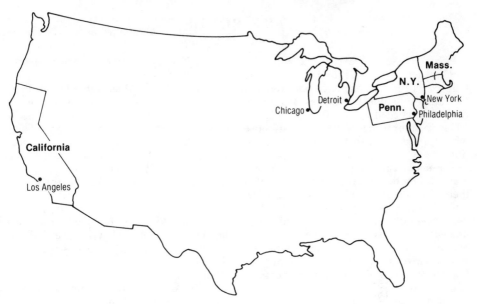

	1821–1830	25,079	1901–1910	525,950
	1831–1840	75,810	1911–1920	341,408
	1841–1850	267,044	1921–1930	330,213
	1851–1860	523,974	1931–1940	29,378
	1861–1870	606,696	1941–1950	131,592
	1871–1880	548,043	1951–1960	195,498
(Peak Decade)	1881–1890	807,357	1961–1970	210,028
	1891–1900	271,538	1971–1975	59,588

Total (1820–1975):   4,851,806

(England: 3,136,572;   Scotland: 817,018;   Wales: 94,709;   Unspecified: 803,507)

1970 Census

Foreign-born British	686,099
Native-born, 2nd generation	1,778,951
Total Foreign-stock Population	2,465,050
Estimated British-American Population	30 million

*Main Ethnic Epicenters**		*U.S. Cities*** with Most British*	
California	373,495	New York City	207,524
New York	334,424	Los Angeles	142,705
Pennsylvania	198,190	Philadelphia	104,139
New Jersey	172,308	Detroit	95,059
Massachusetts	152,741	Chicago	81,354

*States with largest foreign-stock populations—i.e., foreign-born residents and their children
**Standard Metropolitan Statistical Areas

THE POLES

Poland ceased to exist as a nation in 1795, when Austria, Prussia and Russia finished partitioning the once-powerful Polish Empire among themselves. Naturally, the Poles rebelled against foreign rule, but when their uprisings were crushed those who were able began fleeing to other nations.

The upper classes were the first to emigrate, and by the time the Civil War erupted there were almost 30,000 Poles living in the United States. The peasants began their mass migrations about 1870, and although immigration statistics are not accurate, it has been estimated that some 2.5 million Polish citizens found their way to the United States by the turn of the century. Listed variously as Austrians, Russians, Germans, Slavics, Slovaks—and even, occasionally, Poles—by immigration officials, the 1910 census registered almost 1,700,000 foreign-stock Poles living in America.

Poland did manage to reappear on the map of Europe in 1918, but decades of separation made it impossible for the Polish people to present a unified front, and their nation once again vanished between 1939 and 1945. The ravages of World War II brought many new Polish immigrants to the United States, under the Displaced Persons Act, which opened our doors to the survivors of Nazi concentration camps and Soviet labor camps.

Hardworking and used to a life of deprivation, the Poles struggled to attain the "American dream." They became politicians, athletes, actors, artists and businessmen. Their best scientific minds developed vitamins, theories of general semantics, and lunar land-roving vehicles. The Poles even introduced the painted toenail to the women of America.

The Poles gave their names to America, too: Sandusky, Ohio, is named for a Polish immigrant, Jacob Sadowski—the first European to descend the Mississippi River; there is a Poland, New York; at least thirty landmarks and cities are named Pulaski; and Warsaws galore are found in New York, Illinois, Indiana, Kentucky, Missouri, North Carolina, Ohio and Virginia.

The Poles gave America plenty of good things to eat, too. For breakfast, the Polish immigrants brought us rolls with holes (bagels), bialys (fancy rolls from Bialystoker, Poland), and babka coffeecake. For lunch, they gave us potato knishes, brand-name frozen fish sticks, and Coney Island's most illustrious hot dogs.

The Poles filled our days and nights with music and brought us the polonaise and the mazurka—but, contrary to popular belief, they didn't invent the polka.

"Firsts" and Facts About the Polish Experience in America

Polish Workers   In 1609, the first Polish settlers to the United States arrived on board the ship *Mary and Margaret*. They were pitchmakers, glassblowers and soap makers specially recruited for the Jamestown colony to supply the settlement with products for export. The Jamestown colony had to import Polish laborers because the original settlement only has 12 working men out of the 92 "gentlemen" who settled in Virginia in 1608.

The Poles have come a long way occupationally since then. According to a 1972 survey on the employment status of six different ethnic groups, only 4.3 per cent of all Polish workers were employed as laborers.

He Did It for Love   Tadeusz Kosciuszko helped the Americans defeat the British at Saratoga in 1777 with his brilliant military plans. He was commissioned as a colonel in the Continental Army, and must have served his "second country," as he called

America, for sheer love. It certainly couldn't have been for the money—he was paid only $60 a month, and never collected a cent until twenty-one years after his enlistment.

In recognition of his services, he was also granted 500 acres of land near Columbus, Ohio. When Kosciuszko died, his will dictated that the land be sold and the proceeds used to establish a school to educate slaves.

O Promise Me The Polish immigrants who came to America did not always find the "Promised Land" quite to their liking. When an entire village from Polish Silesia, led by Father Leopold Moczygemba, arrived in the Texas wilderness in 1854, the dry, parched land which abounded only with rattlesnakes and brush was so disappointing that some of the eight hundred newcomers wanted to hang Father Moczygemba from the nearest tree. Fortunately for the priest, the nearest tree was several miles away and he managed to escape unharmed.

This portrait of Thaddeus Kosciuszko was painted by Clayton Braun. (Courtesy: New York Historical Society)

The villagers eventually resigned themselves to a life in this desolate countryside and established the town of Panna Maria. Other Polish settlements in Texas followed. including: Czestochowa, Kosciuszko and Polonia.

Pulaski Day Parade In 1946, President Truman decreed that henceforth the memory of the Polish Revolutionary War hero, General Casimir Pulaski, would be honored on October 11. Polish New Yorkers, however, didn't need a presidential decree to celebrate Pulaski's memory, since they had been marching in annual parades ever since 1937.

Each year since then, some 100,000 Polish-Americans march from 26th Street to 52nd Street with an array of floats, bands, folk dancers, and buttons that say "Kiss me, I'm Polish."

Ethnic Pride When the late 1960s ushered in a dawn of ethnic pride in America, the Polish-American Congress initiated a major fund-raising drive to protect the Polish people from continued slander. Perhaps it was planned to combat the glut of "Polish jokes" that had suddenly blossomed around the nation, but, as it turned out, the drive was something of a joke itself. Its original goal was $500,000, but a year later only $5,000 in contributions had been raised.

Better success was achieved by "Project Pole," a well-publicized and privately financed campaign designed to educate the general public about the contributions Polish men and women, such as Copernicus and Mme. Curie, had made to the world. Launched in 1971 by businessman Edward Piszek to enhance the image of Polish-Americans, the campaign featured full-page ads in national magazines extolling the role of the Pole in history. That same year a chair in Polish language and literature was endowed at Harvard, sponsored by the Jurzykowski foundation of New York.

Mighty Atom That's what they called Joseph L. Greenstein (1892?–1977), a five-foot, four-and-a-half inch vaudevillian who weighed in at 145 pounds. Despite his small stature, Greenstein could pull a 32-ton truck, bite iron chains in half and crush steel bars over his body.

Born in Suvalk, Poland, the "atom" ran away from home at the age of fifteen and traveled with a Russian wrestler who helped him train for his Herculean feats. He emigrated to the United States in 1911, and attained national fame via "Ripley's Believe It or Not" columns. In 1976, the *Guinness Book of World Records* noted that he possessed the "world's strongest bote."

*After bagels leave the proofing ovens they are boiled and then sent to the baking ovens.
(Courtesy: Lender's Bagel Bakery, Inc.)*

Bagel? What's a Bagel? Until recently, unless you lived in the East, you probably never heard of a bagel—those round rolls that look like doughnuts and chew like three-day-old bubble gum (when they're made properly). In 1960 there were only 40 bagel bakeries in the United States, and 30 of them were in New York. But the "roll with a hole" caught the national fancy, and by 1977 there were 360 bakeries coast to coast.

The "hole" truth about bagels: Boiling makes the bagel chewy, and baking makes the crust crunchy, so a bagel is always boiled first before being sent to the oven. According to legend, the bagel was invented in 1683 by a grateful Viennese coffeehouse owner, who shaped the role to resemble the king's stirrup (*buegel*), in recognition of King John Sobiesky's role in driving off hordes of Turkish invaders.

The "buegel" changed shape slowly over the years until it became a ring, and soon Polish, German and Austrian bakers were making "bagels."

The bagel came to America and flourished in Jewish neighborhoods, but it was Harry Lender, a Jewish immigrant from Lublin, Poland, who introduced bagels to the general American populace. Lender came to America in 1927 and opened what proved to be a very successful bagel bakery at New Haven, Connecticut. In 1963, Lender launched a line of frozen bagels — so that Americans of every ethnic variety could enjoy the rolls that began as a tribute to a Polish king.

Polish Butchers Have the Biggest Kielbasa When Phil Nowicki of Rogers City, Michigan, had his sausage measured on September 7, 1977, he had to be the proudest Polish-American butcher alive. His kielbasa measured 8,773 feet and weighed more than 1.5 tons. That was over a mile and a half of garlic-laden sausage and it beat the existing *Guinness Book of World Records* figure by 1,353 feet.

Once Nowicki's sausage had been devoured, the next largest kielbasa in existence was a 25-footer from the Chicopee Provision Company. Weighing in at a hefty 107 pounds, the kielbasa was stolen while on display at the annual Chicopee, Massachusetts, World Kielbasa Festival, but company manager Leon Partyka refused to offer a ransom for its return. He did volunteer, however, to donate a loaf of rye bread and some horseradish to go with the sausage if the thief ever stepped forward.

When people tell you that in America the gold lies in the streets, don't you believe it! Here everybody has to work . . . This is no Golden Land, but it is a new land; here you break your back for 12 hours a day . . . In America, you will spill more sweat in one day than in a week back home . . . But I will not go back if someone was to give me the master's estate . . . Once you have tasted America, there is no way to go back to those old miseries.

> Polish immigrant, 1870s
> from: *My Name is Million,*

The Other Side

Country:	**POLAND**
Capital:	Warsaw

According to legend, Warsaw was named after two poor fishermen, Wars and Sawa, who were favored by the sirens of the Vistula River. The two fishermen helped a lost prince, sent to them by the sirens, and in gratitude the monarch rewarded their assistance with a large tract of land known today as Warsaw.

Official Name:	Polska Rzeczypospolita Ludow (Polish People's Republic)
Official Language:	Polish
National Anthem:	Jeszcze Polska nie Zginea (Poland has not yet perished)
National Flag:	Horizontal bands of white over red. Dates to 1919, when Poland became an independent republic, after it had been totally absorbed by Austria, Prussia and Russia in 1795.
National Poem of Poland:	Pan Tadeusz
Major Religions:	Roman Catholic, Autocephalous Polish Orthodox, Lutheran or Evangelical Augsburg Church
National Holiday:	July 22

POLISH IMMIGRATION TO THE UNITED STATES

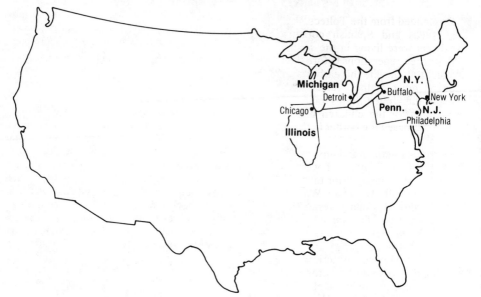

1821–1830	16	1901–1910*		
1831–1840	369	1911–1920*	4,813	
1841–1850	105	1921–1930	227,734	(Peak Decade)
1851–1860	1,164	1931–1940	17.026	
1861–1870	2,027	1941–1950	7,571	
1871–1880	12,970	1951–1960	9.985	
1881–1890	51,806	1961–1970	53,539	
1891–1900	96,720	1971–1975	16,808	
		Total (1820–1975):	502,659	

1970 Census

Foreign-born Poles	548,107
Native-born, 2nd generation	1,826,137
Total Foreign-stock Population	2,374,244
Estimated Polish-American Population	Estimates range from 5,150,000 to 12 million.

*Main Ethnic Epicenters***		*U.S. Cities*** with Most Poles*	
New York	557,478	New York	385,631
Illinois	299,316	Chicago	284,289
Pennsylvania	243,752	Detroit	159,643
New Jersey	217,509	Philadelphia	87,813
Michigan	214,085	Buffalo	74,801

*The Polish Government estimates that 2,122,504 Poles emigrated to the United States prior to World Ear I. Most were listed as citizens of other nations.
**States with largest foreign-stock populations—i.e., foreign-born residents and their children
***Standard Metropolitan Statistical Areas

THE MEXICANS

Descended from the Toltecs, the Aztecs, the Mayas and Spanish conquistadores, Mexicans were living in the southwest for almost three generations before the Pilgrims arrived. But, despite this early start in "our" country, most of the Mexican-Americans living in the United States today are recent immigrants, or the children of immigrants who first crossed the border in the twentieth century.

Like the American Indians, the Mexicans made the fatal mistake of welcoming the Anglos to their land. Prior to the outbreak of the Mexican-American War, Don Pio Pico, the last Mexican governor of California, wrote: "We find ourselves suddenly threated by hordes of Yankee emigrants . . . whose progress we cannot arrest."

When the Mexican-American war ended in 1848, the southwest territory was ceded to the American government according to the treaty of Guadalupe-Hidalgo and the Mexicans found themselves second-class citizens in a foreign land that had once belonged to them. Losing legal control wasn't the worst part—rich Mexicans soon found themselves losing their land as well through technicalities in the Anglos' laws. The *ricos* could not comprehend the need to pay property taxes on land that had been held by their families for centuries, and they often failed to file title claims or were cheated outright by unscrupulous deed keepers who either stole or failed to record their property titles.

The Mexican Revolution (1910–1920) brought thousands of Mexicans north of the border. By 1920 half of the migratory labor force of the Imperial Valley was Mexican; by 1930, there were 250,000 Mexicans living in California, and today the Mexican-American population is approaching 7.5 million. They are our youngest, fastest-growing minority, with an average age ten years younger than that of most other ethnic groups.

Besides giving us their land, the Mexicans contributed much to the culture of America. They showed gold-hungry Californians how to pan for gold, and introduced the technique of using mercury to separate silver from worthless ores. They gave us poinsettias, the Mexican hat dance. Mexican jumping beans, the Mexican hairless (chihuahua), and tacos, tortillas and the fiery hot food that people in the Southwest love to eat.

Like other ethnic Americans, the Mexicans have managed to distinguish themselves as actors (Anthony Quinn, Gilbert Roland), musicians (Trini Lopez, Joan Baez), dancers, choreographers (José Limón), judges (Harold Medina), politicians (Joseph Montoya) and sportsmen (Lee Trevino, Jim Plunkett, Joe Kapp). They've joined the ranks of successful businessmen and millionaires, too, despite the stereotyped image of a race of lazy banditos and revolutionaries that television commercials and the press have only recently put to rest.

Mexicans emigrating to the United States in the early 1900s. (Credit: Culver Pictures)

"Firsts" and Facts About the Mexican Experience in America

What's In a Name? Once considered a derogatory term, "Chicano" attained a new respectability in the late 1960s and is now used with pride by many young Mexican-Americans, although the older generation often prefers "Mexicano." Chicano comes from the Aztec pronunciation of "Mexicano" (*meshicano*) which was corrupted to "Xicano" (*shicano*) and finally to "Chicano."

Others prefer the term "Hispano"— especially if they are descended from colonial Spaniards and do not have Indian ancestry. The term "Mestizo" is used for Mexicans of mixed Indian and European background. But no matter what their individual heritage, all Mexican leaders are working to promote *la raza* (the race)—a feeling of fraternity and community spirit that binds together all people of Mexican descent.

Mexican Jumping Beans Known as "leapers" in Mexico, these bronco beans often make quick movements because of a moth larva living inside. When *Laspeyresia saltitans* moves inside his bean "house," the bean "jumps" up and down.

No Phony Mexican Anthony Quinn (1910–   ) was born during the Mexican revolution in Chihuahua to a Mexican mother and an Irish father. No one was keeping accurate records at the time, and for years Quinn was looked down upon by his Mexican brethren as a "pocho" (a derogatory term for a "gringoized" Mexican). But in 1961 Quinn determined to stop the Mexican tongues from wagging once and for all: "When I made a picture down in Durango, the people accused me of being born in America—and called me a phony Mexican." When the governor of Chihuahua visited the set, Quinn asked him for a birth certificate. After talking to witnesses who remembered Quinn's family and the circumstances of his birth, the governor complied with the actor's request.

Crossing the Barriers Mexican-born actor Ricardo Montalban has played plenty of Latin lovers in his career, but he's also been a Kabuki actor in *Sayonara*, a Frenchman in the musical comedy *Seventh Heaven*, a Jamaican in the Broadway musical *Jamaica*, and an Indian on the 1978 television series *How the West Was Won*.

Poinsettia Known as the Mexican flame leaf in England, this red-leafed plant has become synonymous with the Christmas season ever since Joel Robert Poinsett (1779–1851), the American minister to Mexico, sent the first specimens to friends in the United States way back in the early 1800s.

Mexican Name Shortener Vicki Carr shortened her name from Florencia Bisenta de Castillas Martinez Cardona Moss. Born in El Paso, Texas, Vicki started her career in high school, singing with Pepe Callahan's Mexican-Irish band.

Political Firsts The first Chicano elected to the U.S. Senate was Joseph Montoya in 1964. Montoya was also the youngest person ever seated in the New Mexico state legislature when he was elected to that state's House of Representatives in 1936.

The first Mexican-American elected to the U.S. Congress was Henry B. Gonzales of Texas. First elected to public office in 1953, he became a member of the San Antonio city council, and in 1956 he was elected to the state senate. His election was a first in the 110-year history of the Texas government.

The first Chicano elected as Governor of Arizona was Raul Castro. The Mexican-born Castro was elected in 1974.

The Bane of Banuelos Ramona Acosta Banuelos (1925–   ), a successful California businesswomen, was nominated as Treasurer of the United States by Richard Nixon on September 30, 1971. She had started her business career (Ramona's Mexican Food Products) with a $400 tortilla stand, and mushroomed it into a $5-million enterprise. A few days after her nomination, however, the food packaging plant she owned in south Los Angeles was raided by immigration officials who netted 36 illegal aliens working on the premises. Despite the controversy, Banuelos was confirmed and went on to become the highest-ranking Mexican-American in government office, serving as Treasurer from 1971 to 1974.

Television First The first Mexican-American to portray a Mexican-American in the title role of a television series was Gabriel Melgar. Melgar replaced Freddie Prinze in *Chico and the Man* with Jack Albertson, during the fall 1977 television season.

Discovered at the age of twelve on Olivera Street in Los Angeles' Mexican-American community, Melgar has been performing with his family's music group since the age of four. Although he had never acted before, he was a natural for the part of a Mexican immigrant, since he himself had emigrated to California with his parents at the age of fifteen days.

Publishing First The first Mexican-American prison guard to write a book about her work experience was Janey Jimenez, the U.S. marshall who guarded Patty Hearst for over 350 hours over a two-year period. Her book, entitled *My Prisoner*, was published in 1977.

From Migrant to Management The first American of "Latin origin" to enter a Presidential primary in the United States was fifty-three-year-old Benjamin Fernandez, the son of Mexican immigrants.

Fernandez, a millionaire management consultant, threw his hat into the ring on November 29, 1978, for the Republican nomination in 1980. His parents had emigrated from the pueblo of Tanganzicuaro in the State of Michoacan, and for many years his family lived in a railway car (where he was born) at the Kansas City rail yards because they were too poor to afford any other housing.

Fernandez began picking sugar beets at the age of five to aid his parents, but his migrant-farming days ended when he graduated with a bachelor's degree in economics from the University of Redlands in California; he later earned an MBA from New York University in 1952.

Illegal Aliens A Texas police officer commented on the "wetback" situation by stating, "the only way we're going to stop them is to build a Berlin Wall." Even that might not help, because there are over 9 million unemployed people in Mexico, and they keep coming north seeking work no matter how low the wages or how terrible the conditions. Some Mexicans have been apprehended twenty times, and one man was arrested five times in a single day. Estimates of the illegal alien population are between 3 to 5 million in the United States.

Why do they come? According to one illegal alien who used to earn only $500 in a good year as a tenant farmer in Jalisco, "Coming to the U.S. was a question of economics." Here he can earn $160 a week with overtime as a metals factory worker in Los Angeles and he has managed to save over $2,000 in the past six years. "I love Mexico. It is very beautiful, but you can't live there." (*Time*, Oct. 16, 1978, p. 61)

Do illegal aliens take jobs away from taxpaying American citizens? The evidence is not clear. In some industrial areas the illegal aliens might displace U.S. citizens, but according to Leonel J. Castillo, the first Mexican-American appointed as Commissioner, Immigration and Naturalization Service, "As best we can tell, there is no great rush of unemployed persons on the East Coast to go pick onions in 100-degree heat for three weeks," and in the agricultural field he believes they are not draining jobs from Americans.

The Other Side

Country:	MEXICO
Capital:	Mexico City
Official Name:	Estados Unidos Mexicanos (United Mexican States)
Official Language:	Spanish
National Anthem:	Himno Nacional de Mexico (National Hymn of Mexico)
National Flag:	Vertical bands of green, white and red with coat of arms in the center. Adopted in 1821. Green stands for independence, white for religion, and red for unity. The coat of arms depicts an eagle battling a snake. According to legend, the bird was sighted by Aztec Indians at Tenochtitlán (now Mexico City) and was taken as a sign to build their capital there.
Major Religion:	Roman Catholic
National Holiday:	Independence Day, September 16

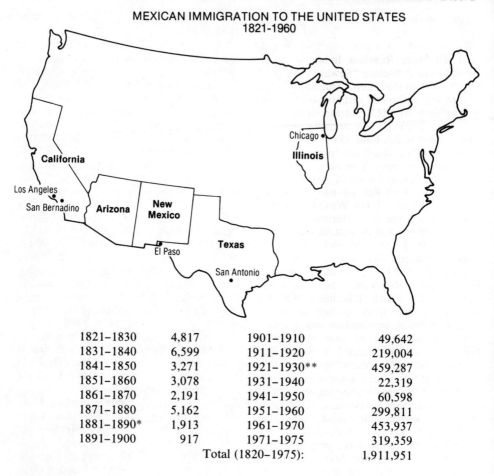

MEXICAN IMMIGRATION TO THE UNITED STATES
1821-1960

1821–1830	4,817	1901–1910	49,642
1831–1840	6,599	1911–1920	219,004
1841–1850	3,271	1921–1930**	459,287
1851–1860	3,078	1931–1940	22,319
1861–1870	2,191	1941–1950	60,598
1871–1880	5,162	1951–1960	299,811
1881–1890*	1,913	1961–1970	453,937
1891–1900	917	1971–1975	319,359
		Total (1820–1975):	1,911,951

1970 Census

Foreign-born Mexicans	759,711
Native-born, 2nd generation	1,579,440
Total Foreign-stock population	2,339,151

Estimated Mexican-American Population 7.5 million (The estimated number of illegal immigrants ranges between 3 and 5 million.)

*Main Ethnic Epicenters***		*U.S. Cities**** with Most Mexicans*	
California	1,112,008	Los Angeles	509,342
Texas	711,058	San Antonio, Tx	121,986
Illinois	117,268	El Paso, Tx	116,470
Arizona	113,816	Chicago	107,652
New Mexico	37,822	San Bernadino, Ca	71,651

*No statistics are available for the period between 1886 and 1893.
**Though technically the peak decade, the 1921–1930 period has been surpassed by the years between 1966 and 1976.
***States with largest foreign-stock population—i.e., foreign-born residents and their children
****Standard Metropolitan Statistical Areas

THE RUSSIANS

There were Russians living in Alaska long before it became "Seward's Folly" in 1867 and passed into American hands. There was a Russian settlement in California as early as 1812, but the Russians did not begin to emigrate in record numbers to the United States until 1880, when worldwide economic conditions triggered an outpouring of the poor from almost every nation in Europe and parts of Asia.

Settling in such Russian-named places as Odessa, Texas; Odessa, Washington; Moscow, Idaho; and St. Petersburg, Florida, over 200,000 Russians entered our country between 1881 and 1890, and over 1.5 million more found their way to America between 1901 and 1910. Not all of them were technically "Russians," however — some were Jewish, Polish, Ukrainian, Byelorussian or Carpatho-Russian — but, for the sake of convenience, immigration officials listed them according to their country of birth or the passports they carried, without regard to their individual "ethnic" heritage.

Attempts have been made over the years to readjust the figures into various subheadings, and the best guesstimate of the "true" Russian population of America stands between 2,000,000 and 2,500,000.

The second great wave of Russian immigrants to the United States came as a result of the 1918 Bolshevik revolution. Many of these immigrants were privileged Russians from the upper and middle classes. They were professionals who came here to *re*make their fortunes. That Revolution gave us the likes of Prince Matchabelli and his perfume; Vladimir Zworykin and his marvelous television; and Vladimir Nabokov, the author of *Lolita,* who helped create a "revolution" of his own in the publishing world.

Besides perfume, the "boob tube" and sexy novels, we have Russia to thank for roller coasters, *Candid Camera* (Allen Funt), helicopters (Igor Sikorsky), Mr. Spock (Leonard Nimoy), ethnic sit-coms on TV (Norman Lear), and the "Paul Revere of Ecology" (Barry Commoner).

The Russians are our leading ethnic group in income and educational attainment, and despite their small size (2.5% of the U.S. population) they are the most

These proud Russian soldiers were photographed at Ellis Island. (Courtesy: American Museum of Immigration)

Jakob Mithelstadt, his wife and their eight children were Russian Germans who came to Ellis Island aboard the S.S. Pretoria *on May 9, 1905. Jakob and his ready-made supply of farm workers were granted admission to the United States and settled near Kuln, North Dakota. (Courtesy: American Museum of Immigration)*

highly represented group in the ranks of professional and technical employment. One might have thought the WASPs enjoyed this distinction in America, but as it turns out the WASPs have fallen on some hard times of late, and are being outdone by the Russians, *proportionately.*

The Russians are still coming today, primarily Russian Jews (or those who claim to be Jewish just to obtain an exit visa). Instead of flocking to Israel as they did in the past, the Russian Jews of the 1970s sought refuge in America with the help of relief organizations to guide them in this new land.

During the 1970s, 110,000 Jews left Russia; almost 8,000 settled in New York City alone between 1971 and 1976, creating a new "ethnic" community in that melting-pot city.

"Firsts" and Facts About the Russian Experience in America

♦ *First Settlements* The first Russian settlement in Alaska was founded in 1784 on Kodiak Island. Called Three Saints Bay, the settlement consisted of 191 men and 1 woman — Natalia Shelikhov, wife of Grigori Shelikhov, the co-owner of a fur trading company and founder of the settlement on Kodiak Island.

The second Russian settlement in America was Fort Ross, California. Established as an agricultural satellite for the Alaskan settlement on Kodiak Island, Fort Ross was manned by 95 Russians and 80 Aleuts. In 1841 they sold their interest in California real estate to John Sutter for $30,000. Unfortunately for Sutter, his mill became the site of the 1848 gold rush and the resultant hordes of squatters killed his livestock, ate his produce and destroyed his property.

♦ *Civil War General* The first Russian immigrant elevated to the status of general was John Basil Turchin (1822–1901). Born Ivan Vasilevitch Turchininoff, he moved to the United States in 1856 after the Crimean War, in which he attained the rank of colonel of the Imperial Guards. When the Civil War broke out, he volunteered his services to his adopted homeland; his plan to capture Huntsville proved so successful that he was made a brigadier general in recognition of his efforts.

♦ The first Russian-language newspaper published in the United States was *Novoye Russkoye Slovo,* founded in New York in 1910. However, as early as 1868, a bilingual, English and Russian biweekly newspaper was published in San Francisco to reach the Russian-speaking peoples who had settled in Alaska and California.

♦ *Oldest U.S. Paratrooper* During World War II, Serge Obolensky (1891–1978) became the U.S. Army's oldest paratrooper when he took to the skies at the age of 53. He earned the rank of colonel during that war, and went on to become one of the nation's leading public relations men. A contemporary once remarked, "Serge could be successful selling umbrellas in the middle of the Sahara."

Like many of his fellow emigrés, Serge was a Russian prince who fled his native land, but only after battling the Bolsheviks as a guerrilla fighter. He married the daughter of John Jacob Astor, one of America's foremost financiers, and settled down to life as an international socialite, conducting his affairs from his Grosse Pointe, Michigan, home in his later years.

♦ *From Russia, With Love* Where did the first roller coaster do its first loop-the-loop? Coney Island? Six Flags over Texas? No, it was in St. Petersburg, Russia, during the seventeenth century.

Roller coasters originated in the late 1600s as ice slides built on wooden frameworks. Passengers would sit atop a two-foot sled and shoot down a 50-degree slope at heights up to 70 feet in the air. The French adapted the Russian idea by putting wheels on the sled to make it a year-round attraction. In recognition of their Eastern neighbors, they called the ride "Russian Mountains."

♦ *To Russia, With Love* According to Craig Whitney, the Russian language has been in a bind recently because of the large influx of products from the western world. The problem? There aren't enough Russian words to go around: the standard Russian dictionary has about 120,000 entries, compared to a whopping 450,000 found in your friendly giant-sized Webster's. (Quite a gap or *defitsit* that needs to be filled for the technological advances, sports, foods and other goods now being imported by the U.S.S.R.) How is the problem being solved? By creeping Western *infiltratsiya* (infiltration) into the Russian language.

"Lenin said that we mar the Russian language by using foreign words unnecessarily," wrote Vladimir Vailyev in the Soviet daily paper *Komsomolskaya Pravda*. "Isn't it high time to declare war on the torture of the Russian tongue?" But still the Russians insist on playing *futbol* and *basketbol*. They're dancing the outdated *tvist*, listening to *rok* music when they can, buying black-market Levis that they call *dzhinzy* (jeans), and drinking *viski* instead of vodka. Quite frankly, many Russians are worried about the effect that newspaper *zhurnalisti* will ultimately have on their beloved language, with their constant introduction of so many western words to the Russian vocabulary. With so much linguistic contamination already apparent, can ideological "contamination" be far behind?

♦ *The Russian Bakke* Rita Clancy paid her registration fees and entered medical school at the University of California at Davis in September 1977. What was so unusual about Mrs. Clancy's admission? It was only made possible after she sued the school, claiming "that she would have been admitted had not the minorities program blocked her, and that she was excluded because she was white."

A Russian-born Jew, Mrs. Clancy emigrated to the United States in 1970, and although she is now married to an American lawyer, she cited her family's poverty, the fact that she had lived on public assistance, and her deficiency in English as just cause for her to be admitted to one of the 16 places reserved for minorities. (The taskforce criteria for minority admissions include language and economic disadvantages as well as race.)

Her suit was the second against a California medical school (Allen Bakke's challenge of the minority admission rules was the first). When Bakke's case was decided in October 1977, both he and Mrs. Clancy were granted the right to admission; they are currently on their way to doctorhood.

The Other Side

Country:	RUSSIA
Capital:	Moscow
Official Name:	Soyuz Sovekskikh Sotsialisticheskikh Respublic (Union of Soviet Socialist Republics)
Official Language:	Russian
National Anthem:	Gosudarstveny Gimn Sovetskogo Soyusa (National Anthem of the Soviet Union)
National Flag:	The red field of the Russian flag represents the revolution. The hammer and sickle stand for the unity between the peasants and the workers. The star represents the Communist Party.
Coat of Arms:	The Russian coat of arms bears the motto "Workers of all countries unite." The hammer and sickle in this instance stand for the spread of Communism and the rising sun symbolizes a new day dawning for worldwide Communism.
Ethnic Mix:	Russian, 53%; Ukrainian, 17%; Byelorussian, 4%; others, 26%*
Religions:	Russian Orthodox, Islam, Roman Catholic, Judaism, Lutheran

*These percentages are changing rapidly as the birth rate of ethnic Russians continues to decline.

RUSSIAN IMMIGRATION TO THE UNITED STATES

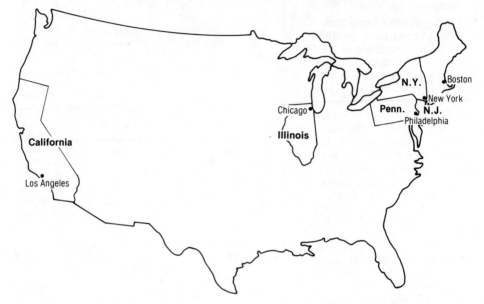

1821–1830	75	1901–1910	1,597,306 (Peak Decade)
1831–1840	277	1911–1920	921,201
1841–1850	551	1921–1930	61,742
1851–1860	457	1931–1940	1,356
1861–1870	2,512	1941–1950	548
1871–1880	39,284	1951–1960	584
1881–1890	213,282	1961–1970	7,229
1891–1900	505,290	1971–1975	2,336
		Total (1820–1975):	3,354,026

1970 Census

Foreign-born Russians	463,462
Native-born, 2nd generation	1,479,733
Total Foreign-stock Population	1,943,195
Estimated Russian-American Population	2 million to 2.5 million

Main Ethnic Epicenters*		U.S. Cities** with Most Russians	
New York	569,813	New York	512,773
California	221,198	Los Angeles	128,693
Pennsylvania	157,348	Philadelphia	120,453
New Jersey	143,234	Chicago	104,835
Illinois	110,321	Boston	76,966

*States with largest foreign-stock populations—i.e., foreign-born residents and their children
**Standard Metropolitan Statistical Areas

THE IRISH

The Irish didn't begin their mass migration to America until the 1830s, but their presence had been felt in the New World from the earliest days. The first Irishman to find his way to our shores was one of Columbus's crew—William Ayers, from Galway. One Francis Maguire was listed among the inhabitants of Jamestown, Va. in 1607 and another Irishman, named John Coleman, accompanied Henry Hudson on his trip up the Hudson River in 1609. Coleman was killed by Indians at a spot named Coleman's Point (now Sandy Hook), and was buried at Coney Island.

As early as 1776 there were some 200,000 sons of Erin living in America out of a total population of 2.5 million, and some sources claim they comprised anywhere from one-third to one-half of Washington's army. Many of the "Irish" counted in the 1776 figures were really "Scotch-Irish"—descendants of Scottish Protestants who had been installed by the English on confiscated lands in Northern Ireland. They considered themselves Scots, the Irish considered them Scots, but the English insisted on counting them as Irish all the same—so the *true* number of Irish in America before the Revolutionary War was probably closer to 40,000.

Still, the Irish figured strongly in America's early history. One of the first Minute Men killed at Lexington Green in 1775 was of Irish descent; there were four Irish-born signers of the Declaration of Independence and at least nine Irish-American signers of that hallowed creed. The Declaration was also printed by an Irishman, John Dunlap—a Philadelphia printer who had the dubious honor of *losing* the original copy of the document.

The Flight From the Blight The peak decade of Irish immigration to the United States came in the wake of the Great Potato Famine (1845–1848) which caused the social and economic structure of Ireland to collapse. Small tenant farmers were driven across the sea to escape from crop failure, excessive rents and poverty so dire that it was said, "Generations of Irishmen have lived and died without ever tasting meat." With their main staple, the potato, destroyed by *Phytophthora* fungus, 25% of

This 1855 woodcut, "The Lure of American Wages," was made during the peak period of Irish immigration. In the decade between 1846 and 1855, some 1,288,307 Irishmen fled the Emerald Isle. (Courtesy: Museum of the City of New York)

the Irish population either emigrated or starved to death during the blight years.

Between 1820 and 1840 about 700,000 Irish immigrants came to the United States. Between 1840 and 1860, that number more than doubled, to somewhere between 1.7 million and 2 million, and Irish immigration did not begin to drop sharply until 1930, when the first U.S. quota laws went into effect and admissions from the Emerald Isle were cut to 6,600 per annum.

In 1930 there were almost 750,000 Irish-born residents of the United States. By 1970, their ranks had dwindled to 250,000 —but despite the fact that most of the 13 million to 16 million estimated Irish-Americans have never seen the "old country," they still remain spiritually attached to Ireland, and always "break out the green" on St. Paddy's Day.

The Irish have made their mark on American politics (no less than twelve presidents have had Irish blood coursing through their veins), American letters (Eugene O'Neill, F. Scott Fitzgerald, Marianne Moore), and in such diverse business ventures as international shipping lines, meat-curing plants and pizza parlor chains.

From the other side, the Irish gave us

Donegal tweeds, Waterford crystal, Beleek china, shamrocks, shillelaghs and the Irish brogue; they gave us the Irish Sweepstakes, so we could gamble before there were legal state lotteries, and they gave us Irish linen, Irish whiskey, Irish stew, Irish wolfhounds and Irish terriers – but not the Irish potato (that tuber is sorely misnamed).

"Firsts" and Facts About the Irish Experience in America

Fleeing the "Great Lord Protector" When Oliver Cromwell began confiscating Irish land in 1652 many Irishmen were sent to the West Indies as laborers and slaves. In 1678 one hundred Irish families came to Virginia and the Carolinas via Barbados to establish new lives for themselves in America as indentured servants.

New York Politics The first Irish governor of New York was Sir Thomas Dongan (1634–1715), a native of Kildare who was appointed to that post in 1682 and served as governor for six years. New York City didn't get her first Irish Catholic mayor until 1880, when William R. Grace, the shipping magnate, occupied Gracie Mansion.

Religion Although many of the Irish immigrants of the 1800s were Catholics, the Irish were also responsible for establishing the first American Presbytery and the first Methodist Church in America. Rev. Francis Makemie (1658–1708) organized the first American Presbytery in Virginia in 1706. A native of Donegal, Makemie emigrated to Virginia in 1683, and earned the title "Founder of Presbyterianism in America." The first Methodist Church in America was founded on John Street in lower Manhattan in 1768 by a group of Irish Methodists led by Philip Embury (1728–1773).

America's Gift to Ireland Eamon De Valera (1882–1975), the son of a Spanish father and an Irish mother, was born in New York City and educated in Ireland. He joined the Irish volunteers and participated in the Easter uprising of 1916. As president of the Dail Eireann (the Irish Parliament) in 1919, he raised almost $5 million from Irish-Americans to support Ireland's fight for independence. He served as prime minister three times, and was elected president of Ireland in 1959 and again in 1966.

Legendary Leaper The only man, until recent times, to survive a leap from the Brooklyn Bridge was Steve Brodie, an Irish-American bartender, who took the plunge in 1886. There has been some speculation that twenty-three-year-old Brodie pushed a dummy into the East River instead of taking the plunge himself, but the truth will never be known. Brodie won his $200 wager and emerged as something of a folk hero in New York City.

Unsinkable Molly Brown Another Irish-American legend was the "Unsinkable" Molly Brown, who managed to become the title character in a play and a movie about her exploits. A wealthy traveler aboard the *Titanic* during her ill-fated maiden voyage, Margaret "Molly" Tobin Brown kept everyone's spirits afloat after the ship sank on that "night to remember." Her steady patter of jokes, songs and lively chatter lifted the spirits of her fellow lifeboat passengers. How did she get her nickname? After her ordeal she was quoted as saying "I'm unsinkable" when she came ashore and greeted the press.

Father of the Homeless Newsboys John Christopher Drumgoole (1816–1888) had his last name immortalized on Drumgoole Boulevard in Staten Island. He was an Irish immigrant who went from church janitor to Catholic priest in his later years. As a religious "Father," Drumgoole began to realize his lifelong desire to help homeless children, a mission that earned him his nickname, the "Father of the homeless newsboys."

In the late 1800s the tenements of New York were overcrowded, disease-laden hovels where life was often "nasty, brutish and short" for the poor, unskilled immigrants who lived there. Without any agencies to care for them, numerous homeless orphans roamed the streets, seeking whatever jobs there were (typically selling newspapers). They slept in alleys and unused stairwells, living hand-to-mouth from their meager earnings. They smoked habitually and were exploited by bartenders who sold them whiskey for 3c a glass. In 1871, Father Drumgoole opened St. Vincent's Newsboys home with one hundred beds. By 1873, the facility was expanded to house 300 children, and in 1883 he established Mount Loretto on Staten Island –

In the absence of any welfare agencies to care for homeless children, many newsboys sold papers during the day, and slept in back alleys at night. (Credit: Culver Pictures)

one of America's largest child-care institutes, still in existence today.

Patron of the Arts James McCreery came to America from Ireland in 1845 at the age of twenty. He made his fortune in New York selling Irish lace, and became a generous benefactor to philanthropic and artistic causes. It was McCreery's sizable donations that helped found New York's Metropolitan Museum of Art.

The Other Side

Country:	IRELAND
Capital:	Dublin
Official Name:	Republic of Ireland
Also Known As:	Eire, Erin, the Emerald Isle
Official Languages:	English, Gaelic
National Anthem:	"The Soldier's Song"/"Amhrán na bhFiann"

National Anthem: Written in 1907 by Peadar Kearney, who composed the music in collaboration with Patrick Heeney, the anthem consists of three stanzas and a chorus. First published in the *Irish Freedom* newspaper in 1912, it was formally adopted in 1926, replacing the old anthem, *God Save Ireland*.

National Flag: Vertical bands of green, white and orange. Green represents the Roman Catholics, Orange stands for the Protestants, and White represents the unity between them. (No comment.) First introduced by Thomas Francis Meagher during the Young Ireland movement of 1848, it was adopted as the national flag in 1916.

Major Religion: 95% of the Irish are Roman Catholic.

IRISH IMMIGRATION TO THE UNITED STATES

	1821–1830	50,724	1901–1910	339,065
	1831–1840	207,381	1911–1920	146,181
	1841–1850	780,719	1921–1930	220,591
(Peak Decade)	1851–1860	914,119	1931–1940	13,167
	1861–1870	435,778	1941–1950	26,967
	1871–1880	436,871	1951–1960	57,332
	1881–1890	655,482	1961–1970	37,461
	1891–1900	388,416	1971–1975	6,559
		Total (1820–1975):		4,720,427

1970 Census

Foreign-born Irish	251,375
Native-born, 2nd generation	1,198,845
Total Foreign-stock Population	1,450,220
Estimated Irish-American Population	13 million

Main Ethnic Epicenters*		*U.S. Cities** with Most Irish:*	
New York	386,403	New York	315,061
Massachusetts	218,798	Boston	147,324
New Jersey	122,600	Chicago	91,514
Pennsylvania	118,174	Philadelphia	83,793
California	109,888	San Francisco	35,744

*States with largest foreign-stock populations—i.e., foreign-born residents and their children
** Standard Metropolitan Statistical Areas

THE AUSTRIANS

The Austro-Hungarian Empire reached its greatest size in 1914. Encompassing such regions as Bohemia, Moravia, Galicia, Bucovina, Styria, Bosnia and Herzegovina, the empire contained almost 52 million inhabitants, of whom 23 million were Slavs, 12 million were Germans, 10 million were Magyars (Hungarians) and 3 million were Rumanians. When the Austro-Hungarian Empire was divided after World War I, the nations of Austria, Hungary and Czechoslovakia were formed, while the remainder of the land was divided among Italy, Poland, Rumania and Yugoslavia.

A small nation, Austria nonetheless has contributed over 600,000 of her citizens to the United States since 1911. Austrian immigrants and their descendants contributed brand-name bathtubs, topless bathing suits and *The Sound of Music* to America. They also gave Milton Friedman to the world of economics, Felix Frankfurter to our justice system and Luise Rainer, Paul Henreid and Hedy Lamarr to the entertainment world.

From the other side, the Austrians gave the world "Ave Maria" by Franz Schubert, "Silent Night," Freudian analysis, Mozart, Bambi and Wiener schnitzel.

The true number of Austrian immigrants to America will never be known because the Bureau of Immigration categorized all the inhabitants of the Austro-Hungarian Empire together between 1861 and 1910. Between 1901 and 1910 over 2.1 million citizens from Austria-Hungary sought refuge in the United States. Most of them were poor, landless peasants who took advantage of the Empire's relaxed emigration laws enacted in 1867. A large number of the Austrians who emigrated to the United States between 1870 and 1914 found employment as miners, servants or common laborers. They flocked to the cities and industrial centers of the northeastern United States, and according to the latest census figures (1970) the largest concentrations of first- and second-generation Austrian-Americans are still found in New York, Chicago and Pittsburgh.

"Firsts" and Facts About the Austrian Experience in America

Kohler Bathtubs　One of John Michael Kohler's (1844–1900) most popular items was a combination horse trough-bathtub coated with enamel. An immigrant from Vorarlberg province in Austria, Kohler founded a machine shop and foundry in Sheboygan, Wisconsin, in 1873. Ten years later he began manufacturing cast-iron plumbing fixtures, and today the company that bears his name is one of the largest plumbing supply manufacturers in the United States. His son, Walter J. Kohler, was Governor of Wisconsin from 1929 to 1931.

Spingarn Medals　Awarded each year to the Black American leader who has been of "greatest service to his race," the Spingarn Medals were first bestowed in 1913 by Joel Elias Spingarn (1875–1939), one of the founding fathers of the National Association for the Advancement of Colored People. Spingarn himself served as president of the NAACP between 1930 and 1939; after his death his brother, Arthur, assumed the presidency until 1965. Born and raised in New York City, Spingarn was the son of an Austrian immigrant father and an English mother.

Supreme Frankfurter　Born in Vienna, Felix Frankfurter (1882–1965) emigrated to America with his family in 1894. After graduation from the City College of New York and Harvard Law School he established a private practice in New York. Appointed to the Supreme Court in 1939 as an associate justice, Frankfurter was awarded the Presidential Medal of Freedom in 1963, a year after ill health forced him to retire from the bench.

Love Is Not Enough　Bruno Bettelheim (1903–　　), Vienna-born psychologist, escaped death in Nazi concentration camps at Dachau and Buchenwald and turned his interviews with fellow prisoners into the classic study "Individual and Mass Behavior in Extreme Situations," published in 1943 in the *Journal of Abnormal and Social Psychology*. His greatest professional recognition, however, has come from his treatment of autistic children and others who had previously failed to respond to therapy. His books include: *Love Is Not Enough* (1950), *Puberty Rites and the Envious Male* (1954) and *The Empty Fortress* (1967).

Music, Music, Music   The Sound of Music, the 1965 Academy Award-winning movie, was based on the early life of Maria von Trapp (1905–   ). An Austrian-born novice who left the convent before taking her final vows, Maria married Baron Georg von Trapp in 1927. After fleeing Nazi Austria in 1938, the singing Trapp family toured America until 1955.

Some of the composers Austria has contributed to the United States over the years include: Arnold Schönberg, Julius Bittner, Erich Korngold, Ernst Toch, Paul Pisk, Fritz Kreisler and Arthur Schnabel.

Topless Swimsuits   Vienna-born Rudi Gernreich (1922–   ) made fashion history in the early 1960s when he introduced his famous "topless" bathing suit for women. That gimmick earned him notoriety, but his fashion designs earned him a place in the Coty Hall of Fame—a major achievement in the world of design.

The Machine That Reads With a "Scandinavian" Accent   Before the advent of the Kurzweil Reading Machine, blind or visually impaired students had to wait for textbooks to be translated into Braille or recorded on magnetic tape. But in 1978 Ray Kurzweil, (1948–   ), an Austrian-American, opened up a whole new world to blind readers.

His machine, which is capable of recognizing each letter of the alphabet by measuring its geometric shape, can "read" the printed material aloud in a computer-generated voice. (Some claim the machine has a Scandinavian accent, while others think it is German or Swedish, but it is definitely "European.") This machine makes it possible for a blind person to "read" *any* and all printed material—from personal letters, utility bills and best-selling books, to the latest edition of the daily newspaper hot off the printing presses. No longer is it necessary to wait months or years for a Braille translation.

The machine can also repeat any phrase and spell out entire words with the push of a button. It takes about twelve hours to learn to use the machine, which currently sells for $50,000. Kurzweil hopes that mass production will lower the cost to the $5,000–$10,000 range over the next three to five years, and that the size of the machine will be reduced considerably so it may be carried in an attaché case. The prototype model weighs in at a hefty 80 pounds and is too bulky to be considered "portable."

Kurzweil was a 1965 national winner of the Westinghouse Science Talent Search; he graduated from MIT in 1970.

The Other Side

Country:	AUSTRIA
Official Name:	Republik Österreich (Republic of Austria) (Österreich means "eastern empire")
Capital:	Vienna
Official Language:	German
National Anthem:	"Land der Berge, Land am Strome" (Land of Mountains, Land at the River)
	Words by Paula von Preradovic, Music by W. A. Mozart
National Flag:	Horizontal bands of red, white and red, with the Austrian coat of arms in the center. The flag was adopted in 1945.
Major Religions:	Roman Catholicism. A concordat between the Pope and the Government of Austria provides for financial support of the Roman Catholic Church of this nation. Freedom of worship is, however, guaranteed by the constitution.
National Holiday:	October 25, Flag Day. This holiday has been celebrated as "flag day" every year since 1955 to commemorate the evacuation of foreign troops and the official signing of the State Treaty.

AUSTRIAN IMMIGRATION TO THE UNITED STATES

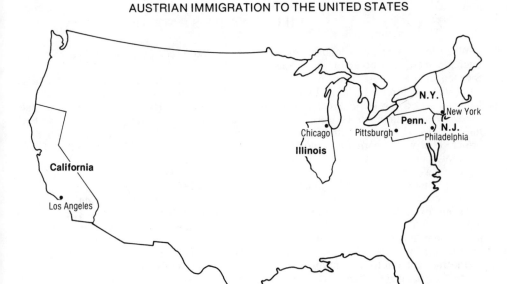

	1861–1870	7,800	1921–1930	32,863
	1871–1880	72,969	1931–1940	3,563
	1881–1890	353,719	1941–1950	24,860
	1891–1900	592,707	1951–1960	67,106
(Peak Decade)	1901–1910	2,145,266	1961–1970	20,621
	1911–1920	453,649	1971–1975	6,961

Total (1820–1975): 4,312,252*

1970 Census

Foreign-born Austrians	214,014
Native-born, 2nd generation	761,311
Total Foreign-stock Population	975,325

*Main Ethnic Epicenters***		*U.S. Cities*** with Most Austrians*	
New York	237,836	New York	197,524
Pennsylvania	145,815	Chicago	56,524
New Jersey	83,165	Pittsburgh	45,996
California	77,382	Los Angeles	37,514
Illinois	65,026	Philadelphia	33,569

*This figure is misleading in a number of respects. Immigration data were combined for Austria and Hungary between 1861 and 1905, and between 1899 and 1919 Polish figures were included with those of the Austro-Hungarian Empire. On the other hand, between 1938 and 1945, immigrants from Austria were listed as Germans.

**States with largest foreign-stock populations—i.e., foreign-born residents and their children

*** Standard Metropolitan Statistical Areas

THE SWEDES

When low wages, crop failures, massive unemployment and other disasters rocked Sweden in the 1840s, many of her finest citizens were forced to leave their homeland and seek a new life in America. Among these Swedish immigrants were so many lumberjacks and farmers that the Swedes are credited with clearing and plowing under more acreage in America than there is in all of Sweden.

Unlike most other immigrants, many Swedes chose to return home when conditions improved: between 1880 and 1920 almost 160,000 returned to Sweden. But many more stayed and continued to farm the virgin soil of the Midwest, which had first attracted them to our nation.

The Swedes were a hardworking people, and through their influence manual training was introduced in our educational system. They also started the concept of 4-H clubs, where youngsters could learn practical skills useful for farm life in the Midwest.

From the other side the Swedes brought gingersnaps, smorgasbords and rutabagas. They built the first log cabins and gave us Greyhound buses for the highways and zippers for the "fly"-ways of America. Their sons and daughters became newspaper columnists (Jack Anderson), beauties of the silver screen (Greta Garbo, Ann-Margret, Candice Bergen), big names in the art world (Thomas Hoving), and Olympic gold medal winners (Donald Schollander). They crossed the Atlantic (Charles Lindbergh), became poets (Carl Sandburg) and even ventured into outer space (Buzz Aldrin).

Gustavus Unonius established the first "modern" Swedish colony at Pine Lake, Wisconsin, in 1841, but the Swedes had been present in America for more than two hundred years by that time. In 1638, a group of 50 Swedes led by Peter Minuit sailed from Gothenburg in two ships, *Kalmar Nyckel* (The Key of Kalmar) and *Vogel Grip* (Bird Grip). They arrived in Delaware four months later and established Fort Christina, on the Christina River—both named in honor of the Swedish queen.

When the Dutch suffered defeat at the hands of the British at New Amsterdam, the Swedes in the former Dutch colonies came under British rule. By 1790 it was estimated that there were 21,500 persons of Swedish ancestry living in the United States. By that time, however, intermarriage had almost eliminated the old-country ways and the Swedish language was in serious decline.

The peak period for Swedish immigration to America was 1877 to 1888, when 97,534 people (almost 2 percent of the entire population of Sweden) emigrated to the United States. By 1930, almost 1.3 million Swedes had sailed the ocean to the New World, and there were over 1.5 million first- and second-generation Swedish-Americans living here at that time. Immigration to the New World began to decline after the quota laws went into effect, and between 1931 and 1940 only 3,960 Swedes found a home in the United States.

"Firsts" and Facts About the Swedish Experience in America

Log Cabins The early residents of New Sweden built the first log cabins in America sometime between 1634 and 1654. Built in the region around the Delaware River, these one-room cabins, about 12 feet by 14 feet, served as kitchen, dining room, bedroom, etc. for the settlers and their livestock during the winter months.

Swedish Monthly The first Swedish magazine published (on a monthly basis) in America was *Vårt Nya Hem,* which debuted in 1873 and died a little over a year later. The first Swedish newspapers had been published as early as 1855.

Illinois's First Swede The first Swedish settler in Illinois was Raphael Wilden, a businessman who first emigrated to New York and made his fortune there before trekking out to Illinois in 1814. By 1890, Illinois had the second largest population of foreign-stock Swedes (200,032); it was outdone only by Minnesota, with 225,990.

The Man Who Put Women Behind the Wheel Thanks to Vincent Bendix (1882–1945), the son of a Swedish clergyman, millions of American women can now drive cross-country or across town whenever they want. This Swedish-American inventor was responsible for the "Bendix drive" —a device that made self-starters practical in automobiles. Prior to the invention of Bendix drive only strong men could risk driving automobiles, because they had to be cranked by hand. Bendix's invention made it possible for the "weaker" sex to sit in the driver's seat, but he didn't stop there. He used his genius to build the Bendix Aviation Corporation, and to manufacture automotive and household appliances.

Female Labor Organizer Mary Anderson (1872–1964), an immigrant from Lidköping, Sweden, joined her older sister in America at the age of 16 after reading her letters about the marvelous new life she had found in the States. After learning English, Mary found a job in a shoe factory near Chicago, and for eighteen years earned her living by stitching shoes. Her interest in union activities led to her appointment as president of Local 94 of the International Boot and Shoe Workers Union and she later became a founding mother of the National Women's Trade Union League.

Oldest College Augustana College, founded in 1860 at Rock Island, Illinois, is the oldest institute of higher learning established by Swedes in America. Swedish immigrants are also responsible for founding three other colleges—Gustavus Adolphus in Minnesota, Bethany College in Kansas, and Upsala College in New Jersey —and two junior colleges—Luther College, at Wahoo, Nebraska, and North Park College in Chicago.

Helping the Gushers Flow Johan August Udden (1859–1932), a geologist born in Uddabo, Vestergötland, Sweden,

was a graduate of Augustana College and the University of Minnesota. He later taught geology at his alma mater in Rock Island, Illinois, but his greatest contribution to America was made in Texas. His development of a technique for examining subsurface strata helped to open the Texas oil fields and develop the economy of that state. For his distinguished work in America, he was decorated with the Order of the North Star by the King of Sweden during a visit to his homeland in 1911.

Bucket Seats and Birth Control Harold W. Bostrom (1908–   ) has contributed over $1 million to the National Planned Parenthood Federation. A self-made millionaire, Bostrom first entered into business with his immigrant uncle, a journeyman upholsterer from the King of Sweden's household, in 1935. He made his first fortune manufacturing suspension seats for farm tractors, and his second fortune by developing molded bucket seats for automobiles.

Working with another Swedish-American, Claes Nobel, the great-grand-nephew of Alfred (the man who started the Nobel prizes), Bostrom is trying to persuade the board of directors of the Nobel foundation to set up a new prize for excellence in the field of ecology. Concerned with the effects of pollution and overpopulation, Bostrom is also working on setting up an equivalent prize for environmental research in the United States. Despite all his contributions to Planned Parenthood, think of the progress Bostrom might have made in that field if he had only thought of putting bucket seats in the *backs* of automobiles, instead of only in the front.

The Other Side

Country:	SWEDEN
Capital:	Stockholm
Official Name:	Konungariket Sverige (Kingdom of Sweden)
	(*Sverige* means "land of the Svear," early Scandinavian people who settled there about 6000 B.C.)
Official Language:	Swedish
National Anthem:	"Du gamla, du fria." (Thou ancient, thou free-born)
National Flag:	A yellow cross on a blue field. The flag dates back to the mid-1400s and was officially adopted in 1663.
National Holiday:	June 6, Flag Day
Major Religion:	Almost 98% of the population is Lutheran.

SWEDISH IMMIGRATION TO THE UNITED STATES
1861-1960

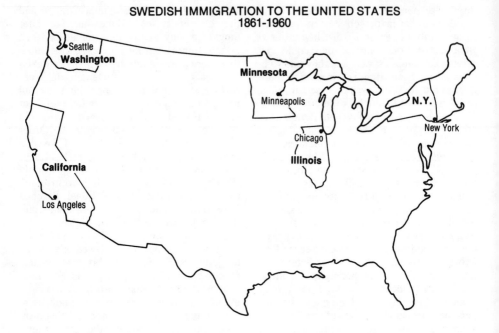

	1861–1870	37,667	1921–1930	97,249
	1871–1880	115,922	1931–1940	3,960
(Peak Decade)	1881–1890	391,776	1941–1950	10,665
	1891–1900	226,266	1951–1960	21,697
	1901–1910	249,534	1961–1970	17,116
	1911–1920	95,074	1971–1975	3,043
			Total (1820–1975)	1,269,969

1970 Census

Foreign-born Swedes	127,070
Native-born, 2nd generation	697,068
Total Foreign-stock Population	806,138
Estimated Swedish-American Population	12 million

*Main Ethnic Epicenters**		*U.S. Cities** with Most Swedes:*	
Minnesota	114,512	Chicago	66,438
California	103,913	Minneapolis	55,910
Illinois	98,254	Los Angeles	36,403
New York	52,058	New York City	30,737
Washington	45,251	Seattle	22,119

*States with largest foreign-stock populations—i.e., foreign-born residents and their children
**Standard Metropolitan Statistical Areas

3 THE UNWILLING IMMIGRANTS

BRIEF CHRONOLOGY OF THE
BLACK EXPERIENCE IN AMERICA

1492 ♦ Pedro Alonso Niño, a member of Columbus's crew, is believed to have been the first black man in the New World. He came here a free man, even though fifty years earlier Portuguese sailors had brought captive Africans back to their homeland as slaves for the first time.

1517 ♦ Catholic bishop Bartolome de Las Casas petitioned Pope Leo X to permit African slaves in the mines of Central and South America. Bishop Las Casas was hoping to alleviate the suffering of the Indians, who had been enslaved by the Spanish and Portuguese. Instead the Indians continued their decline and the enslavement of the Black race began in earnest.

1619 ♦ Twenty Africans were sold into slavery at Jamestown, Virginia, by a Dutch ship which had veered off course on the way to the West Indies. That mistake began what was the eventual enslavement of millions of West Africans from diverse tribal groups such as the Fulani, Mandingo, Wolof and Ashanti.

There is evidence to suggest that the first Africans brought to America were not considered slaves but were merely indentured servants — until legislation passed in Virginia made all "non-Christian servants from overseas" slaves for the rest of their lives.

1639 ♦ An act passed in Maryland spoke of rights for "all Christian inhabitants (slaves excepted) . . ." So, starting this year, not even Christianity could save one from a life of slavery.

1662 ♦ The Virginia legislature decreed that the child of a slave woman and a white man would inherit the status of his mother and be considered a slave.

1670 ♦ Virginia ruled that Christians would not be liable to *lifelong* servitude, and could possibly live as free men and free women without waiting for "judgment day."

1675 ♦ Englishman John Eliot declared, "to sell soules for money seemeth to me a dangerous merchandize."

1682 ♦ In twelve years' time, the state of Virginia found that its stand on Christianity was cutting into the profits of slave owners, and the 1670 law which exempted Christian converts from lifelong servitude was repealed.

1743 ♦ John Woolman began preaching about the evils of slavery to Quakers throughout the colonies.

1773 ♦ Phillis Wheatley (1753?–1784), a slave belonging to Boston merchant John Wheatley, published her *Poems on Various Subjects, Religious and Moral*. The first black woman poet in America, Phillis was brought to Boston from Africa in 1761 and taught to read and write by John Wheatley and his wife. After their death in 1778, Phillis was a free woman, but poverty and ill health plagued her for the rest of her short life.

1775 ♦ Operating under an Irish constitution, Masonic Lodge 441 initiated a black member, Prince Hall, on March 6. He formed the first African Lodge in July 1775, but neither Hall nor his lodge were ever recognized by the American Masons.

Phillis Wheatley. (Courtesy: New York Historical Society)

1777 ◆ Vermont declared that all slaves would be free when they reached "the age of majority."

1781 ◆ Using simple logic, Quork Walker, a former slave, won his freedom in Massachusetts by making a statement of fact before the court. According to the State's constitution, "*all* men are born free and equal." Finding no fault with Quork's reasoning, the court declared Walker a free man.

1787 ◆ The Constitutional Convention met and decided that three-fifths of the slaves would be counted to determine the number of Congressmen a state would have, and the African slave trade would be allowed to continue for twenty years.

1790 ◆ According to the U.S. Census, there were 697,681 African slaves and 59,538 free men and women of color living in the United States this year. The largest slave-owning state was Virginia, with a black population of more than 304,000.

1794 ◆ The Bethel African Methodist Episcopal (A.M.E.) Church for Negroes was established by Richard Allen (1760–1831), a former slave, at Philadelphia, Pennsylvania. Allen broke away from the Methodist church in the belief that Blacks should have their own churches. Allen rose to the rank of A.M.E. Bishop when the Bethel Church merged with several others in 1816.

1800 ◆ Gabriel Prosser led a slave revolt in Virginia, the first major uprising of the nineteenth century.

1802 ◆ The first non-Indian child born in North Dakota was born to black parents.

1808 ◆ The importation of slaves was officially prohibited by Congress starting January 1, but the illicit sale of slaves continued until the Civil War. It has been estimated that 54,000 "illegal" slaves entered the United States between 1808 and 1860.

Most of the American slave population came from the West Coast of Africa.

1817 ◆ The American Colonization Society was founded to solve the problem of slavery in America. Their solution was to send all Africans back to Africa. Land was purchased near present-day Monrovia in Liberia, but only about twelve thousand Afro-Americans made it to the colony by 1822. There were simply too many language and cultural differences to overcome, and blacks born on American soil felt little patriotism for their "homeland," never having had the opportunity to maintain their cultural heritage in America.

1830 ◆ The first National Negro convention was held at Bethel Church in Philadelphia this year. The Black population at this time included 319,000 free persons and 2,009,034 slaves.

1831 ♦ Nat Turner led a slave revolt in Virginia; it eventually resulted in his death and the death of 55 to 70 whites. The last major slave rebellion before the Civil War, Turner's movement led to stricter state legislation against slaves.

1833 ♦ The Philadelphia Negro library was organized.

1850 ♦ The Fugitive Slave Law was passed, requiring the return of runaway slaves to their owners. One of the most dramatic fugitive slave cases was that of Anthony Burns. Before he was returned in 1854, the U.S. government had spent $100,000 for his capture. Despite the Fugitive Law, an estimated twenty thousand slaves were able to escape via the Underground Railroad to freedom in Canada and the Northern United States.

since slaves were not citizens and were not guaranteed any rights under the U.S. Constitution. In the end Scott was given his freedom by a generous man who bought him and freed him a few months after the court decided against Scott.

The same year that this "Reward" was offered, Dred Scott attempted to win his freedom in the courtroom. The Supreme Court Justices ruled that Scott was merely a piece of property, and as such was not eligible to file suit in any court. (Courtesy: New York Public Library)

Slave woman, circa 1850. (Courtesy: National Archives)

1857 ♦ Dred Scott filed suit in Missouri in 1857 in an attempt to win his freedom. He claimed that his residency in free territory for four years made him a free man, and beseeched the court to release him from bondage. The court evaded the issue by ruling that as "a piece of property" Scott could not bring suit in a U.S. court,

1859 ♦ John Brown (1800–1859), a white Abolitionist, conducted a raid on the Federal Arsenal at Harpers Ferry, West Virginia, with 16 white men and 5 black men. Brown intended to set up a republic of fugitive and freed slaves in the Appalachians, and to declare war on the Southern slave states. He was caught, convicted of treason and hung, thereby becoming a much sung-about martyr for the Abolitionist cause.

1860 ♦ There were, 3,953,760 slaves and 488,070 free men and women of color living in the United States. Almost 45 per cent of the free blacks were now living in Southern states.

1861 ♦ Start of the Civil War.

1863 ♦ President Lincoln issued the Emancipation Proclamation, which freed

Thomas Nast drew his vision of the past and future of American Blacks following the Emancipation Proclamation in 1863. (From Harper's Weekly. *Courtesy: Schomburg Collection, New York Public Library)*

slaves *only* in the states fighting against the federal government. The four slave states which sided with the Union were not affected until 1865, when the 13th Amendment to the Constitution was passed, freeing all slaves and abolishing slavery in the United States.

1864 ◆ The first black daily newspaper, the bilingual (French and English) New Orleans *Tribune,* began publication on October 14.

◆ Congress passed a bill equalizing pay, equipment and medical services for black troops fighting in the Civil War.

1869 ◆ Hiram R. Revels of Mississippi was the first black U.S. Senator. He was elected to fill an unexpired term between 1870 and 1871. Blanche Kelso Bruce (1841–1898) was the first black man to serve a full term in the U.S. Senate, from 1875 to 1881. He, too, was from the state of Mississippi.

1873 ◆ The real-life John Henry, a black railroad worker whose awesome strength inspired legendary tales, died this year while working on the construction of the Big Bend Tunnel in Virginia. He became the "Negro Paul Bunyan" and a symbol of the manual workers' last stand against

Hodgeman County, Kansas, recruitment poster. (Courtesy: New York Public Library)

the machines of the coming Industrial Age.

1881 ♦ Tuskegee Institute in Alabama was founded by a former slave, Booker T. Washington (1856–1915). Tuskegee, which was without funds or even a single building that year, grew to become a model technical and agricultural training institute within fifteen short years.

1882 ♦ The modern segregation movement began with the enactment of Tennessee's first "Jim Crow" railroad car law, which provided "separate but equal" facilities for Negroes.

1891 ♦ The National Colored Farmers Alliance had one million members this year.

1893 ♦ The world's first successful heart operation was performed at Chicago's Provident Hospital on July 9 by a Negro physician, Dr. Daniel Hale Williams.

1895 ♦ W. E. B. Du Bois became the first Negro ever to receive a Ph.D. from Harvard. He also became a militant spokesman against Booker T. Washington, whom he regarded as an Uncle Tom for his "Atlanta Compromise" speech made this year.

In the compromise speech, Washington had pledged, to the delight of Atlanta's white citizens: "In all things that are purely social, we can be as separate as the fingers, yet one as the hand in all things essential to mutual progress."

1896 ♦ Ragtime music came of age in the Midwest. A blend of West African and European musical forms, ragtime's syncopated rhythm began to decline about 1910 and was not revived until 1974 when the hit movie *The Sting* made Scott Joplin's (1868–1917) piano music famous once again.

♦ In the Plessy *v.* Ferguson case, the Supreme Court upheld the constitutionality of "separate but equal" facilities. Although the case originally applied to intrastate transportation, the decision was applied to schools, restaurants and other public facilities.

1905 ♦ Bob Marshall of the University of Minnesota was the first Black American selected for the All-American football team.

1909 ♦ Matthew Henson, Commander Perry's Negro assistant, discovered the North Pole along with Perry and four Eskimo guides. Henson accompanied

Perry on all of his Arctic explorations after 1891 and served as translator, hunter, sled builder and dog trainer for the expeditions.

This poster in a Harlem storefront in 1948 urged Black Americans to join forces and fight discrimination by joining the NAACP. Founded in 1909 by a group of black and white citizens, the NAACP originally devoted its energy to passage and enforcement of anti-lynching laws. After World War II, the NAACP stepped up its fight against discrimination and worked toward eliminating "separate but equal" facilities as well as unjust legal penalties for crimes committed by blacks. Today the NAACP has over 405,000 members, with over 700 youth council groups. (Courtesy: Museum of the City of New York)

♦ The National Negro Committee was founded this year on Lincoln's birthday. In 1910 the organization changed its name to the National Association for the Advancement of Colored People (N.A.A.C.P.). Their objectives were to promote equality before the law, and justice in the courtrooms of America.

1910 ♦ The National Urban League was founded to seek employment opportunities for Black Americans.

1910–1920 ♦ Just like the landless peasants from Europe who flocked to the industrial centers of the United States during the early twentieth century, Black Americans began migrating North to seek employment. In this decade more than 300,000 Blacks left Dixie, and joined other immigrants in the struggle to survive in the slums and tenements of the Northeast.

During the 1920s some 1,300,000 Black immigrants left their Southern "homeland"; they were joined by some 4 million more over the next twenty years.

1921 ♦ Marcus Garvey (1887–1940), a Jamaican immigrant to the United States who believed that Negroes would never receive true justice in a white-majority nation, started a "Back to Africa" movement that attracted 2 million followers. He is credited with leading the only real mass exodus of Blacks from the United States, a movement financed by a string of all-Black businesses set up by Garvey with the aid of supporters. The movement declined after Garvey was convicted of mail fraud and began serving a five-year sentence in 1925. President Coolidge commuted Garvey's sentence in 1927 and deported him to Jamaica.

1928 ♦ The first Northern Black elected to Congress was Oscar De Priest, a Republican from Chicago.

1931 ♦ The Scottsboro Boys case was tried. Although the "boys" were found guilty and incarcerated for years before they were vindicated and released, their case established the right of Blacks to serve on juries.

1936 ♦ Jesse Owens (1913–1980) "heiled right in the Führer's face," so to speak, when he won four gold medals in track events at the Berlin Olympic Games. Hitler had hoped the Olympics would be a showcase for the Nazi system and the "Aryan race," but Owens proved that Black was beautiful, talented and, definitely, a winning race.

1940 ♦ Hattie McDaniel (1895–1952) was the first Black American to win an Academy Award. She garnered the coveted Oscar statue as Best Supporting Actress of 1939 for her portrayal of Mammy in Gone With the Wind. Although she was criticized for accepting racist roles, she never minded playing slaves or domestics. She just reflected on the days when she had performed domestic chores for a living, compared the vast differences in salaries and was quite content with her "demeaning" roles on the screen.

1947 ♦ Jackie Robinson (1919–1972) broke through the "color barrier" when he put on a Brooklyn Dodgers uniform and became the first Black athlete to play baseball for the National League. There were states where he had to put that uniform on in a separate locker room, sleep in a different hotel, or dine apart from his teammates, but he struggled through and drove himself to the top of his profession. He paved the way for capable athletes of all races to participate in "mixed" leagues, rather than limit their talents to segregated organizations.

1949 ♦ The first Black-owned radio station, WERD, began broadcasting in Atlanta, Georgia.

1950 ♦ Gwendolyn Brooks (1917–   ) became the first black to win a Pulitzer Prize—for Annie Allen, her second collection of poems. Brooks was raised in Chicago's "Bronzeville" section, and is the poet laureate of the state of Illinois.

♦ Dr. Ralph Bunche (1904–1971) became the first black to receive the Nobel Peace Prize for his efforts in the Middle East.

1952 ♦ For the first time in 71 years of gruesome record keeping, there were no lynchings reported in America.

1953 ♦ A commemorative half-dollar was issued by the United States Mint in honor of Booker T. Washington and George Washington Carver.

♦ Linda Brown was forced to ride two miles each way to an all-Black elementary school in Topeka, Kansas, even though a school for "whites only" was four blocks from her home. Her parents, believing that the segregated school system deprived Linda of her constitutional rights, filed suit against the Topeka Board of Education. In a landmark decision, the Supreme Court reversed its "separate but equal" stance, adopted in the Plessy v. Ferguson case, and ordered schools to desegregate "with all deliberate speed."

1955 ♦ Rosa Parks (1914–   ), too "bone weary" to move on Thursday evening, December 1, refused to stand and let a white man take her seat on the bus.

Although she was seated in the back of the bus, local custom in Montgomery, Alabama, dictated that when the "white section" of the bus was full, blacks had to vacate their seats and allow whites to sit in the rear.

Rosa Parks refused to yield, was arrested, and started the whole civil rights movement rolling as the Black citizens of Montgomery banded together and boycotted local buses for more than a year. Though the boycott required a great deal of organization, effort and cooperation from both blacks and whites, it resulted in desegregation of public transportation and a new career for Dr. Martin Luther King, Jr. King came to national attention as a leader of the boycott, and went on to organize peaceful demonstrations throughout the country, preaching nonviolence and practicing it in the face of bombings and ugly, senseless violence.

1955 ◆ "A voice like hers comes once in a century." That's what Arturo Toscanini said about contralto Marian Anderson, who became the first Black opera singer to debut at the Metropolitan Opera House this year in Verdi's *Un Ballo in Maschera.*

1960 ◆ Black students at Woolworth's lunch counter in Charlotte, North Carolina, sat down to eat despite the local custom of serving blacks *only* if they stood. In response to the "sit-in," eight lunch counters in Charlotte closed down. Before the 1960s drew to a close there would be "wade-ins" at public beaches, "pray-ins" at churches, and "sit-ins" at lunch counters and offices all over the nation.

1962 ◆ James Meredith entered the University of Mississippi as the first official black undergraduate. When he graduated Dick Gregory wrote: "Negroes looked a little different and acted a little different when James Meredith was graduated because they all graduated with him, graduated from the derogatory stigma that all Negroes are ignorant, that all Negroes are lazy, that all Negroes stink."

1963 ◆ Martin Luther King led the "March on Washington" and revealed his "dream" that one day his people, and all people, would be judged by their character and not their color.

1964 ◆ The Civil Rights Act, signed by Lyndon Baines Johnson this year, was the most comprehensive ever enacted. Initiated in 1963 by John F. Kennedy, it integrated public accommodations and prohibited job discrimination on the basis of race, religion or sex.

◆ Martin Luther King received the Nobel Peace Prize for his leadership in the Civil Rights movement and his unending belief in nonviolence as the best means of obtaining equal justice for his people.

1966 ◆ Dr. Robert Clifton Weaver (1907–) became the nation's first Black cabinet member. A graduate of Harvard University, Weaver had been the head of the Housing and Home Finance Agency from 1961 to 1966. On January 17, Lyndon Johnson appointed him Secretary of the Department of Housing and Urban Development (HUD).

NINE MAYORAL "FIRSTS" FOR BLACK AMERICANS

Mayor	City	Date
Walter E. Washington (1915–)	Washington, D.C.	1967
Carl B. Stokes (1927–)	Cleveland, Ohio	1967
Richard G. Hatcher (1933–)	Gary, Indiana	1967
Kenneth A. Gibson (1932–)	Newark, N.J.	1970
James H. McGee (1918–)	Dayton, Ohio	1970
Theodore Berry (1905–)	Cincinnati, Ohio	1972
James Floyd (1922–)	Princeton, N.J.	1971
Thomas Bradley (1917–)	Los Angeles, California	1973
Maynard Jackson (1938–)	Atlanta, Georgia	1974

1966 ◆ Bill Russell became the first Black coach of a major pro-basketball team. Under his tutelage, the Boston Celtics went on to win the NBA Championship in 1967.

◆ "Black power" came of age when Stokely Carmichael was elected chairman of the Student Non-Violent Coordinating Committee (SNCC).

1967 ◆ Walter E. Washington became the

mayor of Washington, D.C. – the first Negro to head a major city government. This same year, Edward Brooke of Massachusetts was elected as the first Black senator since Reconstruction, and Thurgood Marshall became the first Black Supreme Court justice.

1968 ♦ Henry Lewis became the first Black to head an American symphony orchestra when he was appointed director of the New Jersey Symphony.

1970 ♦ Joseph L. Searles III became the first Black to own a seat on the New York Stock Exchange.

♦ Fifty per cent of Black Americans now lived in northern cities; most of them moved from the "old country" – Dixie – in the past 70 years.

1974 ♦ Hank Aaron (1934–   ) broke Babe Ruth's 47-year-old record of 714 home runs when he hit number 715 on April 8, 1974, for the Atlanta Braves. By season's end, Aaron had chalked up 733 home runs.

1979 ♦ Charlie Smith, a former slave who lived in a Bartow, Florida, nursing home, died this year at the age of 137. Believed to be the oldest person in the United States, Smith was born in Liberia in 1842. According to his account, he was coaxed onto a slave ship docked in a Liberian port by a man who promised there were "fritter trees on board with lots of syrup."

When he arrived at New Orleans in 1854, his name was changed from Mitchell Watkins to Charlie Smith, the name of the Texas rancher to whom he was sold into slavery.

Although Social Security officials once verified Smith's story, some critics believe he was no more than 104 years old at the time of his death.

"FIRSTS" AND FACTS ABOUT BLACKS IN AMERICA

Booker T. Washington once facetiously remarked that his people were the only "immigrants" who had their passage to the New World paid for. Despite the many obstacles placed in their path, as early as 1700 some Blacks were on their way to attaining the American dream. Despite discrimination, they were able to make their mark on America as doctors, lawyers, inventors, educators, businessmen and writers, chalking up accomplishments in every field of endeavor.

EDUCATIONAL "FIRSTS":

♦ *First School* One year after the first shipload of captive Africans landed at Jamestown, a school was established to educate both Blacks and Indians in Virginia. In 1704, a Frenchman, Elias Nau, opened the first school for Blacks in New York City, and in 1787 the African Free School was established in New York to provide educational advantages for poor Blacks.

♦ *College Graduate* The first black man to graduate from an American college was John Russwurm (1799–1851). Born in Jamaica and raised in Maine, Russwurm graduated from Bowdoin College in 1826. He later rose to fame as editor of the first Black newspaper in the United States, *Freedom's Journal*, a four-page weekly published in New York City from 1827 to 1829.

♦ *Women and Minorities* In 1834 a vote was taken concerning "the practicability of admitting persons of color" to Oberlin College. The vote was favorable, and Oberlin became the first college in the West to admit both blacks and women as students. That same year the legislature of South Carolina passed a law which prohibited the teaching of black children, either free or slave.

The first black to graduate from a theological seminary in the United States was Theodore S. Wright, a Princeton man, class of 1836.

♦ *No Thanks* That was the reply received by a donor who bequeathed a sum of money to the University of Wisconsin with the stipulation that the funds be used only for white students. Even though the year was 1839, the fair-minded university officials declined the donor's "generous" offer.

Howard University is the largest predominantly Black university in the United States today, but it wasn't our nation's first. That honor belongs to Lincoln University, originally chartered as Ashmond Institute in Chester, Pennsylvania. It was established in 1854, three years before Howard University (which was named for General Oliver Otis Howard, the post-Civil War head of the Freedmen's Bureau, who also served as Howard's president from 1869 to 1873).

♦ *Public School System*   The first public school system for Blacks was opened in the District of Columbia in 1864.

♦ *Top-Notch*   The first black graduate of Harvard University was Richard Greener, 1873. In 1876, Edward Bouchet became the first black man to earn a Ph.D. (in physics) from an American university, when he received his doctorate from Yale. West Point's first black graduate was Henry O. Flipper, a former slave from Georgia, who graduated from the Military Academy in 1877. The first black to graduate from Annapolis Naval Academy was Wesley A. Brown in 1949.

Harvard's first black Ph.D. was W. E. B. Du Bois (1868–1963), the militant black leader of the early 1900s. Du Bois graduated in 1895, and was probably the first black American to express the idea of Pan-Africanism, a belief that all people of African descent should work together to conquer prejudice and promote their common interests. Of French, Indian, Dutch and Negro ancestry, William Edward Burghardt Du Bois became increasingly dissatisfied with the slow progress of race relations in the United States, and moved to Ghana in 1961, two years before his death.

♦ *Rhodes Scholar*   The first black Rhodes Scholar was Alaine L. Locke of Harvard, 1907.

♦ *Degreed Women*   In 1921, three black women received Ph.D. degrees: Evan B. Dykes (Radcliffe); Sadie Mossell (University of Pennsylvania); and Georgiana Simpson (University of Chicago).

♦ *Phi Beta Kappa*   The first black institution of higher learning in the United States to receive a Phi Beta Kappa chapter was Fisk University in 1953.

♦ *Passing Grade*   Most Black American history books list James Meredith as the "first Black man to graduate from the University of Mississippi." According to Stephen Birmingham, the author of *Certain People,* James Meredith was actually the *second* man of color to become an alumnus of "Ole Miss." The first black man was Harry Murphy of Atlanta. The son of a printer, Harry had entered the University of Mississippi many years earlier without any fuss by "passing" as a white man. Because his skin color was so fair, he graduated without attracting the least bit of attention.

MORE "FIRSTS" AND FACTS ABOUT BLACK AMERICANS

♦ *The Man Who Founded Chicago*   Since Chicago is known today as the "capital of black business," it's not too surprising that the city's founding father was a black man — Jean Baptiste Pointe du Sable (1750–1819), a native of Haiti who described himself as a "free Negro."

Du Sable emigrated to New Orleans and sailed up the Mississippi until he reached Illinois. Noting that there was a natural crossroads between the Mississippi and the Great Lakes where Indians and Europeans might exchange goods, Du Sable established the "Windy City's" first trading post at the "place of the wild onions," Shi-kai-o, as it was called by the local Potawatomi Indians.

Chicago's founding father later sold his holdings to a Frenchman, Joseph La Lime, in 1800, who in turn sold out to John Kinzie in 1804. Du Sable died a poor man in St. Charles, Missouri, nineteen years later, but he fared better than either of his successors: Kinzie stabbed La Lime to death and later lost his holdings through gross mismanagement of his business affairs.

The Du Sable Museum was started by Margaret Burroughs, a black Chicagoan who stored the collection in her home from 1961 to 1974, until museum space was donated by the city of Chicago. In addition to supplying information about Chicago's founding father, the museum suggests African names for expectant parents who want to keep in touch with their "roots"; demonstrates techniques for African turban- and skirt-wrapping; and provides information for those desiring wedding ceremonies with an African flavor.

♦ *The Apollo Theater*   Opened as the Hurtig and Seaman theater in 1913 with a white-only admission policy, the Apollo Theater on Manhattan's 125th Street was taken over by Frank Schiffman and Leo Brecher in 1934. They opened the Apollo's doors to mixed audiences, but only blacks were allowed to perform. Every Wednesday night was "amateur night" and unknown hopefuls would appear on the chance that they might be discovered.

The Apollo, Harlem's showplace for black entertainers, drew thousands of whites to Harlem for an evening's entertainment. Some of the greats who appeared on stage include: Bessie Smith, the "Empress of the Blues"; Huddie "Leadbelly" Ledbetter; Duke Ellington; Count Basie; Thelonius Monk; Arethra Franklin; and James Brown.

♦ *Big Band's Black Man* Benny Goodman may have been the "King of Swing," but he never would have earned his crown without the help of black musician Fletcher Henderson (1898–1952).

Goodman's first success at the Palomar Ballroom in Los Angeles on August 21, 1935, was with a Henderson arrangement. That arrangement and the "big band" sound originated by Henderson in the 1930s propelled the twenty-five-year-old Jewish boy from Chicago to the heights of fame and fortune, and brought Henderson fame as Goodman's arranger.

♦ *Name Changer* Thurgood Marshall (1908–   ) who in 1967 became the first Black American appointed to the Supreme Court, was a victim of the "name game." When he was born his parents saddled him with a twelve-letter name that probably expressed their hopes for his future endeavors – Thoroughgood. As he explained, "By the time I reached the second grade, I got tired of spelling all that out and had it shortened to Thurgood." (Still quite unusual, but at least it fits on computerized application forms.)

Thurgood lived up to his original name scholastically, and graduated at the top of his Howard University Law School class. He was admitted to the Maryland bar in 1933, but a year after he hung out his shingle, he found that he was $1,000 in debt. The reason? He kept taking civil rights cases for little or no compensation, and although he didn't bring home the bacon during that first year, his generosity and his cleverness in court battles earned him the title, "Mr. Civil Rights."

♦ *FBI Manhunt* In 1977 the FBI launched one of its biggest stakeouts ever. Descending upon the National Urban League's conference, held in Washington, D.C., federal agents attempted to enlist dozens of black recruits to their organization. Despite gains over the past decade and frequent attempts to solicit agents from the black community, fewer than 2 per cent of the FBI's 8,500 agents are Black Americans – so the G-men hoped to appeal to the National Urban League for help in recruiting more Blacks for the Bureau.

♦ *Philanthropic Postman* Thomas Cannon lives in a poor section of Richmond, Virginia, in a house with a leaking roof and obsolete electrical wiring. He drives a fourteen-year-old car back and forth to his job as a postal worker, where he earns $16,000 a year. What's so unusual about Tom Cannon? Between 1972 and 1977, Mr. Cannon gave away more than $33,000 to strangers less fortunate than himself, or to others, in better financial circumstances, whose deeds he admires.

Some of the people Cannon has helped include: a nine-year-old orphan from South America; a black couple who served as foster parents to over forty children; an honest high school boy who was tormented by his classmates for returning money found on a school bus; and an Egyptian child who came to Richmond for abdominal surgery.

He and his wife prefer to deny themselves life's small luxuries so that they can help others. As he puts it, "I have chosen a way of life over a way of living. We've deliberately kept our standard of living low so that we can free our money to do these other things." Cannon adds, "I've been called a weirdo and crazy for what I do, but it's my form of religion in action."

THE URBANIZATION OF BLACK AMERICANS 1950–1970
Cities with Largest Proportion of Blacks

	1970	1960	1950
Atlanta, Ga.	51.3%	38%	37%
Baltimore, Md.	46.4%	35%	24%
Chicago, Ill.	32.7%	23%	14%
Cleveland, Ohio	38.3%	29%	16%
Detroit, Mich.	43.7%	29%	16%
Memphis, Tenn.	38.9%	37%	37%
Newark, N.J.	54.2%	34%	17%
New Orleans, La.	45.0%	37%	32%
Philadelphia, Pa.	33.6%	26%	18%
St. Louis, Mo.	40.9%	29%	18%
Washington, D.C.	71.1%	54%	35%

TEN BEST CITIES FOR BLACKS

Which cities are considered the best places for Black Americans to live? According to *Ebony* magazine, the ten cities blacks should consider prime targets for relocation, based on economic, political, environmental, social and educational criteria, are:

Atlanta; Baltimore; Chicago; Dallas; Denver; Houston; Indianapolis; Los Angeles; Minneapolis; Washington, D.C.

TOP TEN BLACK-OWNED OR BLACK-CONTROLLED BUSINESSES IN U.S.

Each year since 1973, *Black Enterprise* magazine has surveyed the top Black businesses in the United States. When the first survey appeared, the total revenue for the top 100 Black companies was $473 million. In 1979, total sales for the top 100 Black businesses topped $1.2 billion.

For the eighth consecutive year, Motown Industries of Los Angeles, the entertainment conglomerate, ranked in first place.

Rank	Company	Location	Sales*
1	Motown Industries (entertainment)	Los Angeles	$64.8
2	Johnson Publishing Company (publishing)	Chicago	6.10
3	Fedco Foods Corp. (supermarkets)	Bronx	45.0
4	H. J. Russell Construction Co. (construction and development)	Atlanta	41.0
5	Johnson Products Co. (hair care)	Chicago	35.5
6	Vanguard Oil & Service Co. (oil distribution)	Brooklyn	35.0
7	Afro International Corp. (exports)	New York	32.0
7	Smith Pipe and Supply Inc. (oilfield supply)	Houston	32.0
9	Grimes Oil Company (petroleum)	Dorchester, Ma.	30.0
10	Wallace & Wallace Enterprises (fuel oil sales)	St. Albans, NY	25.9

* 1979 figures, in millions of dollars

BLACK WOMEN

Victims of double discrimination because of their gender and their skin color, black women have been "first" in many fields of endeavor:

♦ The first woman bank president in the United States was Maggie Lena Walker (1867–1934), a native of Richmond, Virginia, who founded the St. Luke Bank and Trust Company in 1903.

♦ The first woman millionaire in the United States was Madame C. J. Walker (1867–1919), who developed a new hair conditioner in 1905. She started by peddling her product door-to-door and ended up with her own manufacturing plant in Indianapolis. At the time of her death in May 1919 her estimated worth was in excess of $1 million.

♦ The first Negro ever accepted for entry into the National Tennis Championships was Althea Gibson (1927–   ). The daughter of a sharecropper who moved to Harlem, she won the women's singles title at Forest Hills and at Wimbledon in 1957–1958. The British *Evening Standard* wrote of her triumph: "More than the Negro people should benefit from Miss Gibson's victory . . . it shows that somewhere in the great American dream there is a place for black as well as white."

♦ The first black YMCA was established on January 3, 1853, but it wasn't until 1967 that a black woman became president of the "Y." In April 1967, Mrs. Robert W. Claytor (Helen Natalie Jackson Claytor, b. 1907) became president of the national YWCA.

♦ The first black Congresswoman was Shirley Chisholm (b. 1924), who was elected in November 1968 to represent the 12th Congressional District in Brooklyn, New York.

♦ Mrs. Emma Clarissa Clement of Louisville, Kentucky, was selected by the Golden Rule Foundation Mother's Committee as "American Mother of the Year" in 1946. The granddaughter of a slave, she was the first black woman to receive this honor.

♦ The first Negro woman to receive a medical degree was Rebecca Lee, an 1864 graduate of the New England Female Medical College of Boston, Massachusetts.

♦ In 1872, Charlotte E. Ray became the first black woman lawyer. She was a former graduate of Howard University Law School, where she chalked up another first by being their first female law student.

♦ The first black woman admitted to practice before the U.S. Supreme Court was Mrs. Violette A. Johnson, born in 1882.

♦ *Rasin in the Sun* was the first major Broadway play written by a black woman. Lorraine Hansberry's play debuted in 1959, became a smash hit, and went on to lead three lives: as a play, as a movie and as a musical (*Raisin*) in the 1970s.

♦ The first U.S. Representative ever granted maternity leave was Yvonne Brathwaite Burke (1932–   ). The first black woman elected to the California General Assembly, she was also the first to represent California in the U.S. Congress. An outspoken proponent of social welfare programs, Burke has said: "I see Congress as a great opportunity. I want to be able to look back and say there are people whose lives are better because I served there."

♦ The career of Judge Jane M. Bolin (1908–   ) has consisted of one "first" achievement after another. The daughter of a Poughkeepsie lawyer, she was the first black woman graduated from Yale's Law School, the first black woman admitted to the Bar Association of the City of New York and the first black woman judge in the United States.

Appointed by Mayor Fiorello La Guardia in 1939 to the Domestic Relations Court (precursor of Family Court), Jane Matilda Bolin had graduated from Wellesley College with honors in 1928, and despite her father's objections she enrolled in Yale's Law School soon afterward. "He was very opposed to the idea at first," she said. "He assumed I'd be a schoolteacher. He didn't think that women should hear the unpleasant things that lawyers have to hear."

Any problems in her career? Other than being turned away from hotels in New England during the 1930s, 40s and 50s because of her color, the only problems she had to face were mixing motherhood and a high-pressure career: "I don't think I short-changed anybody but myself. I didn't get all the sleep I needed, and I didn't get to travel as much as I would have liked, because I felt my first obligation was to my child . . . But professionally, I've never had any disappointments. I've always done the kind of work I like. I don't want to sound trite, but families and children are so important to our society, and to dedicate your life to trying to improve their lives is completely satisfying."

♦ The first Black woman to earn a commission in the U.S. Army National Guard as a first lieutenant was Julia J. Cleckley, in June 1978.

BLACK AMERICAN FEMINIST

Sojourner Truth (1797–1883)

Sojourner Truth was born a slave on January 30, 1797, in Hurley, N.Y. She became a preacher, an Abolitionist and an outspoken advocate of women's rights, and was the first Black woman to lecture against slavery.

In 1851, she appeared at an Ohio woman's convention presided over by Frances Gage. At that time it was not always simple for blacks and whites to cooperate in joint activities, and when Sojourner asked for the right to speak, there were many women who did not want to grant her request.

Slowly she rose to her almost six-foot height; Frances Gage announced her as she approached the speaker's podium. Sojourner Truth bared her arms to show the audience her muscles, and in her deep voice she told of a life of hard work on the farm to dispel the notion that women are weak.

She asked the audience: "And a'n't I a woman? I could work as much and eat as much as a man — when I could get it — and bear the lash as well! And a'n't I a woman? I have borne 13 chilern, and seen 'em mos' all sold off to slavery, and when I cried out with my mother's grief, none but Jesus heard me. And a'n't I a woman? . . . Den dat little man in black dar, he say women can't have as much rights as men 'cause Christ wa'n't a woman! Whar did your Christ come from? From God and a woman! Man had nothin' to do wid Him." She returned to her seat amid roars of applause, leaving many women with tears in their eyes.

Sojourner Truth died a free woman on November 26, 1883, in Battle Creek, Michigan.

Sojourner Truth (1797–1883) was one of the first Black American women to speak out for women's rights. (Courtesy: New York Historical Society)

EVERYONE COMES FROM SOMEWHERE

THE ARMENIANS IN AMERICA

Soviet Armenia, one of the fifteen republics of the U.S.S.R., is all that remains of a nation that once stretched between the Black, Caspian and Mediterranean Seas. Over the centuries, Armenia has been fought over and ruled by Persians, Romans, Mongols and Ottoman Turks. Armenia did become an independent nation briefly in 1920, but independence lasted only a few months before Russian and Turkish troops invaded and claimed control. Eastern Armenia became the Armenian Soviet Socialist Republic in 1921, and today Armenia's territory is divided between Iran, Turkey and the Soviet Union.

Haikistan, Not Armenia Armenians call their homeland Haikistan, and refer to their people as Hai, after their legendary leader, Haik. The reputed great-great-grandson of Noah, the Biblical ark-builder whose ship came to rest on Mt. Ararat (in what was Armenia), Haik founded a dynasty that lasted until the third century B.C., when Armenak gained control. Subsequent generations called the country Armenia in his honor.

The Great Massacre After almost 400 years of Turkish control, a strong nationalistic movement and cultural renaissance swept across Armenia during the nineteenth century. Revolutionary organizations, intent on freeing Armenia from the yoke of Turkish rule, sprang up and were quickly squelched by the government. Abdul Hamid, the Sultan of Turkey, ordered the first massacres and began a campaign to drive Armenians from their homeland in 1894. As a result the number of Armenian immigrants to the United States jumped from a mere 69 in 1870 to almost 15,000 by 1899.

Turkey prohibited Armenian emigration between 1899 and 1907, but a new constitution under Mustapha Kemal's regime restored their rights to emigrate in 1908. Under Kemal's regime, the Young Turks began wholesale massacres of the Armenian people in 1915, causing thousands to flee to Syria, Egypt, Greece and the United States. "No Armenian breathes whose life has not been touched by that genocide," one immigrant noted. "We all lost relatives—parents, grandparents, uncles or cousins." The actual number of Armenians killed at the hands of the Turks will never be known, but estimates as high as 1,800,000 have been quoted.

The true number of Armenians who emigrated to the United States will never be known, either, because they were listed as Turks or Russians by immigration officials. Others entered the country via Greece, Canada and South America. Today, there are an estimated half million Armenians living in North America, with sizable communities in Massachusetts, California, New York, New Jersey and Chicago.

◆ ◆ ◆

◆ The Armenian Church is the oldest national Christian church in the world, dating back to A.D. 301, when the first church in Armenia was founded at Mt. Ararat by the Apostles Thaddeus and Bartholomew. The church has been the center of Armenian life and culture in the United States ever since the close of the nineteenth century, when the first Armenian church in America was built to serve the community of Worcester, Massachusetts.

◆ *Adapting to Life in America* In their homeland, Armenians made pilaf, shish-kebab, lahmajoon (lamb meat pies seasoned with green peppers and tomatoes) and dolmas (stuffed grape leaves). But, being an adaptable people, the Armenians and their descendants in America gave the masses food we could all enjoy: Peter-Paul Almond Joy, Mounds bars and fried chicken (the Chicken Unlimited fast-food chain was founded by Kegham Giragosian). One Armenian, George Vartanian, even made his living as owner of the Supreme Tamale Company in Chicago.

♦ The first Oriental rug merchant in America was probably Hagop Boghigian, an Armenian who settled in Boston, Massachusetts, in 1885.

♦ The first Armenian newspaper in America was *Arekag* (the Sun), first printed in May 1888. Published at Jersey City, New Jersey, the newspaper contained editorials and news from the other side for the 1,000 or so Armenians who were living in America at the time.

♦ *By a Nose* The Futurity Foto-Finish Camera, installed at some of the nation's finest racetracks in 1936, was perfected by a Boston rug merchant, Captain G. Harry Adalian. Adalian invented the high-speed camera to eliminate disputes and needless bickering over which horse finished in the money.

♦ *Money Man* Christopher Der Seropian, an Armenian student who came to America in 1843, discovered the black and green dyes that are used on all U.S. paper currency today. Designed to prevent counterfeiting, Der Seropian's dyes patents were purchased by the Treasury Department for a nominal fee.

♦ *Melon Man* Armenian immigrants to California introduced Persian melons and casaba melons to the United States. One grower, who produced most of the melons grown near Fresno, California, was an Armenian named Arakelian, later dubbed the "Melon King" by his neighbors. Arakelian was also a prominent grape producer in the U.S. during the 1950s.

♦ *"Come On A My House"* A popular song of the 1950s, "Come on a my house" was recorded by Kay Armen, an Armenian-American singer and daughter of the famous wrestler Robert Manoogian (Manogoss). She dedicated the song to her own mother, who was always telling family, friends and strangers to "com-on-ah-mya-

howze." Once inside, her mother would proceed to welcome all guests with that gregariousness that is common among immigrants to America. She would cajole them into eating everything she set before them—nothing was too good, or too much trouble, for a guest in her home.

♦ *Cymbals of Success* The Zildjian family has been making world-famous cymbals for generations, according to a secret process handed down in their family. The family business started in Constantinople, and the secret later traveled across the sea with family members who emigrated to America.

♦ *Immigrant Surgeon* Dr. Varazted Kazanjian (1879–1974), a world-famous plastic surgeon, emigrated to America in 1895. He lived in Worcester, Massachusetts, and worked in a local wire mill for the grand salary of 95¢ per week. Kazanjian was able to enter the Harvard Dental School in 1902 and graduated four years later.

During World War I he became interested in plastic surgery as a means of helping soldiers whose faces had been shattered in battle. His miracle surgery helped many soldiers return home to lead normal lives. (Besides his achievements in plastic surgery, Dr. Kazanjian's other claim to fame was as Arlene Francis's uncle.)

Arlene Francis was the center of attention when she visited the Paramount Theatre in New York for a showing of the movie "Three Sailors and a Girl." Culver Pictures.

Facts About the Other Side:

Official Name:	ARMENIAN SOVIET SOCIALIST REPUBLIC
Capital:	Erevan

Who's Armenian?

Business and Industry:	Tycoons Alex Manoogian (1901–), cited by *Fortune* magazine as one of the 139 richest men in America, and Kirk Kerkorian (1917–), the grandson of an Armenian immigrant from Harput, who built the International Hotel in Las Vegas and worked his way up the ladder of success from millionaire to billionaire.
Show Business:	Arlene Francis (born Arlene Kazanjian), Mike Connors (Krekor Ohanian) and David Hedison.
Music:	Opera stars Lili Chookasian and Lucine Amara; pop singer Cher Sarkisian Bono Allman; musicians Edward Costikyan and Alan Hovhaness, a composer of Armenian and Scottish ancestry, who was the first composer to incorporate songs of the humpback whale into a symphony: "And God Created Great Whales."
Sports:	Football's Ara Parseghian and Garo Yepremian.
Letters:	Pulitzer Prize winner William Saroyan.
Art:	Sculptor Reuben Nakian (1897–).

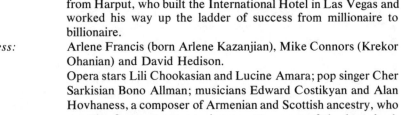

Ten years prior to the publication of his best-selling book, My Name Is Aram, *William Saroyan had been employed as a messenger boy in San Francisco. To celebrate his rise from messenger to best-selling author, Saroyan gave copies of his book to messengers in San Francisco and took one for a spin on his bike. Culver Pictures.*

ASIAN INDIANS IN AMERICA

Between 1820 and 1830, a total of 9 Asian Indians entered the United States. It wasn't until the turn of the century, when severe drought conditions brought widespread starvation to the Punjab region of India, that almost 5,000 Indians left their homeland to seek a new life in California.

Most of these newcomers were members of the Sikh religion, an amalgam of Hindu and Moslem beliefs. A distinguishing trait of all male Sikhs is their uncut hair and beards. Because of this and the use of the turban, they were easily identified and subjected to discrimination by local residents, who were quick to dub these Punjabis "rag heads."

Thumbu Sammy, a 17-year-old "Hindoo" (as he was categorized by immigration officials) arrived at Ellis Island aboard the S.S. Adriatic *on April 14, 1911. (Courtesy: American Museum of Immigration)*

Restrictive immigration laws and changes in naturalization requirements (aimed primarily at the Chinese) denied all Asians citizenship, and quickly reduced the flow of Indians to the United States. In the decade from 1931 to 1940, only 496 Asian Indians came to our shores.

Times have changed, and in recent years India and Pakistan have been major contributors of immigrants to the United States. Most are "brain drain" young peo-ple who come to America for an education, find employment with a large American corporation, and return home only to marry or to visit their relatives periodically.

From the other side, the Indians brought Americans yoga exercises, sitar music, beautiful silk saris, Nehru jackets and curries for the dinner table. They gave us religious leaders for the 1960s (Maharishi Mahesh Yogi and Maharaj Ji), musicians (Ravi Shankar, and conductor Zubin Mehta), meditation, mantras, ragas and passive resistance. But, they didn't give us Indian ink — despite it's name, that writing fluid was invented in China.

◆ ◆ ◆

◆ *The First Swami* Even before Maharishi Mahesh Yogi became a cult figure of the 1960s, America had fallen under the spell of religious leaders from the Far East. The first Swami to visit America was Swami Vivekananda, who came to America in 1893 to attend the Parliament of Religions at the Chicago World Columbian Exposition. The following year, Swami Vivekananda founded the first Vedanta Center in New York. With the funds collected in America he was able to establish missions in his homeland to educate and provide medical care for his people.

◆ *Aryans Are "White"* Dr. Sakaram Ganesh Pandit was born in Gujarat in western India in 1875. After receiving his doctorate in education and philosophy at the Hindu University at Dharwar, Dr. Pandit emigrated to the United States in 1906. He became a naturalized citizen in 1914, but when the U.S. revised its naturalization laws in 1923, the government attempted to revoke Dr. Pandit's citizenship, claiming that he was not "white."

Pandit argued that he was indeed "white" on the grounds that Asian Indians belong to the Aryan race. His argument was accepted and his citizenship upheld, but the decision was overturned at a later date when the court decided that "white" did not encompass Asian Indians, no matter what race they belonged to! By this time, Pandit was a lawyer and was married to an American-born woman. He owned property in the United States and had recently relinquished all title to land he once had owned in India. If he were declared not to be a citizen, he would lose his license to practice law, as well as his property, and according to the oppressive laws at that time, his wife would lose her citizenship, too.

Fortunately for Pandit, he won his case in 1927 and was able to remain a U.S. citizen. But it wasn't until 1946, when the Luce-Celler bill was passed under President Truman's administration, that Asian Indians were allowed to become citizens, own property or bring their relatives into America.

♦ Gobind Behari Lal (1889–   ) won a Pulitzer Prize for scientific writing in 1937. Lal was a feature writer for the *San Francisco Examiner* and a science editor for Universal Service.

♦ Sabu Dastagir (1924–1963), better known to the movie-going public as just plain Sabu, was discovered in his native India at the age of twelve. His most famous film was *The Thief of Bagdad,* produced in 1940. Sabu became a naturalized citizen in 1944; he earned the Distinguished Flying Cross for his military service during World War II.

♦ The first Asian Indian elected to Congress was Dalip Singh Saund, a native of the Punjab. Saund ran for Congress in 1956 and was elected to the House of Representatives from the state of California. Ill health forced Saund to retire from politics in 1958.

♦ *Solar Diet*   Rev. Matthew P. Thekaekara (1914–   ), a native of India, proved that the solar constant, previously believed to be 2 calories per square centimeter, was incorrect. Instead of 2 calories, the solar constant was only 1.940 calories/cm^2. A Roman Catholic priest and a physicist, Rev. Thekaekara became a naturalized citizen in 1962.

♦ Har Gobind Khorana (1922–   ), an Indian-born American chemist, shared the 1968 Nobel Prize for Medicine and Physiology for his work in unraveling the genetic code.

♦ Maharaj Ji, the child-guru, became a naturalized American citizen at the age of 19. Because he was married to an American woman, he was able to file citizenship papers after three years instead of the usual five-year waiting period. As Ji put it, "now was as good a time as any" to give up his Indian citizenship and become an American, especially in view of the fact that his Divine Light Mission, with its 30,000–50,000 adherents, was based in Denver.

♦ In 1977, Queens, New York, became the first of the five boroughs to have a Hindu temple. The building is a testimony to the large influx of Indians to the New York metropolitan area, most of whom have come here since the liberalization of immigration laws in the 1960s. There are now an estimated 110,000 Indians living in New York, and area officials expect that number to double in the early 1980s.

Facts About the Other Side

Country: INDIA
Official Name: Bharat (Union of India)
Natinal Anthem: *Janagana-mana* (Thou art the ruler of the minds of all people.)
National Flag: Horizontal bands of saffron, white and green represent courage and sacrifice; truth and purity; and faith and chivalry. An ancient symbol of law, the Dharma Chakra, adorns the middle band of the flag.

Country: PAKISTAN
                        Pakistan was established in 1947 when India was partitioned according to religious lines. In 1971, East Pakistan declared itself independent of West Pakistan, and it eventually became Bangladesh — but not without a bloody civil war.
Official Name: The Islamic Republic of Pakistan. (Pakistan means "land of the pure.")
National Anthem: *Quami Tarana*
National Flag: The colors of the flag are white and green. Green represents the Moslem majority of the nation; the white star and crescent are traditional symbols of Islam.

Facts About Indian-Americans

Immigration to the United States (1820–1975):   107,446
Recent Immigration (1966–1975):   91,237

As the above figures point out, almost 85% of all Indians who have emigrated to the United States are recent arrivals. The McCarran-Walter Act ended all racial barriers to naturalization in 1952, finally permitting Indians and other Asians to apply for citizenship. And when immigration laws were liberalized in 1965, removing all racial and ethnic quotas, there was a tremendous surge in the number of both highly educated and unskilled Asian immigrants to the United States.

Immigration statistics from Pakistan have been tabulated since 1948. During the decade 1948–1958, an average of 150 Pakistanis per year came to America. Between 1958 and 1975, 9,136 Pakistanis emigrated to the United States.

Foreign-stock population   According to the latest U.S. Census, there were 75,533 first- and second-generation Indian-Americans and 9,308 Pakistani-Americans living in the United States in 1970. Of these, 51,000 Indians and 6,182 Pakistanis were foreign-born.

INDIA'S NATIONAL ANTHEM
"Janagana-mana" was adopted as the national anthem on January 24, 1950. First sung on December 27, 1911, the song was originally entitled "Bharat Vidhata" as a poem by Rabindranath Tagore.

> *Jana-gana-mana-adhinayaka, jaya he*
> *Bharata-bhagya-vidhata.*
> *Punjab-Sindhu-Gujarta Maratha-Dravida-Utkala-Banga*
> *Vindhya-Himachala-Yamuna-Ganga Uchchhala-Jaladhitarnga*
> *Tava subha name jage,*
> *Tava subha asisa mage,*
> *Gahe tava jaya-gatha.*
> *Jana-gana-mangala-dayaka, jaya he*
> *Bharata-bhagya-vidhata*
> *Jaya he, jaya he, jaya he,*
> *Jaya jaya jaya, jaya he.*

The following is Rabindranath Tagore's English rendering of the stanza:

> *Thou art the ruler of the minds of all people, dispenser of India's destiny.*
> *Thy name rouses the hearts of the Punjab, Sind, Gujarat and Maratha, of the Dravid and Orissa and Bengal; it echoes in the hills of the Vindhyas and Himalayas, mingles in the music of the Jamuna and Ganges and is chanted by the waves of the Indian sea. They pray for thy blessings and sing thy praise. The saving of all people waits in thy hand, thou dispenser of India's destiny.*
> *Victory, victory, victory to thee.*

(Source: Information Service of India, 3 E. 64th St., New York, NY 10021)

THE BELGIANS IN AMERICA

When Spanish troops invaded Belgium in 1567, almost 200,000 Protestant Walloons were forced to flee their homeland. Many settled in England and the Netherlands, where they established more than seventy Walloon churches during the next fifty years.

After the Dutch West India company was formed, Jesse de Forest led the first shipload of Walloons to the New World in 1624. They sailed aboard the ship *New Netherland* and settled in Manhattan, Albany, and Brooklyn, New York, and further south in Gloucester, New Jersey. They were the first settlers in the Middle States, the first to till the soil of New Netherland, and the first to introduce the daisy and the peach, pear and quince trees to the New World.

At that time the Middle States were known as *Nova Belgica,* or New Belgium, but within a few generations the Walloons, with their customs and traditions, had been "intermarried" out of existence, thanks to the presence of a growing Dutch population.

Over the past 155 years, some 200,000 Belgians have found their way to America. But, despite their relatively small numbers, the Belgians who emigrated to American shores contributed much to our nation. Belgian-Americans gave us the plastics industry, the Atlas missile, a history of science and the Panama Canal.

◆ ◆ ◆

◆ Michael Pauw, a Belgian immigrant, was quite a land tycoon in the early seventeenth century. In 1630, he bought Staten Island from the Indians for some kettles, axes, hoes, wampum and other tools and trinkets. He later purchased what is now Hoboken, New Jersey, and Jersey City.

◆ *The First Trolley* Karel Vandepoele, a native of Lichtervelde, was the man who introduced trolley cars to Detroit, Michigan. As early as 1869, Vandepoele's trolleys were whizzing up and down the streets of Detroit. Some historians claim Vandepoele's experiments with electric light were the basis for Edison's discoveries.

◆ The only Flemish newspaper published outside of Belgium is *De Gazette van Detroit,* which has been published in Michigan since August 1914. This was not, however, the first Flemish newspaper in America.

George Washington Goethals, the Belgian-American in charge of constructing the Panama Canal. (Courtesy: New York Historical Society)

That honor belongs to the *Gazette van Moline,* which was published in Moline, Illinois, in 1907.

♦ George Washington Goethals (1858–1928), the American army officer and civil engineer who spent seven years of his life overseeing the construction of the Panama Canal, was born in Brooklyn, New York, to Belgian immigrant parents. A graduate of the City College of New York and West Point, Goethals was the first civil governor of the Canal Zone.

♦ *Belgian Place Names in America* Antwerp, New York, Ohio and Michigan; Brussels, Illinois, Wisconsin and Missouri; Flanders, New York and New Jersey; Fleming, Georgia, New York and Ohio; Ghent, Massachusetts; Hoboken, New Jersey and Alabama; Ostend, Pennsylvania; Wallonia, Kentucky.

Facts About the Other Side

Country:	BELGIUM
Capital:	Brussels
Official Name:	Royaume de Belgique (French)
	Koninkrijk België (Flemish) (Kingdom of Belgium)
Official Languages:	French, Flemish
National Flag:	Vertical bands of black, gold and red. The colors represent the three provinces that led the revolution of 1789. The flag was adopted in 1831.
National Anthem:	La Brabaconne (The Braband Song)
National Holiday:	July 21, Independence Day
Major Religion:	Roman Catholic

Facts About Belgian-Americans:

Immigration to the United States (1820–1975):	200,575
Peak Decade (1901–1910):	41,635

1970 Census

Foreign-born Belgians	41,412
Native-born, 2nd generation	89,238
Total Foreign-stock Population	130,650

Belgians constitute 0.4% of our nation's foreign-stock population.

Who's Belgian?

Science Karel-Jan Bossart (1904–1975), the "Father of the Atlas Missile."

Invention Leo Baekelandt (1863–1944), pioneer plastics formulator who developed the first synthetic resin, Bakelite, in 1909.

Letters George Sarton (1884–1956), author of the monumental work *Introduction to the History of Science.*

Medicine Father Joseph Damien De Veuster (1840–1889), better known as Father Damien, was the Roman Catholic priest who devoted his life to the care of lepers on the Hawaiian island of Molokai. A Belgian immigrant to Hawaii, Damien ministered to the bodies and the souls of the lepers until he contracted that dread disease himself in 1885.

THE CHINESE IN AMERICA

Some historians claim there were Chinese shipbuilders plying their trade in America as early as 1571; others claim Chinese laborers were living in the West around 1788. Immigration records were not kept until 1820, and that year only 1 Chinese immigrant ventured to our shores.

Between 1821 and 1830, 2 more immigrants from China came to America, and by 1850 there were 758 Chinese residents of the United States. Extended periods of drought in Canton Province between 1847 and 1850 contributed to large-scale immigrations of Chinese peasants to Mei Kwok, or "the Beautiful Land," as the peasants called America. During the 1850s more than 41,000 Chinese made their way across the Pacific Ocean to settle in the United States. Many came here during the

"gold rush," seeking the nuggets that were reputed to be lying in the rivers and streams for the taking. But, like the Southern and Eastern Europeans who followed them later in the century (seeking the gold that lay in the *streets* of America), the Chinese found only hard work and discrimination in Gum Shan ("the Mountain of Gold" — America's new nickname).

"Coolie" labor was in great demand during the 1850s, when cheap workers were needed to build the transcontinental railroad systems. In 1852, the Governor of California, John Mac Dougall, called the Chinese: "[the] most desirable of our adopted citizens." It was estimated that 9,000 out of the 10,000 laborers who built the Union Pacific railroad were Chinese. Continued Chinese emigration to America

An affluent Chinese family who resided in New York City at the turn of the century. (Courtesy: Museum of the City of New York)

was met with great favor by the railroad builders of America—*until* 1869 when the Central Pacific met the Union Pacific at Ogden, Utah, and thousands of Chinese were thrown out of work.

The Panic of 1876 brought economic collapse to many parts of our nation, and the Chinese were seen as a threat to the "native American" workingman. According to the 1870 census, there were more than 105,000 Chinese living in America, many residing in California, and the slogan "The Chinese must go" began to echo around the nation.

Most of the Chinese immigrants in the nineteenth century were unskilled, uneducated peasants who came to the States hoping to earn a "nest egg" for their families in China. But, like so many other immigrants, the Chinese found themselves transplanted here permanently; despite the discrimination and hardships they had to endure, they stayed in America and began to call it home.

◆ ◆ ◆

◆ The "Father of the Chinese student movement" was Yung Wing, the first Chinese to become a naturalized American citizen. Wing came here in 1847, attended Yale and was naturalized in 1849. He later returned to his native land to recruit students for study at American universities. His autobiography, *My Life in China and America,* was published in 1909.

◆ Why are there so many Chinese laundries? When the 49ers went to work in the mines, they traveled light and left their womenfolk behind. Since laundry, tailoring and cooking were considered "women's work" in the 1850s, there weren't many he-men in the mining camps who were willing (or able) to do these chores. But, for thousands of Chinese, barred from many jobs, "women's work" was a golden opportunity to make the quantum leap from hired hand to "boss" and become an entrepreneur. With an iron, ironing board, bucket and washboard, a Chinese laborer did not have to work for "coolie" wages. Washing and ironing was hard work in those days, to be sure, but it had to be less hazardous than laying railroad ties and digging underground tunnels.

◆ The first Chinese newspaper published in America was *Kim Shan Jit San Luk* (San Francisco Golden Hills News), which debuted in 1854. By 1891, San Francisco had its first bilingual (English and Chinese) daily, *China World.* In 1900, the first all-Chinese daily newspaper, *Shung Sai Yat Po* (The Chinese Western Daily) appeared.

◆ The first Chinese woman to graduate from an American medical school was Dr. Mary Stone (real name: Shih mai-yu), who graduated from the University of Michigan in 1896.

◆ The derisive term for a Chinese born in the United States is *jook-sing,* meaning the hollow part of a bamboo pole; this indicates that Chinese-Americans are "empty" of the culture and traditions of China.

◆ The Chinese remained "without a Chinaman's chance" of swaying politicians to their cause until 1943. Since they were barred from becoming American citizens, they had no votes to exchange for political favors; hence, no candidates would champion their fight for civil rights.

◆ In 1947, President Harry S. Truman named Eddie Gong, the grandson of an immigrant launderer, the "Boy President of the United States." Not to be outdone in the area of goodwill toward the Chinese-Americans, Mrs. Truman named Mrs. Toy Len Goon of Maine "America's Mother of the Year" in 1952.

◆ In 1940 there were 28 "Chinatowns" in the United States. By 1955, the number had dwindled to 16, reflecting the "Americanization" of the Chinese-American population.

◆ Republican Hiram L. Fong, the son of sugar plantation laborers who emigrated to Hawaii from China in 1872, became Hawaii's first Senator in 1959. But, he was not the first Chinese-American to serve as an elected official—that honor belongs to Wing F. Ong, who was elected to the Arizona state legislature in 1946.

◆ The first Chinese-American to become a judge was Delbert E. Wong. Appointed by California's Governor Edmund Brown in 1959, Wong served on the Los Angeles municipal bench.

◆ The first Chinese-American to become a member of the New York Stock Exchange was Whalen Lou. Mr. Lou purchased his seat, in September 1979, for $205,000.

Facts About the Other Side:

Country:	CHINA
Capital:	Peking
Official Name:	Chung-hua jen-min-kung-ho-kuo
	(People's Republic of China)
Official Language:	Mandarin dialect, Chinese
National Anthem:	"The March of the Volunteers"
National Flag:	Adopted in 1949 when the Communists drove the Nationalists from the Mainland. Red field with yellow stars representing the Communist party and the four classes that make up the party.

Country:	TAIWAN
Capital:	Taipei
Official Name:	The Republic of China
	Established in 1949 when Chiang Kai-shek moved his Nationalist Government to Taiwan, formerly known as Formosa.
Official Language:	Chinese
National Anthem:	"National anthem of the Republic of China"
National Flag:	Dates back to 1906 when Dr. Sun Yat-sen chose the design of a white sun in a blue sky over a crimson ground. It was officially adopted in 1928. Blue stands for equality, justice and *min chuan,* or democracy; white is for fraternity, frankness and *min sheng* (People's livelihood); and crimson is for liberty, sacrifice and *min tsu* (nationalism).

Facts About Chinese-Americans:

Immigration to the United States (1820–1875):	487,803
Peak Decade (1871–1880):	123,201
Recent Immigration, from China and Taiwan (1971–1975):*	85,645
(1966–1975):	181,393

Recent changes in the ties between the United States and China have caused a surge in emigration from the People's Republic in 1979. More than 2,000 applications are being submitted in Hong Kong each month, versus 100 applications per month during the same period in 1978.

1970 Census:

Foreign-born Chinese	172,132
Native-born, 2nd generation	167,111
Total Foreign-stock Population	339,243

Chinese constitute 1.0% of our nation's foreign-stock population.
Estimated Chinese-American Population (third generation and beyond)   500,000

There are 135 Chinese in West Virginia; 589 in Atlanta; 672 in Dallas; and none in Gary, Indiana.

*Taiwan has been included since 1957

Main Ethnic Epicenters:		***U.S. Cities with Most Chinese*	
California	136,860	San Francisco	71,585
New York	66,407	New York	62,061
Hawaii	20,939	Los Angeles	32,684
Illinois	11,833	Honolulu	19,452
Massachusetts	11,324	Chicago	9,985

More than one-third of all Chinese-Americans reside in either San Francisco or New York. In San Francisco, the Chinese constitute 10 percent of the city's population and have more political clout there than in any other city in the United States.

Who's Chinese?

Business and Industry An Wang, an electronics specialist, founded Wang Laboratories in 1955 . . . The Manhattan Fund was started in 1964 by Gerald Tsai, Jr., a Changai-born naturalized citizen who amassed $270 million from 150,000 investors to start his financial venture . . . The Li Foundation, which provides fellowships for advanced students, was established by K. C. Li, an industrialist who founded the Wah Chang Corporation and built it into the world's largest tungsten refinery by 1953 . . . National Dollar Stores, founded by Joe Shoong and his family in 1907, had grown to a 54-store chain by 1928.

Entertainment Bruce Lee, deceased star of martial arts movies; Kam Fong, regular star of television's only major employer of Oriental actors—*Hawaii Five-O;* Chang and Eng, the original "Siamese twins."

IN THEIR OWN WORDS . . .

Leslie Wong talks about finding his "roots" in the People's Republic of China in 1977:

"I may look Chinese. Certainly, the roots of my ancestry are in China. My father was born in Hong Kong, my mother in Shanghai. I was born in Oakland, California, and spent most of my life there. . . . I am still conspicuously American in culture—a result of growing up in a middle-class, multi-ethnic neighborhood.

"My friends envied me in being able to go to China to get a firsthand look at 'my' culture. But my friends were wrong. I found, after my 30-day visit, that despite the fact that I look Chinese, know how to use chopsticks and cook a few Chinese dishes, I felt unconnected with the flow of life in China. My culture wasn't in China, of course. My culture is the one in which I grew up."

"I did find that while the roots of my ancestry were Chinese, they have been lost . . . my life is inextricably rooted in America."

"One of my aunts was curious to know why I didn't speak Chinese. My mother told her that she had tried to teach me when I was a child, but one day when I was playing in front of our house with some friends, an airplane roared over our heads. I shouted with excitement, using the Chinese word for airplane, *fei chi.* When I realized that my friends didn't understand what I was saying, I didn't want to speak Chinese any more, at all."

Smithsonian, April 1977, pp 116–120.

THE CUBANS IN AMERICA

With the exception of the descendants of the few immigrants who came to America in the 1830s to work in cigar factories and a trickle of Batista-era refugees, most of the Cubans living in America today are recent arrivals. Unlike their Spanish-speaking neighbors from other islands in the Caribbean, the Cubans were welcomed to America with open arms as political refugees from communism. Almost 700,000 Cubans came to America after Fidel Castro seized power in 1959, and most of them were admitted to the country without regard to rigid quota systems or long waits for permanent visas, which other immigrants were subjected to.

During the airlift sponsored by the U.S. government between 1965 and 1973 the Cuban population of Dade County, Florida, increased so rapidly that the area earned the nickname "Little Havana." Today, Cubans are the single largest ethnic group in Miami's public schools, and they have a strong desire to maintain their cultural heritage.

Of all the Spanish-speaking ethnic groups in America, the Cubans are the most highly educated and earn the most money. Almost 25% of the Cuban families living in Miami have an annual income of at least $15,000. Cubans own more than 8,000 businesses and small industries in the area, as well as five banks in Dade County.

One of Miami's most famous immigrants is Juanita Castro, Fidel's sister. A fervent anti-Communist, Juanita left her native land and fled to Miami in 1964. Six years later she entered into a partnership with two Cuban refugees and bought a drugstore in the Miami area, where she works and leads a rather reclusive life. Of her relationship with her brother, Juanita says: "I have nothing to discuss with Fidel."

The most recent wave of Cuban immigration began in April, 1980, when a flotilla of private boats began ferrying refugees from Cuba to Key West, Florida. By the middle of June, more than 110,000 Cuban refugees had settled in the United States.

Unable to control the flow of illegal Cuban aliens, President Carter bowed to humanitarian pressures and granted the refugees political asylum.

Many of the recent Cuban immigrants had relatives in the United States, whom they joined in the ethnic communities of Southern Florida and Northern New Jersey. But, unlike the Cuban immigrants of the 1960's, who were upper class professional and technical workers, the refugees of the 1980's are penniless exiles. Many are factory workers, farm laborers, or unskilled workers seeking entry level jobs at the minimum wage.

In West New York, New Jersey where Cubans account for 55 percent of the town's 52,000 residents, and in Elizabeth, New Jersey, where Cubans make up about 20 percent of that city's 103,000 residents, local relief organizations have been successful in finding employment for many of the newcomers.

Facts About the Other Side:

Country:	CUBA
Capital:	Havana
Official Name:	República de Cuba (Republic of Cuba)
Official Language:	Spanish
National Flag:	Horizontal bands of blue (3) and white (2) with a red triangle on the left-hand side. A white star within the triangle stands for independence. The flag was adopted in 1902, after Cuba became a republic.
National Anthem:	"La Bayamesa"
National Holiday:	July 26, anniversary of Castro's attack on the Moncada Army Barracks.
Major Religion:	Roman Catholic

Facts About Cuban-Americans

1970 Census

Foreign-born Cubans	439,048
Native-born, 2nd generation	121,580
Total Foreign-stock population	560,628
Estimated Cuban-American population	800,000

Cubans represented 1.7% of the foreign-stock population of the United States in 1970.

Main Ethnic Epicenters:
   According to the latest census report in 1970, there were 252,520 Cubans living in Florida; 98,479 living in New York; 71,233 in New Jersey; 47,699 in California; and 19,649 in Illinois. The states with the least number of Cubans were Vermont with only 7 and Montana with 45.

Who's Cuban?

Entertainment Desi Arnaz, bandleader and comedy star for more than two decades on *I Love Lucy.*

Dance Fernando Bujones (1955–   ), Miami-born dancer with the American Ballet Theater.

Sports baseball's Tony Oliva, Luis Tiant, Pedro Ramos; featherweight boxer Kid Chocolate.

Business Former president and current chairman of the board of the Coca-Cola Company, Cuban-born Roberto C. Goicueta.

THE CZECHS IN AMERICA

In the 1600s Czech Protestants fled their homeland because of religious persecution following the Thirty Years War. Some settled in Sweden, Holland and England, and from there they made their way across the sea to colonies established in America.

The first Czech in America was probably Augustine Herrmann (1605–1686), who arrived in New Amsterdam in 1633. Herrmann later settled in Maryland, and in the early 1920s one of his descendants, U.S. Senator Thomas F. Bayard of Delaware, built his home on the tract of land where Herrmann, Bayard's first American ancestor, had once lived.

During the 1730s members of the Moravian Brethren religious sect began emigrating to America in fairly large numbers. Although their first colony was in Georgia, they eventually settled in the towns of Bethlehem, Nazareth and Lititz in Pennsylvania.

The Czechs didn't start mass migrations until the 1840s when a potato famine, poor economic and social conditions and political uprisings in 1848 led many disgruntled Czechs to seek greener pastures in the New World. There were large Czech settlements in Iowa, Wisconsin, Nebraska, Oklahoma and Texas. Even today, there are almost 90,000 Czechs (still speaking the language of their ancestors) scattered throughout 100 Texas towns.

Modern Czechoslovakia was formed in 1918 when the Czechoslovak national council was recognized by the Allied Powers. The movement for Czech independence from the Hapsburg Empire was directed, from the United States, by Thomas Masaryk. During the war, Masaryk did research work at the New York Public Library with the help of his American-born wife, and in 1918 he was installed as President of a "new" Czechoslovakia that was basically identical in territory to the original Czech kingdom destroyed in 1620. There was one addition, however: Carpathian Russia, or Ruthenia, requested transfer to Czech jurisdiction in 1918. Ruthenia was ceded to Russia in 1945, and in 1948 Communists gained control of the Czechoslovak government.

♦ ♦ ♦

♦ The first Czech-language newspaper in America was *Slovan Amerikansky*, published in Racine, Wisconsin, in 1855.

♦ The first American Sokol organization, dedicated to physical, mental and cultural development, was founded in 1865 at St. Louis, Missouri. It was an outgrowth of an 1862 movement that originated in Prague. (*Sokol* means "falcon.")

♦ The Gothic pinnacles of St. Patrick's Cathedral in New York City were designed by Joseph Svak, an immigrant architect from Czechoslovakia.

♦ In 1880 there were over 85,000 Bohemians living in the United States. Thirty years later, in 1910, there were almost 500,000 first- and second-generation Americans of Bohemian and Moravian stock.

♦ The first Czech congressman was Adolph Sabath, a Jewish lawyer who came to America in 1881 at the age of fifteen.

♦ Antonin Cermak, the Czech-born mayor of Chicago, died as a result of an assassination attempt made on the life of President-elect Franklin D. Roosevelt in February 1933. An unemployed bricklayer mortally wounded Cermak instead of his real target, FDR.

♦ *First American Man Canonized* Bohemian-born Jon Nepomucene Neumann, the Bishop of Philadelphia from 1852 to 1860, was the first American male to be canonized as a saint. On June 19, 1977, Pope Paul VI declared "that Jon Newmann . . . is in heaven and is worthy of honor and imitation by all the faithful."

♦ Chicago is the most "Czech-ered" city in the United States, with over 79,000 first- and second-generation Czech-Americans. Milwaukee, one of the oldest Czech communities in America, was first settled by immigrants because the climate was similar to that of the old country, the soil was suited for the crops they were familiar with and the land was cheap at $12.50 for 10 acres. (There were almost 5,000 foreign-stock Czechoslovakian Americans living in Milwaukee at the time of the 1970 U.S. Census.)

♦ *Places With Czech Names* Bohemia, New York; New Prague and Moravia, Minnesota; Prague, Nebraska; Moravia, Texas; and Slovaktown, Arkansas.

Facts About the Other Side:

Country:	CZECHOSLOVAKIA

A 1968 amendment to the Czech constitution divided Czechoslovakia into two sections: the Czech Socialist Republic, consisting of Bohemia and Moravia; and the Slovak Socialist Republic.

Capital: Prague

Motto: *Pravda vitezi* (The Truth Will Win)
Adopted by the Czech Republic in fifteenth century.

Official Name: Ceskoslovenska Socialisticka Republika (Czechoslovak Socialist Republic)

Official Languages: Czech and Slovak

National Anthem: "Kde domov muj?" (Where Is My Homeland?) and "Nad Tatrou sa blyska" (Lightning Flashes over the Tatra)

National Flag: A blue triangle on the left intersects two horizontal bands of white over red. The three colors represent the regions of Bohemia, Moravia and Slovakia.

Major Religions: Roman Catholic, Czechoslovak National Church and Czech Brethren.

Ethnic Mix: When the independent state of Czechoslovakia was formed in 1918, it incorporated Bohemia, Moravia, Silesia, Slovakia and Carpathian Russia (Ruthenia). Formerly, Bohemia, Moravia and Slovakia had been part of the Austro-Hungarian Empire. Today, Czechs comprise 65% of the population and Slovaks 30%. In addition, there are Hungarians, Germans, Gypsies, Ruthenian-Ukrainians and Poles living in Czechoslovakia.

Facts About Czech-Americans:

Immigration to the U.S. (1920–1975): 135,995

Figures are only available for Czechoslovakia since 1920. Prior to that, immigrants were recorded as Austro-Hungarians.

Recent Immigration:
The peak decade for Czechoslovakia was 1921–1930, when 102,194 immigrants reached our shores. Between 1941 and 1950, 8,347 Czechs came to America, but after Communist control began in 1948 only 918 immigrants came between 1951 and 1960. Czech immigrants numbered 3,444 between 1971 and 1975.

1970 Census

Foreign-born Czechs	160,899
Native-born, 2nd generation	598,628
Total Foreign-stock Population	759,527
Estimated Czech-American Population	1,750,000

Main Ethnic Epicenters:		*U.S. Cities with Most Czechs:*	
Pennsylvania	118,855	Chicago	79,982
Ohio	93,187	New York	66,466
New York	90,641	Cleveland	53,049
Illinois	88,259	Pittsburgh	50,447
New Jersey	51,599	Los Angeles	21,110

Who's Czech?

Entertainment Betsy Palmer (Betsy Hrunek); Walter Slezak; Jon Voight, the grandson of an immigrant coal miner from Czechoslovakia.

Art Andy Warhol, the artist who turned soup cans into money-making canvases, was born sometime between 1927 and 1932 in Pennsylvania. His father was a Czechoslovakian coal miner and his mother was an immigrant from Mikova.

Sports George Blanda, pro-football player.

Politics Ralph H. Perk, former mayor of Cleveland, Ohio; Richard Bassett, a signer of the Constitution.

Science Carl and Gerty Cori, 1947 Nobel Prize winners for Physiology and Medicine; Zdenek Kopal, astronomer.

Astrology Svetlana Godilla, President Carter's astrologer.

Theater Martin Beck (1867–1940), a theatrical manager born in Lipto, Szent Miklos (now a part of Czechoslovakia), is no longer with us, but his name lives on: it identifies a Broadway theater that he built in 1924 on 45th Street.

THE DANES IN AMERICA

Immigration statistics were not kept until 1820, so there aren't any records of the Danes who came to our shores between 1600 and 1820. It is certain, however, that Danish immigrants came to America as early as the seventeenth century—one of them being Jonas Bronck, the man who gave his last name to one of New York City's five boroughs.

By 1850 the U.S. Census reported 1,837 Danes living in America. During the 1850s, almost 3,700 Danish immigrants were recruited to American shores by Mormon missionaries, and at the time of the next U.S. Census in 1860 there were more than 10,000 Danes living in America. The majority lived in the Midwest, on farms in Wisconsin, Illinois, Iowa and Minnesota.

By 1920 there were almost half a million first- and second-generation Danish-

Americans in the United States, concentrated mainly in Iowa and Minnesota. According to the 1970 census there were 325,561 foreign-stock Danes living in the United States — 61,410 were born in Denmark and 264,151 were born in America. While Minnesota is still the second-largest population center for Danish Americans, Iowa has fallen to fifth place, behind California, Illinois and New York.

◆ ◆ ◆

◆ The first Danish newspaper in the United States was *Den Danske Pioneer,* which was published for the first time in 1872.

◆ Racine, Wisconsin, once nicknamed "Dane City," was founded by Danish immigrants in 1834. To this day, Racine has a large percentage of German- and Scandinavian-Americans of third generation and beyond.

◆ The first Danish fraternal organization, The Danish Brotherhood, was established in 1882 at Omaha, Nebraska. Still in existence today, the Danish Brotherhood had more than 250 lodges in 1930.

◆ One of the most famous Danish-American journalists was Jacob Riis (1849–1914). Often called "America's first photojournalist," Riis used his camera to verify the truthfulness of his newspaper stories. His book, *How the Other Half Lives,* published in 1890, aroused public sympathy and support to improve the wretched living conditions that many of our nation's poor immigrants were subjected to in urban slums. An immigrant himself, Riis was born in Ribe, Denmark, and came to the United States at the age of 21.

◆ In 1917, the United States purchased the Danish West Indies (later renamed the Virgin Islands) for $25 million. Ten years later, the people of the Virgin Islands, including approximately 3,200 Danes, were granted U.S. citizenship.

Jacob A. Riis was named "the most useful citizen in New York" by McClure's *magazine in 1901. (Courtesy: New York Historical Society)*

Facts About the Other Side:

Country:	**DENMARK**

Capital: Copenhagen
Official Name: Kongeriget Danmark (Kingdom of Denmark)
Official Language: Danish
National Flag: A white cross on a red field. According to legend, the flag appeared in the sky in 1219 to King Valdemar II as a victory sign during a battle.
National Anthem: Der er et yndigt land (There is a lovely land)
National Holiday: June 5, Constitution Day
Major Religion: Evangelical Lutheran Church

Facts About Danes in America:

Immigration to the U.S. (1820–1975): 362,833
   Peak Decade (1881–1890): 88,132

1970 Census
Foreign-born Danes   61,410
Native-born, 2nd generation   264,151
Total Foreign-stock Population: 325,561

Main Ethnic Epicenters:

California	62,757
Minnesota	22,762
Illinois	22,021
New York	20,911
Iowa	20,024

In 1970, 194,462 Americans claimed Danish as their mother tongue. Estimated Danish-American population: 2 million.

Who's Danish

Education Martha Elizabeth Peterson (1916–   ), former President of Barnard College and the granddaughter of a Danish immigrant; Arthur Jensen (1923–   ), educational psychologist of Danish and German ancestry who has gained notoriety for his theories about human intelligence.

Letters Peter Matthiessen (1927–   ), naturalist, explorer and writer; Jacob Riis, journalist and crusader for legislation to protect immigrants and children.

Business Semon Knudsen (1912–   ), chairman of White Motor Company; William Knudson, Vice-President of General Motors.

Religion Rev. Howard A. Johnson (1915–   ), Clergyman of Danish, English and Irish descent who was appointed as Canon Theologian of the Episcopal Cathedral of St. John the Divine in New York City in 1954.

Music Victor Borge fled Denmark during the Nazi invasion and arrived here in 1940. He learned English at the movie theaters, and consequently his first English sentence was "You'll burn for this, you rat."

Dance Peter Schaufuss, principal dancer with the New York City Ballet.

Art Gutzon de la Mothe Borglum, the sculptor of Mount Rushmore.

THE DUTCH IN AMERICA

The First Wave of Dutch Immigration

Basing their claims to the New World on Henry Hudson's explorations in America, the Dutch established New Netherland in 1621. They settled Fort Orange (now Albany) in 1624, and colonized New Amsterdam (now New York City) in 1625.

Most of the early Dutch settlers were fur traders, and despite repeated attempts by the government to lure farmers to New Netherland, the conditions at home were simply too comfortable to force many Dutchmen to seek their fortunes in America. The Netherlands was experiencing its "golden age" of prosperity, and the Hollanders were not about to trade the peace and security of home for an American adventure.

In 1640, the Dutch West India Company agreed to pay the passage of anyone willing to settle in New Netherland, and it was only then that the colony became viable by enticing a few Dutch, Norwegians, English, Germans, Huguenots and Swedes to the New World.

The second wave of Dutch immigration to the United States began in the 1800s when economic distress, religious persecution and the Napoleonic Wars uprooted thousands of Dutch citizens from their homeland. Although the Dutch preceded the Puritans to America, they have never emigrated here in large numbers, preferring to begin their second chance at life in the capitals of Europe and the German Rhineland. From 1820 to the present, only about 360,000 Dutch immigrants have reached

Peter Mortier engraved this scene of New Amsterdam sometime around 1673. (Courtesy: New York Historical Society)

our shores—a mere trickle when compared to the floodtide of Irish (more than 4 million) and Germans (more than 3 million) who emigrated to America between 1820 and 1920.

Dutch influence in the United States far outweighs the relatively small number of immigrants Holland contributed to our nation. There is no need for Americans of Dutch ancestry to scour obscure history books in search of forebears who made their mark on America: the Dutch were a visible part of our nation's history, contributing such well-known names as Stuyvesant, Roosevelt, Van Buren and Vanderbilt.

The Dutch gave us place names such as Amsterdam, Missouri (and New York); Verboort, Oregon; Holland, Michigan (and Nebraska); Nederland, Texas; Vandervoort, Arkansas; and South Holland, Illinois. Most of the Dutch place names are found in the region surrounding the Delaware River, and in the Hudson River Valley of New York: Kill van Kull, Peekskill and Catskill come from the Dutch *kil*, meaning "creek" or "channel." Barnegat, and the ominous-sounding Hell Gate come from the word *gat*, meaning a pass in the channel. Other Dutch-inspired names have been changed over the years: Rikers Island, a prison facility in New York, was originally named in honor of a Dutch man named Reigers, and Coney Island started out as Konijn Eiland (Rabbit Island)—a descriptive name given because of the wildlife that once abounded at that seaside resort.

Although most of the 17 million Americans of Dutch ancestry are far removed from the immigrant experience, there are more than 383,000 foreign-stock Hollanders living in America, primarily in Michigan, California and the New York metropolitan area.

◆ ◆ ◆

◆ The first Dutch immigrant ship to land in America was the *Niew Nederlandt,* which docked here in 1624 with 30 families and some single men, plus livestock, seed grain and farming tools. Most of the new arrivals were Protestant refugees (Walloons from the Spanish Netherlands and Huguenots from France) who came to America to escape religious persecution.
◆ The first Indian War was accidentally started by William Kieft, Director-General

of the Dutch West India Company from 1637 to 1646. The war not only proved catastrophic to the colony of New Netherland (the population was reduced from 3,000 to 1,000) but also ruined Kieft's career—he was fired and replaced by Peter Stuyvesant in 1646.
◆ The first police force in America, consisting of 8 men, was established in New Amsterdam in 1658. It wasn't until 1693, when the British controlled the region, that they were first issued uniforms.
◆ The first cabbage grown in America came from a cabbage patch planted by Dutch colonists near Setauket, Long Island. The Dutch also introduced the cultivation of beets, endive, spinach, dill, parsley and chervil to America.

DUTCH NAMES THAT HAVE BEEN "CORRUPTED" OVER THE YEARS

Old Dutch Name	What It Became
Bloemendael (vale of flowers)	Bloomingdale
Boswyck	Bushwick
Breucklen (broken land)	Brooklyn
Gravezande	Gravesend
Heemstede	Hempstead
Niew Haarlem	Harlem
Tarwe Town	Tarrytown
Vlack Bos (flat woods)	Flatbush
De Kromme Zee	Gramercy
Vliessingen	Flushing

◆ New York's Dutch Politicians. Since New York City start out as a "Dutch" settlement, it's only fitting that she's had her share of politicians with Dutch ancestors. There was De Witt Clinton, Cornelius Van Wyck, and more recently, John V. Lindsay, one of New York's most dashing mayors, who served from 1966 to 1973.
◆ Germantown, Pennsylvania. A group of Dutch Mennonites living in Krefeld and Kriesheim, Germany, emigrated to Pennsylvania in 1683 and purchased 5,000 acres of land from William Penn. Despite their

Dutch heritage, they called their settlement Germantown; it remained predominantly Dutch until 1709. By that time massive German immigration and intermarriage with the Hollanders had served to erase most traces of Dutch customs and traditions in the area.

♦ Joseph Ellicot (1760–1859) was a Dutch-English engineer nicknamed the "Father of Buffalo" for founding that New York city in 1803.

♦ Castle Garden became the compulsory landing place for immigrants in 1855 due to the efforts of Gulian Verplanck, the Dutch-American who served as Commissioner of Emigration in the mid-1800s. Verplanck hoped the centralized arrival gate would lessen incidents of exploitation, whereby newly arrived immigrants were cheated out of the few dollars they had by unscrupulous railway agents and boarding house owners.

♦ When the 1920 Census was tabulated there were 6.9 million persons of Dutch ancestry living in America. When national immigration quotas went into effect in 1924, the Netherlands National Origins Quota was fixed at 3,136, preventing unrestricted Dutch immigration to the United States.

Facts About the Other Side:

Country:	HOLLAND (the name means "woodland")
Official Name:	The Kingdom of the Netherlands (Du Koninkrijk der Nederlanden)
Official Language:	Dutch
National Anthem:	"Wilhelmus van Nassau" (William of Nassau)
National Flag:	Red, white and blue vertical bands; until 1630, the flag's colors were orange, white and blue.

Facts About Dutch-Americans:

Immigration to the U.S. (1820–1975):   356,282
   Peak Decade (1881–1890):   53,701

1970 Census
Foreign-born Dutch   110,570
Native-born 2nd generation   273,139
Total Foreign-stock population   383,709
Dutch-Americans are 1.1% of America's foreign-stock citizens.

Main Ethnic Epicenters:		U.S. Cities with Most Dutch:	
Michigan	72,763	Grand Rapids, Mich.	43,334
California	63,772	Los Angeles	23,844
New York	32,043	Chicago	21,579
New Jersey	28,440	Paterson, N.J.	16.585
Illinois	27,189	New York	14,530

Estimated Dutch-American population: Some sources claim that there are 17 million Americans with some Dutch blood coursing through their veins. In 1930 there were a total of 413,966 foreign-stock Dutch-Americans living in the United States. By 1970, that total had declined to 383,709.

You poor, who know not how your living to obtain;
You affluent, who seek in mind to be content;
Choose you New Netherland, who no one shall disdain;
Before your time and strength here fruitlessly are spent.

—Jacob Steendam, 1662

(a verse to encourage immigration to his colony on the Delaware)

Who's Dutch?

Letters: Pearl Buck; Herman Melville; Walt Whitman; Jerald Terhorst, presidential press secretary to Gerald Ford.

Entertainment: Cecil B. De Mille, motion picture director; actor James Caan; Walter Cronkite, TV newsman. (Cronkite's first American ancestors on his father's side were Wyntje Theunis and Hercks Siboutszen *Krankheydt*. They married in 1642 in New Amsterdam. His mother's forebears were German immigrants who came to this country in the mid-nineteenth-century.

Dance: Agnes De Mille, choreographer.

Money: The many monied Vanderbilts.

Medicine: Dr. Benjamin Spock.

Invention: Lee De Forest, "Father of Radio Broadcasting."

Sports: Johnny Vandermeer, pitcher for Cleveland and Chicago during the 1950s. Norm Van Brocklin, coach for Minnesota Vikings and Atlanta Falcons.

The life and times of pioneers were not easy, and it isn't any wonder that most Hollanders were unwilling to leave the safety and comfort of home to emigrate to America when one considers the plight of Penelope van Princis.

Penelope was only 18 years old when she and her husband sailed from Holland in 1640 for New Amsterdam. The weather was fine during the long voyage across the ocean, but a storm wrecked Penelope's ship just off the New Jersey coast near Sandy Hook. The passengers and crew who made it ashore decided to walk to Manhattan Island where there were fortifications to protect them from Indian attacks, but Penelope's husband was seriously ill and unable to travel, so she was forced to remain behind and care for him.

Raritan Indians attacked and killed her husband and left Penelope for dead with a fractured skull and serious abdominal wounds. Somehow she managed to crawl into a hollow tree where she hid for several days, living only on bark and frozen tree gum.

Two Indians found her and took her to their village, where she was nursed back to health. News of Penelope reached New Amsterdam, and she was ransomed for some beads, bracelets, cloth and scissors. She started a new life among the Dutch and later married an Englishman, Richard Stout, with whom she had ten children. When she died at the ripe old age of 90, she left behind 502 direct descendants.

THE FRENCH IN AMERICA

The French were among the earliest explorers and settlers of the Southeastern portion of the United States. The first French Huguenot settlement in America was established at Parris Island, South Carolina, in 1562. However, extreme hardships caused the colony to be abandoned two years later. The French Calvinist settlers who went to Florida in 1564 didn't fare much better when they founded Fort Caroline on the St. Johns River—they were slaughtered by Spanish troops in 1565.

But, despite these early setbacks, the French kept coming to the New World.

They were first lured here, in the sixteenth and seventeenth centuries, by the lucrative fur trade. Later, when the Edict of Nantes was revoked in 1685, thousands of French Huguenots fled their homeland, seeking religious freedom, and settled in South Carolina, Virginia, Massachusetts and New York.

Other Huguenots emigrated to the American colonies via Holland, England and Germany, and although there aren't any hard statistics on the number of French settlers who came ·to America in the early 1700s, estimates have placed the number at about 15,000 refugees between 1685 and 1760.

No one will ever know how many French citizens have made America their new homeland, but since 1820 over three-quarters of a million Frenchmen have said "Oui" to America and entered our immigration gates. Other Americans of French ancestry are descended from French-Canadians (Quebec was settled by the French in 1608), or settlers of the Louisiana territory who became "inadvertent" citizens when the U.S. purchased that tract of land in 1803.

◆ ◆ ◆

◆ New Paltz, New York, founded by French Huguenots in 1678, is one of the few remaining Huguenot settlements in America. Some of the first stone houses built over 300 years ago are still standing, and many of the local residents are descended from the orginal settlers of New Paltz.

◆ French explorer Robert Cavelier, Sieur de la Salle, claimed the entire Mississippi Valley for France in 1682 and named the region "Louisiana" in honor of Louis XIV, the king of France. Although a colony was established at Ocean Springs, Mississippi, in 1699, there was a general lack of interest in emigrating to the Louisiana territory on the part of Frenchmen. To help populate the region, the French government began a policy of forced migration: beggars, vagabonds, prisoners rescued from the gallows, mental patients and prostitutes were all dumped upon Louisiana in the early 1700s,

and although the Regent of France put an official end to the practice in 1720, the next year witnessed the importation of 25 French prostitutes to Louisiana to lure the settlers away from Indian women.

◆ The first French newspaper printed in America was the *Courrier de L'Amerique,* published in Philadelphia in 1784. By 1794 the French-speaking population had a daily newspaper, the *Courrier Français,* also published in Philadelphia; it lasted for four years.

◆ Jean Lafitte, the pirate, was offered $30,000 by the British to aid them in capturing New Orleans. A civic-minded soul, Lafitte sided with the Americans, and even earned a Presidential pardon for his efforts in defending that city in 1815.

◆ The development of dental science in America was largely due to the efforts of two French dentists, Joseph Le Mayeur and James Gardette, who taught their oral techniques to dentists during the American Revolution. Among those educated by Le Mayeur and Gardette was Washington's personal dentist, John Greenwood.

◆ Du Pont is one of the most famous French names in American business today. But, in 1978, for the first time since the company was founded in 1802, Du Pont de Nemours and Company found itself without a Du Pont in top management. When Irenee Du Pont retired at the age of 58, he handed over the reins to Irving S. Shapiro, a Jewish-American from Minneapolis. Although the Du Ponts are not represented in management, they still own 35–40% of the company stock, which is valued at $4–$7 billion. Commenting on his own rise to the top, Irenee remarked that being a Du Pont "must have been an enormous advantage . . . it would be highly unusual for a B.S. chemical engineer to reach the level I did other than by pull."

◆ American places with French names: Louisiana is named for King Louis XIV; Maine is named after a French province; Vermont comes from the French words *vert mont,* meaning "green mountain." There are also: La Grange, La Salle and Paris, Kentucky; Joliet, Illinois; and Lake Champlain, named after the French mapmaker-explorer, Samuel de Champlain (1567–1635), who explored that region in 1603.

Facts About the Other Side

Country:	FRANCE

Capital:	Paris
Official Name:	Republique Française (French Republic)
Official Language:	French
National Anthem:	"La Marseillaise" (1792). Originally sung by a group of Marseilles soldiers as they marched into Paris before the French Republic was proclaimed.
National Flag:	Vertical bands of red, white and blue. The tricolor was first used by Louis XVI to represent France in 1789.
Major Religion:	Roman Catholic. Separation of Church and State was decreed in 1905.
National Holiday:	July 14, Bastille Day—commemorates the capture of the Bastille prison by the People of Paris in 1789.
National Motto:	Liberté, Égalité, Fraternité (Liberty, Equality, Fraternity)
National Symbol:	"Marianne"—a young woman dressed in red, white and blue—symbolizes the French Republic. Her name was taken from that of a secret society which labored to restore the Republic during the Second Empire.

Facts About French-Americans:

Immigration to the U.S. (1820–1975): 742,442
    Peak Decade (1841–1850):   77,262

1970 Census
Foreign-born French   105,385
Native-born 2nd generation   237,982
Total Foreign-stock Population 343,367

Main Ethnic Epicenters:
California   63,449
New York   56,861
New Jersey   22,152
Illinois   19,266
Pennsylvania   18,484

Who's French?

Heroines: Priscilla Mullins, originally Molines, was a French Huguenot who sailed on the *Mayflower*. The object of devotion of both John Alden and Miles Standish, she made the phrase "Speak for yourself, John" famous.

Food: Some of America's greatest chefs have been of French birth or ancestry. Louis Sherry, whose name lives on as a brand of ice cream and sweets today, was the son of a French carpenter who opened his own restaurant in New York in 1881. Charles Ranhofer, an immigrant from Denis, France, joined the famed Delmonico's Restaurant in 1862 and created such delights as "Baked Alaska." Philip Armour of meat-packing fame was also descended from French ancestors, as is Frank Perdue, the man who brought "brand-name chickens" to the poultry cases of America. A descendant of Henri Perdeux, a French Huguenot who came to America in 1657 to escape religious persecution, Frank let himself in for some "persecution" during the early 1970s when his slogan, "Is your husband a breast man or a leg man?" attracted the ire of women's groups.

Politics: John Jay was a French Huguenot, as was Paul Revere, the famous midnight rider. Revere's father, also a silversmith, was named Apollon Rivoire. Pierre Salinger, former press secretary to President Kennedy, is of French descent on his mother's side. Mike Gravel (1930–), U.S. Senator from Alaska, is of French-Canadian descent; William Simon (1927–), former Secretary of the Treasury, is the grandson of French immigrants; Anne Armstrong (1927–), former U.S. Ambassador to Great Britain, is of French-Creole ancestry on her paternal side.

Entertainers: French-born Claudette Colbert settled in the U.S. in 1910; Rod Steiger (1925–) is of French, Scottish and German ancestry; Joan Crawford (1908–1977) was of French and Irish extraction. Charles Boyer (1899–1978) was a famous "imported" leading man born in France.

French aerialist Philippe Petit entertained crowds that gathered below the World Trade Center in 1974 as he teetered on a thin cable slung between the twin 110-story buildings for over 45 minutes.

Letters: Henry David Thoreau; John P. Marquand (1894–1960), a 1937 Pulitzer Prize winner for his novel *The Late George Apley;* Oliver La Farge, a 1929 Pulitzer Prize winner for his first novel about American Indians, *Laughing Boy;* R. H. Dana, Jr., an American of Huguenot ancestry, who wrote *Two Years Before the Mast.* John Greenleaf Whittier's mother was French (her maiden name was Feuillevert, French for "green leaf"). Stephen Vincent Benét won a 1929 Pulitzer Prize for his epic poem, *John Brown's Body.* Will Durant, the historian, is of French-Canadian ancestry.

Science: Alexis Carrel, 1915 Nobel Prize winner in Medicine and Physiology; André Cournand, 1956 Nobel Prize winner in same field. René Dubos (1901–), microbiologist.

Beauty: French-born beauty expert Nicole Ronsard made cellulite a household word among diet-conscious Americans in the early 1970s when she introduced her exercise regimen, designed to eliminate this purported by-product of fat from the body.

THE GREEKS IN AMERICA

The first Greek to explore America was probably a sailor named Theodore who sailed with a Spanish expedition to Florida in 1637. Some scholars claim there may have been Greek sailors aboard Columbus's ship on his first voyage to the New World, while other scholars contend that Columbus was not Italian, but Greek!

One of the first Greek settlements in the New World was the Colony of New Smyrna, Florida, established in 1767 by Andrew Turnbull and his Greek wife. Turnbull named the colony after his wife's hometown of Smyrna, and the couple recruited almost 1,400 destitute Greeks and Italians to cultivate vineyards and olive orchards,

which they believed could flourish in the warm Florida sun. New Smyrna did not turn out to be the agricultural paradise that Turnbull had hoped. Instead of lush orchards and fat, juicy grapes, the settlers found only hardship, hostile Indians and unyielding Florida swampland. Ten years after New Smyrna was founded the last of the 600 remaining colonists departed, searching for greener pastures and more profitable farmland.

Greek immigration to the United States did not begin on a large scale until the 1890s, when political oppression, economic hardship, crop failures and droughts forced thousands of Greeks to flee their homeland.

Between 1891 and 1920, more than 367,000 Greeks entered the United States. Thirty years earlier, between 1861 and 1890, the number of Greek immigrants to the United States had been fewer than 13,000.

Most of the immigrants who came to America at the turn of the century were young, single men. They came here with the sole intent of earning enough money so they could return to Greece at a later date with a "nest egg" to use toward building a home, purchasing farmland or starting their own business. Like so many other immigrants, though, the Greeks became caught up in America. They put down roots here, married, had children and became American citizens.

When strict immigration quotas went into effect in the 1920s, Greek immigration plummeted sharply, and from 1930 to 1950 an average of only 900 Greek immigrants came to our shores each year. When immigration quotas were lifted in the early 1960s, immigration from Greece soared once again to more than 122,000 new arrivals between 1966 and 1975.

Many of these new immigrants were medical school graduates, engineers and other professionals who found the political climate of their native land oppressive, or else believed there was more opportunity for career advancement in the United States. Along with the droves of well-educated Greeks were scores of uneducated village dwellers who managed to carve a piece of the American dream for themselves by running successful businesses. In the words of one third-generation Greek-American whose family owns four large supermarkets in northern New Jersey, "My grandfather came here in 1919 with nothing, and managed to build up his business with hard work and brains."

Like Americans from almost every ethnic group, the Greeks have found that it's easier to make your way in America as your own boss. For that reason it seems that Greeks have a monopoly on the luncheonettes, diners and even pizza parlors in the Northeast, where they serve *souvlaki* and *gyro* sandwiches along with Italian specialties. There aren't any hard facts on the number of Greek-owned food stores and restaurants, but in one suburban county near New York City, there are at least 12 super-markets, 6 diners and 5 restaurants owned by Greeks within a 10-mile radius.

◆ ◆ ◆

◆ The first Greek newspaper, *Atlantis,* was established in New York in 1894 by Solon John Vlasto (1852–1927). *Atlantis* was the first paper in the world to use typesetting machinery for the Greek alphabet.

◆ Greeks were greeted with the same open arms that "native" Americans (those who had been here for two or three generations) extended to every new ethnic group. In 1909, the Greek community of Omaha, Nebraska — some 1,200 men, women and children — were driven out of town. Anti-Hellenic sentiments of the townsfolk turned to violence, a riot ensued and much of the Greek community's property was destroyed.

◆ In Greece, life revolves to a great extent around the Church. By the end of World War I, there were 130 Greek Orthodox churches in the United States, attesting to the deep roots of the Greek community. One of the most famous of the Greek Orthodox churches is Annunciation Church in Milwaukee, which was designed by architect Frank Lloyd Wright.

◆ Although it was only performed once, New York opera buffs were able to see the Greek opera *Perouze,* by Theodore Sakellarides, in 1925.

◆ Maria Anna Cecilia Sofia Kalogeropoulos (1923–1977), better known as Maria Callas, was a beloved opera star both here and abroad. The daughter of a Greek immigrant druggist, Callas grew up on the streets of Hell's Kitchen, a tough New York City neighborhood. She later renounced her American citizenship. Callas made her debut in Athens in the leading role of Santuzza in *Cavalleria Rusticana* at the age of fifteen. At the peak of her career, Callas's voice was able to stretch almost three octaves. Of her early start in opera Maria once complained, "The worst thing in the world is a child prodigy. I had to sing and take care of the family. I feel I have been robbed of my youth."

◆ During the "brain drain" of the early 1960s, almost one-third of all Greek medical school students, and 20% of Greek engineering students were seeking employment in the United States after graduation.

♦ The only privately operated Greek Orthodox school in the United States is St. Andrew's Academy in Queens, New York. St. Andrew's has an enrollment of more than 500 pupils, ranging in age from nursery school level to high school.

♦ Spiro Agnew was the first American Vice-President of Greek descent. However, many Greek-Americans looked upon him as primarily "American": 1) His mother was a Virginian; 2) he converted to Episcopalianism from Greek Orthodoxy; and 3) he could not speak the language of his father—Greek. Spiro was only a second-generation Greek-American (his father emigrated to the United States in 1897) but in one short generation he had lost many of the old-world ways. Still, when he was elected on the Nixon ticket in 1968, he was promptly dubbed "Zorba the Veep" in honor of his Greek heritage.

♦ *Done In By Miss Liberty* In 1975 a TV news team featured a story on the redecorating that was going on inside the Statue of Liberty. There in the background, painting the walls of the national monument, were two Greek brothers—Athanasios and Georgios Plessias.

Like other illegal aliens in the New York City area, the brothers were earning a living in America as housepainters (or, in this case, monument painters)—their non-union wages, no doubt, enabling the contractor to bid low for the job of painting Miss Liberty. Unfortunately, that television show proved to be the brothers' undoing, for Maurice F. Kiley, District Immigration Officer, spotted them and became suspicious. As it turned out, both were in the country on the sly—Athanasios had jumped ship in 1969 and his brother had entered the United States on a visitor's permit in 1971 and never left. As a result of their television debut, the brothers were arrested and faced deportation back to Greece.

♦ *Places With Greek Names* Ypsilanti, Michigan, is named after General Demetrios Ypsilanti (1793–1832), a hero of the Greek war of independence. The Straits of Juan de Fuca, between Washington state and Vancouver, Canada, are named after a Greek navigator who sailed for Spain. Juan de Fuca discovered the sea passage in 1592 and named it after himself, believing that it was a connecting waterway between the Atlantic and Pacific oceans.

Facts About the Other Side:

Country:	**GREECE**
Official Name:	Elliniki Dimokratia (Hellenic Republic)
Capital:	Athens
Official Language:	Greek
National Anthem:	"Imnos pros tin Eleftherian" (The Hymn to Liberty) The Greek national anthem, written by the poet, Solomos, has 158 verses. Most Greeks only know the first four, and the first two are sung at official gatherings. The music for the anthem was composed by Matzoros.
National Flag:	The Greek flag, adopted in 1822, consists of five blue and four white horizontal stripes, interrupted in the upper left-hand corner by a white cross on a blue field.
Coat of Arms:	Adopted in 1973, the phoenix symbolizes the rebirth of Greece as a republic after the abolishment of the monarchy.
Major Religion:	Over 95 percent of the population belongs to the Greek Orthodox Church, the official state religion. The church is supported by government funds and religion is taught in public schools, although freedom of worship is guaranteed by the constitution.

Facts About Greek-Americans:

Immigration to the U.S. (1820–1975):   629,349
    Peak Decade (1911–1920):   184,201
    Recent Immigration (1966–1975):   128,924

1970 Census
Foreign-born Greeks   177,275
Native-born, 2nd generation 257,296
    Estimated Greek-American population: 3 million

Main Ethnic Epicenters:		*U.S. Cities with Most Greeks:*	
New York	90,886	New York	79,131
Illinois	48,669	Chicago	45,014
California	43,645	Boston	23,137
Massachusetts	39,669	Lost Angeles	16,219
New Jersey	25,703	Detroit	14,047

Who's Greek?

Entertainers Telly Savalas became a household word in the early 1970s as that lollipop-sucking cop, Kojak. He was born in Garden City, New York. His mother was a former Miss Greece, and Savalas himself contributed a lot to the world of "beauty" by proving that "bald can be beautiful." John Cassavetes, actor and director; George Maharis; George Chakiris; Betty White; Spyros Skouras, co-founder of 20th Century-Fox; Alexander Pantages, theater owner.

Sports Baseball's Milt Pappas; Gus Triandos; and football's Alex Karras, an All-American defensive tackle with the Detroit Lions.

Politics Spiro Agnew (former Governor of Maryland and Vice-President of the United States), whose immigrant father changed his name from *Anagnostopoulos;* Michael Dukakis, Governor of Massachusetts; Peter Peterson (a.k.a. Petropoulos), U.S. government official.

Fashion Designers George Stavropoulos and James Galanos; Christie Brothers furriers.

Advertising George Lois.

Science Nicholas Christofilos, nuclear physicist.

Medicine George Papanicolaou (1895–1963).

Food Industry John Zervas, onetime "hot dog king" of New York City who owned the concession rights for 60 vending sites in Central Park. He employed recent Greek immigrants to sell pretzels, hot dogs and soda.

"I think in time the people will come to know what a warm, sweet, lovable person I really am." — Spiro Agnew, 1971. (Courtesy: Culver Pictures)

THE GYPSIES IN AMERICA

It has been estimated that the Gypsy population of the United States is somewhere between 500,000 and 1,000,000. However, since ethnic origins were not usually recorded in past national censuses and many gypsies are continually on the move, no one will ever know for certain how many Americans have some "Gypsy in their souls."

According to the 1970 census figures, there were only 1,588 persons living in America who claimed Romani (the universal language of the Gypsies) as their native tongue. Although the majority of the world's Gypsies make their home in Europe, it was from India that the Romany people began their never-ending migrations in the fifth and eleventh centuries. They fled first to Persia, then to Turkey and Egypt and finally to the nations of Europe. The name "Gypsy" comes from a corruption of "Egyptian"—Egypt was one of their last stopovers on the way to England, Russia, Hungary and other nations.

Gypsies call themselves "Rom," which means "man" in Hindi. Their language is derived from a Hindi dialect related to Sanskrit. All non-Gypsies, be they Americans, Hungarians or Mexicans, are lumped together as "gajo"—meaning "barbarian."

The most famous gypsy in America is Yul Brynner. Born on Sakhalin Island, Russian territory north of Japan, Yul is Romany on his mother's side and Mongolian on his father's. In 1978, Brynner was appointed honorary president of the World Romany Congress, and as such addressed the United Nations with a proposal to end worldwide discrimination against all Gypsies. He also wanted recognition for his people as a national minority, claiming "I am a Gypsy through my mother and through my soul" (even though he's been the "King" of Siam for more than twenty years).

Stereotypes and Discrimination The stereotype Gypsy is a con artist, fortune-teller, and tambourine or violin player who travels around the country in a caravan. According to one Gypsy living in Chicago, "The Gypsy race has been persecuted. If one Gypsy committed a crime, it was the entire race that was blamed."

Even in America, in the late 1970s, there were still discriminatory, anti-Gypsy laws on the books in many states:

The state of Maryland required that "Gypsies, fortune tellers and nomads" pay $1,000 for a license to do business in that state.

Tennessee charged Gypsies $2,000 for the privilege of living in the "Volunteer State."

These Serbian Gypsies were detained at Ellis Island pending admission to the United States. (Courtesy: American Museum of Immigration)

Texas law referred to "Prostitutes, gypsies and vagabonds" in the same breath, and charges the Romany people $500 to live there.

Many Gypsies shun the mainstream of American life, hoping to maintain their identity by insulating themselves from the "gajos." In the words of one self-styled

"King": "The melting pot is not for my people. The secret of the Gypsies is that they hold onto their culture separate and apart from the American way. The melting pot will destroy the Gypsy culture."

Other Gypsies disagree, and are slowly putting down roots in American towns, intermarrying with non-Gypsies, and getting "gajo" educations at colleges and universities. Gypsy spokesman, Professor Ian Hancock, an English professor at the University of Texas, maintains, "We've got to change with the times without sacrificing anything of our culture." He says, "The non-Gypsy world could learn much from the Gypsies, especially in the area of respect for elders and understanding between the generations."

THE HUNGARIANS IN AMERICA

Between 1870 and 1920 almost 2 million immigrants from Hungary crossed the sea to America. Since Hungary was a multi-national state there is no way of knowing how many "Hungarians" emigrated to the United States in the past 155 years, especially since the figures for the Austro-Hungarian empire were combined between 1861 and 1905.

Forced to emigrate because of war, famine and persecution at home, the Hungarian immigrants came from all social classes, The Hungarians and their descendants contributed widely to the fields of science (the atom bomb was the cooperative effort of no less than four Hungarians), music, entertainment, religion and literature in America.

Hungarians gave us Pulitzer prizes, Twentieth Century-Fox, the diagnostic Schick test and, from the other side, they contributed Labanotation (a script method for preserving ballet and other dance movements, invented by Rudolf Von Laban), and their wonderful goulash and paprika.

◆ ◆ ◆

◆ As early as 1840 a Hungarian tailor, Attila Kelemen, made a fortune selling "tincturus papricus" as a miracle drug for the treatment of cholera. Actually, it contained nothing more than Hungarian paprika and whiskey.

◆ One of the first Hungarian settlements in America was New Buda, Iowa, founded in 1849. Almost 4,000 refugees from the upper and middle classes settled in Decatur County, under the leadership of Laszlo Ujhazi.

◆ The first successful American newspaper published in Hungarian was *Amerikai Magyar Nepszava*. It started as a weekly in 1899, and was elevated to daily status in 1904. It was not the first Hungarian newspaper in the New World, however—other publications had come and gone since 1853.

◆ The "most Hungarian city in the United States" was the title once given to New Brunswick, New Jersey. Proportionately, it had more Hungarians than any other city in America. In 1915 there were 5,572 Hungarians living in New Brunswick out of a total of 30,019. According to the latest census, there were 41,885 Hungarians living there in 1970.

◆ *Pulitzer Prizes* The "founder of modern journalism," Joseph Pulitzer (1847–1911), was born in Mako, Hungary. He founded the St. Louis *Post-Dispatch* in 1878 and the New York *World* in 1883. Pulitzer was one of the first publishers to print a Sunday edition, and in 1896 he introduced the Sunday supplement section as a gimmick to attract readers. His name has been immortalized as a result of the $2.5 million he bequeathed to Columbia University's School of Journalism to establish the Pulitzer Prize awards, which are bestowed each year to America's outstanding journalists and writers.

◆ *Carousel* The Rodgers and Hammerstein Broadway play of 1945 was inspired by the 1921 play *Liliom,* written by Hungarian playwright Ferenc Molnar, who emigrated to America in 1940.

◆ In 1962 Istvan Serenyi, draped in the colors of the Hungarian flag, walked across

When Hungarian patriot Louis Kossuth rode up Broadway in 1851, he was cheered by more than 100,000 Americans. (Courtesy: New York Historical Society)

the country from San Francisco to New York. It took him 74 days to complete his journey.

♦ *Music, Music, Music* The Hungarian contribution to American music ranges from the sublime to the ridiculous. Hungarians in America have been represented by composer Bela Bartok; conductors George Szell, of the Cleveland Symphony, and Eugene Ormandy of the Philadelphia Symphony Orchestra; violinist Eugene Fodor; trumpeter Herb Alpert (half Russian Jew, half Hungarian), and the Kabuki-faced rock guitarist of KISS, Gene Simmons, whose mother is a Hungarian immigrant.

♦ The leading American firm handling foreign banknote transactions is Deak-Perera, founded by Hungarian-born Nick Deak in 1939. Business was abruptly halted by World War II, but after serving in the Office of Strategic Services for the duration, Deak resumed his foreign exchange trade and established convenient offices at airports and in the financial districts of America. To keep pace with the postwar travel boom, Deak-Perera introduced such innovations as currency vending machines and ready-made "tip" packages of $10 or $15 so travelers would have cash on hand when they arrived in a foreign country.

♦ The Crown of St. Stephen, the symbol of Hungarian nationhood, was brought to America for safekeeping in 1945. When President Carter decided to return the 978-year-old crown to its homeland in 1978, he chose Ted Weiss, the only Hungarian-born member of Congress, to accompany the crown on its return trip. Weiss, who had emigrated to America at the age of ten, represented a New York City district in the House of Representatives.

♦ Hungarian place names in America: Buda, Illinois and Texas; Kossuth (named after the exiled Governor of Hungary), Indiana, New York, Mississippi and Pennsylvania.

Facts About the Other Side

Country:	HUNGARY
Capital:	Budapest
Official Name:	Magyar Népköztársaság (Hungarian People's Republic)
Official Language:	Magyar
National Anthem:	"Isten áldd a Magyart" (God Bless the Hungarians)
National Flag:	Horizontal bands of red, white and green
Major Religions:	Roman Catholic, Calvinist, Lutheran
National Holidays:	March 15, Independence Day
	April 4, Liberation Day (communist holiday)

Facts About Hungarian-Americans

Immigration to the U.S. (1911–1975):   530,163*
   Peak Decade (1911–1920):   442,693

1970 Census
Foreign-born Hungarians   183,236
Native-born, 2nd generation   420,432
Total Foreign-stock Population   503,668

*Immigration from Austria-Hungary totaled 4,312,252 between 1861 and 1975. Austria and Hungary have been reported separately since 1905.

Who's Hungarian?

Dance: Ivan Nagy, former principal dancer for the American Ballet Theater, applied for resident alien status in the United States in 1968.

Medicine: Bella Schick, the man whose name lives on as the "Schick test" for diphtheria.

Musicians: Coloradan Eugene Fodor (1950–   ) was the first Western violinist ever to share the top honors at the International Tchaikovsky Competition, held in Moscow every four years.

Entertainment: Tony Curtis; the Gabor family; Ernie Kovaks; Harry Houdini (real name Erich Weiss; he was the son of a Hungarian rabbi); Cornel Wilde; horror-movie stars Peter Lorre and Bela Lugosi.

Movie Moguls: Adolph Zukor of Paramount Pictures; Hungarian-born William Fox of 20th Century-Fox.

Letters: Joseph Pulitzer; Edna Ferber.

Beauty: Mickey Hargitay, Mr. Universe 1950.

Sports: Larry Csonka; Charlie and Pete Gogolak; Joe Namath; Don Shula.

Science: John Von Neumann (1903–1957), a Hungarian immigrant, has been called the "greatest mathematician of the age." A recipient of the Fermi Award in 1956, Von Neumann developed the mathematical science of "game theory" in 1928. George V. Bekessy, 1961 Nobelist in Medicine and Physiology; Albert Szent-Gyorgyi, 1937 Nobel laureate for Medicine and Physiology; and Eugene Wigner, 1963 Nobel Prize winner in Physics.

THE JAPANESE IN AMERICA

The first Japanese in America were sailors who were either rescued at sea by American fishing ships or washed ashore on the Pacific Coast. Between 1782 and 1876, almost fifty Japanese ships were beached on the Aleutian Islands, Alaska, Hawaii and the Pacific Coast of the mainland. The first Japanese rescued was Nakahama Manjiro, who was brought to New Bedford, Massachusetts, by a whaling ship in 1843. In 1850 Hikozo Hamada, who entered the United States in a similar fashion, stayed here and became America's first naturalized citizen of Japanese birth.

There were a few Japanese immigrants to Hawaii in 1868, although the Japanese government did not pass legislation permitting its citizens to emigrate until 1885, and even then, only 2,270 Japanese ventured to our shores in the decade between 1881 and 1890.

Japanese contract laborers began entering Hawaii in 1885, and that started the momentum toward America. During the 1890s, the number of Japanese immigrants increased tenfold over the previous decade to 25,942. Between 1901 and 1910, 129,797 Japanese entered American immigration gates. Increasingly they began to be viewed as a second "Yellow Peril" by residents of the West Coast, who feared they would lose their jobs to Japanese workers.

The Gentleman's Agreement of 1907 limited the number of Japanese who entered the United States. The restrictive immigration quotas of the 1920s almost eliminated the flow completely by denying entry to large numbers of Asians and of Southern and Eastern Europeans.

The Japanese contributed "Japanese cherry trees," Japanese beetles, sukiyaki, sake, bonsai trees and kimonos from the other side, while their American cousins gave us instant coffee, "Tokyo Rose," a Nobel prize winner, scientists, musicians, actors and Benihana restaurants.

How did we repay the Japanese for their generous contributions to America? Well, let's put it this way — we treated them with the same enthusiasm we reserved for members of every recognizably different ethnic group (blacks, Chinese, Mexicans, Turks): we discriminated against them and tried to keep them out of the country. The Japanese suffered the indignity of not being able to own property; and at one time if a native-born American woman married a Japanese immigrant, the law took away her citizenship. Perhaps the worst indignity was the detention of almost 70,000 native-born Americans of Japanese ancestry in so-called "relocation centers" during World War II. It would be hard to imagine a similar roundup of Italian-Americans or German-Americans ever taking place.

Despite these early hardships, the second- and third-generation Japanese Americans have managed to overcome many social and economic barriers in a relatively short period of time.

GUIDE TO JAPANESE-AMERICAN GENERATIONS

ISSEI   First generation (Japanese-born immigrant to America)
NISEI   Second generation (American born)
SANSEI   Third generation
YONSEI   Fourth generation

♦ George Shima (1870–1926), a Japanese immigrant who came to our shores in 1889, earned the title "Potato King" for his efforts in the field of agriculture. By the time of his death, he had amassed an estate valued at $15 million.

♦ In 1899, after Hawaii was annexed as a U.S. territory, some 2,850 Japanese came to the mainland and established the first Buddhist temples in America. (The oldest Japanese Christian church in America is the *Pine United Methodist Church* in San Francisco.)

♦ Satori Kato, an immigrant chemist from

Japan, invented instant powdered coffee. Kato first sold his product in 1901 at the Buffalo, New York, Pan-American Exposition.

♦ By 1910, there were 80,000 Japanese living in Hawaii, and over 72,000 on the mainland. That year, the first American of Japanese ancestry was admitted to the bar. Arthur Kenzaburo Ozawa was able to practice law in both Michigan and Hawaii.

♦ Japanese cherry trees attract thousands of visitors to our nation's capital each year as tourists crowd to Potomac Park to see the cherry blossoms emerge. The trees were planted in 1912 as a gift from the people of Tokyo. The first shipment actually arrived in 1909, but had to be destroyed because of insect infestation.

♦ Japanese beetles (technically known as *Papillia japonica*) came to this country as "illegal aliens" in the early 1900s. First discovered about 1915 near Riverton, New Jersey, the beetles were found hiding inside the root of a nursery plant that had been imported from Japan—hence their name.

♦ As early as 1900 the Japanese comprised almost 39% of Hawaii's population. They peaked in 1920 at 48% but with the latest influx of "haoles" (whites) to the islands, the Japanese population has dwindled to a mere 28%, according to the 1970 census.

♦ The first Japanese-American to fight professionally was James Yoshinori, who appeared in the ring at Madison Square Garden in 1927. Unfortunately, the bout proved disastrous for Yoshinori, whose eyesight was permanently damaged as a result of severe blows to his head.

♦ The first Japanese-American in the U.S. Senate was Daniel Ken Inouye. Elected in 1962, at the age of 38, Inouye was also the first Japanese-American in the House of Representatives (1959).

♦ The first Japanese-American woman prominent in Hawaiian politics was Patsy Takemoto Mink. She was elected to the U.S. House of Representatives in 1964 after having been the first Nisei woman in the Hawaii State legislature and the first Nisei woman to practice law in Hawaii.

♦ Samuel Ichiye Hayakawa (1906–   ), U.S. Senator from California who claims, "I've been all my life the kind of intellectual highbrow I disapprove of," is not quite as stuffy as he would have us believe. According to a recent magazine article, Hayakawa "plays a mean harmonica, picks at guitar and mandolin, tap dances, collects jazz records and African art" and took up scuba diving at the age of seventy. Born in Canada to Japanese-American parents, Hayakawa was president of San Francisco State College during the turbulent 1960s, and also wrote a widely used college textook on semantics.

♦ Benihana of Tokyo advertises American favorites prepared "according to a 1,000-year-old Japanese recipe," though many food critics consider Benihana's fare strictly "American." But, no matter, the food is edible and it comes with a "floor show." Specially trained chefs slice, dice and fry beef, shrimp and chicken with lightning-fast speed, and a rhythm that rivals the world's best xylophone players.

The man behind all this dicing and slicing is Rocky Aoki, a Japanese immigrant wrestler who came to the United States in 1960. He was on his way to the Olympic Games in Rome, but liked America so much that he decided to come back after the games. He started out selling ice cream cones, and was able to open his first restaurant after he had saved $10,000. Today he is a multi-millionaire. Although his restaurants serve "Japanese" food, Rocky professes to dine on American-style food at home with his wife, Chizuru, and his two children, Kevin and Grace.

♦ Today there is a growing population of Japanese nationals residing in major American cities. New York City alone has more than 20,000 Japanese businessmen and their families, who represent some 450 companies; and in Gardena, California, there are almost 24,000 Japanese on assignment from Japanese-based firms. For these Japanese, who know that they will return home and do not choose to adopt American ways, life can be difficult. Many wives are unable to communicate with their neighbors, and there is much isolation and loneliness—so much, in fact, that the Reverend Justin Haruyama of the Japanese-American United Church of Christ in Manhattan is considering a "hot-line" telephone program with counselors fluent in Japanese, to minister to the needs of a growing affluent community which is scattered and isolated, and does not enjoy the benefits that many impoverished immigrants had of living within a supportive ethnic neighborhood.

Facts About the Other Side

Country:	JAPAN
Official Name:	Nippon or Nihon (the name means "Source of the sun")
	Also known as "The land of the rising sun"
Official Language:	Japanese
National Anthem:	"Kimigayo" (The Reign of our Emperor)
National Flag:	Red sun on a white field
National Holidays:	February 11, National Foundation Day
	May 3, Constitution Memorial Day

Facts About Japanese-Americans

Immigration to U.S. (1861–1975):*	391,389
Peak Decade (1901–1910):	129,797
Recent Immigration (1971–1975):	26,005

*No records of immigration from Japan were kept until 1861.

1970 Census

Foreign-born Japanese	120,235
Native-born, 2nd generation	273,554
Total Foreign-stock Population	393,789
Estimated Japanese-American Population	600,000

Main Ethnic Epicenters:		*U.S. Cities with Most Japanese:*	
Hawaii	217,307	Honolulu	79,759
California	213,280	Los Angeles	64,071
New York	20,351	San Francisco	24,048
Washington	20,335	New York	13,864
Illinois	17,299	Chicago	10,999

72% of all Japanese-Americans live in Hawaii and California.

Who's Japanese?

Tokyo Rose One of President Ford's last official acts before leaving the White House in 1977 was to pardon "Tokyo Rose." Born in Los Angeles on the Fourth of July, Iva Ikuki Toguri (1916–) earned her nickname during World War II when she was one of 13 women announcers who narrated Radio Tokyo's English-language programs. Accused of broadcasting treasonous remarks to

Tokyo Rose being interviewed by American war correspondents in 1945. (Courtesy: Culver Pictures)

American troops stationed in the Pacific, Tokyo Rose was a victim of circumstance—trapped in Japan when the war erupted, she could not return home, and as an alien was required to find any employment available. For her broadcasts, Mrs. d'Aquino (she had married a Portuguese in the interim) was convicted of treason in 1949, and sentenced to 10 years in prison and a fine of $10,000. She was paroled in 1956. As he signed the pardon President Ford remarked: "The pardon has been expected for some time, with a growing feeling that Mrs. d'Aquino had been caught in an unfortunate web of circumstance."

Median family income for Japanese-Americans is almost $3,000 higher than that of the mythical "average American family."

Many hold professional occupations, and their level of education is higher than that of any ethnic group except the Russian-Americans, according to the U.S. Census Bureau. Seventy percent of all Japanese males over the age of 16 have completed high school, and 19% have completed college—compared to the U.S. averages of 54% and 13% respectively.

The majority of Japanese-Americans, almost 58%, do not live in "ethnic neighborhoods." They have moved away from their "roots" and are dispersed in the cities and suburbs of America.

The Japanese-Americans have a high degree of "out-marrying." While the first generation (Issei) married outside of their own ethnic group only about 1% of the time, the second generation (Nisei) out-marries 10% of the time, and the third generation (Sansei) about 40%.

Actors: Sessue Hayakawa (1890–1973) emigrated to the United States in 1909 and studied drama at the University of Chicago. One of his most famous roles was in the 1957 Academy Award-winning film, *The Bridge on the River Kwai.*

Sports: Tommy Kono won an Olympic gold medal for weight lifting in 1956.

Music: Seiji Ozawa is conductor of the San Francisco Symphony Orchestra.

Comedy: John Yune is America's first half-Korean, half-Japanese stand-up comedian. He debuted on national TV in 1978, claiming his friends call him "Ko-Jap."

Science: Dr. Leo Esaki, a Japanese immigrant, received the 1973 Nobel Prize in Physics for his electron tunneling theories. Makio Murayama (1912–   ) has conducted basic research on sickle-cell anemia; and Hideyo Noguchi, a Japanese immigrant who came to America in 1899, was the first to isolate the syphilis germ.

THE JEWS IN AMERICA

Although the Jews in America come from many different nations, their religion binds them together as an "ethnic group." Their customs, culture and even religious traditions may vary from country to country, but the synagogue and the Jewish faith are the ties that bind.

There have been three major "waves" of Jewish immigration to the United States. The first Jews, the Sephardim, were descendants of Spanish and Portuguese Jews driven from the Iberian peninsula at the time of Columbus's first voyage to the New World. Given a choice between conversion to Christianity or expulsion, many Spanish and Portuguese chose to resettle in Dutch Brazil rather than convert. When the Portuguese reclaimed the area, some of these Jews fled from Brazil to New Amsterdam in 1654.

Although there had been Jews in America as early as 1492 (Luis de Torres, one of

Columbus's crew, was believed to be a "Marrano"—a Jew who outwardly adopted Christianity in order to live peacefully in Iberia), the 23 Sephardic Jews who ventured to New Amsterdam in 1654 formed the backbone of the Jewish community and paved the way for all who followed. The Sephardim won for all Jews the right to serve in the militia, the right to travel and trade freely, and the right to own property. They established North America's first Jewish cemetery and its first congregation, Shearith Israel (Remnant of Israel), still in existence today. (The building no longer stands, but the Jews of New York City have been worshipping continuously as a community since 1655.)

Drawing of the first Jewish synagogue in America, Shearith Israel. (Courtesy: New York Public Library)

Although the Sephardim were the smallest wave of Jewish immigrants to America, they continued to dominate the religious life of America's Jewish community until the nineteenth century. It wasn't until 1802 that the first Ashkenazic (Eastern European Jewish) congregation was founded, despite the fact that German Jews had outnumbered the Sephardim as early as 1720.

Large numbers of German-Jewish immigrants came to our shores following the Revolution of 1848, and at the time of the Civil War there were almost 150,000 Jews living in America. Some 6,000 or so served the Union cause during the War, and about 1,000 Jews took the side of the Confederacy.

After the pogroms of 1881, Eastern European, Yiddish-speaking Jews began to arrive in record numbers. By 1914, more than 2 million Jewish immigrants had arrived to fill the tenements and sweat shops of major American industrial cities. Altogether some 3 million Ashkenazi came to America between 1880 and 1910. Most were listed by immigration officials not as Jews, but as Germans or Russians, so the exact total will never be known.

What did the Jews contribute to American life? Most of the food we consider "Jewish"—corned beef, chopped liver, gefilte fish, pastrami, bagels and lox—is actually Eastern European in origin, but it was introduced to the masses via the Jews who emigrated from Poland, Lithuania, Russia and other lands. (The "Jewish" food of the Sephardim is virtually unknown to non-Jews.) Besides all those delicious matzo balls, blintzes, potato pancakes and thick, heavy cream-cheese cheesecakes, the Jews gave America some of its most outstanding scientific and medical minds. Jewish doctors invented cures for polio and other dreaded diseases. Many of our department stores, clothing manufacturing firms, cosmetics firms and book publishing houses were founded by Jews. There are Jewish-American representatives among the movie moguls, actors, actresses, comedians, writers, newspaper publishers, sportsmen, politicians and beauty queens of the United States.

♦ ♦ ♦

♦ *17th Century Firsts:* The first Jewish settler in New Netherland was Jacob Barsimson, an immigrant from Brazil who arrived here in August 1654. A month later, he was followed by 23 more Jews from Brazil, and together they formed the first Jewish community in America. In 1657 Barsimson and Asher Levy, the first kosher butcher in the New World, won their struggle to obtain citizenship rights from the council of New Amsterdam.

♦ *Religious Firsts:* First congregation in America: Shearith Israel. Although the original building no longer stands, the congregation is currently worshiping at Seventieth Street and Central Park West in New York City. First Ashkenazic congregation: Rodeph Shalom, founded in Philadelphia in 1802. Oldest existing synagogue: The

Touro Synagogue, located in Newport, Rhode Island, is the oldest Jewish synagogue in America. Named after the first officiating rabbi, Isaac Touro, it was built in 1763.

♦ The first Jewish doctor in America was Jacob Lumbrozo, a native of Lisbon who settled in Maryland in 1656.

♦ The first Young Men's Hebrew Association (YMHA) was established at Baltimore in 1854.

♦ The first American rabbi to serve as an Army chaplain was Jacob Frankel. Prior to his admission, Jews in the Union Army were refused religious services because the law provided only for ministers "of some Christian denomination" to tend to the soldiers' spiritual needs. After Rabbi Fischel of New York complained to President Lincoln, the law was changed to include all "regularly ordained ministers of some religious denomination."

♦ Yeshiva University, the oldest Jewish university in the United States, was founded in New York City in 1886.

♦ Yonah Schimmel developed the first American version of *kasha knishe* in 1910 on the Lower East Side of New York. Today, potato knishes come fresh and frozen, and are sold in cities and suburbs across the country.

♦ The first Jewish Supreme Court justice was Louis Brandeis (1856–1941). Appointed by Woodrow Wilson, Brandeis was sworn in on June 3, 1916.

♦ The first secular university founded and sponsored by Jews was Brandeis University. Opened in the fall of 1948 with 108 freshmen, Brandeis has more than 3,400 students and 360 faculty members today. The school, in Waltham, Massachusetts, also boasts a $50 million endowment, a 250-acre campus, and a library of over 660,600 volumes.

♦ Hank Greenberg became the first Jewish-American in the Baseball Hall of Fame when he was admitted in 1956.

♦ When President Nixon appointed Henry Kissinger as Secretary of State he boasted to Golda Meir, the Prime Minister of Israel, that now both the United States and Israel had Jewish foreign ministers. Golda's response? "Yes," she said with a grin, "but mine speaks English," referring to Henry's German accent. Despite popular belief, Henry Kissinger was not the first Jew to hold a U.S. Cabinet-level position, nor was he the first Jewish Secretary of State. Oscar S. Straus, Secretary of Commerce and Labor, appointed by Theodore Roosevelt in 1906, was the first Jewish-American to serve as a Cabinet advisor. The first Jewish Secretary of State was Judah P. Benjamin (1811–1884) who served the Confederacy as At-

Young boy examining pickle vats on First Avenue, circa 1934. (Courtesy: Culver Pictures)

torney General, Secretary of War, and finally, Secretary of State.

♦ Betty Robbins of Massapequa, New York, became the first woman cantor in 1955 when she sang at Temple Avodah on the eve of Rosh Hashanah. In 1972, Sally Priesand (1948–   ) became the first female ordained as a rabbi in America. As an Associate Rabbi of the Stephen Wise Free Synagogue in New York City, Rabbi Priesand served her congregation for more than six years before she resigned her position.

♦ The first Jewish-American to head the American Bar Association was Bernard G. Segal (1907–   ). He was president of that organization 1969–1970.

♦ Every Friday evening the famed Grossinger's Hotel, which has been family-owned for almost seventy years, is sold! But, every Saturday evening, the Grossinger family buys it back again. This "sale" has been going on every weekend since the 1940s to permit the hotel to allow dancing, music, recreation and entertainment on the Jewish Sabbath. Each Friday before sundown, Henry Speckhardt, the non-Jewish master chef of their kosher kitchens, buys the hotel until sundown on Saturday. No money changes hands, but by technically transferring ownership, the Grossingers are not deviating from the strict practices associated with the Jewish Sabbath.

Who's Jewish?

Comedians: Milton Berle, the Marx Brothers, Eddie Cantor, Mel Brooks, Gabe Kaplan.

Entertainers: Al Jolson (real name, Asa Yoelson), born in Russia (1886–1950); Theda Bara; Paul Muni; Zero Mostel; Edward G. Robinson; Lauren Bacall; Dustin Hoffman; Walter Matthau.

Department Store Names: Bamberger's; Altman's; Gimbel's; the Straus family (who bought out R. H. Macy's interest in 1896); the Lazarus family; and Abraham Abraham, the founder of Abraham and Straus.

Notable "Fathers": Abraham Goldfadden, the "Father of the Yiddish Theater"; Abraham Flexner, "Father of Modern Medical Education"; Albert Einstein, "Father of the Atomic Age."

Movie Moguls: Warner Brothers; Louis Mayer; Samuel Goldwyn.

Letters: Fanny Hurst, Susan Sontag, Nobel Prize winner Edna Ferber, Irwin Shaw, Norman Mailer, Lillian Hellman, Walter Winchell, Lionel Trilling, Moss Hart, Arthur Miller.

Music: Eddy Duchin, George Gershwin, Jascha Heifetz, Jerome Kern, Frederick Loewe, Jan Peerce, Richard Rodgers, Richard Tucker.

Medicine: Samuel A. Levine, the Polish-Jewish heart specialist who made coronary thrombosis a household word; Jonas Salk; Albert Sabin; Abraham Jacobi; Selman Waksman.

Politics: Arthur Goldberg, U.S. Ambassador to the United Nations under President Johnson's administration; Herbert Lehman, Governor of New York three times and U.S. Senator twice; Ed Koch, Mayor of New York; Abraham Beame, Mayor of New York; Jacob Javits, N.Y. State Senator; Golda Meir (1898–1978), prime minister of the state of Israel.

60% of all American Jews live in the Middle Atlantic states.

80% are residents of only ten American cities: New York, Los Angeles, Philadelphia, Chicago, Boston, Miami, Washington, D.C., Baltimore, Cleveland and Detroit.

95% of the Jewish-American population lives in urban areas.

Jewish-Americans constitute 8% of the college-educated population of the United States. In 1964, 80% of America's Jewish youth attended college.

According to 1960 estimates there were approximately 5.5 million Jews living in the United States. Estimates for 1969 were almost 5.9 million.

Almost 50% of the world's Jewish population lives in the United States.

According to the 1970 Census, there were 1,593,993 Americans who claimed Yiddish as their mother tongue. There were also more than 59,000 foreign-stock Israelis living in America at that time (a number that has increased dramatically over the last decade as more and more Israelis have sought the relative security of the United States).

IN THEIR OWN WORDS . . .

(Memories of Boston's North End in the early 1900s)

Sam Gurvitz was born in the North End and spent most of his early years there.

"My grandparents came here about 1897 and they settled in the North End of Boston, where I was born in 1904 . . . At the time my family moved here, the North End was a predominantly Russian-Jewish community. The German and early Jewish people usually settled in the South End area where they had their synagogue. The Russian, Lithuanian and Polish-Jewish people opened their own synagogues in the North End . . .

"My home was a strictly kosher home. My people ran a strictly kosher restaurant in the North End for over 20 years, Gurvitz's Kosher Restaurant. We only served meat foods. In a strictly kosher restaurant you cannot mix dairy foods with meat foods. My father worked early in the morning 'til 8 or 9 at night. He would do the buying, so he'd have to get up early and the restaurant would open at 11 A.M. and close at 7 at night. All the kids helped out. We washed dishes. We would wait on table. I would take the cash on certain days. My mother did all the cooking. The biggest restaurant we ever had accommodated about 50 people. But I would say we served between 100 and 120 meals a day. The most expensive meal I remember was 65 cents, and that was for a five-course meal.

"I was born on North Margin Street in 1904 and at that time my father tells me he was paying $2 a week rent. You paid your rent by the week, because nobody could accumulate a month's rent. Different Jewish people owned the apartment buildings that we lived in. Very little of the real estate in the North End now is owned by Jewish people . . .

"The days I lived there, the young non-Jewish people were still pulling the beards of the old Jewish men. It was very dangerous, in a sense, to cross certain lines. The Jewish people had their area, the Italian people had their area, and the Irish had their area.

"We more or less recognized the different areas and walked with caution should we have to go through there. We all went to school together, the Italian kids and the Irish kids . . . There was always a certain amount of friction. You can't prevent this. I imagine the same friction that exists between the blacks and the whites today, that same friction existed among the Italians and the Jews and the Irish in the North End.

"Well, when the Italian kids called me, they used the phrase, 'Mazza Christo,' which meant we were Christ-killers. That's how they referred to Jewish kids and we in turn would call them 'Dagos' and 'Wops,' and we would call Irish people 'Micks.' Every once in a while somebody would call them 'potato head' because of the potato famine that drove the Irish in large numbers to the United States. But all of these things completely disappeared as we grew older. When I got to be, say 18 or 19, it had all disappeared. They accepted us, we accepted them. Most of the storekeepers were Jewish and learned Italian to be able to sell to the Italian people that were coming in in large numbers. In 1926, when my family moved out, there were only 12 Jewish families left in the whole North End."

THE LATVIANS IN AMERICA

Conquered by Russia in 1795, Latvia has remained under Russian domination ever since, except for a brief period of independence following World War I. In 1940 Latvia became a Soviet Socialist Republic.

Most of the Latvians who have emigrated to America came here out of dissatisfaction with foreign rule. During the first two decades of the twentieth century, some 30,000 Latvians found their way to the United States. But, while Latvia enjoyed freedom as an independent nation between 1918 and 1940, only 666 Latvians saw any reason to leave their homeland for America. After

World War II, many of the 200,000 displaced Latvians sought refuge in the United States under the displaced Persons Act of 1948.

♦ ♦ ♦

♦ In 1638, four Latvians settled in a Swedish colony that had been established at Delaware Bay. Throughout the seventeenth, eighteenth and nineteenth centuries, scattered groups of Latvians settled on the eastern shores of the United States.
♦ It wasn't until the late 1880s that there were a sufficient number of Latvians in America to establish their own cultural societies and newspapers. The Boston Lettish Society was founded in 1889 by Jacob Seeberg, and the first Latvian newspaper, *Amerikas Vestnesis* (The American Herald), was published in Boston in 1896.
♦ The oldest Latvian civic group still in existence today is the Philadelphia Society of Free Letts, established in 1892.
♦ In 1900 there were 4,309 Latvians in the United States, many of whom sought their fortunes in the gold mines of the American West. One of them, August Krastins (1859–1942), patented his "Krastin Gasoline Automobile" in 1901, seven years before Henry Ford began working on his "better idea," the Model T.

Facts About the Other Side:

Country: LATVIA

Capital: Riga

Facts About Latvian-Americans:

1970 Census

Foreign-born Latvians	41,707
Native-born, 2nd generation	44,706
Total Foreign-stock Population	86,413

According to a 1974 survey conducted by the American Latvian Association: 55% of all Latvian-Americans 19 years and older have some college education (95% between the ages of 19 and 35); 70% own their own homes; 95% vote in political elections; there are almost 600 physicians and dentists in America of Latvian ancestry; there are also about 600 scientists and scholars of Latvian descent teaching in American universities.

The five states with the largest Latvian populations are: New York (16,433), California (9,769), Illinois (8,318), New Jersey (5,164), Massachusetts (5,100).

Who's Latvian?

Military: Martin Bucin, one of the first casualties of the Civil War.
Science: Peteris Otto Krumins (1898–1964), a chemical engineer, developed the standard method for determining the CO_2 content of coal in 1961.
Business: Leon Swirbul, former president of Grumman Aircraft.

Government: Karlis Ulmanis graduated from the University of Nebraska in 1909 before becoming President of Latvia in 1918.
Sports: Māra Kristberga-Culp (1941–) won the 1969 Powder Puff Derby.
Beauty: Mārīte Ozers, Miss USA of 1963.

THE LITHUANIANS IN AMERICA

One of the earliest Lithuanians in America was Dr. Aleksandras K. Kursius, a physician who became New York City's "first secondary school teacher." Dr. Kursius lived in New York from 1659 to 1661 and taught at a schoolhouse in the financial district (at the corner of Broad Street and Exchange Place) for the grand salary of 500 florins.

Most of the Lithuanians who settled in America during the seventeenth and eighteenth centuries were noblemen or craftsmen who came here individually, not as part of a massive migration. After the 1831 Rebellion, the famine of 1850 and the second Polish-Lithuanian insurrection, which ended in failure in 1863, thousands of Lithuanians began the trek to America. They settled in Pennsylvania mining towns and on the farms of New England. It has been estimated that a total of about 500,000 Lithuanians emigrated to the U.S. between 1868 and 1914. However, the true figures will never be known, since all incoming Lithuanians were listed either as Poles or Russians; they did not receive their own immigration category until 1931.

By 1884 there were 15,000 Lithuanians in America. By the turn of the century, their ranks had blossomed to 275,000 Almost 75,000 Lithuanians lived in the coal-mining regions of Pennsylvania and West Virginia; 10,000 inhabited the cities of Philadelphia and Baltimore; and 30,000 were living in Chicago by 1904.

Following World War II, Lithuanians were admitted to the United States from displaced persons camps. Over 37,000 were admitted between 1948 and 1953 under this special dispensation granted by Congress.

♦ ♦ ♦

♦ The "Apostle of the Alleghenies," Reverend Demetrius Augustine Gallitzin, was the first Roman Catholic priest to study and take vows in the United States. Gallitzin, who was a descendant of Lithuanian immigrants, founded the town of Loretto, Pennsylvania, in 1795.
♦ During the Civil War there were 373 Lithuanian soldiers fighting for the Union cause and 44 serving the Confederacy.
♦ The first woman army nurse in the Civil

War was a Lithuanian-American, Sister Mary Veronica Klimkiewicz.
♦ The first Lithuanian language newspaper in America, *Lietuwiszka Gazieta,* was published in Shamokin, Pennsylvania, in 1874.
♦ The first Lithuanian woman to graduate from medical school was Joanna Baltrusaitis. She received her degree in 1896 from the Women's Medical College in Baltimore, Maryland.
♦ *The Man Who Made "Cents"* Victor D. Brenner (1871–1924), who was known as Victor Baranauskas in his native Lithuania, designed the Lincoln penny in 1909. That first year of issue, some 28 million cents were minted with his initials, VDB, engraved on the front.
♦ The Federal Bureau of Investigation's first director was Alexander Bruce Bialaski, who called himself a "Lithuanian of Poland." Bialaski served as director of the FBI from 1912 to 1919.
♦ *Green Pastures* was written by Peretz Hershbein (1881–1948), a Lithuanian Jew.
♦ *Miles of Aisles* The Strand Book Store, one of the largest secondhand bookstores in the United States, with over 8 miles of books, has been operating in New York

City since the 1920s. Strand's founder was Benjamin Bass (1901–1978), a Lithuanian immigrant raised in Hartford, Connecticut. Bass started in the secondhand book trade with a small stall, and built the Strand into a business that occupies three floors and covers some 32,000 square feet.

♦ Lithuanian Day has been an annual event at Lakewood Park, Pennsylvania, since 1913. Almost 20,000 people attend the festivities each year.

♦ A Lithuanian prize fighter, Jack Sharkey (Juozas Zuhauskas) was the World's Heavyweight Boxing Champ in 1932.

♦ In 1967, the Keistutis Loan and Building Association of Chicago, the first Lithuanian-American savings and loan institution, changed its name to the Union Federal Savings and Loan. It was founded in 1897.

♦ The first Lithuanian community in America was established at Danville, Pennsylvania, in 1869 by four men. Three years later, Danville's population had increased to more than 200 Lithuanian-Americans, and to this day Pennsylvania is one of the main population centers for foreign-stock Lithuanians. It has been estimated that there are more than 500,000 Lithuanian-Americans of the third generation and beyond living in Pennsylvania today.

Facts About the Other Side:

Country:	LITHUANIA
Capital:	Vilnius
Official Name:	Lietuva (Lithuanian Soviet Socialist Republic) (Although Lithuania became a republic of the USSR in 1940, Soviet jurisdiction is not recognized by the United States)
Official Language:	Lithuanian
National Anthem:	"Lietuva, Tèvyne Mūsu" was composed in 1898 by Dr. Vincas Kudirka (1858–1899), a physician and musician.
National Flag:	Three horizontal stripes of equal width: yellow at top, green in middle, red at bottom. Yellow stands for the fields of ripening rye or wheat, and symbolizes freedom from want; green stands for the beautiful forests of Lithuania, and symbolizes hope; red, the color of flowers, symbolizes love of country. The flag was adopted in May 1920.
Major Religion:	In 1940, approximately 80% of the population was Roman Catholic.
National Holidays:	February 16, Day of Restoration of Lithuania's Independence (1918); September 8, Lithuanian Kingdom Day
State Emblem:	Vytis, a mounted knight in white on a field of red. It is the coat of arms of the Grand Duchy of Lithuania and dates back to 1440. ●

Facts About Lithuanian-Americans:

Immigration to the United States (1931–1975):*	3,782
Peak Decade (1931–1940):	2,201

1970 Census

Foreign-born Lithuanians	76,001
Native-born, 2nd generation	254,976
Total Foreign-stock Population	330,977

There are 37 Black Americans who claim Lithuanian as their mother tongue. All are naturalized citizens.

Utah had only 112 Lithuanians in 1970; Wyoming had only 82.

Lithuanians comprise 1.0% of the foreign-stock population of the United States.

*Immigration statistics for Lithuania began in 1931.

Main Ethnic Epicenters:		U.S. Cities with Most Lithuanians	
Illinois	58,285	Chicago	51,249
Pennsylvania	43,183	New York	31,099
New York	42,863	Philadelphia	15,148
Massachusetts	32,617	Boston	14,426
New Jersey	22,658	Los Angeles	12,903

Other cities with large Lithuanian populations are: Worcester, Massachusetts; Detroit, Michigan; Baltimore, Maryland; Pittsburgh, Pennsylvania.

Estimated Lithuanian-American Population:
According to a 1969 estimate, there were some 1,650,000 Americans of Lithuanian ancestry. Most of these were third-, fourth- and fifth-generation Americans, and not included as "foreign stock" by U.S. Census officials.

Who's Lithuanian?

Entertainers: David Brenner, comedian; Joanna Shimkus; Laurence Harvey (real name Laurynas Skinkis); Charles Bronson (Casimir Businskis); Ruta Lee (Ruta Kilmonis); and Walter Matthau, the son of a Jewish-Lithuanian mother and a father who had been a Catholic priest in Czarist Russia.
Music: Elizabeth Swados, composer.
Sports: Tennis: Vitas Gerulaitis; *Pool:* Jean Balukis, top female pool player in America, winner of U.S. Open five years in a row; *Football:* Johnny Unitas, Ed Krause, Dick Butkus, B. Lazolaskus, Jim Katcavage; *Baseball:* Johnny Podres, Ed Miksis.
Playwright: Murray Schisgal.
Film Makers: Jonas and Adolphus Mekas.
Business: The Hyatt Corporation, which includes a chain of luxury hotels, was started by the Pritzker family, descendants of Nicholas J. Pritzker, a Jewish immigrant from Lithuania, who arrived in Chicago in 1880 at the age of nine.

"LIETUVA, TEVYNE MUSU"
National Anthem of Lithuania

Lithuania, our country,
Land of might you'll ever be;
Through the ages your fond sons
Have gathered strength from thee.

Lithuanian, your children
Paths of righteousness shall tread;
For their native land they'll labor
Earth's aspiring aims they've bred.

Fount of light, may your bright sun
Pierce all that's in darkened sheen,
Show us Truth's noble way,
And we'll follow in your gleam.

In our hearts, Lithuania,
Love for you will dwell fore'er
Spirit of the world is soaring
Caught in your exalted glare.

THE NORWEGIANS IN AMERICA

Although Norwegians didn't begin their mass migrations to the United States until the 1820s, there were a few Norwegians present in New Amsterdam in the early 1600s. One early Norwegian settler was Tryn Jonas, a native of Marstrand, who was employed by the Dutch West India Company as the first professional midwife in New Netherland. Another settler was Anneken Heriksen of Bergen, Norway, who married Jan Arentzen Van Der Bilt in 1650 and started the rich and powerful Vanderbilt family.

In 1825 the ship *Restauration,* loaded with a cargo of iron and household supplies, docked at New York on October 9 with 52 Norwegian passengers. Later, these immigrants purchased farmland in western New York state and established a settlement known as Kendall.

When Ole Rynning published his *True Account of America* in 1837, his fellow Norwegians were intrigued by his descriptions of the land and of the crops that could be grown in abundance here. Besides whetting the Norwegian appetite for adventure, Rynning also included practical tips on how to get here, when to travel, and what to expect from daily life in the United States.

In the 1840s, 13,903 immigrants from Norway and Sweden found their way to our shores, compared to only 1,201 for the previous decade (1831–1840). During the 1860s, Norway alone supplied more than 71,000 new citizens to America, thanks in part to rave reviews from immigrants like Rynning.

For the most part, successive waves of Norwegian immigrants maintained their ties to the land, and as late as 1920 more than half of all Norwegian-Americans resided in agricultural areas, especially on the farmlands of Minnesota.

From the other side, Norwegians gave America the Norway maple, the Norwegian elkhound, Leif Ericsson and, unfortunately, the Norway rat. The Norwegians in America gave us outboard motors, the cyclotron, the Holland Tunnel and the "fighting Irish."

◆ ◆ ◆

◆ The first Norwegian newspaper published in the United States was *Nordlyset* (the Northern Light), which debuted in 1847. Knud Langeland founded the paper four years after he had emigrated from Bergen, Norway.

◆ *Norwegian Utopia* Ole Bull (1810–1880), a violinist from Norway, came to America in 1843 and was so impressed with this new land that he decided to invest in a "Utopian" community, known as Oleana. He bought land in Pennsylvania and invited hundreds of Norwegians to come to Oleana and clear the land, farm, build houses and make a new life for themselves as Americans.

Unfortunately, Bull was a violinist, not an agricultural specialist, and the land he chose was difficult to clear and not quite as fertile as the American plains. Lastly, Bull's title deed to some 120,000 acres of land was questionable. Considering the hardships of Oleana too much to bear, the Norwegians packed up their belongings and headed farther west to richer soil that was waiting to be farmed.

◆ *Ancestral Courage* In 1856, Frederik Mundal, a farmer, with his wife and his sixteen-year-old son, Ole, set sail from Bergen, Norway, in search of a new life in America. One hundred twenty-three years later, Ole's grandson, Walter F. Mondale, Vice-President of the United States, returned to the village of his forebears, also named Mundal. In tribute to his ancestors, Mondale praised their adventuresome spirit: "What a challenge that must have been. Leaving their friends, their home, their church, their farm, everything they knew, to go to America, to a new land they knew little about. What brave people they must have been! I wonder how many members of my generation would have as much courage as they did."

◆ *Cure for Pellagra* Dr. Conrad Elvehjem, a Norwegian-American biochemist at the University of Wisconsin, discovered that nicotinic acid would cure the dreaded vitamin-deficiency disease, pellagra. Lest the public believe that nicotine or tobacco leaves would effect a cure for pellagra, the name of this B vitamin was changed to niacin.

♦ *Mama's Bank Account* In 1979, *I Remember Mama* debuted on the Broadway stage as a musical comedy starring Norwegian actress Liv Ullmann. The basis of the musical was a collection of stories, first published in *Reader's Digest* and later bound together as a book, *Mama's Bank Account*, in 1943. Written by Kathryn Forbes, the stories were true-life reminiscences of her childhood in San Francisco, as part of a large family of Norwegian immigrants. *I Remember Mama* was produced as a dramatic play on Broadway in 1944, as a movie in 1948, and as one of tele-vision's first ethnic sit-coms from 1949 to 1957.

♦ *First Lady's Hairdresser* Elvind Bjerke, a native of Grue-Solor, a small town seventy miles north of Oslo, came to America in 1964 and found employment at a beauty salon owned by a fellow Norwegian, Per of Georgetown. By 1977, Bjerke was a regular "guest" at the White House, each Monday and Friday, as he performed his hairdressing skills on Rosalynn Carter. When President Carter toured Latin America on an official visit, Bjerke went along to keep the wives of top government officials looking their best. His services were paid for by the State Department.

Facts About the Other Side:

Country: NORWAY

Capital: Oslo
Official Name: Kongeriget Norge (Kingdom of Norway)
Also Known As: The Land of the Midnight Sun (One-third of the country lies north of the Arctic Circle, and the sun shines day and night here from late May through July.)
Official Language: Norwegian
National Anthem: *Ja vi elsker* (Yes, We Love with Fond Devotion)
National Flag: Adopted as the national flag in 1898, the blue cross outlined in white on a red field was first used by merchant ships in 1821.
Major Religions: The official church is the Evangelical Lutheran Church, to which 96 percent of the Norwegian people belong. There is freedom of worship, however, for other religious groups.
National Holiday: May 17, Constitution Day

Facts About Norwegian-Americans:

Immigration to the U.S. (1820–1975):   855,337*
   Peak Decade (1901–1910):   190,505

1970 Census
Foreign-born Norwegians	97,243
Native-born, 2nd generation	517,406
Total Foreign-stock Population	614,649

Main Ethnic Epicenters:		*U.S. Cities with Most Norwegians:*	
Minnesota	114,221	Minneapolis-St. Paul	40,335
California	69,278	New York	39,522
Washington	60,427	Seattle	32,579
Wisconsin	52,681	Chicago	27,737
New York	47,605	Los Angeles	23,249

*From 1820 to 1868 the totals for Norway and Sweden were combined; hence this figure is inflated.

Who's Norwegian?

Business: Arthur Anderson, founder of a national accounting firm which dates back to 1913, the year when the Internal Revenue Service was inaugurated; Conrad Hilton, hotel-chain founder; C. W. Larsen, founder of Larsen Baking Company in Brooklyn in the early 1900s; Ole Evinrude, inventor of the first practical outboard motor.

Government: Minnesota Congressman Andrew Volstead, who introduced the National Prohibition Act of 1919; Bob Bergland (1928–   ), U.S. Secretary of Agriculture under President Carter—he was the first farmer to hold that position since 1945; Dr. Roger Egeberg, Assistant Secretary of Health and Scientific Affairs in 1969.

Science: 1939 Nobel Prize winner Ernest O. Lawrence, inventor of the cyclotron.

Law: Allan Bakke, medical student who won court battle for admission to University of California Medical School in 1978 as a victim of "reverse discrimination."

Journalism: Eric Sevareid, CBS news an-alyst; Victor Lawson, co-founder of the Associated Press in 1894.

Entertainment: James Cagney; James Arness; Sonja Henie; Celeste Holm; Risë Stevens; Judith Blegen; Sally Struthers (Scottish and Norwegian ancestry); Peter Graves; the Andrews Sisters (Greek and Norwegian ancestry).

Politics: Karl Rolvaag, son of author Ole Rolvaag, was Governor of Minnesota in the 1960s; Hubert H. Humphrey (1911–1978) was of Welsh and Norwegian ancestry.

Engineering: Ole Singstad, engineering genius who created the world's first tunnel designed for motor cars—the Holland Tunnel.

Sports: Knute Rockne, head football coach of Notre Dame University's "Fighting Irish" from 1918 to 1931. Over the years his teams scored 105 victories, 12 losses and 5 ties.

Letters: Caroline Bird (of English and Norwegian descent), author of *Enterprising Women*.

THE PORTUGUESE IN AMERICA

Over the past three hundred years, Portugal has given America over 411,000 of her native-born sons and daughters. The peak decade for immigration was between 1911 and 1920, when 89,732 Portuguese emigrated to our shores. Many were farmers and fishermen by trade and chose to settle in the agricultural and fishing centers of Hawaii, California and Massachusetts.

Recently Portuguese immigration has been on the upswing; from 1971 to 1975 over 52,000 Portuguese have settled in the United States. Many joined friends and relatives in the "Ironbound" section of New-ark, New Jersey, or in the Portuguese enclaves of New England—Fall River and New Bedford, Massachusetts. Others settled in neighboring states, and in 1974 the Department of Motor Vehicles in Rhode Island published the first driver's manual ever issued in the Portuguese language, attesting to the large influx of immigrants from Portugal, Madeira and the Azores.

From the "other side" the Portuguese contributed Madeira wine, Castile soap, sardines, and cork for bottle caps and bulletin boards. The Portuguese introduced the sweet potato to California, the ukulele to

Hawaii, and gave us the words *cuspidor* ("spitter") and "Canada." Although their ranks are small compared to the millions of German and Italian immigrants, the Portuguese managed to contribute quite a bit to America: they discovered California, helped found the New York Stock Exchange and donated famous authors, musicians, athletes, actors and statesmen.

♦ ♦ ♦

♦ On Thursday, September 28, 1542, Joao Rodrigues Cabrillo, a Portuguese sailing under the flag of Spain, entered San Diego harbor and landed near Ballast Point, becoming the first European to set foot on the Pacific coast. Further explorations by Cabrillo led to his discovery of Santa Catalina, San Pedro Bay and the Santa Barbara Channel.

♦ According to one legend, a group of Portuguese sailors with the Gaspar Côrte-Real expedition sailed down the St. Lawrence River in 1500, believing it to be a passage to the Pacific Ocean. Upon discovering their mistake, they shouted out in disgust, "Ca nada," meaning "Here, nothing!" Natives on the banks of the river heard their shouts and, believing them to be a greeting, repeated the words when Jacques Cartier's expedition arrived in 1534. (Cartier's journal carries a different version of the story and claims Canada was derived from a Huron-Iroquois word, "kanata," meaning "village.")

♦ During the first week of September in 1654, 23 Portuguese Jews from Brazil arrived in New Amsterdam. They founded the congregation Shearith Israel with Saul Brown as their first rabbi; services continued to be conducted in Portuguese until the mid-eighteenth century. Shearith Israel is the oldest Jewish congregation in the United States; its services are currently conducted at Seventieth Street and Central Park West in New York City.

♦ The first meeting of what eventually evolved into the New York Stock Exchange took place at the Merchants Coffee House on May 17, 1792. One of the founders of the New York Stock Exchange was Benjamin Mendes Seixas, the son of a Por-

tuguese immigrant, Isaac Seixas, who had arrived in New York in 1730.

♦ Mass migration of Portuguese to Hawaii began in 1878 when the sailing ship *Priscilla,* which has been called the "*Mayflower* of the Portuguese," landed at Honolulu with 120 citizens from Madeira. Over the next 20 years almost 13,000 Portuguese came to the Islands seeking employment as farm laborers. By 1930 there were 167,891 Portuguese-Americans living in the continental United States, and 27,588 on the islands of Hawaii, where they comprised 7.5% of the total population.

♦ Although the ukulele was popularized in Hawaii about 1877, this small guitar originated on the island of Madeira. Known as the "machete" in Portuguese, this four-stringed instrument took its new name from a nineteenth-century British army officer, Edward Purvis. Purvis was a petite, lively man whose antics reminded his Hawaiian friends of a leaping flea—so they nicknamed him "ukulele" (jumping little flea). Purvis learned to play the machete and was responsible for the instrument's popularity throughout the islands, so when local craftsmen began to manufacture their own instruments, they began marketing them as "ukuleles" in honor of the lively little man who loved to play and dance.

♦ The first Portuguese school in America was established in Santo Christo Parish at Fall River, Massachusetts, in 1910. By 1973, almost 20% of the teachers in Fall River were of Portuguese descent, due to the large Portuguese-American population of that New England town.

♦ The first Portuguese-American elected to the House of Representatives was Frank B. Oliveira, the son of immigrants from the Azores, who served as a congressman from the State of Massachusetts from 1944 to 1958.

♦ The first U.S. soldier killed in World War I was a Portuguese-American, Walter Goulart.

♦ The first Portuguese newspaper published in the United States was the *Journal de Noticias,* which appeared in 1877.

♦ The first recorded Festival of the Divine Holy Ghost (Festa do Divino Spirito Santo), an annual event in California, was held at Sausalito, on San Francisco Bay, in 1887.

Facts About the Other Side:

Country:	PORTUGAL
Capital:	Lisbon
Official Name:	República Portuguesa (Republic of Portugal)
Official Language:	Portuguese
National Anthem:	"A Portuguesa" (The Portuguese). Words by Henrique Lopes de Mendonça; music by Alfredo Keil.
National Flag:	Vertical bands of red and green represent the blood of Portuguese heroes and hope for the future. Unfortunately blood seems to outweigh hope, as the red band is twice the width of the green. The coat of arms represents the Christian faith and a never-ending search for true knowledge.
Major Religions:	Most Portuguese embrace Roman Catholicism, although church and state have been separate since 1910.
National Holidays:	June 10, Day of Portugal

Facts About Portuguese-Americans:

Immigration to the U.S. (1820–1975):   411,136
   Peak Decade (1911–1920):   89,732
   Recent Immigration (1966–1975):   120,508

1970 Census
Foreign-born Portuguese   91,034
Native-born, 2nd generation   149,532
Total Foreign-stock Population   240,566

Who's Portuguese?

John Philip Sousa (1854–1932), the "March King"

John Dos Passos (1896–1970), author

Billy Martin (1928–   ), baseball manager

Tony Lema (1934–1966), golfer

Harold Peary (1908–   ), "the Great Gildersleeve"

Benjamin Nathan Cardozo (1870–1938), Supreme Court Justice

Humberto Sousa Medeiros (1915–   ), Archbishop of Boston

Jacques Loeb (1859–1924), biologist

Robert le Roy Ripley (1893–1949), compiler of odd facts and other trivia in "Ripley's Believe It or Not"

THE PUERTO RICANS IN AMERICA

Columbus landed on the island of Puerto Rico on his second trip to the New World in 1493, but the Spanish didn't settle on that island until 1508. For more than 400 years Puerto Rico was part of the Spanish Empire – until 1898, when it became a protectorate of the United States. The Foraker Act of 1900 made Puerto Rico an American territory, with an American governor, and the Jones Act of 1917 granted U.S. citizenship to all Puerto Ricans.

In 1910 there were only 500 Puerto Ricans living in New York. Thirty years later their ranks had swelled to 70,000, most of whom settled in the section of Manhattan that came to be known as "Spanish Harlem." The peak year for Puerto Rican immigration to the U.S. was

1946, when almost 70,000 Puerto Ricans made the plane trip to the mainland. By 1969 there were over 1.5 million Puerto Ricans living in the United States, with more than 977,000 living in New York City, where they comprised about 11% of that city's population.

The Puerto Ricans became America's first "airborne" immigrants. Instead of sailing past Miss Liberty into New York Harbor, they flew into Idlewild airport. They did not have to suffer agonizing weeks of steerage-class travel aboard sailing ships; they were not isolated at Ellis Island detention centers; and there was no need for them to wait five years before applying for citizenship papers.

Almost 70,000 Puerto Ricans came to the mainland in 1946 to seek a brighter future for their children; many found that extreme poverty awaited them instead. (Courtesy: Culver Pictures)

Since the end of World War II almost one-third of the island's population, some 800,000 "immigrants," have found their way to the United States. During the 1970s a trend toward "reverse" immigration began, as many "Neoricans" (as they are called by their island-bred relatives) returned to Puerto Rico. Most either were born in the United States or had spent most of their adult life there, and now were returning to their native land. These "reverse immigrants" are for the most part skilled workers in their mid-thirties, and their average educational level was about tenth grade. In 1972, more Puerto Ricans re-turned to the island than emigrated to the mainland, making the net flow minus 34,000 that year.

◆ ◆ ◆

◆ New York City's French Hospital was founded in 1869 by a Puerto Rican immigrant, Dr. José Julio Henna (1848–1924). Dr. Henna became a U.S. citizen in 1872.
◆ The first Puerto Rican to play big-league baseball was Hiram Gabriel Bithorn (1916–1952). Born in Santurce, Puerto Rico, Bithorn played for two Chicago teams—the Cubs and the White Sox—in the 1940s.
◆ The First Catholic church in the United States to minister to the needs of the Puerto Rican community was La Milagrosa, located at 114th Street and 7th Avenue in Manhattan. A former synagogue, the building was "converted" in 1926 to meet the growing needs of the community, reflecting the ever-changing ethnic mix of the neighborhood.
◆ The first popularly elected governor of Puerto Rico was Luis Muñoz Marín, who took office in 1948. The Crawford-Butler Act, signed by President Truman in 1946, permitted Puerto Ricans to elect an official of their own choosing rather than having to accept an appointed governor.
◆ Herman Badillo (1929–) was the first Puerto Rican-born American to serve as a U.S. congressman. Over the years, in addition to earning degrees as an accountant and a lawyer, Badillo has served as Commissioner of the Office of Relocation in New York City (1962), Bronx Borough President (1965), and as a member of the House of Representatives.
◆ In 1977, Maria Fernanda Hernández ("Marifé" for short) was appointed as U.S. Deputy Chief of Protocol for New York. Born in Puerto Rico, Marife has a mixed ethnic heritage—she is descended from Puerto Rican and French ancestors, was raised in South America, and was educated in British schools.
◆ In 1978, Dionisia Perez celebrated her 118th birthday. A native of Peñuelas, in southwestern Puerto Rico, Mrs. Perez did not claim to know the secret of long life, but she advised the young to "Sing, sing, and be happy." Of her 14 children, only 4 were still living in 1977, but she also had 60 grandchildren, 40 great-grandchildren, and 20 great-great-grandchildren.

"GEE, YOU DON'T *LOOK* PUERTO RICAN"*
By Irma Alvarado

There was a time when hearing that gave me a high that lasted all day. How proud I was that others had not guessed I was of Puerto Rican heritage! What an ego trip to be able to speak without an accent!

Unfortunately, it went deeper than that. I can't remember how or when I "learned" that it was wrong to be Puerto Rican. I must have been a small girl, because my memories of answering questions relating to my nationality never included "Puerto Rican." In grammar school in the 50s, I was Spanish (very vague). In junior high school, I was either Spanish or combination Spanish/South American. By high school (a parochial girls' school in the Bronx, N.Y.) I had narrowed it to Spanish father/Colombian mother . . . who knows *where* I picked up the "Colombian" part.

I'd like to be able to say that by the time I started college, I'd smartened up, but it didn't happen that way. I did, however, become a bit more generous. I admitted to a Puerto Rican mother, but quickly added that *her* parents were from Spain!

It's very sad when I think now of all the effort I put into avoiding any shame or embarrassment. I realize that my conditioning was the result of many different factors; growing up in a neighborhood where we were the only "Spanish" family didn't help. Would I have been better off if I'd grown up in El Barrio? Who knows. But how I wish I could have shared my pride in being bilingual, learned to mambo earlier, appreciated my mother's cooking sooner.

When did I change? I don't know. I think meeting my husband-to-be had a lot to do with it (yes, a genuine P.R.!). For some reason, I always knew I'd marry a Latino; maybe my roots were working on me all along, or maybe I didn't think anyone else would "accept" me. Most probably it was a combination of both. At any rate, he introduced me to a culture I hadn't known. He took me to Latin dances where I met lots of young Puerto Ricans, most working and many in college. They were bright, exciting. I wished I'd had friends like that as I'd grown up.

Looking back, I see myself mostly as having been a victim of the society around me as I grew up; somehow I got it into my head that being Puerto Rican was wrong. By the time I was old enough to understand that this notion was wrong, look at how much time had passed. I get angry when I think about it too much – at "them" for making me feel that way and at myself for not being able to overcome it sooner.

That's why it's so important to me that *my* kids feel a pride and dignity in their heritage. I want them to know about and see Puerto Rico (one has); I'd like them to speak the language (I admit to getting lazy about this at home). The danger of not instilling a sense of pride and love for their heritage in our children is that, in later generations, many of the traditions we take for granted now will become memories and trivia for our grandchildren. I don't want my grandchildren to miss out on the *fun* of being "different," as I did.

What do I say now to people who say I don't look Puerto Rican? It depends on my mood. If I'm feeling low, I'll hit back with, "Just what *does* a Puerto Rican look like?" More often than not, I realize that someone who makes a statement like that is either innocent or ignorant, so a smile of affirmation is enough. But don't knock it – that affirmation, in my case, was a long time coming.

Irma Alvarado is a New York Puerto Rican housewife.

Nuestro magazine, September 1977. Reprinted by permission.

Who's Puerto Rican?

Sports: Angel Cordero (1942–   ), top jockey who rode 345 winners in 1968; Chi Chi Rodriguez (1935–   ), golfer; José Santiago, Roberto Clemente, Orlando Cepeda (the "Puerto Rican Babe Ruth"), Carlos Ortiz, baseball stars; pro boxers José Torres (1965 medium heavyweight champ) and Sixto Escobar, the first Puerto Rican boxer to win the bantamweight world championship in 1936.

Music: José Feliciano (1945–   ), has been blind from birth, a victim of congenital glaucoma, but he was determined not to let blindness interfere with his musical career. José gave his first public appearance at El Teatro Puerto Rico in New York at the age of 9; Tito Puente, Tito Rodriguez—leading Latin musicians.

Entertainment: Freddie Prinze, the late star of the TV series *Chico and the Man,* was of mixed Puerto Rican and Hungarian Gypsy ancestry; Tony Orlando; Chita Rivera is one-fourth Puerto Rican; Brunilda Ruiz, ballerina; Liz Torres, actress of Venezuelan and Puerto Rican ancestry; Erik Estrada, star of NBC's *Chips* series, and newscaster Geraldo Rivera. José Vincent Ferrer (1912–   ) made his New York theater debut in 1935 despite his father's objections that "It is not the career I would have picked for you, but it's your own life, not mine. Do what you must with it." His father was a successful lawyer, and hoped his Princeton-educated son would follow in his footsteps, but the lure of the stage was too strong for José. Raul Julia (1940–   ), a San Juan-born actor, has been performing in New York theaters for more than 14 years. His recent Broadway roles include *Dracula, Three-Penny Opera* and *Betrayal.* Julia has also appeared as Othello and in the 1978 film *The Eyes of Laura Mars.*

THE ROMANIANS IN AMERICA

Although Romanians trace their language and ancestry directly to the Romans, they are descended from several tribes, including the Goths, Huns, Slavs and Dacians, as well as the Romans who ruled their nation in the second century A.D.

Romania did not become an independent, unified nation until 1861, when Moldavia and Wallachia merged, and it wasn't until after World War I that Romania gained the provinces of Banat, Bucovina and Transylvania.

The first immigrant to America from what is now Romania was a Transylvanian priest, Samuel Damian, who came to our shores in 1748. The first major wave of immigration from Transylvania, Banat and Bucovina, the Austro-Hungarian provinces that were to become Romania, was triggered in 1900 by a series of economic, social and political upheavals. Altogether some 53,000 refugees entered the United States in the first decade of the twentieth century.

By 1905, America had its first Romanian Orthodox Church, St. Mary's in Cleveland; its first Romanian Catholic parish, St. Helen's on Cleveland's East Side; and its first Romanian language newspaper, *Tribuna* (the Tribune), as well as its first Romanian mutual aid society.

Another 13,000 Romanians sought refuge here between 1911 and 1920, and in the first part of the 1920's over 60,000 Romanians settled here. The flow was stopped by the immigration law of 1924, which limited their quota to 603 new arrivals each year.

Facts About the Other Side:

Country:	ROMANIA
Capital:	Bucharest
Official Name:	Republica Socialista Romania
	(Socialist Republic of Romania)
Official Language:	Romanian
National Anthem:	"Te slăvim Românie, pămînt stramoşesc"
	(We praise thee, fatherland Romania)
National Flag:	Vertical stripes of blue, yellow and red, with the coat of arms in the center of the flag. The red star in the coat of arms symbolizes communism.
Major Religion:	Romanian Orthodox (75% of population)

Facts About Romanian-Americans:

Immigration to the U.S. (1880–1975):	165,747
Peak Decade (1921–1930):	67,646

1970 Census

Foreign-born Romanians	70,687
Native-born, 2nd generation	146,116
Total Foreign-stock Population	216,893

In 1970, 56,590 Americans declared Romanian as their mother tongue.

Who's Romanian?

Military: During the Civil War, George Pomutz, a Romanian from Iowa, was elevated to the rank of brigadier general for his services at the battles of Vicksburg, Atlanta and Savannah.

Entertainment: During the 1940s the Metropolitan Opera House in New York had two principal singers of Romanian extraction: Stella Roman and Christina Caroll; actress Lauren Bacall is one-fourth Romanian.

Science: Dr. George Palade, Nobel Prize winner.

Art: George Zolnay, Saul Steinberg.

Sports and Games: Charles Stanceu and Johnny Moldovan, baseball players in the 1940s; Ely Culbertson (1891–1955), bridge player.

Letters: Dagobert Runes, founder of The Philosophical Library, a New York publishing house; Mircea Eliade, Professor, History of Religions, University of Chicago.

Business: Ben Zuckerman (1890–1979), the "dean of the American ready-to-wear coat and suit industry."

THE SPANISH IN AMERICA

Between 1820 and 1975, a mere 246,334 Spanish immigrants came to America, yet the Spanish-speaking population of the United States is one of our largest minority groups. Most of these Hispanic Americans have Spanish ancestry that has been filtered through the cultures of other lands, such as Mexico, Puerto Rico and the rest of Latin America.

The Spanish were the first settlers in Florida and the Southwest; they introduced the horse to North America, gave their language to some 12 million Americans, gave us place names in the West and Southwest, and lent their good name to such things as the "Spanish flu" (which spread wildly in 1918, killing almost 20 million people worldwide), Spanish fly (a reputed aphrodisiac made from beetles), and Spanish Moss (an epiphytic plant that hangs from trees in the Southern U.S.). They gave us Spanish mantillas and flamenco dancers, but *not* José Greco (who is Italian).

◆ ◆ ◆

◆ Ponce de Leon discovered Florida in 1513 and claimed it for the King of Spain. In 1565, Spanish forces founded the first permanent European colony in America at St. Augustine, Florida, and did not relinquish their claim to that state until 1763, when they traded Florida for the return of Cuba and the Philippines following the French and Indian War.

◆ In addition to the horse, the Spanish also introduced cattle, sheep and swine to North America between 1540 and 1565.

◆ The first Catholic parish was founded by Father Martin Francisco Lopez de Mendozo Grajales at St. Augustine, Florida, in 1565, to tend to the religious needs of the Spanish settlers.

◆ Los Angeles is not the original name of that California town. It was shortened from El Pueblo de Nuestra Señora la Reina de Los Angeles de la Porciuncula, "The Town of Our Lady, Queen of the Angels of the Porciuncula." There are more than 400 cities and towns in California with Spanish-origin names. The state itself is named for an imaginary island in Spanish folklore, meaning "an earthly paradise."

◆ Other Spanish place names: Texas (from *tejas,* land of tile roofs), Nevada (land of snow), Colorado (red land).

◆ The first Spanish newspaper ever published in the United States was *El Redactor,* which debuted on July 1, 1827, in New York City.

◆ The first opera ever produced in Spanish at New York's Metropolitan Opera House was Enrique Granados' *Goyescas,* in 1916.

Facts About the Other Side

Country:	SPAIN
Capital:	Madrid
Official Language:	Castilian Spanish
National Anthem:	Himno Nacional (National Anthem)
National Flag:	Horizontal bands of red bordering a yellow field twice their width
Major Religion:	Roman Catholic

Facts About Spanish-Americans:

Immigration to the U.S. (1820–1975):	246,334
Peak Decade (1911–1920):	68,611

1970 Census

Foreign-born Spaniards	57,488
Native-born 2nd generation	97,668
Total Foreign-stock Population	155,156

Who's Spanish?

Music: Carlos Montoya (1903–   ), flamenco guitarist.

Government: Elwood Quesada (1904–   ), first head of the Federal Aviation Agency, and former vice-president of Lockheed Aircraft Corporation.

Letters: Truman Capote (1924–   ), born in New Orleans of Spanish descent; Anais Nïn (1903–1977), the diarist, was of Spanish-French descent.

Entertainment: Martin Sheen (1940–   ), of Spanish and Irish parents; Raquel Welch (1940–   ), whose real name was Raquel Tejada—her father was a Bolivian immigrant of Castilian extraction; Imogene Coca's father was a musician of Spanish descent; Xavier Cugat (1900–   ), the "Rhumba King" was born in Barcelona.

Sports: Rosemary Casals (1948–   ), top tennis player, is the grandniece of cellist Pablo Casals.

Science: Severo Ochoa (1905–   ), biochemist.

Politics: Joseph Montoya (1915–1978), U.S. Senator from New Mexico whose parents were descended from eighteenth-century Spanish immigrants.

THE SWISS IN AMERICA

Some 350,000 Swiss people found their way to the United States between 1820 and 1975. The Swiss are one of America's smaller foreign-stock groups: according to the 1970 census they comprised 0.7% of our foreign-stock population.

Despite their rather small numbers, the Swiss have managed to make their mark on America in many different fields of endeavor. From the other side, the Swiss gave us: Swiss chard, a leafy green vegetable that was first cultivated here in 1806; dotted Swiss fabric, for curtains and party dresses; Swiss cheese; and the Brown Swiss cow, first brought to New England in 1869 as a dairy breed.

The Swiss immigrants and their descendants in America gave us: Hershey's milk chocolate; Sutter's mill; the Chevrolet; Waldorf salad; Lobster Newburg; the Lincoln Tunnel; and an assortment of Nobel Prize winners, diplomats, pioneers and military men. There were even two U.S. presidents of Swiss-German extraction—Hoover and Eisenhower.

The first Swiss citizen in America was Diebold von Erlach, a mercenary soldier in the service of Spain who fought and died in Florida in 1562. But despite the early arrival of a few scattered Swiss citizens, it wasn't until 1670 that the first Swiss settlement in America was established, near Charleston, South Carolina. In 1683, Swiss immigrants settled in Pennsylvania at the behest of William Penn, who assured them of religious freedom. It has been estimated that almost 25,000 Swiss came to America in the 1700s, during which period they established colonies at Germanna, Virginia; Purysburg, South Carolina; and New Bern, Dakota, a settlement founded by Christopher de Graffenried (1661–1743) in 1710.

According to the 1970 census, there were over 49,000 Swiss-born residents and almost 169,000 children of Swiss immigrants living in the United States.

◆ ◆ ◆

◆ Colonel Henry Louis Bouquet (1714–1765) was the hero of Fort Pitt, and a military genius during the French and Indian War.

◆ Albert Gallatin (1761–1849) served as Secretary of the Treasury under both Jefferson and Madison, and enjoyed a full career as a diplomat, senator, U.S. Representative and, later, banker. He also founded the American Ethnological Society and New York University.

◆ Ferdinand-Rudolph Hassler (1770–1843) was the first Superintendent of the U.S. Coast and Geodetic Survey.

◆ Swiss-born Louis Agassiz (1807–1873)

Capt Sutter's account of the first discovery of the Gold

PORTAIT OF Mr MARSHAL, TAKEN FROM NATURE AT THE TIME WHEN HE MADE THE DISCOVERY OF GOLD IN CALIFORNIA

VIEW OF SUTTER'S MILL OR PLACE WHERE THE FIRST GOLD HAS BEEN DISCOVERED

Lith & Pub. by Britton & Rey San Francisco. Cal.

John Sutter's account of the discovery of gold on his property in 1848. (Courtesy: New York Historical Society)

and his son, Alexander, came to America in 1848. While the father taught natural history at Harvard University, the son studied there, and together they contributed much of our basic knowledge about the natural sciences, by studying animals, fossils and geological structures.

The senior Agassiz established the Museum of Comparative Zoology at Harvard and, after his death, his son was appointed curator.

♦ The Swiss brothers Peter and John Del-Monico, founded their famous restaurant, Delmonico's, in 1827 in the financial district of New York City. It was here that Americans first became acquainted with elegant Continental dining, and such dishes as Baked Alaska, pie á la mode and Lobster Newburg. Lobster Newburg started as Lobster à la Wenberg when it was first concocted by Charles Delmonico, a nephew of John and Peter, in 1876. He named it after his seafaring friend Ben Wenberg, who gave him his inspiration for preparing lobster with heavy cream, egg yolks, cognac and sherry. When Ben and Charles had a falling out, Delmonico changed the name on his menus to read Lobster à la Newberg, by reversing the first three letters of Ben's name.

♦ John A. Sutter was a Swiss-German immigrant who gave not only his name but his fortune to the Gold Rush of 1848. When gold was discovered at Sutter's mill in Sacramento, California, on January 24, thousands of gold prospectors, half-crazed with visions of dollar signs dancing in their heads, trampled Sutter's crops, slaughtered his livestock and squatted on his land, plunging Sutter to the depths of poverty.

♦ Henry Clay Frick (1849–1919), the industrialist who was influential in the 1901 merger that formed the United States Steel Corporation, left his home and art collection to New York City as a museum after his death.

♦ James William Good (1866–1929) was Secretary of War under Hoover's administration.

♦ Ernest Bloch (1880–1959), a Swiss Jew from Geneva, came to the United States in 1916 and became a naturalized citizen in 1924. His musical contributions include: *Macbeth,* an opera first produced in Paris in 1910; *Solomon* (1916), music for cello and orchestra; and *America,* a symphonic poem, first performed in New York on December 28, 1928, for which he won a $3,000 prize.

♦ *Oscar of the Waldorf* . . . Another famous "inventor" of Swiss origin was Oscar Tschirky, better known as "Oscar of the Waldorf." He was maitre d'hotel at the Waldorf Astoria in New York City from 1893–1943, and it was there that he first combined apples, celery, lettuce and mayonnaise — better known to the world as Waldorf salad.

♦ Felix Bloch (1905–   ), a Swiss-American physicist, won the 1952 Nobel prize in physics for developing a method of probing atomic nuclei with radio waves.

♦ Walter John Stoessel, Jr. (1920–   ), former United States Ambassador to Poland, is a third-generation descendant of Swiss immigrants who came to America in 1860.

Facts About the Other Side:

Country:	SWITZERLAND
Capital:	Bern
Official Name:	Schweiz (in German); Suisse (in French); and Svizzera (in Italian). The name, *Switzerland,* is derived from "Schwyz," one of the three founding cantons. Helvetia, the Latin name of Switzerland, is used on coins and stamps to avoid having to print it in three languages.
Official Languages:	German, French, Italian. In addition, 1% of the population speaks Romansch, a Swiss dialect.
National Anthem:	"Swiss Hymn"
National Flag:	A white cross on a red background; each arm of the cross is one-sixth longer than its width.
National Holiday:	August 1, Swiss National Day
Major Religions:	Roman Catholic (49.4%); Protestant (47.8%)

Facts About Swiss-Americans:

Immigration to the U.S. (1820–1975):   346,468
   Peak Decade (1881–1890):   81,988

1970 Census
Foreign-born Swiss   49,732
Native-born, 2nd generation   168,976
Total Foreign-stock Population   218,708

Main Ethnic Epicenters:		U.S. Cities with Most Swiss:	
California	44,483	New York	15,281
New York	23,773	Los Angeles	10,153
Wisconsin	14,316	San Francisco	9,968
New Jersey	13,219	Chicago	7,207
Ohio	12,337	Paterson, N.J.	4,729

There are only 160 Swiss-Americans of the first and second generations living in the state of Mississippi.

THE SYRIANS / LEBANESE IN AMERICA

It has been estimated that the total Arab-American population is somewhere between 1.5 million and 2 million persons. The immigration records are vague, however, since many Syrians and Lebanese who emigrated to the United States in the late nineteenth and early twentieth centuries came here with Turkish passports. Their nations were part of the Ottoman Empire until 1918.

The term "Arab-American" is not a racial or religious designation, but a cultural one, applying to anyone who is from an Arabic-speaking country. However, the majority of the Arab-Americans in the United States today are Christians from the portion of Syria which became Lebanon in 1941. They belong mainly to the Maronite and Melkite Rites of the Catholic Church, or to the Syrian Orthodox religion. In recent years the number of Arabic-speaking Moslems has been on the rise, but the majority of second- and third-generation Arab-Americans are Lebanese Christians.

♦ ♦ ♦

♦ The first Lebanese immigrant to America was Anthony Bishallany, who arrived in the United States in 1854.

♦ The first Arabic newspaper in America was *Kawkab Amerika* (The Star of America), founded in 1892 by Ibrahim and Najeeb Arbeely. The first daily newspaper was *Al-Hoda,* founded in Philadelphia in 1898 by Naoum Anthony Mokarzel. It became a daily in 1902 when the paper's offices were moved to New York.

♦ In 1915 the first Melkite Catholic Parish, St. George's, was established in New York. By 1931 there were also 34 Maronite-rite churches, with more than 9,000 members.

♦ In 1919, there were an estimated 400,000 Syrians and Lebanese living in America. One of the largest colonies was centered on Washington Street in New York, and encompassed almost seven city blocks of lower Manhattan. When the financial district began to expand the Arabs were forced to move, and many journeyed across the Brooklyn Bridge to Atlantic Avenue. This is still one of the largest Arab communities in the United States.

♦ When immigration quotas were imposed in 1921, the quota alloted for Syrians and Lebanese was 925 per year, three percent of the Arabic population enumerated in the 1910 census. The Immigration Act of 1924 lowered the quota to 2% of the 1890 census, and with legal avenues to America closed to the thousands who wanted to emigrate, many Arabs began entering the U.S. through Canada or South America. Some immigrants resorted to "buying" birth certificates of deceased Brazilians or Colombians, and thus entered the United States on another country's quota.

♦ St. Jude's Hospital in Memphis, Tennessee, is one of the foremost institutions for the treatment of leukemia-stricken children. The hospital was built as a thanksgiving from Danny Thomas for show-business success. ALSAC, a national organization previously known as the American Lebanese Syrian Associated Club (the acronym now stands for "Aiding Leukemia Stricken American Children"), is a nonprofit charitable organization devoted to fund raising for St. Jude's.

♦ For more than 52 years Jimmy Jemail made his living by photographing people on the sidewalks of New York and asking them to reveal their opinions on a variety of subjects. Born in Biblos, Lebanon, Jemail emigrated to the United States with his parents at the age of five. He attended the Naval Academy and was a halfback in the first Rose Bowl game played between Brown University and Washington State in 1916.

♦ Elizabeth Halaby, the granddaughter of an immigrant from Aleppo, Lebanon, changed her name to Queen Noor in 1978 when she married Jordan's King Hussein. Educated at Princeton, the twenty-six-year-old Arab-American married the forty-three-year-old monarch after a three-month courtship. Her father, Najeeb Halaby, was a former chairman of Pan-American World Airways.

The flavor of the Syrian colony on Washington Street in lower Manhattan was captured by the artist Bengough in the early 1900s. (Courtesy: Museum of the City of New York)

Facts About the Other Side:

Country:	SYRIA
Capital	Damascus
Official Name:	Al-Jamhouriya al Arabiya As-Souriya (Syrian Arab Republic)
Official Language:	Arabic
National Flag:	Three horizontal stripes of red, white and black. A golden hawk, the coat of arms, adorns the white stripe.
National Anthem:	*"Homal El Diyar"* ("Guardians of the Homeland")
National Holiday:	April 17, Evacuation Day
Major Religions:	Islam, 83%; Christian, 17%

Country:	LEBANON
Capital:	Beirut
Official Name:	Al-Joumhouriya al-Lubnaniya (Republic of Lebanon)
Official Language:	Arabic
National Flag:	Horizontal stripes of red and white with a green cedar tree in the center. The flag, adopted in 1943, symbolizes holiness, eternity and peace.
National Anthem:	*"Kulluna lil watan lil 'ula lil 'alam"* ("All of Us for the Country, Glory, Flag")
National Holiday:	November 22, Independence Day
Major Religions:	Islam, Maronite Rite of Roman Catholic Church, Greek Orthodox.

Facts About Arab-Americans

1970 Census
Foreign-born
Syrians	14,962
Lebanese	22,396

Native-born, 2nd generation
Syrians	44,527
Lebanese	62,985

Total Foreign-stock Population
Syrian	59,489
Lebanese	85,378

Who's Syrian / Lebanese?

Business Two of America's best-known names in men's slacks — Farah and Haggar — are of Lebanese origin. Mansour Farah started his company in El Paso, Texas, in 1920, and his sons, William and James, built it into a $165-million business. Maroun Hajjar changed the spelling of his name when he started selling brand-name slacks to department stores over 55 years ago; Robert Aboud, former vice-chairman, First National Bank, Chicago; Najeeb Halaby, former chairman of Pan-American.

Entertainment Danny Thomas; Marlo Thomas; Jamie Farr; Paul Anka; Tige Andrews; Rosalind Elias; Paul Jabara, Oscar-winning songwriter (1978 – "Last Dance").

Letters Philip Hitti; William Blatty; Kahlil Gibran.

Sports Joe Robbie, owner of the Miami Dolphins; Abe Gibron, former coach of the Chicago Bears football team.

Medicine Michael De Bakey.

Government Philip Habib, Assistant Secretary of State for East Asian and Pacific Affairs; James Abourezk.

Consumer Affairs Ralph Nader.

THE YUGOSLAVS IN AMERICA

Yugoslavia was formed in 1918 through the incorporation of several Balkan states and territories previously under the domination of the Hapsburg Empire. Serbia, Croatia, Slovenia, Montenegro, Dalmatia, Macedonia, Bosnia and Herzegovina.

The first immigrants from Croatia settled at Ebenezer, Georgia, about 1698. They introduced silkworm cultivation to that state, and their colony flourished until its destruction in battle shortly after the outbreak of the Civil War. It has been estimated that some 700,000 Croatians emigrated to the United States prior to 1914. Most settled in the industrial centers of Pittsburgh, Chicago and New York, but when Yugoslavia was formed after World War I almost 30% returned to their homeland.

Three peasants from the Balkans posed for this "official" Ellis Island *photograph prior to admission to the United States. (Courtesy: American Museum of Immigration)*

Facts About the Other Side:

Country: YUGOSLAVIA (the name means "Land of the South Slavs")

Capital: Belgrade

Official Name: Socijalisticak Federativna Republika Jugoslavija (Socialist Federal Republic of Yugoslavia)

Official Languages: Slovene, Macedonian, Serbo-Croatian

National Anthem: Hej Sloveni (Hey, Slavs)

National Flag: A red star (which represents Communism) bordered in gold centered on three horizontal stripes of blue, white and red.

Major Religions: Orthodox, Catholic, Moslem.

Major National Groups: Serbs (Serbia, Banat, Herzegovina, Bosnia); Croats (Croatia); Slovenes (Slovenia); Montenegrins (Montenegro); and Macedonians (Macedonia).

Facts About Yugoslav-Americans:

Immigration to the U.S. (1911–1975): 106,108*
    Peak Decade (1921–1930): 49,064

(Since 1922, Serbs, Croats and Slovenes have been recorded as part of Yugoslavia's total.)

1970 Census
Foreign-born Yugoslavians 153,745
Native-born, 2nd generation 293,526
Total Foreign-stock Population 447,271
Estimated Yugoslav-American Population: 1 million

Main Ethnic Epicenters:		U.S. Cities with Most Yugoslavs:	
Ohio	73,843	Chicago	51,219
Illinois	59,280	Cleveland	41,301
Pennsylvania	54,424	New York	32,795
California	53,868	Pittsburgh	31,624
New York	41,756	Los Angeles	24,477

There were only 84 Yugoslav-Americans of the first and second generations living in Vermont in 1970.

In 1970 there were 239,455 Americans who claimed Serbo-Croatian as their mother tongue, and 82,321 whose first language was Slovene.

Who's Yugoslavian?

Entertainment Karl Malden, the actor who used to haunt *The Streets of San Francisco* and now travels the world extolling the virtues of a major international credit card. Milos Forman, the Serbian film director who defected to the United States, recently produced the tribal rock musical of the 1960s, *Hair*. Movie director Peter Bogdanovich (1939–   ) is of Serbian, Austrian and Jewish ancestry.

Science Michael Pupin, a Serb, was famous for his inventions in the field of wireless telegraphy. Nikola Tesla (1856–1943) was born in Smiljan and emigrated to the United States in 1884. In 1888 he sold to George Westinghouse his patent for a rotating-field motor, which made alternating-current induction motors possible.

Letters Louis Adamic (1899–1951), born in Blato, Slovenia, emigrated to the United States in 1913 and became a citizen in 1918. His major works include: *A Nation of Nations* (1945), *The Eagle and the Roots* (1952), *The Native's Return* (1934).

Sports Gary Beban (1946–   ), of Yugoslavian and Italian descent, was a Heisman Trophy winner in 1967. During his last year of collegiate football at the University of California, he was known as "the Great One" for setting new team records for rushing, passing and touchdowns.

Government Helen Bentley (1923–   ) chaired the Federal Maritime Commission during President Nixon's administration.

*Immigration statistics do not accurately reflect the true number of Yugoslavs in America, since the total number of foreign-born citizens outnumbers the number of Yugoslav immigrants: 153,745 *vs.* 106,108.

PART II

Contributions,
or Everyone Gave Something

5 LANGUAGE AND LITERATURE

THE AMERICAN LANGUAGE

ENGLISH vs. AMERICAN

Over the past centuries, British-English and American-English have diverged quite a bit. Many of our common, everyday gadgets are unheard of in England, or else they are known by other names.

An American cook uses a *spatula* to turn pancakes, while an Englishman uses a *fish slice*.

Americans use *suspenders* to hold up their pants, but the British prefer *braces*, because suspenders are women's garters in England.

American men have long *sideburns* down their cheeks, but British men have *sideboards*.

Rubbers are waterproof shoes or contraceptives in America, but merely erasers in England.

English children suck on *dummys* and *iced lollys* while ours enjoy *pacifiers* and *popsicles*. The British eat *baps, joints* and *sultanas* while we dine on *hamburger buns, roasts* and *raisins*. In some parts of England they smoke *fags* after dinner, instead of *cigarettes*. You can't even trust the numbers in England to be the same! In America, a *billion* is a "thousand million," but in England it's inflated to a "million million." Even the *elevator*, excuse me, *lift*, doesn't stop in the same place, because the *first floor* in England would be on the *second floor* in America.

If an Englishman raves about a blind date he might claim she was quite *homely*, which isn't "ugly" over there, but "pleasant." And don't be surprised if an Englishman recommends a play that *bombed*, because that means it was "successful," as opposed to being a "disaster" on this side of the Atlantic.

There are some things, however, that sound infinitely better in England: while we merely have *tractor-trailers* and *moving vans* rolling down *divided highways*, the British have *articulated lorries* and *pantechnicons* rolling down *dual carriageways*. Now that's class!

The American language began to diverge from the Queen's English within hours after the first colonists stepped off the Mayflower. It was inevitable that the two languages should take separate paths of evolution — there were simply too many new plants, animals and geological structures in the New World, and too few English words to describe them. To remedy the situation, the colonists were forced to invent new words, borrow them, or adapt them from other languages.

Also, since the colonists were separated from the mainstream of British life, they tended to keep obsolete words in circulation, and began to develop their own rules for syntax and pronunciation. As early as 1781, scholars were noting that Americans got "mad" instead of "angry," and they were always insisting that they "wouldn't" or "couldn't" do certain things, while the British always "would not" or "could not."

In 1783, Noah Webster published his *American Spelling Book* and freed us from all those laborious "u's" in *colour, labour* and *favour,* but he didn't stop there. Web-

ster devoted his life to capturing all our "American words" on paper for inclusion in his dictionaries. In the preface to his 1806 *Compendious Dictionary of the English Language,* Webster predicted that "In fifty years . . . the American-English will be spoken by more people than all other dialects of the language."

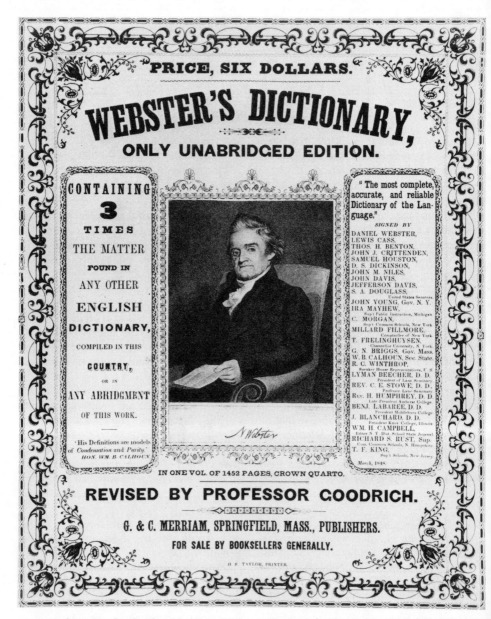

An early poster for the first Merriam-Webster dictionary. (Courtesy: C. and G. Merriam Co.)

ETHNIC CONTRIBUTIONS TO THE AMERICAN LANGUAGE

Every ethnic group that settled in America had at least a few words to contribute to our language. While some contributions have managed to appear on both sides of the Atlantic and are commonly used in English and American conversations, other words are strictly "American" or else they have passed from American usage into English usage as our two cultures merge closer and closer thanks to increasingly rapid avenues of communication.

Over the years Americans have taken *pizza* from the Italians, *cuspidor* from the Portuguese, and *cookies* from the Dutch. Each day our language evolves, adding more and more "foreign" words (such as *sputnik*) and loan-words that have become "American" by omitting the italics and accent marks from print (divorcee and depot came from the French *divorcéê* and *dépôt*). We also continue to garner new contributions from every ethnic group that seeks refuge here.

Some of the major contributions to the American language have come from the Indians and the Spanish, Dutch and German settlers — but almost everyone who settled here had a kind word or two to offer!

Indian Givers

We took everything else from the Indians, and since they were the first to show the colonists what to eat, how to cook it and what to call it, it was logical that we would take their words for the local animals and edible wild plants that abounded in North America.

The Crees gave us *woodchuck*, the Micmac contributed *toboggan* and the Sioux and Ojibwa showed us their *teepees* (tipi) and *totems* — but forget all those old cowboy and Indian movies, because the Indians never gave us warpath, war paint, paleface, medicine man, peace pipe or firewater. Those words were invented by "forked tongue of the white man."

We took over 500 Indian words as our own, but it was the Algonquins of the Eastern woodlands who contributed the most. Their language was the most widespread Indian tongue in America, and over 125 Algonquian words are still in common use today: *moose, skunk, chipmunk, opossum,* *raccoon, caribou, hominy, pecan, persimmon, squash, succotash, pemmican* and *terrapin* are just a few.

INDIAN WORDS WITH A SPANISH TWIST: Some words came directly from the Indians, while others developed a Spanish accent along the way. From the natives south of the border we took *coyote, mesquite* and *avocado* (from *ahuacatl,* meaning "testicle," which describes the appearance of the fruit). They also contributed *chocolate, tomatoes, chicle, chili* and *peyote.*

Other words that crossed the border and became part of the English language include: *corral, ranch, rodeo, lasso, lariat, locoweed, stampede, bronco, adobe, alfalfa* and even "ten-gallon hats." Some authorities believe that the ten-gallon hat, which actually holds about two quarts, got its name from the Spanish *sombrero galon* which means a "hat with braids."

The Spanish gave us *bodega, cabana, fiesta, hacienda, hombre, macho* and *mañana.* We also took *padre, peon, señorita, tequila, bonanza, siesta* and *barbecue.* The word *barbecue* comes from the Spanish *barbacoa,* a term that refers to a method of cooking employed by the Carib Indians of the West Indies. The Caribs used open-pit fires to preserve meat and fish, but as early as 1700 Americans were roasting calves and sides of beef outdoors for on-the-spot consumption. Even the "father of our country" liked barbecues — Washington's diary entry for September 18, 1773, notes: "Went to a Barbicue of my own giving at Accatinck."

Dutch Contributions

Hollanders have contributed some very important words to the American language. Without the Dutch, we wouldn't be able to *smoke, snoop, hoist, spatter, loiter* or *frolic* at will. There wouldn't be any *cider* or *brandy* to drink; and what would American cuisine be without *potatoes, pickles* and *cranberries?*

The Dutch put the *pits* in apricots, the *spooks* in Halloween and *filibusters* in the Senate. They gave us *bedspreads, bedpans, bosses* and *patroons;* garbage *scows, wagons, railroads, yachts* and the *skippers* who sail them. We have the Netherlands to thank for *luck, business, spools, earaches, bottles, bother* and *belong;* as well as "yes, ma'am" and *"good-bye."*

KEMO-WHO?

There is an old joke about Tonto and the Lone Ranger that has the dynamic duo surrounded by hostile, scalp-hungry Native Americans. The Lone Ranger turns to his trusty Indian friend and says, "Tonto, I think we're in trouble," to which Tonto replies, "What you mean 'we,' Kemo sabe?"

For years, American children have accepted the fact that "kemo sabe" meant something like "friend," "faithful white companion" or "trusty scout." But what does *kemo sabe* really mean?

According to research conducted by Dr. Martha Kendall, an anthropologist with a specialty in American Indian languages, *kemo sabe* is about as Indian as "Hi-yo Silver." There isn't one Indian language in which kemo sabe means "faithful friend." So Dr. Kendall began rooting around to see how Francis Striker, the creator of the Lone Ranger, might have derived his famous phrase.

The worst possibility is that *kemo sabe* is a corruption of the Spanish *quien lo sabe* (who knows?) or *el que lo sabe* (he who knows). If *kemo sabe* is Spanish, then it comes to mind that *tonto* is also a Spanish word for "stupid" or "crazy"; according to Dr. Kendall, this creates a curious "relationship between our two heroes; one habitually calls the other 'he who knows' and is addressed as 'stupid' in return. If we accept a Spanish etymology for *kemo sabe,* then the Lone Ranger becomes a racist and Tonto a red-skinned Stepin Fetchit."

Alan Shaterian of Berkeley has theorized that *kemo sabe* might be a corruption of a Yavapai word. If Striker had asked a Yavapai Indian the word for "one who is white" the answer would be *kinmasaba,* or *kinmasabeh,* "one who wears white clothing." It's close to *kemo sabe* and it fits the description of the Lone Ranger's lone costume of white pants and white shirt.

Following Shaterian's "word corruption" logic, Dr. Kendall found a few other Indian words that might have been mispronounced into *kemo sabe:*

kemoo'tisew	Cree for "he is secret, concealed"
qima	Southern Paiute for "stranger"
kema; sabe	Tewa for "friend"; "Apache"

Other Indian words yielded meanings such as "dumpling," "stink beetle" and "red breasted turtle," making it a good bet that Striker simply made up the phrase. After all, he was a writer from Buffalo, New York, not an Indian language scholar, and the farthest west he ever traveled in his pre-Lone Ranger days was to Detroit.

The Dutch are responsible for *towns, bush* (meaning wilderness), *landscape* paintings and *dope.* And, although they gave us *dikes* and made flowering bulbs famous, we actually should thank the Turks for *tulips. Tulip* is the Turkish word for turban and refers to the flower's shape.

French Contributions

The English language began to acquire a decided "French accent" after the Battle of Hastings in 1066, when Norman rule was established throughout England. By the time the Puritans docked the *Mayflower* at Plymouth Rock, thousands of French words had found their way into the English language — but there were still some new contributions to be made in America.

Most of the French words, or French-inspired words that entered the American language came to us courtesy of the Louisiana French and their fur-trapping brethren to the North, in Canada, who frequently crossed the border in search of prey. They gave us *sashay* (from the verb *chasser*, to chase) and *camouflage* (from *camoufler*, to disguise), as well as *prairie*, *levee* and *bayou*, to describe the geography in different parts of the country.

We imported some of their words from the "other side," but we could never quite make up our minds on how it should be done. Hence, we took *negligee* and *resume*, dropping the accents from the end, but when it comes to *canapé*, *attaché*, and *naïveté*, the accents remain.

German Contributions

English is basically a Germanic language, containing thousands of German-origin words. Still, when the "new" immigrants came to America in the late 1800s they managed to add a few more terms to our American vocabulary.

They gave us *wanderlust* and *klutz; hoodlums*, *bummers* (loafers) and *shysters*. They brought us *cookbooks, coathooks, concert masters, yesmen*, and *kindergarten* teachers who played *pinochle*. They gave us a lot of *flak* (which really isn't a word, it's an acronym for *Flieger abwehr kanone* — an antiaircraft gun that fires fast and furiously), and they sometimes played *dumb*, but it was all worth it because they gave us *noodles, pretzels, sauerkraut, hamburgers, frankfurters* and *delicatessens*.

They gave us *seltzer* and *lager* beer to wash down all that food, and they gave us *Octoberfests*, song*fests* and fun*fests* so we would have an excuse to celebrate everything.

There is only one doubtful contribution that the Germans made: they gave us *pumpernickel* bread, which is quite delicious, but the word itself is derived from *pumpen*, "to fart," and *nickel*, "the Devil," indicating that the bread is quite difficult to digest and might give you a devil of a time after you ate it. And who needs trouble like that, *bub?* You'd be better off eating your *liverwurst* on *zwieback*.

Irish Contributions

Yes indeedy, the Irish gave us *boycotts, hooligans, limericks, leprechauns, teetotal-*ers and *lynch* mobs. They even gave us *quiz, bog* and *bard*, and as you'd expect they donted *blarney, whiskey, shillelagh, shamrock* and *colleens* with *brogues* from the other side.

Boycotts were named for Captain Charles Cunningham Boycott, b. 1832, a retired British army officer who became a land agent for an absentee landlord. Boycott was so despised by the tenant farmers who worked on his boss's land that they mounted organized reprisals against him, and boycotted Boycott by refusing to buy any goods from him, or pay him his taxes or rent.

As the English tell it, the *Hooligans* (or Houlihans) were an Irish family living in London, who earned their despicable reputation by beating, robbing and exploiting their fellow man.

Quiz began as a nonsense word invented by a Mr. Daly who managed a Dublin theater. He wrote the four letters Q U I Z all over walls and buildings in 1780, convinced that he could make the public adopt this meaningless string of letters as a new "word."

Lynching took its name from the unfortunate Mayor of Galway, who was forced to "lynch" his own son, a convicted murderer sentenced to die by hanging.

Italian Contributions

Some Italian contributions retained their original form (*pizza, spaghetti, ghetto*), while others were anglicized (*sonnet, gazette, balcony*) when they crossed the ocean.

The Italians gave us musical words (*concert, opera, serenade, sonata, aria, finale*); musical directions (*adagio, allegro, crescendo*); musical performers (*tenor, diva, soprano*); the musical scale (*do, re, mi*) and musical instruments (*piano, piccolo, viola, mandolin*, and *Stradivarius* (1644–1737), the famous *violin* maker).

The Italians gave us architectural and artistic words such as *fresco, profile, impasto, model, studio, torso* and *bust*.

Thanks to the Italian language, we can attend *gala* balls, throw *confetti*, wear *costumes* and dance the *tarantella*. We can attend a *carnival* or *masquerade* at the *marina*, or pay a *compliment* to our *escorts* at the *casino*. We hope that our evening won't be ruined by *vagabonds, charlatans, ruffians,* or *bandits* brandishing *stilettos*.

The Italians contributed *catacombs, limbo, madonnas; monsignors, cardinals* and the *cassocks* they wear to our religious language. And in the military field, they made it possible for *corporals* to fire *cannons, carbines* and *muskets* when attacked by *squadrons, regiments, battalions* or the *cavalry*.

Italy gave us *laundries, cafeterias* and *saloons,* as well as *banks, cashiers, credit* and *debt,* but the best Italian contributions are found on a menu—*zucchini, ravioli, macaroni,* and *vermicelli* (even if it does mean "little worms").

Black Contributions to the American Language

In 1842, Charles Dickens wrote: "All the women who have been bred in slave states speak more or less like Negroes, from having been constantly in their childhood with black nurses."

The true extent of Negro influence on the white Southern dialect is unknown, but some African linguistic patterns still survive to this day in the rural South and inner-city neighborhoods. For years many scholars maintained that Black English was merely ungrammatical, but today it is recognized as a true American dialect—the result of speaking English with an African accent.

Black contributions to the general American language come from several sources—some words were borrowed directly from the African languages spoken by early slaves, others evolved from American Negro dialects, and some were born in the consciousness-raising 1960s.

Americans have Africa to thank for *bananas, goobers, gumbo, okra* and *yams,* as well as *voodoo, hoodoo, zombies, juke-*boxes, *banjos, hepcats* and all that *jazz*.

Banana was a West African word. *Goober* (peanut) comes from the Bantu word *nguba; gumbo* from the Angolan *'ngombo;* and *okra* from its West African namesake *nkruma. Yam* came into popular American usage from *njam,* a Gullah dialect word which was derived from *nyami,* meaning "to eat."

Voodoo, a syncretic religion that combines elements of Christianity and African religious beliefs, comes from Dahomey *vodu* (spirit or demon). (*Hoodoo* is a variation of the word that emerged in American usage in the 1870s.) *Zombie* comes from Kongo, a Bantu language, and combines the words *zumbi* (fetish) and *zambi* (god).

Juke is derived from a Wolof word *dzug* (to misbehave) and was originally used in the Gullah dialect of coastal Carolina Blacks to refer to a house that dealt in liquor and was frequented by loose women. It later came into slang usage for places that featured coin-operated music (*juke joints*) and eventually the music machines themselves came to be known as *jukeboxes*.

Banjo probably comes from *mbanya,* a Kimbundu word meaning "stringed instrument." The word was brought to America by slaves from the West Indies and is derived from *bandore,* an ancient guitar-like instrument brought to Africa by the Portuguese.

The slang terms *cat, hip* and *hepcat* were first used in the entertainment subculture in America, and may very well have come from the Wolof word *hipicat,* meaning "a man who is aware or has his eyes open."

There is considerable controversy over the origin of the word *jazz,* but it is generally credited with Black origins. The *Oxford English Dictionary* notes that jazz is "generally said to be Negro" and *Webster's New International* claims jazz is a Creole word of West African origin, although attempts to trace the etymological roots of *jazz* to Africa have failed.

The Civil Rights movement and emerging Black pride of the 1960s increased the number of Black English words in common American usage. The first *sit-in* was conducted by CORE in Chicago in the 1940s, but it wasn't called that—the term only came into popular use in 1961 when demonstrators in the South sat at "white only" lunch counters and refused to move until they were arrested, so that they could challenge segregation laws in the courts.

"Tell it like it is," a civil rights slogan, was replaced by *"right on"* in the 1960s to indicate audience approval of a speaker's remarks. Black Americans also gave us *"rap"* and *"soul,"* which has been defined as the "uninhibited self-expression that goes into every Negro endeavor." The term

evolved from the 1950s soul music, and has since spawned other terms such as *soul brother, soul sister, soul session,* and *soul food.*

Other phrases attributed to Afro-American slang are: "my man" (1930s); "make the scene" (1950s); and "let it all hang out" (1970s).

"BLACK IS BEAUTIFUL"

" 'Black is beautiful' was a motto of genius which uplifted us far above its first intention. Once Americans had thought about it and perceived its truth, we began to realize that so are brown, white, red and yellow beautiful. When I was young, a Sunday-school teacher told us that the beauty of Joseph's coat was its many colors. I believe Americans are beautiful — individually, in communities, and freely joined together by dedication to the United States of America."*

*Gerald R. Ford, President of the United States, July 5, 1976 (The Washington Post, 7-6:(A)3). In *What They Said in 1976* (Beverly Hills, Calif.: Monitor, 1977).

Word Contributions from Other Lands and Languages

ARABIC — *algebra, alcohol, alchemy, alcove, albatross, arsenal* and *assassin* (the last comes from the Arabic word meaning "hashish addict").

CHINA — *yen, flophouse, tea, typhoon, tong, kumquat, kaolin, kowtow* and the verb *"to shanghai."*

CZECHOSLOVAKIA — *robot* comes from the Czech word meaning "work." The term was first introduced by Czech writer Karel Capek in his 1923 play, R.U.R. (Rossum's Universal Robots), about a factory revolt by robot workers.

HEBREW — *Amen, hallelujah, cherub, sabbath, satan, rabbi, kosher, kibbutz* and *manna* from heaven.

HUNGARY — When Cinderella arrived at the prince's ball in her pumpkin *coach,* it was courtesy of the Hungarians. The word originated from the village of Kocs, where the first horse-drawn vehicles capable of carrying several passengers were designed many centuries ago.

INDIA — *loot, thug, juggernaut, bandana, dungaree, teak* wood, *atoll, copra* meat (from coconuts) and *khaki* (from the Urdu *khak,* meaning dust).

MALAYSIA — *orangutan, sarong, bamboo, rattan, kapok* and to run *amok.*

PERSIA — *pajama, shawl, taffeta, divan, lilac, bazaar,* mint *julep, checkmate* and whirling *dervish.*

POLYNESIA — *Tattoo* is one of the few donations the Polynesians have made to the American language. "Tatau" marks were tribal or professional emblems used as a sign of rank, caste or marital state.

SRI LANKA — The country that used to be called Ceylon gave us *tourmaline* and *beriberi* (a vitamin deficiency disease).

TONGA ISLAND — *taboo.*

TURKEY — *caviar, yogurt, shish kebab, tulip* and *meander* (after the Menderes River, which twists and turns its way through Western Turkey).

YIDDISH — *schmaltz, schlemiel, lox, blintz, matzo, schlep* and *schnook.*

Top Ten Foreign Languages Spoken in America

When the 1970 U.S. Census was taken, more than 160.7 million Americans, or 79.1%, claimed English as their mother tongue. Almost 27 million Americans claimed one of the following ten languages as their mother tongue:

Spanish	7,823,583
German	6,093,054
Italian	4,144,315
French	2,598,408
Polish	2,437,938
Yiddish	1,593,993
Swedish	626,102
Norwegian	612,862
Greek	458,699
Czech	452,812

Mother Tongue of the Population

English	160,717,113	Russian	334,615
American Indian Languages	268,205	Ukrainian	249,351
Norwegian	612,862	Lithuanian	292,820
Swedish	626,102	Finnish	214,168
Danish	194,462	Romanian	56,590
Dutch	350,748	Yiddish	1,593,993
French	2,598,408	Greek	458,699
German	6,093,054	Italian	4,144,315
Polish	2,437,938	Spanish	7,823,583
Czech	452,812	Portuguese	365,300
Slovak	510,366	Japanese	408,504
Hungarian	447,497	Chinese	345,431
Serbo-Croatian	239,455	Arabic	193,520
Slovene	82,321		

HAND JIVE
or
HOW TO BE OFFENSIVE WITHOUT OPENING YOUR MOUTH

Sometimes you don't even have to say a word to offend someone in another country — your hands can say it all. In America, our most insulting gesture is the middle finger of one's hand extended solo, but in other countries the gesture is meaningless. That's because they have other "hand language" that serves the same purpose — so always be careful how you hold your hands in the presence of immigrants or ethnic Americans, because you might be saying something insulting.

♦ In Greece the ultimate in insulting messages is conveyed by placing the thumb between the index finger and the middle finger. This signifies the genitals and is insulting to the Greeks, but in Latin America it is known as the sign of the "fig" and is used to ward off the effects of the evil eye.

♦ What is "okay" in North America, is not always okay in South America, because the "okay" sign — made by joining the thumb and index finger in a circle with the other three fingers extended upright — is "dirty" in Brazil and other South American countries.

♦ Never hitchhike in Sardinia. Not only is the practice equally dangerous in all countries, but it is especially hazardous there because an upturned thumb is considered obscene — and no one likes a rude passenger.

"DIRTY" WORDS AND SLURS

Just like women's hemlines, the styles in dirty words also change with the times. At various points in the 1800s our forebears deemed different words taboo for one reason or another and began changing the names of things so they wouldn't be offensive. They took the *cock* out of *roaches,* made *donkeys* out of *asses,* transformed *stockings* into *hose,* and always *retired* instead of *going to bed.* Well, the times are a-changing again, and so are our taboo words.

In the early 1960s the Rolling Stones had to change the lyrics to one of their songs from "Let's spend the night together" to the nonsensical "Let's spend the tonight 'gether" in order to receive air time in many states; Jack Paar was once chastised for saying "W.C." (British slang for a toilet) on television. Today, few Americans would be shocked by the Stones or Parr, but, unbeknownst to the admen and moviemen of the past who tried so hard to keep the airwaves of America "clean," ethnic Americans all over the nation managed to find some "innocent" words quite offensive. That's the funniest part about taboos in an eclectic society such as ours—they are meaningless to many ethnic segments of the population, while the *innocent* words are shocking:

♦ When Procter and Gamble first marketed *Biz* detergent booster in the early 1960s they had no idea how their ads titillated the Arab-American community. How could they know that "biz" is a common term for a woman's breasts in Arabic. There probably wasn't any market research conducted to cover such a biz-zare turn of events.

♦ When Josh Logan directed his 1960 movie *Fanny,* with Leslie Caron in the leading role, he probably didn't have any Australian friends. While "fanny" is a perfectly decent woman's name in America (or a slang term for a "rear end" at worst), in Australia it is a "dirty" term used to describe a female's sexual apparatus.

♦ While no offense was intended, whoever dreamed up the name Spic and Span for the floor cleaning product? Do you think it's a big seller in Hispanic neighborhoods? It sounds like someone's idea of a bad joke for a new television ethnic sit-com, or an old vaudeville comedy duo.

♦ American women traveling alone in England might be offended if a gentleman offered to "knock you up" on the telephone. Of course, it's merely a slang expression for telephoning a friend over there, but it has different connotations on this side of the Atlantic.

Names We Call One Another, or "Mick" Is Just a Four-Letter Word

Once upon a time, all "four-letter words" were excluded from print. No one ever read "hell" or "damn" in the newspaper, and when characters in a novel got angry they usually said, "f--- you!" In a recent article, Anthony Burgess, author of *A Clockwork Orange,* commented on the changing patterns of acceptability for some four-letter words:

> "In 1960, I published a novel that had the sentence: 'He looked him up and down from his niggerbrown shoes to his spinsterishly tightset lips and then said quietly: "---- off.'" In the new edition of 1975, the shoes and lips are more generally and less offensively characterized and the dirty word is set out in full."

In the 1970s a new group of unprintable "dirty" words emerged as a result of our nation's new aura of self-consciousness. Suddenly it was all right to use four-letter words for bodily functions, but please!—never use "dago," "kike," "coon," "mick," "turk" or even "WASP" to describe a fellow American.

Why do ethnic slurs offend us? "Sticks and stones may break our bones but names will never hurt us." "That which we call a rose by any other name would smell as sweet..." But that's not the point. What offends us is the *intent* behind the word—the communication of the idea that being Irish, Jewish or Puerto Rican is "less than and not equal to" the speaker's own ethnic heritage.

Many second- and third-generation ethnic Americans don't find terms such as "Bohunk" or "Chessie" offensive. The more removed one is from the immigrant experience the less sting these slurs have, and the more easily they are sluffed off as childish retorts. But, although it may be all right for an Italian to jokingly refer to himself as a "wop" or a "dago," it is not usually acceptable for others to use the term unless they are *coumads.*

This listing of ethnic slurs is dedicated to everyone who ever wondered why Puerto Ricans are called *spics,* why Mexicans call Americans *gringos* and how the word *kike* originated.

I'm a Dutchman If I Do!

Centuries before there were "Polish jokes," the English managed to insult the Dutch royally. Warfare between Holland and England in the seventeenth century led to anti-Dutch traditions among the early colonists, who perpetuated an abundance of disparaging remarks and expressions aimed at the Dutch. In fact, the people of the Netherlands have been so maligned by the English language over the past three centuries that officials of Holland were once ordered to drop the word "Dutch" and substitute "Netherlands" whenever possible.

Pejoratives such as "Dutch treat" (no treat at all, since each person pays his own way); "Dutch feast" (a party where the host gets drunk first); "Dutch defense" (a surrender); "Dutch courage" (courage gleaned from alcoholic beverages); and phrases such as "I'm a Dutchman (liar) if I do" all hint that the Dutch are cheap, cowardly and of low moral character.

Even the word "Yankee" was originally intended as a slur against the Dutch. "Yankee" was derived from "Jan Kees" (John Cheese), a disparaging name the British gave to the cheese-loving Hollanders of New Amsterdam. However, the Dutch in New York managed to turn the British insult around and used the term "Yankee" to refer to their English neighbors in New England. Soon the British were using "Yankee" to refer to all English settlers in America, and today the term is used as a nickname for all New Englanders, with or without British ancestors.

MORE DUTCH PEJORATIVES

Dutchman's Drink	the last one in a bottle
Dutchman's Headache	one caused by a hangover
Dutch Medley	when everyone plays a different tune
Dutch Nightingale	a frog
Dutch Praise	condemnation
Dutch Reckoning	pure guesswork, no skill involved
Dutch Widow	a prostitute
Dutch Route	suicide
Dutch Lap	an economical method of shingling
Dutch Gold	an alloy of copper and zinc used for imitation gold leaf
Dutch Uncle	a critical person who administers stern lectures

Confusion between Dutch and *Deutsch* (German) gave rise to additional Dutch insults intended for the Germans: "To get into Dutch," meaning to get into *trouble;* and "to get one's Dutch up," meaning to be *angry.*

The Dutch also gave their name to plants, a disease, a game and household items.

Dutch door	a two-sectioned door that opens at the top and bottom
Dutch oven	a heavy covered kettle for pot roast and stew
Double Dutch	a children's game that uses two jump ropes simultaneously, moving in opposite directions
Dutchman's breeches	*Dicentra cucullaria;* the flowers of the plant resemble baggy britches hanging upside down
Dutch elm disease	fungus disease transmitted by bark beetles (first observed in Holland in 1919, it spread to America in 1930 and devastated the tree-lined streets of New York)
Dutch two hundred	a bowling score of 200 points obtained by alternate strikes and spares

The Luck of the Irish

In America, the Irish even insult one another — the "lace-curtain" Irish (poor immigrants who worked their way up the ladder of success) look down on the lower-middle-class or "shanty" Irish. The term "shanty" comes from the Gaelic words *sean tig* ("old house") and refers to the tumbledown shacks where the poor lived.

America contributed "mick," "paddy wagon" and "Irish banquet" to the Irish lexicon. Mick is used disparagingly for Irish Americans, and was derived from a common name for many of Erin's sons — Michael. The paddy wagon, a police van used to transport criminals, takes its nickname from another favorite Irish given name — Patrick — and makes reference to the fact that the Irish dominated the police forces of many major cities, such as Boston and New York, during the early 1920s.

What does one serve at an Irish banquet? Corned beef and cabbage? Mutton stew? Irish soda bread? No need to get that fancy: an Irish banquet is merely a potato and a six-pack — another jibe at the Irishman's stereotyped love of a good brew.

The British began the assault on the Irish by christening cobwebs "Irish draperies" and calling a sack of potatoes "Irish mail," but try as they might, none of the insults they invented could ever compare to the colorful ones Americans devised:

Irish beauty	a colleen with two black eyes
Irish clubhouse	a police station
Irish apple or apricot	potato
Irishman's dinner	a fast
Irish buggy	a wheelbarrow
Irish promotion	a demotion
Irish pennant	a loose thread on one's clothing
Irish diamond	a rock

On the positive side there is Irish moss, the seaweed from which carrageenin is extracted; Irish stew, properly made with mutton; Irish whiskey, Irish coffee and beautiful Irish linen.

Black, Beautiful and Slurred

"Nigger" is probably the most bitterly resented epithet aimed against Blacks. Derived from the dialectal pronunciation of Negro in Northern England and Ireland, the term was used quite commonly until 1825, when Blacks and Abolitionist leaders lobbied against the word on the grounds that it was demeaning.

In his 1964 autobiography, *Nigger*, political activist Dick Gregory dedicated his book with these words:

> "Dear Momma, Where ever you are, if ever you hear the word 'nigger' again, remember they are advertising my book."

Offshoots of "nigger" include: "nigger-toes" (Brazil nuts); "nigger heaven" (the top row of a theater balcony); and "nigger driving" (forced hard labor).

"Coon" entered popular American usage about 1862. A Black songwriter, Ernest Hogan, further popularized the term in his 1896 song, "All coons look alike to me."

The terms Black, Mulatto, Quadroon, Octoroon, and Griffe comprise a complex nomenclature system that was actually employed by the U.S. Census Bureau until 1891 to denote the percentage of Negro ancestry a citizen had. Blacks were 100% Negro; mulatto was reserved for persons of half Negro and half Caucasian ancestry; quadroons were persons of one-quarter Negro ancestry; octoroons were only one-eighth Negro; and griffe was a reserved for anyone "lighter" than an octoroon.

Commenting on the absurdity of assigning special categories to people on the basis of their racial ancestry, Wallace L. Ford II, President of the Harlem Lawyers Association, had this to say in a letter to the editor of *New York* magazine in 1978, after an article on "Mulatto Pride" appeared in that weekly publication:

"I would like to take the opportunity of this letter to praise Orde Coombs and *New York* magazine for the recent article on mulattoes ('Mulatto Pride,' June 26). I am heartened to see that an item of such monumental and crucial importance to the black community was included in the magazine rather than an article dealing with such insignificant issues as directionless black youth, unemployment, black-infant mortality, *Bakke,* racism in New York, etc.

"Unfortunately, there is one small note of criticism that I must add. Since Mr. Coombs and *New York* magazine saw fit to write and publish an article dealing with an important and outspoken minority within the black community, it is only fitting that other minorities within our community also be given similar recognition, including quadroons, octoroons, macaroons (the descendants of black-Irish unions) and kangaroons (the descendants of black-Australian unions)."

WALLACE L. FORD II
President
The Harlem Lawyers Association,
   Manhattan
New York. July 24, 1978

Other epithets for Black Americans include: jigaboo, jig, shine, spade, pickaninny and jungle bunny. In fact, at various times Black, colored, Negro and Afro-American have been regarded by succeeding generations as inappropriate descriptions for Americans of African ancestry. In the 1960s a bitter national controversy emerged in the press concerning the proper designation for identifiable Americans with African roots. (Some scholars claim that in addition to the 20 million *identifiable* Black Americans in the United States, some 15 million "White" Americans have African ancestors.)

When the debate had ended, Black emerged victorious, took on a new aura of pride and began to replace Negro as the preferred term of identity for many young Americans.

Actually, the controversy over the proper designation for Americans of African descent is not a new subject, and it has flared up several times in the United States since the beginning of slavery.

The English word *Negro* is derived from the Spanish and Portuguese *negro,* meaning black, and although the reaction of the first African-Americans to the word "negro" has never been studied, it would appear that they preferred the word "African" and named their organizations accordingly: African Free School (1787), First African Baptist Church (1788), African Methodist Episcopal Church (1794), African Episcopal Zion Church (1821).

In the nineteenth century, when the American Colonization Society organized a movement to send free Negroes back to

---

WHAT'S IN A NAME? —
BLACK vs. NEGRO vs. COLORED vs. AFRO-AMERICAN

"Names are the essence of the game of power and control, and . . . a change in name will shortcircuit the stereotyped thinking patterns that undergrid the system of racism in America." That was the view put forth by Lerone Bennett, Jr., in a 1967 article that appeared in *Ebony* magazine. Critics who opposed changing the form of identification for Americans of African descent from "Negro" to "Black" or "Afro-American" argued that "A Negro by any other name . . . would be as black and as beautiful . . . and as segregated."

Both sides agreed that the times were too crucial to waste valuable energy arguing over nomenclature, but many people believed the word "Negro" was not culturally specific and only served to perpetuate the "slave-master mentality" in the minds of both Blacks and Whites. In response to this controversy, the editors of America's leading Black publication, *Ebony,* decided to poll their readers and ask them to select the term of ethnic identification they preferred. When all the ballots were counted, the vote was tied between Afro-American and Black, and the editors opted in favor of Black as the magazine's choice for future use.

Africa, the Black community responded by abandoning the word "African" in favor of "Colored" and "free person of color." In 1835 the Fifth National *Negro* Convention recommended that Blacks remove the words "colored" and "African" from their organization mastheads, but despite the convention's recommendations, the rest of the nineteenth century was dominated by "colored."

Colored vs. Negro

Blanche Kelso Bruce (1841–1897), the first Black man to serve a full term in the United States Senate, refused to use the word *colored*. He said, "I am a Negro and proud of my race." James Walker Hood, a Black delegate to the North Carolina constitutional convention of 1868, countered by saying, "The word Negro has no significance as to color, but can only be used in a reproachful or degrading sense." Hood further stated that no one knew where the term originated, "since it was not found in ancient history, inspired or profane." Clearly, the controversy was only beginning.

Up until the late 1880s Black was considered a slave term and colored was preferred, but as the nineteenth century drew to a close, Negro began supplanting "Colored" and "Afro-American" as witnessed by the founding of the American Negro Academy (1897) and the National Negro Business League (1900). The founding of the NAACP (National Association for the Advancement of Colored People) in 1909 marked the last major usage of the word "colored," and by 1919 *The Negro Year Book* reported, "the word Negro is more and more acquiring a dignity that it did not have in the past."

With a Capital "N"

The NAACP launched an aggressive campaign to have the word Negro capitalized, and on June 7, 1930, the New York *Times* announced that the "n" in "Negro" would in future be capitalized "in recognition of racial self-respect for those who have been for generations 'in the lower case.' " The U.S. Government Printing Office followed the example set by the *Times* and began to capitalize Negro in 1933.

In the 1930s, Negro had become the generally accepted designation for Americans of African descent, but there were still those who disagreed: Adam Clayton Powell continued to use the word Black, and although W. E. B. DuBois founded the American Negro Academy, he wrote *The Souls of Black Folk; The Gifts of Black Folk;* and *Black Folk Then and Now.*

The controversy reemerged in the 1960s, and many organizations began changing their names in response to appeals from their constituency. The Negro Teachers Association of New York City became the African American Teachers Association, and in 1967 the New York *Amsterdam News,* the nation's most influential Black newspaper, announced that the word "Negro" would no longer be used by their writers.

Today, Black seems to be firmly established in the publishing world, and most book indexes will refer a reader to headings under "Black" instead of "Negro" or "Afro-American."

Despite the gains made by proponents of "Black," the 1979–1980 Manhattan Telephone Directory listed the Negro Action Group, Negro Actors Guild of America, Negro Digest, Negro Ensemble Company, Negro Labor Committee, Negro Radio Stories, Afro Arts Cultural Center, Afro-American Total Theater Arts Foundation, and the National Association for the Advancement of Colored People, indicating that the matter may merely have been laid to rest for a while.

Other European Epithets

Germans are slurred as "Sauerkrauts" — or "Krauts" for short — in reference to their love of fermented cabbage. Kraut became a common term in the United States in 1869 when Joseph Heister, a candidate for the office of Governor of Pennsylvania, was nicknamed "Old Sauerkraut" by friends and foes alike.

Another derogatory name for Germans is "Heinie," which is derived from the common given name Heinrich. We call rubella "German" measles — blaming the German immigrants for bringing the disease with them to the new world at a time when epidemics raged throughout Europe during the mid-nineteenth century.

Scandinavians are Herring Chokers; natives of Poland are Poles or Polaks; Hungarians are Hunks, and Bohemians are Bohunks or Bohos. A Litvak is a Lithuanian; a Rusky is a Russian; and a Chesky is a Czechoslovakian. All Gypsies have been slurred by the term "to gyp," which condemns them all as a race of cheats, pickpockets and con men. Frenchmen are Frogs, not only because they enjoy the hind legs of those green amphibious creatures, but also because the coat of arms of the city of Paris is embellished with the likeness of toads.

The English are known as "Limeys" due to their astute observation that eating limes (a good source of vitamin C) would prevent scurvy during long ocean voyages. The English slur the French by calling syphilis "the French disease," while the French blame the Italians and call it "the Italian malady."

Italians are slurred as Wops or Dagos. Wop is derived from the Italian word *guappo*, meaning a "dandy," and it was the Italians themselves who were the first to use the term. Immigrants used to mock their pretentious friends by calling them "guappo," which other Americans shortened to "wop."

The slur Dago was originally applied to Portuguese and Spanish immigrants to America, and is derived from the Spanish given name *Diego* (James). When the first wave of Italian immigrants came to America, many Americans believed them to be natives of the Iberian peninsula because of their swarthy skin. Presumed to be Portuguese, the Italians were slurred as "Dagos" and in time, since there were more Italian immigrants than Portuguese, Dago became the exclusive property of the Italian-Americans.

While the Portuguese may have lost "Dago" to the Italians, they do have a namesake of their very own—the Portuguese man of war. A familiar sight in warm ocean waters, *Physalia pelagica* is a floating, colonial organism that was derisively named "Portuguese man of war" when that nation had begun to decline as a world sea power. Despite its pleasant blue-tinged appearance, this wedge-shaped, translucent creature is quite deadly. The gas-filled "float" is harmless, but there are scores of toxin-laden tentacles dangling between the waves that can ensnare unsuspecting fish,

paralyze them with poison and slowly digest them for dinner.

The Arabs and the Jews

Kike was originally a disparaging term used by German-American Jews for the new arrivals from Eastern Europe—the Polish and Russian Jews. Illiterate Jews entering the country refused to sign an X on immigration forms, on the grounds that it resembled a Christian cross. Instead, they signed their legal documents with a circle (*kikel,* in Yiddish), which was soon shortened to kike and applied to anyone who made the sign of the circle.

Sheeny may have originated with the German word for pretty, *schön,* which was commonly used by Jewish peddlers to describe their wares during the early 1820s.

At one time people used to "Jew down" merchants on the price of an item, but a vigorous campaign by American Jews has virtually eliminated the term from print.

Lately even the term Arab has come to be despised by some Americans of Syrian and Lebanese extraction, who complain of cultural stereotyping and evocation of negative images. Hisham Sharabi, president of the National Association of Arab Americans complained, "[We are] one of the few groups still singled out for ethnic and cultural stereotyping, with particular emphasis on a leering figure in desert robes, either squandering money or holding the West hostage over oil, or both. How would Jewish-Americans react to a headline saying 'Jews Buy Bank in California'?"

At one time all Arab-speaking people were lumped together as Turks whether they came from Syria, Lebanon or Iran—since many carried Turkish passports. They are also called Camel Jockeys and Greaseballs; the latter term is applied to almost any dark-skinned foreigner, be he Italian, Greek, Syrian or Palestinian.

Asia and the Orient

Americans called the Koreans Gooks, and not being creative enough to invent another slur for the Vietnamese we called them Gooks, too. The Japanese are called Skibby on the West Coast, a slur derived from the Japanese word Sukebei, meaning lewd.

Filipinos are Gu-gus, and the Chinese are called Chinks. The expression "not a Chinaman's chance" refers to the early days of the California gold rush, when the Chinese in the mining camps had no rights whatsoever and human life was held to be cheap. Even self-defense against a crime was not permitted, and if a case went to court the luckless men from Canton didn't have a "Chinaman's chance" of being acquitted.

Spanish-Speaking Slurs

Latin Americans, Panamanians and Puerto Ricans are called Spics, which comes from the phrase "no speek English." Mexicans are called Wetbacks, in reference to the illegal aliens who enter the southwestern states by crossing the Rio Grande River, which is rather easy to do since it forms two-thirds of the boundary between Mexico and the United States.

Bracero (from *brazo*, arm) is an agricultural worker permitted to enter the United States under contract with the Mexican government. However, the laws permitting seasonal labor expired at the end of 1964, and braceros have to become Wetbacks or *Mojados* ("wet ones") if they want to work seasonally.

The Mexicans in turn have derogatory names for Mexican-Americans, the most prevalent of which is *Pocho. Cholo* is another derogatory term for a Mexican immigrant, but its use is mainly limited to California. *Chicano* (slang for a clumsy person) was once a term applied to lower-class Mexicans by the upper classes of Mexico, but the word has taken on a new aura of self-respect and is used by many young Mexican-Americans, proud of their heritage and not aspiring to be Anglos.

White Slurs

In the same way many people try to lump all Blacks, Indians and Orientals together as a group, Whites have been lumped together and labeled with epithets of their own, without regard to creed or national origin.

The most common derogatory term used by Blacks is Whitey, a creation of the early 1960s. Honkey has been around since the early 1950s, and there are several stories behind the origin of this pejorative term, all of which or none of which may be true. One story claims that Honkey originated in Detroit when White men came calling for their Black girl friends. Instead of getting out of their cars to call for them, they would simply honk the horn of their automobiles. Another story claims Honky refers to the nasal tone evident in so many WASP voices. A third explanation says that Honky originated in the meat-packing houses of Chicago. When Black workers heard white ethnics calling their friends Bohunks or Hunkies (slur terms for Bohemians and Hungarians) the Blacks adopted the term, possibly reasoning that all Whites look the same.

The slang term Ofay may have originated as pig-Latin for "foe" in the mid-1920s. Another source credits French-speaking Blacks with christening Whites as "au lait" (meaning "with milk"), which came to be pronounced ofay.

The acronym WASP stands for White Anglo-Saxon Protestant. Although a WASP is any person of English ancestry, the term is sometimes used in a disparaging way by ethnic Americans to denote Americans of nonspecific ethnic origin.

Mexicans refer to their "north of the border" neighbors as Gringos. According to one source, Gringo originated during the 1846 invasion of Mexico by Zachary Taylor and his troops. As the merry men meandered through Mexico, they sang a jolly tune: "Green grow the rushes, oh. The happiest hours that ere I spent, were spent among the lasses-oh." The Mexicans picked up the first two words of the song, and nicknamed the soldiers Gringos.

SLURRING OURSELVES

When a Black American thinks that his brother is kowtowing to Whites, he disparages him as an "Uncle Tom," or an "Oreo"

— black on the outside and white inside. In a similar vein, American Indians call one another "Uncle Tomahawk," or "Apple"— red on the outside and white on the inside. The Mexicans, too, have a version of "Uncle Tom," known as a "Tio Taco."

ETHNIC ORIGINS OF SOME EXPLETIVES, EXPRESSIONS AND EPITHETS

"boondocks" (Philippines)
The expression "way out in the boondocks" comes from the Philippine word "bundok," meaning mountain. The expression was first used by U.S. troops who were stationed at outposts in remote mountainous regions during the Spanish-American War, in 1898.

"Bring home the bacon" (Black American)
This phrase was popularized by the mother of Jack Johnson, the great Black American boxer. When she was interviewed after Johnson defeated Jim Jeffries for the heavyweight championship title in 1910, Mrs. Johnson said: "He said he'd 'bring home the bacon,' and the honey boy has gone and done it."

"by golly" (Black)
The expletive "by golly" was a popular oath used by Negro slaves prior to the Civil War.

"Dixieland" (French)
"Dixieland" is derived from the French word "dix" (ten). Prior to the Civil War, the Citizen's Bank in Louisiana commonly issued bilingual currency. Printed in both English and French, these ten-dollar bills caused New Orleans, and eventually all of the South, to be nicknamed the "Land of Dix-ie."

"Dunce" (Scottish)
"Dunce," meaning a stupid person, comes to us courtesy of John Duns Scotus (1265?–1308), a Scottish philosopher. It started out as a contemptuous reference to the men who adhered to Duns Scotus' beliefs, who were called "Duns men" and, eventually, dunces.

"the 400" (Scotch-French-American)
"The 400" were considered to be the elite of New York society. The phrase was first coined in 1892 by Ward McAllister, an American lawyer of Scottish and French ancestry, who once commented that New York's social circuit consisted of only 400 people. When asked, "Why only 400?" he replied, "Because Mrs. Astor's ballroom holds only that number . . ."— implying that those not invited to party with the Astors were simply not part of "the scene."

"gesundheit" (German)
The German expression, gesundheit, means "to your health" and is commonly uttered whenever someone sneezes. The expression first gained national exposure via Walt Disney's 1940 animated film, Pinocchio, and soon Americans of all ethnic backgrounds began using the word.

"good-bye" (English)
"Goodbye" is a contraction of the phrase "God be with ye," and it was originally spelled "Godbwye" when the Pilgrims first set foot on American soil.

"gumption" (Scottish)
This word was once a Scottish slang expression for hard cider— the kind of juice that had enough alcohol to give any man courage to stand up to his enemies and foes.

"honcho" (Japanese)
The chief "honcho" is someone important. The word comes from the Japanese han (squad) and cho (leader).

"hunky dory" (Dutch)
When everything is "hunky dory" life just couldn't be better.

"I need that like I need a hole in the head"; "I should live so long" (Jewish)
Both catchphrases are of Jewish origin, commonly employed in jokes by stereotypic "Jewish mothers" who use them when they kvetch (complain).

"Manifest destiny" (Irish-American)
The embodiment of the American concept of territorial expansion, "manifest destiny" was first coined in 1845 by John L. O'Sullivan, a second-generation Irish-American who edited the Democratic Review from 1836 to 1845. Manifest destiny was the belief that the territorial expansion of the U.S. was inevitable because of its

economic and political superiority. It was believed that the United States would one day rule all of North America.

"the melting pot" (Jewish)

Israel Zangwill (1864–1926), a Jewish playwright from England, is generally credited with inventing the term "melting pot" to describe the ethnic mix of the United States. Actually, De Witt Clinton was one of the first to claim, in 1814, that immigrants were being "melted down" in America, but Zangwill popularized the term in his 1908 play of the same name.

"mind your p's and q's" (English)

For years, countless thousands of American children have been listening to teachers and parents tell them to mind their p's and q's. Although they had no idea what their elders were talking about, somehow the message always managed to come across that the children were bordering on trouble.

One theory behind this phrase has to do with "ye old ale shoppes," where generous English proprietors frequently extended credit to their best customers. A scorecard was used to mark down what a customer drank, either a pint or a quart of ale, and the innkeeper frequently abbreviated the amount with a "p" or a "q." The customers, anxious that their bills be correct at the end of the month, frequently reminded the bartender to "mind his p's and q's" so he would be exact when tabulating their tabs.

"muckraker" (Canadian-American)

The term "muckraker" is usually associated with Joseph Lincoln Steffens (1866–1936), the Canadian-born reporter who exposed business/political corruption in his books, notably *The Shame of the Cities* (1904) and in magazine articles such as "Philadelphia: Corrupt and Contented." Actually, President Theodore Roosevelt deserves credit for coining the term in 1906, when he suggested that "men with the muckrake are often indispensable to the well-being of society, if they know when to stop raking the muck."

"mugwump" (American Indian)

The term *mugwump* dates to 1884. Used to deride voters who did not support the party candidate, the term actually comes from an Algonquian word that means "great man."

"mush!" (French)

When the French-Canadians yelled, "Mush, you huskies!" to their faithful sled dogs, it was short for "mushons," meaning "let's go." "Mushons" came from the verb form *marchons,* meaning "let us walk."

"nix" (German)

An emphatic "no," from the German word *nicht* of the same meaning.

"O.K." (American Indian)

Andrew Jackson was called the "father of the O.K." by those who sought to discredit him as an illiterate during the 1838 campaign for the Presidency. Supposedly, Jackson derived the term from the Choctaw word "okeh," which was used to emphasize the validity of a statement or, in a wishful way, in the hope that what one said would come true.

"poppy cock" (Dutch)

"Poppy cock," meaning "nonsense," comes from the Dutch word *pappekak,* meaning soft dung.

"Proud as Punch" (Italian)

When someone is pleased with himself, we say he is as "proud as Punch." The expression comes from the "Punch and Judy" puppet shows, which originated in Naples about 1600.

One of the title characters in this puppet soap-opera was Punch (Pulcinello in Italian), a vainglorious male, who became as pleased and as proud as could be whenever he was victorious over his shrewish wife, Judy.

"put up your dukes" (English)

This call to arms, or rather fists, was inspired by the Duke of Wellington, the military commander who defeated Napoleon at Waterloo and also enjoyed quite a reputation as a ladies' man. Besides being known as a great soldier and a great lover, he was also noted for his enormous nose—a schnozzola which rivaled even the great Durante's. His nasal appendage was so famous that "duke" became a nickname for a nose, and fists became known as "dukebusters," later shortened to "dukes."

"sell down the river" (Black American)

Whenever you take advantage of an unsuspecting friend, you "sell him down the river." The phrase was first used in the 1830s and refers to a punishment that was a constant threat to slaves on the Upper Mississippi River. If they misbehaved, they were in danger of being sold to sugar-plantation owners down the river, where the conditions were supposedly even worse for slaves.

(You can also "send someone up the river," but that phrase originated in New York and refers to Sing-Sing prison, which was supposed to be the pits for prisoners.)

"Sir, I have not yet begun to fight" (Scottish)

These famous words were uttered by John Paul Jones, a Scottish immigrant and founder of our American navy. When a British sea captain demanded that Jones surrender his sinking ship it looked like curtains for the American boys, but somehow Jones came back with the line, "Sir, I have not yet begun to fight," and made it come true. He managed to win that battle at sea and chalked up a victory for the Revolutionary forces in 1779.

"slim chance" (German)

When the prospects are bad for getting a raise, a new job, or a date for the dance on Saturday night, one is said to have a "slim chance" for success. "Slim" is derived from the German word *schlimm,* meaning "bad."

"so long" (German)

The English say "good-bye," but the Germans gave us "so long," from their salutation *so lange.*

"to talk a blue streak" (German)

Whenever someone talks, and talks, and talks, he is said to "talk a blue streak." This comes from the German expression "das Blaue vom Himmel schwatzen"—meaning "to chatter the blue from the skies."

ETHNIC AMERICANS WHO BECAME WORDS

BLACK MARIA   Legend has it that this nickname for a police van was taken from an early nineteenth-century Black American woman, Maria Lee, the proprietress of a waterfront boardinghouse in Boston.

A tough woman who served the American cause in 1798 by running guns and cannons to protect merchant ships at sea, Maria was no cream-puff of a lady—she was as strong as they come, and easily capable of putting sailors in their place with a threat to use her awesome strength on them.

According to the story, she once helped a policeman who was under attack by a thug and, from then on, whenever there was trouble on the waterfront the police would jokingly say, "Send for the Black Maria" whenever they needed assistance. Later, when horse-drawn wagons were introduced to carry suspects to jail, the black-painted wagons were nicknamed in her honor.

BOWIE KNIFE   The man who gave his name to the knife died by the sword at the Alamo. He was Jim Bowie (1799–1836), a Scottish-American hero of the Texas Revolution, and although he was lauded as a "fighter, a fearless and mighty adventuring man," he didn't invent the knife that bears his name—he merely popularized the foot-long hunting blade that was either invented by James Black or designed by Bowie's brother, Rezin, about 1825.

COLT 45   The man who perfected the first handgun with a revolving barrel was Samuel Colt (1814–1862), American born, of Scottish ancestry on both sides. Colt adopted Eli Whitney's mass production ideas and began manufacturing his six-shooters at the Patent Arms Manufacturing Company in Paterson, New Jersey, in 1833.

He kept on improving his revolvers until they could be fired rapidly and carried conveniently, but that wasn't his only contribution to the citizens of America. Besides making bloodshed in the Old West quicker and more efficient, he also was one of the first to experiment with electrical detonators for underwater mines, in 1842.

GERONIMO!   His real name was Goyathlay, or "one who yawns," but the Mexicans called him Geronimo, which is Spanish for Jerome. Born about 1829 in the mountains of what was to become Arizona, Geronimo was a medicine man, prophet and chief of the Bedonkoke tribal group of Apaches. When his people were placed on a reservation in 1876, he began a ten-year hit-and-run war with the white settlers, and his fierce reputation as a warrior led to his immortalization as an Apache battle cry. Today, Americans of all ethnic backgrounds use his name before "charging" into one endeavor or another, and his name is frequently yelled, in motion pictures at least, by people parachuting out of airplanes.

JIM CROW The name "Jim Crow" became synonymous with "Negro" in many parts of the country due to the efforts of song-and-dance man Thomas Dartmouth Rice (1808–1860). Rice, known as the "Father of American minstrelsy" was an Irish-American who toured England and the United States in black-face makeup, singing and dancing "Negro" songs. He patterned his act after a black stablehand named Jim Crow, and popularized a song named in his honor. The song, "Jim Crow," which became a hit in America and the British Isles, contained many different stanzas, all followed by the same chorus:

"First on de heel tap, den on de toe,
Ebery time I wheel about I jump Jim Crow,
Wheel about and turn about and do jis so,
And ebery time I wheel about I jump Jim
Crow."

The name eventually was applied to a set of Southern discriminatory laws in effect until 1956 when Congress banned "Jim Crow" railroad cars from interstate traffic.

MACADAM The technique for paving roads and driveways with small stones, bound together with tar, was invented by an ingenious Scottish immigrant—John L. MacAdam (1756–1836), who settled in New York about 1776.

MASON-DIXON LINE Once considered the boundary between the "slave" states and the "free" states, the line that separates Pennsylvania and Maryland was named for Charles Mason and Jeremiah Dixon, two English-Americans who surveyed the land between 1763 and 1767.

PONZI SCHEMES This type of "racket" has made people of all ethnic backgrounds rich in America, but it was invented by and named after an Italian immigrant, Charles A. Ponzi (1882–1949).

Ponzi defrauded hundreds of American investors in the 1920s with his promise of a 50% return on investment after only 90 days. The catch, however, is the fact that there wasn't any product or service to be sold to produce income for investors—all revenues came from new participants. The Ponzi scheme is somewhat similar to the "pyramid" racket that made Glenn Turner of "Dare to Be Great" fame so rich and so prosecuted in the early 1970s.

Ponzi came here from Parma, Italy, at the age of 17 with only "$2.50 in cash and a million dollars in hopes." When he was arrested in 1925, he had boosted his fortune to more than $15 million. He served nine years in prison, and was deported on October 7, 1934, for inventing the ultimate scam.

THE REAL McCOY When people ask for the "real McCoy" they want to be sure they're getting the item they bargained for, and not a cheap substitute. The man who gave his name to that phrase was Elijah McCoy (1844–1929), a Black American inventor born to fugitive slave parents in Ontario, Canada. McCoy held more than 50 patents on lubricating systems, but his first famous invention was for a self-lubricating device which continuously fed oil into heavy industrial machinery. Prior to McCoy's invention, machines had to be shut down every so often to lubricate the moving parts; this prevented them from grinding against one another and wearing out. Whenever a businessman bought a new piece of equipment he wanted to be sure it was the "real McCoy" so he could save himself a great deal of time, money and energy in manufacturing.

RUBE GOLDBERG Whenever someone builds a crazy contraption, it is called a "Rube Goldberg" in honor of the cartoonist, Reuben Lucius Goldberg (1883–1970), a Jewish-American who delighted in drawing "action-reaction" inventions.

In a typical "Rube Goldberg" there are always three or four indirect actions that take place before the intended result occurs.

Besides giving us his own name, Rube also introduced the word "baloney" to the English language, and was immortalized by the Reuben Award, presented annually by the National Cartoonists Society, 9 Ebony Court, New York, New York, to the outstanding cartoonist for the year. (He won it in 1968!)

SEQUOIA These large redwood trees are named after a Cherokee Indian, Sequoya (1760–1842), who attained history book status by inventing an alphabet so his people could learn to read, write and record their history.

The American Indians did not have any written languages, and pronunciation is such an important part of the spoken word that it took Sequoya more than twelve years of steady labor before he was able to systematize the Cherokee language into 85 sounds and symbols.

His work took even longer than it might have, because fellow tribesmen scorned his efforts and began to fear that his work was involved with witchcraft. In a vain attempt to stop his endeavor, they burned his cabin and all his records to the ground, but Sequoya recomposed his work and persevered until the job was done in 1821. The Cherokees were the first Indians to publish a newspaper (the *Cherokee Phoenix,* 1828) and print a hymn book, thanks to the efforts of Sequoya.

SIAMESE TWINS   The originals, the one and only Chang and Eng (1811–1874) were actually misnamed. Since they were of three-quarters Chinese and only one-quarter Siamese ancestry, their name should have been recorded in history accordingly. But everyone makes mistakes, and the term "Siamese twins" has been coined to describe the condition that results from an incomplete division of an ova that should have produced identical twins.

Chang and Eng were joined at the waist and shared some common liver tissue and

Chang and Eng were the original Siamese twins. (Courtesy: New York Historical Society)

hepatic functions, which made separating them an impossible task in the nineteenth century. But their affliction didn't stop them from living a "normal" life. After touring the United States for ten years as a carnival attraction, they became United States citizens and settled down to life on a North Carolina farm, where they proceeded to marry sisters and father 19 children between them.

Not much is known about their thoughts, but in later years Chang became quite fond of drinking and the two argued frequently. (You can't blame Eng for being upset—after all, Chang was destroying his liver, too!) Chang was the first to die, and before a separation operation could be attempted, Eng, too, passed away.

TAMMANY   HALL   The   powerful Democratic political machine took its name from a Delaware Indian chief who lived in Bucks County, Pennsylvania, and signed a peace treaty with William Penn in 1694. Chief Tamanend, once honored with a festival every May 1, has been credited with such glorious traits of virtue, character and ability that there was once a movement to have him canonized as the "Patron Saint of America."

The Tammany Society of New York was founded in 1789 as an outgrowth of Sons of Liberty, but it is best remembered for its most scandalous member—Boss Tweed.

THOMPSON   SUBMACHINE   GUN In 1919, John Taliaferro Thompson (1860–1940), an English-American, and his son Marcellus invented the "Tommy gun." Their weapon was lightweight, semi-automatic and capable of delivering individual machine-gun fire from the shoulder. It was also simply constructed and remarkably free from mechanical malfunctions. The Tommy gun earned the father-and-son team a British prize of 3,000 pounds sterling in 1928.

UNCLE TOM   Although "Uncle Tom" is used by Blacks as a derogatory term for members of their race who act in a subservient or humiliating fashion, the real-life "Uncle Tom," the inspiration for Harriet Beecher Stowe's 1852 novel, *Uncle Tom's Cabin,* bears little resemblance to the fictional character of the same name.

The real "Uncle Tom" was Josiah Henson (1789–?), a slave who escaped with his family via the Underground Railroad and

Advertisement for Uncle Tom's Cabin.
(Courtesy: New York Public Library)

started a sawmill in Canada. Henson not only attained economic success, he used part of the profits to open a manual training school; helped 118 other slaves escape to freedom; and even traveled to England, where he met the Archbishop of Canterbury while trying to raise funds for his school.

WRONG-WAY CORRIGAN Douglas Gorce Corrigan earned his name in 1938 when he took off for California from Floyd Bennett airfield in New York and landed in Ireland the next day.

"They thought I did it deliberately . . ." said the Irish-American pilot, and it *was* rather suspicious, since he had previously been denied a permit to fly across the Atlantic, so the federal aviation authorities suspended his license for five days. Other than losing his license temporarily, Corrigan was featured in a movie, *The Flying Irishman,* from which he earned about $75,000 — enough money to buy an orange grove in Santa Ana, California, where he and his three unmarried sons were still living in 1969.

ETHNIC ORIGINS OF AMERICAN PLACE NAMES

In addition to places named after foreign capitals (Rome, New York) and those christened with descriptive titles (Red Bank, New Jersey) there are millions of names of streets, towns, counties and municipalities in America that have been translated from foreign languages or named after an immigrant. Some of the names are famous, others obscure, but they all represent a little bit of immortality for some ethnic American who passed this way!

AMERICA: First on a list of ethnics who gave their names to America is the Florentine nobleman Amerigo Vespucci (1451–1512) who helped outfit the ships for Columbus's second voyage in 1493 and made four voyages to the New World himself. As early as 1532 most Europeans were calling the new continent "America" — everyone, that is, *except* the Spanish and Portuguese, who refused to call this new land *America* until the eighteenth century out of respect for Columbus.

Amerigo Vespucci gave his name to our nation. (Courtesy: New York Public Library)

BASTROP COUNTY, TEXAS is named for Baron Von Bastrop, the founder of a German settlement on the Colorado River, near Austin, in 1823.

BERING STRAIT Captain Vitus Bering died of scurvy on his way back to Russia in 1741 and was buried on the island that bears his name today. The Bering Sea and the Bering Strait were also named in his honor when he led a fur-trapping expedition to southern Alaska.

BLOCK ISLAND, NEW YORK, is named after the Dutch navigator Adrian Block, who explored that region in 1614.

THE BRONX One of New York City's five boroughs, the Bronx is the only one connected to the mainland of the United States (Manhattan, Brooklyn, Queens and Staten Island are all separated from the mainland by bodies of water). The Bronx is named after Jonas Bronck, a Danish immigrant who purchased 500 acres of land there in 1639. People traveling north would always stop by his farm and visit "the Broncks"—meaning Jonas and his family. The name stuck, and quite possibly that's why it's always referred to as *the* Bronx.

CHISHOLM TRAIL This famous cattle trail of the Old West, now part of Highway 81, was blazed by a Cherokee Indian— Jesse Chisholm. The trail was a favorite of cattlemen, who drove their herds from Texas, through Oklahoma and on to the railroad terminals of Kansas.

COLUMBUS Although America was named for someone else, Christopher Columbus (1451–1506) is remembered for his efforts in no less than 35 states with countless cities, towns, counties and streets named Columbus, Columbia or even Columbiana in his honor. There is a Columbus in Georgia, Illinois, Indiana, Kansas, Kentucky, Louisiana, Missouri, Montana, Nebraska, New Jersey, New Mexico, North Carolina, North Dakota, Ohio, Pennsylvania, Texas and Wisconsin. There is a Columbia in Alabama, California, Connecticut, Florida, Illinois, Iowa, Kentucky, Maine, Mississippi (two), Missouri, New Jersey, North Carolina, Pennsylvania, South Carolina, South Dakota, Tennessee and Virginia. And, last but not least, there is the District of Columbia.

DULUTH, MINNESOTA was named for the French explorer Daniel Greysolon Duluth, who built a trading post in that area and signed treaties with the Sioux and Chippewa in 1679. His named was Anglicized from either *du Lhut,* or *Dulhut.*

GALLATIN, PENNSYLVANIA, was named after Albert Gallatin, the Swiss-born financier who served as Secretary of the Treasury between 1801 and 1811.

GERMANTOWN, TEXAS, was renamed Schroeder, Texas, during World War I in honor of a local soldier of German ancestry who died while fighting for the American cause.

GUFFEY, COLORADO, was named in honor of James McClurg Guffey (1839–1930) a pioneer oil and gas developer responsible for opening the oil fields of Kansas, Texas, California, West Virginia and Indian Territory. Born in Westmoreland County, Pennsylvania, of Scotch-Irish ancestry, Guffey was the largest individual oil producer in the United States with a fortune valued at many millions of dollars during the early years of his business. Yet, when he died at the age of 91, his wealth had dwindled away. A few months before his death, his home in Pittsburgh was sold in foreclosure of a mortgage amounting to over $248,000 with interest penalties.

PORT HERMANN, MARYLAND, was named for a German immigrant, Augustin Hermann, the first colonial citizen naturalized in Maryland in 1666.

"HIGH GROUND," INDIANA Terre Haute ("high ground" in French), Indiana, the manufacturing and coal shipping center of the Wabash Valley, was first founded in 1816 at the site of an abandoned French and Indian fur trading post. The French called it "high ground," or "high land," to indicate that it was elevated above the high-water line and was safe from the flood waters of the Wabash River.

KOSSUTH, PENNSYLVANIA, is named after the Hungarian patriot and statesman Louis Kossuth (1802–1894), who visited the United States as a political exile in 1852.

LANSING, MICHIGAN, is named after an old Dutch family who emigrated to Michigan from Albany, New York.

"LARGE BREAST" NATIONAL PARK The shape of Wyoming's Teton mountains must have reminded some sex-starved explorer of a woman's breasts (tétons) and he named them accordingly. Grand Teton National Park was created in

1929, and expanded to include the Jackson Hole Monument in 1950.

LITTLE ROCK, ARKANSAS, was founded by Bernard de la Harpe, who originally called the town La Petite Roche in his native French. A trading post was established at that site in 1722.

LOUISVILLE, KENTUCKY, was named for King Louis XVI of France in 1780, and MARIETTA, OHIO, for his queen, Marie Antoinette, in 1788 as a token of appreciation for the French effort during the American Revolution.

LYNCHBURG, VIRGINIA, was founded by and named after John Lynch, the son of an Irish immigrant, who settled there in 1760.

"MINE OF SPAIN," IOWA? When Julien Dubuque (1762–1810), a French-Canadian, began mining lead ore along the banks of the Mississippi River in 1788 he named his claim "The Mine of Spain." When the town's founding fathers decided to name that port city in 1833 they chose to call it Dubuque, in honor of Iowa's first white settler, rather than perpetuate the fanciful name that Julien had chosen for his mining claim.

"THE MONKS," IOWA Iowa's capital city takes its name from the Des Moines

20 STATES WITH INDIAN NAMES

State	Meaning	Language
Alabama	"I open the thicket"	Choctaw
Arizona	from *arizonac*, "place of the small spring"	Papagao
Arkansas	"south wind people"	Sioux
Connecticut	from *quinnitukgut*, "at the long tidal river"	Mohican
Idaho	"light on the mountains"	Shoshone
Iowa	from *aijuba*, "the sleepy one"	Dakota
Kansas	"south wind people"	Sioux
Kentucky	from *kentake*, "meadow land"	Iroquois
Massachusetts	"at the big hill"	Algonquian
Michigan	from *mica gama*, "big water"	Chippewa
Minnesota	"sky blue water"	Sioux
Mississippi	from *mici sibi*, "big river"	Chippewa
Missouri	"muddy water"	Algonquian
Nebraska	from *ni-bthaska*, "river in the flatness"	Omaha
Ohio	from *Oheo*, "beautiful water"	Iroquois
Oklahoma	"the red people"	Choctaw
Oregon	"beautiful water"	Algonquian
Utah	"higher up"	Navaho
Wisconsin	"grassy place"	Algonquian
Wyoming	from *mache-weaming*, "at the big flats"	Algonquian

16 INDIAN PLACE NAMES AND THEIR MEANINGS

Chattanooga	rock rising to a point	Shenandoah	daughter of the skies
Chautauqua	foggy place	Spokane	sun warrior
Kalamazoo	boiling pot	Tallahassee	old town
Milwaukee	gathering place by the river	Tuscaloosa	black warrior
Nantucket	the faraway place	Walla Walla	place of many waters
Mohave	three mountains	Winnebago	people of the filthy water
Podunk	neck of land	Woonsocket	at the very steep hill
Poughkeepsie	at the bottom of the water-fall	Yosemite	killer grizzly bear

River, which was originally known to the Indians as the Moingona, meaning "River of the mounds." French explorers who heard the Indian name corrupted the title to *la Rivière des Moines* (the river of the monks). Over the years the name of the river became shortened to Des Moines.

MUSKEGON, MICHIGAN   Founded in 1812, Muskegon was originally the site of a trading post established by Jean Baptiste Recollet. The name is derived from a Chippewa Indian word meaning "river with marshes."

NEW   ORLEANS,   LOUISIANA, started out as Nouvelle Orleans, but after the 1803 Louisiana Purchase the town's name was Anglicized to New Orleans.

NEWPORT   NEWS,   VIRGINIA Daniel Goodkin, a wealthy merchant from Port Newce, in County Cork, Ireland, led a band of settlers to Virginia in 1621. He named the settlement *New Port Newce*, but like so many other names in America, it was corrupted over the years into Newport News.

PAOLI, PENNSYLVANIA   Located just outside of Philadelphia, Paoli, Pennsylvania, is named after Pasquale Paoli (1725–1807), a leader in the Italian struggle for independence who fought for Corsica's freedom in 1768. Benjamin Franklin was so impressed with Pasquale's efforts that he had the town named in his honor.

PRINSBURG,   MINNESOTA,   was founded in 1888 by Martin Prins, a Dutchman from the province of Groningen. Prins represented a Chicago-based firm which encouraged settlements along railroad routes in the United States.

PROVO, UTAH, was named in honor of a French-Canadian trapper, Etienne Provot, who explored that region in the early 1820s.

"RED STICK," LOUISIANA   The capital of Louisiana was established as a French fort in 1719. The name, *Baton* *Rouge* ("red stick" in French) refers to a local Indian custom of using a red-stained post to mark the territorial boundary between hunting grounds of two different tribes.

MT. RICHTHOFEN, COLORADO, is named after Baron Ferdinant von Richthofen, a German geologist.

SCRANTON, PENNSYLVANIA, was named for George W. and Selden T. Scranton, two descendants of John Scranton, an Englishman who emigrated to Boston in 1637. The Scranton brothers first settled their namesake town in 1840.

TITUSVILLE,   PENNSYLVANIA, the site of the 1858 oil strike, was named for Jonathan Titus, the grandson of a German immigrant, Peter Titus, who settled in Staten Island, New York, about 1750.

TONTITOWN, ARKANSAS, is named in honor of Italian-born Enrico di Tonti, the "Father of Arkansas." Also known by the nickname "Man with the iron hand" as the result of a grenade accident, Tonti was the first European to establish a settlement in the lower Mississippi Valley, somewhere near Hot Springs, Arkansas, in 1686.

WILHELMINA, MARYLAND, was named after the Dutch queen, Wilhelmina, who reigned over the Netherlands from 1890 to 1948.

WILKES-BARRE, PENNSYLVANIA, was named in honor of two Englishmen, John Wilkes and Issac Barre, who spoke out in favor of the American cause. The town was founded in 1769.

YONKERS, NEW YORK, is named after Jonkheer Adriaen van der Donck. Adriaen's   journal,   *Description   of New   Netherland,* was   influential   in encouraging immigration from the Netherlands. He settled on a tract of land north of present-day Manhattan in 1646. It is known today as Yonkers—a corruption of his title, Jonkheer. He also established a sawmill there in 1649.

"I have fallen in love with American names,
The sharp names that never get fat,
The snakeskin-titles of mining claims,
the plumed war-bonnet of Medicine Hat,
Tucson and Deadwood and Lost Mule Flat."

STEPHEN VINCENT BENÉT
American Names

SURNAMES: WHERE DO THEY COME FROM AND WHAT DO THEY MEAN?

Like hereditary diseases, heirloom silver and family traditions, your surname is passed on from your ancestors to you. Every surname tells a story, so to speak, about the person who was first to be named Smith, Jones or O'Malley:

Smith is English in origin, and is derived from tradesmen's names, such as blacksmith, arrowsmith, etc.

Jones is another English name; it means "God is gracious."

O'Malley comes from the Emerald Isle and means "one who is descended from the chieftain."

Surnames were usually descriptive of a person's occupation, the father's first name, a place of residence or a nickname. If your surname isn't on the following list you might wish to look it up in one of the many books on the subject, listed below:

Ackerman	a plowman
Bloch	foreigner
Castro	resident near an army camp
Chavez	"key"; nickname for keymaker
Cleaver	user of a spike-studded war club
Disney	place of iron mines
Dreyfuss	three-footed; once used for a man with a crutch
Dunlop	son of the brown man of the mountain
Fabian	bean grower
Gable	young man of God
Hefner	a potter or maker of jugs
Heifetz	"desire" or "delight"
Hoffman	a farmer who owned his land
Kraft	strong or powerful man
Landers	one who bleached flax
Margolis	pearl
Moskowitz	one who came from Moscow
Nixon	son of Nick
Oswald	dweller in the eastern forest
Portnoy	tailer
Rizzo	curly-haired man
Rockefeller	dweller near the rye field
Sandburg	dweller on a sandy hill
Scharfstein	sharpening stone, used for a grinder
Schurz	one who sold aprons
Shapiro	from the city of Speyer in Bavaria
Smucker	one who decorates things
Swoboda	lover of freedom and independence
Tappan	one who purs wines or beer
Tiffany	one to whom God has appeared; once used for children born on the Feast of the Epiphany, January 6
Webster	a weaver
Van Buren	one from the neighborhood
Vargas	home on steep hillside

LOOK IT UP:

Bardsley, C. W.
A Dictionary of English and Welsh Surnames
1901, rept. 1968, Genealogical Publishing Co.

Kaganoff, B. C.
A Dictionary of Jewish Names and Their History
New York: Schocken, 1977

Rule, L. R. and W. K. Hammond
What's in a Name
New York: Jove, 1973

Smith, E. C.
American Surnames
Philadelphia: Chilton, 1969

Smith, E. C.
New Dictionary of American Family Names
New York: Harper and Row, 1973

"I HEAR AMERICANS CHANGING THEIR NAMES . . ."

When Carl Sandburg's father, August Johnson, first emigrated to the United States from Sweden, he found that his surname was much too common in Illinois, so he decided to change it to "Sandburg" to distinguish himself from the hordes of other Swedish immigrants.

For many reasons, thousands of immigrants before him and after him have chosen to change their names (usually from a "-burg" to something like Johnson) because they were "too ethnic," "too difficult to pronounce," or simply "too long" to fit on computer-read forms. So for the sake of convenience and conformity, they "Americanized" them.

It usually starts off innocently: For example, a Romanian immigrant named "Trandafirescu" finds it simpler to give the name "Tranda" when making reservations over the phone, and soon he finds himself lopping off the end of his name legally.

Often, especially in the heyday of immigration, it was the officials at Ellis Island who decided to change a new arrival's name through mispronunciation, misspelling, or the inability to translate a Russian or Greek name into Roman letters.

For various reasons, many people have "whitewashed" or "WASP-washed" their names, but the practice is especially prevalent among Italian-, Jewish- and Polish-Americans.

Polish Name Polishers

One Polish immigrant who should have changed his name was Brigadier General Wlodzimierz Krzyzanowski, the first governor of Alaska. Despite his great contributions to the Union effort during the Civil War, he was twice passed over for promotion. The problem? As Carl Schurz noted, the Senate had rejected Lincoln's appeal for Krzyzanowski's promotion "because . . . there was nobody there who could pronounce his name."

Determined not to let life pass them by because American tongues were easily tied, many Polish immigrants changed their multi-consonanted names:

EDMUND MUSKIE Muskie was the first Polish-American elected as governor of Maine, and as a U.S. Senator. But, would he have been elected with the name Marciszewski on the ballot? Maybe, but his Polish-born father, Stephen Marciszewski, changed the family name to Muskie in 1903 when he emigrated to the United States, giving his son a more pronounceable last name for the ballot box.

BARRY GOLDWATER When Barry's Polish-Jewish grandfather, Michael, fled the 1848 insurrection in his native land, he settled in Sonora, California. Instead of changing his name from Goldwasser to something "more American," he translated his surname, and became known as Michael Goldwater to his new friends.

SAMUEL GOLDWYN A former glove salesman who made it big as a movie mogul, Samuel Goldwyn (1882–1974) changed his name from Goldfish to Goldwyn when he emigrated to America from Warsaw, Poland. The presiding judge approved the decision by commenting, "A self-made man may prefer a self-made

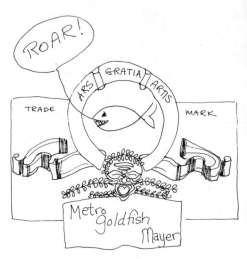

If Samuel Goldwyn hadn't *changed his name, the MGM logo might look something like this.*

name." (And let's face it, Metro-Goldfish-Mayer just doesn't have the right ring.)

STELLA WALSH, who won the Olympic gold medal for track in 1932, was born Stanislawa Walasiewicz in her native Poland. But, a name change alone was not enough to win Stella a place on the U.S. track team. Because she was not an American citizen, Stella had to bring home the gold for Poland, instead of her adopted nation, the United States.

Other celebrities who Americanized their Polish names include: Carroll Baker (Karolina Piekarska); Michael Landon (Michael Orowicz); Stefanie Powers (Stefania Federkiewicz); and Janet Lynn (Janet Lynn Nowicki).

As W. S. Kuniczak noted in his history of the Poles in America: "There are other distinguished actors and actresses who do not care to advertise their Polish descent, and yet others who do the Polish-American community a service by concealing theirs."

More Celebrity Name Droppers

Almost every famous movie star, comedian and announcer in Hollywood has changed his name or at least toyed with the idea. Besides striving for a name that people will remember, stars want names that are euphonistically pleasing. What sounds better, Cary Grant or Alexander Archibald Leach? Would Jack Benny have become one of America's top comedians with the name Joseph Kubelsky? Would Rita Hayworth have made it as a sex symbol with a name like Marguerite Cansino? Probably! But still, many aspiring stars have tried to euphonize or Americanize their names. Krekor Ohanian gave up his Armenian name to become Mike Connors; Vincent Furnier became Alice Cooper; Joe Yule became Mickey Rooney; Michael Igor Peschkowsky became Mike Nichols; and

Delores Consuelo Figueroa del Rivero became Chita Rivera for short.

Recently, many actors and writers have started "keeping" their own names as they climb the ladder of success: Mario Puzo, Al Pacino, Sylvester Stallone and David Wallechinsky (who declined his father's "new" name of Wallace in favor of his grandfather's name) are some of the Italian and Jewish celebrities who refused to participate in the name-change game.

Can you match the following Jewish and Italian "name-changers" with their old monikers?

	New Name		Ethnic Name
1	Robert Alda	a	Leonard Hacker
2	Woody Allen	b	Walden Robert Cassatto
3	Anne Bancroft	c	Anthony Papaleo
4	Vic Damone	d	Belle Silverman
5	Bobby Darin	e	Bernard Schwartz
6	Vince Edwards	f	Alonso D'Abruzzo
7	Tony Franciosa	g	Anna Maria Italiano
8	Rocky Graziano	h	Gary Marscharelli
9	Buddy Hackett	i	Allen Konigsberg
10	Steve Lawrence	j	Joseph Gottlieb
11	Garry Marshall	k	Concetta Ignolia
12	Joseph Papp	l	Rocco Barbella
13	John Saxon	m	Joseph Papirofsky
14	Beverly Sills	n	Vincent Zoino
15	Connie Stevens	o	Vito Farinola
16	Joey Bishop	p	Sidney Leibowitz
17	Tony Curtis	q	Carmen Orrico

Answers:

1-f; 2-i; 3-g; 4-o; 5-b; 6-n; 7-c; 8-l; 9-a; 10-p; 11-h; 12-m; 13-q; 14-d; 15-k; 16-j; 17-e

Black American Name Changers

When Black pride emerged in the United States during the late 1960s, many Black Americans began searching for African names for their newborn children, while others changed their own WASP-sounding names to something more relevant. Some of the most famous Black name changers include: Cassius Clay, who became Muhammad Ali; Le Roi Jones, the playwright, who became Amiri Baraka (which means Prince Blessedness); Robert Poole, the religious leader of the Black Muslims who changed his name to Elijah Muhammad; and Malcolm Little, who first changed his name to Malcolm X and later to the Orthodox Islamic name, El Hajj Malik El Chabazz.

According to *Ebony* magazine, the most common Black family name in America is "Washington." Almost four-fifths of the Washingtons in the United States are Black. (Dinah Washington, entertainer; Walter Washington, mayor of Washington, D.C.; Booker T. Washington, educator.)

All About Name Changing . . .

SOME WHO DID . . .

TONY BENNETT, Italian-American singer: "[I got my] first big break in the music business twenty-five years ago as a youngster. Pearl Bailey was playing at the Greenwich Village Inn. She kept me on when she heard me sing. She said "hold him over because I want him for my show.' So I stayed with her for a while. When Bob Hope came to see her — he was appearing at the Paramount Theater with Jane Russell — he asked: 'What's your name?' I was nervous as hell but I said 'Anthony Dominick Benedetto.' He replied, 'Well, that's way too long for the marquee!' So Bob Hope said, 'Let's Americanize it and call you Tony Bennett.'

"Actually, it's been a very lucky show business name for me, but I always felt a little guilty about it because a lot of Italians ask me why I did it, and ask if I'm not proud I'm Italian and things like that. But, luckily, I paint as a hobby, and now my name as a painter is Benedetto, so you see, I've reverted to my original name."

HARRY GOLDEN, Yiddish author: "Though my mother wore a big red tag which spelled our name when she carried me down the gangplank of the *Graf Waldersee,* for their own convenience and probably through their own ignorance, the immigration officials changed it from Goldhirsch to Goldhurst. Thirty-seven years later, I changed the name again — to Golden . . . I was not, however, putting the past behind me."

RED BUTTONS, Polish-American comedian: Red Buttons (1919–   ) would be funny with any other name, except perhaps Aaron Chwatt, the name he was born with on the Lower East Side of New York. There isn't anything wrong with the name Aaron Chwatt — it just doesn't happen to be right for a vaudeville comedy act, which is how "Red" started his career.

"My real name is Blue Zippers," Red once told an interviewer, "but I had to change it when I went into show business. Think of how that would look on the marquee: 'BLUE ZIPPERS' . . ." Where did Red Buttons really get his name? "Red was easy, it had nothing to do with my hair," claims Buttons, "I was a Communist for ten years." All jokes aside, Red did get his nickname from his once full head of red hair, and "Buttons" came from his onetime job as a bellboy. (Buttons was a common nickname for bellboys in the early 1930s, referring to the large number of buttons on their uniforms.)

GERALDO RIVERA, Puerto Rican-Jewish newscaster: When Geraldo Rivera, the son of a Puerto Rican father and a Jewish mother, was blackballed by Sigma Nu fraternity in his college days because the brothers thought he was Mexican, it proved to be a turning point in his life. He went from being Gerald Rivera to Geraldo.

It happened about the same time that Lew Alcindor saw fit to change his name to Kareem Abdul-Jabbar, and it was a significant moment of truth for the young reporter. Later, Rivera would be accused of changing his name from Jerry Rivers to capitalize on the ethnic chic of the 1970s, but Rivera claims this rumor is untrue. He maintains, "I am now a classless person. I am a raceless person. I'm not a white person, not a black or brown person. I'm a rainbow person."

TED MORGAN, French-American author: When Sanche de Gramont became an American, he decided that he would do away with both his French title (Count) and his French-sounding name.

How did Sanche de Gramont become Ted Morgan? As he explains in his book, *On Becoming American,* he simply threw out Sanche, a contraction of St. Charles (too Gallic) and began scrambling the letters in his last name. He might have chosen to become: Dr. Montage, R. D. Megaton, or Dan Gromet, but he picked the name Ted Morgan because, "Morgan, he felt, was someone you would lend your car to. Dogs and small children would like him."

MICHAEL CRISTOFER, Italian-American playwright: Cristofer is the first Italian-American to win a Pulitzer Prize and Broadway's prestigious Tony Award; he won both in 1977 for his play *The Shadow Box.* He changed his name from Procaccino to Cristofer during what he described as a "period of alienation in his life." But, with his recent success and the climate of the 70s he is considering changing his name back to Procaccino, "to honor my father."

VOWEL DROPPER WITH MISTAKEN IDENTITY:

"When I moved to California from New York, I dropped the vowel at the end of my name so I wouldn't be 'too Italian' in a place full of people with blond hair and blue eyes. I'm proud to be an Italian-American, but I just didn't want to be stereotyped as another 'guinea from New York.'

"Now, ten years later, I'm sorry I did it, because when I changed my name — suddenly I became "Jewish." People keep asking me if I'm Jewish. Who knows? Maybe I do look Jewish, but it really annoys me because there are some people out here who don't like me because they think I'm Jewish. So now instead of being considered just another guinea from Brooklyn, I'm stereotyped as just another Jew from Flatbush."

TV network executive, age 37

NO "SVET" Svetlana Alliluyeva, the daughter of the late Soviet dictator Josef Stalin, caused a stir when she became an American citizen in November 1978 after residing in the United States for almost a dozen years. In addition to changing her citizenship, Svetlana also shortened her name: "I don't want to be Svetlana anymore," she said in an interview. "I like to be Lana Peters. It is easy to spell and now it is legal, through naturalization." Lana was briefly married to American architect W. Wesley Peters in 1970.

SOME WHO DIDN'T . . .

MEYER LANSKY, Jewish gambling czar: "The first time I defended my honor as a Jew was when the Irish kids asked me to play basketball in a schoolyard game. In those days the Irishers would pull the beards of old Jews and open the flies of Jewish kids to check their origins. During the game one of them made an anti-Semitic remark. I slugged him, even though I was a shrimp. The other Irishers liked that: they told me that from now on they'd call me Mike. I said no thanks, the name is Meyer."

LORETTA SWIT, Polish-American actress: "Swit is pronounced 'sweet' in Polish and means 'dawn.' I was never tempted to change it, although several agents tried. I thought it sounded like a punctuation mark."

RICARDO MONTALBAN, Mexican-born actor: Born Ricardo Gonzalo Pedro Montalban Merino, the suave actor resisted all attempts to Anglicize his name when he first broke into Hollywood films in 1947 (playing a Latino, of course, opposite Cyd Charisse in *Fiesta*): "I said, 'Let my accent and name be. It distinguishes me.'"

MERYL STREEP, Dutch-American actress: Meryl's rather unusual last name is of Dutch origin, and over the years she also has resisted suggestions by agents that she change her name to something more melodious. Was she ever self-conscious about her unusual name as a child? Absolutely not. "With Carmine Petriccione, Pancho Solegna and Bozo della Russo around the neighborhood," she recalls, "no one was making fun of *my* name."*

LEONARD BERNSTEIN, Jewish conductor: Although the world of music is replete with Jewish names, conductor Serge Koussevitzky once advised Leonard Bernstein to change his name. Koussevitzky believed the name "Bernstein" might impede young Leonard's progress in the field of music, and he suggested Leonard S. Berns as an alternative.

Bernstein considered Serge's advice, but, in the end, he was determined to keep his ethnic name: "I lost a night's sleep over it, and came back and told him I decided to make it as Leonard Bernstein or not at all."

*Quote from New York *Times* Magazine, Feb. 4, 1979, p 24

ETHNIC WORDSMITHS

JACKSON ANDERSON (1922–) A nationally syndicated newspaper columnist whose columns regularly appear in the *Washington Star,* Jack Anderson was born in Long Beach, California, of Swedish ancestry. Working out of a Victorian townhouse with a staff of 20, Anderson has broken more "big" stories about Washington, D.C., in the past 31 years than any other reporter in the United States. His columns appear in almost 1,000 newspapers, and he is heard over network television and radio. A Mormon missionary in his youth, Anderson has a rather flamboyant speaking style and is a popular speaker on the lecture circuit.

ISAAC ASIMOV (1920–) The son of Russian-Jewish immigrants to Brooklyn, New York, Asimov was born in Petrovich, U.S.S.R., in 1920. He "disappointed" his parents by earning a Ph.D. in chemistry — they were hoping for a medical doctor in the family. But Asimov was hardly a disappointment in his chosen field. One of America's most highly regarded scientific writers (of both science fact and science fiction), Asimov also enjoys a reputation as one of America's most prolific writers: his 201st book was published in 1979.

JIM BISHOP (1907–) A syndicated columnist and author of over two dozen books, Bishop learned his straightforward reporting style from his Irish-Catholic father, John Michael Bishop. As a child, Jim watched his police-lieutenant father file reports that reconstructed crimes in a step-by-step manner, and always included all the details. Three of Bishop's best-selling books were suspenseful hour-by-hour narrations which helped bring historical events to life: *The Day Christ Died, The Day Lincoln Was Shot, The Day Kennedy Was Shot.*

WILLIAM PETER BLATTY (1928–) The first and youngest child of Lebanese immigrants secured his financial future with his best-selling book about demonic possession, *The Exorcist.* A veteran writer of novels and film scripts with a Ph.D. to boot, Blatty sold some 9 million copies of his horror story, which has been translated into a dozen languages. *The Ex-orcist* hovered on the New York *Times* best-seller list for over a year, and when the film version debuted in December, 1973, it attracted record-breaking crowds.

PEARL SYDENSTRICKER BUCK (1892–1973) Born in West Virginia of Dutch extraction, Pearl Buck spent much of her life in China and the Far East, accompanying her parents and her first husband, John Buck, in their missionary work. She wrote over 40 books during her career, and contributed much to Western understanding of the customs, traditions and problems of the Oriental world. She won a Pulitzer Prize in 1931 for *The Good Earth,* and in 1938 she became the first American woman to be awarded a Nobel Prize for literature. In addition to her literary achievements, Buck also founded the East and West Association to promote relations between the U.S. and Asia, and in 1949 she founded Welcome House, an adoption agency for children of Asian-American parentage.

EDGAR RICE BURROUGHS (1875–1950) Burrough's first American ancestor was an immigrant from Ipswich, England, who settled at Salem, Massachusetts, in 1634. Although he became famous as the creator of *Tarzan,* Edgar did not set his sights on a literary career as a young man. He was employed as a cavalry instructor, department store manager, miner, cowboy, storekeeper, publisher and policeman before he considered writing as a career in 1911. He first conceived *Tarzan of the Apes* in 1914, and soon America's first "swinger" was the international star of some 25 books which were eventually translated into 56 different languages.

CARLOS CASTENEDA (1925? 1931?–) The "facts" about Casteneda are clouded with discrepancies. He was either born in Sao Paulo, Brazil, in 1931 and emigrated to the United States at the age of 20, or else he was born in Peru in 1925. No one knows for certain, because he has changed his story on occasion and prefers to remain shrouded in mystery.

His three best-selling books, *The Teachings of Don Juan, A Yaqui Way of Knowledge; A Separate Reality;* and *The Second Ring of Power,* all tell of his adventures with Don Juan, a seventy-year-old Yaqui

Indian in Mexico who introduced Carlos to peyote, jimson weed, sacred mushrooms and other psychedelic plants. Besides earning royalties from his books, Carlos used his research to fulfill the thesis requirements for a degree in anthropology at U.C.L.A.

SAMUEL LANGHORNE CLEMENS (1835–1910) was better known in literary circles as Mark Twain. Born in Florida, Missouri, of Dutch and English stock, Clemens adopted his pen name, Mark Twain, in 1863 when he joined the staff of the Virginia City, Nevada, newspaper, the *Territorial Enterprise*. His most famous works include *Tom Sawyer* (1876), *The Prince and the Pauper* (1882), *Huckleberry Finn* (1885), and *A Connecticut Yankee in King Arthur's Court* (1889). Twain made a fortune from publishing his works, but bad business investments left him bankrupt in 1894. In order to repay his debts, Twain had to make a two-year lecture circuit of the world.

PAUL DE KRUIF (1890–   ) Born in Zeeland, Michigan, of Dutch parentage, Paul De Kruif was a bacteriologist who gained fame as a medical and scientific writer. His most noted works, *The Fight for Life* (1938), *Microbe Hunters* (1926), and *Hunger Fighters* (1928), honor the scientific minds who benefited our world with increased agricultural output and with disease prevention and control measures.

JOHN DOS PASSOS (1896–1970) The son of a well-to-do lawyer, and the grandson of an immigrant Portuguese shoemaker, Manoel dos Passos, John dos Passos not only distinguished himself in the field of literature, but was awarded a U.S. patent for one of his inventions. In 1959, dos Passos was granted a Patent for his "toy pistol that blows soap bubbles."

His trilogy, U.S.A., written in 1937, has been acclaimed as the "great American novel." Dos Passos also wrote *The 42nd Parallel* and *The Big Money*.

WILLIAM JAMES DURANT (1885–   ) A famed historian of French-Canadian ancestry, Durant has taken it upon himself to tackle the history of civilization. He wrote the first six volumes of his monumental *Story of Civilization* by himself, and collaborated with his wife, Ariel, on the next five. Over the years, the Durants' work has been acclaimed as a great literary achievement.

MARILYN FRENCH (1929–   ) Her surname to the contrary, Marilyn French's parents were both Americans of Polish ancestry. Her 1977 novel, *The Women's Room*, was acclaimed as the "women's novel of the year," and enjoyed a long, successful run on both the hardcover and paperback best-seller lists for almost two years.

KAHLIL GIBRAN (1883–1931) Born in Bsharre, Lebanon, Gibran emigrated to the United States in 1895 and settled in Boston, Massachusetts. Gibran's most famous book is *The Prophet*, which has sold almost 4 million copies since its first publication in 1923. *The Prophet* sells steadily, year after year, without any advertising budget, as successive waves of young students form a never-ending "Gibran cult." He published 11 other books, including *The Garden of the Prophet* and *Sand and Foam*.

ALEX HALEY (1921–   ) In Gambia, the family historian who learns the oral history of his fathers and forefathers and passes it on to his sons is called the *griot*. Alex Haley, who recounted his family's history in *Roots*, has to be the most successful *griot* in history—earning well over $4 million for a tale that some critics charge is more fiction than fact. Nonetheless, *Roots* attracted a record television audience when it was first aired in 1977 in addition to being one of the best-selling books of the decade. It's a sad comment on the times we live in, but when NBC was promoting its Easter-time showing of *Jesus of Nazareth* in 1979, the network chose to quote reviews which acclaimed Jesus' story to be "more moving than *Roots*."

MARCUS LEE HANSEN (1892–1938) labored for over 20 years on *Atlantic Migration, 1607–1860*, and won a Pulitzer Prize posthumously for his efforts in 1941. The son of Norwegian and Danish immigrants who settled in the Midwest, Hansen was educated at the State University of Iowa and earned his Ph.D. from Harvard in 1924. His other noted books include: *The Immigrant in American History*, and *The Mingling of the Canadian and American Peoples*.

EVAN HUNTER (1926–   ) When Evan Hunter was growing up he determined, "I'm not going to live in slums all my life. I'm going to get rich and have big houses and expensive cars and beautiful women." Born Salvatore Lombino in 1926, Evan spent his youth growing up in New York City's Italian ghetto during the Depression years. He changed his name to Evan Hunter soon after graduating Phi Beta Kappa from Hunter College in 1950, but that was not the last time he changed his name. After his first successful book, *The Blackboard Jungle,* was published in 1954, Hunter continued to write murder mysteries under three different pen names — Richard Marsten, Hunt Collins and Ed McBain (who has sold 53 million books on his own).

WASHINGTON IRVING (1783–1859) The son of a wealthy New York merchant of Scottish ancestry, Washington Irving published his satirical *History of New York* in 1809 under the pseudonym Diedrich Knickerbocker. After a brief career in importing (and subsequent bankruptcy), Irving returned to the writing life in 1817. Under the pseudonym Geoffrey Crayon, Irving published *The Sketch Book* in 1820; it contains the classic legends of Sleepy Hollow and Rip Van Winkle.

EMMA LAZARUS (1849–1887), a Jewish poet, wrote the words that are engraved on a plaque inside the pedestal of the statue of Liberty Enlightening the World:

"Give me your tired, your poor,
Your huddled masses yearning to breathe
  free
The wretched refuse of your teeming shore,
Send these, the homeless, tempest-tossed,
  to me;
I lift my lamp beside the golden door."

Lazarus' sonnet, entitled *The New Colossus,* was donated at a fund-raising auction to benefit the Statue of Liberty Fund in 1883. She had published her first volume of verse at the tender age of 17, under the guidance of Ralph Waldo Emerson, and although her early efforts were critically well received, Lazarus did not attain the fiery passion that was to become her trademark until 1882, when she published *The Banner of the Jew.* Written after the first Russian pogrom of 1881, it marked the beginning of Emma's devotion to Zionism and the Jewish cause.

JERZY KOSINSKI (1933–   ) was the first foreign-born American writer to receive the National Book Award. The Polish-born Kosinski was awarded the NBA in 1969 for his novel *Steps.*

BETTY MacDONALD (1908–1958) wrote the 1945 best seller *The Egg and I* about a chicken ranch in the Olympic mountains of Washington. Her maternal ancestors were Dutch settlers in New York in the early 1600s, while her father's ancestors hailed from Scotland. Brought up to believe that a wife's place was beside her husband in his life's work, MacDonald painted a humorous portrait of life on a remote, run-down ranch.

MARY McCARTHY (1912–   ) The "first lady of American letters" was born in Seattle, Washington, in 1912. The granddaughter of Irish immigrants, she and her three brothers (one of whom is Kevin McCarthy, the actor) were orphaned in 1919 and forced to live with their greataunt, who, in McCarthy's own words, had a "gift for turning everything sour and ugly." Some of her best-known books are: *Memories of a Catholic Girlhood* (1957); *The Group* (1963); *Birds of America* (1965); and *Hanoi* (1968).

HERMAN MELVILLE (1819–1891) was a descendant of English and Dutch colonial forebears. Melville's mother was a member of one of New York State's oldest families, the Gansevoorts. Melville's paternal ancestors hailed from Fife, Scotland.

Melville's first six books were based on his experiences at sea between 1839 and 1844, when he crewed on whalers and frigates. His seventh book and masterpiece, *Moby Dick,* did not appear in print until 1851, seven years after he had last set foot aboard ship.

WILLIAM HOLMES McGUFFEY (1800–1873) Known as the "schoolmaster to our nation," William McGuffey was born in Washington County, Pennsylvania, to Scotch-Irish Presbyterian parents. *McGuffey's Readers* were standard school texts for almost 100 years in the Midwest, and all told McGuffey sold more than 120 million volumes of his works. Schoolchildren all over America learned to read from his books, the first two volumes of which were written in 1836.

HENRY LOUIS MENCKEN (1890–1956) The son of a German-American businessman, H. L. Mencken began his career in journalism with the Baltimore *Sun* in 1906. His social criticism and satire made

78 McGUFFEY'S FIRST READER

LESSON XLIV.

laid	lamb	where	fol-low
rule	what	fleece	ev-er-y
that	harm	school	wait-ed
love	made	ea-ger	ap-pear
sure	snow	Ma-ry	a-gainst
bind	white	gen-tle	an-i-mal
near	laugh	a-fraid	ling-er-ed
went	makes	teach-er	pa-tient-ly

MA-RY'S LAMB.

MA-RY had a lit-tle lamb,
Its fleece was white as snow,
And ev-er-y where that Ma-ry went,
The lamb was sure to go.

Page from McGuffey's First Reader, *published in 1836. (Courtesy: New York Public Library)*

him famous in the 1920s, but his most lasting contribution to American letters was his three-volume work *The American Language.* It was here that Mencken traced the English slang terms, loan words, idioms and common expressions that evolved in America.

VED MEHTA (1934–   ) A staff writer for the New Yorker Magazine, Mehta has been blind since the age of three, following an attack of meningitis. His father, a distinguished Indian doctor, did not discourage his son from attempting to obtain an education, and at the age of fifteen, after being rejected from 30 schools in foreign countries, Ved was accepted to the Arkansas School for the Blind. He later received a scholarship to Pomona College in Claremont, California.

Although he is no longer an Indian citizen, Mehta has written extensively about his native land in *Face to Face,* his autobiography, which was published in 1957; *Mahatma Gandhi and His Apostles;* and *The New India* (1977).

VLADIMIR NABOKOV (1899–   ) Born in St. Petersburg, Russia, to an aristocratic family, Nabokov inherited wealth equivalent to $2 million only to lose it a short time thereafter when the Revolution rocked his native land. He settled in Europe and lived there until 1940, when he fled to the United States out of concern for the safety of his Jewish wife, Vera. Nabokov became a U.S. citizen in 1945, and in 1958 he was on his way to literary fame with the publication of his novel, *Lolita.* Reviewers, shocked by his story of the nubile nymphet, Lolita, called the book "repulsive" and "disgusting." Nabokov was merely amused at the fuss, claiming: "I rather dislike little girls."

GEORGE O'NEILL (1921–   ) and NENA O'NEILL (?–   ) wrote their best-selling book, *Open Marriage,* in 1972. Despite all rumors to the contrary, they are still together after three decades of marriage and their relationship has definitely been "enriched" by their marital philosophy. Their book, with its cautious endorsement of extramarital sex, sold 3.5 million copies and was translated into 14 languages. Despite George O'Neill's Irish-sounding family name, his roots can be traced to Spanish nobility. He does have some Irish in him, however, since his ancestors moved to Spain from Ireland in 1601.

MARIO PEI (1901–   ) One of the world's leading authorities in the field of linguistics, Pei was born in Rome and became a naturalized citizen in 1925.

Mario began his teaching career at the age of 17 in a New York City parochial school. He later taught at Columbia University, and in 1952 was made a full professor of that esteemed institution. During World War II, Pei created a 37-language course in "War Linguistics" at Columbia, and devised a series of radio-broadcast English lessons for Spanish-speaking citizens. Some of his books include: *The Story of Language, The Story of English, What's in a Word,* and *Invitation to Linguistics.*

EDGAR ALLAN POE (1809–1849) Known as the "founder of the modern detective story" for his ability to instill horror into the hearts of his readers, Edgar Allan Poe is best known for "The Fall of the House of Usher" (1839) and "The Murders in the Rue Morgue" (1841). The great-grandson of a Scottish immigrant, Poe was a master of both prose and poetry. His most haunting poems, *The Bells* (1849) and *Annabel Lee* (1849), were written after his physical and emotional deterioration, which followed in the wake of his wife's death in 1847.

MARIO PUZO (1920–   ) The son of Italian immigrants, Puzo was raised in "Hell's Kitchen," a tough neighborhood on the West Side of Manhattan. His father deserted the family when Mario was 12, and the boy had to take a part-time job to supplement the family income. In his words, "I really thought that I would spend the rest of my life as a railroad clerk. That I was hopelessly trapped by family, by society, by my lack of skills and education." World War II freed Mario from "Hell's Kitchen" and gave him the material for his first novel. But his big killing, so to speak, came when he wrote *The Godfather,* a blatant attempt to cash in on the public's love of Mafia lore. In Puzo's estimation, "I am another Italian success story. Not as great as DiMaggio or Sinatra, but quite enough. It will serve."

WILLIAM SAROYAN (1908–   ) America's best-known Armenian author is William Saroyan, a Pulitzer Prize winner who penned the classic *The Daring Young Man on the Flying Trapeze* in 1934. Saroyan has been turning out a veritable "Black Sea" of ink for almost 50 years, with more than 40 books and plays as well as countless short stories to his credit. When asked to comment on the passing of another year for the December 1977 issue of *Variety,* Saroyan, who was sixty-nine years old at the time, summed up the entire year in two sentences: "1977 was one hell of a year. I didn't die." From the titles on some of Saroyan's other books, it appears that death is constantly on his mind: *I Used To Believe I Had Forever, Now I'm Not So Sure* (1967); and his autobiography, *Not Dying* (1963).

RICHARD SMITH (1941–   ) wrote the best seller, *The Dieter's Guide to Weight Loss During Sex* in 1977, but before you think a roll in the hay is the solution to your weight problem be forewarned that the book is written tongue-in-cheek and is not intended as medical advice. Smith, who claims he was born into "a classical Jewish eating family," believes his passion for food developed when he was two years old and first discovered cake. His next best-selling book was *The Bronx Diet,* a spoof on the 1978 diet book from a classier locale, *The Scarsdale Diet.*

JOHN STEINBECK (1902–1968) Born in Salinas, California, of Dutch and German ancestry, Steinbeck was the sixth American author to receive a Nobel Prize. Steinbeck won his in 1962, joining laureates Sinclair Lewis, Pearl Buck, William Faulkner, Eugene O'Neill and Ernest Hemingway.

His fourth novel, *Tortilla Flat,* was a best seller in 1935. Some of his most famous books include: *Cannery Row* (1945), *Sweet Thursday* (1954), *East of Eden* (1952), *Of Mice and Men* (1937), *The Winter of Our Discontent* (1961), *Travels with Charley* (1962) and *Grapes of Wrath* (1939), for which he won a Pulitzer Prize.

JACQUELINE SUSANN (1926–1974) Although the critics routinely panned Susann's books, the public loved them and she became one of the most successful authors of recent times. Born in Philadelphia, of Dutch-Jewish ancestry, Susann knew how to pen a commercially valuable book — one with high paperback sales and great film potential. Her books include *Valley of the Dolls* (28 weeks on the New York *Times* best-seller list), *The Love Machine, Delores* and *Once Is Not Enough.*

GAY TALESE (1932–   ) Born Gaetano Talese, the son of an immigrant tailor from Calabria, Italy, Gay Talese first gained national attention as a New York *Times* reporter in 1956 when he covered the sinking of the *Andrea Doria* on July 26. He acquired a following for his "nonfiction short stories," which first appeared in *Esquire* in 1963, and by 1969 he had parlayed his popular writing style into the best-selling *The Kingdom and the Power*—a behind-the-scenes look at one of America's most influential newspapers, the New York *Times.*

His next best seller was *Honor Thy Father,* published in 1971 thanks to the cooperation of Bill Bonanno, son of Mafia patriarch Joe Bonanno. Talese's book painted the unglamorous picture of an everyday

Mafioso and his family, who must constantly live in fear.

In 1980, Talese's epic study of American sexuality, *Thy Neighbor's Wife,* was finally published after ten years of exhaustive research.

ALVIN TOFFLER (1928–) Polish-American writer Alvin Toffler propelled himself to the top of the best-seller list with his book, *Future Shock.* His 1970 book was "about what happens to people when they are overwhelmed by change . . . the ways in which we adapt, or fail to adapt, to the future."

BARBARA TUCHMAN (1912–) Jewish-American historian Barbara Tuchman became the first woman ever elected as President of the American Academy and Institute of Arts and Letters in 1979. Twice winner of the Pulitzer Prize, Tuchman was 50 years old before her first book, *The Guns of August,* was published to great critical and popular success. Her latest best seller, *A Distant Mirror,* sold more than half a million copies in less than 6 months, and her other works—*The Proud Tower* and *Stilwell and the American Experience in China*—were both well received critically.

To what does Tuchman attribute her literary success? "I never took a Ph.D. I think if I had taken a doctoral degree, it would have stifled any writing capacity."

LEON URIS (1924–) How does this best-selling Jewish-American writer sum up his literary career to date? "I'm an eight-time Pulitzer Prize loser for my novels. I'm not a member of the critically favored establishment. I have yet to get a kind word from *Time.* I've never received much recognition from the [New York] *Times,* which is big for obscure women poets who've killed themselves. I'm a writer, this is the way I make my living."

Despite Uris' lack of critical acclaim, he has managed to make a rather respectable living as a writer. Some of his best-selling books are *Exodus* (1957); *Q B VII* (1970); *Trinity* (1976).

KURT VONNEGUT (1922–) Vonnegut's inspiration for his best-selling book, *Slaughterhouse Five,* came from his experiences during World War II. Vonnegut, of German ancestry, was captured in Luxembourg during the Battle of the Bulge and detained in a prisoner-of-war camp in the Sudetenland until the war's end. Some of his other best sellers are *Cat's Cradle, The Sirens of Titan* and *Slapstick.*

WALT WHITMAN (1819–1892) was born in West Hills, Long Island, of mixed Dutch and English ancestry. His greatest works include *Oh Captain! My Captain,* a poem written about Lincoln's assassination, and *Once I Pass'd Through a Populous City,* a poem which some critics contend alludes to a homosexual love affair in New Orleans. (Other critics claim it was a heterosexual romance which resulted in the birth of one of his six illegitimate children.) His *Leaves of Grass* (1855) was revised nine times during Whitman's life, yet it was deemed "immoral" by government officials and resulted in his dismissal from a federal job following the Civil War.

PUBLISHING MEN AND WOMEN

Bennett Cerf (1898–1971) Random House
Bennett Cerf started in the publishing field in 1925 when he bought Modern Library, a reprint house, for $215,000. With his profits, Cerf decided to publish original manuscripts from time to time ("at random," in Cerf's words), and in 1927 Random House was born.

Of French-Jewish ancestry, Cerf was noted for his wit and quick humor. He was a panelist for over 17 years on television's *What's My Line.*

Frank Nelson Doubleday (1862–1934) Doubleday & Company
Founded in 1900 as Doubleday, Page and Company, Doubleday is one of the few

Doubleday's logo features a dolphin curled around an anchor, a device first used by printer Aldus Manutius of Venice c. 1500. (Courtesy: New York Public Library)

remaining family-owned publishing houses in America. Born in Brooklyn, New York, of French and Canadian heritage, Frank Doubleday was known to his friends by an Arabic nickname. Rudyard Kipling was the first to call him "effendi" (chief, in Arabic), an acronym for his initials, F.N.D.

Malcolm S. Forbes (1919–   ) Forbes *Magazine*

The son of Scottish immigrants, Malcolm Forbes once stated that his meteoric career rise to the top was due to "sheer ability (spelled i-n-h-e-r-i-t-a-n-c-e)."

Forbes interests are not limited to the world of money and finance. He served as a New Jersey state senator from 1952 to 1958 and in 1973 he became the first man to cross the United States in a hot-air balloon. An attempt to cross the Atlantic Ocean in 1975 was unsuccessful, and the price of Forbes' aborted balloon voyage was high—$1.25 million.

Malcolm Muir (1885–1979) Business Week

Malcolm Muir founded *Business Week* in 1929 to serve the interests of a broad range of corporate executives. Born in Glen Ridge, New Jersey, Malcolm was descended from Scottish immigrants from Kelso who settled in America in 1833. Muir began his business career as a file clerk for James McGraw, and rose to assume the presidency of the McGraw-Hill publishing company in 1928.

Dr. Clilan Bethany Powell (1894–1977) The Amsterdam News

Clilan B. Powell, publisher of the *Amsterdam News* from 1936 to 1971, was one of America's most influential black businessmen. The grandson of slaves, Powell graduated from Howard University Medical School in 1920 and became the first black physician to specialize in X-ray techniques. Half of his $5.11 million estate was bequeathed to his alma mater to provide scholarships and loans to students in financial need.

Harry Scherman (1887–1969) Book-of-the-Month Club

Harry Scherman, the son of Jewish emigré parents from England who settled in Canada in 1882, was the genius behind the book-of-the-month marketing concept.

Once described as the "greatest bookseller in the history of America," Scherman began his literary career as a journalist. The Little Leather Library he founded in 1916 was a forerunner to the Book-of-the-Month club he established in 1926, with only 4,750 subscribers.

Scherman was a pioneer in the direct-mail marketing technique, and a "mathematical wizard" of sorts: Despite his company's name, there are 15, not 12 books sent to subscribers each year.

Gloria Steinem (1934–   ) Ms. *Magazine*

Considered radical when it debuted in 1972, *Ms.* was the first woman's magazine

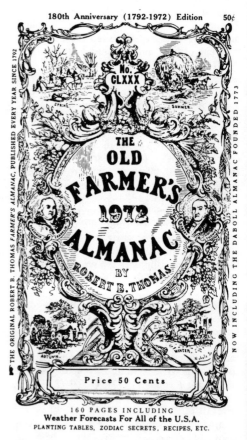

Cover of the 180th anniversary edition of The Old Farmer's Almanac. (*Reprinted with the permission of Yankee, Inc., Dublin, N.H.*)

that did not contain recipes, child rearing hints, beauty tips, or rules of proper etiquette — subjects heretofore deemed to be the only ones of interest to women. Gloria Steinem, the magazine's founding mother, decided that *Ms.* should be "serious, outrageous, satisfying, sad, funky, intimate, global, compassionate, and full of change as women's lives really are." Born in Toledo, Ohio, of Jewish and French Huguenot ancestry, Ms. Steinem has been a leading proponent of the women's movement since 1968.

Robert Bailey Thomas (1766–1864) The Old Farmer's Almanac

Published each year since 1792, *The Old Farmer's Almanac* contains a wealth of interesting tidbits and useful information. The weather predictions for the coming year are usually fairly accurate, too. The almanac was founded by Robert Bailey Thomas, the grandson of a Welsh immigrant, William Thomas, who settled in America about 1718.

THE CHILDREN'S HOUR

For generations, American children have been put to bed with stories of Mother Goose, Peter Pan, Babar the Elephant and, more recently, the fantastic creatures created by Dr. Seuss and Maurice Sendak.

Some of these children's tales were imported from abroad, while others were penned in America by ethnic writers who knew how to capture the imagination of our youth.

Ethnic Roots of America's Favorite Fairy Tales, Stories and Rhymes

♦ MOTHER GOOSE "Mother Goose" is a generic name for numerous collections of nursery rhymes which include such perennial favorites as the careless Three Little Kittens who must forgo pie for dessert until they find their mittens; Old Mother Hubbard, whose cupboard is bare; and other characters such as Simple Simon and Wee Willie Winkie, who is rather "simple" himself, running "uptown, downtown in his nightgown."

The first Mother Goose was the title

character in a collection of tales by Frenchman Charles Perrault (1628–1703). His *Contes de Ma Mére l'Oye* (Tales of Mother Goose), published in 1697, included such traditional stories as *"Cendrillon"* (Cinderella), *"La Barbe Blue"* (Bluebeard), "Puss in Boots," "Sleeping Beauty," "Tom Thumb" and "Little Red Riding Hood."

Although he was nicknamed "the inventor of French fairy tales," his stories were not all French in origin. *"Le Chat Botté"* (Puss in Boots) was probably derived from the Italian tale *"Piacevoli Notti,"* by Straparola, or from the Norse version of the cat's tale ("Lord Peter"), or even from the Swedish ("Palace with Pillars of Gold"). There are even Swahili and Hindi tales about a cat who makes his owner a rich man.

Some sources claim that there was an actual Mother Goose — an American woman, Mrs. Elizabeth Goose, who lived in Boston in the early 1700s. Her daughter married a printer named Thomas Fleet, who printed "Songs for the Nursery" (subtitled "Tales from Mother Goose") in 1719. However, no eighteenth-century manuscript has ever been found to substantiate the rumor which may have been fabricated by one of Fleet's descendants in 1860.

♦ OH, DEM "GLASS" SLIPPERS How did that French lass, Cinderella, ever manage to get her feet into a pair of glass slippers? Glass-molding technology simply wasn't up to such a "feet" in the seventeenth century, so where did Perrault get the idea of putting slippery, frictionless, fragile shoes made of glass on our heroine? Not only would it be impossible for her to boogie the night away in these slippers, but how could she ever be expected to catch her pumpkin coach at the stroke of midnight wearing such impractical shoes?

The answer to this perplexing mystery is simple. Her original footgear was made of "fur." Over the years, oral tradition was responsible for corrupting the French word for fur into a similar-sounding word, *verre* (glass). By the time Perrault set the story down for posterity at the end of the seventeenth century, the slippers had been "miraculously" transformed into glass.

♦ PINOCCHIO Walt Disney made this little wooden boy famous in his 1943 animated film, *Pinocchio,* but the story did not originate at Disney studios. *Pinocchio* was adapted from a nineteenth-century Italian fable about a puppet whose nose grows every time he tells a lie.

♦ PETER PAN Created by Sir James Barrie (1860–1937) in the early 1900s, Peter Pan is the young leader of the "Lost Boys" who refuses to grow up. He made his first appearance in *The Little White Bird* (1902), and graduated to become the title character in his own play, *Peter Pan,* in 1904. Sir Barrie wrote further adventures for Peter, including *Neverland, Peter Pan in Kensington Gardens* and *Peter and Wendy.* But it wasn't until the British-born Peter appeared on Broadway and television in the 1950s, with Mary Martin in the leading role, that he gained a place in the hearts of American children. He, too, was immortalized in a Disney animated film.

♦ BABAR, KING OF ELEPHANTS Babar, that lovable pachyderm who rules his kingdom of elephants with the help of his hefty queen, Celeste, and his able assistants, Monkey Zephir and the Old Lady, has been delighting youngsters with his adventures since 1931. Created by French author Jean de Brunhoff (1899–1937), the Babar stories were continued by Jean's son, Laurent, who has added 21 volumes to his father's original 6. Over 5 million copies of Babar's exploits have been sold in the United States in the past 50 years. The reason for Babar's appeal to young children? Laurence de Brunhoff believes his pachyderm is successful because, "He's heavy, he's slow, he's secure and he is funny."

♦ THE BROTHERS GRIMM Jakob (1785–1863) and Wilhelm Grimm (1786–1859) began writing down folk tales told to them by villagers and farmers near Kassel, Germany, about 1807. They collected 156 stories in all, many of them similar to tales preserved by Perrault, such as "Cinderella" and "Puss in Boots." But the Grimms also gave the children of America and the world new characters to worry about: wicked stepmothers ("Hansel and Gretel," "Snow White"), wicked witches ("Sleeping Beauty"), wolves ("Little Red Riding Hood"), and dwarves ("Rumpelstiltskin").

♦ HEIDI To those Americans who don't read children's books, the name "Heidi" brings to mind a 1968 Sunday night football game which NBC cut off with one minute of playing time left in order to air a television special of Heidi's adventures in Switzerland. As Heidi came on the air, the New York Jets seemed certain of a victory over the Oakland Raiders. Unfortunately for football fans, the Raiders scored two touchdowns during that last 60 seconds and won the game 43–32.

Football fans notwithstanding, Heidi has been a favorite heroine of American children for almost a century. Written by Johanna Spyri (1827–1901), a Swiss author who did not write her first book until the age of 43, Heidi's peaceful life in the Swiss Alps is a perennial "good read" for young girls.

More Ethnic Roots of Our Favorite Fairy Tales, Stories and Rhymes

♦ *THE ARABIAN NIGHTS,* which includes tales of "Aladdin and His Lamp" and "Ali Baba and the Forty Thieves," came to us from the folktales of Asia and Northern Africa.

♦ *THE BLUE FAIRY BOOK,* written in 1889 by Andrew Lang, a Scottish scholar, was the first of 12 "colored" fairy books.

Having been awakened by a kiss, Sleeping Beauty is carried off by her prince to his castle. (Courtesy: German Information Center)

Lang followed his first volume of stories with such hues as Crimson, Yellow and Green.

♦ "THE OWL AND THE PUSSYCAT," who sailed the sea in their beautiful pea green boat, came to America via England. The odd couple first appeared in English author Edward Lear's *Book of Nonsense* in 1846.

♦ *PIPPI LONGSTOCKING*, the young girl who travels around the world in print and movies, was the creation of Swedish author Astrid Lindgren.

♦ "THE THREE LITTLE PIGS" and "JACK THE GIANT KILLER" are two of the tales collected by Joseph Jacobs (1854–1916). An Australian-born Jewish scholar, Jacobs collected traditional English and Irish folktales in the late 1800s to preserve them for posterity.

♦ "TWINKLE, TWINKLE, LITTLE STAR" was a poem written by two English sisters, Ann and Jane Taylor. It was included in their 1804 book of verse, entitled *Original Poems for Infant Minds*.

♦ "WINNIE THE POOH," that "tubby little cubby all covered with fluff" was the creation of England's A. A. Milne.

Ethnic American Authors of Children's Books

LUDWIG BEMELMANS (1898–1962); Born in Meran in the Austrian Tyrol, Ludwig Bemelmans emigrated to the United States at the age of sixteen. He wrote the first of eleven "Madeline" books in 1939, about Madeline and eleven other little girls who lived at a boarding school in Paris. In 1953 he won the Caldecott medal for *Madeline's Rescue*.

MARY MAPES DODGE (1831–1905): An American of Dutch ancestry, Mary Mapes Dodge wrote the story of *Hans Brinker,* the Dutch boy with the silver skates, in 1865. A native New Yorker, Dodge started her literary career at the age of 27 when she became a widow and was forced to support her two small sons. A recognized leader in the field of juvenile fiction, she served as editor of *St. Nicholas* Magazine when it was first published in 1873.

ROSAMOND DU JARDIN (1902–): Although her novels only dealt with such mild adolescent problems as beer drinking and cigarette smoking, thousands of American girls growing up in the 1950s enjoyed Rosamond Du Jardin's books.

Of Scotch, Irish, Welsh and English ancestry, Du Jardin was an all-American WASP, as were the characters in her books: Tobey Heydon in *Practically Seventeen,* Pam and Penny, the two sisters of *Double Date* and *Double Feature*. Although her characters are somewhat old-fashioned, their frustrations and insecurities are timeless, and some of Du Jardin's books have been reissued as paperbacks in the late 1970s.

CAROLYN KEENE Teenage girls have been reading about Nancy Drew's exploits for almost four generations. Television, which helped popularize the female detective and her male counterparts the Hardy boys, also spurred sales of the series to all-time highs. The authors of the Nancy Drew books were Edward Stratemeyer (1862–1930), the son of a German immigrant who ventured to California during the gold rush of 1849, and his daughter, Harriet Adams. Using the pen name Carolyn Keene, the father and daughter wrote scores of mysteries for young Nancy to solve.

Stratemeyer also founded his own Literary Syndicate in New York City in 1906; he employed other writers to elaborate on the juvenile plots he had dreamed up and to create book-length stories out of them. Under this arrangement Stratemeyer was able to publish the Bobbsey twins books as well as the Tom Swift series and the Motor Boys books. During his lifetime he wrote over 150 books and originated the plots for more than 600 others.

ERIC KELLY (1884–1960) An American of English ancestry, Eric Kelly was one of our leading authorities on Polish history and culture. In 1928 he won the Newbery Medal, a prestigious award for juvenile literature, for *The Trumpeter of Krakow*. The Trumpeter, made possible by a grant from the Kosciuszko Foundation, has helped to introduce thousands of American children to Polish culture over the past fifty years.

CLEMENT C. MOORE (1779–1863) Clement Moore, an English-American, wrote "The Night Before Christmas" in 1822 for his own children. One of the most popular Christmas poems ever written, it was also published under the title "A Visit from St. Nicholas."

Born in New York City, Moore taught at Columbia University for almost three decades as a Professor of Oriental and Greek literature. He wrote a book of *Poems* (1844) and even authored a Hebrew dictionary, but his most famous work is the one parents read to their children each year to make "visions of sugarplums dance in their heads" on Christmas Eve.

MAURICE SENDAK (1928–   ) Nicknamed "the Picasso of children's books" for his unique style of illustration, Maurice Sendak is probably best known for his book *Where the Wild Things Are*. He won the Caldecott medal in 1964 for his imaginative and somewhat scary tale of Max and the "wild things" who "roared their terrible roars and gnashed their terrible teeth."

Born in Brooklyn, New York, Sendak is a second-generation Jewish-American whose parents emigrated from a *shtetl* in Poland.

DR. SEUSS (1904–   ) Dr. Seuss is the pen name of German-American writer Theodor Seuss Geisel. The good doctor has been delighting children for more than forty years with his wonderfully lyric works, which seem to roll off one's tongue.

Over the years, Dr. Seuss has written

Dr. Seuss. (Photograph by Antony di Gesu. Courtesy: Random House)

more than forty books for youngsters, including *The Cat in the Hat, Green Eggs and Ham,* and *How the Grinch Stole Christmas.* Like other authors who adopt pseudonyms, Geisel writes under more than one name. If he illustrates the book in addition to writing the verse, he uses the pen name Dr. Seuss. If he hires someone else to draw the illustrations, he uses the name Theo Le Sieg (Geisel, backwards).

BEST ETHNIC WRITINGS

Albanian:

DEMO, CONSTANTINE A.
  The Albanian in America: The First Arrivals.
  Boston: Society *Fatbardnesia* of Katundi, 1960.

ZAIMI, NEXHMIE
  Daughter of the Eagle: The Autobiography of an Albanian Girl.
  New York: Ives Washburn, 1937.
      Written by a twenty-two-year-old Wellesley student, this story is filled with the customs and practices of the author's homeland.

American Indian:

HILL, RUTH BEEBE
  Hanta Yo: An American Saga
  Garden City: Doubleday & Company, Inc., 1979.
      Hanta Yo is the story of four generations of

two Teton Sioux families between the late 1700s and the 1830s. Written in collaboration with Chunksa Yahu, a full-blooded Santee Sioux, Hill's book presents a view of American Indian life prior to the arrival of white settlers.

Armenian:

ARLEN, M. J.
  Passage to Ararat.
  New York: Ballantine Books, 1975.
  QUOTE: "At a particular time in my life, I set out on a voyage to discover for myself what it is to be Armenian. For although I myself am Armenian, or part Armenian, until then I knew nothing about either Armenians or Armenia . . . I felt generally American, or perhaps for a while Anglo-American, but clearly, there was also something missing . . ."

DER NERSESSIAN, SIRARPIE
The Armenians.
New York: Praeger, 1970.

FEDERAL WRITERS PROJECT
Armenians in Massachusetts.
Boston: (American Guide Series), 1975.
(Reprint of 1937 ed.)

HAGOPIAN, RICHARD
Faraway the Spring.
New York: Scribner's, 1952.

HARTUNIAN, VARTAN
Neither to Laugh nor to Weep.
Boston: Beacon Press, 1968.

HOGROGIAN, RACHEL
The Armenian Cooking.
New York: Atheneum, 1971.

HOUSEPIAN, MARJORIE
A Houseful of Love.
New York: Random House, 1957.

HUTCHINSON, E. P.
*Immigrants and Their Children, 1850–
1950.*
New York: John Wiley & Sons, Inc.,
1956.

KHERDIAN, D.
*The Road from Home: The Story of an
Armenian Girl.*
New York: William Morrow & Co.,
1978.

KULHANJIAN, GARY A.
*An Abstract of the Historical and Socio-
logical Aspects of Armenian Immigration to the United States, 1890–1930.*
San Francisco: R & E Research Associates, 1975.

MAHAKIAN, CHARLES
History of the Armenians in California.
Los Angeles: R & E Research Associ-
ates, 1974.

MALCOM, M. VARTAN
The Armenians in America.
Boston/Chicago: The Pilgrim Press,
1919.

MARDIKIAN, GEORGE
Song of America.
New York: McGraw-Hill, 1956.

SAROYAN, WILLIAM
My Name is Aram.
New York: Harcourt Brace Jovanovich:
1940.

SURMELIAN, LEON Z.
I Ask You, Ladies and Gentlemen.
New York: Dutton, 1945.

TASHJIAN, JAMES H.
The Armenians of the U.S. & Canada.
Boston: Armenian Youth Federation,
1947.

WERTSMAN, VLADIMIR
The Armenians in America, 1618–1976.
Dobbs Ferry: Oceana Publications,
1978.

Blacks:

APTHEKER, H. (ed.)
*A Documentary History of the Negro
People in the United States.*
New York: Citadel, 1951 (reprinted
1973).

BENNETT, LERONE, JR.
Before the Mayflower.
Chicago: Johnson, 1969.
Story of the Negro in America, 1619–1968.

BIRMINGHAM, STEPHEN
Certain People.
Boston: Little, Brown, 1977.

CURLEY, E. F.
Crispus Attucks: The First to Die.
Philadelphia: Dorrance, 1973.

DORMAN, J. H. AND R. R. JONES
*The Afro-American Experience: A Cul-
tural History Through Emancipation*
New York: Wiley, 1974.

DOVER, C.
American Negro Art.
Greenwich: New York Graphic Society,
1960.

FRANKLIN, J. H.
*From Slavery to Freedom: A History of
American Negroes.*
New York: Knopf, 1974.

GRAHAM, S.
*Jean Baptiste De Sable, Founder of Chi-
cago.*
New York: Nessner, 1953.

GREENE, R. E.
Black Defenders of America, 1775–1943.
Chicago: Johnson Publishing Co., 1974.

GREGORY, D.
Nigger.
New York: Dutton, 1964.

GUTMAN, H. G.
*The Black Family in Slavery and Free-
dom 1750–1925.*
New York: Vintage, 1976.
Refuting the theories that the family struc-
ture of Americans blacks was destroyed by

slavery, Gutman presents his case from narratives, plantation records and census tracts.

JACKSON, F.
The Black Man in America 1619–1790.
New York: Franklin Watts, 1970.
> Traces anti-slavery movement, and contributions made by outstanding black men from Jamestown on up to 1790.

KATZ, B. & J.
Black Woman: A Fictionalized Biography of Lucy Terry Prince.
New York: Pantheon, 1973.
> Part fact and part fiction, the biography of an early black pioneer woman.

LEWIS, C.
Benjamin Banneker.
New York: McGraw-Hill, 1970.

MELTZER, M.
In Their Own Words. A History of the American Negro 1619–1865.
New York: Crowell, 1964.
> History of American Blacks as revealed through excerpts from books, letters, interviews and government documents.

ORTIZ, V.
Sojourner Truth: A Self-Made Woman.
Philadelphia: Lippincott, 1974.

QUARLES, B.
The Negro in the American Revolution.
Williamsburg: University of North Carolina Press, 1961.
> The role played by Black Americans in the Revolution.

RANSOM, A. (ed.)
America's First Negro Poet: The Complete Works of Jupiter Hammon of Long Island.
Port Washington: J. Friedman Division, Kennikat Press, 1970.

RENFRO, H. G.
Life and Works of Phillis Wheatley.
Miami: 1969.
> Life of Phillis Wheatley, the first black poet to publish a book of poetry. A former slave, she was the first to use the word "Columbia" to describe our nation.

British:

BLACK, GEORGE F.
Scotland's Mark on America.
San Francisco: R & E Research Associates, 1972 (reprint of 1921 ed.).

BRIDGES, H. J.
On Becoming an American.
Boston: Jones, 1919.

GRAHAM, IAN C. C.
Colonists from Scotland: Emigration to North America, 1707–1783.
Ithaca, N.Y.: Cornell University Press, 1956.

HARTMANN, EDWARD G.
Americans from Wales.
Boston: Christopher Publishing House, 1967.

HUGHES, DAVID
The Welsh People of California, 1849–1906.
San Francisco? 1923?

NORTON, MARY BETH
The British Americans: The Loyalist Exiles in England, 1774–1789.
Boston: Little, Brown, 1972.

Chinese:

ARCHER, JULES
The Chinese and the Americans.
New York: Hawthorn Books, 1976.

BARTH, GUNTHER
Bitter Strength: A History of the Chinese in the United States, 1850–70.
Cambridge, Mass.: Harvard University Press, 1964.

HSU, FRANCIS L.
The Challenge of the American Dream: The Chinese in the United States.
Belmont: Wadsworth Publishing Company, 1971.

LEE, C. Y.
Flower Drum Song.
New York: Farrar, Straus and Cudahy, 1957.
> Famous as a book and a play, *Flower Drum Song* made Nancy Kwan a star.

LEE, CALVIN
Chinatown, U.S.A.
Garden City: Doubleday & Company, Inc., 1965.

LEE, ROSE HUM
The Chinese in the United States of America.
Hong Kong: Hong Kong University Press, 1960.

LEE SUNG, BETTY
Mountain of Gold: The Story of the Chinese in America.
New York: Macmillan, 1967.
> Historical look at Chinese immigration and life of the Chinese in America.

LYMAN, S. M.
Chinese Americans.
New York: Random House, 1974.

MILLER, STUART C.
Unwelcome Immigrant: The American Image of the Chinese, 1785–1882.
Berkeley: University of California Press, 1969.

WONG. JADE SNOW
Fifth Chinese Daughter.
New York: Harper and Row, 1950.
Memoir of life and family traditions in San Francisco's Chinatown.

YUNG WING
My Life in China and America.
New York: Holt, 1909.
Life of Yale's first Chinese student.

Croatian:

PREVEDEN, FRANCIS R.
A History of the Croatian People. 2 vols.
New York: Philosophical Library, Vol. 1, 1956; Vol 2, 1962.

PRPIC, GEORGE J.
The Croatian Immigrants in America.
New York: Philosophical Library, 1971.

Cubans:

BLANK, JOSEPH P.
"Escape from Cuba."
Readers Digest, May 1972.

JACOBY, SUSAN
"Miami Sí, Cuba No."
New York *Times* Magazine, Sept. 29, 1974.

NARVEZ, A. A.
"50,000 Cubans Add Prosperity and Problems to New Jersey."
New York *Times,* Nov. 24, 1970.

Czechs:

CAPEK, T.
Czechoslovak Immigration.
New York: Service Bureau for Intercultural Education, 1938.

CAPEK, T.
The Czechs (Bohemians) in America: A Study of Their National, Cultural, Political, Social, Economic, and Religious Life.
New York: Arno Press, 1969 (reprint of 1920 edition).

DVORNIK, E.
Czech Contributions to the Growth of the United States.
Chicago: Benedictine Abbey Press, 1962.

LASKA, V.
The Czechs in America, 1633–1977.
Dobbs Ferry: Oceana Publications, 1978.

MILLER, K. D.
The Czechoslovaks in America.
New York: Doran, 1922.

PSENCIK, L. F.
Czech Contributions to American Culture.
Austin: Texas Education Agency, 1970.

RECHCIGL, E.
Directory of the Members of the Czechoslovak Society of Arts and Sciences in America.
New York: Czechoslovak Society of Arts and Sciences in America, 1969.

ROUCEK, JOSEPH S.
The Czechs and Slovaks in America.
Minneapolis: Lerner Publications, 1967.

Danes:

BILLE, J. H.
A History of the Danes in America.
San Francisco: R. & E. Research Associates, 1971 (reprint of 1896 volume).

DANUS, E.
Danish American Journey.
Franklin, Massachusetts: Gauntlet, 1971.

MORTENSEN, E.
Danish American Life and Letters: A Bibliography.
New York: Arno Press, 1978 (reprint of 1945 book).

NIELSEN, A. C.
Life in an American Denmark.
Des Moines: Bookstore, Grande View College, 1962.
History of Danes who settled in Howard County, Nebraska.

Dutch:

BERTUS, HARRY WABEKE
Dutch Emigration to America, 1624–1860.
New York: Arno Press, 1944.

BOK, EDWARD W.
The Americanization of Edward Bok.
New York: Scribner's, 1920.
  Edward Bok (1863–1930) won a Pulitzer Prize for his autobiography in 1920. Although he was forced for financial reasons to leave school at the age of 13, he became a successful editor of the *Ladies Home Journal*, a position he held for over twenty years, and was praised for his literary talents. His book sold over 250,000 copies and he bequeathed 2 million dollars to charity.

DE JONG, D.C.
Belly Fulla Straw.
New York: Knopf, 1934.
With a Dutch Accent.
New York: Harper, 1944.
  Both books chronicle the author's journey from the Netherlands in 1918, and the difficulty he had becoming "Americanized."

DE JONG, G. F.
The Dutch in America, 1609–1974.
Boston: Twayne, 1975.

JANVIER, T. A.
The Dutch Founding of New York.
Port Washington: Kennikat, 1967.

LUCAS, HENRY S.
Dutch Immigrant Memoirs and Related Writings.
Assen: Van Gorcum's Historische Bibliotheek, 1955.

LUCAS, HENRY S.
Netherlands in America: Dutch Immigration to the United States and Canada, 1789–1950.
Ann Arbor: University of Michigan Press, 1955.

Arnold Mulder's novels, *The Dominie of Harlem* (Chicago: A. C. McClurg, 1913) and *The Outbound Road* (Boston: Houghton Mifflin, 1919), about the Dutch settlers in Michigan, describe the conflicts between the first generation—the immigrants—and their children, the second generation, who strive to be "American."

SINGLETON, E.
Dutch New York.
New York: Arno Press, 1968.

SMIT, J. W.
The Dutch in America, 1609–1970.
Dobbs Ferry: Oceana Publications, 1972.

Other books about the Dutch experience in America: Cobie De Lespinasse's *The Bells of Helmus* (1934) about Dutch set-tlers in Iowa; and Sara Elizabeth Gosse-link's *Roofs Over Strawtown* (1945), about the life of Hollanders in Pella, Iowa.

Estonians:

PENNAR, JAAN
The Estonians in America, 1627–1975.
Dobbs Ferry: Oceana Publications, 1975.

Filipino:

ALCANTARA, REUBEN R.
The Filipinos in Hawaii: An Annotated Bibliography.
Honolulu: Social Science Research Institute, University of Hawaii, 1972.

BUAKEN, MANUEL
I Have Lived with the American People.
Caldwell: Caxton Printers, 1948.

FERIA, BENNY F.
Filipino Son.
Boston: Meador, 1954.

KIM, HYUNG-CHAN
The Filipinos in America, 1898–1974.
Dobbs Ferry: Oceana Publications, 1976.

MUNOZ, ALFREDO
The Filipinos in America.
Los Angeles: Mountainview Publishers, 1971.

Finnish:

HOGLUND, WILLIAM
Finnish Immigrants in America, 1880–1920.
Madison: University of Wisconsin Press, 1960.

JALKANEN, RALPH J.
The Finns in North America.
Hancock: Michigan University Press, 1969.

KOLEHMAINEN, JOHN ILMARI
The Finns in America. A Bibliographical Guide to Their History.
Hancock: Teachers College, 1968.

LOUHI, E. A.
The Delaware Finns: or The First Permanent Settlements in Pennsylvania, Delaware, West New Jersey, and Eastern Part of Maryland.
New York: Humanity Press, 1925.

WARGELIN, JOHN
The Americanization of the Finns.
Hancock: The Finnish Lutheran Book Concern, 1924.

WUORINEN, J. H.
  The Finns on the Delaware, 1638–1655.
  New York: Arno Press, 1966 (reprint of
  1938 book).

French:

ECCLES, WILLIAM J.
  France in America.
  New York: Harper & Row, 1972.

FECTEAU, EDWARD
  French Contributions to America.
  Methven: Soucy Press, 1945.

HIRSCH, ARTHUR H.
  The Huguenots of Colonial South Caro-
  lina.
  Hamden, Conn.: Shoe String, 1973.

KUNZ, VIRGINIA B.
  The French in America.
  Minneapolis: Lerner Publications, 1966.

MORGAN, T.
  On Becoming American.
  Boston: Houghton Mifflin, 1978.
    A former French Count, Sanche de Gra-
    mont, became an American citizen in 1977, at
    which time he shed his title and his old name.

PULA, JAMES S.
  The French in America, 1488–1974.
  Dobbs Ferry: Oceana Publications,
  1975.

RONCIÈRE, CHARLES DE LA
  What the French have done in America.
  Paris: Typographie Lon-Nourrit et Cie,
  1915.

THWAITES, REUBEN G.
  France in America, 1497–1763.
  New York: Cooper Square, 1968.

ZOLTVANY, YVES F.
  The French Tradition in America.
  Columbia: University of South Carolina
  Press, 1969.

Germans:

BILLIGMEIER, ROBERT HENRY
  Americans from Germany. A Study in
  Cultural Diversity.
  Belmont: Wadsworth Publishing, 1974.

BITTINGER, LUCY F.
  The Germans in Colonial Times.
  New York: Russell & Russell, 1901, reis-
  sued 1968.

BOYERS, ROBERT (ed.)
  The Legacy of the German Refugee In-
  tellectuals.
  New York: Schocken, 1972.

FERMI, LAURA
  Illustrious Immigrants: The Intellectual
  Migration from Europe, 1930–1941.
  Chicago: University of Chicago Press,
  1968.

FURER, HOWARD
  The Germans in America, 1607–1970.
  Dobbs Ferry: Oceana Publications,
  1973.

KLOSS, HEINZ
  Atlas of German American Settlements.
  Marburg: N. G. Elwert, 1974.

O'CONNOR, RICHARD
  The German Americans.
  New York: Little, Brown and Co., 1946.

RIPPLEY, LA VERN J.
  The German Americans.
  Boston: Twayne Publishers, 1976.

ROTHAN, EMMET
  The German Catholic Immigrant in the
  United States, 1830–1860.
  Washington, D.C.: Catholic University
  Press, 1946.

SALLET, RICHARD
  The Russian German Settlements in the
  United States. Trans. by La Vern J.
  Rippley and Armand Bauer.
  Frago: Institute of Regional Studies,
  1974.

TOLZMANN, DON HEINRICH
  German Americans: A Bibliography.
  Metuchen: Scarecrow Press, 1975.

WOOD, RALPH (ed.)
  The Pennsylvania Germans.
  Princeton: Princeton University Press,
  1942.

WUST, KLAUS
  The Virginia Germans.
  Charlottesville: University of Virginia
  Press, 1969.

When Gottfried Duden returned to his native Germany in 1829 after a three-year visit to America, he began to write about his wonderful experiences in the New World. His descriptions of the "promised land" lured many Germans to America and earned him the nickname *der Lügenhund* ("lying dog"), because his descriptions were often rosier than the realities of pioneer life on America's plains.

Greeks:

ADAMIC, LOUIS
"Americans from Greece." *A Nation of Nations.*
New York: Harper, 1945.

BURGESS, T.
Greeks in America.
New York: Arno Press, 1975 (reprint 1913 book).

CANOUTAS, S. G.
Christopher Columbus: A Greek Nobleman.
New York: St. Mark's Press, 1943.

CATERAS, S.
Christopher Columbus Was a Greek Prince and His Real Name Was Nicolaos Ypsilantis.
Manchester, NH: 1937.

CUTSUMBIS, MICHAEL
A Bibliographic Guide to Materials on Greeks in the United States, 1890–1968.
New York: Center for Migration Studies, 1970.

FENTON, HEIKE, AND HECKER, MELVIN
The Greeks in America, 1528–1977.
Dobbs Ferry: Oceana Publications, 1978.

SALOUTOS, T.
The Greeks in the United States.
Cambridge: Harvard University Press, 1964.

STEPHANIDES, MARIOS
The Greeks in Detroit.
San Francisco: R & E Research Associates, 1975.

XENIDES, J. P.
The Greeks in America.
San Francisco: R & E Research Associates, 1972 (reprint of 1922 edition).

ZOTOS, STEPHANOS
Hellenic Presence in America.
Wheaton: Pilgrimage, 1976.

Hungarians:

ANTHONY, J.
Golden Village.
Indianapolis: Bobbs-Merrill, 1924.
The difficulties of assimilation in a rural village.

BABO, ELEMER
Guide to Hungarian Studies. A Bibliography. 2 vols.
Stanford: Hoover Institute Press, 1973.

BELL, T.
Out of This Furnace.
Boston: Little, Brown, 1941.
Family problems of workers in Pennsylvania's steel mills.

COOK, HULDA FLORENCE
The Magyars of Cleveland.
Cleveland: Cleveland Americanization Committee, 1919.

GRACZA, REZSOE AND MARGARET
The Hungarians in America.
Minneapolis: Lerner Publications Co., 1969.

HANZELL, VICTOR E.
The Hungarians.
New Haven: Human Relations Area Files, Yale University, 1955.

Hungarians in the U.S.A.: An Immigration Study.
St. Louis: The American Hungarian Review, 1967.

KONNYU, L.
A History of American Hungarian Literature.
St. Louis: Cooperative of American Hungarian Writers, 1962.

KOROSFOY, JOHN
Hungarians in America.
Cleveland: Szabadsag, 1941.

LENGYEL, EMIL
Americans from Hungary.
Westport: Greenwood Press, 1975.

STIBRAN, TEREZ D.
The Streets Are Not Paved with Gold.
Cleveland: Printing Co., 1961.

SZEPLAKI, JOSEPH
The Hungarians in America, 1583–1974.
Dobbs Ferry: Oceana Publications, 1975.

Icelandic:

STEFANSSON, V.
Iceland: The First American Republic.
Westport: Greenwood Press, 1971 (reprint of 1939 edition).

WALTERS, T.
Modern Sagas: The Story of the Icelanders in North America.
Fargo: Institute for Regional Studies, 1953.

Irish:

BYRNE, STEPHEN
Irish Emigration to the United States.
New York: Arno Press, 1969.

COCHRAN, AL. L.
The Saga of an Irish Immigrant Family.
New York: Arno Press, 1976.
  Study of a Midwest Irish family from 1792
  when John Mullanphy left his Irish homeland
  and settled in St. Louis.

DUFF, JOHN B.
The Irish in the United States.
Belmont, Calif.: Wadsworth, 1971.

GRIFFIN, WILLIAM D. (comp.)
The Irish in America, 550–1972.
Dobbs Ferry: Oceana Publications,
1973.

MACLYSAGHT, EDWARD
Irish Families: Their Names, Arms, and
Origins.
New York: Crown, 1972.

MCDONALD, G.
*History of the Irish in Wisconsin in the
Nineteenth Century.*
Washington, D.C.: Arno Press, 1976 (re-
print of 1954 edition).

MCCAFFREY, LAWRENCE
The Irish Diaspora in America.
Bloomington: Indiana University Press,
1978.

MAGUIRE, JOHN FRANCIS
The Irish in America.
New York: Arno Press, 1969.

MURPHY, EUGENE
An Album of the Irish Americans.
New York: Watts, 1974.

O'DONOVAN, J.
*Irish Immigration in the United States:
Immigrant Interviews.*
New York: Arno Press, 1976 (reprint of
1864 book).

O'GRADY, J. P.
*Irish-Americans and Anglo-American
Relations, 1880–1888.*
New York: Arno Press, 1976.

VINEYARD, J. M.
The Irish on the Urban Frontier.
New York: Arno Press, 1976.
  Urban ghetto experience of Irish settlers in
  nineteenth century America: how they main-
  tained their ethnicity and attained success in
  Detroit.

WITTKE, C.
The Irish in America.
New York: Russell and Russell, 1956.
Re-issued 1970, Louisiana State Uni-
versity Press.

Italians:

BARZINI, L.
*O America: When You and I Were
Young.*
New York: Harper and Row, 1977.

CANZONERI, R.
A Highly Ramified Tree.
New York: Viking, 1976.
  Warm account of an American's return to
  Sicily with his eighty-three-year-old father.
  Canzoneri describes meeting his Sicilian rela-
  tives for the first time and recalls his boyhood
  as the son of an immigrant Southern Baptist
  preacher in a small town in the South.

D'AGOSTINO, G.
Olives on the Apple Tree.
New York: Doubleday, 1940.

DELLA FEMINA, JERRY, AND SOPKIN,
  CHARLES
An Italian Grows in Brooklyn.
Boston: Little, Brown, 1978.
  Advertising executive Jerry Della Femina
  grew up in a tough Brooklyn neighborhood he
  describes as "the worst breeding ground for
  lower middle class nonentities in the United
  States." In this book he reminisces about the
  "bad old days"—the neighborhood was poor,
  the family was in need, there was violence everywhere, and anyone who could escaped
  from the neighborhood. "I sometimes wake
  up in the middle of the night in a stone-cold
  sweat saying, 'Jesus, what a close call. They
  almost got me.'"

DE CONDE, A.
*Half Bitter, Half Sweet: An Excursion
  into Italian-American History.*
New York: Scribner's Sons, 1971.

DI DONATO, P.
Christ in Concrete.
New York: Pocket Books, 1978.
  Reissue of 1939 classic about immigrant
  life. Pietro di Donato recounts, in rhythmic
  Italian-American speech, the life of a New
  Jersey bricklayer and his family. When the fa-
  ther is killed in an accident, his eldest son is
  left to support his mother and seven younger
  sisters and brothers. Di Donato himself was a
  bricklayer, the son of immigrants from
  Abruzzi.

FANTE, G.
Dago Red.
New York: Viking, 1940.
An Italian boy grows up in Denver.

FEDERAL WRITERS PROJECT.
The Italians of New York.
New York: Random House, 1938.

FOERSTER, R. F.
The Italian Emigration of Our Times.
Cambridge: Harvard University Press, 1919.

GAMBINO, R.
Blood of My Blood: The Dilemma of the Italian-Americans.
Garden City: Doubleday, 1974.

GAMBINO, R.
Vendetta.
New York: Doubleday, 1977.
Story of the "largest lynching in American history."

IORIZZO, L. J., AND S. MONDELLO
The Italian-Americans.
New York: Twayne, 1971.

Italian Americans: A Guide to Information Sources.
Chicago: Gale, 1978.

LO GATTO, A. F.
The Italians in America, 1492–1972.
Dobbs Ferry: Oceana Publications, 1972.

MANGIONE, J.
Mount Allegro.
New York: Houghton, 1942.
Described by critics as "an Italian *Life with Father,*" Mangione's book described life in Mount Allegro, the "Little Italy" of Rochester, New York.

MOQUIN, W., AND VAN DOREN, C.
A Documentary History of the Italian-Americans.
New York: Praeger, 1974.

NELLI, H. S.
The Italians in Chicago, 1880–1930.
New York: Oxford University Press, 1970.

NULL, G., AND STONE, C.
The Italian Americans.
Harrisburg, Pa.: Stackpole Books, 1976.

PISANI, L. F.
The Italian in America.
New York: Exposition Press, 1957.

PUZO, M.
The Fortunate Pilgrim.
New York: Fawcett, 1978.
Puzo's first book, though critically acclaimed, was a financial failure. That's when he decided to write about Italian-Americans the way the public really wants to read about them: the result of this decision was, of course, *The Godfather.*

SCHIAVO, G.
Four Centuries of Italian American History.
New York: Vigo, 1958.

SORRENTINO, J.
Up from Never.
New York: Bantam, 1971.
Autobiography of an Italian-American from Brooklyn who drops out of high school, is thrown out of the Marine Corps, goes to jail, but conquers all odds by becoming a Harvard Law School graduate.

TOMASI, M.
Deep Grow the Roots.
Philadelphia: J. B. Lippincott, 1940.

Japanese:

CHUMAN, F. F.
The Bamboo People.
Del Mar: Publishers Inc., 1976.
One-hundred-year account of Japanese immigrants, their persecution and their struggle for justice in America.

HOSOKAWA, BILL
Nisei.
New York: William Morrow & Co., 1969.

ICHIHASHI, YAMATO
Japanese in the United States.
New York: Arno Press, 1969.

KITANO, HARRY
Japanese-Americans: The Evolution of a Subculture.
Englewood Cliffs: Prentice-Hall, 1969.

LIGHT, I. H.
Ethnic Enterprise in America.
University of California Press, 1972.
Examines the Chinese and Japanese credit associations and trade guides that helped the Oriental businessman succeed by providing capital to help local store owners and shopkeepers become established. Compares their situation to that of the freed blacks, who lacked such organizations in Northern cities.

MASAKO, H.
The Japanese in America, 1843–1973.
Dobbs Ferry: Oceana Publications, 1974.

MATSUDA, MITSUGU
The Japanese in Hawaii, 1868–1967.
Honolulu: University of Hawaii Press, 1968.

PETERSON, WILLIAM
Japanese Americans: Oppression and Success.
New York: Random House, 1971.

SARASOHN, EILEEN
Issei Means Pioneer.
Sacramento: California Journal Press, 1978 (new edition).

WEGLYN, MICHI
Years of Infamy: The Untold Story of America's Concentration Camps
New York: William Morrow, 1976.

Jewish:

ANTIN, MARY
The Promised Land
Boston: Houghton Mifflin, 1969.

BARON, SALO W., AND BLAU, JOSEPH L. (eds.)
A Documentary History of the Jews of the United States, 1790–1840. 3 vols.
Philadelphia: Jewish Publication Society.
New York: Columbia University Press, 1964.

BIRMINGHAM, STEPHEN
Our Crowd.
New York: Harper & Row, 1967.

BAUM, C., AND P. HYMAN
The Jewish Woman in America.
New York: The Dial Press, 1976.

GAY, RUTH
Jews in America.
New York: Basic Books, 1965.

GLAZER, NATHAN
American Judaism.
Chicago: University of Chicago Press, 1957.

GOLDSTEIN, SIDNEY, AND GOLDSCHEIDER, CALVIN
Jewish-Americans.
Englewood Cliffs: Prentice-Hall, Inc., 1968.

HANDLIN, OSCAR
Adventure in Freedom: 300 Years of Jewish Life in America.
New York: McGraw-Hill, 1954.

HOWE, IRVING
World of Our Fathers.
New York: Touchstone/Simon and Schuster, 1976.
Story of Eastern European Jews and the life they created and shared in America. "This book tells the story of those East European Jews who, for several decades starting in the 1880s, undertook a massive migration to the United States. There were two million of them, and they settled mostly in the large American cities, where they attempted to maintain their own Yiddish culture; then, as a result of both external pressures and their own desires, they made their way into American society. Among the Jews settling in America, the East Europeans were by far the largest complement and thus the most influential. To tell their story is, to a considerable extent, to tell the story of twentieth-century American Jews."

KAZIN, A.
New York Jew.
New York: Knopf, 1978.
Completes a trilogy (*A Walker in the City; Starting Out in the Thirties*) by Kazin about his life in New York; this volume deals with his experiences as editor of *The New Republic,* from 1942 on.

KERTZER, MORRIS N.
Today's American Jew.
New York: McGraw-Hill Book Co., 1967.

MELTZER, M.
Remember the Days.
Garden City: Zenith Books, 1974.
Short history of Jewish Americans.

POSTAL, B., AND FLEET, L. KOPPMAN
Jewish Landmarks of New York.
New York: Fleet, 1978.
Tracing the history of the Jewish community of New York from 1654, Postal and Koppman have assembled a remarkable fact book which includes such information as a list of Manhattan's kosher restaurants; a directory of synagogues, organizations and bookstores; little-known facts about pre-Revolutionary Jews in America; and a borough-by-borough breakdown of Jewish neighborhoods.

ROCKLAND, M. S.
The Jewish Yellow Pages.
New York: Schocken Books, 1976.

ROTTENBERG, DAN
Finding Our Fathers. A Guidebook to Jewish Genealogy.
New York: Random House, 1978.
Deals with the special problems faced by Jews in finding their forebears. Rottenberg

takes the reader step by step through the memories of living relatives, to the examination of existing documents such as marriage licenses, passenger-ship lists, and birth and death certificates both here and abroad. He explains special clues that can be found in family customs, and how you can track down your family's tribal origins through Biblical names.

Includes a guide to 8,000 Jewish names and their origins; a guide to tracing Jewish ancestors abroad; a guide to U.S. resources; and a guide to researching Jewish genealogy in the Mormon collection.

ROTH, H.
Call It Sleep.
New York: Avon Books, 1974.

SHERMAN, BEZALEL
The Jew Within American Society.
Detroit: Wayne State University Press, 1965.

SUHL, YURI
An Album of the Jews in America.
New York: Franklin Watts, 1972.
Jewish contributions to America, from 1492 to present.

TELLER, JUDD L.
Strangers and Natives.
New York: Dell Publishing Co., 1969.

TENNENBAUM, SYLVIA
Rachel, the Rabbi's Wife.
New York: William Morrow, 1978.

YAFFE, JAMES
American Jews.
New York: Random House, 1968.

Latvians:

AKMENTINS, O.
Latvians in Bicentennial America.
Latvju Gramata, 1976.

KARKLIS, M., et al.
The Latvians in America, 1640–1973.
Dobbs Ferry: Oceana Publications, 1974.

Order through:
Latvian Book Shop
27 Miller Place
Hempstead, N.Y. 11550

Lebanese and Syrians:

HITTI, PHILIP K.
Syrians in America.
New York: George H. Doran Company, 1924.

KAYAL, JOSEPH
The Syrian Lebanese in America.
Boston: Twayne, 1975.

KAYAL, JOSEPH M. AND PHILIP M.
The Syrian-Lebanese in America: A Study in Religion and Assimilation.
Boston: Twayne Publishers, 1975.

KAYAL, PHILIP M.
The Arab Christians of America.
Boston: Twayne Publishers, 1974.

RIZK, SALOM
Syrian Yankee.
Garden City: Doubleday & Co., 1943.

WAKIN, EDWARD
The Lebanese and Syrians in America.
Chicago: Claretian, 1971.

Lithuanians:

ALILUNAS, L. J. (ed.)
Lithuanians in the United States: Selected Studies.
San Francisco: R & E Research Associates, 1978.

BALYS, J.
Lithuania and Lithuanians: A Selected Bibliography.
New York: Praeger, 1961.

BUDRECKIS, A. M.
The Lithuanians in America, 1651–1975: A Chronology and Fact Book.
Dobbs Ferry: Oceana Publications, 1976.

GIMBUTAS, MARIJA
The Balts.
New York: Praeger, 1963.

KUCAS, A.
Lithuanians in America.
San Francisco: R & E Research Associates.

MARGERIS, ALGIRDAS
The Lithuanian Americans and a Dictionary of English Loanwords in Lithuanian.
Chicago: 1956.

ROUCEK, J. S.
American Lithuanians.
New York: Lithuanian Alliance of America, 1940.

ST. ZOBARSKAS (ed.)
Lithuanian Folk Tales.
New York: Voyages Press, 1959.

SINCLAIR, UPTON
The Jungle.
New York: New American Library, 1971 (reprint of 1906 book).
  Besides highlighting the abuses of the meat-packing industry in the late nineteenth and early twentieth century, *The Jungle* provides a look at the life of Lithuanian immigrants to Chicago.

SUZIEDELIS, S.
Encyclopedia Lituanica.
Boston: Juozas Kapocius, 1967.

VITKAUSKAS, AREJAS
An Immigrant's Story.
New York: Philosophical Library, 1956.

Mexicans:

BARRIO, RAYMOND
The Plum Plum Pickers.
New York: Canfield/Colophon Books, 1971.

CORTES, CARLOS (ed.)
The Mexican American: Mexican American Bibliographies.
New York: Arno Press, 1974.

GALARZA, ERNESTO, et al.
Mexican Americans in the Southwest.
Santa Barbara: McNally & Loftin, 1960.

GARCIA, RICHARD A.
The Chicanos in America, 1540–1974.
Dobbs Ferry: Oceana Publications, 1977.

GONZALEZ, RUDOLFO
I am Joaquín: An Epic Poem.
New York: Bantam Books, 1973.

HEATHMAN, JAMES E., AND MARTINEZ, CECILIA J.
Mexican American Education: A Selected Bibliography.
University Park: New Mexico State University, 1969.

MCWILLIAMS, CAREY
North from Mexico: The Spanish Speaking People of the United States.
New York: Greenwood Press, 1968.

MARTINEZ, J.
Mexican Emigration to the U.S.
San Francisco: R & E Research Associates, 1971.

The Mexican Immigrant: His Life Story.
New York: Arno Press, 1969.

MIER, MATT S., AND RIVERA, FELICIANO
The Chicanos: A History of Mexican Americans.
New York: Hill and Wang, 1972.

MOQUIN, WAYNE, AND VAN DOREN, CHARLES (eds.)
A Documentary History of the Mexican Americans.
New York: Bantam Books, 1971.

NAVARRO, ELISEO A. (comp.)
The Chicano Community: A Selected Bibliography for Use in Social Work Education.
New York: Council on Social Work Education, 1971.

NOGALES, LUIS (comp.)
The Mexican American: A Select and Annotated Bibliography.
Stanford: Stanford University, 1969.

PAREDES, AMERICO
With His Pistol in His Hand.
Austin: University of Texas Press, 1971.

PINCHOT, J.
The Mexicans in America.
Minneapolis: Lerner Publications, 1973.

STEINER, STAN
La Raza: The Mexican Americans.
New York: Harper & Row, 1968.

VASQUEZ, R.
Chicano.
Garden City: Doubleday & Co., 1970.
  A newspaperman examines the struggles of three generations of Mexicans who strive to enter the mainstream of American life. Vasquez depicts the problems, progress and general difficulties encountered by Mexican-Americans in the Southwest.

VILLARREAL, JOSE ANTONIO
Pocho.
New York: Anchor Books, 1970.

VILLASENOR, EDMUND
Macho.
New York: Bantam Books, 1973.

Norwegians:

ANDERSON, ARLOW WILLIAM
The Norwegian-Americans.
Boston: Twayne, 1975.

BLEGEN, THEODORE CHRISTIAN
The Norwegian Migration to America, 1891–1969. 2 vols.
New York: Arno Press, 1969.

ROLVAAG, O.
Giants in the Earth.
New York: Harper and Row, 1965.
  Tale of a Norwegian immigrant farmer and his wife, who eventually succumbs to madness; shows the difficulties they faced as pioneers on the South Dakota plains.

RYGG, ANDREW NILSEN
Norwegians in New York, 1825–1925.
Brooklyn: Norwegian News Company, 1941.

SUNBY-HANSEN, HARRY
Norwegian Immigrant Contributions to America's Making.
San Francisco: R & E Research Associates, 1970.

Polish:

ALGREN, NELSON
The Neon Wilderness.
Garden City: Doubleday & Co., 1947.

BANKOWSKY, R.
Glass Rose.
New York: Random House, 1958.
    Story of the rise and fall of a Polish immigrant family in New Jersey, told through recollections of family members and friends at the wake of Stanislaw Machek.

BOLEK, F., AND SIEKANIEC, L. J.
Polish American Encyclopedia.
Buffalo: Polish American Encyclopedia Committee, 1954.

BOLEK, F.
Who's Who in Polish America.
New York: Arno Press, 1970 (reprint of 1943 issue).

DWORACZYK, E. J.
The First Polish Colonies of Americans in Texas.
San Francisco: R & E Research Associates, 1969 (reprint of 1936 work).

GREEN, V.
For God and Country: The Rise of Polish and Lithuanian Ethnic Consciousness in America.
State Historical Society, Wisconsin, 1975.

GRONOWICZ, ANTONI
An Orange Full of Dreams.
New York: Dodd, Mead, 1971.

KUNICZAK, W. S.
My Name is Million.
Garden City: Doubleday & Co., 1978.

LOPATA, H. Z.
Polish Americans.
Englewood Cliffs: Prentice-Hall, 1976.

Poland and the Poles in America.
Chicago: Polish American Congress, 1971.

RENKIEWICZ, F. A.
The Poles in America, 1608–1972.
Dobbs Ferry: Oceana Publications, 1973.

REYMONT, WLADYSLAW
The Peasants.
New York: Knopf, 1924.

THOMAS, WILLIAM I., AND ZNANIECKI, FLORIAN
The Polish Peasant in Europe and America.
New York: Dover Publications, 1958.

WANDYCZ, D. S.
Register of Polish American Scholars, Scientists, Writers, and Artists.
New York: Polish Institute of Arts and Sciences in America, 1969.

WIECZERZAK, J. W.
A Polish Chapter in Civil War America.
New York: Twayne, 1967.

WOOD, ARTHUR EVANS
Hamtramck, Then and Now: A Sociological Study of a Polish American Community.
New York: Bookman Associates, 1955.

WYTRWAL, J. A.
America's Polish Heritage.
Detroit: Endurance Press, 1961.

Portuguese:

ANDRADE, L. C.
The Open Door.
New Bedford
    Story of Portuguese immigrant to Massachusetts who started working in the local cotton mills, and later instituted the first high school language courses in Portuguese ever conducted in the United States.

CARDOZO, MANOEL DA SILVEIRA SOARES
The Portuguese in America, 590 B.C.–1974.
Dobbs Ferry: Oceana Publications, 1976.

EELLS, E. S.
The Islands of Magic.
New York: Harcourt, Brace and Co., 1922.
    Collection of folk and fairy tales and legends from the Azores, including "why dogs sniff" and other "true" tales which have been passed down orally for generations.

LEY, CHARLES DAVID
Portuguese Voyages, 1498–1663.
New York: Gordon, 1977.

"Portuguese in America."
Literary Digest, vol. 63, November 22, 1919.

MAZZANTENTA, O. LOUIS
"New England's 'Little Portugal.'"
National Geographic 147: Jan., 1975, pp. 90-109.

MORISON, SAMUEL ELIOT
Portuguese Voyages to America in the Fifteenth Century.
New York: Octagon, 1965.

PRESTAGE, EDGAR
The Portuguese Pioneers.
London: A. & C. Black Ltd., 1933.

TAVERS, B.E.
Portuguese Pioneers in the United States.
Fall River, Massachusetts.

VAZ, AUGUST MARK
The Portuguese in California.
Oakland: I.D.E.S. Supreme Council, 1965.

Puerto Ricans:

CADILLA DE MARTINEZ, MARIA
Costumbres Y Tradicionalismos De Mi Tierra.
San Juan: Imprenta Venezuela, 1938.
Origin of customs and traditions of Puerto Ricans—dance, religion, superstition, etc.

CHENAULT, LAWRENCE
The Puerto Rican Migrant in New York City.
New York: Russell, 1970.

CORDASCO, FRANCESCO, AND BUCCHIONI, EUGENE
The Puerto Rican Experience.
Totowa: Rowman & Littlefield, 1973.

CORDASCO, FRANCESCO
The Puerto Ricans, 1493-1973.
Dobbs Ferry: Oceana Publications, 1973.

FITZPATRICK, JOSEPH P.
Puerto Rican Americans: The Meaning of Migration to the Mainland.
Englewood Cliffs: Prentice-Hall, 1971.

GLAZER, NATHAN, AND MOYNIHAN, DANIEL PATRICK
Beyond the Melting Pot.
Cambridge: Harvard University Press, 1963.

HANDLIN, OSCAR
The Newcomers.
Cambridge: Harvard University Press, 1959.

HAMILL, PETE
"Coming of Age in Nueva York."
New York, II, pp. 33-44, 47. November 24, 1969.

HANSEN, TERRENCE LESLIE
The Types of the Folktale in Cuba, Puerto Rico, the Dominican Republic, and Spanish South America.
Berkeley: University of California Press, 1957.
Folktales of Hispanic America.

LARSEN, RONALD J.
The Puerto Ricans in America.
Minneapolis: Lerner, 1973.

LEWIS, OSCAR
La Vida.
New York: Random House, 1965.

MARDEN, CHARLES F., AND MEYER, GLADYS
Minorities in American Society. 3rd ed.
New York: American Book Co., 1968.

PADILLA, E.
Up from Puerto Rico.
New York: Columbia University Press, 1959.
Plight of New York City's Puerto Rican population. An anthropologist's description of the life and changing cultural patterns of Puerto Ricans living in Spanish Harlem.

SENIOR, CLARENCE
Strangers—Then Neighbors.
New York: Freedom Books, 1961.

WAKEFIELD, DAN
Island in the City.
Boston: Houghton Mifflin Co., 1959.

Romanian:

ANISOARA, S.
They Crossed Mountains and Oceans.
New York: William Frederick Press, 1947.

The Romanian Cooking.
New York: Citadel Press, 1969.

GALITZI, CHRISTINE AVGHI
A Study of Assimilation Among the Romanians in the United States.
New York: Columbia University Press, 1929.

NEAGOE, PETER
Easter Sun.
New York: Coward-McCann, Inc., 1934.

RADU, F., AND MCNALLY, R.
In Search of Dracula: A True History of Dracula and Vampire Legends.
Greenwich: Graphic Society, 1972.
Scholarly study of the Romanian prince, Vlad the Impaler, who came to be known as "Dracula." It was Vlad's life that inspired British writer Bram Stoker to pen his famous chiller *Dracula* in 1897.

RAVAGE, M. E.
An American in the Making.
New York: Harper, 1936.

VASILIU, MIRCEA
Which Way to the Melting Pot?
New York: Doubleday & Co., 1963.

Russians:

ARGUS, M. K.
Moscow on the Hudson.
New York: Harper & Row, 1951.
A newspaper writer for *Novoye Russkoye Slovo,* Argus describes his humorous adventures as a Russian immigrant married to an "American."

BERGMAN, M.
The Russian American Song and Dance Book.
New York: A. S. Barnes and Co., 1947.

DAVID, J.
The Russian Immigrant.
New York: Macmillan, 1969 (reprint of 1922 edition).

EUBANK, N.
The Russians in America.
Minneapolis: Lerner Publications, 1973.

HUTCHINSON, E. P.
Immigrants and Their Children: 1850– 1950.
New York: John Wiley and Sons, 1956.
Social and economic aspects of Russian immigration.

NABOKOV, V.
Pnin.
New York: Doubleday and Co., 1957.
Satiric novel of the life of an emigré Russian professor at a New York State college.

WERTSMAN, V.
The Russians in America: A Chronology and Fact Book.
Dobbs Ferry: Oceana Publications, 1977.

Scandinavians:

FONKALSRUD, ALFRED O.
The Scandinavian-American.
San Francisco: R & E Research Associates.

FURER, HOWARD B.
The Scandinavian in America, 986–1970.
Dobbs Ferry: Oceana Publications, 1972.

NEIDLE, CECYLE S.
The New Americans.
New York: Twayne, 1967.

NELSON, O. N.
History of the Scandinavians and Successful Scandinavians in the U.S.A.
New York: Haskell House, 1969 (reprint of 1904 work).

Scottish and Scotch-Irish:

BLACK, G. F.
Scotland's Mark on America.
San Francisco: R & E Research Associates, 1972 (reprint of 1921 book).

FORD, HENRY JONES
The Scotch Irish in America.
New York: Arno Press 1969 (reprint of 1915 edition).

GREEN, SAMUEL SWETT
The Scotch Irish in America.
San Francisco: R & E Research Associates.

REID, WHITELAW
The Scot in America and the Ulster Scot.
San Francisco: R & E Research Associates, 1970 (reprint of 1911 address).

Slaves:

GIMBUTAS, MARIJA
The Slavs.
New York: Praeger, 1971.

PEHOTSKY, BESSIE OLGA
The Slavic Immigrant Woman.
San Francisco: R & E Research Associates.

PORTAL, ROGER
The Slavs.
New York: Harper & Row, 1969.

ROUCEK, JOSEPH S.
Slavonic Encyclopedia.
Port Washington: Kennikat Press, 1969 (reprint of 1949 edition).

VJEKOSLAV, MELER.
The Slavonic Pioneers of California.
San Francisco: R & E Research Associates, 1972 (reprint of 1932 book).

WERLING, JOAN
History of the Slavs in Arizona: 1864–1912.
San Francisco: R & E Research Associates, 1968.

Slovak:

Panorama: A Historical Review of Czechs and Slovaks in the United States of America.
Cicero, Illinois: Czechoslovak National Council of America, 1971.

MILLER, K. D.
The Czecho-Slovaks in America.
New York: Doran, 1922.

ROUCEK, J. S.
The Czechs and Slovaks in America.
Minneapolis: Lerner Publications, 1967.

STASKO, J.
Slovaks in the United States of America.
Cambridge: Dobra Kniha, 1974.

Slovenian:

PRISLAND, MARIE
From Slovenia to America.
Chicago: Slovenian Women's Union of America, 1968.

PRPIC, GEORGE P.
On South Slav Immigrants in America and Their Historical Background.
Cleveland: John Carroll University, 1972.

ROUCEK, JOSEPH S., AND PINKHAM, PATRICIA
American Slavs: A Bibliography.
New York: Bureau of Intercultural Education, 1944.

Spanish / Hispanic:

ALFORD, HAROLD J.
The Proud Peoples: The Heritage and Culture of Spanish Speaking Peoples in the United States.
New York: David McKay Company, Inc., 1972.

EISEMAN, A.
Mañana Is Now.
New York: Atheneum, 1973.

GONZALEZ, NANCIE L.
The Spanish Americans of New Mexico: A Heritage of Pride.
Albuquerque: University of New Mexico Press, 1967.

NATELLA, ARTHUR A., JR. (comp. & ed.)
The Spanish in America, 1513–1974.
Dobbs Ferry: Oceana Publications Inc., 1975.

PIKE, FREDERICK B.
Spanish America, 1900–1970: Tradition and Social Innovation.
New York: Norton, 1973.

PINERO, M.
Short Eyes.
New York: Hill & Wang, 1975.
Winner of the New York Drama Critics Circle Award for 1973–1974 season. Pinero's play portrays daily life in a house of detention.

Swedish:

BENSON, ADOLPH B., AND HEDIN, NABOTH
Americans from Sweden.
Philadelphia: Lippincott, 1950.

JANSON, FLORENCE EDITH
The Background of Swedish Immigration, 1840–1930.
New York: Arno Press, 1970 (reprint of 1931 edition).

KASTRUP, ALLAN
The Swedish Heritage in America.
Minneapolis: Swedish Council of America, 1975.

LEIBY, A.
The Early Dutch and Swedish Settlers of New Jersey.
Princeton: Van Nostrand, 1964.

NELSON, HELGE
The Swedes and Swedish Settlements in North America. 2 vols.
New York: 1943.

Ukrainian:

CHYZ, YAROSLAW J.
The Ukrainian Immigrants in the United States.
Scranton: Ukrainian Workingmen's Association, 1940.

HALICH, WASYL
Ukrainians in the United States.
New York: Arno Press, 1970 (reprint of 1937 edition).

KUBIJOVIC, VOLODYMYR
Ukraine: A Concise Encyclopedia.
Toronto: University of Toronto Press, 1963.

KUROPAS, M.
Ukrainians in America.
Minneapolis: Lerner Publications, 1972.

SHTOHRYN, D. M.
Ukrainians in North America: A Biographical Directory of Noteworthy Men and Women of Ukrainian Origin in the United States and Canada.
Champaign: Assoc. for the Advancement of Ukrainian Studies, 1975.

STECHISHIN, SAVELLA
Traditional Ukrainian Cookery.
Winnipeg: Trident Press, 1959.

WERSTMAN, V.
The Ukrainians in America, 1608–1975: A Chronology and Fact Book.
Dobbs Ferry: Oceana Publications, 1976.

Yugoslavs:

ADAMIC, L.
Laughing in the Jungle: The Autobiography of an Immigrant in America.
New York: Arno Press, 1969 (reprint of 1932 book).

ADAMIC, L.
The Native's Return: An American Immigrant Visits Yugoslavia and Discovers His Old Country.
New York: Harpers, 1934.

COLAKOVIC, B. M.
Yugoslav Migrations to America.
San Francisco: R & E Research Associates, 1972.

ETEROVICH, A. S.
A Guide and Bibliography to Research on Yugoslavs in the United States and Canada.
San Francisco: R & E Research Associates, 1975.

ETEROVICH, ADAM S.
Yugoslavs in Nevada, 1859–1900.
San Francisco: R & E Research Associates, 1973.

GOVORCHIN, G. G.
Americans from Yugoslavia: A Survey of Yugoslav Immigrants in the United States.
Gainesville: University of Florida Press, 1961.

VUJNOVICH, MILOS M.
Yugoslavs in Louisiana.
Gretna, La.: Pelican, 1974.

Immigrant Experience

AGUEROS, JACK
The Immigrant Experience: The Anguish of Becoming American.
New York: Dial Press, 1971.

COPPA, F. J., AND T. J. CURRAN
The Immigrant Experience in America.
Boston: Twayne, 1976.

DOLAN, JAY P.
The Immigrant Church.
Johns Hopkins University Press, 1977.
    A look at the conflicts between Irish and German Catholics during the mid-1800s, as both groups struggled to maintain their ethnic identities while living in a Protestant environment.

FAST, HOWARD MELVIN
The Immigrants.
New York: Dell, 1978.

GREELEY, ANDREW M.
Why Can't They Be Like Us?
New York: Dutton, 1971.

GREENLEAF, B. K.
American Fever.
New York: Four Winds Press, 1970.
    Story of American immigration.

HANDLIN, OSCAR
The Uprooted.
Boston: Little, Brown, 1951.

HANSEN, M. L.
The Atlantic Migration, 1607–1860.
New York: Harper, 1940.

HANSEN, MARCUS LEE
The Immigrant in American History, 1892–1938.
Cambridge, Mass.: Harvard University Press, 1940.

HARNEY, ROBERT F.
Immigrants.
Toronto: Van Nostrand Reinhold, 1975.

KATZ, W. L. AND J. H.
Making Our Way.
New York: Dial, 1975.
    "America at the turn of the century, through the eyes of the poor and powerless."

KENNEDY, J. F.
A Nation of Immigrants.
New York: Harper and Row, 1964.

NOVAK, M.
The Rise of the Unmeltable Ethnics.
New York: Macmillan, 1971.

NOVOTNY, A.
Strangers at the Door.
Riverside: Chatham Press, 1971.

PEOPLE'S BICENTENNIAL COMMISSION
Early American Almanac.
New York: Simon and Schuster, 1974.
    Contains dates, maxims, recipes and anec-
    dotes about early days in America.

TYLER, POYNTZ (ed.)
Immigration and the United States.
New York: Wilson, 1956.

Useful Directories:

AMERICAN COUNCIL FOR NATIONALITIES
*Foreign Language Radio Stations in the
U.S.A.*
New York: 1970.

FISK, MARGARET, et al. (eds.)
Encyclopedia of Associations.
Detroit: Gale Research Company, 1975.

WYNAR, LUBOMIR
*Encyclopedic Directory of Ethnic News-
papers and Periodicals in the United
States.*
Littleton, Col.: Libraries Unlimited, Inc.,
1972.

Ethnic Joke Books

For those who haven't heard enough Polish, Italian or Irish jokes, there is a series
of paperback books written by Larry
Wilde, entitled *The Official Ethnic Joke
Books.* Included are jokes about blacks
and whites—and, of course, Polish, Italian, Jewish and Irish jokes.

The Ethnic Prejudice in America Series

*Chink!—Anti-Chinese Prejudice in Amer-
ica,* edited by Cheng-Tsu Wu.
Kike!—Anti-Semitism in America, edited
by Michael Selzer.
Mick!—Anti-Irish Prejudice in America,
edited by Joan McKiernan and Robert
St. Cyr.
Wop!—Anti-Italian Prejudice in America,
edited by Elihu Smith.

San Francisco: Straight Arrow Books.
Each book reviews the history and development of prejudice, stereotypes
and discrimination that every group
experienced when they arrived in
America. Includes editorials, news
clippings and other writings about the
ethnic experience, and laws that were
passed to exclude various groups.

THE COMIC STRIPS IN AMERICA

Art imitates life, and the comic strips are
no exception. Over the years, the funnies
have managed to parallel the changing ethnic mix of the United States and chronicle
the "new" ethnic consciousness that has
arisen in America. Some of the old favorites
are gone—such as "Li'l Abner" and "Terry
and the Pirates"—but they've been replaced by black comic strips, American Indian comic strips and strips about Jewish
mothers.

Our comic characters reflect every segment of history, from the "new" immigration of the 1880s to the space-age superheroes of the 1970s.

1880—THE DECLINE OF PURITAN INFLUENCE

Due to a strong Puritan influence and the
existence of blue laws to regulate Sabbath
observance, it wasn't until 1880 that newspapers in America even published a Sunday
edition. The large influx of "new" immigrants, especially the Germans, who
wanted to enjoy their day of rest with some
relaxing music and a few beers, began to
exert a stronger and stronger influence over
the general public. Immigrants were invad-
ing the publishing field, too. Joseph Pulitzer,
a Hungarian immigrant who bought the fail-

ing *World* newspaper in 1883, was the first to dream up the "Sunday supplement" to attract readers to his weekend paper. He also published the first color cartoon on February 16, 1896.

Other newspapermen were quick to realize the appeal of comics. In 1897 William Randolph Hearst introduced *The American Humorist* magazine, and ten years later he printed the first daily comic strip—"Mutt and Jeff."

1897—THE RISE OF THE GERMAN STEREOTYPE

The oldest comic strip still printed in America is "The Katzenjammer Kids," first drawn in 1897 by Randolph Dirks (1877–1968), a German immigrant to Chicago. For over 80 years now those two brothers, Hans and Fritz, have been raising hell on the pages of America's leading newspapers. "Katzenjammer" is German slang for a "hangover" and the kids, true to their name, are always raising a ruckus and making their poor, fat Momma and der Captain sick with their antics.

"The Katzenjammer Kids" was based on a German strip, "Max und Moritz." The kids, Momma, der Inspector and der Captain, a boarder (a likely story) who lives with the fatherless family, were the main characters in this non-ending series of tricks, trouble and buffoonery which usually ended with the kids having the last laugh. All of the characters spoke English with a German accent, but when anti-German sentiment reached a peak during World War I, the name of the strip was changed to "The Shenanigan Kids" in an attempt to pass off Hans and Fritz as Irish!

One of the "founding fathers" of American comics, Dirks was the first to create a strip complete with frames, talk balloons and a permanent cast of characters who were probably similar to some of the German immigrants he encountered in his ethnic Chicago neighborhood in the early 1800s.

1913—MADE IN AMERICA, THE PLIGHT OF THE FIRST GENERATION

Jiggs has made it in America. An Irish immigrant and the title character in "Bringing Up Father," Jiggs aspired to and attained the "American dream," rising from hod carrier to nouveau riche American in a relatively short period of time.

Therein lies the problem and the running gag for the strip. Although Jiggs has struck it rich, he is still an immigrant at heart. He is not cultured or refined and has no desire to attend polo games and dine on caviar with his rich neighbors. Jiggs' idea of a night out is to play cards with the boys at Dinty Moore's tavern and feast on "Irish soul food"—corned beef and cabbage. Though not ashamed of his activities, Jiggs has to hide them from his snobbish wife. Maggie is an incessant social climber who aspires to a life of conspicuous consumption and social acceptance by their "old money" neighbors. Maggie also happens to be quite handy with a rolling pin, and she is inclined to use it on Jiggs whenever he steps out of line.

Created in 1913 by George McMannus (1884–1954), "Bringing Up Father" was the first comic strip to attain world-wide fame. Translated into 16 languages in 46 countries, Jiggs and Maggie also inspired movies and television and radio shows based on their life together.

McMannus was born on January 23, 1884, to an Irish immigrant father who managed the St. Louis Opera House. It was there that the seeds of inspiration for "Bringing Up Father" were sown, when *The Rising Generation*, a play about a newly rich Irish family, was produced at his father's theater.

1930—THE SECOND GENERATION AND BEYOND

Dagwood Bumstead's ancestors came over on the Mayflower in the seventeenth century, and according to a theory espoused by Marshall McLuhan, Dagwood's plight is typical of second-generation Americans. Unlike their immigrant fathers who came to America with a zeal for success, the second generation is more complacent about accumulating wealth. They are not driven by the same demons as their parents, and are content to live the good life and enjoy the benefits of wealth rather than push themselves to accumulate even more money.

Dagwood, created in 1930 by "Chic" Murat Young, was the playboy son of a railroad tycoon who was disinherited from the Bumstead fortune when he married his pert, golden-haired wife, Blondie. Rather than striking out on his own, Dagwood works in Mr. Dithers' law office, taking both browbeatings and physical abuse from his boss when things don't run smoothly. McLuhan belives Dagwood takes Mr. Dithers' guff because he is comfortable. He has no desire to start his own business—he just wants to be able to relax when he goes home, and generally leaves it up to Blondie to rescue him from any domestic entanglements.

One of the most successful international strips, Blondie is the most widely circulated comic in the world. In Latin America, Dagwood is known as Lorenzo; in France, he's called Emile; and in Sweden, he's Dagobert.

1950S — IMMIGRATION RESTRICTION

When the comic strip "Dondi" debuted in September 1955, Dondi, the son of an Italian woman and a deceased American G.I. father, was desperately trying to enter the United States. Immigration restrictions imposed by the McCarran-Walter legislation of the 1920s prevented Dondi's quick entry to America, and soon the whole nation was enthralled by the fate of this poor orphan boy, created by Gus Edson (1901–1966). Dondi's plight was typical of that of most ethnics from Southern or Eastern Europe, who were turned away from our doors by restrictive "quota" laws.

Ethnic Stereotypes in the Comics

Like the population of America, our cartoonists and the characters they created come from every ethnic group and cross section of the socio-economic sphere. There are privileged WASPs, Irish immigrants, Italian war orphans, Blacks, Mexicans and American Indians gracing our funny pages.

Of course, the comics usually present only stereotypical behavior in an attempt to make us laugh through exaggeration—so, all the Germans are fat, pipe-smoking sausage eaters and all the Chinese are wise old philosophers.

THE WORLD ACCORDING TO CHING CHOW   True to the stereotyped image of Chinese wit and wisdom are the characters Charlie Chan (who graduated from books to films and comic strips) and Ching Chow. Chow was originally drawn more than fifty years ago by Stanley Link, and later by Henri Arnold and Rocco Lototo (all Occidentals). This syndicated single panel has changed considerably over the years. Instead of wearing his hair in an outdated "queue" (pigtail), Ching Chow now sports a Western-style haircut. His kimono is shorter, and his face has become less "Oriental" over the years. His name has even changed. When he debuted as a character in "The Gumps" during the 1920s his name was Ching Chew, but his surname became Chow when he graduated to top billing in his own panel.

The only thing that hasn't changed over the years is Chow's cozy philosophy. He still spouts such homilies as "Do unto others," "Don't cry over spilled milk," and "A fool and his money," etc.—all with an Oriental touch.

THE ORIGINAL POLISH JOKE   Joe Palooka was a dumbbell prizefighter who was long on punches but rather short on brains when he first appeared in 1928. Modeled after a real-life Polish-American prizefighter from Wilkes-Barre, Pennsylvania, Palooka mellowed somewhat over the years and became more refined and eloquent than he had been in the early years of the strip.

Created by Ham (Hammond Edward) Fisher (1900–1955) in the 1920s, the strip's title character was originally called Joe Dumbelletski. But even in those pre-Polish-joke days, newspapers refused "Dumbelletski" until Fisher rechristened him Palooka—a common boxing term for a third-rate slugger.

THE FIGHTING IRISH   Joe Palooka wasn't the only comic strip character who started out as a real-life American. Flip Corkin, a leading character in "Terry and the Pirates," was modeled after Philip Cochran, a World War II fighter pilot and old friend of Milton Caniff (1907–1979), the strips' creator.

Phil and Flip had a lot in common—both came from Erie, Pennsylvania; both were handsome Irishmen in their early thirties; both had prematurely gray hair, square jaws, two false front teeth and a documented penchant for "hat-check chicks."

When Caniff stopped drawing "Terry and the Pirates" in 1946, due to contractual disputes, he took Phil Cochran with him and made him General Philerie in "Steve Canyon."

PRIVILEGED WASP AVENGER
Batman was created in May 1939 (the
year after Superman's comics debut) by
Bob Kane and Bill Finger for Detective
Comics. The alter ego of WASP millionaire
Bruce Wayne, Batman began his devotion
to crime-fighting as a child when his parents
were brutally murdered by thugs. Unlike
Superman and other superheroes who followed (Spiderman and the Hulk), Batman is
just a normal, average American millionaire. He fights crime with only his wits and
the aid of his .007-type inventions—he receives no aid from Kryptonic powers, no
supernatural strength from radioactive spi-
derbites or chemical blasts.

MEXICAN ROBIN HOOD Based on
a character from an O. Henry story, "The
Caballero's Way," the Cisco Kid became a
successful film character, a television series
and, eventually, in 1951, a syndicated daily
comic strip drawn by Argentinian artist
José-Luis Salinas.

This Mexican doer of good deeds waged
a never-ending battle for truth, justice and
the "American" way in turn-of-the-century
New Mexico. Times changed, however,
and in the 1960s cowboy-and-Indian stories
fell by the wayside." The Cisco Kid" was
discontinued as a strip in 1968, because he
was no longer deemed "relevant" to the
Chicano experience in America.

MEXICAN SUPER HERO The Mexican-American prototype hero of the 1970s
is Relampago ("lightning" in Spanish).
Created by Judge Marbarito C. Garza of
Corpus Christi, Texas, Relampago is not
yet a commercial success, but the judge
hopes his books will become a symbol for
Mexican-American children of the Southwest.

In his comic books, Relampago uses supernatural powers to break up drug rings,
foil robberies and battle motorcycle gangs.
An old witch used "sorcery" to transform
him from Marcos Zapata, a common petty
criminal, into the Southwest's first super
hero.

Garza, a second-generation Mexican-
American, hopes his books will help
Spanish-speaking youngsters increase their
English vocabulary skills (Garza claims that
he himself learned to read English from
comic books). Garza's main ambition is to
eliminate some of the stereotyped images
Mexican-Americans have about the "glam-

The mild-mannered WASPs have Clark
Kent's alter ego, Superman, to admire,
the Mexican-Americans have Relampago—
America's first Chicano superhero. (Courtesy: Judge M. Garza)

orous" life of banditos and of fancy
caballeros like the Cisco Kid.

BLACKS IN THE COMICS No other
ethnic group in America has been stereotyped as mercilessly as the American
Negro. For years the only blacks who appeared as comic strip characters were wide-
eyed, with "unbelievably big lips and solid
black skin ovaled into a stupid-looking
face." That's what Ponchitta Pierce thought
about the situation when she wrote,
"What's Not So Funny About the Funnies," in *Ebony,* in November 1966.

It wasn't until the end of World War II
that black organizations began complaining
about their limited horizons in the comics.
The only Negroes found in strips were either servants, subordinates or jungle inhabitants. Joe Palooka had a black valet named
"Smokey" who disappeared one morning
after the NAACP complained. Instead of
instituting a change in the role blacks played
in the comics, strip writers found it easier to
exclude them altogether. Fear of a "no win"
situation spurred many to avoid blacks, for
as Alfred Andriola, creator of "Kerry

Drake" noted at the time, "Let's face it. You can't deal with race or color in comics. A colored maid or porter brings on a flood of letters. And if we show the Negro as a hero we get angry letters from the South [and elsewhere]." Another cartoonist noted: "If I draw a lazy-looking white guy lounging around in his underwear, it's all right. But if that same guy happens to be a Negro, there would be letters."

The first strip to feature a Black in a major role was "On Stage," written by Leonard Starr, who patterned his theater character, Philmore, after a well-known New York music coach, Phil Moore. That was in 1961, and at the time Starr received only positive letters from readers for his action. Four papers did cancel his strip but, as he noted, "It would be hard to prove" that they canceled because Starr used a Black in his strip.

When CORE complained to Ken Kling, an Alsatian-American cartoonist and racing expert, who frequently left "hot tips" for bettors in his daily strip "Joe and Asbestos," Kling was happy to comply with their requests concerning the latter character. He had first started drawing Asbestos in 1925 and modeled him after a famous black jockey, Isaac Murphy. CORE objected to Asbestos' "rubber lips" and black face, and overnight Asbestos became lighter, with normal lips, and even started to speak with a better command of the English language. "I made him look like a regular person, less grotesque. When we draw cartoons we make all kinds of silly caricatures. We don't mean any harm."

The first "integrated" comic strip was 'Wee Pals," by black cartoonist Morrie Turner (1923–   ). Although Turner became the first black to find success with black comic strip characters, he was not the first successful black cartoonist—that distinction belongs to E. Simms Campbell, who drew "Cuties" in the 1940s.

After Turner's strip was nationally syndicated in 1965, other black characters and strips followed in the wake of his success: 'Luther" debuted in 1968, and that same year, Franklin, a black tyke, joined the 'Peanuts" gang. In 1970, Lt. Flap enlisted in Beetle Bailey's unit with the line, "How come there's no blacks in this honky outfit?" "Quincy," drawn by Jamaican artist Ted Shearer, was syndicated in 1970. And,

in 1971, "Butter and Boop" became nationally syndicated after starting out in 1969 with only 10 black newspapers supporting it.

OTHER "MINORITIES" In 1967, "Redeye," created by Gordon Bess (1929–   ) brought the comic misadventures of an Indian tribe to daily and Sunday papers. And, in 1970, "Momma," the first nationally syndicated comic strip starring a stereotyped Jewish mother, was created by Mel Lazarus (1927–   ).

ETHNIC AMERICAN CARTOONISTS

Max Fleisher (1885?–1972) "Betty Boop"

Born in Vienna, Austria, Max Fleischer emigrated to America with his parents as a child of four. Max and his brother Dave started an animation studio called Out-of-the-Inkwell Films, which featured such early stars of the animated screen as Ko-Ko the Clown (1915), Popeye the Sailor, and Betty Boop (1931). Boop was a Kewpie-doll type character with an oversized head, spit curls, flirtatious eyes and an hourglass shape.

Popular during the 1930s, Boop graduated from celluloid to print and became a strip character in 1934. During her heyday, actress Helen Kane sued the Fleischer brothers, claiming they had modeled Betty's face after her own. In the 1940s the popularity of the comic strips and the animated films began to decline, but as late as 1957 it was still possible to hear a "book-boop-e-doop" emanating from your TV screen.

Jules Feiffer (1929–   ) "Feiffer"

Born in a Jewish neighborhood in the Bronx to Polish immigrant parents, Feiffer always believed ". . . it was some awful mistake that I was living there. I should have been living in the Manhattan of the movies I saw as a kid."

Famous for his satirical cartoons, for his Broadway production Little Murders, and as screenwriter for the award-winning film Carnal Knowledge, Jules Feiffer decided to become a cartoonist during a two-year stint in the Army. He had always drawn comics as a hobby, ". . . but," he claims, "the army changed my ambition from that of being a comic cartoonist to a satirist. I had to do something to counteract the sense of continual oppression I felt."

He got his first "break" in 1956 when the *Village Voice* allowed him to draw for them, without pay. More than twenty years later, his work is nationally syndicated, though he still contributes his weekly panel to the *Village Voice* free in appreciation for their support during those lean years.

Harold Foster (1892–   ) "Prince Valiant"

Born in Halifax, Nova Scotia, Foster emigrated by bicycle from his home in Winnipeg to Chicago, where he attended art classes at the Chicago Art Institute. Before embarking on his career as an illustrator, Foster worked as a boxer, gold prospector and fur trapper. In his own words, "I was no darn good at a lot of things but I was always good at drawing." When he tired of illustrating other people's strips and stories in 1937 (he had worked on early "Tarzan" comic strips), Foster created Prince Valiant. He wrote and illustrated the strip for more than thirty years, until 1971, when, at the age of 79, Foster ceased illustrating Prince Valiant to spend his time solely on the story line.

George Herriman (1880–1944) "Krazy Kat"

Although Herriman claims to have been born in New Orleans of Greek immigrant parents, recent evidence suggests that he might have been the first successful black cartoonist to "pass." He despised working in his family's bakery, and after he put salt in the doughnuts instead of sugar and planted a dead mouse in a loaf of bread, his parents agreed that he should choose another career. That's when Herriman took off for the coast to become an office boy for a Los Angeles newspaper.

His first published comic strip was "The Family Upstairs," which debuted in 1910 in the *New York Journal*. But the characters he is best remembered for are Krazy and Ignatz, the cat-and-mouse team with the love-hate relationship. "Krazy Kat" debuted in 1911, after starting out as a "running gag" in "The Family Upstairs."

Stan Lee (1922–   ) "Spiderman."

When Stanley Lieber (a.k.a. Lee) was growing up in New York City he "read ev-

erything." According to Stan, "I would read the labels on ketchup bottles while I was eating if there was nothing to thumb through. I read Dickens, Mark Twain, Edgar Rice Burroughs," – and, of course – "all the comic strips."

He began his literary career as an assistant comic book editor at the age of seventeen. He was promoted to editor in 1942, and for the next thirty years he wrote adventure comics, romance comics and the superhero adventures that made him famous. Lee created the Fantastic Four in 1961, and followed those heroes with Spiderman and other fantastic creatures.

The son of Rumanian Jewish immigrants, Lee has been called the "Homer" of twentieth-century mythology.

The Hulk is the only member of the Fantastic Four to graduate from the printed page to become a media superstar with his own weekly television series. A former Mr. America, Italian-American Lou Ferrigno, portrays the Hulk after his transformation. (Courtesy: CBS Entertainment)

Charles Monroe Schulz (1922–   ) "Peanuts"

With the exception of Disney's rodents and ducks, there aren't any better known and loved characters in cartoondom than the cast of "Peanuts." This crew of tykes, who recently celebrated their thirtieth year in print, includes Charlie Brown—the great American "un-success" story, who can't seem to excel at anything. Charlie is a failure at kite flying, ball playing, and making the red-haired girl notice him. His antithesis in the strip is Snoopy—his debonair, intelligent, sensitive dog—and his nemesis is Lucy, the shrewish sister of the blanket-hugger, Linus.

Based on Schulz's "unhappy memories" of his childhood in Minneapolis, the "Peanuts" strip has been estimated to rake in over $50 million a year from syndication rights, books, feature films and other ventures which bear the Peanuts trademark. That's not bad for a cartoonist who was originally turned down by half a dozen syndicates, and even had his drawings rejected from his high school yearbook.

"Peanuts" was originally titled "Li'l Folks." Schulz was desperate to see his characters in print and agreed to change the name to "Peanuts" when United Features offered him a chance to appear in 7 daily newspapers in 1950. By 1960, that number had grown to more than 1,200 newspapers, while Charlie Brown, Lucy and Snoopy made their way across the ocean to over 60 foreign countries.

Pat Sullivan (1887–1933) "Felix the Cat"

Pat Sullivan emigrated to the United States from his native Australia in 1914. He worked as a prizefighter and vaudeville comedian for almost three years before he opened his own cartoon studio and animated his first Felix film in 1917.

Felix was an immediate success. Over the next 16 years, Sullivan cranked out over 100 feature films, including the first sound cartoon and the first televised cartoon, which appeared over NBC in 1930. "Felix" graduated to print in the 1920s, appearing as a Sunday feature in 1923 and a daily strip in 1927.

Garry Trudeau (1948–   ) "Doonesbury"

Unlike some of America's starving immigrant cartoonists, Garretson Beekman Trudeau can trace his ancestry back to the 1650s, when his family emigrated from France to Montreal. One branch stayed in Canada and fostered the forebears of Canada's Prime Minister, Pierre Elliott Trudeau. The other branch of the family emigrated from Montreal to New York, where Garry was born in comfortable circumstances.

Financially secure, Trudeau did not have to struggle for years to have his daily strip syndicated. The 1974 Pulitzer Prize winner began drawing cartoons under contract at the ripe old age of 22, shortly after he graduated from Yale. Trudeau had created the strip, originally entitled "Bull Tales," as an undergraduate, and he was a regular contributor to the *Yale Record*. Currently "Doonesbury" is carried by more than 440 newspapers and has an estimated following of more than 60 million readers in the United States.

THE ETHNIC PRESS

Arabic

ARAB JOURNAL
(Organization of Arab Students U.S. and Canada)
2929 Broadway
New York, N.Y. 10025

Features articles on political, cultural and economic aspects of life in various Arab countries, to promote Arab-American understanding.

Established   1953
Language   English
Circulation   7,000
Frequency   Quarterly

AL-ALAM AL JADID (The New World)
25720 York Road
Royal Oak, Michigan 48067

News of life in Arab countries and in the United States.

Established   1962
Language   Arabic
Circulation   1,000
Frequency   Weekly

AL-HODA (The Guidance)
16 West 30th Street
New York, New York 10001

Oldest Lebanese newspaper in the United States.

(Courtesy: New York Historical Society)

Established   1898
Language   Arabic
Circulation   5,400
Frequency   Semi-weekly

LEBANESE AMERICAN JOURNAL
16 West 30 Street
New York, N.Y. 10001

   With the decline of Arabic-reading Americans, the second and third generation can still keep up with events happening in Lebanon and in Arabic neighborhoods in the United States.

Established   1952
Language   English
Circulation   10,000
Frequency   Weekly

SYRIAN AMERICAN NEWS
811 South Sierra Bonita Ave.
Los Angeles, California 90036

   International affairs and local community news.

Established   1932
Language   English
Circulation   7,400
Frequency   Semi-monthly

Armenian

BULLETIN FOR THE ADVANCEMENT OF ARMENIAN STUDIES
(National Association for Armenian Studies and Research)
175 Mount Auburn Street
Cambridge, Massachusetts 02138

Information on grants and Armenian studies programs in the United States.

Established   1955
Language   English
Circulation   2,500
Frequency   Semi-annually

Bulgarian

MAKEDONSKA TRIBUNA (Macedonian Tribune)
542 South Meridian Street
Indianapolis, Indiana 46225

   News of affairs in the Balkans, as well as social and cultural activities of Bulgarians in America. Objective: to preserve the cultural and religious heritage of the Macedono-Bulgarians in America.

Established   1927
Language   Bulgarian/English
Circulation   2,501
Frequency   Weekly

Byelorussian

BELARUSKAYA   DUMKA   (Byelorussian Thought)
34 Richter Avenue
Milltown, New Jersey 08850

   Surveys Byelorussin life in U.S. and abroad.

Established   1960
Language   Byelorussian/English
Circulation   1,000
Frequency   Semi-annual

Chinese

THE CHINESE AMERICAN WEEKLY
199 Canal Street
New York, N.Y. 10013

   Cultural magazine sponsored by the Chinese-American press.

Established   1942
Language   English
Circulation   9,000
Frequency   Weekly

MEI JO JIH PAO (The Chinese Journal)
7 East Broadway
New York, N.Y. 10038

   World and national news and reports from Chinese communities in America.

Established 1928
Language English
Circulation 15,525
Frequency Daily

LIN HO JIH PAO (The United Journal)
199 Canal Street
New York, N.Y. 10013
News from China, Asia and local communities.

Established 1952
Language Chinese
Circulation 15,000
Frequency Daily

Croatian

CROATIA PRESS
P.O. Box 1767
Grand Central Station
New York, N.Y. 10017
Current affairs of interest to Southern Slavs and Americans of Croatian descent. Covers political, economic and cultural activities.

Established 1947
Language Croatian/English
Circulation 500
Frequency Quarterly

Czech

AMERICAN BULLETIN
(Czechoslovak National Council of America)
2137 South Lombard Avenue
Cicero, Illinois 60650
News of interest to Americans of Czech and Slovak descent.

Established 1954
Language English
Circulation 3,050
Frequency Monthly

C.S.A. (Czechoslovak Society of America)
JOURNAL
2138 South 61 Court
Cicero, Illinois 60650
In 1967 switched from a newspaper format to a magazine; still includes editorial section, sports, family page.

Established 1892
Language Czech/English
Circulation 18,500
Frequency Monthly

Dutch

THE HOLLAND REPORTER
3680 Division Street
Los Angeles, California 90065
Dutch-American weekly with news from Holland and the U.S.

Established 1960
Language Dutch/English
Circulation 8,200
Frequency Weekly

D.I.S. MAGAZINE (Dutch Immigrant Society)
2216 Edgewood, S.E.
Grand Rapids, Michigan 49506
Information on D.I.S. activities and on the Dutch-American community.

Flemish

GAZETTE VAN DETROIT (Detroit Gazette)
11243 Mack Avenue
Detroit, Michigan 48214
General news and reports about activities of Flemish organizations.

Established 1914
Language Flemish
Circulation 2,855
Frequency Weekly

French

FRANCE-AMÉRIQUE
1111 Lexington Avenue
New York, N.Y. 10021
Oldest French language newspaper in the United States, France-Amérique recently celebrated its 152nd anniversary. Descended from Le Courrier des Etats-Unis (1827), the 16-page weekly has a reputation for thorough coverage of national and international news of interest to French-Americans.

Established 1827
Language French
Circulation 20,000
Frequency Weekly

German

DER DEUTSCH-AMERIKANER
4740 North Western Avenue
Chicago, Illinois 60625
Includes organizational news of German-American National Congress

and articles on German language, customs and culture, in an effort to preserve the heritage of German-Americans.

Established   1959
Language   German / English
Circulation   12,200
Frequency   Monthly

KONTINENT
601 West 26th Street
New York, N.Y. 10001

Established   1964
Language   German
Circulation   30,000
Frequency   Monthly

STAATS-ZEITUNG UND HEROLD
36-30 37th Street
Long Island City, N.Y. 11101

Established   1834
Language   German
Circulation   23,500
Frequency   Weekly

Greek

ETHNIKOS KERIX (The National Herald)
134-140 West 26th Street
New York, N.Y. 10001

Covers international, national and local news of interest to Greek-American population.

Established   1915
Language   Greek / English
Circulation   18,942
Frequency   Daily

Hungarian

"WISCONSINI MAGYARSA 'G" HUNGARIAN
NEWSPAPER
609 North Plankinton Avenue
Room 508
Milwaukee, Wisconsin 53203

Primarily news articles of interest to Hungarians residing in Wisconsin.

Established   1924
Circulation   18,700
Language   Hungarian
Frequency   Semi-monthly

Indian (American)

INDIAN AFFAIRS
Association of American Indian Affairs
432 Park Avenue South
New York, N.Y. 10016

Established   1949
Language   English
Circulation   25,000
Frequency   Bi-monthly

Irish

IRISH WORLD AND GAELIC AMERICAN
84 Fifth Avenue
New York, N.Y. 10011

Articles and news of interest to Irish-Americans.

Established   1970
Language   English
Circulation   100,000
Frequency   Weekly

Italian

IL PROGRESSO ITALO-AMERICANO
(Italian-American Progress)
260 Audubon Avenue
New York, N.Y. 10033

Only Italian daily in the U.S.; stresses news of events in Italy.

Established   1880
Language   Italian
Circulation   70,548
Frequency   Daily

THE ECHO
243 Atwells Avenue
Providence, Rhode Island 02903

Family-oriented weekly concentrating on Italo-American life-styles, accomplishments and heritage. Covers international, national and local news; sections on the arts, education and sports.

Established   1896
Language   English and Italian
Circulation   29,000
Frequency   Weekly

THE ITALIAN TRIBUNE NEWS
427 Bloomfield Avenue
Newark, New Jersey 07107

Focuses on the Italian people and the culture of their homeland. Weekly features include: Italian language lessons; Italian settlers in America; Italian heritage in the United States.

Established   1931
Language   English
Circulation   20,000
Frequency   Weekly

Japanese

PACIFIC CITIZEN
125 Weller Street
Los Angeles, California 90012

Published by the Japanese American Citizens League, *The Pacific Citizen* contains articles on achievements, contributions and issues of importance to persons of Japanese descent.

Established   1930
Language   English
Circulation   18,969
Frequency   Weekly

RAFU SHIMPO (Los Angeles Japanese Daily News)
242 South San Pedro Street
Los Angeles, California 90012

Specializes in news concerning Americans of Japanese descent and highlights national and international news.

Established   1903
Language   Japanese / English
Circulation   19,669
Frequency   Daily

KASHU MAINICHI (California Daily News)
346 East First Street
Los Angeles, California 90012

Established   1931
Language   English / Japanese
Circulation   5,610
Frequency   Daily

Jewish

DER TOG-MORGEN JOURNAL (The Day-Morning Journal)
183 East Broadway
New York, N.Y. 10002

General, national, international and local news of interest to Yiddish readers.

Established   1914
Language   Yiddish
Circulation   43,340
Frequency   Daily

JEWISH PRESS
2427 Surf Avenue
Brooklyn, New York 11224

National and international news of interest to the Jewish community.

Established   1951
Language   English
Circulation   162,250
Frequency   Weekly

JEWISH DAILY FORWARD
175 East Broadway
New York, N.Y. 10002

Oldest Jewish daily in the United States.

Established   1897
Language   Yiddish
Circulation   50,000
Frequency   Daily

Lithuanian

NAUJIENOS
The Lithuanian Daily
1739 South Halsted Street
Chicago, Illinois 60608

Emphasis on news of Lithuanians in America and the Soviet Union.

Established   1914
Language   Lithuanian
Circulation   13,000
Frequency   Daily

DRAUGAS
Lithuanian Daily "Friend"
4545 West 63rd Street
Chicago, Illinois 60629

News coverage of Lithuanian communities in America and the Soviet Union.

Established   1909
Language   Lithuanian
Circulation   13,000
Frequency   Daily

You don't have to know Yiddish to read the Jewish press. In 1977, President Carter's staff became concerned about the possibility of a backlash within the American Jewish community, so they began printing a weekly news roundup of Jewish publications in the United States. Similar to the daily news wrap-up that is prepared for the President, this one carries a blue "Star of David" logo and is sent only to Carter and some of his senior staff members.

Polish

POLISH AMERICAN WORLD
3100 Grand Boulevard
Baldwin, New York 11510

Coverage of news happenings in Polish-American communities and events of interest in Poland.

Established 1959
Language English
Circulation 5,000
Frequency Weekly

ZGODA (Unity)
1201 North Milwaukee Avenue
Chicago, Illinois 60622

Official publication of the Polish National Alliance; features news about prominent Polish Americans.

Established 1881
Language English/Polish
Circulation 160,000
Frequency Semi-monthly

(The first Polish language newspaper published in America was *Echo z Polski* (The Echo of Poland), 1863–1864.)

Portuguese

DIARIO DE NOTICIAS (The Daily News)
93 Rivet Street
New Bedford, Massachusetts 02742

News of interest to Portuguese Americans.

Established 1919
Language Portuguese
Circulation 7,263
Frequency Daily

VOZ DE PORTUGAL (Voice of Portugal)
370 A. Street
Hayward, California 94541

News of interest to Portuguese Americans.

Established 1960
Language Portuguese
Circulation 3,970
Frequency 3 times/month

LUSO AMERICANO
88 Ferry Street
Newark, New Jersey 07105

Local news, plus features of interest to Americans of Portuguese descent.

Established 1928
Language Portuguese
Circulation 5,250
Frequency Weekly

Russian

NOVOYE RUSSKOYE SLOVO
(New Russian Word)
243 W. 56th Street
New York, N.Y. 10019

Established 1910
Language Russian
Circulation 33,000
Frequency Daily

Scandinavian

THE AMERICAN DANE MAGAZINE
3717 Harney Street
Omaha, Nebraska 68131

News items and articles of interest to Danish-Americans.

Established 1926
Language English
Circulation 9,500
Frequency Monthly

NEW YORKIN UUTISET
4418-22 Eighth Avenue
Brooklyn, New York 11220

Finnish-American news and reports on cultural and social activities.

Established 1906
Language Finnish
Circulation 2,580
Frequency Semi-weekly

SVENSKA   AMERIKANAREN   TRIBUNEN
(Swedish American Tribune)
916 West Belmont Avenue
Chicago, Illinois 60657

General news of interest to Swedish-Americans.

Established 1876
Language Swedish
Circulation 19,435
Frequency Weekly

NORDSTJERNAN SVEA (The North Star— Svea)
4 West 22nd Street
New York, N.Y. 10010

Oldest Swedish newspaper in the United States.

Established   1872
Language   English/Swedish
Circulation   11,000
Frequency   Weekly

NORDEN (The North)
4816 Eighth Avenue
Brooklyn, N.Y. 11220

News from Finland; it is the only newspaper that caters to the needs of Swedish-speaking people from Finland.

Established   1896
Language   Swedish
Circulation   1,720
Frequency   Weekly

NORDISK TIDENDE (The Norwegian News)
8104 Fifth Avenue
Brooklyn, N.Y. 11209

General news of interest to Norwegian-Americans.

Established   1891
Language   Norwegian/English
Circulation   10,500
Frequency   Weekly

WESTERN VIKING
2040 N.W. Market Street
Seattle, Washington 98107

Contains "News of Norway," from the Norwegian Information Service, and reports on latest happenings in Norwegian clubs and societies in the U.S.

Established   1889
Language   Norwegian/English
Circulation   3,080
Frequency   Weekly

THE AMERICAN SCANDINAVIAN FOUNDA-TION
127 East 73rd Street
New York, N.Y. 10021

Articles of interest to Americans of Scandinavian ancestry; covers all aspects of life in Scandinavia and America.

Established   1913
Language   English
Circulation   7,000
Frequency   Quarterly

Spanish

AZTLAN INTERNATIONAL JOURNAL OF CHI-CANO STUDIES RESEARCH
405 Hilgard Avenue
Los Angeles, California 90024

Scholarly journal sponsored by the Chicano Studies Center; contains articles on politics, sociology, history and culture of Chicanos in America and Mexico.

Established   1969
Language   Spanish/English
Circulation   2,000
Frequency   3 times/year

EL DIARIO-LA PRENSA (The Daily Press)
181 Hudson Street
New York, N.Y.

Serves the Hispanic community of New York: El Diario and La Prensa were merged in 1948.

Established   1918 (La Prensa)
Language   Spanish
Circulation   100,000
Frequency   Daily

AMERICAN SPANISH NEWS
2448 Mission Street
San Francisco, California 94110

National, interntional and local news of interest to Spanish-speaking Americans.

Established   1953
Language   Spanish/English
Circulation   25,000
Frequency   Semi-monthly

Ukrainian

AMERYKA (America)
817 North Franklin Street
Philadelphia, Pennsylvania 19123

Emphasis on developments within the Ukrainian Catholic Church; includes news of Ukrainian communities both here and abroad.

Established   1912
Language   Ukrainian/English
Circulation   6,500
Frequency   Daily

KRYLATI (The Winged Ones)
315 East Tenth Street
New York, N.Y. 10009

Articles on Ukrainian history and culture, as well as current events.

Established   1963
Language   Ukrainian
Circulation   6,000
Frequency   Monthly

THE NEW ETHNIC AMERICAN MAGAZINES

The recent rise of interest in our ethnic heritage has spurred the publication of several new magazines designed for the second generation and beyond. As readership of foreign-language newspapers literally dies off with the older generation, there aren't enough sons and daughters to carry on the subscriptions – simply because they never learned to read the language of their parents or grandparents.

With the new "ethnic consciousness," many Americans are curious to learn about their "roots" and the culture of the "other side"; this opens up a whole new market for ethnic magazines that don't require knowledge of a second language.

Hispanic Magazines

There are Spanish editions of *Cosmopolitan* and of *Popular Mechanics,* as well as the Hispanic magazines *Vanidades,* but until recently there weren't any magazines written in English for Hispanic Americans. During the Seventies *Latin New York, Latin Times* and *Nuestro* magazines debuted in an effort to tap the market of Latins born and raised in the United States.

Latin New York was founded in 1973, mainly as an entertainment guide for Puerto Ricans living in New York. The magazine lists clubs that play *salsa,* reviews *salsa* records, and profiles Latin artists who play *salsa,* because as publisher Izzy Sanabria puts it, "[Salsa] is everything we are about: culture, values, everyday reality, all reflected through our music."

Latin Times, on the other hand, is not directed at the young "Saturday night Salsa Set," but at the "upwardly mobile Puerto Ricans" of New York. Issues contain a mix of fashion, art, music and culture, with articles on politics and current events.

While *Latin New York* and *Latin Times* are aimed primarily at the New York market, *Nuestro,* introduced in 1977, is a national magazine.

Nuestro, published by Dan Lopez, a Chicano born in Chicago, is the first magazine that attempts to reach Hispanic Americans of every ethnic origin – Cuban, Mexican, South American, Spanish, Puerto Rican, Caribbean – some 9 million Americans in all. As difficult as this task sounds, Lopez

(Courtesy: Nuestro *Magazine)*

was able to attract 150,000 subscribers after a direct mail campaign, and circulation was up to 200,000 copies in 1979.

Nuestro is a pleasant, easy-to-read, well-illustrated mix of entertainment, fiction, news and commentary. A fan had this to say: "It makes me feel good to read about my own people making it." But detractors insist, ". . . it doesn't say much. It's like a movie with beautiful color that doesn't have much of a message."

Italian-American Magazines

Not to be outdone, the Italian-American publishers had their own entrants into the "slick" ethnic magazine race for subscribers in 1977. Unfortunately, the publications were underfinanced and did not manage to garner widespread support from the 25 million-plus Italian-Americans of the third generation and beyond. *I-Am* and *Identity* magazines were short-lived, but in 1979 the former editor of *I-Am,* Ron de Paulo, came back with a similar (and this time well financed) publication called AT-TENZIONE . . . USA which he hopes will attract more attention than his last venture.

6 CUSTOMS AND TRADITIONS

A CALENDAR OF ETHNIC FEASTS, FESTIVITIES, AND CELEBRATIONS

Each year thousands of ethnic festivals take place in America. There are Italian *carnevales*, Mexican *fiestas*, Steuben Day parades, and festivals for almost every race, religion and nationality represented in the United States.

The people who came to America brought their feast days, saint's days, religious holidays and special ways of celebrating Christmas and New Year's Day. They gave us Groundhog Day, Leap Year, and Valentine's Day Traditions, and their descendants instituted Labor Day and Arbor Day to honor the workingman and to plant new trees.

You don't have to be Irish to march in the St. Patrick's Day Parade (as the Yiddish Sons of Erin prove each year in New York), and you don't have to be a Christian to celebrate Christmas — atheists and agnostics alike have Christmas trees, and there are a growing number of Jewish Americans who erect "Chanukah bushes" decorated with candy canes and dreidels. Our holidays are beginning to blend into one another as Americans find new ways to celebrate traditional holidays, and new reasons to celebrate the holidays of their ethnic friends and neighbors. Where else but in America could a local St. Patrick's Day parade committee (from Westhampton, New York) hold a German Octoberfest at a Middle Eastern disco?

The following calendar contains both fixed holidays and "movable feast days" which are often shifted to weekends for convenience. For further information about local celebrations, contact the Chamber of Commerce or Office of Economic Development in the town where the festival is held.

JANUARY

1 New Year's Day
Americans celebrate the arrival of a new year with a Mummer's parade in Philadelphia, football games all over the nation, and news stories about the first baby born after midnight on January 1. There isn't any special significance to the football games, but what about our other New Year's traditions? Where did the Mummers and "Baby New Year" come from? Well, it certainly wasn't from the early Puritans — they didn't even call the month January, because it was named after a pagan god, Janus. They preferred to call it "first month," thank you, and they didn't care to celebrate anything about it.

Mummers Strutting to the tune "O Dem Golden Slippers," the Mummers make their way through the streets of Philadelphia led by King Momus, the leader of the parade. The Mummers' method of celebrating is a combination of English, Swedish and German traditions. The English custom of "mumming" on New Year's Day (going from house to house dressed in costumes and presenting plays) was combined with the

German tradition of welcoming the New Year with street festivals, marching bands and the pagan tradition of wearing animal skins. The Swedes introduced the German traditions to the Delaware River Valley, and soon everyone in the region was parading together, making music and shooting off firearms as noisemakers.

Baby New Year The symbol of a baby to represent the birth of a new year comes to us from the Greeks, who used to carry babes in baskets on New Year's Day. The custom, however, came to America via the Germans, who adopted the Greek tradition in the fourteenth century.

6 Greek Cross Day
On the feast of the Epiphany, January 6, Greek Orthodox prelates gather to bless the sponge fleet at Tarpon Springs, Florida. The waters are blessed and a white dove is released during the ceremony to symbolize the appearance of the Holy Ghost at Christ's baptism. A blessed cross is then thrown into the water, and the diver who retrieves it is blessed by special indulgences for the entire year.

11 de Hostos' Birthday, Puerto Rico
de Hostos (1839–1903) was a Puerto Rican educator, writer, and social philosopher who worked for democratic reform in Spain and throughout the Americas and for inter-Caribbean cooperation and federation.

15 Martin Luther King's Birthday
In many communities (Washington, D.C., Illinois, Kentucky, Maryland, Massachusetts, New Jersey) the birthdate of slain Black American civil rights leader Martin Luther King (1929–1968) is celebrated as a legal holiday.

17 Feast of St. Anthony
On this day Mexican pets are blessed in church.

30 FDR's Birthday
Ever since 1958, the birthday of Dutch-American president Franklin Delano Roosevelt has been celebrated as a legal holiday in Kentucky. The man behind the move to honor him was Ed Overbey, Sr., who believed: "FDR, in my opinion, ranks among the greatest of the other Presidents such as Lincoln and Jefferson. He brought about the biggest revolution this century has ever seen—deficit spending."

MOVABLE FEASTS

Tet Vietnamese New Year is celebrated on the first day of the first month of the lunar calendar.

Chinese New Year begins at the time of the first new moon after the sun enters Aquarius, sometime between January 21 and February 19. The Chinese lunar calendar dates back to the twenty-seventh century before Christ.

Each year is named in honor of one of 12 animals: horse, ram, monkey, rooster, dog, boar, rat, ox, tiger, hare, dragon, serpent. (Our year 1981 is the Chinese year of the rooster, 4679.)

Chinese New Year celebrations begin on 24th day of the 12th month and culminate seven days later (New Year's Day) with the traditional fireworks, dragon dances, food, music and colorful costumes. The most important part of the New Year's celebration occurs during the week prior to the street festivities—a time devoted to spiritual and physical purification of the home. This week is considered a "lucky" time for house-cleaning, and most of the 500,000 Chinese-Americans in the United States use this week to dust, sweep and remove the dirt and "evil influences" that have been accumulating throughout the year in the corners and dark recesses of the home.

This is also a time to pay homage to the household gods who protect the family. Old images of gods, such as those who protect the hearth, kitchen and front door, are burned and new images are purchased to honor the gods for their good work in protecting the home during the past year.

Where to find Chinese New Year celebrations: In the Chinatowns of Philadelphia, New York, San Francisco and Boston; Americans of all ethnic backgrounds can take part in New Year's festivities.

FEBRUARY

2 Groundhog Day

Originally a religious day known as Candlemas, February second marked the purification of the Virgin Mary 40 days after the birth of Christ, as was required by Jewish tradition. It is the only day of the year when sunshine is considered a "bad" omen by those who dislike wintry weather.

It was the British who gave us this bit of superstition that a pleasant, sunny Candlemas meant six more weeks of winter, but it was the Germans who contributed the folklore about the groundhog. In Germany the official animal who sees his shadow and is frightened back into his hole for the duration is a badger, but since there aren't any of those here in America we elected the groundhog as our official weather-predicting animal. Each year Americans wait with bated breath, snow shovels in one hand and suntan oil in the other, for the results from the official groundhog sighting town — Punxsutawney, Pennsylvania.

4 Ceylon Independence Day

6 Mexican Constitution Day

11 Japanese Founding Day

12 Lincoln's Birthday

Ever since 1866, Americans have been celebrating the birthdate of Abraham Lincoln (1809–1865), our 16th President and a descendant of one Samuel Lincoln, an Englishman from Norwich who settled at Hingham, Massachusetts in 1638. What was Honest Abe's opinion on the subject of genealogy? "I didn't know who my grandfather was; I am much more concerned to know who his grandson will be."

14 Valentine's Day

This romantic holiday is the delight of greeting card manufacturers and candy makers in the United States. It is the fourth largest candy-selling holiday (after Christmas, Halloween and Easter), and in 1979 Americans bought 485.3 million valentines to send to their sweeties. Named after an Italian priest who was martyred in 270 A.D., the holiday actually had its origins as a pagan fertility festival and not as a tribute to "romantic" love.

Known as the Lupercalia, it was the Roman day of tribute to Lupercus, the wolf-god in charge of fertility. When Christianity began to spread, the church decided to rededicate the Lupercalia to St. Valentine,* thereby turning a pagan feast into a religious occasion.

Americans inherited the tradition of sending greetings and love letters on this day from the English and the French. During the fourteenth century, British villagers would draw the names of unmarried men and women and write one another "mash" notes on February 14. A Frenchman — Charles, Duc d'Orleans — was the first to send a love note to his wife on this day in 1415 when he was imprisoned in the Tower of London, and gradually the custom changed until letters were exchanged solely with loved ones instead of with strangers. By 1840 there were elegant, ready-made ribbon-and-lace-bedecked "valentines" to send to your sweetheart on this special day. In 1847 Esther Howland of Worcester, Massachusetts, set up the first assembly-line production of valentines and sold almost three million cards her first year in business.

Want to add a special touch to your valentine card? Mail it from Loveland, Colorado — the zip code is 80537.

* He was canonized in 496 and decanonized in 1969.

Harper's Weekly *viewed Valen-tine's Day, 1861, as the perfect time to declare one's true love. (Courtesy: New York Public Library)*

22 (Traditional) Washington's Birthday

Lately, this holiday has been celebrated on the third Monday in February to give millions of Americans the pleasure of a three-day weekend. But, no matter, George Washington, an English-American, probably wouldn't have cared when the nation celebrated his birthday because he was actually born on February 11. And although most history books list 1732 as the year of his birth, he was actually born in 1731.

How did this mix-up happen? It all started in 1750 when the British Parliament discarded the Julian calendar in favor of the more accurate Gregorian calendar invented in 1582 by Pope Gregory XIII. The Julian calendar, which dated back to 46 B.C., was about 11 minutes and 14 seconds longer than the true solar year. By 1580 (after it had been used for over 1,500 years), the seasons had become misaligned. That year, the spring equinox fell on March 11 — ten days sooner than the traditional calendar date, March 21. To restore the equinox to its correct solar date, ten days were dropped from the calendar between October 4 and October 15, 1582, in most European countries. By the time the British got around to accepting the Julian calendar, they had to subtract 11 days from their year to catch up with the rest of Europe — hence, the calendar jumped from September 2 to September 14 in 1752.

According to the Julian calendar, New Year's day was celebrated on March 25. In order to make a smooth transition to a January-December year, the British simply omitted the days between January 1 and March 24, 1751 (that year had only 282 days), and started the new year, 1752, on January 1. The net result of all these changes was that George Washington was 19 years old in 1750, 20 years old on February 11, 1752, and 21 years old on February 22, 1753.

24 Mexican Flag Day

28 Kalevala National Day, Finland

29 Leap Year Day

February usually only has 28 days, but every fourth year it leaps to 29. Back in pre-liberation days, before women began asking men for dates, women were only allowed to ask men to marry them during leap years—for the next three years polite women would have to wait for their "fellows" to pop the question.

Where did this custom originate? According to some sources it started in Ireland, and it was first dreamed up by a group of nuns who wanted to marry priests. In the fifth century, when St. Patrick ruled the Church in Ireland, it was "legal" for priests and nuns to marry—they didn't have to leave the convent or priesthood to live together then, because they weren't required to take the vow of celibacy. As it happened, the priests weren't always quick enough to suit the sisters, and St. Bridget petitioned St. Patrick for the right to have the sisters ask the priest of their choice for his hand in marriage.

After much pleading, St. Patrick finally agreed to allow the women the right to ask the priests to marry them once every seven years—but Bridget and her troops weren't satisfied, and soon whittled Patrick down to once every four years. St. Bridget didn't waste time and proposed to St. Patrick immediately after the decree went into effect, but he declined her offer. He preferred to remain single, and devoted his life to "chasing the snakes out of Ireland" instead of chasing after a bride.

MOVABLE FEASTS

Shrove Tuesday, the day before Ash Wednesday, ushers in the solemn season of Lent and falls between the middle of February and the beginning of March (February 19, 1980; February 10, 1981; February 23, 1982; February 15, 1983; March 6, 1984; February 19, 1985; February 11, 1986; March 3, 1987).

Mardi Gras in New Orleans   The Mardi Gras is New Orleans' most festive occasion, and ethnic Americans of all races and religions take part in the four-day street celebration that culminates on Shrove Tuesday evening with parades, balls and general revelry.

The words "Mardi Gras" mean "Fat Tuesday" in French, and refer to the French custom of feasting heartily the night before Lent begins. The next day, Ash Wednesday, marks the beginning of the 40-day penitential season preceding Easter, during which certain foods are forbidden. The thrifty French want to make sure they use up all the rich, delicious foods that would spoil over the next month or so.

Fastnacht in Germany   The Germans call "Shrove Tuesday" *Fastnacht,* or "Eve of the Fast." And, like the French, the Germans know how to live it up before Lent. They do a better job of it, however, and usually celebrate with six weeks of fun-filled activities before Ash Wednesday rolls around.

In America, the Pennsylvania Dutch, who are really descended from German ancestors despite their name, don't celebrate for six weeks prior to *Fastnacht,* but they do have their traditions. On Shrove Tuesday *everyone* must eat *Fastnacht Kuchen,* rectangular-shaped doughnuts fried in deep fat. Even dieters don't dare to refuse *kuchen* on this day, because failure to eat them could result in some pretty dire consequences. For the rest of the year one might suffer from boils, buy chickens that don't lay eggs, or risk failure of the flax crop, according to local superstitions. Good luck and a plentiful harvest are promised to everyone who munches *Fastnachts Kuchen* on this day, so everyone enjoys them without a thought about the calorie count.

One note of caution: Despite the best influences of the *Fastnacht Kuchen,* if you sew on this day, your chickens will not reproduce; and if you happen to cut yourself with an ax, the wound will not heal properly.

Black History Month   Since 1978, February has been celebrated as Black History Month in the United States. Originally the observance only lasted a week, sometime around the February 14 birthday of Frederick Douglas (1817–1895), the black Abolitionist and ex-slave. The celebration originated in 1926 at the suggestion of Carter G. Woodson, a

Black historian who is often called "the father of Negro history." The theme for the week, or month, differs each year, and in the past historians have used the occasion to draw attention to the history of African art, music and literature, or the progress that Blacks have made in America during the past century.

MARCH

1 **St. David's Day**
St. David is the patron saint of Wales and the Welsh honor him on this day by wearing leek blossoms on their hats. The leek became the national symbol of Wales after a famous battle between the Welsh and the Saxons in the sixth century. At St. David's suggestion, the Welsh troops wore leeks in their caps to distinguish themselves from the enemy and went on to a resounding victory.

3 **Feast of St. Cunegund,** Queen of Bavaria in 1033
Bulgarian National Holiday, celebrating liberation from the Turks in 1878.

5 **Boy's Day in Japan**

11 **Decoration Day, Liberia**

17 **St. Patrick's Day**
St. Patrick, the patron Saint of Ireland, was probably born in Kilpatrick. Scotland, sometime between 373 and 395. Some scholars have claimed his place of birth as England, Wales or France, but one thing is certain: he was not born in Ireland.

Captured by Irish slavers as a youth, he spent six years of his life in captivity tending sheep. His given name was Maewyn, but after his release from slavery he entered the priesthood and chose the name Patrick. Eventually elevated to the rank of bishop, Patrick was sent to Ireland as a missionary after studying in France. Through St. Patrick's efforts the Irish people were converted from Druidism to Christianity.

The first recorded observance of his feast day occurred in 493 A.D. As early as 1737 there was a St. Patrick's Day celebration in America. Today, parades, the wearin' of the green, drinking green beer and dining on corned beef and cabbage are American traditions for "Irishmen" of every ethnic background on March 17.

20 **Tunisian Independence Day**

22 **Abolition Day, Puerto Rico**

23 **Pakistan Day,** national holiday since 1956

26 **Kuhio Day, Hawaii**

29 **Youth Day, Taiwan**

MOVABLE FEASTS

Purim   Also known as the Hebrew Feast of Lots, Purim occurs on the 14th day of the Jewish month Adar, approximately one month before Passover.

Purim commemorates the Old Testament story of Queen Esther, a clever woman who persuaded her husband, King Ahasuerus of Persia, to spare her people from an intended slaughter at the hands of his minister Haman. The intended slaughter was supposed to occur on the thirteenth day of Adar, a date chosen by lot (*pur* in Persian). Later, after Haman's treachery was revealed and the Jewish people were saved, Esther wrote the story down on a scroll or *megillah,* so it could be read on the 14th day of Adar every year afterwards.

Jewish Americans celebrate Purim by reading the *megillah* and making loud noises whenever the villain of the story, Haman, is mentioned. Special poppy seed pastries, known as Hamantashen (shaped like Haman's tricornered hat) are served on this day to recall the triumph of good over evil.

Dutch Heritage Festival   In March of each year, the town of Nederland, Texas, hosts a Dutch Heritage Festival. There is a carnival, a flea market and a crafts show. For more information, write in care of the Chamber of Commerce, Nederland, Texas 77672.

JEWISH CALENDAR OF MOVABLE HOLIDAYS

	1981	1982	1983	1984
Purim	March 20	March 9	Feb. 27	March 18
1st day of Passover	April 19	April 8	March 29	April 17
1st day of Shabuoth	June 8	May 28	May 18	June 6
1st day Rosh Hashana	Sept. 29	Sept. 18	Sept. 8	Sept. 27
Yom Kippur	Oct. 8	Sept. 27	Sept. 17	Oct. 6
1st day Sukkoth	Oct. 13	Oct. 2	Sept. 22	Oct. 11
Simhath Torah	Oct. 21	Oct. 10	Sept. 30	Oct. 19
1st day Hanukkah	Dec. 21	Dec. 11	Dec. 1	Dec. 19

APRIL

1 April Fool's Day
This custom came to America via the early English settlers, who enjoyed playing pranks on one another on the first of April. The custom actually began in France in 1564, when Charles IX adopted a new calendar for his country. Prior to 1564, the New Year began in the spring and April 1 was celebrated with festivities appropriate to New Year's Day. When the new calendar shifted New Year's Day to January 1, a small group of diehards who opposed "progress" continued to celebrate, as they always had, on the first of April. They were called "April Fools," and by the early 1600s the practice of fooling one's friends had spread throughout other parts of Europe.

5 Chin Ming Festival: the Chinese visit the graves of their deceased relatives.

8 Buddha's Birthday in Korea and Japan (India celebrates April 9).

14 Pan American Day

15–22 Italian Culture Week, New York (1978)

16 De Diego's birthday, Puerto Rico

17 Flag Day, Samoa
Verrazano Day, New York State – in honor of the Italian explorer who discovered New York Harbor in 1524.

19 Independence Day in Venezuela

21 Independence Day in Ecuador

22 Lenin's birthday, Russian national holiday

22 Arbor Day
The man behind Arbor Day was Julius Sterling Morton, a politician and descendant of Richard Morton, an Englishman who came to America on the "second Mayflower," *Little Ann.* (Julius's son, Joy Morton, later made the family name a household word with his salt company's slogan that promised. "When it rains, it pours.")

In 1872, when Julius was serving his country as Governor of Nebraska, he began offering prizes to the county agricultural society that planted the most trees each spring. Soon, the practice of planting trees on a special day in the springtime spread throughout the nation and in 1885, when the legislature decided to make Arbor Day a legal holiday in Nebraska, they chose Morton's birthday, April 22.

25 Anzac Day in Australia to honor war dead
26 Tanzania Union Day
29 Annual Fair, Focsani, in Romania
Hirohito's Birthday, Japanese national holiday

MOVABLE FEASTS

Easter The traditions associated with Easter in America, such as the Easter bunny, Easter ham and egg-rolling contests come to us from the English and German settlers.

Egg rolls This custom, which came from England may be symbolic of the stone that was rolled away from Christ's tomb on Easter morning. The most famous egg-roll in America is the one held each year on the White House lawn. President James Madison started the tradition when he invited the nation's children to roll eggs there in 1809.

Easter bunny The rabbit who hops down the bunny trail with his baskets full of eggs and candy is a native of Germany, brought to America by immigrants from the Palatinate. Their children would build nests for the bunny, where he would "lay" colored eggs for them to find on Easter Sunday morning.

Ham and all the trimmings Americans eat turkey on Thanksgiving and ham on Easter Sunday. The tradition of dining on cured pork meat originated out of spite. The English originally consumed a gammon of bacon on Easter as a display of contempt for the Jewish practice of abstaining from pork. William the Conqueror (1027–1087) preferred ham to bacon, and when he conquered England, he had the customary Easter meal changed to suit his taste.

(Easter varies between late March and mid-April. In 1981, Easter Sunday falls on March 29; in 1982, April 11; in 1983, April 3; in 1984, April 22; in 1985, April 7.)

Easter, Greek Style On Holy Saturday, Greeks attend midnight Mass and after services gather at the home of friends for a late-night supper. During the religious service, a flame is passed from one candle to another, held by the parishioners, until the entire church is ablaze with light. Everyone receives a red Easter egg as they leave the church to signify the start of a new life — symbolic of the arrival of spring and the resurrection of the Lord.

The traditional meal which breaks the Lenten fast is *Mageritsa,* a soup made with the intestines, heart, liver and stomach of the baby lamb which has been slaughtered in preparation for Easter Sunday's meal. Thick with egg and lemon sauce and seasoned with dill and scallions, the soup represents both the suffering of Christ and the joyfulness of his resurrection.

Easter, Eastern European Style *Pysanky* is the Ukrainian tradition of painting Easter eggs, but the custom is practiced in most other Eastern European and Baltic countries, too. Hot wax is applied in designs to certain areas of the egg, and then removed after the egg is dipped into the first color. Successive layers of wax protect "yellow" from becoming "green" when the egg is dipped into blue dye, and as a result the egg emerges with an intricate network of lines and colors.

Why do Ukrainian women practice this tedious custom each year? Aside from the beauty of the eggs and their value as an art form, legend claims that the fate of the world depends upon the maintenance of this custom. If the tradition ever ceases, a chained monster will be unleashed upon the earth to devour us all.

Passover This Jewish celebration, which occurs on the 15th day of the Hebrew month Nisan, commemorates the liberation of the Hebrew people from Egyptian bondage. It takes its name from the Biblical story of the angel of death who, at the Lord's command, descended upon the homes of the Egyptians, killing all firstborn children, while passing over the homes of the Jews.

During their hasty flight to freedom, the Jews had no time to wait for bread to rise, and therefore had to eat unleavened bread. For this reason, a flat *matzoh* is the traditional bread consumed by Jews all over the world during this eight-day celebration.

Hispanic Festival   During the month of April, the town of Tucson, Arizona, salutes its multi-cultural heritage with a series of festivals featuring Spanish, Mexican and Indian themes.

MAY

1 May Day

Although maypoles seem to be going the way of "white gloves and hats" for ladies, there was a time when young American girls would dress in flowing white gowns and dance around a pole festooned with ribbons on the first day of May.

The first recorded maypole in America was erected in 1627 by Thomas Morton, an English Anglican, who lived in Plymouth Colony. When the Puritans saw Morton and his men dancing and frolicking with Indian maidens aroud the maypole, the governor ordered the pole to be chopped down. Morton was later shipped back to England on trumped-up charges of selling arms to the Indians.

MOVABLE FEASTS

Mother's Day, First Sunday in May

Although an American, Anna M. Jarvis (1864–1948), is credited with originating the idea of Mother's Day, the holiday is steeped in English tradition. In England it is known as "Mothering Sunday."

At the time of her death, Anna Jarvis was heartbroken at the rampant commercialism that had overtaken the holiday tradition she started. Rather than expensive presents, cards and gifts, Jarvis would have preferred a celebration more in keeping with the English custom of taking over Mother's chores for the day and gathering around Mom for a family Sunday dinner.

REGIONAL FESTIVALS

Dutch   May is tulip time, and there are many towns in the United States that host annual tulip festivals each year. The festival held at Holland, Michigan, probably the best known, has been drawing Americans from all over the United States for more than fifty years. In addition to the tulip farms and flower shows, attractions include a wooden-shoe factory, a Netherlands museum, street scrubbing rituals, dances and parades.

Although tulips are grown strictly for beauty today, there once were enormous profits to be made on the tulip market. When the flowers were first introduced to Europe from Constantinople in the 1500s their popularity grew so rapidly that all of Europe was overcome with a desire to possess these lovely bulbs. "Tulipomania" raged through Holland between 1634 and 1637, as thousands of businessmen invested their life savings in rare bulbs, much as we invest in oil and steel stocks today. Fortunes were made and lost on the tulip market until the government was forced to step in and regulate the trade of flowering bulbs.

French   Port Arthur, Texas, holds an annual Cajun Festival complete with crawfish races to celebrate the heritage of the region.

German   McCook, Nebraska, hosts German Heritage Days in early May to commemorate the town's heritage. Other German festivals this month can be found in Hermann, Missouri, and Brenham, Texas.

Latin American   Each year since 1966, the Spanish-Speaking Citizens Foundation of San Francisco has hosted a fiesta in that California city. Features include a coronation ball, Latin music, dancers, floats and marching bands.

Mexican   Mexican fiestas are held in May at Bakersfield, California; Lompoc, California; and Goliad, Texas.

Norwegian   The residents of Poulsbo, Washington, celebrate Norwegian Independence Day each May with folk dancing, arts, crafts and a smorgasbord. *Syttende Mai Fest* celebrations can also be found in Spring Grove, Minnesota; Stoughton, Wisconsin; and Petersburg, Alaska.

JUNE

6   **Korean Memorial Day**
    Swedish National Day, since 1893
7   **Norwegian Flag Day**
9   **Danish Constitution Day** — annual festival held at Minneapolis, Minnesota
11 **Birthday of King Kamehameha the Great.** The annual celebration held in Honolulu features hula contests, parades, luaus and canoe races.
12 **Helsinki Day, Finland**
15 **Farmer's Day in Korea** — time for rice transplanting
18 **Salusalu Festival in Fiji Islands**
19–20   **Czech Days in Tabor, South Dakota**
    Each year since 1848 the town has saluted its Czechoslovakian heritage.
22 **National Tree Day, El Salvador**
23 **Wainiki Holiday, Poland**
24 **Midsummer Day, England**
26 **Independence Day, Malagasy Republic**

REGIONAL FESTIVALS

Filipino   Honolulu hosts an annual Filipino Fiesta to honor the many Filipinos who inhabit the Hawaiian Islands. The fiesta includes traditional folk dances, crafts, songs and theater presentations from the Philippines.

German   Each year since 1959, the citizens of Frankenmuth, Michigan, host their annual Bavarian Fun Time Festival. Held during the second week of June, the Festival features German bands, polka contests, craftsmen, sausages and quantities of beer.

Swedish   Each June, Geneva, Illinois; Minneapolis, Minnesota; Stromberg, Nebraska; Philadelphia; and Cambridge, Minnesota, all host an annual Swedish festival.

JULY

6   **Constitution Day, Cayman Islands**
8   **Unity Day, Zambia**
14 **Shinto Festival of Fans, Japan**
17 **Constitution Day, Korea**
    Muñoz Rivera's Birthday, Puerto Rico
20 **Independence Day, Colombia**
22 **Polish National Day**
25 **Constitution Day, Puerto Rico**
26 **Liberian Independence Day**
27 **Barbosa's Birthday, Puerto Rico**

REGIONAL FESTIVALS

Basque The National Basque Festival held each year at Elko, Nevada, attracts the many Basque residents of the western United States. Highlights of the festival are the sheep herding and sheering contests, which attest to the most prevalent occupation of our citizens from the Basque region, on the border between France and Spain. Another Basque festival is held each July at Sun Valley, Idaho.

Dutch Edgerton, Minnesota holds an annual two-day Dutch festival in mid-July.

French An annual French Festival held at Cape Vincent, New York, honors the heritage of the region, with French foods, handicrafts, band concerts, parades and a festival queen.

Pennsylvania Dutch One of the most famous ethnic festivals is the Kutztown Folk Festival, an annual event in Pennsylvania since 1949. For two weeks in early July, one can enjoy food from the Amish country (shoo-fly pie, scrapple, chow-chow and funnel cakes); hear lectures on folklore; enter a quilting contest; or watch craftsmen weave and paint "hex signs."
For more information, contact:
Kutztown Folk Festival,
College Boulevard & Vine,
Kutztown, Pa. 19530.

Spanish/Mexican Each year since 1951, the Mission of San Luis Rey in Oceanside, California, has conducted a Hispanic festival featuring entertainment, games, street dancing, music, a barbecue, and the Blessing of the Animals.

AUGUST

1 Lammas Day in England, start of the whest harvest
7 Battle of Boyaca, National Holiday in Columbia
15 Wedding of the Sea, Atlantic City, New Jersey.
  Each year Italian-Americans gather at this seaside resort to honor Christ's mother, Mary, on the feast of the Assumption. The "Wedding of the Sea" has been a tradition for hundreds of years in Venice, and in keeping with the Old World traditions, the ceremony begins with Mass, and is followed by a parade of the faithful carrying a statue of the Blessed Mother to the shoreline. The water is blessed by a priest, and the mayor of the city tosses a wreath of flowers and a wedding band into the sea. Afterwards, the sick and elderly bathe in the blessed waters, and collect samples of seawater to bring home for its "curative" effect.
17 Independence Day, Indonesia
24 Flag Day, Liberia
26 Harlem Day, New York City
27 Lyndon Baines Johnson's birthday is celebrated as a holiday in Texas.
31 Malaysian Day

REGIONAL FESTIVALS

American Indian The Festival of the Americas, held in New York City, honors the first residents of North, Central and South America. Festivities include: basket weaving demonstrations, costumes, crafts, puppet shows, dances and other entertainment.

Belgian Each August, Belgian American Day is celebrated at Ghent, Minnesota. There are thick Belgian waffles laden with whipped cream, parades, music and a prysbolling contest (the national sport of Belgium). For more information contact the Department of Economic Development, 480 Cedar Street, St. Paul, Minn. 55101.

English   Renaissance fairs have gained popularity throughout the United States since the early 1960s. Striving to recreate the splendor that was Elizabethan England, each fair features jousting competitions, horse races, costumes and appropriate music. The most famous fair is held each year at San Rafael, California. Other fairs can be found at Agoura, California, and Shakopee, Minnesota.

Italian   Each year Clinton, Indiana's "Little Italy" hosts its annual Italian festival. There are strolling musicians, Italian food, songs and dancing. There is also a grape stomp, and the chance to take a gondola ride down the Wabash River.

Japanese   Nisei Week, in Los Angeles' "Little Tokyo" has been an annual event in mid-August since 1942. This week-long celebration features judo, karate and kendo demonstrations; parades; Japanese food; and music.

Polish   Bronson, Michigan, and St. Paul, Minnesota, both feature Polish festivals in early to mid-August. There is kielbasa (Polish sausage) to eat; music; wycinanki (Polish paper cutting art) demonstrations and contests such as tractor pulling, horseshoe pitching and polka dancing.

Scandinavian   Junction City, Oregon, holds a four-day festival in early August to celebrate the town's Scandinavian heritage. One day each is set aside to honor the Finns, Danes, Swedes and Norwegians with appropriate food, crafts, music, and dancing.

Scottish   August witnesses annual Scottish games festivals in Syracuse, New York, and at Old Westbury Gardens on Long Island. Sports and entertainment include caber tossing, sheaf pitching, hammer throwing, piping, soccer and Highland flings. The Long Island Scottish Clans Association sponsors their games in late August. For more information call (516) 333-0048.

Spanish   August is *the* month for Spanish festivals in America. Old Spanish Days, held at Santa Barbara, California, commemorate that city's Spanish heritage; St. Augustine, Florida, honors its 1565 founding by the Spanish with a festival that features Spanish food, handicrafts and amusements. And, in late August, there is the Fiesta de Santa Fe in New Mexico, honoring the peaceful conquest of New Mexico by Don Diego de Vargas in 1692. Held every year since 1713, the Fiesta de Santa Fe is the Southwest's oldest celebration.

Swiss   Swiss Independence Day is celebrated at Waterville, New Hampshire, on the Saturday closest to August 3. Squaw Valley, California; Tell City, Indiana; and Berne, Minnesota, also feature Swiss celebrations this month, with Swiss wrestling competitions, yodeling, alpine horn blowing, arts and crafts, and food such as pear bread (*berrebrot*), rabbit ears (*musli*) and *küchlis* ("big nothing" cookies).

Swiss folk dancers. (Courtesy: Swiss National Tourist Office)

CELEBRATIONS FOR ALMOST EVERYONE

The Garden State Arts Center at Holmdel, New Jersey, hosts ethnic festivals for almost every nationality in the Northeast. Here's a partial listing of their annual events; for more information write in care of the festival of your choice, New Jersey Highway Authority, Woodbridge, New Jersey 07095.

Polish Festival	early June
Ukrainian Festival	early June
Jewish Festival of the Arts	mid-June
Irish Festival	late June
Italian Festival	late June
German-American Festival	early September
Puerto Rican Heritage Festival	September
Hungarian Festival	mid-September
Scottish Heritage Festival	mid-September
Grecian Arts Festival	late september

SEPTEMBER

5 **Cherokee National Holiday**
10 **African American Day, New York City**
15 **Independence Day in Mexico, Nicaragua. Costa Rica and Honduras**
16 **Cherokee Strip Day, Oklahoma**
17 **Steuben Day** honors the memory of General Baron Friedrich Wilhelm von Steuben, a Revolutionary War hero. The first parade in New York City honoring Steuben was held in 1958 when the son of a German immigrant (Robert F. Wagner) presided as Gotham's mayor. Each year more than 12,000 German-Americans and friends of German-Americans march to honor the many contributions German immigrants made to America. Just as shamrocks are the symbol of St. Patrick's Day marchers, cornflower garlands have become the symbol of the Steuben Day Parade.
28 **Portuguese-Americans in San Diego, California,** celebrate the discovery of California on this day. In 1542, a Portuguese explorer named Juan Cabrillo became the first European to spot San Diego Bay.
29 **Michaelmas,** the feast of the Archangel St. Michael. (In England, the day is celebrated by eating Michaelmas goose.)

MOVABLE FEASTS

Labor Day   First Monday in September
The workingman's holiday, Labor Day was the brainchild of an Irish-American leader of the Knights of Labor — Peter J. McGuire. The tenth child born to hardworking Irish immigrants, McGuire first suggested a holiday to honor the common workingman of America in 1882. That year the first Labor Day celebration was held on September 5 as 10,000 workers from the Central Labor Union marched around Union Square in New York City. The parade and celebration were such a success that McGuire suggested that Labor Day be repeated each year on the first Monday in September.
American Indian Day   Fourth Friday
Indian Day, Oklahoma   First Saturday after full moon

Sixth annual Labor Day Parade at Union Square in New York City. (Courtesy: New York Historical Society)

Rosh Hashanah, the Jewish New Year, occurs in mid or late September, on the first day of the Jewish month Tishri. And since the Hebrew calendar is 3,761 years ahead of ours, 1981 will be the Jewish year 5742.

Yom Kippur, the Day of Atonement, is a Jewish holiday that falls on the 10th day of the month Tishri (late September–early October). It is characterized by fasting and by prayers beseeching God's forgiveness for human errors.

REGIONAL FESTIVALS

Asian   The Asian-American Outdoor Festival, held in New York City's Chinatown, draws the overflow crowd from "Little Italy's" Feast of San Gennaro which occurs during the latter part of September. The Asian festival features Chinese, Japanese, Vietnamese and Korean arts, crafts, music and food.

Italian   The Festival of San Gennaro lasts 10 days, and usually occurs during the second half of the month (the Saint's actual feast day is September 19th). The days and nights are full of food, drink and merriment, in honor of a third-century Bishop (St. Januarius) who saved Naples from destruction by stopping the eruption of Mt. Vesuvius.

During September, the town of McAlester, Oklahoma, also hosts its annual Italian festival, in honor of Italian coal miners who lived in the town during the 1880s.

Japanese   Since 1970, San Francisco has hosted a three-day festival (Aki Matsuri) at the Japan Center each September. There are *bonsai* (dwarfed tree) displays, Japanese music and dance, *origami* (paper folding) demonstrations, *ikebana* (flower arranging) instructions and demonstrations of the martial arts. The festival is an outgrowth of the harvest festivals which have been held in Japan at this time for hundreds of years and play such a vital role in the cultural and social life of the Japanese people.

Mexican   Stockton, California, is home to the annual Mexican Independence Day celebration in mid-September. There are *mariachi* bands, *folklorico* dancers, and drum and bugle corps performers. Other Mexican celebrations are found in Scottsbluff, Nebraska, and Toledo, Ohio, where the residents gather to pay tribute to our southern neighbor.

Syrian / Lebanese St. Elias Orthodox Church in Toledo, Ohio, hosts an annual Syrian-Lebanese-American Family Festival in late September. There are stuffed grape leaves and shish kebabs to eat, as well as music, dancing, entertainment, raffles and other festivities.

OCTOBER

2 **Gandhi's Birthday, India**
3 **National Foundation Day, Korea**
9 **Leif Ericson Day**
Norwegians at Jensen Beach, Florida, host a special celebration on the Sunday closest to this day.
11 **Pulaski Day** is a tribute to the Polish general who served the American cause during the Revolutionary War and died of wounds he suffered during the siege of Savannah, Georgia. This day is an official holiday in the state of Indiana.
12 **Traditional Columbus Day,** when Italian-Americans march in honor of their *coumad* who discovered America in 1492. The first Columbus Day was celebrated on October 12, 1792, on the 300th anniversary of the discovery of America. The next celebration took place in 1892, when Columbus Circle was dedicated in New York City. (Incidentally, the monument that adorns Columbus Circle was the work of a Sicilian sculptor, Gaetano Russo. The total height of the column is 75 feet, including the statue, which stands 14 feet tall.)

Columbus Day began to be observed widely on an annual basis in 1893, when the Chicago World's Columbian Exposition was held. (That Exposition celebrated the 400th anniversary of Columbus' discovery, albeit a year late.)
13 **Thanksgiving Day, Canada**
28 **Greek National Day**
29 **Republic Day, Turkey**
31 **Halloween**
Although it isn't a legal holiday, Halloween is first in the hearts of many young children who enjoy dressing up as goblins, spooks and ghosts to beg for treats on "All Hallows Eve."

Like most other traditions, "trick or treat" has religous origins. The poor would beg for "soul cake" in Ireland on the night when the spirits, witches and ghosts walked the earth; and those who contributed food to the poor were blessed while the tightwads were threatened with bodily harm.

Later on, the children took up the habit of dressing in one another's clothing and begging for treats on Halloween — as "protection" or "insurance" against evil deeds.

The Irish also gave us the Jack-o'-lanterns we carve from pumpkins on this night. Designed to scare away "evil spirits," the jack-o'-lantern is named for a miserable Irishman named Jack. A greedy, stingy man when he was alive, Jack was not welcomed in Heaven when he died. But, since he had always played tricks on the Devil,* Jack was not welcomed in Hell, either, and he was forced to roam the earth until Judgment Day, carrying a lantern to light his way.

Other Irish traditions, not as well known in the United States, include two traditional foods served on Halloween to foretell the future: barmbrack and colcannon.

*Jack had once tricked the Devil into climbing a tree for an apple. Once the Devil was up the tree, Jack drew the sign of the cross on the trunk — thereby trapping Satan. Jack released him, but only after the Devil promised never to hound him for his soul when he was dead. When Jack was refused admission to Heaven, the Devil was duty bound to keep his word and could not take Jack into Hell.

Similar to the custom of carving pumpkins into jack-o'lanterns is the Swiss tradition of Räbenlichter. Swiss children hollow out turnips and place lit candles inside. The children parade through town, carrying their turnips and singing folksongs. (Courtesy: Swiss National Tourist Office)

Barmbrack is an unleavened (barm) sweet bread that has coins, rings and buttons baked inside. If you are lucky enough to receive a ring baked in your slice, you will be married within the year. Coins symbolize wealth and buttons indicate general good fortune.

Colcannon is a mixture of spinach or kale and mashed potatoes with a lucky coin placed inside. The colcannon is placed on the table with a pool of butter in the center and everyone starts eating it at once, from the outside in, dipping their forkfuls in the liquid butter. If you find the "lucky" coin, you will be blessed throughout the coming year.

REGIONAL FESTIVALS

French The heritage of the Louisiana French is celebrated at the International Acadian Festival at Plaquemine, Louisiana, and the Bridge City Gumbo Festival. The latter features entertainment, eating contests and, naturally, a gigantic 4,000-gallon potful of gumbo.

German The Germans invented the "Octoberfest"—an annual festival where good food, beer and German music abound. Most festivals feature oompah bands, sauerkraut and plenty of wursts—knockwurst, bauernwurst and bratwurst, to name a few. You can find Octoberfests in South Amana, Iowa; Waterville, Maine; Bowie, Maryland; and La Crosse, Wisconsin.

Irish San Francisco's Convention Center conducts an annual Irish festival for one week in mid-October. There is music, and traditional Irish crafts are displayed.

Norwegian Jensen Beach, Florida, features Viking boat races, Norwegian folk dances, and a reenactment of the Viking landing in celebration of Leif Erickson's Day, October 9.

Russian Sitka, Alaska, celebrates its "Russian roots" with an annual parade and festival in mid-October to commemorate the sale of Seward's Folly.

Scottish Balboa Stadium in San Diego, California, is the home of Scottish highland games during the middle of this month. There are tugs-of-war, caber tossing contests, hammer throws and rugby matches. A similar festival is held at this time at Stone Mountain Park in Atlanta, Georgia.

Swedish In odd-numbered years, Lindsborg, Kansas (nicknamed "Little Sweden, U.S.A."), hosts a week-long celebration in honor of the town's early Swedish pioneers. Held every other year since 1941, the *Svensk Hyllningfest* features ethnic foods, exhibits and entertainment.

NOVEMBER

1 National Holiday, Algeria
3 Panama Independence Day
11 Remembrance Day, Canada
22 Independence Day, Lebanon
23 Rice ceremony, Kyoto, Japan
29 Republic Day, Yugoslavia
   National Holiday, Albania
30 Independence Day, Barbados

30 **St. Andrew's Day**
Andrew is the patron saint of Scotland, and on this day every self-respecting Scotsman eats *haggis* – the national dish. Made of sheep's liver (or calf's liver) and other vital organs, such as the heart and lungs, *haggis* is boiled in a bag made from the animal's stomach.

MOVABLE FEASTS

Thanksgiving Fourth Thursday in November
The winter diet of colonial America was agonizingly boring. Day after day there were few vegetables to be eaten, save for the root crops (turnips, potatoes, carrots) which could be stored in root cellars for several months without decaying. Thus, before the advent of canned, frozen and dehydrated foods, Thanksgiving had an even greater meaning than it does today. Besides being a day of thanks for the bountiful harvest, it was also the last "big" meal of the autumn season. After Thanksgiving, the colonists would have to tighten their belts and eat sparingly to make their supply of potatoes, carrots and turnips last through the winter, until new vegetables could be grown in the spring.

The first Thanksgiving was held in 1621 when Governor Bradford of Plymouth Colony invited Chief Massasoit and his tribesmen to a three-day feast to celebrate their plentiful harvest and the "peace" that reigned between the two groups. It wasn't until 1783 that the Thanksgiving ritual became official, when Elias Boudinot (1740–1821). President of the Continental Congress, proclaimed: ". . . the second Thursday in December next as a day of public thanksgiving . . ."

Known as the "Father of Thanksgiving," Boudinot was descended from early French-Huguenot settlers of New York. In 1789, Boudinot changed the national observance of Thanksgiving from December to the last Thursday in November, but the holiday was not nationally observed until after the Civil War, with the date shifting between late October and mid-December.

Three Facts About Thanksgiving Dinner:
1 The Aztec and Zuñi Indians were the first to domesticate the wild turkeys that are native to North America.
2 Although turkey is the traditional fare for Thanksgiving feasts today, in colonial times the bird of choice was Thanksgiving goose with all the trimmings. Before the poor bird was slaughtered, his feet were bound and he was thrown down the chimney. His fiercely flapping wings removed all the soot and grime from the walls of the flue as he struggled to gain altitude.

THE TURKEYS' HOLIDAYS.

Butcher shop interior at Thanksgiving time in 1866. (Courtesy: New York Historical Society)

3 In 1630, four shillings would buy a 40-pound bird. If any of the 141.4 million turkeys sold in 1980 had weighed 40 pounds, the going rate would have been close to $35.

REGIONAL FESTIVALS

Onion Festival   Florida, New York, a town with a large Polish population, hosts an annual onion harvest festival complete with floats, an "Onion Queen" and a "Maypole" decorated with — you guessed it — onions! Similar onion festivals have been held in Europe on the fourth Monday in November for hundreds of years.

Onions on parade. (Courtesy: Swiss National Tourist Office)

DECEMBER

4 National Day, Burma
13 Feast of St. Lucia. On this day, young Swedish girls, dressed in white with candles atop their heads, traditionally serve St. Lucia buns to their parents.
21 Forefathers Day commemorates British landing at Plymouth Rock in 1621.
25 Christmas Day
26 Boxing Day in Europe—a time to exchange Christmas gifts.
   St. Stephen's Day. The Irish reenact the pagan custom of dressing up in disguises and going from house to house "trick or treating" while singing the "Wren Song."
28 All Fool's Day in Mexico. If a person is "foolish" enough to lend a friend something on this day it does not have to be returned.
31 New Year's Eve.
   "Touch a pig for luck" Day in Austria. (Barring the availability of a swine in your neighborhood, many delicatessens and food shops sell marzipan pigs for you to nibble on at midnight for "good luck" during the coming year.)

MOVABLE FEASTS

Hanukkah This joyous festival commemorates a Jewish military victory over 2,000 years ago. In the second century B.C., Syrian forces under King Antiochus conquered Jerusalem and desecrated its Temple. Their victory was short-lived, however, as Judah Maccabeus led the Jews to a great triumph over Antiochus. When the Jewish forces entered the Temple, they found only a one-day supply of lamp oil. Thanks to divine intervention, however, this oil lasted for eight days, thus enabling the Jews to celebrate their victory and the rededication of the Temple. To commemorate this miracle, a new candle is lit for each night of the eight-day Hanukkah period, and children are given gifts on each night of the holiday. The "Feast of Lights" falls on the 25th day of the Hebrew month Kislev.

CHRISTMAS

To the dismay of religious leaders, Christmas in America is no longer strictly a religious holiday — Americans from every ethnic background and religious upbringing can find some reason to rejoice over this season of "peace on earth and good will toward mankind." Retail merchants rejoice because those presents under the Christmas tree represent billions of dollars in sales; there is increased employment for street-corner Santas, increased revenues for caterers and an increase in traffic for the churches of America.

Where else but in America could one of our best-loved Christmas songs have been written by a Jewish immigrant from Russia? "White Christmas" only goes to prove that you don't have to be Christian to have "Christmas spirit."

Where did all our customs and traditions associated with Christmas come from? It certainly wasn't from the Puritans — rather than celebrating Christmas, they passed a law in 1659 that made it illegal! Anyone caught celebrating Christmas in Massachusetts would be fined 5 shillings. The English immigrants who came to our shores later on brought us Christmas goose, holly boughs, plum pudding, and the tradition of placing lit candles in our windows as a symbol of peace and good cheer. Like our citizens, our Christmas customs and traditions come from all over the globe.

ETHNIC CONTRIBUTIONS TO CHRISTMAS IN AMERICA

Christmas Seals The use of Christmas seals originated in Denmark in 1904. A postal clerk named Einar Holboell first thought up the idea of selling special stamps at Christmas time to show that money had been donated to a worthy cause.

Christmas Trees   The first recorded Christmas tree was erected at Strasbourg, Germany, in 1604. The first person to bring the Christmas tree *inside* was Martin Luther, who chopped down a tiny fir tree and decorated it with lighted candles to represent the stars, thereby starting the tradition that was brought to America by early German settlers in the 1800s.

There are two contenders for the "first Christmas tree in America": some scholars claim that August Imgard, a German immigrant from Hesse, was the first to set up a tree at his Wooster, Ohio, home in 1847; but there is some evidence that the honor might belong to Charles Follen of Cambridge, Massachusetts, who supposedly decorated a Christmas tree as early as 1832.

Kissing Under the Mistletoe   We have to thank the Scandinavians for the myth that surrounds this poisonous, epiphytic plant. According to legend, Baldur the Beautiful (the god of light and spring) became convinced that his life was in danger. He asked his mother, Frigga (the goddess of love) to travel all over the world and ask every living thing that inhabited the air, earth, water and fire to spare his life. Unfortunately for Baldur, Frigga was a little sloppy in accomplishing her task and neglected to ask the lowly mistletoe not to harm her beloved son. Loki (the god of fire) fashioned a dart from this parasitic plant and slew Baldur because of Frigga's mistake. As a result, Frigga decreed that mistletoe would never again be used as a weapon, and declared that she would kiss anyone who passed beneath the plant. Her tears were transformed into the white berries that are characteristic of the plant, and mistletoe became a symbol of peace and love.

Christmas Stockings   The real Saint Nicholas was the Bishop of Myra in Asia Minor (now Turkey) during the fourth century. He was a real-life "Santa Claus" who saved a poor man's daughters from slavery by providing a gift of golden coins for their dowry. He threw the coins down the chimney and they happened to fall into the girls' stockings, which had been hung by the fireside to dry. That started a tradition, and soon children all over the world were hanging up stockings "in hopes that Saint Nicholas soon would be there," to deposit candy, oranges or toys in the toes of their hose.

Gifts on Christmas Day   St. Nicholas died on December 6, 345, and for centuries it was a Christian tradition to give presents on his feast day *and* on Christmas morning.

Economics probably forced the two customs to merge as St. Nicholas gradually became associated with Christmas Eve.

Through the influence of the Dutch and the Germans, all Americans adopted the custom of exchanging gifts on December 25, rather than on the date originally preferred by the English, January 1.

From Christmas to "Xmas"   Ever wonder why Christmas is abbreviated as "Xmas?" It all started with the Greeks who used their letter χ (chi), (the first initial of Christos), as an abbreviation for Christ's name.

Lazy Christians of all nationalities began to follow their example, and ever since the 16th century "Xmas" has been used as an abbreviation for the birth of Christ.

Poinsettias   Legend claims a poor Mexican girl who had no gift for the Virgin Mary placed some scrawny flowers at Mary's feet. Miraculously the sorry flowers were transformed into the brilliant red poinsettia plant which blooms in December. They were first brought to the United States by Joel Poinsett (hence their name), American minister to Mexico in the early nineteenth century.

Christmas Cards   Christmas cards were first sent in England as messages of good cheer to mark the birth of hope, peace and good wishes for the new year. The first entrepreneur to make a "killing" in the Christmas card market was Sir Henry Cole, who hired John Calcott Horsely to design a commercial Christmas card in 1843. He sold one thousand copies that first year, but more importantly, he planted the seeds for the billion-dollar greeting card industry of the twentieth century.

The first commercial Christmas cards in America were produced by a German immigrant, Louis Prang. He opened a plant in Roxbury, Massachusetts, in 1874, but he exported all of his inventory to England, where "Christmas card fever" was firmly established. The next year he set his sights on the United States, and by 1882 Christmas cards had become the bane of the U.S. Postal Service. That year the *Washington Star* reported, ". . . a few years ago a Christmas card was a rare thing. The public then got the mania and the business seems to be getting larger every year." The Superintendent of the Washington, D.C., post office had to hire 16 extra mailmen that year, and he commented, "I don't know what we'll do if it keeps on."

Prang's idea was obviously one whose time had come! Puritan influence was declining; free mail delivery had been authorized by Congress in 1863 and service was improving; the Civil War generated a new prosperity in the North; and the cards provided a bit of inexpensive "art" in every home.

Away in a Manger   In many American homes, a nativity scene is set up beneath the Christmas tree and a figure of Christ is placed in the manger after midnight Mass. The custom originated in Greccio, Italy, with St. Francis of Assisi (1182–1226), who assembled a live tableau of animals and people to portray the story of Christ's birth.

The custom spread throughout Europe, but eventually the live nativity scenes were replaced by the carved images that still grace Christmas trees around the world.

Sint Klaas to Santa Claus   The Dutch called him Sint Klaas (or Sinter Klaas), a form of Saint Nicholas, and introduced the tall, thin, elegant man to America in the 17th century. Gradually, though, this Christmas icon underwent a transformation in English-speaking America. By 1823 he was known as Santa Claus, but his name wasn't all that changed over the years. He went from being a stately figure dressed in a red bishop's robe astride a horse to a fat, roly-poly gentleman who flies through the sky on a sleigh pulled by eight reindeer. When Washington Irving first described him in *Knickerbocker's History of New York* (1809), Saint Nicholas was riding over the treetops of New York in a wagon and tossing presents down the chimneys.

By 1822, when Clement C. Moore got finished with him, Santa was a round, jolly old fellow whose stomach jiggled like a bowl full of jelly. Moore also added the reindeer in his poem, "A Visit from St. Nicholas." Thomas Nast's famous 1866 drawing, "Santa Claus and His Works," sealed Santa's fate as a tubby, reindeer-riding checker of good and bad deeds, whose rotund body somehow managed to fit down tiny chimneys without the slightest problem. Though the figure has remained fairly constant since then, Santa has changed a bit over the past 100 years. For a complete recap of Santa's three hundred years in America, see E. Willis Jones' *The Santa Claus Book,* Walker, 1977.

"Merry Christmas to all and to all a good night." This Christmas drawing by Thomas Nast was the first to depict Santa "flying" through the air on a sleigh drawn by reindeer. (Courtesy: New York Historical Society)

Santa Claus Specialist   America is the land of the "specialist," so why shouldn't there be a Santa Claus *maven?* Shouldn't there be one man who knows more about how to portray Santa than anyone else; someone who is so expert that he can train more than 300 Santas every year in the kindly art of Christmas giving and listening.

That specialist is Stan Solomon, a Jewish-American who has even written a book on the subject. Solomon's been playing Santa himself for over 10 years, and trains the kindly helpers for Manpower, Inc., a temporary agency that farms out Santa Clauses to over 100 department stores and shopping malls in cities across the United States. His book, *The Santa Training Manual,* contains strict guidelines for would-be Santas: Santa never smokes; Santa never drinks while on duty; Santa never eats garlic; and Santa always pays attention to personal hygiene (it gets pretty hot inside that suit!). And most important of all, Santa never, never promises bicycles, expensive toys or baby sisters or brothers.

Two laps, no waiting. Macy's department store in New York City, the largest store in the world, has *two* Santas to reduce the Christmas crush. Little tykes are ushered through one of two doors so they never see the *other* jolly man in the red suit, only the one to whom they present their lists.

CELEBRATING CHRISTMAS IN OTHER LANDS

Everyone celebrates with their own unique customs and traditions, so if you'd like to add a bit of "ethnic color" to your next Christmas you might want to try some of these customs from the "other side."

Bulgaria On Christmas morning, after mass, the children open the presents brought to them by Grandpa Koleda (the Bulgarian version of Santa Claus). The traditional food for the day is a large round cake (*kravai*) decorated with the figures of a flower, a bird and a cross—topped with a lit candle.

Denmark Danish children put out porridge on Christmas night for the *nisse*, gray-bearded creatures some 4,000 years old and similar in some respects to our elves. The *nisse's* portrait appears on Christmas posters, on Christmas decorations and even as a nursery character.

Lately, though, he's been getting some stiff competition from *Julemand* (the Danish Santa) for the affections of young Danish children, and over the past fifty years fewer and fewer children have been leaving porridge out for the *nisse* on Christmas night.

France On Christmas Eve, also known as "layette night" in France, women gather together to make baby clothing for their expectant friends, or clothing that can be distributed to the poor on Chirstmas morning. One of the prettiest desserts for the holiday season is a *buche de Noël*, a rolled-up cake shaped like a Christmas log and decorated with mushrooms made of meringue.

Germany Many of our "American" customs at Christmastime come from Germany: the Christmas tree, the Advent wreath, the Yule log, *pfeffernüsse* cookies and Kris Kringle-German for Santa Claus. The name comes from the word *Christkindl*, meaning "Christ child."

Italy On Christmas day children write letters to their parents (not to Santa Claus) to express their love and appreciation for their kindness throughout the year. The notes are then read aloud prior to the Christmas feast.

Traditional foods include: *panettone* (cake filled with candied fruit), *torrone* (nougat with nuts), *panforte* (Siennese gingerbread made with hazelnuts, honey and almonds). Christmas Eve is "fish night" and includes such delicacies as *capitone* (female eel), squid and other, more mundane creatures from the sea, such as shrimp, octopus, and anchovies.

The Italian answer to the Christmas tree is the *ceppo*, a triangular framework made of wood, with three or four shelves used to hold candy, nuts, gifts and a nativity scene of baby Jesus surrounded by angels and shepherds. Each child has his own individual *ceppo*, but Santa has nothing to do with the presents they find there. In Italy, the *Befana* climbs down the chimney on January 5 and leaves presents to be opened by Italian children on January 6, the feast of the Epiphany (12 days after Christmas).

According to legend, the three wise men met an old woman on their way to Bethlehem. She wanted to go with them, but insisted on cleaning her house first. Well, she waited too long, and ever since then *Befana* (a corruption of *Epiphania*) has been wandering the earth at Twelfth Night in search of the Christ child.

Mexico The Mexicans begin celebrating *posadas* (lodgings) on December 16. For nine nights they commemorate the difficult journey of Mary and Joseph from Nazareth to Bethlehem and their exasperating search for lodging on that fateful night.

Piñatas come to us from Mexico, where they are traditionally associated with the Christmas season. Made of clay and covered with bits of colored paper to represent animals, birds, etc., the piñata is suspended above the heads of the children, who take turns swinging a stick at the not-so-fragile crock. When it breaks, its candy, money and tiny toys spill onto the floor where every child, except the blindfolded "batter," has an equal chance of raking in some goodies to take home.

Netherlands Santa Claus—or Sint Klaas, as he is known in Holland—doesn't have elves to help him at Christmas time. A little boy, known as "Black Pete," helps him distribute toys to good little girls and boys. Instead of finding goodies in their stockings, Dutch children find either treats or coal in their wooden shoes. In return they must be good for the whole year and leave some water for St. Nick and some straw for his horse to "refuel" them before their next house stop.

Norway The traidtional Christmas cookie from this country is "Fattigman"—little pastry cookies tied into knots.

Poland Christmas Eve dinner begins when the first evening star appears. There are 12 courses served (one for each of the Apostles), and one empty seat at the table. This seat is saved for any "unknown strangers" who might happen by, because on this night the Poles say, "Our hearts are open to stranger, kith and kin."

The "Vigilia" or Vigil Supper begins with *Oplatek,* a thin, unleavened wafer, blessed and stamped with the figures of the holy family, known as the "bread of love." There are two "superstitions" surrounding the feast: 1) if you expect to stay healthy throughout the new year you must taste each one of the courses; 2) an even number of people must not be seated at the table, or else some of the feasters might not live to see another Christmas.

A traditional Polish Christmas feast might include: apple pancakes; Polish "pasta" —pierogi; fish in several forms; potato salad; baked sauerkraut; and nut torte for dessert.

Romania At Christmastime young boys travel from house to house singing carols. The leader of the group carries a large wooden star (*Steaua*) atop a long pole, above the heads of the crowd. This *steaua* is illuminated with a candle and has a picture of the Holy Family in the center.

Russia The Russian *Baboushka* (similar to Italy's *Befana*) brings presents to boys and girls on the Epiphany.

Sweden Swedish Christmas Eve dinner includes *lutfisk,* boiled cod fish treated with lime. (Not the citrus fruit, but lime as in calcium oxide—the substance used in concrete. It can blind you if it gets in your eyes.) Needless to say, the dish has remained popular only with Swedes in America!

Most Americans prefer the Swedes' other contributions to the Yule table—delicious cookies and *glögg* (punch made from wine and brandy, seasoned with cinnamon, cloves and cardamom).

The Swedes want to make sure every living creature rejoices on Christmas Day, so they dip a sheaf of wheat in some suet, attach it to a pole, and place in outside as a "feast" for the birds.

Almost all religions of the world have had a special celebration sometime in December. The Feast of the Frost King was celebrated by Scandinavians before Christianity took hold; the Romans celebrated the Saturnalia, which Catullus described as "the merriest festival of the year," on December 17; the Egyptians honored Horus in midwinter; the Druids cut mistletoe; and the Jews celebrate Hanukkah, the Festival of Lights.

CHRISTMAS AROUND THE WORLD

English	Christmas
Czechoslovakian	Vanoce
Italian	Natale
Spanish	Navidad
Russian	Rozdestvo Khristova
Greek	Kristougenna
Esperanto	Kristnasko
Polish	Boze Narodzenie
Swedish	Julklapp
Serbo-Croatian	Bozic

CHRISTMAS GREETINGS

Portuguese	Feliz Natal, Boas Festas
German	Fröhliche Weihnachten
Danish	Glaedelig Jul
Dutch	Hartelijke Kerstgroeten
French	Joyeux Noël
Swedish	God Jul
Italian	Buon Natale
Finnish	Hauskaa Joulua
Spanish	Feliz Navidad
Romanian	Nosteria Lui Christos Sa Va Die (May the birth of Christ bring you happiness)
Norwegian	Gledelig Jul

WHO BRINGS THE GIFTS – SANTA BY ANY OTHER NAME

Brazil	Sao Nicolau or Papa Noël
Bulgaria	Grandpa Koleda
Czechoslovakia	Svaty Mikulas
Denmark	Julenissen (the yule gnome)
Finland	Wainomoinen, or Ukko (Old man Christmas)
Germany	Christkind, or Pelznickle (Nicholas dressed in fur)
Netherlands	Sint Niklass
Norway	Jule-nissen
Italy	Befana (a woman!)
Switzerland	Christkindli (Christ child, who arrives in a sleigh with 6 reindeer)

NEW YEAR'S EVE

What Are You Doing New Year's Eve? Our custom of meeting at a friend's home to ring in the new year comes to us from Norway and Sweden, where people gather on the last night of the old year to reaffirm mutual friendships for the next 12 months. The loud, boisterous parties, à la Times Square in New York City, come to us via the fun-loving Dutch, who also introduced the custom of having "open house" on New Year's Day, so friends could feel free to visit without an invitation.

Sometimes we throw confetti at the stroke of midnight, but in Italy they throw dishes out the windows at the "witching hour." This custom is a way to rid the house of "evil" influences which have accumulated over the past year. All chipped and cracked dishes are tossed out as "noise makers" for a clean start.

The custom of throwing confetti also started in Italy, but originally the Italians threw small hard candies during celebrations. When the cost began to rise and the demand increased, the thrifty-minded switched to lime pellets—but this, too, proved expensive and, most of all, dangerous. The French adopted the Italian custom of throwing small things, and were the first to toss paper scraps instead of candy at their Mardi Gras celebrations.

In Austria and parts of Germany the way to begin the new year is by munching on a marzipan pig. Marzipan is a candy made from almond paste, so sweet that one can usually eat only a small bite. Tradition calls for the host and guests to take a bite of the pig at the stroke of midnight. The pig holds a gold coin in his mouth, and signifies good luck for the coming year. His presence echoes the traditional New Year's dinner in Austria: roast suckling pig, complete with apple in mouth.

Chimney sweeps really clean up on New Year's Eve as they go from house to house in Austria so revelers can touch them and get soot on their fingers. It's supposed to bring good luck, and no doubt the good citizens are willing to pay well for the privilege of touching a sweep on December 31.

Another tradition for this last night of the old year is the Austrian habit of eating *Faschings Krapfen* (carnival fritters) — apricot-jelly doughnuts covered with powdered sugar.

Greeks are fond of serving an orange-flavored cake, known as St. Basil's Cake since his feast day is on January 1. A gold coin or other charm is baked in the cake and whoever finds it is said to have good luck in store for the coming year.

People also like to predict what the new year will bring, and in Sweden and other countries "casting lead" is a favorite new year's eve pastime. A small amount of lead is placed in a spoon and held over a flame until the lead melts. The melten lead is quickly thrown into a container of cold water, which causes the lead to assume rather unusual forms. Everyone present then tries to interpret the meaning behind the shapes, much like reading tea leaves, to discern what the future will bring.

What Year Is It? It all depends upon whose calendar you consult. In America, it is 1981, but according to the Japanese the year is 2641. Other calendars vary as follows:

Japanese	2641
Byzantine	7490
Jewish	5742
Roman	2734
Nabonnassar	2730
Indian	1903
Grecian	2293
Diocletian	1698
Mohammedan	1402
Chinese	4679

ETHNIC SUPERSTITIONS, OMENS AND BELIEFS

"We are all tattooed in our cradles with the beliefs of our tribe."

— *Oliver Wendell Holmes* (1809–1894)

Whether we claim to believe in superstitions or not, there is some nagging doubt that keeps many Americans from walking under ladders, buying black cats or making plans for Friday the 13th.

There are an estimated 50 million superstitions currently in circulation throughout the United States — some are domestic creations, but the majority were imported from the other side, brought here by the immigrants who sought refuge on our shores.

Some ethnic groups agree about what brings good luck and bad luck, but in many cases superstitions contradict one another: In England it is considered a bad omen to spill wine on your clothing, but in Ireland spilling alcoholic beverages is always "lucky" — it indicates that you are sharing your drink with the fairies, who will no doubt reward your kindness with some "good luck" in the future.

For what they're worth, here's a sampling of the beliefs, omens and superstitions perpetuated by ethnic groups from the four corners of the earth.

Knock On Wood

When the Dutch "knock on wood" to prevent bad luck, it has to be on *un*painted wood for the invocation to be effective. In keeping with the Dutch traditions, most Americans knock on the underside of the table, where the 'wood is free from oil, lacquer, varnish or paint.

Take Your Chances — Good Luck Or Bad Luck!

In Denmark breaking a mirror can either bring you seven years of good luck or seven years of bad luck. Unfortunately there's no way to predict the outcome before the glass is shattered.

Black Americans don't always consider a black cat crossing their path to be a bad omen. If the cat veers off to the right he will bring you good luck, but if he goes off to the left the luck will be all bad.

Itches and Twitches

To the superstitious every itch, twitch, scratch and tingle has a meaning. If your ears tingle, it means someone is talking about you. If it is the left side that tingles — it's malicious gossip; if the right side tingles — it's praise. This belief is one of the few that knows no ethnic boundaries — it is popular in England, Germany, France, Greece, Armenia, Bohemia, India and other parts of the world.

Jamaicans believe that if your nose itches someone is spreading evil gossip about you.

The Armenians interpret a twitch in your right eye to mean "good news." An itch on your left palm means "you will receive money," but an itch on your right palm means you will have to pay money to someone else.

If your foot itches, Armenians believe you will take a long trip; and if a spoon falls off the table during dinner, set an extra place, because it means you'll be having company soon.

Sometimes Superstitions Come True

Before Amelia Earhart left Hawaii in 1937 to complete her around-the-world flight with Fred Noonan, a plaque was dedicated in her honor. After she departed the plaque was set in place, but the stone it was attached to broke off and fell, causing the plaque to shatter. According to an old Hawaiian superstition, that meant Amelia would never return to the island. Her plane was lost somewhere between New Guinea and Howland Island on July 2, 1937, and no trace of either aviator has ever been found.

Death and Beyond

Please don't bring daisies In Japan, it's considered very poor taste to bring a sick friend cut flowers as a present. Cut flowers are technically "dead," since they have been severed from their roots and it is only a matter of time before they will wither and die. A living plant is the only "polite" gift for a friend, as it symbolizes your hopes for a speedy recovery.

Howl of the banshee, hoot of the owl In Ireland or Scotland you can tell when you are going to die because you will hear the "banshee" (a female spirit in Gaelic folklore) howling outside your window. The Pima Indians of North America have a similar belief. They believe owls carry the souls of the dead to another world, and the hooting of an owl has always been regarded as a sign of impending death.

Hanging tree Bohemians believe that Judas hung himself from a willow tree after he betrayed Christ, and ever since, Bohemians contemplating suicide have had an affinity for the willow tree.

Hard to "swallow" In Albania, it is believed that the souls of the dead often return to life disguised as birds. If a swallow, or other bird, flies over a sick person it is an omen of death in the near future.

Don't sneeze at the table   Early American Negroes of the North Carolina coast believed that sneezing during a meal meant you would soon hear of a death.

Don't bring it in the house   The Scotch never carry spades or shovels into the kitchen because it symbolizes "death coming into the house." If by chance someone waves a shovel at you—the only way you can protect yourself from this threat of imminent death is by throwing a handful of dirt at the person to negate the effects of this bad omen.

"No Animals Allowed"   If a cat jumps on a recently deceased body, that person will become a vampire. That's what the Greeks believe, and (for once) the Turks agree with them! They believe that both the cat and the person will become vampires and spend eternity sucking blood from the necks of unwitting victims.

The Jews don't allow animals near the dead for fear their souls will enter the body of the animal instead of departing for heaven.

Avoiding Bureaucratic Red Tape   When a Russian dies, his body is buried with a certificate that can be presented to St. Peter to prove his worthiness on this earth, and thereby speed up his entry through the "pearly gates."

Better a widow than the wife of a Gypsy   In times past the Gypsies were a bit more strict about their funeral practices than they are today. They believed in disposing of all a deceased man's belongings so the departed would never be tempted to return to the world of the living. They used to build a large funeral pyre and burn his wagons, jewelry, horses, money and all of his "possessions"—including, at one time, his wife.

Courtship

The power of dots   In Hungary, when a woman wants to attract a certain man, she sometimes resorts to wearing polka-dotted clothing, which supposedly possesses magical powers for winning the affections of stubborn suitors.

Marriage

Recipe for a Happy Marriage in Scotland   If you want to be happy for the rest of your life there are five things you should avoid, according to Scotch superstition:

1 never give your beloved an engagement ring with an opal or an emerald;
2 never see your betrothed prior to the ceremony on your wedding day;
3 never give your fiancee a Bible as a present before you are married;
4 don't marry in an "a" month, such as April, May or March; and
5 don't allow guests at the wedding to wear green or black.

Wait until June   According to early American Negro superstitions, May is an unlucky month in which to be married.

Old shoes and tin cans   The Scotch and Irish believe it is "good luck" to throw boots or shoes after a friend who is about to embark on a long journey. That's why we tie old shoes and tin cans (to scare away evil spirits) to the back of a newlywed couple's car. Ben Jonson once wrote: "Hurl after me a shoe, and I'll be merry whatever I do."

Shoo away evil spirits   At Jewish weddings, the bridegroom breaks a glass at the end of the ceremony to divert the evil spirits from spoiling this happy occasion, and the congregation shouts "Mazel Tov" (good luck), for extra protection for the couple during their married life.

Pregnancy and Birth

"Imprinting" before birth   Before the science of genetics explained hereditary diseases and ailments, people were hard-pressed to explain physical deformities of the newborn, so they attributed them to "imprinting" or evil influences that affected the mother during her pregnancy. For this reason Jewish grandmothers always advised pregnant women against visiting the zoo (lest one give birth to a monster); Icelandic grandmothers advised pregnant women not to drink from a cracked cup—it might cause a harelip; and not to eat the speckled eggs of the ptarmigan—that would doom the unborn child to a face full of freckles.

Touch your backside   That's what superstitious Italian women recommend for pregnant ladies with a craving. According to folklore, if a pregnant woman has a craving that is not satisfied, and she touches her body, the child will develop a birthmark on a similar part of his body. That's why superstitious Italian-Americans advocate touching your bottom when you have a craving, lest you mar the face of your unborn child with a strawberry mark or mole.

Sneezing together In Estonia, when two pregnant women sneeze simultaneously it is a sure sign that they will both give birth to girls. If their husbands sneeze together, the babies will be boys.

Feline Fertility Rite In Transylvania, Romanian farmers bring a cat into the home a month or so after their wedding and rock it in a cradle to ensure that the newlywed couple will soon bring forth children.

Ravishing ravens If the afterbirth of a baby boy is given to the ravens, Kwakiutl Indians of British Colombia believe he will be able to forsee the future. The future life of a baby girl doesn't quite match the expectations of the Kwakiutl boys, and her afterbirth is usually buried at the high-water mark to insure that she will become an excellent clam digger later on in life.

In Bolivia, the Indians bury a girl's afterbirth with cooking pots and a boy's with miniature farm tools to ensure them success in their future domestic endeavors.

Sprinkling of salt Sicilians ensure fertility by sprinkling salt around the bed of a newly married couple.

Rich Man, Poor Man, Beggarman, Thief

According to American Negro folklore, if you cut a child's fingernails before the age of one year, he or she will become a thief. The Pennsylvania Dutch also advise against using an old diaper for a newborn baby. Unless he is given a brand new diaper to wear as his first item of clothing, he too will grow up to be a thief.

The Spanish ensure good luck for their newborn children by brushing their faces gently with the bough of a pine branch.

If you want your child to grow up with a voice like Caruso's, the Pennsylvania Dutch advise saving his baptismal water. If he drinks it later on in life, he will become an excellent singer.

The Anglo-Saxons and the Jews agree that a child should not be allowed to gaze at his own image for quite some time after birth. Hard luck will fall upon the English baby who sees his reflection before he is a year old, but the Jewish baby only has to wait until his first tooth emerges before he can "safely" look into the mirror.

Sneezing

In Germany, when you sneeze everyone says "Gesundheit" (health) in the hope that no sickness will come to you as a result of the sneeze. In Spain, they say "Jesus," and ask him to protect you from any harm, but in Nigeria, a simple sneeze reaps blessings of "health, wealth, prosperity and children" upon the sneezer.

Insuring a Good Harvest

If you eat apples on Christmas night in Germany, the wine will be of excellent character next year.

If you have a young tree that is bearing fruit for the first time and want to ensure that it will be prolific, the Germans believe you should find a woman who has produced many children and ask her to pick the first apple (or cherry, etc.) and eat it. From then on your tree will produce abundant crops every year.

Numbers, Numbers

Seven is lucky to the Scottish, English and Irish, and the seventh child born to a family is reputed to be "gifted." In Romania, seven children isn't such a joyful accomplishment, and the seventh child is doomed to become a vampire after death. Gypsies favor the number seven, and the seventh daughter of a seventh daughter is reputed to have great fortune-telling abilities.

If 13 is an unlucky number, no wonder the American dollar is in so much trouble. The back of the buck not only has 13 stars over the eagle's head; but there are 13 arrows in his left claw, 13 leaves and 13 olives on the branch in his right claw; and a pyramid with 13 rows of building blocks on the left side.

Sail Away—Superstitions of Sailors and Fishermen

Right foot first Spanish sailors always put their right foot on board ship first. Stepping aboard with the left foot first spells disaster for the voyage.

Beware of Mermen Norwegian sailors fear "mermen," those half-fish, half-man creatures who appear on the waves once every seven years. If they catch sight of your ship passing by, it will sink before it reaches port.

Destination unknown Swedish sailors never discuss the port for which they are bound, as it is considered unlucky to do so.

No tweeds, dogs or barefoot women In Scotland, the sailors never wear Harris Tweed jackets or caps while at sea. Why? The wool in Harris Tweed is dyed with a lichen (crotal) which grows on sea rocks in the New Hebrides Islands and local fishermen maintain that "crotal always returns to the rocks" which spells disaster for anyone wearing crotal-dyed fabric while at sea.

Other rules observed by Scottish fishermen include: never passing a bare-footed woman before boarding ship and never speaking about a four-legged animal while at sea — both scare the fish away.

The Power of Animals

In Silesia and the Tyrol, if bees build a hive in your house, it is a sign that it will catch on fire.

Swedes don't (or at least shouldn't) kill swallows, robins or storks, because it brings bad luck; and if you kill a wren, you'll break a bone.

In Poland, the goat is considered a lucky animal, but the wolf, crow and pigeon are omens of bad luck.

American Indian tribes believe a chipmunk living near your home is a good omen.

In Bohemia, if you carry the right eye of a bat in your waistcoat pocket, you will become invisible.

Adding insult to injury In some parts of the world, vulture, swallow and pigeon droppings are considered omens of bad luck. In Nigeria, vulture droppings falling on your head destine you to a life of poverty; in China, bird droppings of any kind are an omen of misfortune in the future.

Cats The English warned us about black cats crossing our paths, but in Japan, where they say *Kureneko wa mayoke in u,* or "Black cats keep the devils away," they are quite acceptable.

Pigs Cats aren't the only animal to fear in England. If you happen to see a lone pig crossing the road before you embark on a journey, it will be a disappointing one. But, if the pig happens to be a sow traveling with her young, your luck is reversed, and the trip will be a success.

Rabbits The Arabs carry the ankle bone of a rabbit for protection against the devil and ghouls of all kinds, but our practice of carrying a rabbit's foot for good luck comes from American Negroes. The hare figures in many African folktales, where he is usually a hero or a cunning, smart creature who outwits all would-be predators.

Is It True What They Say About Friday the 13th?

The Pennsylvania Dutch consider "Friday the 13th" to be an unlucky day, but the superstition of bad luck connected with this day has ancient origins. It is believed to be a combination of superstitions concerning Fridays and the number 13.

What's so bad about Friday? The sixth day of the week, Friday has been called "Hangman's Day" because it was once reserved for executions. According to the Bible, Adam was tempted by Eve on Friday; the great flood began on Friday; the Temple of Solomon fell on Friday; and Christ was crucified on Good Friday.

What's wrong with the number 13? According to Polish traditions and those of other cultures, it is "bad luck" to seat 13 people at the dinner table. It is a sure sign that one guest will die before the year is over. There were 13 men present at Christ's last supper, and according to Norse mythology, when Loki, the god of mischief, turned up uninvited at a banquet for 12 other gods, the death of Baldur, a favored god, was the unpleasant result of the evening.

The English government once set out to prove how ridiculous the superstitions connected with Friday were. They began constructing a new vessel on Friday; named it the HMS Friday; launched it on a Friday; and sent it out on its maiden voyage on a Friday. The ship was never heard from again.

Obviously Americans do not have the dread "triskaidekadophobia" (a fear of the number 13). There were 13 original colonies; George Washington took command of the Revolutionary armed forces on a Friday the 13th; and construction of the White House began on a Friday the 13th.

Have no fear—Scandinavians consider Friday their lucky day; and if you were born on the 13th day of any month, then Friday the 13th is your lucky day.

The "Eyes" Have It

According to a recent study, no less than 67 different peoples of the world have a belief in the power of the "evil eye." That's over 36% of the world's population, including such scattered and diverse ethnic groups as Egyptians, Hebrews, Irish, Basques, Fijians, Micmac and Zuñi Indians, Haitians and Italians. Almost all countries that border the Mediterranean Sea have a belief in the eye, but different cultures have different methods of dealing with its ill effects:

Greeks wear a round, glassy blue bead with black concentric circles to represent the "eye" and thwart its evil effects. Italians have several avenues of protection afforded to them. The effects of the *Mal occhio* can be negated by 1) touching iron, 2) extending the index finger and pinky of one's hand into the "sign of the horns" and thrusting it towards the ground three times, 3) wearing the *cornicelli,* a charm shaped like a horn, which is capable of "piercing" the eye, 4) hanging peppers and other pointed vegetables over the door (these are also capable of "piercing" the eye), 5) wearing a replica of the *gobbo* or hunchback (This charm, made of red and white plastic, features a hunchback with a horn-shaped body, making the sign of the horns.)

Slovaks never return a weaned baby to the bottle or the breast. They believe that doing so will cause the child to develop the "evil eye."

Italian-American educator Richard Gambino talks about "protection":

As was common practice, the entrance to my grandparents' home was adorned with a protective device. Over the door hung a pair of real bull's horns, painted bright red as a warning to all malignant forces that might threaten, whether human, natural or supernatural. I remember my grandparents taking special note of the fact that in the cowboy movies they saw on television the ranch homes often had steer horns ornamenting a wall or fireplace. They once asked me why it was that cowboys attended to the evil eye when other Americani did not.

My fellows at P.S. 142 had a typical assortment of pagan and Christian amulets hanging side by side or in little sacks from necklaces worn under their clothing or attached to their undershirts with safety pins. In addition to those already mentioned, I saw pictures of saints, little fish (the ancient Christian symbol for Christ), and tiny scissors and daggers to cut or impale powers of evil. My grandmother was uneasy about the lightness of the protection I enjoyed as a small child. It came from a gold crucifix I wore on a chain under my shirt —the only amulet my mother would use. At times when I was ill, my grandmother placed little sacks next to the crucifix and replaced them almost as soon as my mother removed them. The sacks were sewn tightly closed, and to this day I don't know what they contained except that I could tell from feeling them that their contents included paper and solid objects. In the generation preceding mine some Italian-American children were sent to school wearing toothlike cloves of garlic under their garments. I leave the reactions of their teachers to the reader's imagination. (*Blood of My Blood.* Doubleday, p. 200).

GOOD LUCK IS . . .

. . . being born in the month of January if you're Sicilian – it protects you from the effects of the evil eye.

. . . meeting a chimney sweep first thing in the morning in Germany, France, Bohemia or Great Britain.

. . . spilling *dry* salt in Denmark.

. . . seeing a pin and picking it up in England. (All that day you'll have good luck!)

. . . tying a red bow around the steering wheel of your new car, if you're an Italian-American. If you're Romanian, good luck comes from tying a red bow around your child's ankle.

. . . hanging herbs over the doorway if you're Chinese.

. . . throwing candy in your new home to "sweeten" it if you're a Greek Jew living in America.

. . . rainwater from the merry month of May. In Cuba this water is considered to have special beneficial qualities.

. . . being born with one or two teeth in your mouth. In France, Italy and other Latin countries this is considered a sign of a wonderful future and has been accepted as such since Roman times.

. . . meeting an old man or a hunchback on New Year's Day in parts of Italy, where it is considered a sign of good fortune for the coming year. Old men signify living to a ripe old age, and hunchbacks are always supposed to bring good fortune. (To whom? Certainly not the poor hunchback?)

. . . dying on your birthdate. The Jews consider it "lucky." (If you have to go – it may as well be under "lucky" circumstances!)

. . . wearing red clothing; it's the color of good omens in China.

BAD LUCK IS . . .

. . . trimming your toenails prior to a business trip if you are Japanese.
If the clippings are thrown into the fire, death can result, and if the deed is done at night, the next morning your nails will have grown back as cat's claws.

. . . stirring your food with a knife if you are a Navaho Indian.

. . . using zippers or "hooks and eyes" to fasten your clothing if you are Pennsylvania Dutch. All of these newfangled contraptions are merely devices for Satan to hang on.

. . . a Korean woman crying after sunset.

. . . ashes flying from a burning log into the room. It is a sure sign of trouble to come if you are Greek.

. . . spilling *damp* salt in Denmark.

. . . wearing red and green together in some parts of Scotland.

. . . mailing a letter on Christmas Day, February 29, or September 1 – all unlucky mailing days in Scotland.

. . . breaking a mirror in England – it can mean death for your best friend.

. . . being born with a tooth in Finland – it is considered a sign that the child will become a vampire or a sorcerer. Asians, Africans, Hungarians, Bohemians and Moravians also consider it an ill omen in contrast to the people of the Mediterranean region, who consider it a sign of good luck.

. . . sneezing in Germany while putting on your shoes.

. . . giving an English friend a knife, scissors or other sharp cutting tool as a present. It indicates that the relationship will be "severed."

. . . seeing a priest in Paris. Street urchins considered this extremely unlucky and therefore carried pieces of iron in their pockets to negate all ill effects of a priest sighting.

. . . passing one nun on the streets of Austria. (Two nuns were considered lucky.)

ORIENTAL VS. OCCIDENTAL—
9 Differences in "Culture"

Americans sometimes forget that what we regard as "normal and customary" is done quite differently in other parts of the world. According to Jack Seward, in his book *The Japanese,* there are at least nine subtle differences between Japanese and American "culture."

1 In America, black is the color of mourning, but in Japan, white is normally worn by the family of the deceased.
2 When Americans mount a horse it's always from the left side; the Japanese approach a horse from the right.
3 When we travel or give directions we always say "northeast" or "southwest." The Japanese refer to the equivalent directions as "eastnorth," and "westsouth."
4 American men sometimes whistle at women, but the Japanese (rightly so) whistle only at dogs.
5 American hospitality dictates filling someone's glass almost up to the brim, but the Japanese consider it impolite to fill a guest's cup too near to the top.
6 When the Japanese count on their fingers they open the hand and bend in the fingers one by one as they count. Americans usually start with a closed fist and extend the fingers as they count from one to five.
7 When a Japanese carpenter cuts wood he pulls the saw toward himself, while American woodworkers usually push the saw away from their bodies.
8 American rowing teams usually move the oars in a backward motion, while the Japanese row forward.
9 When we use the "john" we face away from the tank, but the Japanese usually face the back of the toilet when seated.

CELEBRATING EVENTS ETHNIC STYLE

WEDDINGS

At a typical "American" wedding, the bride wears a white gown and a veil (with something blue hidden away for good luck). She and the groom exchange wedding bands at the ceremony. Afterwards, at the wedding reception, there is a multi-tiered wedding cake, and traditionally the bride's bouquet and garter are tossed to the unmarried guests.

Where did these "American" traditions come from? The Romans, among others, believed June was the best month in which to marry; they introduced the bridal veil to shield the bride from any evil spirits that might mar her happiness; and they traditionally prepared a wedding cake of salt, water and barley flour to assure that the newlyweds' future would be free from want. Sometime in the fourteenth century the French introduced the custom of tossing the bride's bouquet, to determine the next maiden to be married. It is also believed that a modern-day Frenchman started the tradition of tossing the bride's garter to the unmarried male guests for the sole purpose of getting them involved in the festivities.

Blue is the color of love, purity and fidelity. It was the ancient Hebrews who first encouraged brides to wear blue ribbons on their wedding day. Although the Egyptians were the first to portray large "wedding rings" (which represented eternity) in their hieroglyphics, the Romans and early Christians made them "finger-sized" for the bride to wear. Early German settlers introduced the custom of wearing wedding bands to America.

Here's a sampling of other wedding customs from around the world:

Protective Awning Jewish couples get married under a special canopy (*chupa*) which protects the couple and their happiness together from being ruined by "evil spirits."

The Greeks have to pay According to general American tradition, the father of the bride or the bride herself is responsible for wedding expenses such as the wedding

Godey's Lady's Book *featured the latest wedding fashions in 1850. (Courtesy: New York Public Library)*

gown, reception and entertainment. Not so in the Greek tradition—the man has to pay for the reception, and for his intended's wedding gown as well.

Nuts to you At Italian weddings, guests are usually served sugar-coated almonds, which symbolize hopes of "fertility" for the newly married couple.

Sawing wood In parts of Germany, after the wedding ceremony the bride and groom are given a log of wood to be sawn by them. The success with which they meet this task is an indication of the success or failure of their married life.

Breaking cake together At a Norwegian wedding, the bridal couple "breaks" off pieces of wedding cake for their guests to enjoy. The wedding cake, made of almond paste, is baked in rings and decorated with icing and bon-bons; tradition dictates that it not be sliced with a knife.

Ensuring Fertility To ensure the fertility of a newly married couple, it is a Yugoslavian tradition that the couple's oldest living relative enter their new home with gifts of bread and salt.

"Taxi" dancing At Swedish and Lithuanian weddings it is customary for guests to "pay" for the privilege of dancing with the bride. Known as the *acziavimas* in Lithuanian, the custom was chronicled in Upton Sinclair's *The Jungle:*

"The *acziavimas* is a ceremony which, once begun, will continue for three or four hours . . . the guests form a great ring, locking hands, and when the music starts up, begin to move around in a circle. In the centre stands the bride, and, one by one, the men step into the enclosure and dance with her."

When each male guest has had his turn dancing with the bride, he drops a sum of money into a hat, and the money is used by the newlyweds to pay for the reception and to defray the expenses of setting up a new household.

Jumping the broom Early American slaves didn't have any clergymen to minister to their souls or salvation, so when they wanted to get married they simply jumped the broom. In front of all their friends, the couple would declare their decision to remain together (as long as possible, considering the way slave families were ummercifully torn apart) and jump over a broomstick together. The ceremony was described by Alex Haley in *Roots:*

As Matilda's missis had planned it, the wedding would combine some of the white Christian wedding service with jumping the broom afterward. Guiding her rapidly sobering groom by one yellow sleeve, Matilda positioned them before the preacher, who cleared his throat and proceeded to read a few solemn passages from his Bible. Then he asked, "Matilda and George, do you solemnly swear to take each other, for better or worse, the rest of your lives?"

"I does," said Matilda softly.

"Yassah!" said Chicken George, much too loudly.

Flinching, the preacher paused and then said, "I pronounce you man and wife!"

Among the black guests, someone sobbed.

"Now you may kiss the bride."

Seizing Matilda, Chicken George crushed her in his arms and gave her a resounding smack. Amid the ensuing gasps and tongue-clucking, it occured to him that he might not be making the best impression, and while they locked arms and jumped the broom, he racked his brains for something to say . . .

Other wedding traditions After a Hopi Indian woman is married she braids her hair to resemble a ripened ear of corn. Prior to her marriage, she is supposed to wear it whorled high on the sides of her head to resemble squash blossoms, the symbol of chastity.

In Persia, it was customary to send a bride-to-be certain gifts on her wedding day: a tray full of 100 kinds of drugs and herbs, a mirror and 10 yards of white cloth to cover her during the wedding ceremony.

In Uganda, it is customary for a new bride to be allowed a month's vacation after the ceremony. Her relatives bring food as wedding gifts, and once this is consumed, in about a month's time, the bride must start to gather food and cook for herself and her new husband.

Koreans generally have three names. The family name comes first, followed by a name to identify the generation, and the given or personal name is placed third. A woman does not change her name after marriage. In Korean conversation, she will be referred to as "Park's wife," etc., or by her full name.

ETHNIC WEDDING RESEARCHER

Tired of the same old white gown, veil, and tuxedoed groom weddings? Arthur A. Giger, proprietor of Ancient Wedding Fables, 350 South Street, Morristown, New Jersey, will provide information and personnel to put together an authentic ancient wedding ceremony from the country of your choice.

A Persian wedding would be complete with roses, curly headpieces for the men to wear, the scent of saffron in the air and a gift for the bride of a golden necklace with the groom's profile engraved on it.

An American Indian of the Lenni Lenape tribe would favor peppermint-scented candles and a chamois gown for the bride to wear.

Greek and other Eastern Rite churches feature a walk around the altar for the newly married couple as a reward for their "chastity."

"Everyone gets married here and there," says Giger, and he reasoned that many young couples might be interested in an unusual ceremony, reception or wedding apparel for that important occasion.

Giger's service will provide instructions for making gowns, headpieces, authentic wedding feast foods and music to dance to, so your "once in a lifetime" event can be ethnically correct.

OTHER SPECIAL EVENTS

Birth of a baby Instead of passing out cigars when a baby is born in the family, the sweets-loving Belgians offer friends "dragées" — almonds coated with a soft layer of sugar.

Baby's first tooth Syrian and Lebanese Americans serve a sweet drink known as *Qamhiyyi* to celebrate the emergence of a baby's first tooth. *Qamhiyyi* is made from whole wheat kernels, nuts, raisins and rose water.

Baby's first birthday At the time of a Korean child's first birthday, he/she is dressed in a traditional costume and seated amidst piles of rice cakes, cookies and fruits. Friends and relatives offer the child objects that symbolize his future career — such as a pen for a writer or a coin for a banker or businessman — and the first one he grabs indicates his future occupation.

Becoming a man On his 13th birthday, a Jewish boy officially enters adulthood. At that age he is considered old enough to understand the meaning and purpose of the Jewish faith. A traditional ceremony (Bar Mitzvah) solemnizes the boy's passage into manhood.

The Japanese celebrate a boy's passage into manhood a little later. At a ceremony known as "new cap," or *Uikamuri,* a fifteen or sixteen-year-old boy is given a man's cap for the first time, symbolizing the fact that from this day on he may dress as a man, instead of as a child.

Sweet 16 Rich WASPs have always had debutante balls to celebrate a young woman's passage into "society," and for thousands of less wealthy American girls there was always the "Sweet 16" party to tell the world that she was ready to begin dating. Today, many Jewish girls have "Bas Mitzvah" celebrations, similar to the Bar Mitzvahs of thirteen-year-old boys. And in Hispanic communities all over America, a girl's fifteenth birthday is celebrated with a bash known as the *quince.*

Derived from the Spanish custom of celebrating a girl's passage into womanhood, *quinces* were once limited to the well-to-do and the upper classes. But now they are quite common in Miami, Union City, New Jersey, and other Cuban communities, and they are gaining in popularity with Mexican-Americans as well.

The *quince* is more than just a "Sweet 15" party: it signifies that the woman is now ready to begin looking for a husband. Naturally, in America, the event became bigger and more extravagant than it had been in the old country. Many señoritas emerge from a cloud, or step out of a parted seashell to greet their guests. Often the *quince* requires the services of a choreographer to see that the young lady is introduced with style.

Many *quinces* cost upward of $10,000, more than a fancy wedding reception, but unlike many a wedding today, a *quince* only comes once and many parents want to be sure to give their daughters an affair to remember.

Moving into a new home When Jewish families move into a new home, many place a *mezuza* outside the front door to remind them of God's presence within. The *mezuza* is a small metal case which contains a prayer from Deuteronomy 6:4–9 and 11:13–21. The Torah commands all Jews to nail the *mezuza* "upon the doorpost" to remind them that the home should be kept pure.

Starting a new business When a Japanese businessman enters into a new venture, a friend usually gives him a Daruma san, or good luck charm. This small, doll-like figure represents an Indian philosopher who meditated in one position for so long that he lost the use of his eyes, arms and legs. If the business is successful after the first year, the friend returns to paint eyes on the Daruma san. This is a very happy occasion, since the Daruma san is no longer blind — success has given him back his sight. The doll is designed so that no matter how many times you knock it over, it always returns to an upright position. Despite his handicaps, you can't keep a good "Daruma san" down.

RELIGION IN AMERICA

America has traditionally been a haven for victims of religious persecution. Huguenots, Shakers, Hutterites, Schwenkfelders, Quakers, Baptists, Amish, Mennonites, Dunkers, Lutherans and countless others have been attracted to our shores by the promise of religious freedom. Even today, Jewish immigrants from Russia, prohibited from practicing their religion in their native land, are being admitted to the United States under an emergency refugee policy.

In addition to importing all manner of religious persuasions from abroad, America has also served as a crucible for vast numbers of new religions, sects and cults, ranging from the mainstream to the bizarre. Following is a brief and selective chronology of the religious spirit in America.

1493 ♦ Roman Catholic priests accompanied Columbus on his second voyage to the New World and began spreading their faith throughout the Americas.

1607 ♦ When the first Charter of Virginia was issued, King James I of England wrote that "the true word and service of God [should be] preached, planted and used" in the New World. Although James believed that all inhabitants of English colonies should conform to "the doctrine, rites and religion now professed and established within our realm of England" this policy was never enforced.

1620 ♦ Separatist Congregationalists sailed from Leyden and established a colony at Plymouth with full permission of the Virginia Company.

1634 ♦ St. Mary's Catholic Church was founded in Maryland this year; this was the beginning of continuous Catholic worship in English-speaking North America.

1639 ♦ The first Baptist church in America was organized by Roger Williams at Providence, R.I.

1654 ♦ The first Jewish congregation, Shearith Israel, was founded in New York City.

1663 ♦ The first commune founded on American soil was established in 1663 by Pieter Cornelis Plockhoy, a Dutch Mennonite who espoused universal brotherhood, popular government, religious freedom, social and economic justice for all.

Plockhoy had traveled to England in 1658 to meet with the Great Lord Protector himself, Oliver Cromwell. Although Cromwell had expressed interest in Plockhoy's proposal to establish several utopian communities in England, he died before the plans could be finalized. Forced to seek other means of financing his venture, Plockhoy began negotiating with the Amsterdam burgomasters to establish a cooperative community in the Delaware Valley. The city council approved Plockhoy's scheme and even gave each family 100 guilders toward defraying the expenses of passage to the New World.

In his pamphlet, *Kort en Klaer Ontwerp*, Plockhoy set down the rules and regulations for his community. Each person was required to work for a certain number of hours each week for the community, and any money obtained through cooperative efforts would be divided according to the size of each person's family. The society was not totally communistic, since private ownership was permitted. There was freedom of religion, and complete separation of church and state. Although communal living was encouraged, it was not mandatory.

Plockhoy hoped to attract 100 families to his utopia, where all men and women would live as one "familie or household government," but when the *St. Jacob* set sail from Holland in May 1663, it carried only 25 Dutch Mennonite families bound for America.

The commune arrived at the mouth of the Delaware Bay in July and settled near Swanendael (now Lewes, Delaware). Unfortunately, their community was shortlived: most members of the colony were killed in an attack by the British in 1664.

1682 ♦ The British soon realized their best recruits for the colonies might be found among the oppressed religious minorities of Europe, whose zeal and enthusiasm were greater than that of "immigrants" recruited from debtors' jails and prisons. Accordingly, in 1682 King James II (a Roman Catholic) instructed the governor of New York to "permit all persons of what religion so ever quietly to inhabit" that region.

♦ This year, William Penn, a convert to Quaker principles, arrived in America and began recruiting settlers for his Pennsylvania colony.

1733 ♦ The first Catholic parish in the British colonies was established in Philadelphia. There were only 37 parishioners—22 were Irish and 15 were German.

1740–1750 ♦ The Amish began arriving in considerable numbers during this decade, settling in Berks and Lancaster counties in Pennsylvania about 1727. Many came from Switzerland, where Jacob Amman (1644–1730), a Mennonite preacher from Bern, had founded their sect.

1774 ♦ Ann Lee Standerin (1736–1784) led the "Shakers" from England to Watervliet, New York. Known as "Mother Ann," Standerin claimed that the Second Coming of the Messiah would be in the form of a woman. Properly called the United Society of Believers in Christ's Second Coming, Ann's followers were nicknamed "Shakers" because they chose to worship the Lord through singing, dancing and speaking in tongues.

All property was owned communally, and although the community lived as one, they remained celibate because they believed "the end" was near—hence, there was no need to reproduce. When the end failed to arrive, the Shakers increased their ranks by adopting children; prior to the outbreak of the Civil War they reached their highest membership—almost 6,000.

The Shaker community produced the first commercial seed in the United States and the first metal pen points, and invented the circular saw. After the Civil War their ranks began a decline that continued throughout the twentieth century. By 1979 only a handful of aged members remained.

1775 ♦ 98.4% of the population of colonial America belonged to one Protestant sect or another. Only 1.4% of the population embraced Roman Catholicism, and only .0015% embraced Judaism. This year there were 6 Jewish congregations, 56 Catholic, 65 Methodist, 120 Dutch Reformed, 150 Lutheran, 159 German Reformed, 310 Quaker, 494 Baptist, 495 Anglican, 588 Presbyterian, and 668 Congregational churches in America.

1803 ♦ Johann Georg Rapp (1757–1847), a minister from Württemberg, Germany, founded the Society of Rappists in 1787 after a split with the Lutheran Church. In 1803, the Rappists bought land near Pittsburgh, Pennsylvania, and established the settlement of Harmony.

Dedicated to preparing themselves for the second coming of Christ, the members of Harmony were totally opposed to the distractions of the flesh, and celibacy was advocated for all members.

The society was financially quite successful. At the time of Rapp's death in 1847, the church fund contained almost $500,000 in gold and silver. Over the next 50 years the Harmonists invested heavily in oil, and built pipelines and railroads which further increased their wealth. But, despite their resounding financial success, the Harmonists disbanded at the turn of the century for lack of leadership and members.

1826 ♦ This year, Frances Wright (1795–1852), an attractive, well-educated young Scotswoman, purchased 2,000 acres of land near Memphis, Tennessee and started the communal colony of Nashoba. It was here that Wright brought together slaves and whites, settled them in village cooperatives and taught them skills necessary for survival and self-sufficiency.

A staunch believer in equal rights for women, Fanny Wright was blessed with an adventurous spirit and a large inheritance. It was her dream to help slaves relocate in Africa, after teaching them the skills necessary for survival.

Nashoba did not last long. Beset with economic problems and the condemnation of the surrounding community for their liberal sexual practices, Nashoba was disbanded in 1830. The remaining Blacks were taken to Haiti and given their freedom.

For her radical and outspoken views on abortion, atheism, miscegenation and women's rights, Frances Wright went down in history and her name passed into the language. During the 1800s any woman who dared to address a public audience, on any topic, was ridiculed as a "Fanny Wrightist."

1827 ◆ In 1827, an angel named Moroni led Joseph Smith (1805–1844), an American of part-Scottish ancestry, to Cumorah Hill, near Palmyra, New York. It was here that Smith unearthed "golden tablets" and set down their message in the Book of Mormon before the tablets were taken up into heaven.

Smith organized the Church of Jesus Christ of Latter-day Saints in 1830 in accordance with the word of God he received through revelations. He introduced polygamy, and tithing (members must donate 10% of their gross income to the church), but in 1890 the Supreme Court ruled the former illegal. The practice of tithing has continued, however, and made the Mormon church very successful over the years. Mormons own much of downtown Salt Lake City; over 326,000 acres of land throughout the United States; insurance companies with more than $383 million worth of assets; a newspaper, 11 radio stations and two TV stations; $36 million worth of *Times Mirror* stock; a sugar beet company; and a department store chain.

A rift among church members occurred in 1844, resulting in two branches of the Mormon church. The larger, with over 2.3 million members, is headquartered at Salt Lake City; the smaller, the Reorganized Church of Jesus Christ of Latter-day Saints, has only 185,000 members, and is headquartered at Independence, Missouri—the site, according to Joseph Smith, of Christ's Second Coming.

1843 ◆ Christian Metz led 800 members of a German pietistic sect to Ebenezer, New York, in 1843, in search of religious and political freedom. His followers were Swiss, French and Germans who believed in divine revelation through "inspired prophets" or *Werkzeuge,* and they called their religion the Community of True Inspiration.

In 1855, the community moved to Amana, Iowa, where all land and industries were held in common and managed by church elders. By 1908, seven Amana

Souvenir postcard from the Mormon Church. (Courtesy: New York Public Library)

colonies had been founded (Amana, East Amana, Middle Amana, West Amana, South Amana, High Amana and Homestead), and all were flourishing. The church owned some 26,000 acres of land, valued at $1.8 million.

When the Depression caused hard times in 1930, Amanaites voted to separate church and business affairs. All members of the commune received one free share of Class A common stock (valued at almost $81 in 1932, and over $20,000 in 1975) plus a number of shares of lesser value distributive stock, according to the number of years each had spent in the community.

In 1934, the Amana Corporation began manufacturing beverage coolers, and from there expanded their operation to produce refrigeration units. Today,

Amana is one of the nation's largest manufacturers of microwave ovens.

There are almost 2,000 Amanaites living in Iowa today, descendants of the German, Swiss and French settlers who followed Christian Metz to the United States.

1848 ◆ John Humphrey Noyes (1811–1886), a descendant of Nicholas Noyes, who emigrated to Massachusetts from England in 1633, founded the Oneida community in 1848 as a religious and social society.

Noyes believed that spiritual equality was necessary for the "perfect" life. He and his followers advocated that all personal property be given over to the community interest, and that all parts of one's personal life be lived communally. Convinced that monogamy was not compati-

When this woodcut, entitled "The Children's Hour," ran in Frank Leslie's Illustrated Newspaper, Noyes' utopian community was described as the Oneida Community of Free Lovers. (Courtesy: New York Historical Society)

ble with his doctrine (called Perfectionism) Noyes wrote about free love in the famous "Battleaxe letter" of 1837.

The community began at Putney, Vermont, in 1846, but when their "complex marriage" system, whereby everyone was married to one another, aroused indignation among the local residents the Perfectionists were forced to move, and settled at Oneida, New York.

Birth control was enforced at Oneida, and the number of babies to be born each year was predetermined by the community. Parents were "chosen" to provide the best offspring possible — according to the community's standards — and after one year of age, all babies were reared in common at the Children's House. They remained here until the age of twelve, and were only allowed to visit with their parents once or twice a week.

Between 1848 and 1880, the Oneida community lived, worshiped, worked and played together. But, faced with increased attacks from the local clergy, and the fact that their leader, Noyes, was now almost seventy years old, the three hundred members agreed to dissolve their communal way of life and marry among themselves. Oneida ended as a commune, but a joint-stock company was formed to carry on the community's industries and many of the former members became "employees" of Oneida Silversmiths — the same company that manufactures tableware today. Many of these descendants, to the third and fourth generation, still live and work in Oneida, New York.

1870s ♦ Followers of Jacob Hutter, a clergyman who was burned at the stake in Innsbruck, Austria, in 1536, began emigrating to South Dakota during this decade. Most of these "Hutterites" were descended from Swiss immigrants who had fled Moravia in 1526 and later emigrated to Russia about 1777.

1872 ♦ Charles Taze Russell (1852–1916), a native of Pittsburgh, whose parents were both of Scotch-Irish ancestry, founded the Jehovah's Witnesses in 1872. According to Russell, the Second Coming of Christ occurred, in invisible form, in the autumn of 1874, and since that time the world has lived in the "Day of Jehova."

According to Jehovah's Witnesses, a worldwide revolution of the working classes will occur shortly and will reduce society as we know it to chaos. This will be followed by a resurrection of the dead and a judgment period lasting one thousand years.

Russell's life was marked by several scandals, including the bushels of ersatz "miracle wheat" sold by his church in 1911, but scandals did not dissuade his followers, and membership increased each year. Today there are more than 577,000 members of the Jehovah's Witnesses in the United States. Their main publication, *The Watchtower,* is printed worldwide in over 70 languages.

1879 ♦ The Church of Christ, Scientist, was founded in 1879 by Mary Baker Eddy (1821–1910), an English-American who could trace her ancestry back to seventeenth century settlers of Massachusetts.

Eddy published the first edition of *Science and Health, With a Key to the Scriptures* in 1875, and formally chartered her church, which stresses spiritual healing, four years later. In 1908, Eddy founded the *Christian Science Monitor,* a respected daily newspaper. Headquartered in Boston, Massachusetts, the Christian Science religion boasts some 3,200 branches worldwide.

1897 ♦ In a dispute with the hierarchy in Rome, some 80,000 Roman Catholics of Polish ancestry fell away from the church and formed the Polish National Catholic Church with Reverend Francis Hodur as their first bishop. The religious rift occurred because the Polish-Americans felt their special needs were not being met by the local dioceses. In 1886 there were 69 Catholic bishops in America — 35 Irish, 15 German, 11 French, 5 English and one each of Dutch, Scottish and Spanish heritage. But, despite a sizable Polish Catholic community, there was not a single Polish-American bishop. Today there are almost 140 parishes of the Polish National Church in America, with some 300,000 members.

1906 ♦ There were only about 30,000 Roman Catholics in the United States in 1790 — less than 1% of the population. But, by 1906, 17% of America's population was Catholic, thanks in part to a large influx of Catholic immigrants from Ireland and Southern Europe during the nineteenth century.

1920–1930 ♦ During this decade the Monophysite Church of Armenia, the oldest established national Christian church, founded several American branches.

1921 ♦ Father Edward Joseph Flanagan (1886–1948), a native of Ballymoe, Ireland, established Boys Town, 10 miles west of Omaha, Nebraska, as a home and educational facility for homeless and delinquent boys. Father Flanagan, whose motto was "There are no bad boys," maintained that given a good home, an education and job training, all boys could mature into productive adults despite an early "bad start" in life.

Only about 20% of the 12,000 boys who have passed through Boys Town were ever "in trouble"; the rest were homeless boys in need of someone who cared. Incorporated as a village in 1936, the facility now covers some 1,700 acres. The original "Boys Town" was a rented house in Omaha where Father Flanagan first cared for five boys in 1917.

1931 ♦ Wali D. Farad founded the Nation of Islam in Detroit, Michigan. Farad proclaimed himself a prophet from Mecca, the reincarnation of Allah, who had come to urge American Blacks to create a separate all-Negro state. According to Farad's belief, all Black Americans were members of the tribe of Shebazz, whose long-lost language, literature and religion he had come to restore.

When Farad disappeared in 1934, Elijah Muhammad (born Robert Poole in 1897 at Sandersville, Georgia) became the head of the Black Muslims, and built it into an organization with 100,000 followers and mosques in 42 cities. Muhammad preached the virtues of the "Protestant ethic"—thriftiness and hard work—to his followers, and advocated that they abstain from pork, drugs, tobacco and alcohol.

1932 ♦ Norman Vincent Peale (1898–) became pastor of the Marble Collegiate Reformed Church in New York City in 1932. Of part-Irish descent, Dr. Peale is famous for his radio broadcasts and books which extol "the power of positive thinking." His church, now known as Dr. Norman Vincent Peale's Marble Collegiate Church, maintains a 24-hour "help line" of volunteers who are always available to discuss your problems: 212-281-1070.

1940 ♦ Billy Graham (1918–), one of America's most successful evangelists, was ordained a Southern Baptist minister this year. Born near Charlotte, North Carolina, of Scottish ancestry, Graham has conducted his spiritual campaigns and "Youth for Christ" movements across the globe.

A shy youth in high school, Graham became a Fuller Brush salesman at the age of sixteen and managed to outsell every representative in North Carolina that year. It was that experience that allowed him to overcome his shyness; it taught him how to talk to people and how to sell. Today, the Billy Graham Evangelistic Association, Inc., headquartered at Minneapolis, Minnesota, has an annual operating budget of more than $20 million.

1946 ♦ Frances Xavier Cabrini (1850–1917) became the first American citizen to attain sainthood in the Roman Catholic Church. Known as the "Patron Saint of Immigrants," Mother Cabrini was an immigrant herself—born in Lombardy, Italy, the youngest of 13 children.

Cabrini established the Missionary Sisters of the Sacred Heart in 1880, emigrated to the United States in 1889 and proceeded to establish 65 orphanages worldwide. Four miracles were credited to her intercession, but before Cabrini could be declared a saint it was necessary for Monsignor Salvator Natucci to play the "Devil's advocate" and cross-examine witnesses about her supposed "cures." Pope Pius XI declared her a saint in 1946, and a limb was severed from her corpse for use as a first-class relic.

1947 ♦ Following in his father's footsteps, Martin Luther King Jr. (1929–1968) was ordained a Baptist minister. A Black American who preached nonviolence as a means to achieve full civil rights for all Americans, King won a Nobel Peace Prize in 1964.

1953 ♦ Fulton J. Sheen (1895–1979), an Irish-American bishop in the Catholic

Church, became one of the few religious leaders to enjoy a full career in the media. During the 1920s he broadcast The Catholic Hour over the radio; and during the 1950s he starred in his own weekly TV series, Life Is Worth Living—a show that grew out of the title of his best-selling book published in 1953. Sheen published more than 50 books, and was the director of the Society for the Propagation of the Faith for many years.

1961 ◆ John Joseph Krol (1910–   ), a native of Cleveland, Ohio, became the first American of Polish ancestry to lead a major Catholic diocese when he was ordained Archbishop of Philadelphia. In 1967 he was elevated to the rank of Cardinal, and in 1971 he became president of the National Conference of Catholic Bishops.

1965 ◆ This year marked a peak in religious history—64.3% of the American population belonged to one of the more than 200 religious groups in the United States.

1966 ◆ Swami Prabhupada (1896–   ), a native of Calcutta, founded the International Society for Khrishna Consciousness in 1966, at the height of American interest in Eastern religions and mysticism. The Swami, born A. C. Bhaktivedenta, came to the United States at the age of 69 with only 5 dollars to his name and a box of vedic scriptures. In 1979, there were an estimated 40 communal Khrishna centers in the United States and Canada.

1966 ◆ Bishop Harold Perry (1916–   ) became the first Black Roman Catholic bishop elected in the United States during the twentieth century. Born in Lake Charles, Louisiana, Perry was not the first Black American to rise to such heights in the Catholic church. That honor goes to James Augustine Healy, an American of Irish and Negro ancestry who was born a slave near Macon, Georgia, in 1830.

1970 ◆ King Efuntola, a native of Detroit, Michigan, founded the community of Ovotunji in 1970. Tucked into a pine forest in South Carolina, just off Route 17, this community of 90 black Americans follows the Yoruba way of life, much as it has been lived in Africa for thousands of years.

The King was ordained a Yoruba priest in Cuba more than twenty years ago. He once ran a temple in Harlem, in addition to selling trinkets on the sidewalks of New York to support himself during the lean years. Tourists may visit Ovotunji to experience life in a "real African community." (There is an admission charge as well as an extra fee to watch ceremonial dances.) For an offering of $25 and up, a chicken or a goat can be sacrificed in one's name by King Efuntola, who is also a voodoo priest.

1971 ◆ Maharaj Ji, a pudgy Indian guru of 13, came to the United States to found the Divine Light Mission.

1975 ◆ This year there were 72.5 million Protestants, 48.7 million Catholics, 5.8 million Jews and 5.2 million members of other religious bodies in the United States. Catholics accounted for 24% of the population, while Protestants had fallen from 98.4% of the population two centuries ago, to 36%.

1977 ◆ Three women were ordained as Reform Jewish rabbis in the United States, and 35 others were enrolled at rabbinical schools throughout the country.

1977 ◆ According to the 1979 *Yearbook of American and Canadian Churches,* overall church membership in the United States grew .7% to 132,812,470 persons, or 60.8% of the population in 1977. (That percentage was down from the 1965 peak of 64.3%.

In 1977 the two largest Protestant bodies reporting membership gains were the Southern Baptists (America's largest Protestant group), which increased 1.24% to 13,078,239 members; and the Mormon Church, which increased its tithing rolls 3.9% to 2,486,261 members.

Despite the large influx of Catholic immigrants to the United States from the Dominican Republic, Colombia and Puerto Rico, the Roman Catholic church witnessed a decline of 233,144 members. Total Catholic membership in 1977 was 49,602,035, or 22.59% of the population.

Other church memberships that declined during 1977 included: Lutheran Church—Missouri Synod, down 3.04%; Episcopal, down 2.19%; United Presbyterian Church, down 1.77%; United Church of Christ, down 0.87%; United

Methodist Church, down 0.77% and the Lutheran Church in America, down 0.25%.

1978 ◆ Joseph Freeman, 25, became the first known Black American to serve as a Mormon priest. This year marked a milestone for the Mormon church in America — a church that had once preached that people were born into the black race as a "punishment" for failing God in a prior existence, and was once sued by the NAACP for refusing to allow Blacks into Mormon Boy Scout troops. All of that changed in June 1978 when a revelation occurred to members of the church hierarchy. From that date forward, "all worthy males," no matter what their race, were allowed to serve as priests.

◆ Metropolitan Theodosius (1933–) became the head of the Orthodox Church in America. He was born in Cannonsburg, Pennsylvania, to the Lazor family; his ancestors hailed from Galicia, a patch of Eastern Europe that has been ruled by Austria, Poland and Russia over the years.

The Metropolitan is the first American-born leader of the Orthodox Church in America. Once associated with the Russian Orthodox Church, the American Orthodox church is now independent. There are dozens of national and ethnic branches, such as the Greek Orthodox (1,950,000 members), Russian Orthodox (51,500) and Syrian Orthodox (50,000) churches in America, which share a common heritage of liturgy and hymns.

◆ When Cardinal Karol Wojtyla became Pope John Paul II in 1978, his American relatives, members of the Wojcik family from Hamtramck, Michigan, boarded an Alitalia plane to witness their famous cousin's installation as Pontiff of the Roman Catholic Church. (John Paul II was the first non-Italian pope in 455 years — the last being Pope Adrian VI, who was poisoned in 1523.)

1979 ◆ Charles E. Bradford became the first Black to head the Seventh Day Adventist Church of North America. The Seventh Day Adventists have a religious following of 550,000 in North America, and more than 3 million members worldwide.

7 FUN AND GAMES

PLAYTHINGS OF THE WESTERN WORLD

Rag dolls and home-whittled toys have gone the way of home-baked bread and hand-dipped candles. Except for a few craftsmen who turn out high-priced nostalgic toys, most of the playthings American children line their shelves with are mass-produced by large manufacturing companies. "Child's play" has become big business in America, accounting for more than $4 billion in annual sales; a really "hot" item can make millions for its manufacturer during one Christmas season.

Most of the best-selling toys and games in America are variations of those that have been enjoyed by children the world over for hundreds of years. Toy animals, balls and pull toys were favorite playthings in ancient Egypt; kites and tops are believed to have originated in China; and the ancient Greeks and Romans made miniature boats, rocking horses and hoops for their children to play with.

Although many of the toys, games and gimmicks American children like best have been imported from the other side (boomerangs, yo-yos and checkers, for instance), each Christmas season brings a new crop of playthings to capture a child's imagination. And the dream of every toy manufacturer is to invent an item that will have the lasting power of—

The Barbie Doll

Before Mattel swooped into the marketplace with its "full-figured" Barbie doll and captured the minds, hearts and purses of millions of American girls, all of the dolls

sold in this country were as "flat as a board." But when Barbie burst on the toy scene in 1959, little girls were finally free to fantasize about a woman who had it all—a real figure, a successful modeling career, designer clothes, furs, boats, airplanes, jewels, townhouses, and a handsome male companion, Ken. No longer were the tots limited to mundane dreams of cleaning up after Betsy-Wetsy or wiping Tiny Tears' eyes—Barbie was a swinging adult, and she had the anatomical features to prove it.

There are two women behind the success of the Barbie doll: Ruth Handler, cofounder of the Mattel Company, and her own daughter, Barbie, who inspired the doll.

When Ruth noticed that her own daughter preferred teenage paper dolls to the baby dolls that wet, burped and cooed, she decided to fill a void that existed in toyland by marketing an adult fashion doll "with all the trimmings." The result was outstanding, and Barbie has been a maverick in Mattel's toy stable for almost two decades.

Born in 1917, Ruth was the youngest of ten children born to Polish immigrant parents in Denver, Colorado. She married her high school sweetheart, Elliot Handler, a designer who began making furniture for doll houses from scraps of wood and plastic, and together they founded the Mattel toy company in 1945.

Besides Barbie, the other factor that made Mattel one of the great names in children's playthings was the decision to buy network television time in 1955. By designing toys that children wanted and advertising them, the Handlers were able to turn Mattel into the world's largest toy manufacturer, with sales in excess of $280 million per year.

Anatomically Correct

For decades, thousands of brotherless American girls have felt cheated on Christmas morning when Santa Claus brought them baby boy dolls, which, when disrobed, turned out to be identical to baby girl dolls. At one time, all dolls were made from the same "neuter" mold, possessing neither male nor female sex organs, but all that changed in 1967 when the French introduced Little Brother to America.

Petit Frère, as he was known in his native land, was designed by Claude Refabert and his wife to represent an average 4-month-old baby boy. The Parisian toy manufacturers were inspired by their own young grandson, who picked up a doll dressed as a boy and asked, "Is it a boy or a girl?" after examining its anatomy more closely.

When Petit Frère went on sale in Europe in 1966 it created quite a stir. The English disapproved, whereas the Scandinavians clutched Little Brother close to their sexually liberated hearts. People in the United States were likewise divided when they received word that Creative Playthings would soon be importing the tyke. Upon his arrival at U.S. Customs after his steerage-class journey from France, Little Brother was apprehended by officers who had been alerted that an obscene doll was being shipped into America. When the Customs officials examined the little guy, they brushed the complaint aside, finding the 4-pound, 21-inch infant a perfectly acceptable teaching aid for young, curious children.

The climate of the 1970s was a bit more receptive to "correct" baby dolls, and other companies jumped on the bandwagon, manufacturing their own versions of baby boys to satisfy the curiosity of little girls who don't have brothers.

The producers of the popular television show, *All in the Family,* even made a deal with a toy company to market a "baby boy" doll named after the grandson of that lovable conservative, Archie Bunker. However, the Joey Stivic doll (the first Polish-American doll) never became a commercial success.

Ethnically Correct

For years white dolls tried to "pass." They attempted to conceal their Caucasian features and straight hair behind a layer of brown pigment, but Black consumers able to see beyond that layer of "brown wash," were reluctant to buy white dolls that had merely been dipped in brown paint.

The climate of the 1960s and more sophisticated marketing research, taught toy manufacturers that Blacks were not going to buy unrealistic baby dolls, and the thought of racking up sales to 11% of the population sent them back to the drawing board. Black artists were hired to make dolls as "ethnically correct" as possible, and soon Remco and Mattel were marketing Black dolls throughout the United States.

One of the most successful manufacturers of Black toys and games is Shindana Toys, a Los Angeles-based organization which was privately funded and established by Mattel executives in 1968 to promote industry in the ghetto. Appropriately enough, the word *shindana* means "competitor" in Swahili, and the Black-managed company has been quite successful in selling toys designed for Black consumers. Some of their best selling items include: Baby Nancy, their first doll, who came complete with Afro or twin ponytail hairstyles; Flip Wilson and Rodney Allen Rippy dolls; and games such as The Jackson Five, The Black Experience, and Captain Soul.

Teddy's Bear

Possibly the most beloved American toy is the Teddy Bear. Each night millions of American children fall asleep with their arms wrapped around their stuffed bears, never giving a thought to the Russian immigrant who started it all, Morris Michtom (1870–1938), the "father of the Teddy bear."

Michtom was inspired to create his stuffed bear by a 1902 cartoon that appeared in the *Washington Star.* Clifford Berryman's illustration showed Theodore Roosevelt, rifle in hand, standing with his back turned from a cowering bear cub. The caption read, "Drawing the line in Mississippi," and referred to a trip the President had taken to the South to settle a border dispute between Louisiana and Mississippi and to take in a little hunting on the side. Local residents, informed of Teddy's hunting trip, wanted the President to return home with a trophy. To facilitate matters, they trapped a young bear cub for the President to shoot. Roosevelt refused and the cartoon that told the tale was reproduced by news services across the nation.

Prompted by the cartoon, Michtom quickly produced a small stuffed bear which he placed in the window of his Brooklyn, New York, candy store next to a sign that read "Teddy's Bear." Soon, besieged by anxious customers with orders for similar pets, Michtom decided to petition Roosevelt for permission to use his name on the stuffed bears. Roosevelt gave his consent, but confessed he "couldn't see what use my name would be in the stuffed animal trade." The result is history, and by 1906 the country was overpopulated with teddies. Michtom was so successful at selling toys that he decided to give up his candy-novelty store in Brooklyn, and went on to found the Ideal Toy Company in 1903. The original Teddy bear also went on to bigger and better things: it now has a permanent home in the Smithsonian Institution in Washington, D.C.

Stuffed by Steiff

The first stuffed bear was probably fashioned by Margaret Steiff, a polio victim confined to a wheelchair, who began sewing felt animals in her native Germany in the 1880s. Today, Steiff is one of the world's most respected names in the animal kingdom, selling stuffed carnivores, herbivores and omnivores of every size and shape. Tiny mice can be purchased for a few dollars, but 5-foot-tall giraffes and life-size tigers command price tags between $500 and $900. Steiff also manufactures bears in many sizes, shapes and species, and although they were probably first to stuff them, Michtom was the first to call them "Teddy."

Silly Putty

Like so many other brainstorms and great inventions, Silly Putty started life as a mistake. After all, would a business-minded corporation such as General Electric deliberately spend hard-earned research dollars to develop a substance whose only function

in life was to bounce, stretch, snap and transfer color when placed on the Sunday comics?

The answer is "Yes!" — if they had only known what a great toy Silly Putty would make and that annual sales would average $6.5 million per annum over the past two decades.

The year was 1945 and industrial researchers all over America and Europe were feverishly competing to develop a synthetic rubber for wartime use. James Wright, a Scottish engineer at General Electric's New Haven facility, inadvertently mixed boric acid with silicone oil and dropped the test tube to the floor. Much to his surprise, he discovered that the mixture bounced! Not only did it bounce: it had a rebound capacity 25% greater than that of rubber, it could withstand wide variations in temperature without deteriorating and it was impervious to rot and decay. Unfortunately, it wasn't of any strategic or industrial value, but it did make a great conversation piece at local cocktail parties in the New Haven area.

That's where Peter Hodgson was first introduced to the liquid-solid substance that was to make him a millionaire. A recent immigrant from Montreal, Hodgson was working as a copywriter for a New Haven toy store when he attended a local party in Connecticut. While muching hors d'oeuvres in the corner, he noticed how much adults enjoyed playing with the useless, putty-like substance one of the researchers had brought along. Acting on a hunch, he made a deal with G.E. and his boss agreed to include "Silly Putty" in the toy store catalog. That year, Silly Putty outsold every other item in the catalog except for those perennially popular drawing tools — crayons. Peter's boss was pleased with sales, but considered the item a fad that would fade, and decided not to include Silly Putty in the following year's catalog.

Hodgson thought differently, and decided to manufacture Silly Putty himself. His instincts were right — kids everywhere were crazy about the stuff, and bought it by the carloads. Unfortunately, parents found it stuck to rugs, chairs, furniture and hair, and sales soon began to slack off in the wake of ruined furnishings. A new, non-sticky formula was introduced in 1960, and Silly Putty became a bestseller once again with sales averaging $6.5 million each year since then, as kids of all ages bounced it, stretched it and made grotesque faces from comic strip imprints.

Spirograph

A relative newcomer to the American toy chest, Spirograph can keep a child going around in circles for hours. On paper, that is. This deceptively simple system of plastic gears that rotate inside a fixed ring can make anyone, even an adult, a whiz at producing complex designs and op-art patterns.

The man who invented Spirograph is Denys Fisher, a British electronics engineer who first conceived the idea while designing bomb detonators whose patterns incorporated numerous epicyclic curves. Fisher spent a long time perfecting his perfectly meshed gears, and although the toy was slow in catching the public eye in his native England, once it was distributed properly sales exploded.

Since Spirograph was first imported from England in 1967, sales have amounted to several million dollars in the United States alone, as budding young artists everywhere develop small-muscle control by guiding their pens through some pretty fancy maneuvers.

Erector Set

Poor people often say "Money can't buy happiness," but in his autobiography, *The Man Who Lives in Paradise,* Alfred Carlton Gilbert (1884–1961) claimed to be the happiest millionaire alive: "I've never worked at anything that wasn't fun. If I had my life to live over I don't think I'd change it. Except maybe to take up mountain climbing."

Descended from Thomas Gilbert, an Englishman who settled in Massachusetts about 1640, A.C. Gilbert was a man who wore many hats. Not only was he a rich toy inventor, he had a medical degree from Yale, an Olympic gold medal for pole vaulting (1908), and a successful magic trick business under his belt by the time he was 28 years old.

In 1912, while gazing out a railway window, Gilbert was intrigued by crewmen constructing a high tension tower by the side of the railroad tracks. As he commuted to work each day he watched with fascina-

tion as the tower grew higher and higher. That tower was the inspiration for his best-selling toy, the Erector Set, a miniaturized steel building kit complete with girders, nuts, bolts, and washers that eager little hands, and big ones, too, could assemble into Ferris wheels, bridges, towers or motorized elevators.

Lego

One of the most popular building toys sold in America today is a Danish import known as Lego. A contraction of two Danish words, *leg godt,* Lego means "play well," and that's just what Ole Kirk Christiansen and his son Godtfred had in mind when they invented these colorful plastic building blocks. With these child-sized interlocking bricks that really hold together, youngsters can build police stations, hospitals, ambulances and even windmills without parental aid, simply by following the step-by step instructions.

First marketed in 1954, Lego quickly became a best seller with children all over the world. If you're ever in Billund, Denmark, you might want to visit the Lilliputian-sized village that adjoins the Lego factory, where a whole town of 600 buildings has been created from Lego bricks.

Lincoln Logs

In a world full of polystyrene, polyethylene, and polypropylene playthings it is comforting to know that some things haven't changed. Lincoln Logs, those notched wooden rails that young hands can use to build log cabins and frontier-type towns, still look pretty much the same as they did 60 years ago. Oh, a few changes have been made, such as plastic chimneys instead of wooden ones, and newfangled plastic gables that make it easier to attach the green roofing slats, but the logs are still made of wood, and every time you open the familiar cardboard canister that great "wooden" smell fills your nostrils and brings back childhood memories.

Billed as "America's national toy," Lincoln Logs were invented in 1916 by John L. Wright, a Welsh American, who inherited his love for building from his famous architect father, Frank Lloyd Wright (1869–1959).

John was always fascinated by stories of America's pioneer days. On a business trip to Japan with his father, watching workmen haul huge rough-hewn timbers for construction of the Imperial Palace Hotel in Tokyo, he conceived the idea for a building toy that would allow young people to recreate a part of America's past by building their own forts, log cabins and covered bridges. He started marketing his toy as soon as he returned home to Merrill, Wisconsin, but it wasn't until 1924 that Lincoln Logs caught the fancy of American children. Manufactured today by Playskool, who purchased rights to the toy from Wright in 1943, Lincoln Logs have been a steady seller for the past six decades.

Parker Brothers' Monopoly

When Charles Darrow first presented his new board game, Monopoly, to George and Charles Parker in 1933, they told him to "take a walk on the Boardwalk." The Parkers, who were descended from English ancestors, thought Monopoly was too long, too complicated, and contained at least 52 weak points they usually tried to avoid when producing a new game.

Discouraged but still determined, Darrow picked up his playing pieces, went home and began printing Monopoly sets by himself. After he sold 5,000 sets to Wanamaker's in Philadelphia during the 1934 Christmas season, the Parker Brothers changed their tune and offered Darrow a contract. The game of Monopoly was so successful that Darrow, a former engineer from Germantown, Pennsylvania, was able to retire at the age of 46 – a millionaire from his Monopoly royalties.

Some 80 million sets have been sold throughout the world in English, French, Italian, German, Dutch, Flemish, Swedish, Danish, Norwegian, Greek, Potuguese, Japanese, Chinese and Hebrew. There are also three different Spanish versions marketed in Colombia, Spain and Venezuela. Each game has its own famous equivalents of Boardwalk and Park Place, which are called Mayfair and Park Lane in London; Paseo del Prado in Spain; and Rue de la Paix in France.

You'd be correct if you guessed that a game with a name like Monopoly would be banned in the Soviet Union as too capitalistic, but that hasn't stopped the Russian people from indulging. When the American National Exhibition opened in Moscow in 1959 there were 6 samples of the game on display. By the time the exhibition was over, all of the games were missing, so there is reason to believe that somewhere furtive Russians are shelling out 25 rubles for a ride on the Reading.

As of 1974 the Parker Brothers have manufactured over 2,560,000,000 little green houses, 720,000,000 red hotels, and $56,392,000,000. That's more money than the U.S. Mint produced in its entire history (a mere $2,897,080,000).

Milton Bradley

Another big name in the toy and game business is Milton Bradley (1836–1911). Descended from Daniel Bradley, a Londoner who disembarked at Salem, Massachusetts, in 1635, Milton was raised in a home where playing cards were not permitted, and chess and checkers were the only form of entertainment allowed, since they were games of skill, not of chance.

Bradley started his career as a lithographer, and one of his first widely sold portraits was of Abraham Lincoln. One day, however, a man strode into Milton's office and demanded his money back – the lithograph was a fraud! It turned out that Lincoln had grown a beard, so Bradley was forced to destroy thousands of prints. The surviving copies eventually became valuable collector's items.

His first best-selling game was The Checkered Game of Life, which he touted as a moralistic game to teach children the advantages of living a good, clean life. Today the company that bears his name is not quite as fervent about upholding the Puritan ideal: Milton Bradley is responsible for such games as Twister – in which everyone ends up on all fours in some rather awkward positions.

Othello

During the early 1970s Othello took Japan by storm. Some 25 million devoted fans took up the game before the craze spread to America. Invented by a Japanese salesman, Goro Hasegawa, in 1971, the game was named after the Shakespearean play by Goro's father, who noted that Othello's appeal lay in the "dramatic reversals" that can occur when the dual-colored playing pieces are flipped. Since one misplaced piece can cost a player as many as 18 men, in a game where 33 wins, you can never really be sure of a victory until the final piece is laid.

Unfortunately, not much is really new under the sun: Othello bears a startling resemblance to a nineteenth century English board game called Reversi. Reversi was also a fast-moving game with dramatic changes that utilized a board with 64 squares and dual-colored playing pieces. The only difference is that Reversi wasn't patented.

More Facts About Toys and Games in America

♦ Bavarian maple from the Black Forest of Germany is the only wood used to manufacture the letter tiles in Scrabble word games. Its tightly pressed grain makes it more difficult for the backs of the letters to be "marked" by unevenness and defects that might give gamesters with good memories an unfair advantage when picking tiles.

♦ The Milton Bradley game Chutes and Ladders, popular with preschool children all over America, is a variation of an ancient Hindu game, *Moksha-patamu* (Snakes and Ladders), which represents man's treacherous journey through life on the road to Nirvana. Virtuous acts are rewarded by climbing the ladder toward heaven, while evil deeds earn one a trip down the chute, or snake, to reincarnation as a lower form of animal life.

♦ Chess, which probably originated in India or China during the sixth century, is played the world over under different names. An early prototype chessboard was even discovered in the tomb of King Tutankhamen in Egypt.

In America we call the game *chess*, but in Old English the name of the game was *check*. The Persians called it *shatranj*, the Chinese dubbed it *chong ki*, the Irish knew it as *fifth cheall* and the Welsh called their game *tawlbwrdd*. In India the game is known as *chaturanga*, in Italy it's *sácci alla rabiosa*, in France it's *echecs* and in Spain the game is called *ajedrez*.

♦ Checkers is almost universally slurred as a "woman's" game. During the middle ages it was called chess for ladies. In France, it was *jeu des dames;* in Germany, *damenspiel:* in Italy, *giuoco della dama;* in Spain, *juego de damas;* in Arab-speaking nations it's known as *la-ab eddama.* The English call the game draughts, but in America we call it checkers, referring to the pattern of the game board.

♦ Chinese checkers has a somewhat "checkered" past. Despite the name, it is not an ancient Chinese game, nor was it even invented in the Orient. Chinese Checkers is actually a modern version of an old English game, halma, which originated about 1880. It was introduced to China by the Japanese. It reached its peak of popularity in the United States in the 1930s, and is now standard game room fare in America.

♦ Almost every nursery has a cradle gym hanging over baby's crib. These wooden and plastic beads, sometimes adorned with mirrors, ropes and bells designed to keep baby amused, were introduced to the first colonists by the American Indians, who invented the toy.

♦ Backgammon, from the Welsh *back gammon,* meaning "little battle," was invented by an Indian sage named Qaflān. Qaflān designed the game to represent the solar year. The 24 points on the game board represent the hours in each day; 30 playing pieces represent the days of the month (well, at least 4 of the months have 30 days); the two dice represent day and night; and the seven spots that appear on opposite ends of the dice represent the days of the week.

♦ The first darts in America were brought here by the Pilgrims. Although they considered playing cards evil, they saw nothing wrong in passing a few idle hours throwing darts at a bull's-eye. Thanks to our Puritan forefathers we can all enjoy a game of 301 now and then at the corner pub.

♦ Mah-Jongg is an Occidental version of an ancient Chinese game that was first brought to America in 1920 by Joseph Babcock, an American businessman. Babcock changed the rules a bit and added Arabic numerals to the playing tiles before he began importing games from China under the trade name Mah-Jongg.

Mah-Jongg became the hot fad of the 1920s (more than 1.5 million sets were sold in 1923) until it was displaced by the Contract Bridge craze that began in 1930.

♦ *Two Toys That Originated As Weapons* The Boomerang is a lightweight version of a weapon once used in battle by Australian aborigines. Another "harmless" toy that started out as a method of destruc-

tion is the "yo-yo." Sixteenth-century hunters in the Philippine Islands used to tie two heavy objects together with a long length of rope. When the weapon was hurled through the air it could catch an animal by the neck and ensnare its legs in the long length of rope. Donald Duncan modified the design and introduced the yo-yo to America in 1929.

THE SPORTING LIFE

Like everything else that is "American," our best-loved sports, games and street games were either appropriated from other cultures or invented by ethnic Americans.

BADMINTON   In its native India the name of the game was *poona,* but when British army officers brought the game home to England it was doomed to remain nameless until 1873. The Duke of Beaufort and his aristocratic friends popularized the sport at his country estate, Badminton, in Gloucestershire, England, and players everywhere began referring to the sport as "the game at Badminton."

The name stuck, and when the rules of badminton became formalized in 1887 it became official. The first U.S. match was played in New York City in 1878, but badminton did not gain national prominence until 1920, when soldiers returning home from England gave the game a new boost that started Americans batting shuttlecocks from coast to coast.

BASKETBALL   If Dr. James Naismith (1861–1939), the Canadian-born inventor of basketball, had had his way, the Boston Celtics would be a "boxball" team today.

Shortly before the first basketball game was to begin at the International YMCA Training School in Springfield, Massachusetts, Naismith asked the janitor to tack up two boxes on either side of the gymnasium. When the resourceful custodian was unable to find two large cartons, he substituted the peach baskets that eventually gave the sport its name.

Naismith invented the game in 1892 specifically to meet the need for an indoor sport that would keep athletes in shape between football season and spring training for baseball and lacrosse. Many of Naismith's original 13 rules are still used in modern play,

but many other new regulations have been added—some out of necessity. For example: the need for a backboard first became apparent when overzealous fans seated in the gym's balcony took to snatching the ball out of the basket before the opposing team could score.

Besides developing one of the few sports that originated on American soil, Naismith also designed the first headgear ever used in football and wrote several books on basketball and physical education.

BOWLING   Bowling originated in ancient Germany—not as a sporting event, but as a religious rite. Christians were required to prove their virtue by knocking down the *heide,* or heathen, represented by a club. A direct hit was proof that the bowler was leading a chaste and honorable life, but any parishioner who failed to knock down his *kegel* (club) was retested until proved virtuous.

Though the practice was abandoned by the Church in the fifth century, bowling's popularity spread beyond the monastery walls. Eventually, wooden balls were substituted for the rounded rocks that were first used, and specially shaped pins were fashioned for the game. Even religious leader Martin Luther found time to bowl a few games of "nine pins" now and then, helping to popularize the sport in Germany during the early 1500s.

The Dutch introduced bowling (known as "nine pins" until the 1840s) to America, with the pins arranged in the shape of a diamond. When the burghers of Connecticut, concerned about the inordinate amount of gambling associated with the game, banned "bowling at nine pins" during 1840s, a resourceful Yankee managed to sidestep the law by inventing the game of

The Ex-Champion

ROUND 21
SULLIVAN'S VAIN ATTEMPT TO RISE.

Gentleman Jim whips the Boston Strong Boy at
New Orleans on September 7, 1892.

The Boston Strong Boy, John L. Sullivan, was the first fighter defeated under Queensberry rules. (Courtesy: New York Public Library)

"ten pins." He arranged the pins in the shape of a triangle, and we've been playing with that configuration ever since.

BOXING   Bare knuckles were the weapons of choice in the boxing rings of Europe and America until 1867, when the Marquis of Queensberry, a British nobleman, invented the boxing rules that bear his name. According to the new, civilized "Queensberry Rules," boxers were required to wear gloves, and rounds were limited to three minutes each with one-minute rest periods in between.

The rules, compiled by J. G. Chambers, spread to America in 1892. One of our most famous Irish-American fighters, John L. Sullivan, had the dubious honor of being the first fighter defeated under the Queensberry regulations. He lost his heavyweight title to James J. Corbett in New Orleans when he was knocked out in the 21st round.

HANDBALL   The rules of the game have changed quite a bit since handball was first introduced to the United States in 1882: the court is shorter, the ball is softer and kicking your opponent is no longer allowed.

We call it "handball," but the original

name for the Irish national sport of the 1800s was "fives," so named because all five fingers are used to smack the ball against the wall. Invented in old Eire during the 10th century, the sport was introduced to America, fittingly enough, by an Irishman.

Phil Casey, who arrived in Brooklyn, New York, in 1882, had been an avid handball player in his native land, and as much as he loved living in New York he had two complaints about his newly adopted land: "Not enough handball players, and no handball courts."

Casey began to teach the game to his neighbors, and when they clamored for more he built the first handball court in 1886. In 1887 he became America's first International Handball Champion when he defeated Ireland's leading player, John Lawlor, 11 games to 6. One of the world's best handball players, Phil Casey remained undefeated against all challengers until 1900 when he retired from professional sports.

JAI ALAI   An ancient game from the Basque region of the Pyrenees, on the border where France meets Spain, jai alai was first played in America at an exhibition game during the St. Louis World's Fair in 1904. By 1924, jai alai was Miami's number one tourist attraction, due to the influence of its large Cuban population. Today, jai alai betting is legal in four states. In Nevada alone the sport attracted 2,000 spectators and generated $50,000 in bets per night during the first year of operation in 1974, proving that the appeal of the game was not limited to the Hispanic community alone.

In Spain the game is known as pelota, but when the game was imported to Havana in 1900 it was first played at a facility known as the *Frontón Jai Alai*. Today, jai alai (from the Basque for merry festival) is played on three-walled courts called *frontóns*.

Promoters claim that the costs of jai alai are so high that gambling is necessary to make the game profitable. And profitable it must be! The average take per night in Bridgeport, Connecticut, between November and May, 1977, was $400,000. That adds up to almost $150 million yearly, with the state receiving 5%, or $7.5 million. The city of Bridgeport receives a paltry $375,000, while the *frontón gets $18 million* plus profits from ticket, program, food and liquor sales.

Ostensibly the rest of the money is used to pay off bets with exotic names like Quinielas, in which bettors pick two teams to finish first or second; Perfectas, where you must pick the first and second teams in order; and Trifectas, where you must pick the teams that win, place and show, in order. The Trifecta can pay up to four figures for the right bets, but for many bettors the four figures are all zeroes due to the complexity of pitting eight teams against one another in a round-robin situation.

Most of the players in the United States are Basque, with the exception of Joey Cornblit, a Jewish-American born and bred in Miami, one of the few Americans who have mastered the sport.

LACROSSE The Indians of North America had been playing lacrosse for centuries before Europeans ever set foot on the continent. Known to the Ojibwa tribe as *baggataway,* the forerunner of modern lacrosse was rougher and bloodier than the current game.

The Indians often played an intertribal game with as many as 2,000 braves taking part in the melee. And brave one had to be to play the game, which often lasted up to three days, and had only one objective: "To disable as many opponents as possible." The Cherokees, who made no bones about their version of the game, called the sport "Little brother of war" and considered it an endurance test similar to combat training.

One of our nation's most memorable lacrosse games took place at what is now Mackinaw City, Michigan, at Fort Michilimackinack, when the Ojibwa and Sac Indians staged a demonstration game to celebrate King George III's birthday in 1763.

The French and Indian War had ended in February of that year, and on a beautiful day in June all the hostilities between the British and the Indians were forgotten (by the British, that is). The gates to the fort were opened in a gesture of peace, and tranquillity was in the air as the British troops relaxed their guard to enjoy the day's festivities. Many soldiers even left their posts and climbed to the top of the fort to watch the game.

Suddenly, without warning, the Indians rushed through the gates with concealed weapons garnered from conspirators in the crowd and slaughtered all but 20 of the fort's British inhabitants. Despite this bloody start, Canadians and Americans developed a fondness for the game that became the national sport of Canada in 1867.

The name Lacrosse was given to the game by a French priest, Francois Xavier de Charlevoix, who likened the stick to a bishop's crozier—*la crosse* in French. But, it was a Canadian physician, Dr. W. George Beers, nicknamed "the father of lacrosse," who popularized the game and wrote down the first set of rules and regulations in 1859.

Today, the only authentic lacrosse sticks are those manufactured on the St. Regis Indian reserve in Canada. Craftsmen hand-fashion the sticks from hickory, and then shape, wire and cure them for over a year before they are shipped to the United States.

JUDO The gentle art of self-defense was invented by a young Japanese man, Jigoro Kano, in 1882. Like Charles Atlas, who developed his body building course in self-defense, Kano invented judo after being repeatedly attacked by local bullies.

First he learned the ancient art of combat, ju-jitsu, to develop his reflexes and teach him how to deliver death-blows to opponents; he later evolved judo (the gentle way) from this aggressive sport. He wanted to condition young men, and provide them with a means of self-defense, without necessarily teaching them to harm their opponents.

To prove the effectiveness of his new method of defense, Kano staged a showdown between the top Japanese judo and jujitsu artists in 1886. Judo won hands down, and business has been flourishing ever since then. Even President Theodore Roosevelt earned a brown belt for his *judogi,* as the white pajamas are called.

POLO   First introduced to England in

Gymnastics as a sport was introduced to America by German immigrants. This 1854 print by Fr. Venino depicts an excursion of the New York Turners. (Courtesy: J. Clarence Davies Collection, Museum of the City of New York)

1869, polo originated in India, where once again British Army officers transformed a native game into a pastime for the rich. It started when native horsemen staged an exhibition, at which riders hit an odd-looking "ball" up and down a field. When the show was over, an officer pointed to the unusual "ball" and asked what the game was called. The answer was *pulu,* referring to the willow root from which the "ball" had

been carved. The British added goal posts, boundary lines, and corrupted the game's name to polo, but the balls are still made from willow roots.

In 1876, James Gordon Bennett, publisher of the New York *Herald,* brought the game to America.

TABLE TENNIS   Table tennis is another popular sport that originated on Indian soil, but unlike polo and badminton, table tennis was purely an English innovation, dreamed up by bored army officers in 1881.

Parker Brothers, the gamesmen from Salem, Massachusetts, began importing nets, paddles and balls, under the trademark Ping-Pong, at the turn of the century. Within a short time, Ping-Pong became the first American fad of the twentieth century, sweeping the nation for two years, 1902–1904. But, alas, Americans are a fickle race, and Ping-Pong faded from the limelight almost as quickly as it ascended. It did retain a modest number of fans, and sales remained constant until a recent surge in popularity spurred on by President Nixon's 1972 visit to mainland China, where table tennis is one of the leading indoor activities.

WATER SKIING Fred Waller (1886–1954), the grandson of English immigrants who settled in New York City in 1815, introduced the sport of water skiing to America in 1924 and patented the first wide water ski in 1927.

In addition to giving Americans the thrill of riding on top of water, Waller also attained fame by inventing the Cinerama movie technique.

TENNIS Although the origins of the game are obscure, the terminology is definitely French. When the game score is 15 to 0 it is announced as "15–Love" which makes very little sense, unless you consider that "love," meaning "no score," "zero," "zilch," or a big, fat "goose egg" is derived from the French word for egg—*l'oeuf.*

SWIMMING Yes, the Australian Crawl did originate in Australia. It was introduced to the world by Richard Cavill in 1902, who learned the stroke in his native Australia and revolutionized the art of swimming. The crawl stroke is one of the speediest methods of getting from one end of a pool to another, and although it was once considered too exhausting for long competitions, the crawl stroke is the choice of long-distance and marathon swimmers the world over.

TRAPSHOOTING began in England about 1830, and made its way to the United States in the late 1870s. Americans then invented another version of the game called "round the clock shooting" where marksmen shoot at clay pigeons from 7 or 8 stations arranged in a semicircle.

Known today as skeet shooting, the sport got its new name when *National Sportsman* magazine conducted a competition to name the shooting game in 1910. Mrs. Gertrude Hurlbutt of Dayton, Montana, won $100 for choosing the name "skeet" from a Scandinavian form of the word "shoot," thus making the title as redundant as "pizza (meaning pie) pie."

STREET GAMES

The names of the inventors of our best-loved street games have been forever lost to history, but their games live on, and we can justly give credit where credit is due to the people who gave us the raw materials to play with. After all, you need a stoop for stoopball; bottle caps for skullsy; and aggies to play marbles.

♦ Stoopball was made possible by the Dutch settlers of New Amsterdam, who introduced the *stoep* as an architectural feature of New York City townhouses. In Holland, where flooding is a constant thread, stoops (front stairways) are necessary to prevent water from seeping into the parlor.

Stoopball is one of the most versatile and inexpensive sports available to city dwellers: it can be played almost anywhere, there are no expensive court fees, and no special equipment is required other than a "spaldeen."

♦ Spaldeens are lively pink rubber balls that bounce the highest and last the longest, giving a player most bounce per ounce. Always 5¢ or 10¢ more expensive than cheap "pinkies" or white "pimple" balls, a good "spaldeen" might last a whole summer, and could frequently escape harm even after being run over by a slow-moving car. (There is no sadder sight than a "spaldeen" that has been split in two by the wheels of a fast-moving truck.)

"Spaldeens" are actually the guts of Spalding brand tennis balls, which have been bounced out of their tin cans and polyester coverings for being off-spec. First manufactured about 1900, they are named after Albert Goodwill Spalding (1850–1915), a descendant of early English settlers, who founded the sporting goods firm that bears his name in 1876.

THE WORLD SERIES OF BOCCE

Every year since 1974 the World Series of Bocce has been held at the Rome, New York, Bowling Center.

According to legend, the first authentic bocce balls were designed of willow tree roots by an Italian named Luigi Boccahrini, nicknamed Bocci. The game spread throughout Europe, becoming *pétanque* in France and lawn bowling in England.

The game is played with 8 large balls (boccies) and one small ball (pallino); the goal is to roll the big balls as close to the pallino as possible.

Today there are almost 200 bocce leagues in Rome, New York, alone and some 104 teams from nearby states signed up to compete in the 1978 World Series.

For entry rules, regulations and information, write to World Series of Bocce, Inc., 1009 Franklin Street, Rome, New York 13440

More Street Game Facts

♦ Hopscotch is not "Scotch" in origin, but an old English game popular during the seventeenth century. Also known as Potsy in America, our version of the game is a little bit easier. In America, players toss a token into a numbered box and hop on one foot into the remaining boxes; in England the player has to jump on both legs, holding the token between his feet.

♦ Double Dutch Rope, which employs two jump ropes moving in opposite directions, was invented in the Netherlands and came to this country almost 200 years ago with the first New World settlers.

♦ Skullsy or Skellys, a game played by flicking bottle caps into consecutively numbered squares, owes its existence to the genius of William Painter (1838–1906), a machine shop foreman descended from seventeenth-century English Quakers, who patented the disposable bottle cap in 1892.

A good skullsy cap should be heavy, and many children of the past used to weigh down their caps with wax or lead solder to provide better flicking control. The advent of modern screw-top bottles with lightweight aluminum tops has taken its toll on the game, causing it to decline in popularity in recent years.

♦ Marbles are to country kids what bottle caps are to city kids. They can be made of glass, clay or stone, and are usually nicknamed according to their composition or appearance. There are rainbow marbles, cat's-eye marbles, immys and aggies. At least there used to be aggies. Aggies came from the agate mills of Oberstein, Germany, but in recent years the Germans "lost their marbles" due to material shortages and were forced to close down their production plant. That left the United States as the world's largest supplier of glass marbles: one West Virginia plant turns out close to a billion marbles each year.

SPORTS SHORTS ABOUT ETHNICS WHO WERE "FIRST," BEST OR JUST GOOD SPORTS

SOCCER   Besides being America's first American-born soccer star, Shep Messing was also the first Jewish soccer star to stretch out his nude body for the centerfold of *Viva* magazine.

BEFORE SPITZ   Before Mark Spitz won 5 gold medals in swimming at the 1972 Olympics, the most gold garnered by an American swimmer was 4 medals, won by Donald Arthur Schollander (1946–   ) at the 1964 Olympics.

After Spitz's victory a sportswriter asked the Jewish-American how it felt to be a "conquering Jew in Munich." His tasteful reply: "I always liked this country, even though this lampshade is probably made out of one of my aunts."

JESSE   OWENS   James   Cleveland Owens' (1913–1980) initials, J.C., eventually became slurred into "Jesse." One of the greatest black athletes of all time, Jesse Owens was born on an Alabama farm in 1913, but moved with his family to Cleveland, Ohio, soon afterward. He started setting running records in junior high school, when he ran the hundred-yard dash in 10 seconds flat.

Known as the Brown Bombshell and the Buckeye Bullet, Owens set three new world records and walked off with 4 gold medals at the 1936 Olympic Games, which were supposed to be a showcase for Hitler's "superior Aryan race."

Did Jesse ever beat a racehorse? Yes, he ran several 100-yard races against thoroughbreds in the late 1930s, but there was a "trick" to winning. When the starter's gun went off, the horse would rear back, giving Jesse enough time to run 50 yards or more. Even though the horse could cover 21 feet for every 7 Jesse ran, the head start was always enough of an edge to make Jesse a winner.

HORSE PAINTER One of the legendary figures in horse-race fixing was Peter Christian (Paddy) Barrie, an Irish immigrant who started his career in England and later plied his trade in the United States. His skill with a paintbrush could turn a lightning fast horse into a double for a slow-moving nag whose odds were 40-1. He used bleach, paint, henna, and even drilled his equine subjects' teeth in an attempt to duplicate markings. He also carried a package of ice in his little black bag—strategically placed, an ice pack can make a colt look like a gelding.

Paddy fixed about $6 million worth of races in Britain and the United States before he was deported in the 1930s.

SAUK AND FOX OLYMPIAN Jim Thorpe (1888-1953) was proclaimed the world's greatest all-around athlete in 1912 when he won the pentathlon and decathlon at the Olympic games held in Stockholm, Sweden. A member of the Sauk and Fox tribes, Thorpe might have cleaned up had there been television in 1912: he might have been the Bruce Jenner of his day, hawking Indian Walk brand shoes; Pemmican, "the breakfast of champions"; or even endorsing a new brand of cigarettes—"I'd walk a mile for a Buffalo."

POLISH RUNNER Stanislawa Walasiewicz is better known as Stella Walsh (1911-   ). Born in Wierzchownia, Poland, Stella came to the United States at the age of 2 and desperately wanted to compete in the Olympic games for her adopted na-

tion. But, because she was not a citizen of the United States, she had to do the honors for Poland in the 1932 Olympics. She won a gold medal for her record-breaking 100-meter dash and won more than 40 U.S. championships in track and field.

INDIAN ALL-AMERICAN John Levi, an athlete at Haskell Institute, became the first American Indian named All-American Football Player in 1921.

GERMAN SWIMMER The first woman to swim the English Channel was Gertrude Ederle, the American-born daughter of a German immigrant delicatessen owner. She completed her famous swim in 1926, beating the best time of the five men who had completed the swim previously by 2 hours and 2 minutes—it only took Trudy 14 hours and 31 minutes to cross from Cap Gris Nez, France, to Dover, England. But, the price of victory is sometimes high, and the rough seas buffeted her head about so much that her hearing was permanently impaired.

JERSEY JOE WALCOTT, a Black American, was the oldest prize fighter ever to hold the World's Heavyweight Championship title. Born in Merchantville, New Jersey, Arnold Raymond Cream (1914-   ) changed his name in 1936 in honor of a famous welterweight of the early twentieth century.

At the age of 37, Joe kayoed Ezzard Charles in the 7th round and held his title from July 1951 to October 1952, when he was defeated by Rocky Marciano in the 13th round.

ARTHUR ASHE (1943-   ) is of Mexican, Negro and American Indian ancestry, but he is technically listed as the "first Negro" to capture the U.S. Open Singles Championship. He won his title at Forest Hills, New York, in 1968 and established himself "as the Number 1 star in one of the most segregated U.S. sports." How did he feel about his victory? Ashe proclaimed, "I am a sociological phenomenon."

Ashe's victory was the first American win in 13 years of our nation's most coveted tennis title. Prior to his "first" victory at Forest Hills, Ashe was also the first Black member of the U.S. Davis cup team in 1963.

YOGI'S RACQUET Former catcher for the New York Yankees and Mets, Italian-American Yogi Berra has a new "racquet," so to speak. Instead of opening bowling alleys, batting practice ranges, and restaurants as sports figures were wont to do in the past, Yogi opened a racquetball court in Fairfield, New Jersey, in 1978 to cash in on the fast-growing craze.

ROOKIE OF THE YEAR The first pro golfer to become Rookie of the Year, and Player of the Year, as well as Female Athlete of the Year, was Mexican-American Nancy Lopez. She was also the leading prize winner of the Ladies Pro Golf tour circuit in 1978 — her rookie year.

GREATEST THIEF IN HISTORY Call Lou Brock (1939–) a thief and he'll probably smile, because Brock is a thief who's proud of his handiwork. In 1974 he set an all-time single season record of 118 stolen bases, 14 more than the previous season record set by Maury Wills in 1962.

In 1977, Black American Brock broke Ty Cobb's lifetime record of 892 steals, but even more significant was the fact that Ty took 24 seasons, from 1905 to 1928, to build his reputation as a thief, while it only took Brock 16 seasons, 1962–1977, to beat that record.

At the end of the 1979 baseball season Brock had 938 steals to his credit. Will he try for 1,000? "I'm not thinking in terms of 1,000," Brock once said. "Every stolen base over the years has been a challenge of the moment and not a number."

THE MAN WHO STOLE FIRST BASE The only ballplayer in history to steal first base was a German-American, Herman "Germany" Schaeffer of the Detroit Tigers. The year was 1908; the opposing team was the Cleveland Indians. Schaeffer was on first, Davy Jones on third, and Sam Crawford was at bat.

Schaeffer flashed a signal to indicate a double base-steal, but Davy clung to third as Schaeffer slid into second. The pitcher was getting a bit anxious now, and kept his eyes trained on Jones trying to prevent him from stealing "home." In an attempt to outsmart the opposite team, Schaeffer ran backward to first base on the next pitch, hoping to give Jones time to steal home plate. That maneuver only served to confuse everyone — even Jones — and the Tigers were back where they started with a man on first and a man on third. But on the next pitch, the catcher threw to second, Jones

ran home and Schaeffer was "safe." Everyone had been surprised by "Germany's" maneuver, but there wasn't anything in the rule books that said it couldn't be done. That move caused the rules of the game to be rewritten, and from that day onward, the American League declared that all players had to run in a counterclockwise direction.

RIGHT OUT OF THE BALL PARK Lou Gehrig (1903–1941), the son of German immigrants, was raised in the Yorkville section of Manhattan, where he played the game of baseball in vacant lots. He joined the High School of Commerce baseball team and won a trip to Chicago when his team won the New York City championships. He was only 15 at the time, but he managed to hit his first pitched ball right out of the stadium.

POLISH SPORTS PROMOTER Michael Strauss Jacobs (1880–1953) made his living not by playing sports, but by promoting them. With a knack for sensing attractions that could sell out at the box office, Jacobs became a partner in Madison Square Garden in the 1920s and promoted famous boxers such as Joe Louis. How did this Polish-American start his career as a sports promoter? By "scalping" tickets. Before he began putting on "sellout" shows, he would buy large blocks of tickets for attractions he thought the public wanted to see, and sell them for a higher price when all of the box office seats had been sold.

INDIAN PITCHER Charles Bender, a Chippewa Indian, began his major league baseball career with the Philadelphia Athletics, an American League team, in 1903. Considered one of the all-time great pitchers, he won a total of 212 games and lost only 28 throughout his career.

NOK-A-HOMA The Atlanta Braves "mascot" is called Nok-a-homa (pun intended). In 1969, Levi Walker, an Ottawa Chippewa from Charlevoix, Michigan, played the part of Nok-a-homa at home games in the Atlanta stadium, and danced to celebrate every Brave home run.

PUERTO RICAN PITCHER In 1978, Ed Figueroa of the New York Yankees became the first Puerto Rican pitcher to win 20 games in one season.

NORWEGIAN FORWARD PASSER Norwegian immigrant, Knute Kenneth Rockne (1888–1931) made his way to the United States at the tender age of five.

Despite his parents' objections that football was a "system of modified massacre" he became captain of the Notre Dame football team, and introduced the forward pass in 1913, in a game against West Point. He was generally acknowledged as the greatest football coach in America, and was made an honorary Irishman by the "Fighting Irish" of Notre Dame.

PERFECT JEWISH PITCHER Sandy Koufax (1935–   ) pitched one of baseball history's ten pefect games (in which no opposing runner reaches base), on September 9, 1965. Pitching for the Los Angeles Dodgers, the three-time Cy Young Award winner beat the National League Chicago Cubs with a final score of 1–0.

ONLY THE PRIEST KNEW Mario Andretti (1940–   ) admits that when he began racing stock cars in the 1950s, "None of my relatives even knew [that I raced] ex-cept my old priest uncle, and . . . I told him in confession so he couldn't tell." When his father, an Italian immigrant textile worker, found out about Mario and his twin brother Aldo, he was so enraged that Mario had to leave home in order to pursue his career choice. The warm Italian family could not remain divided forever, though, and a rec-onciliation took place later on.

At the age of 25 Mario Andretti became the youngest driver to win the national championship. He won the Indy 500 in 1969 in 3 hours, 11 minutes and 14.71 sec-onds with an average speed clocked at 156.867 miles per hour.

THE LADY IS A JOCK The first fe-male professional jockey to ride a winning horse was Barbara Jo Rubin (1949–   ). Barbara's father is Jewish, and her mother is of English, Scotch, Irish and German an-cestry.

THE ALL-TIME ALL-STAR ARGUMENT STARTER*

BY HARRY STEIN

The Latins

Latins began having a serious impact on [baseball] only after the color line fell. Since 1949, they've come on with a rush. Below is a balanced unit, with speed and power in abundance, and an enviable defense. But with players from no fewer than five coun-tries, plus Puerto Rico, it would probably take a Latin John McGraw to keep order in the clubhouse.

JUAN MARICHAL, R.H.P., 1960–75: The Dominican Dandy. Topped twenty vic-tories six times; career E.R.A. never rose above 2.76.

MIKE CUELLAR, L.H.P., 1959–   : Has averaged twenty victories a year since coming to Baltimore in 1969; 181 career wins. Cuban.

LUIS ARROYO, R.P., 1955–63: In 1961, he was 15–5 for the Yankees, with a league-leading 29 saves. Puerto Rican.

MANNY SANGUILLEN, C., 1967–   : Can hit anything within three feet of the plate. Runs like an outfielder. Career average of .308. Panamanian.

ORLANDO CEPEDA, 1B, 1958–74: The Baby Bull. Terrifying hitter who carried whole teams on his broad back. Puerto Rican.

BOBBY AVILA, 2B, 1949–59: Strong defen-sive infielder, once batted .341 to lead A.L. Once named by *Sport* magazine the best-looking man in baseball. Mexican.

LUIS APARICIO, SS, 1956–1974: Speed on the bases and great defensive skills. Ven-ezuelan.

TONY PEREZ, 3B, 1964–   : The R.B.I. ma-chine, 90 or more each of the past nine seasons. Cuban.

TONY OLIVA, L.F., 1962–   : Perhaps the best natural hitter of recent years. Won three A.L. batting titles. Cuban.

CESAR CEDEÑO, C.F., 1970–   : The only player ever to hit 20 homers and steal 50 bases in three different seasons. Potential unlimited. Dominican.

ROBERTO CLEMENTE, R.F., 1955–72: The perfect ballplayer. Hall of Fame, 1973. Puerto Rican.

The Poles

The distinguishing characteristic of the Polish team is brawn. The average weight of their *infielders,* for example, is two hundred pounds!

* From *Esquire* (July 1976). Reprinted by per-mission of *Esquire* magazine. Copyright © 1976 by Esquire, Inc.

The Polish lineup is a bit short on speed, but it has plenty of power and is strong defensively. The team's backbone is its outfield, good enough to keep Greg Luzinski, the best of the new generation of power hitters, off the squad.

STAN COVELESKI, R.H.P., 1912–28; Coveleski was an overpowering pitcher who won 216 games during his 17-year career. Hall of Fame, 1969.

HARRY COVELESKI, L.H.P., 1907–18: Stan's brother. Was a fine pitcher in his own right, stringing together three successive 20-win seasons (1914–16). Career E.R.A. of 2.39.

RON PERRANOSKI, R.P., 1961–73: Mr. Clutch for the Dodgers in the early Sixties. In '63, went 16–3, 21 saves. E.R.A. of 1.67.

CARL SAWATSKI, C., 1948–63: Good defensive catcher and a fair hitter, makes the team by default. Name a better Polish catcher.

TED KLUSZEWSKI, 1B, 1947–61: Owner of the biggest biceps in baseball history, plus 279 career homers and a .298 lifetime average.

BILL MAZEROSKI, 2B, 1956–72: For seventeen years a steady hitter and the anchor of the Pirate defense. Made more double plays than any other second baseman in history.

TONY KUBEK, SS, 1957–65: Did the job, day after day, season after season, for last eight years of Yankee dynasty.

WHITEY KUROWSKI, 3B, 1941–49: A lifetime .286. Edges out Ray Jablonski and Hank Majeski for hot-corner spot.

CARL YASTRZEMSKI, L.F., 1961– : Ask any Bosox fan.

AL SIMMONS, C.F., 1924–44: Born Aloysius Harry Szymanski. One of the greatest hitters in history; leader of the Athletics team that won three consecutive A.L. pennants (1929–31). Hall of Fame, 1953.

STAN MUSIAL, R.F., 1941–63: The Man. Ranks third all-time in hits, second in extra-base hits and total bases. Hall of Fame, 1969.

The Jews

There haven't been many Jewish ballplayers, let alone Jewish ballplayers of quality, and this creates problems: anyone who is left off the team is likely to feel slighted. A couple of years ago, when a New York sportswriter picked his Jewish all-stars, he was inundated by letters from readers demanding the inclusion of all manner of bums.

Of course, there are a couple of superstars among the Jewish all-stars, and most of the rest of the players on the team are highly competent. The problem, were this a real baseball team, would be one of depth. God forbid someone should get hurt!

ED REULBACH, R.H.P., 1905–17: Led N.L. starters in winning percentage and four times posted E.R.A.'s of under 2.00.

SANDY KOUFAX, L.H.P., 1956–66: Such a boy! The dominant pitcher of his time — and handsome! Wouldn't pitch on Rosh Hashanah.

LARRY SHERRY, R.P., 1958–68: Hero of the '59 World Series, in which he won two games and saved two others for Dodgers.

JOHNNY KLING, C., 1900–13: Strong defensive backstop and a .271 lifetime hitter. First catcher to move in close to the batter and the first to throw from a crouch.

HANK GREENBERG, 1B, 1930–47: Original Hammerin' Hank. Devastating hitter, led the A.L. in H.R.'s and R.B.I.'s four times each. Hit 58 homers in '38. Hall of Fame, 1956.

ROD CAREW, 2B, 1967– : A.L. batting champion 1972–1975: converted after marrying a Jewish woman.

BUDDY MYER, SS, 1925–41: Only half Jewish, but given lifetime .303 average, who's counting?

AL ROSEN, 3B, 1947–56: One of the great sluggers of the early fifties. Mainstay of the strong Indian teams. Twice led the league in H.R.'s and R.B.I.'s.

SID GORDON, L.F., 1941–55: Not flashy, but a solid everyday ballplayer who consistently hit close to .300 and between 20 and 30 H.R.'s.

BENNY KAUFF, C.F., 1912–20: Hit .273 in rookie year for the Yanks, then jumped to new Federal League. Led the Feds in both batting and stolen bases, prompting comparisons with Ty Cobb. Later joined the N.L. Giants; ended career with lifetime mark of .311.

GEORGE STONE, R.F., 1903–1910: Using one of the most unorthodox batting stances ever, compiled lifetime average of .301. In '06, led A.L. with .358 average.

BONUS FACTS: Johnny Klippstein, the pitcher, is not Jewish. Mel Allen, the broadcaster, is.

The Blacks

If you came up with a general all-star team for the last quarter century, it would look very much like the black all-star team named here. The team includes the number one, three and four all-time home-run leaders, the all-time leader in runs batted in and the most successful base stealer in the history of the game. It is fair to say that a Black "B" team would be as strong as any other team on these pages.

BOB GIBSON, R.H.P., 1959–75: Bullet Bob. Second only to Walter Johnson in career strikeouts. A sure thing to be elected to Hall of Fame in 1980, the year he's eligible.

VIDA BLUE, L.H.P., 1969–   : With 92 victories after only four complete seasons, has equipment to become biggest winner of current pitching generation.

SATCHEL PAIGE, R.P., 1948–53: Our one concession to sentiment. Did not reach the majors until age 42.

ROY CAMPANELLA, C, 1948–57: Campy. Solid backbone of the Dodger's *Boys of Summer* team. Hall of Fame, 1969.

FRANK ROBINSON, 1B, 1956–   : Baseball's first black manager ranks fourth in career home runs. Was M.V.P. in both leagues.

JOE MORGAN, 2B, 1963–   : Excellent speed, good power, enormous defensive ability. One fierce ballplayer.

ERNIE BANKS, SS, 1953–71: Mr. Cub. The most powerful hitter ever to play shortstop. Hall of Fame, 1976.

JACKIE ROBINSON, 3B, 1947–56: Are words necessary? Hall of Fame, 1962.

LOU BROCK, L.F., 1961–   : Greatest base runner ever, stole a record 118 bases in '74.

WILLIE MAYS, C.F., 1951–73: Say Hey. Hall of Fame, 1978.

HANK AARON, R.F., 1954–   : Career totals: first all-time in home runs. First in R.B.I.'s. Hall of Fame, 1981.

Special Treat:
The Italian All-Stars

Did you ever notice how many Italian catchers there are? It seems that every other Italian ballplayer is short and fat and runs funny. There was Pignatano and Garagiola and Lombardi and Romano and Canizzaro. And, the best of them all, Yogi Berra.

A lot of Italian greats were Yankees, and their strength was up the middle – catcher, second base, shortstop and center field. All of them were "money" ballplayers; it is a measure of their skills that, during the thirty-six consecutive years that one or another of them played for the Yankees, their team won twenty-five pennants.

EDDIE CICOTTE, R.H.P., 1905–20: Banned for life after taking part in the fixed Series of '19, he's seldom recognized as the great athlete he was. In 16-year career won 210 games, posted a 2.37 E.R.A.

JOHNNY ANTONELLI, L.H.P., 1948–61: Reliable starter for more than a decade. In best season – the Giant championship year of '54 – won 21 games and lost but 7.

DAVE GIUSTI, R.P., 1962–   : Since move to the bullpen in '70, has saved an average of 20 games a season for the Pirates. Especially tough in the clutch.

YOGI BERRA, C, 1946–63: You don't have to be pretty to swing a bat. Hall of Fame, 1972.

DOLF CAMILLI, 1B, 1933–45: Could be counted on to produce 25 H.R.'s and 100 R.B.I.'s a season and play solid defense.

TONY LAZZERI, 2B, 1926–39: Played on such great Yankee teams that his contributions are sometimes overlooked. A brilliant performer. Once hit .300 five of six years; drove in more than 100 runs 7 times.

PHIL RIZZUTO, SS, 1941–56: Scooter. The consummate defensive shortstop. Did all the little things right: executed the hit and run, took the extra base, advanced the lead runner, made things happen.

JOE TORRE, 3B, 1960–   : One-time catcher, still knocks down grounders with his body. Fabulous hitting makes up for it.

DOM DIMAGGIO, L.F., 1940–53: The Little Professor. Lead-off hitter par excellence, twice led the A.L. in runs scored. In eleven years, never hit below .283 and was superb in the field.

JOE DIMAGGIO, C.F., 1936–51: Poetry. Hall of Fame, 1955.

CARL FURILLO, R.F., 1946–60: Skoonj. A lifetime .299 – with power. Had a gun for a right arm.

ETHNIC SPORTS HALLS OF FAME

There is an Italian American Sports Hall of Fame located in Bensenville, Illinois and a Polish Sports Hall of Fame at Orchard Lake, Michigan. In 1979, television producer Joseph Siegman started the Jewish Sports Hall of Fame, and despite the fact that the Hall will be located in the Wingate Institute outside of Tel Aviv, Israel, many Jewish-American sportsmen are included. Siegman started this venture because "it strikes people's funnybones when you think of Jewish athletes. Some people even laugh almost uncontrollably at the very subject."

Who's in the Jewish Sports Hall of Fame? Swimmer Mark Spitz; baseball greats Hank Greenberg and Sandy Koufax; boxing champ Barney Ross; horse trainer Hirsh Jacobs; and Abe Saperstein, the founder of the Harlem Globetrotters, to name a few.

I'LL BET ON THAT!

A Look at Legal and Illegal Gambling in America

Unlike our Puritanical forefathers, who frowned upon all games of chance, whether or not a wager was involved, modern Americans seem willing to bet on almost anything — tennis matches, horse races, dog races, a roll of the dice, or a spin of the roulette wheel.

According to a recent survey conducted by the National Gambling Commission, 80% of all Americans regard gambling as an acceptable activity, so it shouldn't be surprising that legalized gambling has been on the rise in the United States for the last decade. Numbers games and lotteries are legal in 14 states; parimutuel betting on horses is legal in 21 states; 13 states have dog races; and four states have jai alai games where patrons can bet on the frantic activity on the *fronton*. Casino games such as roulette, craps and slot machines are legal in two states, and hotel owners in Miami and the Catskills are bucking to make Florida or New York the third in hopes of revitalizing lagging resort business.

Based on recent success figures in Atlantic City, legalized gambling promises to become one of our fastest-growing "industries." In 1977 Americans spent almost $15 billion pursuing that elusive lady — Luck. "We fled her down the nights and down the days, we fled her down the labyrinthian ways" of the legal gambling casinos, race

tracks and off-track betting parlors of the United States.

We even sought her in the after-hours joints and dropped an estimated $75–$100 billion into the coffers of illegal gambling czars by playing back-room crap games and roulette wheels, or betting on the numbers and the ponies with our favorite bookies.

For years the government has been trying to get a piece of that $100 billion action, and in the 1960s legal lotteries and numbers games were organized by some states in an effort to capture some of "the mob's" business.

"There should be a legal outlet for those who want to play the numbers game," was the sentiment expressed by New Jersey Governor Brendan Byrne in 1973 when he authorized the State's "Pick-It" Lottery game. A blatant attempt to capitalize on the citizenry's love affair with the "numbers" game, New Jersey officials took a tip from "the boys" and patterned their new lottery game after the illegal racket which allows bettors to pick their own three-digit number for a daily jackpot drawing.

The state was also hoping to fatten its tax coffers and cut down on illegal gambling revenues, but despite the fact that legal numbers games and lotteries took in almost $1.6 billion nationwide in 1977, it seems unlikely that state officials will ever be able to put illegal operators out of business – the competition is just too strong. Illegal operators give credit; allow bets as small as 25¢; provide "neighbor hoods" to collect your wager; and, best of all, if you do strike it rich, the IRS won't come knocking on your door for a share of the profits.

Who Runs the Numbers? At one time, the numbers racket was considered a cohesive network run by "organized crime." According to a recent study of gambling in New York City, Jonathan B. Rubenstein and Peter Reuter, of the Policy Sciences Center, claim a drastic change in bookmaking has occurred over the past decade or so. The big-time operators of the past – Al Adams, who ran 1,000 policy shops in the 1880s while Tammany Hall looked the other way, and Madam St. Clair, who once reigned in Harlem – are legends not likely to be outdone in the future. Bookmaking is now a relatively small bananas operation carried on by independent "policy makers."

According to the report, preliminary data supports the theory that numbers was "an Italian-run racket until quite recently," but now Blacks, Cubans and Puerto Ricans are rising in the ranks. Where have all the Italians gone? Over to the more lucrative fields of sports betting! They've left the "poor man's lottery" to the less affluent minorities and are making "book" on the games the middle class loves to watch – baseball, basketball and tennis matches.

Lest you believe that all organized crime members are Italians, Blacks or Hispanics, remember that gamblers come in every size, shape, color and ethnic background. When you're engaging in illegal activities it's always easier to trust "one of your own kind," so it makes good business sense for bookies to "take care of their own": Black bookies in Black neighborhoods, Italian bookies in "Little Italy," Irish bookies in Kerry Patch, and Syrian bookmakers in Arab neighborhoods.

According to a 1975 study conducted by the Survey Research Center of the University of Michigan, 68% of all American men and 55% of the women, age 18 and over, consider themselves to be "gamblers." Broken down according to race, 62 percent of the white population and 52 percent of the non-white population questioned considered themselves "men and women of chance."

"Who would have believed when I was shooting craps on the sidewalks of Newark that someday I would control gaming."

JOSEPH P. LORDI (Italian-American)
New Jersey Chairman of Casino Control Commission

The Sport of Kings While numbers are the "poor man's lottery," horse racing is the "sport of kings." But as racetrack promoters are finding out, horse racing is also the sport of the middle-aged. The largest proportion of grandstanders is in the 50-to-60-year-old age group, with the 40-to-50-year-olds running a close second.

In order to attract younger people to replace those fans who literally die off, the tracks have been promoting rock and roll concerts; reduced or free admissions for those patrons under 25; and Cap Day and Jacket Day promotions to lure young marrieds and singles to the track.

The shift away from horses has also cut into the need for illegal wire services. At one time, back-room bookie operations were a multi-million-dollar business, and in the heyday of horse betting, Moses Annenberg (1878–1942) earned the title "Father of the Bookie Wire Service."

According to his obituary, "Moses L. Annenberg, capitalized, as much as any man, on two American traits: the desire for daily newspapers and the willingness to make a bet."

Born in Insterberg, East Prussia, Moses emigrated to America in 1885 with his parents and was raised in a slum on the south side of Chicago. Moe's first job was as a Western Union messenger – in the days

Thousands of neighborhoods across the United States have a local "bookmaker." No, he's not a white-haired, wizened old man who restores ancient copies of first edition books —he's a middleman for "organized crime" who places daily bets on local horse races and numbers games. Why do people bet? In the words of a sixty-one-year-old Italian-American grandmother from Brooklyn, "It's fun!"

"I've been playing the numbers for twenty years—25 cents on weekdays and 50 cents on Saturday and Sunday. I never won much until last year; then I won five or six times, and this year I've already won twice. I'll never come out ahead, because you'll never win the horses and you'll never beat the numbers. But I don't smoke, and I don't drink, and I get a thrill when I open the paper and find out my number won. It's a lot of fun."

---

when they still delivered each and every telegram. An enterprising young man, he managed to succeed in whatever he tried, and eventually worked his way up to a $50,000-a-year position as circulation manager with the Hearst Corporation in the 1920s. He left the Hearst fold in 1926, four years after he purchased the *Daily Racing Form* newspaper, and decided to devote all of his energies to the horse-racing field.

Through deals with racetracks across the nation, Annenberg set up a national leased wire service which furnished information on betting odds and payoff prices to poolroom operators. He became the fifth largest customer of AT&T, with annual telephone bills topped only by the three nationwide news services and RCA. Over the phone lines of America, race results were sent from 29 tracks to 233 cities in 39 states of the union.

There was nothing illegal about his wired radio organization, Teleflash, which provided "sporting news and bulletins for restaurants, cafes, and . . . private offices, homes, clubs." But records of the New York Police Department showed dozens of seizures of Teleflash equipment taken during gambling raids.

Weekly rentals paid by bookmakers in poolrooms ran between $300 and $800, with the average fee of $500 paid by 2,000 outlets across the nation. Annenberg's estimated annual income was in excess of $50,000,000 (according to F. B. Warren in *The Nation*, August 8, 1938), but after he was indicted for income tax evasion (to the tune of $9,500,000 worth of back taxes plus interest) in 1939, his Nation Wide News Service was dissolved.

More Ethnics Who Contributed to the Sport of Horse Racing:

Parimutuel Pierre Oller, a perfume sho owner in Paris, France, developed the first parimutuel calculation system in 1865. This system of betting on races allows winners to divide the total amount bet at the track, minus management expenses, in proportion to the amounts they have wagered. (*Pari mutuel* means mutual stake in French.)

By a Nose Thanks to Gustavus Town Kirby (1874–1956), the world can tell whether or not a horse is really a winner at the wire. A descendant of Michael Kirby, an English settler of Talbot County, Maryland, about 1700, Gustavus Kirby invented the first photo-finish camera ever used in horse-racing events.

August Belmont (1816–1890) was born in the Rhenish Palatinate, and emigrated to America in 1837 at the age of 21. Apprenticed at the Rothschild's bank in Frankfurt from the age of 13, Belmont rose to become one of America's top private bankers in three short years after his arrival.

He fell away from the Jewish faith, married a Christian woman (Caroline Slidell Perry, the Commodore's daughter), and converted to the Episcopalian Church. He even raised pigs on his farm near Babylon, Long Island, and was known to feed them Jerusalem artichokes to improve the flavor of the bacon.

In 1866, Belmont and Leonard Jerome organized the American Jockey Club and established a racetrack in New York— Jerome Park.

Belmont Park, the Long Island racetrack, was named in his honor by the Westchester Racing Association, but the Belmont Stakes, one leg of the "Triple Crown," was instituted by his son, August Belmont (1853–1924), chairman of the Jockey Club and President of the Westchester Racing Association.

Beyond the Ponies

What else do Americans bet on other than the ponies? Well, there are dog races, cockfights, card games, sporting events and casino games. The slot machines, roulette wheels, crap games and keno parlors of America all owe their existence to the ethnics who brought their favorite games of chance to America and gave us new ways to vent our "gambling fever."

One-Armed Bandit The slot machine, or "one-armed bandit," as it is known to thousands of losers, was invented in 1895 by Charles Fey, a Bavarian immigrant. Having studied to become a mechanic in his native land, Fey used his mechanical know-how to invent the Liberty Bell slot machine shortly after he arrived in San Francisco. The Liberty Bell paid nickels to fortunate winners, but jackpots were rare and most of those nickels were kept by the house. In return for the space used to house the machine, Fey split the profits 50–50 with the store and restaurant owners.

Fey was moderately successful throughout the San Francisco Bay area, but it was Herbert S. Mills of Chicago who popularized slot machines nationwide. His "fruit" machine, which he called the "'kalamazoo," was the prototype of the modern one-armed bandits that display pictures of cherries, lemons and oranges.

Roulette Supposedly, the roulette wheel was invented by Blaise Pascal (1623–1662), the French mathematician, as a "spin-off" of his studies and experiments with perpetual motion. French roulette first appeared in England in 1820, and became popular in the United States thanks to French immigrants to New Orleans.

Another game that became popular in New Orleans was Craps, a descendant of the old English game of Hazards. In 1800, an unknown Black American from New Orleans changed the game a bit and simplified the rules, creating what we know as craps. Despite its illegality (except, of course, in the gambling casinos of Nevada and New Jersey), craps has been immortalized in song ("Stagger Lee") and expressions ("seven come eleven" and "snake eyes") familiar to gambling and non-gambling Americans alike.

A FRIENDLY GAME OF CARDS? THAT SUITS ME FINE:

Origin of the Four Suits We have to thank the French for the spades, clubs, diamonds and hearts found on our playing cards. The four suits originated in France during the 1500s and were designed to represent the four main classes of French society at the time. Hearts (*coeurs*) stood for the bishops and the clergy; spades (*pique*) for the military; clubs (*trefle*) for the peasants and farmers; and diamonds (*carreau*, meaning "square") for the rest of the populace, who were middle class.

According to Hoyle Edmund Hoyle (1679–1769), the ultimate arbiter of card game disputes, has been the last word in cards for over 230 years. An English whist teacher, he published *Hoyle's Games* in 1746, including rules and helpful hints for five different games, including whist and backgammon. It was the *only* book he ever published, but it became so popular that other authors began to publish books in his name. Since then, "According to Hoyle" has become synonymous with the proper way of doing things.

Poker Poker probably derives from the ancient Persian game *As-nas,* a favorite

Ever since Irish-American Wild Bill Hickok was shot to death in a Deadwood saloon, aces and eights (his last hand) has been known as the "Dead Man's Hand."

with New Orleans sailors in the nineteenth century. The name, first given to the game by Mississippi River boat gamblers, is probably a corruption of either the tenth century French game *pogue* or the German card game *Pochspiel*.

Whist Developed some four hundred years ago in England, whist was the inspiration for bridge (invented in 1896), and for contract bridge, invented in 1925 by Harold S. Vanderbilt.

Bridge The man who made bridge popular throughout the United States was Ely Culbertson, a Rumanian bridge player who challenged the British to a match and won honors for his American team in 1931. After that challenge match was played, bridge became the hottest fad in the United States, and it remains a popular game to this day.

Canasta This card game originated in Uruguay in the early 1940s and spread like a revolution throughout the rest of Latin America. It crossed the border about 1948, and became another "fad" card game in America. (Oswald Jacoby sold 330,000 copies of How To Win at Canasta in 1949.) In keeping with its Latin origins, some of the variations of canasta are called: samba, Bolivia, Chilean, Cuban, Brazilian, Uruguay, and Mexicana. (Canasta means *basket* in Spanish.)

Rummy Another game with a Spanish accent, rummy is derived from the Spanish game *¿Con quien?* (with whom?)

Tarot Cards Used to tell the future by fortune tellers, these cards were first adapted by fourteenth-century Italians from a standard deck, but with 22 additional cards bearing symbols of virtue, vice, death and good fortune.

Cassino A card game similar to "steal the old man's pack," cassino is of Italian origin and was probably first played in Cassino, Italy.

4 ETHNIC MEN OF CHANCE

♦ JIMMY THE GREEK   His real name was Demetrios Georgios Synodinos, but school chums in Steubenville, Ohio, dubbed him Jimmy the Greek. He thought up the name of Snyder when he entered business for himself, simply because it was easier to spell than Synodinos.

Married to a German-American, Snyder is nationally known as the "Las Vegas odds maker." His football predictions are widely syndicated.

Why do people gamble? Jimmy thinks it's "the satisfaction of winning, the disappointment of losing. Some people gamble to punish themselves, too. They feel guilty about something. It's an escape for them."

"I can make odds on anything, but it took 40 years for me to get this experience and to build up a reputation. And you can't do it now like it was then. What can I say about gambling. I've won a lot . . . and I've lost a lot."

♦ JOHN   SCARNE   This   Italian-American earned his fame as the foremost gambling authority in the world back during World War II when he served as a "gaming adviser" to the U.S. Armed Forces, teaching the troops how to avoid being taken by crooked gamblers. Over the years Scarne has served as consultant to the FBI, to the Puerto Rican government and to various hotel chains, overseeing their casino operations.

♦ NICK THE GREEK   Nicholas Andrea Dandolos (1883–1966) was born on the isle of Crete, but it was at Las Vegas gaming tables that he became a legend. His career winnings were estimated at $500,000,000, but his losses were high, too (as much as $40,000 on a single roll of dice).

While escorting Einstein on a tour of Las Vegas casinos, Jimmy once introduced him as "Little Al from Princeton—he controls a lot of the action around Jersey."

♦ MEYER LANSKY   One of the most famous men in the gambling hall of fame is Meyer Lansky (1902–   ), one of only two Jews ever refused a home in Israel. The seventy-eight-year-old Russian-born racketeer, who has been called the "Horatio Alger" of the underworld, once directed Murder, Inc.; held the Mafia franchise for Havana; and brought organized gambling to the Bahamas.

Born Maier Suchowljansky in Grodno, Poland, Meyer emigrated to the United States at the age of nine. Because he was a non-Italian, Lansky was ineligible for membership in La Cosa Nostra of the 1930s, but his financial genius made him an ex-officio member.

Today, Meyer lives in Miami Beach and claims, "There is no such thing as organized crime."

8 FOOD AND DRINK

ETHNIC AMERICAN FOOD

The food America loves to eat has been seasoned in the melting pot by representatives from every immigrant group that set foot upon our shores. Some ethnic groups contributed to American cuisine by introducing national foods and traditional recipes, while other immigrants and their descendants made their mark on the American waistline by manufacturing snack food or opening nationally known restaurants and fast-food chains.

Here's a sampling of some ethnic foods that are "as American as apple pie," which, incidentally, is an English contribution to the American way of eating.

American Indian

POTATO CHIPS The potato chip was invented in 1853 by an American Indian chief, George Crum. Employed as a chef at a posh resort hotel in Saratoga Springs, New York, Crum one day ran into a pompous guest who complained about the French fried potatoes: they apparently weren't thin enough for this gourmet tastes and he insisted that the chef slice a new batch for him.

George complied with the guest's wishes, but the second batch was also returned for being too thick. Finally, in an exasperated attempt to stop the patron's nit-picking, George sent out paper-thin slices fried to a crisp, and much to his surprise the guest liked them. From that night on "Saratoga Chips" became a popular menu item at Moon's Lake House, and every year their popularity continued to grow.

Today, potato chips are America's number one snack food: over 816 million pounds are consumed in the United States annually. That's over 4 pounds per capita, which is equivalent to 17 pounds of fresh potatoes. A grand total of 3,468,000,000 pounds of spuds (or 11% of the total U.S. potato crop) are fried, bagged and munched as snacks each year.

Bohemian

BIG MACS The man who made "two all-beef patties, special sauce, lettuce, cheese, pickles, onions on a sesame seed bun" a lunchtime habit proudly describes himself as a Bohunk, an ethnic slur for Americans of Bohemian-Hungarian descent. Raymond Albert Kroc (b. 1902) is proud of his heritage and of his grandparents who emigrated from Austria-Hungary to find a better way of life for their family.

Born in a lower-middle-class neighborhood on the West Side of Chicago, Ray learned the religion of hard work at an early age. A successful salesman of paper cups in the 1920s, he was constantly in and out of restaurant kitchens, where he was appalled by the problems associated with food service. Inefficiency, waste, lack of portion control, product variability — all of these factors spelled decreased profits for food managers, and led Ray to believe that if he ever opened a restaurant it would be managed much more efficiently to eliminate these common errors.

Though he left the paper cup trade to hawk milk shake machines in the 1930s, his dream of a waste-free, consistently good food product never left his mind. In 1954 he received an intriguing order for 8 multi-mix-ers, capable of mixing 48 shakes at one time. Why, he wondered, would a small store in San Bernardino, California, need to whip up 48 milk shakes at one time? He decided to pay a visit to the restaurant, and that's where he met the McDonald brothers, Maurice and Richard.

When Kroc witnessed their operation, he realized that it was the business of his dreams. The brothers' restaurant was a fast operation with rapid turnover. They offered only one food item on their menu, a hamburger with special sauce; there were no plates, no waste, no choices to boggle the mind—and the food was cheap and good. The wheels began to turn in Kroc's head as he put cars, highways, rapid postwar expansion and brand-name recognition together. He bought rights to the brothers' operation, expanded on their formula for success and opened the first McDonald's fast-food restaurant in Des Plaines, Illinois.

He decided there would be no telephone booths, newsstands, posters, jukeboxes, cigarette machines, pinball machines or vending machines of any kind to delay patrons who stopped there to eat. He also wanted to discourage teenagers from using the place as a "hangout," and stressed cleanliness. Clean floors, windows, restrooms—even the helpers had to be squeaky clean.

The formula worked and Kroc began to expand across the nation. The company went public in 1965, and if you had had the foresight to invest $2,250 in McDonald's stock, you would have earned $104.296 for your trouble by 1975.

Hamburgers are the most popular entree served in American restaurants, and each year McDonald's sells some $2,730,000,000 worth of burgers, fries and shakes.

Black

MORE PARKS SAUSAGES, MOM! In recent years, radio listeners have heard the word "please" added to the little boy's request for more of those delicious Parks sausages, no doubt in response to some parents' group who complained that the commercial in its original form encouraged rude behavior in children.

The man behind the sausages is Henry G. Parks, Jr. (b. 1916). As an honor student at Ohio State University, he was advised by a university placement officer to emigrate to South America, change his name, learn to speak Spanish and then return to the United States. This way he could "pass" as Latin American and have unlimited job opportunities, which did not exist in America for Blacks with marketing degrees in 1939.

Parks resisted the suggestion and was eventually hired by the Pabst Brewing Company as a salesman after World War II. He quickly advanced to national sales representative, responsible for market development among Blacks.

In 1951, after several small business attempts, Parks began bringing home the bacon by making sausages. He ground, mixed and stuffed casings in the morning, and sold his sausage to Baltimore stores in the afternoon. After he had captured the inner-city market of Baltimore, he approached food store chains and began marketing his product for all ethnic groups. "With more than 75% of his company's products being consumed by whites, Henry Parks, Jr., has achieved his American dream . . . He became a success as a businessman who happens to be Black, not as a Black businessman." (*Journal of Marketing, 36*:70–1, July, 1972.)

CHOCOLATE CHIP COOKIES Although Wally Amos didn't invent the chocolate chip cookie, he certainly did invent a new way of promoting them and turning the lowly cookie into a high-priced luxury item. Before Wally made the L.A. scene with his Famous Amos cookies laden with pecans, most of the chocolate chip cookies consumed in the United States were the 89-cents-a-pound variety found at the local supermarket. Bakeries had slightly better versions, but in 1975, if you wanted a really good cookie rich in pecans, chocolate chips and high-quality ingredients, you had to bake them yourself.

Armed with his Aunt Della's recipe and all the knowledge he had culled as a Hollywood press agent and manager, Wally (1937–   ) began to "promote" himself and his wares. He opened a cookie stand on Sunset Boulevard and even printed T-shirts, bumper stickers and posters with his logo.

Los Angelenos gobbled the cookies up and came back for more, despite their $3–$4-a-pound price. Soon "the cookie" had

Famous Amos cookies are "chic" but not cheap.

invaded the East Coast and even had a special grand opening at Bloomingdale's delicacy department. Eventually Wally was baking 6 tons a year, and rolling "in the chips" with his cookies grossing $1 million a year.

Chinese

BING CHERRIES Americans consume over 280 million pounds of cherries each year. One of the sweetest varieties grown in America is the Bing, sought after by cherry lovers everywhere for its young, firm, juicy flesh and deep red color that ranges from mahogany to near-black. Henderson Luelling brought a wagonload of red-skinned beauties clear across the continent to Oregon in 1847 and planted the first sweet cherries west of the Rockies. It was from this stock that a Chinese immigrant, known to history only as Bing, developed the cherry that immortalized his name. Oddly enough, Bing was right in tune with his ethnic heritage when he developed the Bing cherry in 1875, since cherries were first cultivated in China some 4,000 years before they became popular in America.

Danish

The Danes gave us two mighty good desserts, but for some reason they both have confusing names. What we call Danish pastry (airy pockets of dough filled with cheese and fruit) are actually called *Wienerbrød* (Vienna bread) in Denmark.

The second Danish dessert contribution with an unusual name is the "Eskimo Pie." It wasn't invented in Alaska, it wasn't invented by an Eskimo, and it isn't really a pie. These foil-wrapped rectangles of ice cream coated with chocolate were invented by a Danish-born schoolteacher from Iowa, Christian Nelson.

Nelson supplemented his teaching income by managing a candy store after school in Onawa, Iowa. One day a young customer sauntered up to the counter, but couldn't decide how to spend his nickel. "Should I buy a candy bar?" he asked, "Or would I rather have an ice cream sandwich?" Finally, the child realized he wanted them both, but his resources were limited and a decision had to be reached. History didn't record his choice, but the little boy gave Nelson the inspiration to create the dessert that would soon net him upward of $30,000 a week in royalties.

Nelson thought about the little boy's plight and decided that there must be thousands of kids in similar dire circumstances, so he began experimenting with ways to cover ice cream with chocolate.

Unless you've ever tried to coat ice cream with chocolate, you won't believe how difficult it is to do. Nelson began to get discouraged—the chocolate simply would not stick to the ice cream. Finally, a candy salesman suggested the "stickability" of the chocolate might be improved by the addition of cocoa butter, and soon Nelson was on the proverbial road to success.

He had trouble selling his idea at first, but when he teamed up with an ice cream company executive, Russell Stover, things began to click. Stover changed the name from "I Scream" to Eskimo Pie, which he thought had a better commerical sound.

Later, Stover dissolved the partnership and went on to found his own candy company, which is still in existence today. Eskimo Pies are probably the only ice cream bars immortalized in song ("O! My Eskimo Pie" by Dale Wimbrow).

Dutch

The Dutch gave us more fattening breakfast goodies than any other ethnic group: waffles dripping with butter, crullers laden with so much grease they feel cold when you bite into them, hot cocoa and buckwheat cakes for cold winter mornings. They also gave us cookies, chocolate bars, coleslaw, a slew of great cheeses, and that great American dunker — the doughnut.

The Dutch may have invented the fried doughnut, but it was good old Yankee ingenuity that put the hole in the center. The Dutch called them *Olykoek* (oily cake), but when the Pilgrims pirated their recipe and brought it to New England, they began shaping their *dough* into spheres the size of wal*nuts* and the new name, dough "nuts," emerged.

The man generally credited with inventing the doughnut hole is Hanson Gregory, a New England sea captain, who first poked holes in his mother's dough in 1847. As a young boy growing up in Camden, Maine, Hanson's major complaint with Mom's cooking was the soggy centers of her fried doughnuts. He decided that a hole there was thermodynamically necessary to allow hot oil to fry the tender cakes more evenly, and thereby started an American institution.

Today, a bronze plaque stands in the town of Rockport (formerly Camden) Maine, honoring Hanson Gregory and his invention — proof that, in America, you can even become famous for inventing nothing.

German

When it comes to the food that America loves to eat, the Germans are probably our greatest contributors. They gave us plenty of good, nourishing food that really sticks to your ribs — sauerbraten and potato dumplings, sausages and noodles, frankfurters with sauerkraut, liverwurst, pumpernickel bread, zwieback, pretzels and beer to wash it all down. In fact, most of the German words that entered the American language have to do with either eating or drinking.

Besides contributions from their homeland, German-Americans made their mark on American cuisine by making better pickles, producing faster weiners and inventing ice-cream-on-a-stick. Some German-Americans even invented ways to raise better cattle, but they really lost out when it came to the hamburger. They invented it, but let a Bohemian, McDonald's Ray Kroc,

make mincemeat out of them in the marketplace.

HAMBURGERS Russian sailors brought the recipe for Tartar steak to the seaport of Hamburg, where local German cooks improved the recipe by *cooking* the meat. No doubt, the hamburger was probably born when some squeamish soul found the sight of uncooked beef topped with a quivering raw egg unappetizing, and sent it back to the kitchen to be grilled.

The "hamburger steak" was brought to America by German immigrants about 1880 and first placed on a bun at the St. Louis Exposition in 1904. A harried food vendor ran out of plates and began serving ground beef on buns to the starving masses. Soon, everyone at the fair wanted their hamburgers served on rolls, and the fast-food business was on its way.

FRANKFURTERS The first frankfurter sausage was manufactured in Frankfurt, Germany, in 1852. When the Germans arrived in America they brought their love of sausages along with them, and made bratwurst, liverwurst, weisswurst, etc. popular in our country.

Two German immigrants are credited with inventing the frankfurter sandwich, which increased the popularity of the meal by making it portable. One claimant is Antoine Feuchtwanger, a Bavarian, who is said to have introduced the frankfurter sandwich to St. Louis in the 1880s. The other contender for the honor is Charles Feltman, a pushcart peddler at Coney Island who sold frankfurters in toasted rolls to hungry New Yorkers for 10 cents during the 1890s.

Today, Americans spend $600 million a year on nitrate-laden hot dogs (40 franks per person, per year) — enough to stretch from here to the moon and back).

BETTER CATTLE Although no German-American made it big selling "all-beef patties," there is a family who made their fortune selling the raw ingredients.

Descended from German immigrants, the Klebergs manage the largest ranch in the United States today — the King Ranch. Located in Kingsville, Texas, the Kleberg spread is larger than the state of Rhode Island and encompasses some 1.25 million acres of fenced-in land.

Despite the family's current wealth, there was a time when the King ranch was in deep financial straits. In 1918 the ranch was stocked with almost 50,000 purebred Herefords and Shorthorn cattle, but the Klebergs were losing money "hoof over fist."

Since Shorthorns and Herefords are noted for their high beef production, the ranch should have been making a profit, but the cattle were faltering because they couldn't acclimate to the hot Texas sun. They produced few calves, had to be fattened on expensive grain instead of grass and spent most of their time panting in the shade instead of eating their way up the scales to "USDA Prime" condition.

Bob Kleberg, Jr., a recent graduate of the University of Wisconsin, was convinced he could solve the ranch's financial problems by developing a new breed of cattle that produced good beef and was able to withstand the heat. Brahmans seem to thrive on the tough, fibrous grasses of southern Texas and are not bothered by the heat, insects and parasites that abound on the plains. Unfortunately, they are narrow-hipped and produce less beef per carcass than other cattle breeds, so Kleberg decided to cross them with British shorthorns to improve their beef characteristics.

But crossbreeding was only the first step. The process has to be continued over many generations to maintain the desired characteristics.

Finally, twenty years of experimentation paid off: Santa Gertrudis cattle were recognized by the U.S. Department of Agriculture as America's first cattle breed, created specifically for optimal beef production in warm climates.

57 VARIETIES "To do a common thing uncommonly well brings success." That was a favorite motto of Henry John Heinz (1844–1919), but even though Heinz tried uncommonly well to succeed, he had to live through the trauma of bankruptcy in 1875 before his company turned a $15,000 profit in 1879.

Born of German parents in Sharpsburg, Pennsylvania, Heinz knew his fortune lay in peddling food from the time he was 12 years old. His first business experience was selling excess produce from his family's garden, and he later earned a reputation as a horseradish salesman.

In the late 1800s canned and bottled food, frequently contaminated with chalk, sawdust or chemical fillers that often made consumers ill, had a deservedly bad reputation. Heinz made his name by packaging his horseradish in clear glass jars to prove that it was pure and unadulterated by leaves, wood fiber or cheap turnip fillers.

Heinz soon discovered that housewives were willing to pay for the convenience of bottled ketchup, pickles and vinegar, provided the product was wholesome and free from contaminants. Over the years Heinz bottled relish, pepper sauce, apple butter, mincemeat, mustard, chili sauce, pickled onions and baked beans. In all there were over 60 products by 1896, when the slogan "57 varieties" was adopted. It's not that H.J. didn't have a mind for statistics—he just liked the way "57" sounded. Over the years the number has climbed to more than 200 varieties, but the company still prefers the old number.

GOOD HUMOR Christian Nelson was the first to put chocolate on ice cream in 1919, but it was a German-American ice cream parlor operator, Harry Burt, from Youngstown, Ohio, who first put ice cream on a stick. His daughter suggested the stick; after he tried it out, Burt applied for a patent on the Good Humor Ice Cream Sucker in 1920. He then dressed a driver in white, put him in the driver's seat of a white truck, added the bells from the family bobsled and started an American institution.

If you took the wrappers from all the Good Humor bars manufactured last year and laid them end-to-end, they would circle the earth at the equator three and a half times. And (I just love statistics like this) if you took the sticks and laid them end-to-end, they could stretch from New York to Florida, round trip, seven times.

Greeks

CARVEL ICE CREAM Carvel was founded by the man with the "golden voice." Thomas Carvel (1906–   ), a Greek immigrant who played drums, danced and even tried his hand at semi-pro football before he made his fortune selling soft ice cream.

Athanassos Carvelas, as he was known in Greece, took his ice cream on the road in 1940 and successfully sold cones to hungry fairgoers and to army enlistees at Fort Bragg. Today, Carvel holds 13 patents, including one for a high-speed cream freezer essential to making his famous desserts.

Recently, he began voicing-over his own commercials with a voice he describes as "golden going on rusty," which is more honestly described as gravelly! Carvel never writes a script for his television commercials and claims, "I just go right on tape. I leave the flubs in deliberately. There's nothing like someone saying 'uh, uh, uh' — people relate to this. Announcers with perfect diction, perfect poise, perfect appearance — people cut them off." He says, "I'm not an actor, I don't want to be, but who has a better knowledge of my business than I do?"

Irish

Immigrants from Ireland and their descendants popularized corned beef and cabbage (Irish soul food), Irish stew, Irish soda bread and Irish coffee, and brought pizza to middle America. Pizza? Why not? If Jeno Paolucci, an Italian-American, could build his fortune on a pile of Chun King bean sprouts and eggrolls, it stands to reason that two Irish-American brothers could turn mozzarella cheese into gold.

PIZZA HUT   Although Frank Carney (1938–   ) had only tasted pizza once in his life, he and his older brother, Dan, opened a pizza parlor in 1958 and turned it into a multi-million-dollar international chain.

"We had more guts than brains," is Frank Carney's remark about their early days in Wichita, Kansas. At that time there was little pizza to be found between the Rockies and the Adirondacks. Despite the number of GI's who had returned from World War II raving about the food they discovered in Italy, most of the nation's pizzerias were located on the East Coast or the West Coast, where there were high concentrations of Italian-Americans.

Frank Carney was a nineteen-year-old electrical engineering student whose business experience was limited to working evenings and weekends at the family grocery store. The woman who rented the storefront to his parents wanted to evict a tavern operator from another building she owned and suggested that the Carney boys lease the place and open a pizza parlor,

something she had read about in the *Saturday Evening Post*.

The boys agreed, and asked their mother for a $600 loan on a life insurance policy so they could buy some secondhand equipment and lease the old tavern. Luckily they found a friend who knew how to make pizza and promised him a piece of the action for sharing his expertise with them.

They named their place Pizza Hut, because the name fit the existing sign, and the building did seem to resemble a shack. When the Carneys opened for business in June 1958, they had to give away free samples of Kansas's most exotic new food to generate customer interest, but by the time December rolled around the boys were grossing over $1,000 a week, enough to open their second restaurant.

Pizza Hut is the largest pizza chain in America, though the company hasn't been able to crack the "Mom and Pop" pizza parlors of the East Coast. But even without volume from the East, Pizza Hut's annual sales are over $300 million, including revenue from foreign franchises.

In response to local taste, pizza is served with squid in Japan, jalapeño peppers in the Southwest and pineapple in Australia.

Italian

When the Italian immigrants came to America they brought along their eating habits, tastes and regional recipes, as well as a demand for imported and domestic products such as pasta, tomatoes, wine, espresso coffee and other Italian delicacies. Some immigrants opened ethnic restaurants and stores to accommodate their fellow countrymen, and soon Americans of every ethnic persuasion began to frequent the local eateries. Within a short time people all over the United States were eating Italian bread, minestrone soup, lasagna and ravioli, and exotic vegetables such as broccoli, cauliflower, fennel, eggplants, peppers, zucchini and artichokes.

Today, many Italian dishes have crossed that invisible ethnic barrier to become "truly American" fare. No matter where you travel in the United States, some menu is bound to include spaghetti, pizza, macaroni or tomato sauce. But these aren't the only American foods with Italian roots — we also have to thank Italy for bologna sausage,

Anthony Zito's Italian Bakery at 259 Bleecker Street has been catering to hungry New Yorkers for more than 55 years. Founded by Anthony Zito (1885–1963), the bakery is still family-owned and currently is being managed by the third generation. (Courtesy: Museum of the City of New York)

cantaloupes, French fries, Napoleons, Planter's Peanuts and even Chun King Chow Mein.

BOLOGNA Although we've altered the pronunciation and fiddled with the recipe a bit, this spicy lunchbox favorite, which most Americans pronounce "boloney," actually originated during the Middle Ages in Bologna, Italy. Known as *Mortadella di Bologna*, it was originally made with large chunks of white fat distributed throughout the sausage.

CANTALOUPES The seeds for this variety of muskmelon were originally imported from Armenia, but *Cucumis melo cantalupensis* took its name from the Castle Cantalupo in Ancona, Italy, where it was first cultivated in Europe. (In American supermarkets, produce managers use the term muskmelon and cantaloupe synonymously. However, although all canta-

loupes are muskmelons, not all muskmelons are cantaloupes. Cantaloupes are small and round, with a ribbed rind. Other muskmelons are generally more oval shaped, are larger in size, and have netted surface markings.)

FRENCH FRIED POTATOES According to Giulian Bugialli (*The Fine Art of Italian Cookery*), French fries originated, not in France, but in Florence, Italy. The term "French" does not refer to the country of origin, but merely indicates that the potatoes have been cut into thin strips, in the "French" manner.

NAPOLEONS Another fattening food mistakenly attributed to the French is the Napoleon. This popular, rectangular-shaped pastry, which features crisp, flaky layers of custard-filled dough has nothing to do with the Emperor of France. The name is a corruption of the word "Napolitain" and refers to the Neopolitan practice of layering colors and textures in sweets and ice cream.

PASTA Italians make pasta with beans (*pasta e fagioli*), pasta with chick peas (*pasta e ceci*), linguine with clam sauce, and spaghetti with oil and garlic, breadcrums and anchovies, broccoli, cauliflower, and squid. In fact, Italians make pasta with almost everything—*except* meatballs. That dish was invented in Brooklyn, New York.

Much of the cuisine we regard as "Italian" is actually "Italian-American." And the recipes we know and love are not representative of all the regional cuisines of Italy. Rather, they represent the favorite foods of the immigrants from Southern Italy and Sicily who came to America in record numbers during the early 1900s.

The first spaghetti factory in the United States was built in New York in 1767, but it wasn't until the 1880's that spaghetti became common in America. Once considered an "ethnic" food, pasta is now so thoroughly American that we consume over 2.5 billion pounds per year—or an average 10.5 pounds per capita of spaghetti, macaroni and noodles.

In America the word "macaroni" is usually reserved for the thick, tubular pasta that comes in fancy shapes, while the word "spaghetti" is used to describe the long, thin strands of pasta. In Italy, this distinction does not exist, and macaroni is a generic term which includes *fusili, spaghetti, ver-*

micelli, tubettini and pasta of every size and shape.

(Incidentally, when Yankee Doodle "stuck a feather in his hat and called it macaroni" it had nothing to do with food. The term "macaroni" was used in England to describe a dandy or a foppish man who dressed in the latest fashion. During our Revolutionary War there was even a regiment of Maryland militia nicknamed the "Macaronies" because of the magnificently splendid uniforms they wore.)

"*Beloved of newsboys and juvenile messengers, the long-haired Italian who deals in penny ices is an interesting feature in summer street life. His elegant cart, with its green sides and white top and linen awning, is refreshing to look at even. And most pleasant is it to watch the faces of the panting juveniles as they let the cool Neapolitan ices slip down their parched throats.*" *From* Harper's New Monthly Magazine, *September 1858, London, p. 640. (Courtesy: New York Public Library)*

PEANUT KING OF AMERICA
No, that title doesn't belong to Jimmy Carter, our first peanut-farming president. The man who deserved the title "peanut king of America" was Amadeo Obici (1877–1947), the man behind "Mr. Peanut."

Amadeo Obici started his own business at the age of 19 with a used peanut roaster he had purchased for $4.50 and a sign that read, "Obici, the Peanut Specialist." For ten years Obici labored from dawn to dusk roasting and selling nickel bags of peanuts,

peanut candy and salted nuts, until he incorporated the Planters Peanut Company in 1906 and earned the nickname "peanut king of America."

"Friends have been one of my biggest assets," said Obici in 1930. "I have been asked many times how I got from where I was to where I am. I should answer, work and friends. I've worked from 16 to 18 hours a day until recent years, and I have never lacked friends."

One of the "friends" who helped the penniless immigrant from Oderzo, Italy, on the road to riches is Mr. Peanut himself, the company trademark. The original design was created by a Suffolk, Virginia, schoolchild who received $5 for a sketch of a long-legged, peanut-bodied character who was later clothed by a commercial artist in top hat, monocle, spats and gloves. Mr. Peanut has served the Planters company for over 60 years for an initial investment of only five bucks. That's pretty cheap for a company logo these days, when one considers that NBC had to spend $750,000 in 1976 for a red and blue "N."

Mexican

Mexican cookery brings to mind fiery images of hot chili peppers, tortillas, burritos, tamales, enchiladas and chile con carne – good, hot food that can be found in many fast-food chains and luncheonettes across the nation. There is one Mexican dish, however, that managed to cross cultural borders and surface on "continental" restaurant menus all over the United States – Caesar salad.

SALAD SOUTH OF THE BORDER: Caesar Salad was first concocted during the Prohibition era by Caesar Cardini, the proprietor of a small Tijuana hotel. The original salad contained only romaine lettuce, French bread croutons, lemon juice, vinegar, Romano cheese and a coddled egg. Anchovies were probably added to the recipe at a later date by some Californian who wisked the recipe across the border to his home state.

Although Mexico deserves credit for Caesar Salad, some sources claim the country doesn't deserve, and doesn't want credit for, chile con carne. Dale Brown, author of *American Cooking,* quotes a Mexican dictionary which describes chile con carne as "detestable food with the false Mexican title which is sold in the United States."

Historians claim chile con carne was invented about 1880 by Mexican residents of San Antonio, Texas. Suprisingly, the first person to sell canned chile con carne (definitely "detestable") was a German from New Braunfels, Texas, who started his canning company in 1908, six years after he invented chili powder—a spice unknown to true Mexican cooks.

Even tamales can't be labeled uniquely "Mexican," since they were served to Captain John Smith when he landed in Virginia in 1612 and had been served to Cortez by the Aztecs two hundred years earlier when he arrived in what is now Mexico City. Most of the food we "gringos" consider Mexican is actually Indian in origin rather than a combination of Spanish and Indian cuisine. Long before "Mexican" food ap-

peared at the border, John Smith and others were muching "corne roost in the eare green."

Polish

MRS. PAUL'S FISH   The man behind Mrs. Paul's apron strings is a proud Polish-American, Edward J. Piszek (1917–   ). Raised in a tough Philly neighborhood, he never earned more than a dollar an hour before the age of thirty. Despite this late start, Piszek managed to turn his life into a self-made success story as head of a $125-million frozen food processing business.

He started his business in 1946 during a strike at the G.E. plant in Philadelphia, where he was employed. The homemade deviled crabs he made at his "interim" job in a local tavern became the house specialty on meatless Fridays (this was long before a papal ban against the consumption of meat

Nathan Handwerker invested his life savings of $300 to open this fancy seaside stand in 1916. Over the past six decades, Nathan's has sold more than 500 million franks. Today, "the hot dogs that made Coney Island famous" are available at more than 60 Nathan's restaurants in the United States. (Courtesy: Nathan's Famous, Inc.)

by Catholics on that day was lifted). One week there were 100 deviled crabs left over, so Piszek decided to freeze them. When he served them again the following week, they tasted as good as ever, so he and a friend, John Paul, decided to invest $400 to start the frozen seafood business that bears Paul's name today.

Piszek bought out his partner long ago for $50,000, but decided to keep the name. Why didn't he change it to Mrs. Piszek's Kitchens? As he told his mother, "If you don't know the answer to that I can't explain it to you."

Although he declined to name his company after himself, Piszek is proud of his Polish heritage; in the early 1970s he spent $500,000 on an advertising campaign to promote Polish culture in this country.

NATHAN'S FAMOUS Charles Feltman, a German immigrant and one of the first frankfurter pushcart salesmen in New York City, began selling franks in buns for 10¢ each during the 1890s. Later on, he expanded his business to a stand at New York's most famous seaside resort—Coney Island.

A Polish immigrant, Nathan Handwerker, was working at Feltman's stand as an $11-a-week grillman when two entertainers, both unknown at the time, suggested that he open his own place and "sell a frankfurter at a price we can afford—a nickel." Thanks to the suggestion made by Eddie Cantor and Jimmy Durante, Nathan's became the largest and most famous hot dog stand in the world.

Nathan's, one of the few family-owned fast food chains left in America, still uses Ida Handwerker's original 1916 recipe for seasoning and spices. Each year the company sells 15 million frankfurters, more than half at their original Coney Island stand. It has been estimated that over the past 62 years, Nathan's has served hungry Americans more than 500 million franks. That's enough weiners to stretch across our nation from New York to California more than 17 times.

What's the secret of Nathan's frankfurter success? According to Max Rosey, there are several reasons why Nathan and his wife, Ida, succeeded in pleasing America's tastebuds: the meat is 100% beef, with no fillers added; natural sheep-gut casings are used instead of synthetics; and the franks are grilled, not boiled or zapped in a microwave oven.

South America

IRISH POTATOES White potatoes were originally introduced to European explorers in South America by the Inca Indians. The British deemed these white tubers unfit for human consumption and only cultivated them as feed for livestock. Gradually, however, the potato earned a place on European dining tables, and by the eighteenth century *Solanum tuberosum,* a nonpoisonous member of the poisonous nightshade family, had become a staple food in Ireland.

The Irish became so dependent on the lowly spud that when the potato blight struck Europe in 1845 and 1846, starvation spread throughout the Emerald Isle, starting the floodtide of Irish immigration to America.

It was a group of Irish immigrants who first introduced the white potato to fellow colonists at Londonderry, New Hampshire, in 1719. They impressed their neighbors by growing a huge crop of spuds, which they then proceeded to store and eat during the entire winter—quite a feat in the days before canning became a science. Soon other colonists were planting huge crops of "Irish" potatoes to store in their own root cellars and the white potato has been considered Irish ever since.

Americans enjoy potatoes so many ways that over 1.3 million acres of Irish potatoes were harvested in 1974, with a total cash crop value of $1,520,000,000.

Swedish

The Swedes brought their meatballs, rutabagas and the smorgasbord to America, but by far the most popular foods in America with Swedish roots are Howard Johnson's 28 flavors—and puffed wheat and puffed rice, the cereal shot from guns.

THE CEREAL SHOT FROM GUNS Every year the Quaker Oats Company receives hundreds of letters from consumers asking the same question: "Is your cereal *really* shot from guns?" The answer is "Yes," and if you are old enough to remember the 1904 World's Fair, you may have seen Spanish-American War cannons shooting puffed rice kernels into the air.

After rice was placed into breach-loading cannons with recoil mechanisms, the muzzles were capped with plugs. Then the cannons were wheeled into gas-fired ovens set at 550 degrees. Inside the ovens, high heat turned the tiny amount of moisture present inside each grain of rice into steam, which in turn built up tremendous pressure inside the closed cannons. After 40 minutes, the cannons were removed and wheeled out to a mesh enclosure 40 feet wide and two stories high. The "cook" in charged yelled "Fire," and when the cannon plugs were removed the rice exploded into the air, expanding to eight times normal size as a result of the tremendous internal pressure.

The man who made all this possible was a Swedish-American biochemist, Dr. Alexander Anderson, who patented his invention in 1902. He first experimented on rice kernels while doing post-graduate work at the University of Munich. There, colleagues routinely heated grains of rice in open-ended test tubes in order to make them expand; once bloated, the grains could easily be cut apart for analysis. The German scientists warned Anderson never to heat the rice in a closed test tube, but Dr. Anderson, who had an inquiring mind, determined to find out for himself what would happen.

Experimenting with cornstarch, Anderson heated it in a closed test tube at 500 degrees. When he cracked the tubes open, the cornstarch expanded to 10 times its normal size. This delighted Anderson, who hoped that his newly discovered "process" would make wheat and rice easier to digest.

Anderson's discovery coincided with the ready-to-eat cereal craze that started in the early 1900s. A leader in that field, the Quaker Oats Company, made a deal with Anderson for the rights to his process. In 1909, puffed rice and puffed wheat made their appearance on the grocery shelves of the nation. By 1912, the two cereals were hefty contributors to the $2 million annual profit that the Quaker Oats Company raked in that year, and today, more than 70 years later, puffed rice and puffed wheat are still American breakfast favorites.

Syrian and Middle Eastern

The cooking of the Middle Eastern nations has given America much of the "health" food that has become faddish in recent years: bulgur wheat, sesame seed paste (tahini), chick peas, pita bread, rolled apricot "leather," and other good, natural, unadulterated foods that have slowly found their way from Middle Eastern specialty stores to the shelves of health food stores and supermarkets throughout America.

One of the most popular foodstuffs invented by a Syrian-American, however, has nothing to do with nutritious eating. It's just plain old fun food — the ice cream cone:

BIRTH OF A CONE   The ice cream cone was born at the St. Louis Exposition of 1904, when Ernest A. Hamwi, an immigrant from Damascus, rolled a circular Persian pastry into the shape of a cone and placed a scoop of ice cream on top.

Hamwi had come to St. Louis from his native Syria in 1903 and opened a concession stand at the World's Fair in 1904, where he sold, among other things, *zalabia* — a wafer-thin pastry baked on a waffle iron and served with sugar and other sweet toppings.

Business was brisk at the Fair, and one hot summer's day the ice cream concession next to Hamwi's *zalabia* stand ran out of clean dishes. Hamwi saw a great opportunity at hand, quickly rolled a round *zalabia* into the shape of a cone, and plopped a ball of ice cream in the center. The ice cream vendor and Hamwi both profited from their joint venture by selling "World's Fair Cornucopia" (as they were called at the time) and the world gained a new treat — ice cream cones.

Welsh

The Welsh gave America their national dish, Welsh rabbit, and contributed to a great deal of confusion over the actual contents of this cheesy sauce. Made from melted cheese and beer, Welsh rabbit contains neither hide nor hare, and is strictly a dairy dish. How did it get its confusing name? The name was originally intended as a slur by the English, who insinuated that Wales was such a poor nation, the Welsh could not even afford to dine on wild rabbits, which overran the English countryside.

According to another story, the name originated during a hunter's banquet when the chef ran out of meat. Since he did not want the dinner guests to know that there wasn't any game in the cheese sauce, he dubbed it Welsh rabbit.

The name was altered to "rarebit" in 1785, but many restaurants prefer to list the dish by its original name.

HOW SWEET IT IS!

America loves sweets! Each year we gobble up 3,400,000,000 pounds of fudge, chocolate, mints, licorice and candies shaped into canes, kisses, buttons and whips.

We spent almost $5 billion in 1977 for candy bars, boxed candy, penny candy and mints, and another billion dollars for chewing gum. And that figure doesn't include the money spent on dental repairs for teeth cracked on jaw breakers and molars eaten away by sugary residue.

The first candy makers in the New World were the Dutch. They manufactured sugar wafers, macaroons and sugar plums during the days when sweets were a rare treat, and "visions of sugar plums" danced in the heads of children on Christmas Eve, instead of electric racing cars and dolls that grow bosoms before your very eyes. The revolving steam pan, invented in 1851, changed all that: candy makers were now able to mass-produce large amounts of candy at a very low cost, and the era of penny candy and two-for-a-penny treats was upon us.

Some of our favorite candies were invented in America: peanut brittle began life as peanut taffy in 1890, when a New England woman added baking soda to her recipe instead of cream of tartar, resulting in a brittle "taffy." Fudge was also born accidentally. It started out as a batch of caramels that went awry: instead of cooling to a smooth consistency, the mixture crystallized, causing the angry chef to mutter "Fudge," and so a new industry was born.

Of course there were immigrants from the "old country" who brought candy-making recipes with them to the New World and other ethnic Americans who made our life a little bit sweeter by contributing their irresistible cookies, candies and mints to our bulging waistlines.

CHOCOLATE FOR THE MASSES Mention the word "Hershey" and millions of sweet-loving children will immediately respond, "Chocolate!" But, despite the company's long-standing association with chocolate kisses, chocolate bars and chocolate syrup, Milton Snavely Hershey (1857–1945) made his first fortune by manufacturing caramels.

Hershey's great-grandparents, Isaac and Anna Hershey, emigrated to America from Switzerland, and settled in Pennsylvania Dutch country with fellow German-speaking Mennonites. Milton was apprenticed to a printer when he was 14 years old, but when the relationship didn't work out his mother paid Joseph Royer, of Lancaster, Pennsylvania, to teach her son the confectionery trade. Milton spent four years learning to make hand-rolled bonbons, caramels and mints. He then ventured into business for himself in 1876 at the age of 19.

Well, Milton was a failure; not just once, but several times – in Philadelphia, Denver, Chicago and New York. He didn't achieve business success until 1886, when he began exporting milk caramels to England from Lancaster, Pennsylvania. Although business was booming, Hershey believed that caramels were only a fad that would soon fade from the public's fancy. What Milton really wanted was to make chocolate, which at that time was a confection for the rich. Hershey was convinced that by mass-producing just one item in a plain bar shape, he would be able to make it inexpensive enough for everyone to afford.

Hershey produced his first commercial chocolate bar in 1895, after several years of experimentation with milk chocolate formulas. In 1900, he sold his caramel business for a cool million so he could concentrate his efforts on selling chocolate. By 1911, the business had mushroomed to $5 million annually; Hershey was on his way to becoming a household word as sales hit $20 million in 1921. Despite his dream of producing only one chocolate product, Hershey had expanded to include Hershey kisses in 1907, and Mr. Goodbars in 1925 – two delicious ideas.

Milton always said, "Give them quality. That's the best kind of advertising in the world." He must have been right, because the familiar silver and brown wrapper was so firmly entrenched in millions of American minds that executives of Hershey Foods Corporation did not find it necessary to advertise their products to the mass media until 1970.

LIFE SAVERS The man who made "Life Savers a part of living" (according to the television jingle) was Edward John Noble. Descended from Thomas Noble, an Englishman who settled at Westfield, Massachusetts, in 1651, Edward Noble was an advertising salesman and not a candymaker by trade.

He bought the product and trademarks from Clarence Crane of Cleveland, Ohio, in December 1913 for $2,900, but it was Noble's marketing genius that made Life Savers a national success. He asked cigar stores to display Life Savers near the cashier's counter, and to give every customer a nickel with his change to spur impulse purchases of Life Savers at the checkout register. In 1915, over 6,725,000 packs of peppermint-flavored tablets were sold. Fruit drops were added in 1924, and within 20 years sales were approaching $10,000,000 annually. By 1956, sales had doubled to $20,000,000. Noble's partner, J. Roy Allen, who contributed $1,500 of the purchase price, later sold out his share of the business in 1926 for $3,300,000.

CHEWING GUM or THE JOY OF MASTICATION The Mexican general, Antonio Lopez de Santa Anna, who battled Sam Houston in the War of 1836, first brought chicle north of the border and started the American people masticating morning, noon and night.

He approached Thomas Adams, a Jersey City manufacturer, with his new "rubber substitute," but after repeated experiments Adams found that the dried sap of the sapodilla tree was better suited for chewing and patented it as flavorless "Snapping and Stretching Gum" on February 14, 1871.

Soon other gum manufacturers were adding colors and flavors to chewing gum, and a national habit was launched. Gum-making today is a multi-million-dollar industry and, although a pack of bubble gum cards costs twenty-five cents, you can still buy a penny gum ball from a vending machine.

TOOTSIE ROLLS When Leo Hirschfield arrived in America from his native Austria in the late 1800s all he had were the clothes on his back, his dreams of success and a candy recipe.

Leo opened a small candy shop in New York where he painstakingly rolled each piece of chocolate-flavored candy out by hand. As he rolled, his thoughts turned to his young daughter, Tootsie, after whom the confection was named.

Priced at a penny a roll, Tootsie Rolls were an instant success when they hit the candy stands in 1896. By 1919 Tootsie Roll had merged with another firm to become the Sweets Company of America.

Almost 11 million Tootsie Rolls and 5 million Tootsie Pops are produced each day, amounting to over $50 million in sales during 1974 for the candy that has been an American favorite for over 80 years now.

INDESCRIBABLY DELICIOUS When Peter Paul Halajian (1850?–1927) first started selling ice cream and candy in Torrington, Connecticut, he passed out handbills to advertise his wares:

Peter Paul has the very good food
You don't throw any down the chute
His delicious ice cream your dreams will
  haunt
The more you eat it, the more you want

Ice cream soda the year round
No better soda was ever found
His homemade candy will make you fat
To Peter Paul take off your hat.
                              (c. 1900)

His jingles weren't great, but his homemade candy was excellent. Soon demand for his products began to exceed the limits of his small kitchen, and in 1919 he and five other Armenian immigrants founded the Peter Paul Candy Company with a total investment of $6,000.

Like Halajian, who left Armenia in 1870, all of his partners had fled their native land in the late nineteenth century: George Shamlian was the Armenian-born chemist who developed the Mounds formula in 1921; Cal Kazanjian, Peter Paul's brother-in-law; Artin Kazanjian, Cal's cousin; and Jacob Hagopian and Jacob Chouljian, two friends.

Peter Paul died in 1927, but the company that bears his name is still going strong today, producing almost 170 million pounds of candy each year, which amounts to almost 4% of the nation's candy, worth approximately $65 million.

JUJYFRUITS, CHOCOLATE BABIES, AND TENDER JELLIES Remember those great fruit-flavored gummy candies that always stuck to your teeth when you were a kid? Jujyfruits, Mexican hats and red hot dollars are all made from the same sticky formula, somewhere in between gumdrops and their harder brothers, JuJubes. (One box of JuJubes might last an entire week if you just let them dissolve in your mouth!)

The company that makes all these sticky delights, along with chocolate-flavored babies, candy corn, and gum drops dubbed "Tender Jellies" is Henry Heide — a family-owned business that has been making sweets for almost 110 years.

Heide and a partner, both German immigrants, began their business in 1869 in the basement of 175 Spring Street in Manhattan. Since Henry Heide had been here for at least three years, he should have known better than to trust the unscrupulous merchant who sold them their first horse and wagon. The partners paid $60 for the delivery team, and didn't discover the horse was blind until after he had crashed into the pillar of an elevated railway, spilling the day's stock of peppermint sticks, bonbons and coconut cakes all over the sidewalks of New York.

The fourth generation of Heides is entering the business today with Andrew Heide, grandson of the founder, serving as president, and his sons Peter and Philip working their way up the corporate ladder.

CHOCOLATE MATZO BALLS Kosher and Parve candies are a necessity for Jewish-Americans who adhere to strict dietary laws set down in the Torah. At Passover. Barton's sells Honey Cake, Mandel Brodt, Macaroons and Chocolate Matzo Balls in four flavors — smooth chocolate fudge, heavenly marzipan, creamy coconut, and French truffle.

The founder of Barton's Bonbonniere is Stephen Klein, an Austrian immigrant from Vienna who arrived here in the 1940s. Like so many other immigrants before him, Klein was penniless, and he had a wife and three children to support. He began making candy in the family kitchen at night and selling it from office to office in Manhattan. His products were so well received that he soon was able to open his first candy shop in New York.

Today there are over 3,000 agencies in the United States licensed to sell Barton's candy.

REGGIE America's first candy bar named for a Black athlete is the Reggie — a peanut, caramel and chocolate bar manufactured by Standard Brands and introduced in 1978. According to latest sales figures, the bar is still "a rookie." According to Howard Stonesifer, director of corporate affairs for Standard Brands, "It has a ways to go before it catches up with Baby Ruth or Butterfinger." Still, in the first six months of sales in New York, Los Angeles, San Francisco, Chicago, Boston and Philadelphia, the bar has sold a respectable 33 million customers on its taste.

(Courtesy: Heide)

FOREIGN-SOUNDING FOOD INVENTED IN AMERICA

Don't ask for "spaghetti and meat balls" in Italy—that "Italian" specialty was invented in Brooklyn. "Russian dressing" was not invented in the U.S.S.R., and "Baked Alaska" has nothing to do with Eskimos or Aleuts—it was invented in 1867 by a French-born chef, Charles Ranhofer, in New York City.

There are other well-known "foreign" foods that try to pass as exotic fare from other shores, when in reality they were first concocted in the good old U.S.A.

VICHYSSOISE   This cold leek and potato soup with the fancy French name was first concocted by French-born chef Louis Diat in 1910. It was a variation of a recipe his mother used to make, but in those pre-airconditioned, pre-antiperspirant days it was tough to keep your "cool" during the hot summer months, so Diat simply served his Vichyssoise cold to meet the demand for cool refreshing summertime food.

It was first served at the Ritz Carlton Hotel in New York City. (The correct pronunciation, by the way, is vichy-swaz, not vichy-soi.)

LEBANON BOLOGNA   This sausage has nothing to do with the Middle Eastern country of the same name. Lebanon Bologna is an all-beef sausage, smoked for added flavor, that was first made in Lebanon, Pennsylvania.

CIOPPINO   This savory fish stew may have an Italian-sounding name, but it was invented by fishermen along the Monterey peninsula and made famous in the restaurants of San Francisco's Fisherman's Wharf.

CHOP SUEY   Li Hung Chang (1823–1901), a Chinese diplomat of the Manchu government, is known as the "father of Chop Suey." He earned his title during a state visit to New York City, where besides demanding that local policemen carry him aboard a litter to visit Grant's Tomb, he first developed the dish that we know as chop suey, an attempt to recreate authentic Chinese food without the proper cooking utensils, ingredients and seasonings. When friends asked what the dish was called, he combined the words for chop sticks and soya sauce into *chop soya,* which eventually became chop suey.

CHOW MEIN   This is also an American dish, first stewed by Chinese railroad workers in San Francisco.

LIEDERKRANZ   CHEESE   The name is German, but Liederkranz cheese is truly American. In fact, it is one of only two cheeses that have been developed here—the other is Brick cheese, invented by John Jossi, reputed to be a Swiss-American.

Liederkranz is a rather pungent, smelly cheese, in the same odorous family as Limburger. It was invented in 1892 by a Swiss-German-American cheesemaker, Emil Frey, of Monroe, New York. Frey was, in fact, attempting to reproduce a famous German cheese, Bismarck Schlosskäse. Whether he succeeded or not is beside the point. He tested his first batch on a German choral group, the Liederkranz ("garland of song"), which not only loved it but gave its name to the new cheese as well.

ETHNIC SHOPPING LIST

Whether you shop at the A&P (co-founded by George Huntington Hartford, an English-American, in 1869), choose your groceries at Kroger's (founded by Bernard Henry Kroger, an Alsatian-German-American), or buy your weekly supplies at D'Agostino's (founded by two Italians from Abruzzi), you've probably come across one or more of the products listed on the following pages.

BAKER'S CHOCOLATE   Found in the baking section of the supermarket, Baker's chocolate is the stuff that home-made brownies, devil's food cakes, and chocolate fudge frosting are made of. Founded in 1765 by John Hannon, a chocolate maker from Ireland, in partnership with Dr. James Baker, the company has been producing baking chocolate for over 200 years.

In 1769, Hannon disappeared on a business trip to the West Indies, where he had gone to purchase cocoa beans, and the company passed into the control of the Baker family, though the name didn't change until 1895, when James's grandson, Walter,

ETHNIC MENU QUIZ

Ever since those Delmonico brothers popularized "pie à la mode" at their famous New York restaurant, foreign terms have been popping up on menus all over America. See how many foreign terms you can match with their correct description:

1.	à l'Allemande	a.	huntsman's style, with tomato sauce and green peppers
2.	à la broche (brochette)	b.	served with steamed potatoes
3.	à la creole	c.	served with white navy beans
4.	diable	d.	with onions
5.	à la lyonnaise	e.	garnished with blanched almonds sauteed in butter
6.	à la maître d'hotel	f.	baked in the oven until a thin brown crust forms
7.	alla cacciatora	g.	with foie gras, truffles and madeira wine
8.	alla marinara	h.	with peas
9.	alla milanese	i.	garnished with chopped hard-boiled eggs
10.	à la Bourguignonne	j.	Spanish style, with tomatoes, pimientos and oil
11.	aux fines herbes	k.	curried
12.	à la Florentine	l.	served with cooked vegetables
13.	au gratin	m.	served with caviar
14.	à la Hongroise	n.	served with olives, tomatoes and anchovies
15.	à la Provençale	o.	mariner's style, with tomatoes, garlic and spices
16.	à la Russe	p.	German style, served with a white sauce and garnished with sauerkraut or noodles
17.	à la vinaigrette	q.	broiled or grilled on a skewer
18.	suvarov	r.	served with a mixture of parsley, butter and lemon juice
19.	smitane	s.	served with cream sauce and paprika
20.	soubise	t.	Milan style, cooked in butter
21.	polonaise	u.	mixture of fruits or vegetables
22.	moscovite	v.	served with an oil and vinegar sauce
23.	macedoine	w.	cooked with red wine, mushrooms and onions
24.	Amandine	x.	highly seasoned with tomatoes, peppers and onions
25.	à la Bretonne	y.	with finely shredded onions
26.	à l'Espagnole	z.	deviled
27.	à l'Indienne	aa.	served with chopped parsley, chervil, tarragon and chives
28.	à l'Irlandaise	bb.	served with a mayonnaise made with pureed caviar or lobster roe
29.	à la Jardiniere	cc.	rich with garlic and olive oil
30.	à la Niçoise	dd.	served on a bed of spinach
31.	Saint-Germain	ee.	with sour cream

Answers:

1-p; 2-q; 3-x; 4-z; 5-y; 6-r; 7-a; 8-o; 9-i; 10-w; 11-aa; 12-dd; 13-f; 14-s; 15-cc; 16-bb; 17-v; 18-g; 19-ee; 20-d; 21-l; 22-m; 23-u; 24-e; 25-c; 26-j; 27-k; 28-b; 29-1; 30-n; 31-h.

named the chocolate company after himself.

Although the origins of the company were Irish, the trademark that appears on every bar, "La Belle Chocolatière" (beautiful chocolate girl), comes to us via Austria. It was in a quaint Vienna chocolate shop that a certain Prince Dietrichstein met Anna Baltauf, a waitress who soon became his bride. To commemorate their rather offbeat meeting, the Prince had her portrait painted in a serving girl's costume. Walter Baker spied the painting at the Dresden Art Gallery and chose to use it as his company's trademark.

BURRY COOKIES Christina Burry started a small cookie business in Toronto, Canada, in 1888. A widowed Scotswoman, she sold homemade baked goods from a small storefront to support herself and her five sons. As her reputation spread, her business expanded until her small bakery had been transformed into a successful chain of retail stores.

George W. Burry, Christina's grandson, founded the Burry Biscuit Company in Chicago in 1933. Today, the company, a division of Quaker Oats, manufactures such all-time favorites as: Mr. Chips, Fudgetown, Scooter Pie and Euphrates Crackers.

DOLE PINEAPPLE Think about brand-name pineapple products and the first name that comes to mind is Dole. How did James Dole (1877–1958), whose first American ancestor, Richard Dole, migrated from England to Newbury, Massachusetts, in 1639, make his name synonymous with brand-name pineapples in America? All it took was $1,200 and a lot of determination.

When Jim graduated from Harvard in 1899, he set sail for Hawaii, determined "that after two or three years of reasonable effort . . . I would be able to spend the rest of my life in a hammock, smoking cigars." Hawaii had recently become a U.S. Territory and was sorely in need of another cash crop to supplement its sugar cane production. Dole decided to can and export pineapples to the mainland, despite that fact that they previously had been considered unfit to eat.

In their native habitat, Brazil, pineapples were full of seeds, and spoiled rapidly when shipped fresh. Dole's pineapples were seedless, tender, and sweet as sugar, for the simple reason that they were unpollinated. In Brazil, the large blue flowers of the pineapple plant, a member of the Bromeliad family, are pollinated by hummingbirds native to the region. Once pollinated, the pineapple becomes inedible, as it is full of tough seeds. This does not occur in Hawaii, which, fortunately for Dole, lacks hummingbirds.

"RISING" THE LADDER OF SUCCESS Before Charles Louis Fleischmann (1834–1897) came along, most American homemakers relied on homemade "starters" to raise their bread dough. Starting with a soupy batter of potato water, flour, salt and sugar, a homemaker would leave the mixture uncovered in a bowl for several hours in the hopes of attracting "wild" yeast cells that normally float in the air. Relying on such "primitive" methods, the product obtained was never the same twice—not only did the taste vary, but the rate at which the bread could be expected to double in size was also unpredictable.

Fleischmann, an immigrant from Budapest, "rose" the ladder of success in America by patenting a method for the manufacture of compressed yeast. He was awarded U.S. patent #102,387 on April 26, 1870, for an old family method of making yeast from malt. Homemakers were skeptical about his product until Fleischmann proved its usefulness at the Philadelphia Centennial Exposition in 1876.

SI ES GOYA TIENE QUE SER BUENO "If it's Goya it has to be good" —that's the motto of this Puerto Rican company which for two decades has been providing all segments of the U.S. Hispanic population with the foods they like. "Cubans buy our black beans and our long-grain rice; Puerto Ricans don't buy black beans and they want medium-grain rice. Mexicans like our pink beans . . . Caribbeans buy all kinds of beans and hot sauces, and the rest of our market is made up of Spaniards and Portuguese."

Founded in the 1930s by Prudencio Unanue, a Spaniard who emigrated first to Puerto Rico and then to New York, the company sells its products primarily in the heavily populated Spanish-speaking districts of the Northeast—New York City, Hartford, Baltimore, and Washington, D.C., as well as in Miami and Chicago.

Lest you think they only package beans and rice, Goya has over 550 products—enough to stock a large *bodega* with canned fish, packaged desserts, fruit nectars, oils, olives and seasonings.

HÄAGEN-DAZS This extra-rich ice cream with the Scandinavian name was created by Reuben Mattua, a Bronx manufacturer who recreated the expensive ice cream formula of Jan Haagen, a Danish merchant of Dutch ancestry. Made only of natural ingredients, it is one of the heaviest ice creams available. Weighing in at 7½ pounds per gallon, it is three pounds heftier than normal commercial brands with whipped-in air. But beware! Extra richness means extra calories, and Häagen-Dazs can be dangerously addicting to those who must wage a never-ending war against the scales.

HELLMANN'S MAYONNAISE A German immigrant who arrived in New York in 1903, Richard Hellmann opened a deli on Columbus Avenue in Manhattan two years later, and found that the customers kept coming back for sandwiches and salads because they loved the homemade spread he whipped up daily from his wife's recipe. In 1912, Hellmann started bottling his mayonnaise at the request of his customers. Although his deli no longer survives, Americans all over the nation can enjoy the lively sauce that bears his name to this day.

AMERICA SPELLS CHEESE "K-R-A-F-T" Before Canadian-born James Lewis Kraft (1875–1953) and his brother, Charles, started their cheese company in Chicago in 1904, cheese spoiled quickly if it was not kept in cold storage. There weren't any nationwide cheese manufacturers, nor were there any brand-name cheeses; quality varied because continuous bacterial growth changed the flavor of each cheese from day to day.

Kraft was the first cheese processor to experiment successfully with pasteurization. Once the cheese had ripened, he killed off the bacteria, which halted the ripening process and ensured a product that would keep for long periods of time. That first year, Kraft sold $5,000 worth of pasteurized cheese in tin cans, most of it to India and the Orient. The next year, 1916, sales skyrocketed to $150,000, and that was only the beginning. When the United States entered World War II, the demands of the Army and Navy for safe, nutritious canned food grew so large that one single order was placed for 2 million pounds of Kraft products.

To keep up cheese production, Kraft opened cheese factories in 23 states. Previously, Wisconsin produced almost 70% of all cheeses manufactured in the United States, but Kraft enabled one-crop farmers to diversify into cheese production by promising to buy every pound of cheese produced—first in Idaho, then in Montana, Wyoming and Utah—until he was able to produce cheeses near each local market.

Today there are more than 100 Kraft plants around the world, turning out over 6 billion pounds of Kraft products annually.

Although the Kraft brothers emigrated to America from Canada, their family originally hailed from Germany. In 1840 Francis Krafft arrived in North America with his wife and three children and put down roots in Ontario, where the majority of their descendants are still located.

Family tradition maintains that the spelling of the name became "Kraft" when a sign maker erred while painting the first sign for the small, fledgling cheese firm. Unable to afford a new sign, the brothers "resigned" themselves to their new last name.

OATMEAL, STRAIGHT FROM THE HORSE'S MOUTH The giant Quaker Oats Company had its humble beginnings in Akron, Ohio, with Ferdinand Schumacher, a German immigrant who earned the nickname "Oatmeal King" for his efforts in popularizing oats for breakfast. Before Schumacher took oatmeal out of the "horse's mouth" and put it on the breakfast tables of America, most Americans considered the lowly oat suitable only for horse feed. Cartoonists of his time had a field day depicting oat-eating humans wearing feed bags and developing loud "whinnies."

Born at Celle, Hanover, in 1822, Schumacher came to America in 1850 to make his fortune. He opened a small mill for grinding oats in back of a grocery store in Akron, and by 1886 he had built that tiny mill into the largest oat-milling complex in the world. Rebuilt after it was destroyed by fire in 1886, the mill eventually became the basis for the Quaker Oats Company, which has been filling small tummies with hot, nutritious oats for several generations now, thanks to the efforts of the German-American Oatmeal King.

Rival H-O Oats was founded by Alexander Hornby, a retired English leather merchant, who developed a new method for making oatmeal in the 1870s. His "steam-cooked and crushed oats" could be prepared in only 10 minutes, and his H-O (*Hornby Oats*) cereal did much to improve the palatibility of oatmeal for Americans.

PASTA MAKERS One of the leading pasta manufacturers in the nation, the Ronzoni Company, is owned and operated by the third generation of Ronzonis in America.

Emanuele Ronzoni (1870–1956), the founder of the pasta company that bears his family name, was born in 1870 in San Fruttuoso, Italy. He sailed from Genoa at the age of 11 and obtained his first job in America as a helper in a small macaroni factory on New York's Lower East Side. In 1915 he decided to start his own company, just as World War I began disrupting pasta importation from Italy.

At this point "pasta" was almost exclusively an "ethnic food"; it was purchased in bulk and consumed primarily by Italian-Americans. In the 1920s the Ronzoni family began shying away from the traditional twenty-pound wooden cases in favor of consumer-size cardboard cartons. Those small packages made macaroni as American as apple pie, and with the advent of jarred Italian-style tomato sauce, Americans of every ethnic background were able to enjoy a "homemade" meal, straight off the grocer's shelf. Now that's Italian.

Giulio Buitoni started a modest pasta business in San Sepolcro, Italy, in 1827, but his great-grandson Giovanni (1891–1979) turned it into an international company with manufacturing plants in Italy, Paris and the United States.

Giovanni Buitoni emigrated to America shortly after World War II without a lira in his pocket. His wife had to pawn her jewels to finance a plant in Jersey City, New Jersey, and two restaurants in New York City, where Buitoni struck it rich by providing customers with "All you can eat for 25¢." Interestingly, his great-grandmother had to pawn her own wedding jewelry in 1827 to set up his great-grandfather in the San Sepolcro pasta business.

Buitoni's empire was built on hard work, and when he opened a modern $2 million plant in Hackensack, New Jersey, in 1952, Giovanni dedicated it to his parents, ". . . who taught me the religion of God and the religion of work."

SANKA Decaffeinated coffee was first developed in the early 1900s by a German, Dr. Ludwig Roselius, the son of a coffee merchant. Roselius was convinced that the cause of his father's early demise was that old devil, caffeine, so he developed a method that employed steam and a chemical solvent, benzine, to remove the offending substance from green coffee beans prior to roasting.

Calling his new coffee Sanka, from the French "sans caffeine," Roselius marketed it successfully in Europe for several years before bringing it to America in 1910.

THOMAS' ENGLISH MUFFINS In his native London, Samuel Bath Thomas was often awakened by the cries of the local "muffin man" who rang a hand-held bell every morning as he walked from door to door peddling his freshly baked wares.

When Thomas emigrated from London, there weren't any "muffin men" walking the streets of New York, so he decided to start his own bakery in 1875. Armed with his ancestral recipe for "English muffins," Thomas began selling his products to grocery stores and restaurants.

Each day fresh muffins were delivered to local luncheonettes and food markets, where they were displayed in wooden boxes with glass covers that bore the name "S. B. Thomas."

In 1937 sales had passed $1 million, and over the past century millions of Americans have been able to start the day with coffee and an English muffin, full of its butter-catching nooks and crannies, thanks to the genius of Samuel Bath Thomas.

TROPICANA Known in the trade as "chilled orange juice," Tropicana is actually frozen. However, rather than having the water removed from it as in other "frozen" orange juices, Tropicana is frozen "whole" in large slabs and stored in a refrigerated warehouse.

The Tropicana Company was founded in 1921 by Anthony T. Rossi (1900–   ), an Italian immigrant from Sicily who only intended to stay in the States long enough to earn some money so he could explore Africa and produce a movie about the Belgian Congo. Like so many other immigrants, Rossi stayed and stayed and stayed. When the Depression chased him out of New York he began selling gift packages of citrus fruits and juices, which eventually led to the notion of selling "chilled" juice. Today, Tropicana purchases almost 10% of the total Florida orange crop to meet marketing demands throughout the year. In 1978, Rossi sold his company to Beatrice Foods for $488 million.

VAN CAMP   Gilbert C. Van Camp (1817–1900) paved the road to business success with the humble white navy bean. The Van Camp Packing Company began selling pork and beans in 1861 to nourish the hungry armed forces during the Civil War. He fed American troops during the Spanish-American War and by 1900 was selling more than 6 million cans of pork and beans annually.

Descended from Hollanders who settled in New Jersey in the seventeenth century, Van Camp retired in 1898, leaving his namesake company in less reliable hands than his own. The company was soon on the brink of bankruptcy, and in 1933 it was sold to William B. Stokely, Jr., who renamed it Stokely-Van Camp. Stokely upheld the company's tradition of ministering to wartime troops: in 1941 his company developed the "C" ration to feed the men fighting the Second World War.

WORCESTERSHIRE   SAUCE   Lea and Perrins, the makers of "the original and genuine" Worcestershire sauce "from the recipe of a nobleman in the country" (or so it reads on the label), have been manufacturing their sauce since the 1820s.

John Lea and William Perrins, two English chemists from the town of Worcester, in the shire (county) of the same name, were asked to reproduce an Indian sauce by the governor general of Bengal.

Their first attempt produced an unpalatable concoction which was promptly stored in the cellar and forgotten. However, when it had aged, Lea and Perrins found that the flavor had improved greatly, and while the governor general didn't care for the results, other Englishmen savored the sauce.

Today, Worcestershire sauce has become a generic term, although Lea and Perrins is probably the best-known brand name sauce in America.

ETHNIC FOOD SOURCES

Food, food, glorious food! No matter how Americanized the children of im-

migrants become, their stomachs always tend to remember the Old World ways. Polish-Americans who have never seen Krakow wolf down *kielbasa, babka* and *pyrogi;*   Greek-Americans   dine   on *spanākopita, tarama salata* and *baklava;* and almost every ethnic group has its own version of stuffed cabbage. In fact, for many ethnic Americans the only cultural preservation that remains after two or three generations of life in America comes from the kitchen.

Even though the younger generations may abandon their inner-city ghettos and ethnic enclaves for the suburbs, many do "go home again," to stock up on goodies from the ethnic bakeries and food stores in the "old" neighborhood.

On Friday and Saturday afternoons in New York City, when many people do their weekly marketing, you can find Chinese-Americans from Paterson, New Jersey, shopping for bok choy, wonton wrappers and fresh noodles at the corner grocery stores of lower Manhattan's Chinatown district; Lebanese-Americans from as far away as Philadelphia come to Brooklyn's Atlantic Avenue to buy cheese, olives and Syrian bread (pita); and Italian-American transplants to California always visit Little Italy on trips back East, to stock up on provolone or to gorge themselves on pastries, pasta and "real" Italian bread after a year of alfalfa sprouts and yogurt at the health food bars of Los Angeles.

Although many supermarkets all over the country have expanded their "gourmet" food sections in recent years to include Chinese, Mexican, Jewish and Middle Eastern foods, for some reason the food always tastes better when it comes from a corner deli, restaurant or food market in an ethnic neighborhood.

If you don't live near a "source" for your favorite ethnic goodies, you may wish to consult the following directory. Some of these stores will mail small quantities of food, while others deal only in wholesale amounts. Write for details before placing any orders:

Chinese

D. M. Enterprises
P.O. Box 2452
San Francisco, California   94126

D. M. sells Chinese vegetable seeds for home gardeners who want to grow their own bok choy, pea pods and chinese cabbage.

East Wind
2801 Broadway
New York, New York   10025

Oriental Import-Export Company
2009 Polk Street
Houston, Texas   77003

Star Market
3349 North Clark Street
Chicago, Illinois   60657

Tsang and Ma International
P.O. Box 294
Belmont, California   94002

Tsang and Ma sells Chinese seeds for growing coriander, bitter melon, bok choy and snow peas.

Tuck Cheong Company
617 H Street, N.W.
Washington, D.C.   20001

Wing Chong Lung Co.
922 South San Pedro Street
Los Angeles, California   90015

Wing Wing Imported Groceries
79 Harrison Avenue
Boston, Massachusetts   02111

Yuet Hing Market, Inc.
23 Pell Street
New York, New York   10013

Dutch

Vander Vliet's Holland Imports
3245 West 111 Street
Chicago, Illinois   60655

Delftware, wooden shoes; flowering bulbs; biscuits, cakes and pastry; chocolate; cheeses; and rijsttafel spices and condiments.

French

Marin French Cheese Company
P.O. Box 99
Petaluma, California   94952

Accepts mail orders for brie, camembert and other cheeses.

German

Bremen House, Inc.
218 East 86th Street
New York, New York   10028

Located in the heart of New York City's "Germantown," this shop stocks cheeses, cookies, imported honey, ham and wursts galore—leberwurst, blutwurst, bratwurst and more.

Gourmet Food From All Nations

Jamail's
3114 Kirby Drive
Houston, Texas

Called "the Neiman-Marcus of Supermarkets," Jamail's was founded in 1946 by three Lebanese-American brothers and their immigrant father.

Includes regional specialties from all over the United States, as well as imported foods, fresh meat, produce and ethnic takeout foods such as paella, Finnish carrot soup and Danish ham.

Continental Gourmet Shop
210 South Woodward Avenue
Birmingham, Michigan   48011

Epicure Markets
1656 Alton Road
Miami Beach, Florida   33139

Heintzelman's
1128 McKnight Road
Pittsburgh, Pennsylvania   15237

Around the World Food
1149 South Brentwood Boulevard
St. Louis, Missouri   63117

Cardullo's Gourmet Shop
6 Brattle Street
Cambridge, Massachusetts   02138

Zabar's
2245 Broadway
New York, New York

Greek

Poseidon Confectionery Company
629 Ninth Avenue
New York, New York

Founded in 1922 by Demetrios Anagnostou, a Greek immigrant from Corfu, Poseidon specializes in homemade filo dough, and over the past half-century has produced over three-quarters of a million pounds of that thin, translucent dough used for baklava, spanākopita (spinach pies) and tyropita (cheese pies).

Hawaiian

Kemoo Farm Foods, Ltd.
Box 30021
Honolulu, Hawaii 96820

Mail orders taken for guava jelly, macadamia nuts, pineapple and coconut confections.

Hungarian

Lekvar-by-the-Barrel
1577 First Avenue
New York, New York 10028

What is lekvar and why would anyone want to buy it by the barrel? Lekvar is Hungarian prune butter, used primarily in Danishes and in hamantaschen, those delicious triangular shaped pastries traditionally eaten on the Jewish holiday Purim. Besides prune butter, there are other European and Hungarian specialties – poppy seed filling, strudel leaves, hot and sweet paprika, Hungarian salami and ham, and fruit syrups.

Paprika Weiss, Importer
1546 Second Avenue
New York, New York 10028

Specializes in salami, sausage, spices, jams, jellies, preserves and, of course, the Hungarian paprika, which earned the original owner, Mr. Weiss, his nickname "Paprikas."

Indian-Pakistani

Antone's
Box 3352
Houston, Texas 77001

Delmar and Company
501 Monroe Avenue
Detroit, Michigan 48226

Haig's
441 Clement Street
San Francisco, California 94119

House of Rice
4112 University Way Northeast
Seattle, Washington 98105

Kalustyan's
123 Lexington Avenue
New York, New York 10016

Specializing in Indian spices since 1944.

Oriental Foods and Handicrafts
3708 N. Broadway
Chicago, Illinois 60613

Sells rice, grain, dal, chutney, spices and miscellaneous items, such as gripe water, loma oil and henna powder.

Italian

Barzizza Bros. Inc.
351 South Front Street
Memphis, Tennessee 38103

Cappello's
5328 Lemmon Avenue
Dallas, Texas 75209

Conte Di Savoia
555 W. Roosevelt Road
Chicago, Illinois 60607

R. Fazzi and Co.
225 South Spring Street
Los Angeles, California 90027

Guy Montani Fine Foods
12 West 27th Street
Indianapolis, Indiana 46208

Joseph Assi's Imported Foods
3316 Beach Boulevard
Jacksonville, Florida 32207

Manganaro Foods
488 Ninth Avenue
New York, New York 10018

Three generations of Manganaros have been conducting business here since 1893. They have a large mail-order catalog, which includes food, cookware, utensils and imported pasta, cheeses and sausages.

Japanese

Anzen Japanese Foods and Imports
736 N.E. Union Avenue
Portland, Oregon 97232

For over 75 years, Anzen has been supplying the Northwest with everything from tea to rice flour, fermented soybeans, poi, pickled cabbage, rice vinegar, dashi, salted lettuce and shrimp paste. They sell soy sauce by the gallon and rice comes in 50-pound sacks. They also carry a full line of woks, sake sets, books and even Japanese mustard plasters.

Diamond Trading Company
1108 North Clark Street
Chicago, Illinois 60610

Enbun Company
248 East First Street
Los Angeles, California   90012

Katagiri Company
224 East 59th Street
New York, New York   10022

Kinoko Co.
P.O. Box 6425
Oakland, California   94621

Mushroom-growing kits include Japanese enokitake and Chinese wood ears.

Maruyama's
100 North 18th Street
St. Louis, Missouri   63103

Oriental Trading Company
2636 Edenborn Avenue
Metairie, Louisiana   70002

Soya Food Products
2356 Wyoming Avenue
Cincinnati, Ohio   45214

Uwajimaya
P.O. Box 3003
Seattle, Washington   98114

Cookware and specialty foods.

Yoshinoya
36 Prospect Street
Cambridge, Massachusetts   02139

Middle Eastern Foods

Besides cheeses, olives, dried beans and rose water, there are Turkish coffee pots, shish kebab skewers, couscous pots, hookahs (water pipes), backgammon tables, drums and camel saddles for sale in most Middle Eastern stores.

American Oriental Grocery
20736 Lahser Road
Southfield, Michigan   48075

Bezjian Grocery, Inc.
4725 Santa Monica Blvd.
Hollywood, California   90026

Demmas Shish-Ke-Bab
5806 Hampton Avenue
St. Louis, Missouri   63109

Malko Brothers
197 Atlantic Avenue
Brooklyn, New York   11201

Mediterranean and Middle East Import Company
233 Valencia Street
San Francisco, California   94103

Sahadi Importing Co., Inc.
187 Atlantic Avenue
Brooklyn, New York 11201

The first Sahadi family member to emigrate to America was Abraham Sahadi, who settled in Bayonne, New Jersey, in 1890. His great-nephews are running the Atlantic Avenue store while his sons and grandsons manage the A. Sahadi distributorship, which supplies supermarkets, health-food stores and ethnic food shops with their own brand of beans, coffee, olives, tahini and other goods.

The best-selling item in the story is *foul mudammas* (small fava beans). Best-selling olives: Calamata from Greece, split green olives from Greece, Alfonso olives from Chile and Black Salonica olives from Greece. Cheeses include: feta, Kasseri, Syrian braided cheese and lebany (thickened yogurt spread).

Rising postal costs have limited their mail order business to wholesale orders in recent years.

Scandinavian

Nordiska
299 Westport Avenue
Norwalk, Connecticut   06851

Importers of Scandinavian cookware, tools, mixing bowls, trays and cookie cutters.

Food With a Spanish Flavor

If you're searching for Spanish and Latin American food such as chorizo sausages, manioc flour, olive oil, chilies, mango paste, guava paste, masa de harina, queso blanco (white Mexican cheese) and assorted spices, you have a choice: you can buy Goya food products in the supermarket, or you can try one of the following *bodegas:*

Casa Moneo Spanish Imports
210 West 14th Street
New York, New York   10011

La Paloma-Tenorio and Company
2620 Bagley Street
Detroit, Michigan   48216

La Preferida, Inc.
177-181 West South Water Market
Chicago, Illinois   60608

Pena's Spanish Store
1636 17th Street, N.W.
Washington, D.C.   20009

Spanish and American Food Market
7001 Wade Park Avenue
Cleveland, Ohio   44103

Vietnamese

Viet Nam Center, Inc.
3133 Wilson Boulevard
Arlington, Virginia   22201

SAY CHEESE!

Each year the United States imports over 209 million pounds of cheese and cheese substitutes from foreign shores to supplement the 2.8 billion pounds manufactured domestically. According to the Cheese Importers Association of America, the ten most popular imports in 1977 were:

1   SWISS 59.6 million pounds
We call it Swiss (no matter where it's made), but the Europeans refer to this holey cheese as Emmentaler, after the Emmen Tal Valley in Switzerland where it originated in the fifteen century. The characteristic holes in natural Swiss cheese are formed as a result of respiration by those microbial organisms that turn milk into cheese and give each variety its particular flavor. But, be careful, some cheesemakers "cheat" and add carbon dioxide gas to their product to induce rapid hole formation, rather than wait for nature to take its course.

2   GRUYÈRE   15.2 million pounds
Sharper than Swiss, with smaller holes and a higher butterfat content, Gruyère melts easily and is a good choice for making fondue. (The foil-wrapped wedges of processed chesse many Americans are familiar with are made *from* Gruyère, but can't compare to the natural cheese in flavor.)

3   ROMANO, PARMESAN, PROVOLONE   11.1 million pounds
Grated Romano and Parmesan cheeses are the normal toppings for spaghetti sauce, pizza, lasagna and other Italian dishes. The large quantities in which they are imported attest to the popularity of Italian food in America, because unlike "eating" cheeses, a pound of grated romano or parmesan goes a long way.

Romano cheese was first made in the area near Rome, Italy; Parmesan was first made in Parma; and provolone refers to the large (*one*), round cheeses (*prova*) of Naples.

4   PECORINO ROMANO   9.5 million pounds*
Sheep's milk cheese is considered the best topping for a bowl of pasta, but at $5 to $8 a pound in some food stores, it's amazing that we imported so much.

5   CHEDDAR   9.3 million pounds
This cheese was first made in the village of Cheddar in Somerset, England, at the end of the sixteenth century. In addition to the vast quantities imported yearly, many varieties of Cheddars are manufactured, according to the old English process, in various regions of the United States: Longhorn cheddar (Texas, Wisconsin); Colby cheddar, Cooper cheddar (Vermont); and Coon cheese (New York).

6   EDAM and GOUDA   9.3 million pounds
Both are named for Dutch towns: Gouda, near Rotterdam; and Edam, near the capital city of Amsterdam. Both of these contributions from the Netherlands come in red wax skins, but Gouda contains more butterfat per pound.

7 Sheep's milk cheese for eating purposes totaled 6.2 million pounds.

8 BLUE MOLD CHEESES *3.1 million pounds*
Mold is injected into the cheese *on purpose* to give it a characteristic flavor that Americans favor for salad dressings and dessert.

9 BRYNDZA, SBINZ, GJETOST, GOYA *1.7 million pounds*
Although these names are not quite so familiar as the top 8 cheeses, we imported enough to make 27.2 million one-ounce servings. Bryndza is similar to Greek feta cheese, but it is made in the Balkans, Czechoslovakia, Hungary and Romania, where it is used to make *Mamaliga*, the national dish. Sbinz is a gray-green sheep's milk cheese used for grating. Gjetost is a Norwegian goat's milk cheese, brown in color, with a very sweet taste that comes from adding whey. Goya is an Argentinian cheese also used for grating.

10 ROQUEFORT CHEESE *1.6 million pounds*
Roquefort is "blue" cheese, but not all blue cheese can be called "Roquefort." To qualify for this title, cheese must be made from sheep's milk during the lambing season and it must be ripened with Penicillium roqueforti (which comes from moldy bread) in the limestone caverns of Roquefort, France.

Although the top ten imported cheeses have Swiss, Italian, English, Dutch and other European names, the top ten cheese exporting countries are New Zealand, Finland, Denmark, Austria, Norway, Italy, Switzerland, France, Argentina and the Netherlands. Check the label in your supermarket. You may be surprised at the country of origin of your favorite "Swiss" cheese. Of the 60 million or so pounds imported to the United States, only 6.8 million came from Switzerland.

MADE IN AMERICA

There are only two native American cheeses, Liederkranz and Brick. (Cheese connoisseurs totally disregard the pasteurized, processed lumps that deli counters sell as "American" cheese.) American "cheese" is made by boiling two or more varieties of cheese with milk, whey and preservatives. Modern food manufacturers have managed to adulterate a good thing (natural cheese) by turning it into "cheese spread" and "cheese food"—products that contain 50% water, milk and whey solids and therefore cannot legally be called "cheese." Each slice is wrapped in plastic and foil, because the slices are too mushy to be pulled apart once they've been pre-sliced.

DRINK IT UP!

In 1900 the average American consumed about 12 bottles of soda pop a year. It was a treat then, reserved for parties and special celebrations, but soon ice cream parlors began to flourish, along with the American taste for sweet beverages.

By the early 1970s the per capita consumption of soda pop had increased more than 2000%, to 250 bottles and cans per person. (If you figure out how many diabetics, chronic dieters and milk-fed infants that "per person" statistic includes, you'll find there are a lot of Americans who are guzzling down more than 250 cans per year.)

To whom do we owe this consumption of 4,460,000,000 cases of soft drinks each year? Does any one person or ethnic group deserve credit for unleashing 107,040,000,000 no-deposit, no-return bottles and cans on our environment in 1974 alone? Actually, credit for the modern soda

*Figure includes other sheep's milk cheeses used for grating, in addition to Pecorino, which is the most popular.

industry belongs to five men: 1) Joseph Priestly, the English scientist who first invented carbonated water in his laboratory in 1767, and gave plain old water that zing of bubbles that tickle the nose; 2) Torbern Bergman, a Swedish chemist who developed the first commercial method of producing carbonic acid in 1770 so we could fizz large quantities of soda water; 3) John Matthews, an English immigrant; 4) Eugene Roussel, a French immigrant; and 5) Asa Griggs Candler, an English-American.

BRIEF HISTORY OF SODA IN AMERICA

JOHN   MATTHEWS'   "HOLY WATER"   John Matthews was an English immigrant who opened the first soda fountain in New York City in 1832. You might even say that Matthews made his fortune selling "holy water," since the source of his bubbles came from St. Patrick's Cathedral. Matthews used the marble scrap left over from that famous Fifth Avenue church, and mixed it with sulfuric acid to liberate carbonic-acid gas. There was enough scap marble to fizz an estimated 25 million gallons of water—which thirsty New Yorkers began guzzling down, with gusto.

Despite Matthews' success in selling soda water to Americans, he never thought of going beyond the "two cents plain." It wasn't until 1838 that a Frenchman, Eugene Roussel, first mixed soda water and fountain syrup together to make flavored soda for the citizens of Philadelphia.

BOTTLE IT!   Although these "foreigners" helped to whet the American appetite for carbonated beverages, it was an American-born businessman who turned soda into a multi-billion-dollar industry by bottling it! Although Benjamin Silliman, a chemistry professor at Yale, was the first to bottle soda water in the United States, the first person to bottle it successfully was Asa Griggs Candler, the man who made Coca-Cola a household word.

Asa Candler (1851–1929) came to Atlanta in 1873 seeking employment as a pharmacist's assistant. He wore homemade clothes and had only $1.75 in his pocket when he strode into the Pemberton-Pulliam Drug Company seeking a job. John S. Pemberton didn't have an opening available for Candler at that time, but he was to have a

profound effect on Candler's future good fortune.

LEGAL HIGH   Pemberton originated the formula for Coca-Cola in 1886 as an elixir, and named his product for the "untreated" coca leaves and cola nuts it contained.

(Untreated coca leaves are a source of cocaine, and until 1906, when the Food and Drug Act was passed, every single glass of Coca-Cola contained a minute quantity of cocaine. According to a chemical analysis of the soft drink in 1900, the amount of cocaine was so insignificant a person would have had to consume 5½ quarts of Coca-Cola before any noticeable effects could be felt. Today the offending substance is removed before the leaves are used to flavor the world's favorite soft drink.)

Pemberton sold about 25 gallons of his elixir in 1886, but when he became ill in 1888 he sold Candler a one-third interest in Coca-Cola. A few months later, Candler purchased full rights, and in 1890 he closed the drugstore he owned at the time to concentrate all his efforts on marketing the "delicious, refreshing, stimulating, invigorating" drink with the "magic formula."

In 1892 Candler's sales were going strong at 35,360 gallons per year. By 1913, he was selling 6,767,822 gallons per annum, and finding it increasingly difficult to keep up with the ever-increasing demand for his soft drink.

The famous "hobble skirt" Coca-Cola bottle was designed in 1915 by a Swedish-American, Alex Samuelson of Terre Haute, Indiana. Patented in 1915, the swirled green glass bottle went into production late in 1916, and it became almost as famous a trademark as the red sign with white cursive lettering.

By 1919, when Candler sold out for $25 million, some 280,000,000 glasses and bottles of Coke were sold in July, alone. There were 70,000 soda foundtains and 1,500 bottlers dispensing Coke. That year, cola-crazed Americans guzzled almost 20 million gallons of Coca-Cola.

MORE ETHNICS IN THE "SOFT DRINK HALL OF FAME"

HIRES ROOT BEER   "Soothing to the nerves, vitalizing to the blood, refreshing to the brain, beneficial in every way. . . . Hires

Root beer gives the children strength to resist the enervating effects of the heat," or so claimed the *Ladies Home Journal* in 1897.

The man who gave the soft drink his name was Charles Elmer Hires (1851–1937), a New Jersey farmboy-turned-druggist of English, German and Welsh ancestry.

Charles first began experimenting with soft drink formulas in 1875 when the proprietor of a boardinghouse served him a drink made from sassafras bark and herbs. Hires modified the formula, using sarsaparilla root and other ingredients, and began selling his product from a booth at the Centennial Exposition held in Philadelphia in 1876.

Hires eventually sold his root beer to drugstore soda fountains, and even packaged a bag of dried roots, bark and herbs so customers could "brew" their own at home.

SCHWEPPES The man responsible for making Schweppes tonic and seltzer a big seller in the United States was none other than the "living trademark" who appeared in his own television commercials, Commander Edward Whitehead (1908–1978).

As chairman of Schweppes, the Commander (who earned his title in the Royal Navy during World War II) instituted a new policy whereby, instead of exporting the tonic already bottled, he sold the "essence" to licensed bottlers in America who added it to treated water, thus reducing the cost 75% and increasing sales.

He was so successful that Queen Elizabeth awarded Whitehead the Order of the British Empire in 1961 for putting some "Schweppervescence" into the British export market.

CANADA DRY GINGER ALE First manufactured in Toronto by J. J. McLaughlin, Canada Dry brand was the first pale ginger ale on the market in 1904. McLaughlin introduced his product as the "Champagne of Ginger Ales." His sales were so brisk in the United States that he opened a plant in New York in 1921. With talk of Prohibition in the air, this non-alcoholic champagne soon proved a natural.

MALTED MILK MAN Although the fast-food chains of America have tried to replace the old-fashioned malted milk with a quasi-dairy product they hedgingly call a "thick shake," there is no way they can compete with the rich, thick goodness of a malted that has been whirred to perfection in a green metal Mixmaster. Frozen whey-enhanced shakes just can't measure up to the icy goodness of whole milk, fresh ice cream, fountain syrup and that magic ingredient, malted milk powder—served from a stainless steel container that has started to "perspire" due to the temperature differential.

The man who made all these luscious childhood treats possible was an English immigrant, William Horlick (1846–1936), the inventor of malted milk powder.

Born in Ruardean in Gloucestershire, Horlick emigrated to the United States in 1860. He started a food manufacturing firm in 1873 with his brother James; their first successful food product was J&W Horlick's New Food for Infants, Dyspeptics and Invalids, which was made from wheat flour and malted barley.

In 1887, the same year in which he became a naturalized citizen, Horlick registered the trademark "malted milk" for his new product, an extract of malted grain and powdered cow's milk, which was said to "keep indefinitely in any climate, agree with the most delicate stomach." and could be "prepared for use by dissolving in water only."

Horlick attained fame in another way. When Admiral Byrd began his expedition to the South Pole he took along some of Horlick's malted milk tablets, and was so impressed with the product he named an Antarctic island after the manufacturer.

THE SOFT DRINK NAMED FOR A SONG Ever wonder how Yoo-hoo, the chocolate-flavored beverage, got its name? The brand name is said to have been inspired by the "Indian Love Call," a song popularized by Nelson Eddy and Jeanette MacDonald in the 1930s.

BEER IN AMERICA

Throughout the ages beer has always held a special place in the history of man. In Egypt it was used as libation to the gods; in Babylonia, beer was part of a man's daily wages; and in the British Isles, beer was singled out as one of the first commodities subjected to special taxation.

Even the Pilgrims liked a good brew now and then. In fact, according to a diary entry dated December 19, 1620, beer was the real reason that the Pilgrims stopped in Massachusetts instead of continuing on down to their original destination, Virginia:

". . . we could not now take time for further search or consideration, our victuals being much spent — especially our beer . . ."

The first commercial brewery in America was built by the Dutch in 1612. The industry proliferated as the early American colonists took to brewing corn beer, pumpkin beer, potato beer, and even a beer made from persimmons. Yet despite this wild variety, much of the beer consumed in the early days of our nation was imported from England.

Up until the 1840s American beer was mainly of the English type — stronger, darker and fuller-bodied than the beer we drink today. But, thanks to the large influx of German immigrants who came to our shores in the mid-nineteenth century, *lager* became the beer of choice in the United States.

The German-American Brewers

The Germans not only gave their names and skills to the art of brewing in America, they also gave us steins, beer gardens, beer halls, beer cellars and pretzels to munch with our brew. They made Milwaukee, Saint Louis and Cincinnati famous as "brewing towns," and today most of the major breweries in the United States can trace their origins to German founders. Some of the most famous German-Americans who started nationally known brands include: Frederick Miller, Jacob Best, Adolph Coors, Jacob Ruppert, Leopold Schmidt, August Krug, Eberhard Anheuser and Adolphus Busch.

MILLER — "THE CHAMPAGNE OF BOTTLED BEER" When Frederick Miller (?–1888) arrived in America in the mid-nineteenth century, all he brought with him was a small amount of money and his experience as a brewmaster at Hohenzollern Castle in Sigmaringen, Germany. He purchased a small, wooden brewery near Milwaukee's city limits in 1855 and called it "Frederick Miller's Plank Road Brewery" in honor of the street-paving method in his part of town.

That first year of operation, Frederick Miller produced only 300 barrels of beer,

but by the time of his demise in 1888 production has increased to 80,000 barrels annually.

One of the best features of Miller's brewery was the network of storage caves used to cool beer during certain stages of production. Some caves were as deep as 62 feet underground, with walls 44 inches thick. Beer was manufactured here until 1906, and today the caves serve as a museum for brewery exhibits and a starting point for tours of the Miller plant.

No longer a family-owned business, Miller Brewing Company was wholly acquired by Philip Morris, Inc., in 1970 after the purchase of 47% of the company's stock from the DeRance Foundation for $97 million. Philip Morris had previously acquired 53% of the stock from W. R. Grace and Co. in 1969 for $130 million.

PABST BREWING COMPANY In 1844, Jacob Best, a German immigrant, started a brewing company in Milwaukee with the help of his four sons. From 1844 to 1853 the five Bests (Jacob, Jacob, Jr., Charles, Phillip and Lorenz) ran the brewery as a family affair. But when Papa Jacob retired in 1853, three of his sons sold their shares in the brewery business, leaving Phillip in full control.

Captain Frederick Pabst (?–1904), who gained control of the brewery by marrying Phillip Best's daughter, turned what was soon renamed Pabst into the largest brewery in the United States by 1895, with annual sales of almost one million barrels of beer. Pabst revolutionized the brewery industry by introducing regional rather than local distribution channels.

Having survived the Prohibition era by manufacturing soft drinks, malted milk and alcohol-free beer, Pabst continued to grow after the repeal of the 18th Amendment. Between 1960 and 1973, production of Pabst beer jumped from 1.9 million to 13.1 million barrels.

SCHLITZ — "THE BEER THAT MADE MILWAUKEE FAMOUS" Despite its name, the Jos. Schlitz Brewing Company was founded in 1849 by August Krug, an immigrant from Austria. With his wife, Anna, August ran a small restaurant in Milwaukee where he brewed his own beer to serve with his wife's knockwurst and sauerbraten.

The first year, the Krugs sold 150 barrels

of beer. The next year, production jumped to 250 barrels, which so encouraged August that he contacted his father in Bavaria and urged him to finance his brewery in America. With $800 in gold borrowed from his father, Krug was able to begin large-scale production. After Krug died, his assistant, Joseph Schlitz, married his widow. Schlitz changed the name of the brewing company, to his own, in 1874.

The proverbial "big break" for Schlitz beer came after the 1871 Chicago fire. Since the city was low on water, Schlitz volunteered to ship barrels of beer into Chicago for thirsty survivors to drink. The beer caught on in a big way and from then on has continued to make Milwaukee famous.

BUDWEISER – "THE KING OF BEERS" In 1865, Adolphus Busch (1839–1913), an immigrant from Bavaria, joined his father-in-law, Eberhard Anheuser (1805–1880) in the brewery business he had started in St. Louis in 1852. The enterprise was a success, but Busch had a bigger dream—to create a national brand of beer.

Because beer spoiled quickly and could not be kept for long periods of time without losing its flavor, national brands of beer were unheard of prior to the invention of artificial refrigeration and pasteurization. To fulfill his dream, Busch created a network of railside ice houses to cool carloads of beer being shipped long distances, and in 1877 he launched the industry's first fleet of refrigerated freight cars. His invention not only enabled him to sell Budweiser in surrounding states, but it paved the way for the cross-country shipment of perishable foods. In 1879 the Bavarian Brewery changed its name to Anheuser-Busch. Thanks to Busch's dream, Budweiser's annual sales grew from 105,234 barrels in 1879, to better than one million barrels by 1901.

MORE EXPENSIVE IN THE EAST Orphaned at the age of 15, Adolph Coors stowed away on a ship bound for America from Germany when he was 21 and arrived in Baltimore in 1868. Coors settled in Denver in 1872 and began bottling beer and wines. This led in 1873 to the establishment of a brewery in Golden, Colorado, with a partner whom he bought out in 1880.

While many American brewers, like Anheuser-Busch, were eager to increase their sales territory and market national brands in the late nineteenth century, Coors of Golden, Colorado, was content to limit its sales to 11 states: Arizona, California, Colorado, Idaho, Kansas, Nevada, New Mexico, Oklahoma, Texas, Utah and Wyoming. Unlike many other American beers, Coors is not pasteurized after packaging. Although much care is taken to eliminate "weed" microorganisms from the final product, Coors was not willing to risk a flavor change which might result from the rigors of long-distance shipping. Until regional Coors breweries were built, the folks back East were paying almost twice as much for a six-pack as their Western friends.

Beer Drinker's Dictionary:

Ale is a "top fermented" beverage, paler in color and somewhat heavier than beer. Originally, ale was made only from malt, yeast and water, but during the seventeenth century brewers added barley to the recipe, making the formula identical to that of beer. In the 1800s the Germans introduced a new strain of yeast capable of sinking to the bottom of the vat once the fermentation process was completed, and once again ale and beer became two separate brews. "Bottom fermentation" (where the yeast sinks) was used exclusively for beer, and "top fermentation" was reserved for ale.

Porter and *stout* are darker, sweeter variations of ale enjoyed in the British Isles. Their different taste results from the use of dark malt in the brewing process.

Beer The word *beer* comes from the Latin *bibere*, to drink. The Germans call it *bier*, the French *biere*, the Japanese *biru*, but in Spanish it's *cerveza*, which philologists claim is derived from combining the name of the goddess of grain, *Ceres*, with *vis*, meaning *vigor*.

Lager beer is made by aging bottom-fermented beer. Originally mocked as a "woman's drink" because of its pale color, light body and weaker alcoholic content, lager is the major seller in the United States today. Several months of aging are usually necessary to mellow the beer and clear it of any sediments.

Prior to the advent of artificial refrigeration, beer spoiled quickly during the hot summer months and could only be manufactured during the winter, spring and fall. Lager, which was discovered by monks during the seventeenth century, spoiled less quickly during warm weather because it was aged and cleared of sediments. The German immigrants who came to America seeking political freedom during the 1840s and 1850s brought with them their skills for brewing lager, which soon dominated the market.

Pilsner beer The original Pilsner comes from the town of Pilsen in Czechoslovakia, whose water gives the brew its clean, light body. In honor of this great beer, brewers all over the world have adopted the term Pilsner to indicate their smoothest, lightest beer.

Bock beer was first brewed about 1200 in Einbeck, Germany. The name was gradually corrupted to *ein bock,* which means "a goat," hence the trademark which appears in some bock beer ads. Also known as "double beer" because its alcoholic content can be twice as strong as that of lager, bock beer is also darker and sweeter. In Germany, it is made in December and January for spring consumption, but in the United States bock beer is a very heavy brew made from the collected sediments of the fermentation vats when they were cleaned out in the spring. American bock is usually ready for consumption in the fall.

PER CAPITA* CONSUMPTION OF MALT BEVERAGES
(in gallons)

Five States with Highest Consumption		Five States with Lowest Consumption	
1 Nevada	58.1	1 Arkansas	23.5
2 New Hampshire	52.6	2 Alabama	24.7
3 Wyoming	52.3	3 Georgia	27.4
4 Montana	50.3	4 North Carolina	27.4
5 Wisconsin	50.1	5 Connecticut	27.8

*21 years and over; 1976 data compiled by United States Brewers Association, Inc.

TOASTS AROUND THE WORLD

In 1639 the founding fathers of Massachusetts declared "toasting" an illegal act. They considered it a "useless ceremony" that only encouraged the abominable practice of drinking. Despite their disapproval, they found it a difficult law to enforce, and it was stricken from the books in 1645. Today we have toasts in English and other languages, all designed to bring health, luck or cheers to the participants.

American	Bottoms up! Here's looking at you! Here's mud in your eye!
British	Cheers
Swedish	Skøl
Hungarian	Egeszsegere (eggesheeggera)
Russian	Za vashe zdorovie (to your health)
Spanish	Salud
French	Santé (a votre santé) (to your health)
Japanese	Campai
Chinese	Kan Pei (dry your glass)
Yiddish	L'Chaim
German	Prosit
Italian	Cin-cin (Chin-chin)
Greek	Yassou
Irish	May the wind always be at your back

BOCK BIER

Bock beer poster from the late 1870s. (Courtesy: Museum of the City of New York)

Irish   Slainte (to your health)
Lithuanian   Sveika Sviekata
Polish   Na Zdrowie (to your very
             good health)
Romanian   Noroc

WHAT'S IN A NAME?

Every country in the world has its own special wines, brews and liqueurs. Using local plants, shrubs and trees, people have been able to produce vast numbers of tasty alcoholic beverages to suit all occasions.

In the Netherlands, the Dutch have been producing Kümmel since the end of the sixteenth century, flavoring it with caraway seeds and cumin; Yugoslavs make Slivovitz from plums; the Germans and Swiss use cheries for Kirsch; and the Finns use the orange-red fruit of the bramble bush, *Rubus chamaemorus,* commonly known as "cloudberries," to make a liqueur known as Suomurrain or Lakka.

Italians use artichoke leaves for Cynar, gentian root for Campari, and the flowering elder bush for Sambuca Romano. In Jamaica, Tia Maria is made from distilled sugar cane juice and Blue Mountain coffee, while in Mexico the coffee-flavored liqueur is known as Kahlua. Americans even managed to invent some liqueurs, such as Forbidden Fruit, made from grapefruit or shaddock; Rock and Rye, fruit-flavored whiskey sweetened with rock candy; and Southern Comfort, a peach- and citrus-flavored whiskey from St. Louis.

An Ingredient Guide to Ethnic Liqueurs

Since the names of many liqueurs don't give you a clue about their ingredients, let's take a peek under the cap at exactly what goes inside a bottle of ethnic liqueur:

Liqueur: Akvavit
Native Land: Scandinavia

Akvavit, or aquavit, "water of life," has been the national drink of Denmark for over 500 years. Made from grain, potato mash and caraway seeds, which give it its unusual flavor, Akvavit tastes best when it is served well chilled.

Liqueur: Amaretto di Saronno
Native Land: Italy

Named for a small town near Milan, Amaretto is made from apricot pits, although its flavor screams "almonds." Legend claims that a poor, young, beautiful widow (aren't they always beautiful in legends) created the liqueur as a gift for the artist Bernadino Luini in 1525. In return for her favor, Luini immortalized her beautiful face in a fresco that graces the Sanctuary of Santa Maria delle Grazie in Saronno.

Liqueur: Arak
Native Land: Middle East

Arak is a generic name that refers to different spirits made in various parts of the world. Although made from many different substances, arak has a distinct anise or licorice taste. In Syria, arak is distilled from grapes; in Iraq and Egypt, dates are used; and in Turkey, potatoes, plums, molasses or wine may be used, depending upon availability.

Liqueur: Benedictine
Native Land: France

Named after the Benedictine monks, who knew how to keep their spirits up behind those isolated monastery walls, Benedictine was first made at Fecamp, France, in 1510. The formula was devised by Don Bernardo Vincelli, who dedicated his beverage to the greater glory of God. (*Ad majorem dei gloriam*) and even today each bottle bears the letters Dom, an abbreviation for *Deo optimo maximo* ("for the most good and great God").

Although it is no longer restricted to religious consumption (secular production of Benedictine began in 1863), the formula still remains a secret. It is known to contain almost thirty herbs and spices, including: hyssop, myrrh, coriander, pine cones, saffron, nutmeg and maidenhair fern.

Liqueur: Chartreuse
Native Land: France

Made from a secret formula developed at a Carthusian monastery near Grenoble in 1607, Chartreuse comes in two colors — yellow and green. The yellow version contains 187 different herbs and spices, while the green version includes more than 250 exotic ingredients such as palm leaves, peppermint, orange peel and angelica root.

Liqueur: Cognac
Native Land: France

Only brandy that had been made from

grapes grown in the Charente district of France and aged in Limousin oak casks can legally be called "cognac." Just as "champagne" does, the term "cognac" describes an alcoholic beverage made from specific grapes, grown in a specific region of France and aged in a specific manner. Even at that, there are seven different grades of cognac — each noting the location of the grapevine from which the grapes were picked. Those grown in the open fields are more highly valued than those grown near the woods. What makes these grapes so special? It is believed that the high lime content of the soil in Charente is responsible for the highly desirable qualities of the grapes grown in that district.

Liqueur:　　　Galliano
Native Land:　Italy

Made from 80 different herbs and floral essences, Galliano was created at the end of the nineteenth century by Arturo Vaccari of Livorno. Vaccari named this sweet liqueur Galliano in honor of an Italian hero of the Ethiopian war, Major Giuseppe Galliano.

Although Galliano was first imported into the United States in 1925 it did not become popular with the general public until the 1960s, when the Harvey Wallbanger Cocktail (1 part Galliano, 2 parts vodka and 8 parts orange juice) was introduced. Prior to that time, sales had been restricted to the Italian-American community, but Harvey's popularity managed to push annual sales close to the 4-million-bottle mark by 1973.

Liquor:　　　Gin
Native Land:　Holland

First manufactured for medicinal purposes, by a Dutch chemist, Professor Sylvius, gin was originally known as *jenever,* in honor of the juniper berries used to season Sylvius's brew. Jenever was first distributed to apothecary shops as a medicine, but it became so popular that the druggists began setting up their own backroom stills to meet consumer demand.

In the seventeenth century, William of Orange introduced *jenever* to the British, who are responsible for shortening the name to "gin." Today, the gins sold in Holland and in America differ drastically in taste, so much so that Holland gin cannot be used to mix standard drinks. Unlike scotch whiskey, gin does not have to be aged. It's ready to drink the instant it comes down the

condenser tube — hence its popularity with bathtub bootleggers during the prohibition years.

Liqueur:　　　Maraschino
Native Land:　Italy

Made from bitter black Marasca cherries which grow in Dalmatia, on the banks of the Adriatic sea, the word "Maraschino" is derived from the Italian *amarasca,* which means "bitter." The fruit essence is so concentrated in Maraschino liqueur that it takes between 10 and 13 pounds of cherries to make a single quart of this cherry-flavored beverage.

Liqueur:　　　Metaxa
Native Land:　Greece

Metaxa, first produced in 1888, is made from a grape brandy base. Three grades of Metaxa — are sold in the United States. — 5 star, 7 star, and the most expensive, grande fine. This potent brandy represents almost 90% of all the alcoholic exports from Greece to the United States, with the remaining 10% divided between ouzo (an anise-flavored liqueur) and retsina wines.

Liqueur:　　　Millefiori Cucchi; Fior D'Alpi
Native Land:　Italy (Alpine region)

Both of these liqueurs are fairly sweet herbal concoctions with a sugar content approaching 40%. Both are made from various blends of Alpine flowers and herbs and each bottle comes complete with a small twig inside that has been encrusted with sugar crystals. To ensure formation of the sugar crystals on the twig, Fior D'Alpi (Flower of the Alps) must be bottled while warm. Otherwise, as the super-saturated liqueur cools, the sugar precipitates out into the bottom of the mixing vat.

Liqueur:　　　Nocino
Native Land:　Italy

Made in the province of Modena, Nocino is a nut-flavored liqueur made from the shells and meats of green walnuts. The nuts must be steeped in alcohol for two years and then aged in a brown oak cask for another year prior to being distilled and bottled.

Liqueur:　　　Rum
Native Land　　Caribbean Islands

Made from crushed, mangled sugar cane, rum was first distilled in Barbados about 1640. Today, it is one of the most popular liqueurs in America. In 1978, more than

6,200,000 cases of rum were sold in the United States. Most of it was used for such exotic drinks as Mai Tais, Piña Coladas, and Zombies.

Liqueur: Strega
Native Land: Italy

Legend claims that this alcoholic beverage was first brewed by beautiful young maidens in Benevento who disguised themselves as "strega" (witches). Made from over 70 different herbs and barks, romantics claim that two people who drink Strega together will be united forever in love. Some of the herbs and spices in Strega include: angelica seeds, calamus, cinnamon, myrrh, cloves, aloe, vanilla, nutmeg, saffron and sugar. All are mixed together in a brandy base.

Liqueur: Tequila
Native Land: Mexico

Made from the juice of the maguey, or pulque agave plant, tequila is the most popular distilled liqueur sold in Mexico. The agave plant flourishes in the rich, volcanic soil of Tequila, Mexico, where the fermented beverage, called *pulque* by the natives, was first produced.

Its rather strong taste once limited tequila to "he-men" and "macho drinkers" who quaffed their jiggers of tequila with a lick of salt and a piece of lemon. But today, such flavorful concoctions as the Tequila Sunrise and the Marguerita have boosted tequila's popularity in the United States and made it the second most popular liqueur in America with those under 35.

SOUTH AMERICA'S CONTRIBUTION TO THE AMERICAN WAY OF DRINKING

BITTERS   Originally made at Angostura, Venezuela (now Ciudad Bolivar), bitters were invented by a French physician in 1824.

First concocted as a tonic for Simon Bolivar's army, the only earthly use for this bitter-tasting extract of roots, herbs and spices is to spice up such cocktail-hour favorites as the Manhattan (a cocktail that combines bitters, sweet vermouth and whiskey; it got its name from the Manhattan Club in New York City, where it was first mixed in the 1870s) and the Old Fashioned (sugar, bitters, whiskey and lemon peel).

Trinidad is the only country where bitters are manufactured today.

BRAND NAMES IN THE DRINKING HALL OF FAME

OLD CROW This American sour mash Bourbon is named after a Scottish physician, Dr. James C. Crow (c. 1800–1859), who emigrated to Kentucky in 1822 and introduced the "sour mash" method of fermentation to that state.

Sour mash Bourbon is made by "slopping back"—a rather unappetizing term for a process that involves scalding grain and cornmeal with leftover slop from the still.

I. W. HARPER   Mr. Harper was one of liquor merchant Isaac W. Bernheim's best salesmen. Customers seemed to like him almost as much as the liquor he sold, and kept asking Harper to come back with his special stock. Bernheim (1829–?), who was no fool, decided to bottle his Bourbon with Harper's name instead of his own, as vanity would have dictated. But Bernheim's name did not disappear entirely. There is a Bernheim Lane in Shively, Kentucky, and a forest in Bullitt County named in his honor.

SEAGRAM   Seagram's became a famous brand name during Prohibition when the company did a lively mail order business from its Canadian headquarters.

Today, the Chairman and Chief Executive Officer of Seagram's is Edgar Bronfman (1929–   ), a naturalized citizen who emigrated to the United States at the age of 26, leaving behind the Canadian home where his Jewish grandparents from Bessarabia had settled.

SMIRNOFF   The Smirnoff family first began distilling vodka in 1818 in their native

Russia. By 1912, with sales in excess of one million bottles a day, Smirnoff's was the only vodka consumed by the Czar.

When the Russian Revolution came, those members of the Smirnoff family who were not executed fled the nation, and one, Vladimir Smirnoff, sought refuge in Paris, taking only his name and the formula for vodka with him..

A Ukrainian, Rudolph P. Kunett, was responsible for bringing Smirnoff vodka to the United States, where "little water" (*vodka*) did not get off to an auspicious start. Unable to break the popularity of whiskey, Kunett sold his rights to John G. Martin, president of Heublein and the great-grandson of a Bavarian immigrant.

In 1939 sales were a meager 6,000 cases a year, but by the time Heublein got through blitzkrieging the public with advertisements for Moscow Mules, Bloody Marys and Screwdrivers, vodka's reputation was solidly established as an "all-American" drink.

1969 vodka sales reached 2 million cases per year. By 1973 Smirnoff alone was selling 4.5 million cases nationally, and that was only one-third of the vodka sold in the United States. By the late 1970s vodka had become the number-one-selling liquor in the United States, among the under-30 crowd and the 30-to-50-year-old crowd as well.

OLD FORESTER This Kentucky bourbon was first manufactured by Brown-Forman Distillers in 1870. According to one legend founder George Garvin Brown named his Bourbon after the dashing Confederate cavalryman, General Nathan Bedford Forrest (the original spelling of the brew was *Old Forrester*). As it happened, General Forrest went on to attain fame as the first Imperial Wizard of the Ku Klux Klan.

Another legend claims that Old Forester was named after the Catholic "Order of Foresters," but since Brown was a Presbyterian of Scottish and Irish descent and had an ancestor who was beheaded for refusing to follow the Pope, it seems unlikely. Yet another legend suggests that the whiskey was first produced as a private blend for Dr. William Forrester, a prominent Louisville physician. No one knows the truth.

GALLO WINE Born to Italian immigrant parents, Ernest (1909–   ) and Julio (1919–   ) Gallo began their winery in 1933, during the depths of the Depression. Not only did they start their business at a treacherous financial time: there were over 700 American winemakers to compete with in the early 1930s. Still, by making good wine (Julio's job) and pinching pennies (Ernest's job), the brothers were able to turn a handsome profit of $30,000 that first year.

Today Gallo is one of the world's largest wineries, producing almost 30% of all wine sold in this country, clearly dominating the $3 billion domestic wine industry.

One of Gallo's first strokes of marketing genius came in the late 1950s. Like every other major wine distributor in America, the Gallos were aware that many Black Americans bought potent white port wine (with an alcoholic content of 40 proof) and mixed it with lemon juice to cut the harsh taste. Ernest asked Julio and his winemakers to create a new "combination" wine, which they eventually called Thunderbird. By selling this new wine for a few cents less than the combined price of white port and lemon juice, they captured the market, selling 2.5 million cases of Thunderbird the first year.

What a Difference Carbonation Makes The Gallo brothers were also the first on the scene with "pop" wines. In 1969, Julio added carbonation to an old, slow seller, Boone's Farm Apple Wine, which soon was selling to the tune of 720,000 cases per month in 1971. Quite a drastic change for a wine that barely sold 30,000 cases a year before the addition of a little CO_2.

Wine snobs have accused the Gallos of manufacturing wine that lacks "character." Critics contend that the stainless steel tanks used by the Gallos to eliminate the bacteria present in wooden aging vats make each year's wine taste exactly like last year's. Ernest, however, believes that stainless steel vats produce better wine, because it is "more sanitary." No matter what the critics think, the public seems to agree with Ernest — Americans put away almost 100 million gallons of his wine each year.

ALMADEN Etienne Thee, an immigrant from Bordeaux who came to California in 1847 to work the gold mines, established the first Almaden vineyard in 1852. Five years later Thee and his partner,

Charles le France, began planting vine cuttings imported from Europe. Although the experiment was a success, the first grapes harvested from European stock never made it into a wine bottle. Because of a shortage of table grapes that year, they were sold for immediate consumption.

Today, the Almaden winery cultivates some 62 different varieties of grapes on over 6,700 acres of California land. Al-maden's four wineries have a combined aging capacity of more than 26.5 million gallons, making it one of America's largest wine producers.The most famous Almaden plant is located in Cienega, California. It stands directly atop the San Andreas fault, and seismologists from all over the world come to the Cienega winery to view the cleft in its floor, kept open by persistent earth tremors.

What's the difference between California and New York State wines?

California wine comes from European varieties of grapes which have been grafted onto native American rootstocks. New York State wines are made from grapes which have been cultivated and developed from wild varieties of native American grapes — hence the flavor of the two types of wine is quite distinct.

AMERICA'S FIRST PREMIXED COCKTAIL Today there are vending machines and display racks in hotel lobbies where desperate drinkers can purchase ready-mixed Screwdrivers, Bloody Marys and Manhattan cocktails. But the premixed bottled cocktail has been around longer than one might think.

Gilbert and Louis Heublein, Bavarian immigrants who arrived in America in 1856, introduced the first bottled cocktail in 1892. They had prepared a gallon of Manhattans and a gallon of Martinis to be served at a governor's picnic, but when rain cancelled the festivities, the Heubleins found themselves stuck with two gallons of mixed cocktails. That's when they decided to sell them as a convenience item at their hotel in Hartford, Connecticut. However, it wasn't until the era of cheap "disposable containers" that portable drinks became popular in the United States.

"JAPAN" AND SODA, MUD IN YOUR EYE . . . ? Somehow those lyrics just don't sound right — but it remains a fact that the highest-priced whiskey sold in the United States in 1977 came from the Far East.

Suntory, the largest distilling company in Japan, marketed one thousand cases of their Suntory Signature 25-year-old whiskey, at almost $60 a quart.

9 MIND AND BODY

MEDICINE MEN

In the 1880s the average life expectancy for Americans was somewhere between 40 and 45 years. In 1980, thanks to the advances of medical science, the average life expectancy in America had risen to almost 70 years.

The following ethnic Americans contributed to our extra three decades of life expectancy by advancing our knowledge of physical and mental health. Some pioneered in the fields of blood transfusion and nutrition, while others contributed their know-how to combating diseases such as polio, diabetes and cancer.

TRANSACTIONAL ANALYSIS Dr. Eric Lennard Bernstein (1910–1970), better known as Dr. Eric Berne, dropped his allegiance to Freudianism and developed TA in the 1960s – a psychological system of his own, based on the notion that every person has three ego states within him – child, adult and parent. The most visible result of his labor was a popular-style book entitled *Games People Play*, published in 1964. Thanks to word-of-mouth promotion, it began to rack up some pretty impressive sales figures, and wound up on the New York *Times* best seller list for 111 weeks.

Some of the games people play include: Life Games ("See what you made me do"); Marital Games ("Frigid woman"; "If it weren't for you"); Consulting Room Games ("I'm only trying to help you"); and even Good Games ("They'll be glad they knew me" – a variation of "I'll show them").

A Canadian-born psychiatrist who settled in New York and later in Northern California, Berne wrote a number of other best-selling books, including *What Do You Say After You Say Hello* and *Beyond Games and Scripts*.

DAILY INJECTIONS Dr. Charles Herbert Best (1899–1978), a Canadian-American born in Maine, was one of the co-discoverers of insulin, which was first isolated in 1921. Best and his colleagues won a Nobel Prize in 1923 for their work in isolating insulin and demonstrating its beneficial effects in the treatment of diabetes. Best conducted his research at the University of Toronto, and thanks to his scientific genius some 30 million diabetics are able to lead normal lives today.

FIRST WOMAN DOCTOR Elizabeth Blackwell (1821–1910), an English immigrant from Counterslip, England, became the first American woman to graduate from medical school and become a physician.

Her family emigrated to America when Elizabeth was 11, but her father died a few years later, leaving the family destitute. This forced Elizabeth, her mother and her sisters to establish a school to support themselves. In 1845 Elizabeth became interested in medicine and started applying to every medical school in the East. She was duly rejected from each and every school, except one – Geneva College in New York. It turned out that she was accepted at this institution only because her application was assumed to be a spoof.

Ostracized by the townspeople, and often barred from classroom demonstrations "not fit for a woman," Elizabeth earned the respect of her fellow students and professors with her quiet dignity. She was graduated on January 23, 1849, only to realize that the battle had just begun. Blackwell was barred from city hospitals and ignored by her colleagues. In 1857, she founded her own hospital, the New York Infirmary for Women and Children, and hired two female doctors to assist her.

POKER-PLAYING PHARMACOLOGIST When Dr. Bernard Beryl Brodie (1909–), an English immigrant, received the prestigious Albert Lasker Award for basic medical research in 1967 it was said that: "Probably no man has contributed more to the rational use of drugs in the treatment of many diseases than has Dr. Brodie."

How did Dr. Brodie, who was expelled from high school for insubordination, manage to make it to graduate school for a Ph.D. in chemistry? The studying part was difficult, but the finances were easy: During his three-year enlistment with the Canadian Army he won $5,000 playing poker, which he used to "stake" his college education at McGill University in Montreal.

Brodie came to the United States in 1931 to study and conduct research at New York University. In 1950, he was appointed to a position at the National Institutes of Health in Bethesda, Maryland.

MARCH OF DIMES Although Eddie Cantor was a comedian, and not a doctor, he did manage to contribute to the field of medical research in America by coining the slogan "March of Dimes" in 1940.

Cantor was at the White House, discussing ways to raise a million dollars with President Franklin Roosevelt. The comedian, reasoning that people would be quicker to send in a dime rather than a dollar to fight polio, said, "You may lick infantile paralysis with this march of dimes."

Roosevelt knew a good campaign slogan when he heard one, and within 72 hours the White House was flooded with dimes in response to the President's plea for research funds to help fight polio.

CHARLES DREW (1904–1950) was the first Black man to have his portrait hung in the National Institutes of Health at Bethesda, Maryland. He received this recognition in 1976, in honor of his pioneering work in the field of blood preservation.

A graduate of McGill University in Montreal, Drew had the second highest academic rating in his undergraduate class. In 1933 he received his M.D. and a degree in surgery from that same institution.

During World War II, there was a great demand for a safe, pure blood supply for injured and wounded soldiers. Working with Dr. Scudder, Drew created an experimental blood bank in New York, but although the plasma remained fresh indefinitely, the red blood cells spoiled in about a week. That's when Drew realized that whole blood was not needed to treat patients. Red blood cells could be extracted from the plasma; the plasma would keep for months without spoiling; and there would be no worries about typing and cross-matching blood. For his contributions to the science of blood transfusion Dr. Drew was awarded the Spingarn Medal in 1944.

Although he was world-renowned for his scientific contributions, if Drew had wanted to donate a pint of his own blood in the 1940s the army would have refused his generous donation! When the Red Cross began its blood program, the armed forces dictated that only Caucasian blood would be accepted for members of the military. Drew called a conference and stated, "The blood of individual human beings may differ by groupings, but there is absolutely no scientific basis to indicate any difference according to race."

He subsequently resigned from the Red Cross to become medical director of Howard University's medical school.

I.V. M.D. Thanks to Dr. Stanley Dudrick's stubborn streak, thousands of patients' lives are saved every year—patients who would not have recovered from the effects of surgery or disease simply because they were not obtaining adequate nutrition.

In 1961, when Dr. Dudrick was an intern at the University of Texas Medical Center, he saw severe malnutrition take its toll on burn victims, premature infants and patients with severe kidney, liver and bowel diseases. Traditional I.V. (intravenous) solutions were not adequate to nurse these sick people back to health, so the Polish-American doctor decided to work on developing a new method of vein feeding. He calls it intravenous hyperalimentation, or I.V.H., and so far the results from his technique have been impressive.

There were a lot of problems to overcome: veins and blood cells can be damaged if nutrients exceed 5% concentration; more than three liters of fluid can impair heart and lung functions; and veins can collapse through continuous injections. However, by using a larger vein for his I.V.H. and adding diuretics to rid the body of excess fluid, Dr. Dudrick solved many of the problems and made his method safe to use.

WASHINGTON'S DENTIST An English-American, John Greenwood (1760–1819) was the dentist who pioneered the invention of the dental drill by adapting his mother's spinning wheel to make a "dental foot engine." Greenwood was also the dentist who made George Washington's teeth. Actually, he made several pairs of false choppers for our first president – some out of wood, and others out of hippo and elephant tusk. Dr. Greenwood also used live human molars, bought from indigent donors; he set these teeth into the jaws of his rich clients.

HOW MANY JEWISH DOCTORS ARE THERE?

There is an old joke about the stereotyped Jewish mother who laments to her friend Sophie that she has "some good news and some bad news." She goes on to say, "My son just told me that he's gay." "Well, what's the good news?" asks Sophie. "He's going with a doctor!"

Considering the high proportion of jokes about Jewish doctors, and about Jewish mothers who push their sons to become doctors and their daughters to marry them, you might be tempted to guess that at least 50% of all doctors in America are Jewish. Actually, Jewish doctors make up only 9% of the medical population; but since Jews comprise only 3% of the total population in America, they do have a high medical school graduation rate.

LIGGETT-REXALL This drugstore chain was founded by Louis Kroh Liggett (1875–1946), an American of Scottish and Dutch ancestry. The name "Rexall" was suggested by an office boy, as an acronym for *Rx* and *all* – meaning that all prescriptions could be filled there.

MAYO CLINIC Correctly known as the Mayo Foundation for Medical Education and Research, the Rochester, Minnesota, facility was founded in 1889 by the Mayos, two Missouri-born brothers of English ancestry. Patients from all over the world flock to the Mayo Clinic, which is actually several hospitals in one, and even has its own hotel for outpatients and visiting relatives.

BETTY FORD'S "CREATOR" When Betty Ford showed up sporting a new face to go with her brand-new life in 1978, the question asked most frequently of the former First Lady was "Who did it?"

The plastic surgeon who tightened her neck skin, removed her crow's feet and took away the puffiness from her eyes was an Iranian-born plastic surgeon, Dr. Mohammed Reza Mazaheri. But if you're in the market for a new face, please don't call Dr. Mazaheri. "Ever since Mrs. Ford gave out my name I have been swamped with phone calls. I do not want the business . . . if I had known what was going to happen – all these phone calls and letters and telegrams and requests for interviews – I would have thought twice. And maybe I would not have done her." (Quote from *Parade* magazine in Lloyd Shearer's *Intelligence Report*, Nov. 19, 1978)

PAP TEST When it is detected early, cancer of the cervix is 100% curable, so each year millions of American women have a health checkup which includes a Pap smear. Developed and named for Dr. George Papanicolaou (1883–1962), a Greek immigrant who taught clinical anatomy at the Cornell University Medical school for 47 years, "Pap" first began experimenting with the vaginal smear technique in 1923.

As a result of the widespread acceptance of his medical procedure, the death rate for cancer of the uterus in women between the ages of 35 and 44 was cut in half during the decade 1951–1961.

POLIO VACCINE A Jewish comedian helped raise the money for research, and a Jewish doctor was the first to give the world an effective vaccine to prevent poliomyelitis. Dr. Jonas E. Salk (1914–   ), the son of a New York City garment worker, developed the first polio vaccine in 1953, and by 1955 school-age children all over America were receiving their first series of "shots."

Salk's vaccine featured attenuated, or dead viruses, but the oral polio vaccine invented by Russian-born Dr. Albert Sabin (1906–   ) in 1961 contained the live virus germs, and could be taken orally instead of injected into the body.

DR. SCHOLL "Early to bed, early to rise, work like hell and advertise," was the credo by which this third-generation German-American lived. William Mathias Scholl (1882–1968) made his fortune easing tired, aching feet, and by 1976 the company he had started in Chicago in 1904 was racking up almost $200 million in annual sales of moleskins, corn plasters, bunion pads and exercise sandals and shoes.

Dr. Scholl had a "lasting" interest in shoes and leather goods, having first started his business career as a shoe salesman. But when he took a look at what Americans were doing to their feet, he decided to enter medical school and tackle the problem firsthand. His first orthopedic device was the Foot-Eazer, a leather arch support still sold today.

(Courtesy: Public Relations Board)

Scholl's total sales in 1904 were $815.65, but by 1907 he was grossing over $17,000. Today, Dr. Scholl's Foot Comfort Shops, or the company's self-service counters, can be found in virtually every community in the United States and in every major nation of the world, except China and the U.S.S.R.

Jack Scholl, nephew of the founder, and general manager of the company that bears his name, cites the reasons for Dr. Scholl's success: "The key to all this is salesmanship. The doctor may have been an inventor and a physician, but he was also a salesman who never quit pushing his product."

SQUIBB'S ETHER Before the advent of Demerol, nitrous oxide and sodium pentathol (truth serum), patients scheduled for surgery were given heavy doses of opium, alcohol or nicotine to make them delirious and insensitive to the pain of the operation. Unfortunately, emergency operations and amputations often had to be performed before the pain killers could take effect.

Ether was introduced to hospitals in 1846, but surgeons were not eager to administer the gas to their patients. The method of distilling was crude, and toxic impurities often contaminated the ether that was available. The world owes a vote of thanks to Dr. Edward Robinson Squibb (1819–1900) for devising the first safe, practical method for the continuous distillation of diethyl ether in 1852. Squibb's method eliminated the fire and explosion hazards associated with the manufacture of ether and also produced a consistently pure product. Assured of high quality control, surgeons began using ether more frequently, and up until the 1950s it was the anesthetic of choice in most operating theaters of America.

Although E. R. Squibb was descended from an Englishman, Nathaniel Squibb, who sailed to America with William Penn in 1675, the family's roots were originally Spanish. In Spain the name was spelled Esquivel; later, when family members migrated to France, it became Ezquib, and finally, Squibb, when the family reached England.

The Squibb pharmaceutical company was founded in 1858.

THE MAN WHO REARED 50 MILLION KIDS Dr. Spock's Baby and Child Care handbook has sold over 28 million copies since it was first published in 1946.

Translated into 26 languages, it provides a ready reference for those middle-of-the-night earaches, croupy coughs and other childhood emergencies.

Of Dutch ancestry, Benjamin Spock (who has been accused of a permissive attitude toward child rearing) was raised by an extremely strict mother. "Sex to her was a major area of sin. We were brought up with a horrible fear of sexual wrongdoing. If I glanced at a girl on the sidewalk as I sat beside my mother in the car, she would severely reprove me. I couldn't wait to get away from home and her oppressive rule."

Until Spock (1903–   ) came along, many mothers were like his own—strict and inflexible—especially about feeding schedules and cuddling. Many were fearful of "spoiling" children by loving them too much. Spock's teachings have led him to be blamed for everything from long hair to pot smoking and sexual permissiveness among teens, but as Spock says, "I never did preach instant gratification . . . I simply emphasized the emotional needs of children."

Sentenced to two years in prison in 1968 for conspiring to counsel draft evaders, Dr. Spock announced: "There's no point in raising children if they're going to be burned alive."

STILLMAN DIET   Dr. Irwin Maxwell Stillman (1895–1975), author of *The Doctor's Quick Weight Loss Diet* (Prentice-Hall, 1967) is best remembered for advocating large quantities of water combined with high-protein foods, and the avoidance of carbohydrates to attain rapid weight loss.

Over the years, the Jewish doctor from Brooklyn was attacked by colleagues who maintained that his diet was unbalanced and could cause harmful side effects. But Stillman, who went on to write five best-selling books on the same subject, contended that the ill effects of overweight were more harmful than any side effects that might result from his diet plan.

CHARLES R. WALGREEN once threw away the few pennies he had to his name so he could be "flat broke" and thus forced to find employment.

Born in 1873 in Galesburg, Illinois, of Swedish immigrant parents, Walgreen opened his first drugstore in 1901. One of his favorite techniques for impressing customers who telephoned their orders was to repeat their requests aloud so his delivery boy could fill the order and rush it to the customer's home before Walgreen let her off the telephone.

He made his own ice cream to attract customers to his soda fountain, and rather than close up shop in the winter months, he had his wife, Myrtle, brew up a batch of soup and make a few sandwiches—the start of the drugstore lunch counter.

By 1925 there were 65 Walgreens, a number that grew to 397 by 1929. Today there are over 630 Walgreens in 32 states plus Puerto Rico, filling 30 million prescriptions annually. In addition there are 1,860 affiliated agents who handle Walgreen products.

THE MEDICINE CABINET

Americans spend over $10 billion each year stocking up on ethical drugs. We buy vaccines to combat disease, and prescription drugs and over-the-counter remedies to relieve headaches, indigestion, tension, constipation and the scourge of modern man— bad breath.

The Man Who Invented Halitosis   Jordan Wheat Lambert invented Listerine in 1880, but it was his son, Gerald Barnes Lambert (1887–1967), who made Listerine a household word by inventing "halitosis."

Listerine was originally designed as a mild antiseptic for general use, but when Gerald Lambert began searching for a new way to promote his family's product he zeroed in on the touchy subject of "bad breath" and cashed in on our nation's social paranoia. Descended from Welsh, French, Dutch and English ancestors, Lambert began instilling social terror in the minds and hearts of millions of Americans in 1921 with his brilliant ads that warned lovers about the dangers of "halitosis"—the Latin word for unpleasant breath.

Bad breath proved so popular that, by 1923, Lambert was able to sell his share of the business for $25 million. Through careful investments in stocks and government bonds, he survived the Depression and continued to devote his energies to the one true love of his life—sailing.

Taking the Worry Out of Being Close   Ironically, the company that first "took

Listerine ad, circa 1920. (Courtesy: Warner-Lambert)

the worry out of being close" was founded by Gideon Daniel Searle, a descendant of John Searle, an Englishman who sailed to America with the Puritans in 1637.

Enovid was the first birth control pill approved for use in the United States. This orally active steroid, manufactured by G. D. Searle and Company and approved by the FDA in May 1960, has been blamed and praised (depending upon your outlook) for starting the "sexual revolution" that raged through America during the early 1960s. With a supply of pills, which cost about $10 initially, women were freed from the fear of unwanted pregnancy for the first time in history by a compound that prevented conception virtually 100% of the time.

Good old American competition brought the price of "the Pill" tumbling down to about $2 a month in the 1970s as drug companies all over the country began marketing other brands of oral contraceptives, making the Pill one of the most frequently taken drugs in the American medicine cabinet.

A Chocolate By Kiss Ex-Lax is probably the only laxative advertised at the Boston Museum of Fine Arts, where the name figures prominently in a painting by Edward Hopper (1882–1967) entitled *Drugstore*. First offered for sale as "Bo-Bo," Ex-Lax was dreamed up as an acronym for "*Ex*cellent *Lax*ative" when it was discovered that another company owned rights to the name Bo-Bo.

The active ingredient in Ex-Lax is phenolphthalein, a chemical indicator whose laxative properties were first discovered by wine merchants in Hungary. These merchants used to add a small amount of phenolphthalein to their product for identification purposes, but they noticed that when they overindulged in "sampling" their wares, laxation resulted.

A Hungarian pharmacist, Max Kiss, emigrated to New York in 1905 and began mixing phenolphthalein with chocolate as a commercial laxative. Israel Matz (1869–1950), a Jewish drug wholesaler from Kalvarija, Lithuania, incorporated Ex-Lax in 1908 and served as corporate president for 42 years, until his death in 1950.

Laxatives are big business in America, where people rush about and are too busy to wait for nature to take its course. Each year Ex-Lax alone manufactures over 530 million doses of chocolate and unflavored tablets for sale in the United States, making laxatives an integral part of the American medicine cabinet.

"Flesh-Colored" Protection Before the Johnson brothers, descended from English stock, began manufacturing sterile surgical dressings in 1886, physicians commonly covered wounds and surgical incisions with cotton collected from textile mill floors.

No wonder there were so many hospitals with a postoperative mortality rate as high as 90%! The patient would survive the operation, only to die of a serious infection contracted afterward. Even after Lister formulated his theory of antisepsis in 1865, many surgeons found it impossible to believe that they were condemning their own patients to death by operating with their bare hands and using unsterile instruments.

By 1892 Johnson & Johnson had perfected the manufacture of a sterile bandage and in 1921 Band-Aid brand adhesive bandages were introduced. Over the years, Band-Aid bandages have become one of the most common items found in the medicine cabinet, but please, don't refer to all bandages as Band-Aids! Every day of the year,

Ex-Lax ad, circa 1933. (Courtesy: Ex-Lax, Inc.)

Johnson & Johnson fights to keep its trade name proprietary.

Just like Xerox, Jell-O and Kleenex, the trade name Band-Aid is often used to describe similar objects made by Curity and other companies. J&J does not want their trade name to become decapitalized the way some other products have been in the past. Cellophane, aspirin, linoleum and kerosene all started out as trade names and ended up in the dictionary.

Bandages once were advertised as "flesh colored," but manufacturers finally realized that there was more than one shade of "flesh" in America, and advertisements now stress the non-stick attributes of Band-Aids.

A Vitamin a Day Keeps the Doctor Away A Polish immigrant from Warsaw first discovered vitamins. Luckily, he didn't name his compound after himself, or we'd all be taking "multi-funks with iron" every morning.

Casimir Funk (1884–1967), who published his scientific findings in 1912, was the first to suggest that diseases such as scurvy, pellagra and rickets were the result of nutritional deficiencies of substances that he dubbed "vitamines." Funk coined the new word from *vita,* meaning life, and *amino,* for the nitrogen radical group he believed was a chemical component of all vitamines. Later, when it was discovered that not all vitamines contained amino groups, the "e" was dropped and vitamin emerged.

Casimir Funk emigrated to the United States in 1915 and became a naturalized citizen in 1920.

Peanut Butter and "Jelly" When Robert Augustus Chesebrough learned of the 1859 oil strike in Titusville, Pennsylvania, he was convinced it would put an end to his business of refining cannel oil into kerosene. Determined not to be unemployed at the tender age of 22, Chesebrough decided to visit the oilfields and investigate ways to use his refining know-how in the petroleum industry.

At the oil fields, he watched oilmen scraping the pumps to free them from a substance known as "rod wax." This was a terrible nuisance because it constantly fouled the pumps, but Chesebrough noticed that whenever the workers cut or burned their hands they would quickly apply some rod wax to soothe the pain and heal the wound.

Chesebrough began experimenting with a carton full of rod wax he brought back to his rooming house in Brooklyn, and after a few months he had perfected a method of extracting a concentrated residue in the form of a translucent jelly. Over the next few weeks, Chesebrough inflicted scores of sores on his body to test the healing powers of his new jelly. He gave it to ditchdiggers, construction workers and laborers to soothe their occupational cuts and scrapes.

Vaseline became a household word shortly thereafter, and in 1912 both the Army and the Red Cross began recommending petroleum jelly for the treatment of minor cuts and burns.

When an employee once questioned the fact that natives in India reputedly used Vaseline to "butter" their bread, Robert Chesebrough roared: "Young man, our jelly is good to eat—I've eaten pounds of it myself." And, in fact, he had. Each day, Chesebrough consumed a spoonful of Vaseline, considering it a cure-all for the ills of mankind. Apparently it did him no harm, since he died in 1933 at the ripe old age of 96.

Go Gators, Go! Gatorade in the medicine cabinet? Why not? This citrus-flavored drink that kids love to guzzle was actually invented by a doctor as a means to restore some of the body fluids lost through excessive perspiration. Many pediatricians also prescribe Gatorade for their patients after childhood bouts with diarrhea, to help restore proper fluid balance to the body.

A nephrologist, Dr. James R. Cade, invented the new drink in 1965 for the University of Florida football team at Gainesville. It was so popular that he sold marketing rights to Stokely-Van Camp, who began selling Gatorade to kids and adults alike in supermarkets all over America.

Descended from Jack Cade, a ribald Irishman who led Cade's Rebellion and defeated King Henry VI's army at Kent, England, in 1450, Dr. Cade is currently devoting his research energy to finding a "cure" for schizophrenia. Experiments with dialysis, a bloodcleaning treatment used for patients with kidney failure, have been successful in controlling behavior of some patients by filtering out excess amounts of beta endorphine, a blood molecule. So far, over the past six years, 16 out of 25 patients have improved by following a rigid schedule of dialysis under Dr. Cade's supervision.

Although he didn't invent any other compounds for the medicine cabinet, Dr. Cade did invent a hydraulic football helmet and a protein supplement drink he calls Gator-Go.

Calm You Down Two of the best-selling tranquilizers in the United States, Valium and Librium, are manufactured by Hoffman-LaRoche. The New Jersey-based drug company was founded by Fritz Hoffmann, a descendant of Swiss immigrants from Basel who married Adele La Roche at the age of 28 and followed the Swiss custom of adding his wife's name to his own.

Ease the Pain One of the most popularly prescribed pain-killers is Darvon, manufactured by Eli Lilly and Company. The Lilly family originally hailed from Sweden, where the name was spelled "Lillja" in 1450. When they emigrated to France, the family changed its name to Lilly before the ancestors of Colonel Eli Lilly (1838–1898) emigrated to the United States via Holland and England in 1789.

Soothe the Stomach Formulated in Milan in 1880 by an Italian chemist, Achille Brioschi, this pleasant-tasting lemon-flavored powder dissolved in water is just the thing you need after overindulging in pizza, pasta or pesto. The Italian answer to Alka-Seltzer, Brioschi has always been a favorite for speedy relief in the Italian-American community. Now that it is being manufactured here, it is gaining in popularity with Americans of all ethnic backgrounds who suffer from the symptoms of overindulgence, known as the "agony of the feast."

FOLK MEDICINE AND CURES

Good for What Ails You? Admittedly, some old tried and true folk remedies are a bit strange, but others have been proven effective. For centuries, an old English cure for a person suffering from heart disease was to administer a brew made from the foxglove plant. Scientists were perplexed to observe that this remedy did seem to work. The mystery was dispelled by modern chemical analysis of the plant which showed that it contains *digitalis*—a drug widely used today to make the heart beat more regularly

Edward Jenner first thought of inoculating patients with cowpox virus to lessen the ill effects of a bout of smallpox, after hearing an "old wives' tale." According to local folk, milk maids and farmers who suffered from cowpox, a mild form of smallpox, became immune to the dreaded disease.

So when an old aunt from the "other side" gives you her surefire cure for warts, rheumatism, or the hiccups—remember, there may be a grain of truth hidden in the remedy. None of the following, however, is intended as medical advice:

Sure Cures:

♦ *Croup* The Irish cure a childhood case of the croup by making the child drink water that has been poured over arrowheads. The French of Louisiana don't believe in the "power of arrows"—they make their children wear amber necklaces to prevent the croup.

♦ *Headaches* In Sicily a surefire cure for a headache is a crown of lemon leaves worn around the head.

♦ *Whooping Cough* Black Americans once used tea made from white ants to prevent or cure a case of pertussis, commonly called whooping cough.

♦ *Consumption* In Poland, a sure way to cure consumption is to place the skin of a cat on your chest.

♦ *Infections and Inflammations* In Naples, Italy, the way to remove impurities from your bloodstream is with the *cupeti,* or glasses. A coin is wrapped in linen and tied with a string. The point of the cloth is dipped in oil, lit with a match and placed on the sick person's back. A cup or glass is placed over the flame to extinguish it, and as the flame burns out, moisture and "impurities" leave the body.

The Pennsylvania Dutch believe that an inflammation of the skin can be cured by rubbing cow dung on the affected area.

♦ *Rheumatism* The Pennsylvania Dutch cure rheumatism by wearing the eyetooth of a pig as an amulet, but in Holland, the

Dutch prefer to carry a stolen potato in their pockets to cure both rheumatism and sciatica.

♦ *Toothache* In Italy, the way to cure a stubborn toothache is to kiss a newborn infant before it is washed.

♦ *Warts* Everyone in Italy knows that warts are caused by washing your hands in potato water – but, how to get rid of them is another story! In Germany the only way to cure warts and ward off fevers for the coming year is by eating apples on Easter morning.

In India you have one chance each month to remove your warts. Look up at the new moon, remove dust from beneath your left foot, place it on the afflicted area and, magically, the wart will fade with the moon.

♦ *Hiccups* If you want to get rid of your hiccups, repeat the following Finnish "charm" without taking a second breath:

Nikko niineen	*Hiccough to the*
Toinen tuoheen	*heddle (of the loom)*
Kolmas koivun	*Second to the bark*
Neljäs neulaan	*Third to the birch*
Viides viittaan	*Fourth to the needle*
Kuudes kuuseen	*Fifth to the thicket*
Seitsemäs seipääseen	*Sixth to the spruce*
Kahdeksas kantoon	*Seventh to the pole*
Yhdeksäs yllää	*Eighth to the stump*
Kymenes kyllää	*Ninth up!*
	Tenth to the neighbor
	(villager).

(from Folklore in America. N.Y.: Doubleday, p. 104)

♦ *No Frostbite* Here's another Finnish charm used to prevent frozen fingers in the cold winter months:

Pakkanen puhurin poika,	Cold, son of the wind [lit. "puff"].
Aläkylmää kynsiäin'	Don't chill my fingertips
Alä käsiän' palele;	Don't freeze my hands;
Palele ves' pajuja	Freeze the water willows.
Kylmä koivun konkaleita	Chill the birch chunks

(*Ibid*, p. 105)

♦ *Black Buzzard Beliefs* According to folklore of Southern Blacks, wearing a buzzard feather behind your ear will prevent rheumatism; buzzard feathers tied around a baby's neck will ease teething pains; and buzzard grease is a surefire cure for smallpox.

♦ *Sign of Recovery* If the medicine intended for a sick person spills it is a sure sign in Japan that the person will recover from his illness.

♦ *Powerful Placentas* Jews once mixed milk with the ashes of an incinerated placenta to cure any "wasting" diseases of young children. If the ashes from the afterbirth were mixed with snapdragons and tied around the child's neck, he would be protected from evil witchcraft.

♦ *Chinese Demons and Dementia* The Chinese place bundles of Artemesia leaves by the bedside to drive away demons who stalk the night.

Never, never dig up the burrow of a fox – it will cause you to become demented.

MEDICAL MESSIAHS AND QUACKEROOS

There has always been a darker side to American medical history – the quacks from other countries who came here extolling their strange cures for cancer, gout and all the ills of mankind, as well as the "home-grown" variety of medical messiahs bent on giving everyone the "true message."

Think you're immune to the effects of the scientific fringe and its claims of amazing medical cures? If you've ever munched a Graham cracker, eaten Kellogg's cereal or downed a bowl of Post Grape Nuts in the morning – be advised that you were eating, not mere food, but foods invented as cure-alls for such diseases as alcoholism, malaria, consumption and even appendicitis.

The Man Who Went "Crackers" It's hard to believe that those sugar-laden, mass-produced wafers we call Graham crackers once started out as "health food," a vital component of Sylvester Graham's

(1794–1851) vegetarian diet for the cure of alcoholism.

Graham was a second-generation Connecticut Yankee of Scottish ancestry, whose seventy-two-year-old father died in 1796, leaving the two-year-old toddler to be raised at the mercy of various relatives. As a result, Sylvester grew up frail, uneducated and exploited. Always a sickly child, he had begun to study for the ministry in 1823 when tuberculosis threatened to strike him once again. That's when Graham took an interest in nutrition and began to study food and health. A convincing orator, he was soon touring the country and lecturing on chastity, temperance and good nutrition. He advocated putting the bran back in bread for more fiber, and eschewed meat because he believed it led to sexual excess. He likewise advised his audiences to avoid certain condiments (which caused insanity), and never, never to eat chicken pie (a sure cause of cholera).

In addition to Graham bread, which was made from unbolted, coarsely ground wheat (known as Graham flour, and which, according to Graham, should never be eaten before it was at least 12 hours old), Sylvester advocated hard mattresses, open bedroom windows, cold showers, daily exercise, fruits, vegetables and cheerfulness at meals.

By 1835 he had so incensed the local butchers and bakers in Massachusetts with incessant attacks on their products that a riot broke out at the Boston hotel where Graham was to speak.

His influence began to fade in the 1840s, and today the "Father of the public health movement in America" is best remembered for those non-health-food goodies, Graham crackers, that bear his name.

SNAP, CRACKLE, ELIJAH? Before breakfast cereals put Battle Creek, Michigan, on the map, the town was already gaining notoriety as the home of the Battle Creek Sanitarium, headed by Dr. John Harvey Kellogg, an 1874 graduate of Bellevue Medical College in New York. While Kellogg's medical degree was orthodox, his methods for treating patients were not. Depending upon the nature of the illness, patients were seated at various tables in the sanitarium dining room where they were fed only water, only vegetables, or only milk. Patients on milk-only diets were fed 26 glasses of milk each day – a half-pint every half hour. Other patients were immobilized with 20-pound sandbags placed on their abdomens to improve digestion. For these services, Kellogg received hefty sums and donations from America's wealthy industrialists. The most important "medical" discovery to take place in Battle Creek was the invention of the wheat flake, first concocted in 1884 by John and his brother Will K. Kellogg.

Unfortunately, John Kellogg didn't know a gold mine when he saw one, and his brother gained all commercial rights to the flake. Maybe it was because Will Keith Kellogg (1860–1951), of English ancestry, was the "seventh son of a seventh son" that he was able to see such a remarkable future for the humble cereal flake. Today, the company he started has annual sales in excess of $1.4 billion from cereals and other food products.

Other manufacturers saw great potential in the breakfast cereal business and in the years between 1902 and 1904 some 40 breakfast food companies sprang up in Battle Creek, all hoping to get a piece of the breakfast pie. One of the newcomers was Charles William Post (1854–1914), another American of English ancestry, who founded the Post Cereal Company.

Post came to Battle Creek seeking a cure for an undisclosed physical ailment at the "San," as Kellogg's Sanitarium was known to the cognoscenti. A wealthy man who had made his fortune in real estate and manufacturing, he was immediately put into a wheelchair by Dr. Kellogg, and soon found himself without the means to pay for additional treatments. When his wife could no longer earn enough money as a suspender seamstress to support her husband's medical expenses as an outpatient, Post begged Kellogg to keep him on as a patient, in exchange for his services for promoting Kellogg's new cereal coffee product. But Kellogg did not believe in "charity" – he refused to treat patients who could not pay their way.

Post determined to fight back. He kept telling himself "I am well" and eventually he got out of his wheelchair and began waging a full-time war with the Kelloggs. He built his own sanitarium in 1892; began marketing Postum Cereal Food Coffee in 1895, to compete with Kellogg's brand, and started peddling Postum from a pushcart in the streets of Battle Creek to win customers.

In 1898 he introduced the world to Grape Nuts, a breakfast cereal with a difference. According to Post's early advertisements, Grape Nuts was able to tighten loose teeth, feed the brain, and take care of appendicitis, consumption and malaria. Actually, Grape Nuts is nothing more than whole wheat and malted barley flours baked together in the oven for about 20 hours. Long baking converts the starch into dextrose, or grape sugar, partially predigesting the starch and giving the crunchy nuggets their name.

Post's greatest contribution to the breakfast table was the cornflake, which he processed in a similar fashion to Kellogg's wheat flakes, and humbly named Elijah's Manna.

MORE FOOD CURES Besides Kellogg, Post and Graham, there were other Americans who inundated the public with their views on eating and health.

Horace Fletcher (1849–1919), an English-American who was nicknamed the "great masticator," contributed "Fletcherizing" to the great food fads of the late nineteenth century.

A businessman who made his fortune importing silks and other merchandise from the Orient, Fletcher was refused a life insurance policy in 1895 because he was in ill health and at least 50 pounds overweight.

He tried various cures, but he attributed his "recovery" of both his health and his slim physique to the simple procedure of chewing his food thoroughly. Fletcher advised people everywhere to "eat wise and Fletcherize" every bite of food. Each mouthful should be chewed a minimum of 40 times, so that swallowing was not necessary—the food seemed to dissolve into nothingness and "swallow itself."

People all over the nation soon took to "Fletcherizing." Dr. Kellogg hung a large banner with the single word FLETCHERIZE in the San's dining room, where even patients on his milk diet were expected to keep a mouthful of liquid rolling around on the tongue until it seemed to disappear.

LOOK YOUNGER A German immigrant from Württemberg, Helmut Eugene Benjamin Gellert Hauser (1895–   ), was the first person to preach the "religion" of brewer's yeast, powdered skim milk, yogurt, wheat germ and blackstrap molasses in the United States. His 1950 book *Look Younger, Live Longer* sold over 500,000 copies and was translated into 12 languages.

Gayelord Hauser was still walking up to ten miles a day at the age of 82, and traveling around the world lecturing on the benefits of health food. How does he look? According to a 1978 report in the New York *Post,* Hauser looks like a movie star." During a recent tour of Japan, the three most popular questions asked of Hauser were: "How can we grow taller?"; "How can we have sex longer?"; "Is it not true that women's place is in the home?"

WATER WORKS Besides providing a fertile field for food faddists, the United States opened its arms to embrace the medical theories of Father Sebastian Kneipp and Dr. Vincent Preissnitz, two Germans who believed in the power of water. Preissnitz and his American counterparts sprayed patients with water on the outside and effected "cures" by administering as many as 40 glasses of water a day to their patients and denying them any food until they had been "cured." Depending upon your disease, this may or may not have been harmful. If the illness was obesity, it probably worked quite well.

HOMEOPATHY was invented by a German physician, Samuel C. F. Hahnemann (1755–1842) and brought to our country by Constantine Hering (1800–1880), a German immigrant who earned the title "father of homeopathy in America" for his efforts.

The main theory behind homeopathy was that "like cures like" (*Similia similibus curantur*). If you had a migraine headache the best way to cure it was to take some medicine that causes the same symptoms as a migraine headache, and the two would cancel one another out. Any drug that caused symptoms similar to a disease in a healthy person would be able to cure the disease it resembles in a sick person.

Herr Hering founded the North American Academy of the Homeopathic Healing Art in Allentown, Pennsylvania, in 1835 to educate homeopaths, and the "science" enjoyed quite a following during the late 1800s. By 1900 there were some 12,000 practicing homeopaths, with over 15 million followers, but today homeopathy is almost nonexistent in the United States (with the possible exception of California).

SWEDISH MOVEMENT CURE This therapeutic system of body massage was developed by Pehr Henrik Ling (1776–1839), a Swedish poet. He believed that localized movements of the muscles—stroking, kneading and rubbing the body to make blood circulate more freely—would greatly improve one's circulation and increase the secretory action of the body. His greatest success was with women, for whom he devised special "breast massage techniques" and other erogenous therapy to cure headaches and indigestion. Brought to America by German practitioners, movement therapy was quite popular in the late 1800's.

THE MONKEY GLAND MAN That's what they called Dr. Serge Voronoff (1866–1951), a Russian-born surgeon who captured the American imagination in 1940 with his lectures on "the monkey . . . a warehouse of spare parts for the whole human body."

But, Voronoff did more than lecture on his pet theory that anthropoid apes, which are in man's evolutionary tree, could be useful in rejuvenating humans: he actually began transplanting spare parts from apes into human bodies. Why would a man subject himself to being a human guinea pig for a transplant operation in the 1940s? Was it a matter of life or death? Did Voronoff transplant life-sustaining hearts, livers or kidneys? Actually, Voronoff was a rather clever interpreter of human nature and, knowing what men value most, he transplanted apes' testes into old men who believed they needed "rejuvenation."

Voronoff's least expensive operation cost $5,000 in those pre-health-insurance days, yet he performed over 2,000 transplants. Great claims were made that his operation was guaranteed to slow the aging process, but it soon fell into disfavor, for the simple reason that it didn't work. In the end, the donor apes had their revenge on the human subjects who sent them under the knife—many of Voronoff's patients developed simian syphilis, which was transplanted along with the apes glands.

GENETIC DIFFERENCES AMONG ETHNIC GROUPS

There are basic genetic differences among races, ethnic groups and inbred populations. Some are a result of adaptations to the environment where one's ancestors hailed from (such as dark skin and thin noses). Other characteristics, such as straight or curly hair, have no adaptive functions, while others (such as sickle-shaped blood cells) are a result of "survival of the fittest" in a hostile environment.

Let's take a look at some ethnic differences, and some ethnic diseases that afflict the wide variety of *Homo sapiens* who inhabit the U.S.A.

How Racial and Ethnic Characteristics Evolve Before the horse and buggy, automobile, airplane and SST enabled man to move across the continents with ease, people banded together in limited geographical areas and selected their mates from a small circle of friends. Thus, those males and females who survived to adulthood, without the benefits of modern medicine, were those "best" suited to their environment.

Since the "gene pool" from which one could choose a mate was limited to the local inhabitants, this served to intensify and "fix" certain characteristics in a localized area. For example, on the continent of Africa one finds some of the world's tallest humans (Nilotics and Southern Bantus) and some of the world's shortest (Negritos and Bushmen)—each in different areas of the continent.

Contemporary man is extremely mobile, compared to his cave-dwelling ancestors, and the notion of regional physical differences, once called "subraces" of man (Nordic, Mediterranean, Celtic, etc.) is fast disappearing, especially in America, where the peoples of so many nations have gathered together as one.

It's All in the Genes Even though our outward appearances are blending into one homogeneous mass, so to speak, there are some genetic differences to be found among Irish-Americans, Italian-Americans, Chinese-Americans, Basque-Americans and so forth. Whether it be blood types, breast shapes, or variations in their susceptibility to disease, there are distinct differences among America's peoples. Scientists are only beginning to unravel the mysteries of inheritance, and mankind stands to benefit from a better understanding of our physical diversity.

Human Blood Groups Two types of antigens (A and B) and antibodies (a and b) occur in the red blood cells of humans, determining whether their blood type is A, B, AB or O. If your ancestors were Sioux Indians, you probably have Type O blood, as do more than 97% of all native Americans. If your ancestors came from China, there is about 1 chance in 3 that you'll have Type O blood, since the percentage of type O blood among Chinese is only 30.7%.

Wide variation in the frequency of blood group types exists among different races and ethnic groups. Type B is most com-

monly found in central Asia, with the exception of a high frequency in parts of Africa. In Europe, the lowest percentages of type B blood are found in the Scandinavian countries. Until recently, there wasn't any type B blood to be found on the continent of Australia.

Interestingly enough, American Indians, who are believed to have migrated to our continent from Asia over 20,000 years ago, do not exhibit Type B blood, which is fairly common in Asia. Did Type O blood impart some special protective benefits to the first Americans which enabled them to survive in this new land; or did that blood group emerge after the first Indians came to America? Perhaps someday we'll have all the answers.

DISTRIBUTION OF A, B, O BLOOD GROUPS IN SELECTED ETHNIC GROUPS

	%O	A	B	AB
American Indians, Utah	97.4	2.6		
Australian Aboriginies	48.1	51.9		
Basques	57.2	41.7		
English	47.9	42.4	8.3	1.4
Black Americans	51.5	29.5	15.5	3.5
White Americans	42.2	39.3	13.5	5.1
Chinese	30.7	25.1	34.2	10.0
Asian Indians	32.5	20.0	39.4	8.1

OTHER PHYSICAL DIFFERENCES AMONG ETHNIC GROUPS

Rh Factor While Rh negative blood is quite common among European populations, and especially prevalent among the Basques, it is extremely rare in other parts of the globe.

MNS Blood Factors Other antigens (M, N) are present in human red blood cells. M is common to American Indians, but rare among Australian aboriginals and Pacific Islanders, who usually have type N. Among Asians and Europeans, M and N are almost equally distributed.

Color Blindness Middle Easterners have a very high prevalence of red-green color blindness.

Wrist-Bone Fusion Only 0.1% of all Europeans have fused wrist bones, but among West Africans the figure is as high as 6%.

Earwax 99% of Africans and 97% of Germans studied have soft, sticky earwax,

as do most Europeans. However, most members of the Mongolian race – Chinese, Japanese, and American Indians – have a dry, crumbly type of ear wax.

Sickle-Shaped Blood Cells In Africa the prevalence of sickle-shaped blood cells, as opposed to round ones, is as high as 40% in the malarial zones of that continent.

Wisdom Teeth Many Asians lack the extra molars that emerge sometime in the third decade of life, but almost all West Africans have "wisdom teeth."

Breast Shape Caucasian women generally have breasts that are hemispherically shaped, while Black women have conically shaped breasts and Orientals have "saucer-shaped" breasts.

Body Hair Caucasians are the most hirsute race in terms of body hair. Negroids are in the middle and Mongoloids have the least amount of body and facial hair.

Nose Width It is believed that the width of a person's nose is related to environmental conditions. In Africa, where the air is very warm, inhaling a large amount of air is not a problem, but in a cold climate, too much "cold" air might chill the lungs and damage them. Nordic peoples have the thinnest noses and Africans the widest because it was necessary for persons living in an Arctic environment to "warm" the air before it entered the lungs. This theory has been supported by the fact that the Eskimos, who are Mongoloids adapted to the Arctic regions, have a thinner nose than is commonly observed in other Asiatics.

GENETIC DIFFERENCES WITH SERIOUS CONSEQUENCES

An analysis of health statistics in recent years has shown that members of certain ethnic groups are more susceptible to certain debilitating diseases, such as multiple sclerosis, cystic fibrosis, high blood pressure and various anemias.

Jewish Diseases The Ashkenazic Jews, whose ancestors came from Germany and Eastern Europe, comprise almost 85% of the world's Jewish population. Unfortunately, there are at least ten genetic disorders that are known to strike Ashkenazim with a much greater frequency than would be expected in the general population. One of the best known is Tay-Sachs disease, a degenerative disorder that results in abnormal accumulation of lipids (fats) in the cells of an infant. As these lipids accumulate in the nervous system, nerve cells in the brain die off. Blindness and mental retardation result.

Almost 95% of all cases of Tay-Sachs disease are diagnosed in Jewish families, and it has been estimated that 1 out of every 30 Ashkenazic Jews is a carrier. The rate of occurrence of Tay-Sachs disease in Jewish families is once in every 6,000 births, as compared to 1 in 600,000 births for the non-Jewish population.

There is a reliable blood test to screen Tay-Sachs carriers, but unfortunately there is no treatment for this heartbreaking disease.

There are several other disorders which have a high frequency among Ashkenazic Jews. Niemann-Pick disease is a disorder which prevents fats from being metabolized properly, and results in death before the age of three. Gaucher's disease is an adult affliction that results in easy bleeding and fractures due to defective body enzymes which destroy bone and cartilage. This disease was first described in 1882. The rate of frequency in the general population is 1 in 40,000. However, among Jews, the rate is 1 in 2,500 births. The disease is not fatal in childhood, however, and is compatible with a relatively long life-span.

Dysautonomia is a disease that causes recurrent pneumonia and blood pressure problems. When one researcher surveyed 328 cases of dysautonomia, he found that 326 of the afflicted patients had at least one ancestor who came from the Pale of Settlement, an area in the northeastern part of Poland that borders on the Baltic Sea. The Jews were confined to the Pale of Settlement after Russia took over Poland in 1762, and it was probably here that inbreeding helped perpetuate the recessive genes that cause many of these heartbreaking diseases.

Italians, Greeks and Middle Easterners Among the peoples who originally inhabited the area around the Mediterranean Sea, Cooley's anemia, also known as Mediterranean anemia or thalassemia, is fairly common. Untreated, the victim dies in childhood of anemia and liver-spleen complications. In some Italian communities it has been estimated that as many as 20% of the inhabitants are afflicted. Over one million persons are believed to have this disease.

Asians The most common ethnic disease in the world is Alpha thalassemia, a type of anemia in which red blood cells are destroyed. The disease is prevalent in the region between the Mideast, India and the Far East, and is believed to affect some two million persons worldwide.

Irish Phenylketonuria, also known as PKU, is the second most common genetic disease among Caucasians, but it is especially prevalent among the Irish. Immediately after birth, in hospitals across the United States, infants are routinely tested for this inborn error in amino acid metabolism. Careful control of an infant's diet can reduce the severity of the mental retardation which accompanies this disease, so it is urgent that a PKU victim be identified immediately after birth.

Portuguese Thanks to the detective sleuthing of Rose Marie Silva, a new ethnic disease was recently identified by the National Genetics Foundation. Known as the Joseph Family Disease, this crippling affliction had coursed through this single family for over 150 years, dooming many young adults to a slow, lingering death caused by degeneration of the nervous system.

By tracking down members of the family who had dispersed from coast to coast over the past decades, Mrs. Silva (herself a member of the family) was able to discover that the disease was first brought to America by a Portuguese seaman, Antone Joseph, who jumped ship in California in 1845. Through her efforts Mrs. Silva was able to locate more than 600 descendants of Antone and of his brother, John Joseph.

The disease strikes relatively late in life, usually after the victim has unwittingly passed the genetic defect on to his own children. When 80 of the 125 surviving members of the Joseph family gathered together to discuss their common ancestor and their common problem in 1975, it was discovered that 13 had the disease and 26 had a high risk of contracting it.

Dutch Another "family" disorder is Vandenberg's disease, which was first brought to America by Gerrit John Vandenberg, an immigrant from the Netherlands who settled here in 1700. Most of the victims of this neurological disorder live in or around South Dakota.

Blacks The defective gene which causes sickle-cell anemia is carried by almost 8% of our nation's Black population. Almost 1 in 6,000 blacks are affected by this disease, which causes poor health leading to death prior to the age of forty.

Caucasians Cystic Fibrosis is most commonly found among members of the Caucasian race. This hereditary disease results in an abnormal mucus secretion into the lungs, which results in death at about the time of adolescence. Almost 1 child in 2,000 is afflicted.

Multiple Sclerosis is another disease that is more common among whites. According to data released in 1969 by Dr. Geoffrey Dean, who studied African populations, the disease is quite rare among the native Bantu of South Africa. The rate of contraction of the disease was 4 times higher among European immigrants to South Africa than it was among the native-born white *English*-speaking population. Oddly enough, the

rate of contraction of M.S. for European immigrants was 11 times higher than it was among the native-born white *Afrikaans*-speaking population.

ONE MAN'S MEAT IS ANOTHER MAN'S POISON

LACTOSE INTOLERANCE Although the American Dairy Council touts that "you never outgrow your need for milk" there is medical evidence to support the fact that milk is *not* the perfect food for everyone. Past infancy, almost 70% of America's Blacks, Indians and Jews, and about 80% of the Asian and Middle Eastern populations, become increasingly unable to digest milk sugar or lactose. Only in a few population groups from Northern Europe and some African tribes do the majority of adults retain the ability to digest milk sugar. Of course, the sensitivity varies and most people who show a lactose intolerance can handle small amounts of milk and may enjoy cheeses, yogurt, sour cream and buttermilk, where microorganisms have predigested some of the milk sugar.

SALT RETENTION Why are Black Americans almost twice as likely as their white neighbors to develop high blood pressure? Part of the reason may be that their bodies retain more salt, which aggravates hypertension. This is probably an adaptive characteristic for coping with the hot sun of Africa, where it is necessary to conserve body salts that would be lost through excessive perspiration. A study conducted by Dr. James Hunt, chairman of the Department of Medicine at the Mayo Clinic and Medical School in Rochester, Minnesota, showed that 50% of the hypertensive patients in his study were able to bring their blood pressure under control by limiting their intake of salt to one teaspoonful per day. (That's only one-fourth of the average American daily intake of 4 teaspoonfuls, which many scientists believe is excessive.)

ALCOHOL INTOLERANCE Indian alcoholism has been estimated at 12 times the national average for whites and five times the average among Blacks. It is the leading major mental health problem of American Indians. Is there a biological reason for this? Some scientists believe there is.

A study of Eskimos and Indians in Canada, conducted by J. W. Ewing et al. proved that Indians stay drunk longer than Caucasians. Additional data showed that Oriental subjects are more sensitive to extremely low levels of blood alcohol—levels which had little effect on most Occidental subjects.

A popular belief in Taiwan is that those who turn red after the first drink cannot hold their liquor, whereas those who don't turn red can drink much larger amounts.

CANCER   Over the past 25 years, the overall incidence of cancer for Black Americans rose 8%, while the incidence of cancer in whites declined 3%. Over the same period of time, the cancer death rate increased 26% for blacks, a figure that was five times higher than the increase in white deaths.

In 1979 Dr. La Salle D. Leffall, Jr., the first Black president of the American Cancer Society, identified five areas in which the cancer death rate for Blacks was significantly higher than that for whites— cancer of the lungs, stomach, pancreas, esophagus and uterus. (The death rate for uterine cancer in Black women was twice the rate for white women.) The disparity in cancer death rates was mainly attributed to environmental and social factors rather than inherent biological characteristics, since 37% of white men and 42% of white women cancer victims were diagnosed in an early stage, while the corresponding early detection figures for Blacks were only 28% for men and 31% for women.

Since man can't be studied under controlled conditions the way laboratory animals are, it is almost impossible to determine the factors that contribute to the development of cancer—food, air, waterborne organisms or genetic predisposition. However, there are some statistics that suggest large discrepancies in the cancer sites and rates of various nations. For instance, in Japan the average death rate per 100,000 population for cancer of the stomach is 46.6, as compared to only 7.2 in the United States. Americans have the Japanese beat, though, when it comes to cancer of the intestine—our rate is 18.3 deaths per 100,000 population, versus a mere 4.8 in Japan.

What causes these differences? Some scientists believe that the 700,000 new cases of malignancy which are diagnosed each year may be partly attributed to dietary factors—which are culturally set. Some 172,600 new cases of cancer of the digestive tract and 90,000 cases of breast cancer may be related to the high intake of animal fats in the American diet. However, the precise link is not clear. Suffice it to say that the Japanese, whose traditional diet is low in fat, have a bowel cancer rate that is less than one-third that of the American population, but when Japanese-Americans, who consume more beef and butter than their forebears, are surveyed, we find that their risk for bowel cancer is the same as that for other American citizens. Finns, who consume foods high in both fat and fiber, have a relative low rate of bowel cancer; breast cancer in Japan is only 20% as common as it is among Americans, while Japanese-Americans who have been reared on a high-fat American diet have the same incidence of breast cancer as their Caucasian counterparts.

Why do the Japanese develop more stomach cancers than Americans? Possibly this occurs because they consume much nitrosamine-laden smoked fish.

THE GREAT I.Q. CONTROVERSY

When Arthur Jensen (of Danish and German ancestry), a psychologist at the University of California at Berkeley, first published an article on I.Q. differences between blacks and whites in 1969, he was denounced as a "racist" for claiming that the difference of 10 to 20 points between black and white average scores was due primarily to genetic "inferiority." It was basically the old "nature vs. nurture" argument about the formation of intelligence, but Jensen took it a step further by implying that the genes that control intellectual capacity were somehow related to those that determine the color of a person's skin.

Since that time the whole subject of I.Q. tests has been hotly debated. Are I.Q. tests culturally biased so that the middle- and upper-class children of America always attain the highest scores? Are I.Q. tests valid measurements of a person's ability to function within the school environment even if they are "biased"? Some proponents maintain that "Life is unfair, and the tests are un-

Ellis Island officials administering intelligence tests to a newly arrived immigrant in 1917. Considering the testing conditions and the attitude of the officials, it is understandable that most of the immigrants who passed through Ellis Island were considered "subnormal" in their intellectual capacity. (Credit: Culver Pictures)

fair, but they measure the results." Others argue that "gifted" children often do not perform up to expectations, while "dull" children can do well academically despite a somewhat lower than normal I.Q.

Clearly, the debate has no end. However, it is interesting to note that most immigrants who passed through Ellis Island were at one time considered subnormal in their intellectual capacity. When Henry Goddard was commissioned by the U.S. Public Health Service in the early 1900s to administer the Binet intelligence test to newly arrived immigrants, the results were startling: 83 percent of the Jews, 80 percent of the Hungarians, 79 percent of the Italians and 87 percent of the Russians who docked at Ellis Island were "feebleminded." Were all these immigrants really the "bottom of the barrel," so to speak? Or were they simply unable to "take tests"? (For the uninitiated, who don't speak the English language well, "Blue is to sky as green is

to grass" probably doesn't make much sense.)

At the beginning of World War I, when the intelligence of draftees was measured with the Army's Alpha Test, the results again showed that the Latin and Slavic groups performed poorly, yet today, these groups are no longer noticeably different in their general I.Q. scores from the rest of the American population.

Some educators and psychologists attribute this factor to "acculturation" to the American way of life. Following this same line of reasoning, Thomas Sowell, a fellow at the Center for Advanced Study in Behavioral Sciences at Stanford, California, posed the question: "Is there anything peculiar about either the level or pattern of black I.Q.s?" Sowell believes the lower scores are a manifestation of the separate society within which many Black Americans live, and he believes that the data prove that cultural assimilation and upward mobility are the key factors in the higher I.Q. scores for second-generation ethnic Americans. He believes the conditions of the Southern and Eastern European immigrants of the 1920s can be correlated to that of Blacks today, as "outsiders," so to speak, and he is encouraged by the fact that the low I.Q. scores of immigrant groups of the past have now come up to par or exceeded the U.S. average.

THE SEXPERTS

ETHNIC BIRTH CONTROL

Before the IUD, pills and spermicidal jellies and foams invaded the bedrooms of the world, people relied on douches, sponges and magic potions to ward off pregnancy.

Every ethnic group had its own "foolproof" contraceptive technique which was handed down from one generation to the next (an indication of its effectiveness). The I Ching advised Chinese women to swallow quicksilver fried in oil as a means of preventing pregnancy. (Quicksilver is the common name for mercury, and we all know how healthful a daily dose of that can be.) Egyptian women were told to insert a mixture of crocodile dung and honey into the vagina to prevent the active sperm from hitting home. While the sticky honey might have served as a barrier preventing a chance collision between egg and sperm, it is more likely that the crocodile dung was the efficacious agent in this primitive "spermicide"—which worked by keeping the men away!

In the sixth century, the Greek physician Aetius advised women to scoop out the seeds of a pomegranate half and use it as a primitive diaphragm. He was on the right track, but since women and pomegranates both vary so greatly in size his method left room for improvement. Finally, in the eleventh century, probably because everything else had been tried at least once, the Jewish physician Avicenna advised women to jump backward seven times after intercourse, sneezing all the while, in the hopes of dislodging any sperm intent on settling down for a long winter's nap.

When medical science advanced to the point where physicians realized pregnancy *usually* occurred during a certain period of a woman's monthly cycle, some cultures adopted the rhythm method of birth control. But, it too, quickly fell into disfavor as a reliable method because so many couples had trouble agreeing on the rhythm. It wasn't until the seventeenth century that man first invented a fairly reliable contraceptive—the condom.

Credit for this useful device is generally given to the Earl of Condom, a physician knighted by King Charles II (1630–1685) for his invention of the male sheath. Made from sheep membrane, the condom was a godsend that helped poor Charles lessen his monthly benefit payments to illegitimate heirs who dotted the English countryside.

The story may be just a bit fanciful, and in all probability condoms were around long before the Earl gave them his name. As early as the mid-1500s, an Italian scientist, Gabriel Falloppius, had recommended using a linen sheath moistened with lotion to guard against venereal disease. Despite the success of his invention, it wasn't until the eighteenth century that people began to realize that the condom was an effective means of preventing fertilization.

Once the merits of condoms were recognized, the demand for them soared. But, unfortunately, they were so expensive that only the upper classes could afford to use them and the poor peasants still had to "grin and bear it." That is, until good old American ingenuity stepped in!

(Courtesy: Julius Schmid)

American Contributions

When Charles Goodyear (1800–1860), an Anglo-American inventor, first discovered the vulcanization of rubber in 1839, he had no idea his invention would revolutionize the world's sexual relations. When manufacturers began making condoms out of rubber instead of sheep membrane, the price of "rubbers," as they were now called, was so low that the average citizen could easily afford contraceptive protection. When the latex process was developed in the 1930s, the price of condoms dropped even lower and they began appearing in wallets all over the country.

Condoms and rubber diaphragms were some of the best birth control devices available until recent years, but our Puritanical forefathers, who disapproved of sex without procreation, left us a myriad of laws against the sale and display of these items. It wasn't even possible to discuss such matters with a physician until 1918, because lawmakers had labeled sex education "obscene" and relegated it to the back streets and dark alleys of America.

The American Medical Association didn't consider birth control a medical service until forty years ago, and it wasn't until the 1960s that many of our outmoded, though little enforced, sex laws were banished from the books. As late as 1960, contraception was technically a forbidden subject in Boston and other parts of Massachusetts, as well as in Wisconsin, Philadelphia and the Dakotas.

Whom do we have to thank for the revolution in sexual awareness and the declining birth rate in America? Why, the ethnic Americans, of course! An Irish-American nurse, a German immigrant manufacturer and three doctors who devoted their lives to research on birth control—a Chinese immigrant, a Catholic and a Jew. These are just a few of the many crusaders and scientific minds who fought for repeal of antiquated laws, and brought the Pill and prophylactics to the drug counters of America.

An Alternative to Sleeping on the Roof Her own Irish mother had borne 11 children and died at an early age after having had a dreary existence marked by constant pregnancy, childbirth and poverty. When Margaret Sanger (1883–1966) began working as a maternity nurse on the Lowest East Side of Manhattan she was dismayed at the life of a typical tenement wife: pregnancy was a chronic condition; the women of thirty-five seemed old, weary and worn

out before their time; and many women died or seriously injured themselves with self-induced abortions. The hopelessness of their poverty-ridden lives was enough to make Margaret realize that money alone would not create a better life for many of these families.

"I came to a sudden realization," she wrote, "that my work as a nurse and my activities in social service were . . . useless to relieve the misery I saw all about me." Fewer children, spaced further apart, could help many families attain a better standard of living, but when Sanger sought to learn more about "family planning" she discovered there wasn't any information to be found! The Comstock Act of 1873, named after Anthony Comstock, the Postal Inspector and leader of the New York Society for the Suppression of Vice, had labeled contraceptive information "obscene," and as a result there was very little reliable information to be had in the United States.

The Comstock law was responsible for over 700 arrests and $65,256 worth of fines during the 1880s, when more than 64,800 "rubber articles for immoral purposes" were confiscated in the mail. As a result, the doctors Sanger interviewed were reluctant to discuss sex because they feared prosecution under the Comstock Act. In order to learn about the state of the art, Margaret was forced to travel abroad in 1913. She returned to the United States in 1914, armed with literature and methodology, and although she was careful not to offer contraceptive information in her magazine, the *Woman Rebel,* she was still slapped with 9 counts of defying the Comstock law and faced a possible prison term of 45 years. The indictment was eventually squelched and in 1916 she opened a clinic in the Brownsville section of Brooklyn to offer women more helpful birth control advice than the classic remark, "Tell Jake to sleep on the roof."

Once again the Comstock law was invoked. Sanger's diaphragms were confiscated and the clinic was closed after an existence of only 9 days. Fortunately her case won a decision from the U.S. Court of Appeals allowing doctors to provide contraceptive devices to women for the "cure and prevention of disease," and soon public acceptance of "birth control" (a term she coined) began to increase.

Margaret Sanger can safely be called "the Mother of Planned Parenthood," since the two organizations she founded (the National Birth Control League and the American Birth Control League) joined forces in 1939 and were renamed Planned Parenthood Federation of America in 1941.

Margaret Sanger (1883–1966), "the mother of Planned Parenthood." (Courtesy: Planned Parenthood Federation of America)

Rainbow-Colored Birth Control One of Sanger's close friends was Julius Schmid, "a German immigrant with a dream," according to his company's corporate literature, who worked with Margaret and set up the first manufacturing facility in the United States to market diaphragms in the early 1920s.

Schmid was also the first manufacturer of contraceptive jelly in the United States, but for all of his foresight, he probably never would have believed that the company he started in 1883 would one day be able to market multi-colored condoms on open display racks within easy reach of both male and female customers.

No more embarrassing moments trying to find the right words to say to the druggist; no more proof of age or marital status requirements; and imagine, an economy-size package of 36! Multi-colored, ribbed and cheaper by the dozen—that was probably beyond Schmid's wildest "dreams" of the future.

The Pill Revolution Despite their availability, many couples declined to use rubber artifacts because they felt it interfered with the spontaneity of the act. Margaret Sanger dreamed about a truly foolproof method of birth control which would be effortless and effective virtually 100% of the time. She probably didn't believe anything short of sterilization could fulfill those requirements, but medical science was already making astonishing advances in the field of reproductive research as early as the 1930s.

Forty-four years before the first test-tube baby was born in Bristol, England, from an egg fertilized outside the mother's body and implanted in her womb, the groundwork was being laid for the event by Dr. Gregory Pincus (1903–1967) who had successfully fertilized a rabbit ova in a laboratory test tube at Harvard.

That was in 1934, and his later experiments in reproductive research led to the realization that progesterone, a hormone secretion triggered by ovulation, could be used as a birth control device. Progesterone thickens the walls of the Fallopian tubes and of the womb in preparation for the implantation of a fertilized egg, and also guards against overlapping pregnancies by preventing future fertilization. These qualities made progesterone a "natural" birth control agent, and when Margaret Sanger and Mrs. Katherine McCormick, a wealthy heiress, approached Pincus with a request for a "foolproof" method of birth control, his lab began experimenting with hormonal control of a woman's monthly cycle.

Aided by Dr. John Rock, a Catholic physician who specialized in infertility problems, and Dr. Min-Chueh Chang, a Chinese immigrant scientist, and backed by the inherited fortune of the Scotch-Irish inventor, Cyrus McCormick, Dr. Pincus, the son of Russian-Jewish immigrants, began the search for a synthetic birth control hormone in 1951.

After experimenting with over 200 different substances, Pincus and Chang isolated three steroid compounds derived from the roots of the wild Mexican yam, *cabeza de negro*. Human field trials began in 1956, and by 1960 Enovid became the first contraceptive pill approved by the Food and Drug Administration for sale in the United States. By the end of 1961 some 408,000 American women were "Pill" poppers. At the end of 1962 their ranks had grown to 1,187,000; by 1965, 3.8 million women were consuming 2,600 tons of birth control pills each year.

Although some critics blame "the Pill" for the "moral decay" of America, there are others who would give that honor to Hugh Hefner—the man who took girlie magazines out of their "plain, brown wrappers" and added some gloss and class to the art of girl-watching.

THE FLOODGATES OPEN

Hugh Marston Hefner (1926–), a strait-laced Protestant of German and Swedish extraction, started *Playboy* in December 1953. According to *Time* magazine's analysis, he was the first publisher to realize that "the sky would not fall and mothers would not march if he published bare bosoms." By mid-1955 *Playboy*'s circulation had grown to over 300,000 and clearly, as *Time* noted, the "old taboos were going." Twenty years later, *Playboy*'s circulation was 5.5 million copies per month and there were few taboos left to be shattered. But oddly enough, when the 1970s ushered in a new era of permissiveness in printing, suddenly *Playboy* found itself in the position of not being "dirty" enough!

For fifteen years *Playboy* had reigned as king of the newsstands with "sweet-naked-girl-next-door" centerfolds, and the humor and fiction that everyone *really* bought the magazine for. But now the readers wanted more, and they were getting it from magazines like *Penthouse,* which featured more risque models and did not employ air brush artists to obliterate some of womankind's finest features. There was nothing Hef could do except to fight back with *Oui* in 1972, a kinkier version of his *Playboy* success formula which now sells almost 1.5 million copies each month—adding millions in ad revenues to the bunny empire.

Although the Pill didn't change America's morals, what it did do was open up the subject of sex for discussion in newspapers, magazines and popular books. The age-old taboo was lifted and sex emerged as a popular topic in the print medium. Once it was released from the closed doors and backrooms, all hell broke loose, and the public was soon deluged with "how to" books, "how not to" books and "how to do it better" books. Even "how to do it yourself" books soared up the best-seller lists.

One of those sexperts who turned writer was Dr. David Reuben, the son of a Hungarian factory worker who later became a lawyer. Dr. Reuben became an instant celebrity in 1970 when he zoomed to the top of the talk-show circuit by discussing his best-selling book, *Everything You Always Wanted To Know About Sex but Were Afraid To Ask.* Although his book didn't contain "everything," the slack was soon taken up by *The Joy of Sex,* by British-born Alex Comfort. *"Joy"* has been on the best-seller list every week since 1972.

AMERICA THE BEAUTIFUL

BEAUTY CONTESTS

When Miss America parades down the Atlantic City runway, she is the product of no less than 3,000 preliminary contests and the ultimate victor over some 70,000 entrants.

Since the first Miss America, Margaret Gorman, was elected in 1921, to the present day, not one Black, Oriental, Indian, Hispanic, Greek, Turkish or Italian American has been crowned with that coveted rhinestone tiara. Most Miss Americas seem to fit a mold, which makes her almost 5'6" tall, fair-skinned, with brown hair and blue eyes.

According to Frank Deford, author of *There She Is: The Life and Times of Miss America,* the lack of minority candidates and winners has nothing to do with racism —it is a matter of logistics. Beauty contests must be sponsored by local civic groups, such as the Jaycees. Since membership in the Jaycees is predominantly white and middle class, and since "beauty is in the eye of the beholder," the girls invited to file applications are usually friends, daughters, relatives and acquaintances of similar ethnic backgrounds. Between 1921 and 1978 there was only one winner from New York City. That was Bess Myerson, Miss

America 1945, who also happened to be the only Jewish-American ever chosen to represent the nation's beauty ideal at America's state fairs and rotary clubs. There hasn't been a big-city winner since Lee Merriweather of San Francisco was crowned in 1955; most of the Miss Americas are corn-fed country girls or suburban refugees from urban blight.

Whites Only? In Deford's book, reference is made to "Rule Seven" which once stated that "only members of the white race" could enter the Miss America competition. However, such a rule could not have existed legally for the organization to maintain its tax-exempt, non-profit status. Most officials deny such a rule ever existed, but one was quoted as being "pretty sure it was sometime in the middle 1950s when it went out."

In 1967, a group of blacks threatened to picket the pageant, and Roy Wilkins of the NAACP decried the contest as "lily white." Shortly thereafter, Dr. Zelma George, a sociologist, became the first black judge of the pageant, and the next year, 1970, the first black contestant, a Miss Iowa, appeared on stage.

Minorities in Competition Despite the lack of a minority Miss America, there have been a few minority contestants on the runway over the years:

The first Oriental ever to compete in the contest was Yun Tau, Miss Hawaii of 1948.

Cheryl Adrienne Browne, 19, Miss Iowa, was the first black contestant to appear on stage (other than the Negro women originally cast as "slaves" in her majesty's court during early pageant presentations in 1922). A native New Yorker, Cheryl was attending Luther College in Iowa, and qualified to enter the Miss Iowa contest in 1970. Although she did not become one of the ten semifinalists, Browne was awarded a $1,000 scholarship for her talent.

Between 1926 and 1957, the pageant sporadically welcomed an American Indian, sometimes called Princess America or Miss Indian America, to the festivities. These women were not allowed to compete, but rather, they served to represent the "first American beauty." It wasn't until 1941 that a full-blooded Indian, Mifaunwy Shunatona, was elected as Miss Oklahoma. She participated in the Atlantic City contest

and was elected Miss Congeniality, but did not make it to the semifinals.

Miss Puerto Rico was an "official guest" at the pageant in 1937 and between the late 1940s and early 1960s a Miss Puerto Rico was chosen each year to compete at Atlantic City. The rules of the contest were changed in 1961, however, making Miss America a "50 states only" affair.

Although there has never been an Arab-American Miss America, one of the top ten finalists in 1978s contest, Miss Ohio, will go down in history as the first contestant to perform a belly dance for the talent competition.

Minority Winners Even if Miss Puerto Rico, Miss Hawaii, or another minority woman has never won the "big title," they have managed to garner the title Miss Congeniality many times. Miss Hawaii won the title in 1948, 1950, 1951 (tied with Puerto Rico), 1955, 1959; Miss Puerto Rico won in 1951 and 1961, but both times it was a tie (in 1961, the honor was shared with Miss California). Miss Oklahoma, an American Indian, won the award in 1941, and Miss Northern British Columbia won the title in 1945 before Canada was eliminated from the competition.

Black Is Beautiful As early as 1944, there was a nationwide contest held for Miss Sepia, but it wasn't until the 1960s that blacks began competing in "general" beauty contests.

Corrine Huff represented Ohio in the 1960 preliminaries for Miss USA, part of the Miss Universe Contest.

Miss Teenage America had Black finalists in 1967 and 1970.

Valerie Dickinson won the national College Queen Pageant; she was the only Black woman among the fifty contestants in 1968.

David Johns was crowned Mr. America in 1977 by Mae West. A black probation officer from Los Angeles and a former football star, Johns' biceps measured 20 inches around.

Janelle Penny Commissiong, representing Trinidad-Tobago, became the first Black to win the Miss Universe title in 1977. A native of Trinidad, she had moved to New York at the age of thirteen, but returned home in 1976, in time to qualify to represent her native country. The twenty-four-year-old became the first Black winner in the 26-year history of the Miss Universe contest.

Pinky Rings, No; Loving Cups, Yes
Not content to be mere window dressing in someone else's beauty contest, Blacks started their own pageants. Today, there are Miss Black Teenage America and Miss Black America contests held annually. The Miss Black America beauty pageant has been televised since 1972, and since that time the winner has received one of the most highly regarded loving cups in the jewelry world. Tiffany's designed the trophies for Miss Black America, and despite the store's ban on men's pinky rings, which they regard as being in "poor taste," the officials apparently find nothing distasteful about beauty contests.

Indian Beauty The first Miss Indian America title winner was Arlene Wesley James, a Yakima Indian from the state of Washington, who was crowned in 1953 at the annual American Indian Days celebration held at Sheridan, Wyoming.

In 1967, Mrs. Ramona Zephier of Flandreau, South Dakota, a member of the Cheyenne River Sioux, was one of ten finalists in the Mrs. America contest held at San Diego, California. A home economics teacher, she entered the contest to "destroy some stereotypes" about how the Indian lives and works. "I don't go for sit-ins, and I don't presume to speak for the Indian people, but maybe this will show Indians that they can do anything if they really want to do it."

BEAUTY MAKERS

Some of the ethnics who made America more beautiful by providing its women with rouge pots, permanent waves and other means of enhancing their "natural" beauty:

Some Like it Curly Karl Ludwig Nessler (1872–1951), better known to the beauty world as Charles Nestle, brought his permanent waving method to America in 1915. An immigrant from Todtnau, Bavaria, Nestle studied hairdressing in Paris in 1899 under Henri Marcel, the man who gave his name to the fashion world by inventing the "Marcel Wave." Nestle traveled to London after his apprenticeship, and it was there that he invented an improved system of permanent waving. Using borax paste and heat applications, Nestle was able to permanently deform a woman's hair into spiral-shaped "curls," which result from denaturing the protein structure of each hair shaft.

Forced to flee Britain at the outbreak of World War I (Nestle had never applied for citizenship and was declared an enemy alien), he came to New York to ply his trade. By the mid-1920s he had patented his curling devices, hair testing machines, and permanent wave solutions. In 1927, he opened the world's largest beauty salon. He also established the Nestle-LeMur Company, which was once one of the largest manufacturers of permanent wave and hair care supplies.

Although his company suffered losses during the Depression, his invention of the first commercially successful permanent waving machine was the basis for the modern beauty parlor industry.

Some Like It Straight Prior to the consciousness-raising 1960s, there were many Black women in America who sought to imitate WASP standards of beauty by straightening their hair and bleaching their skin. No product can change the color of one's skin, but with enough effort it is possible to straighten curly or frizzy hair—and that's how America's first Black self-made woman millionaire made her fortune.

Sarah McWilliams Walker (1867–1919), better known as Madame C. J. Walker, invented a hair-straightening formula in 1910 that netted her an estate valued at more than $1 million when she died nine years later.

Orphaned at the age of six and widowed at the age of twenty-two, Sarah Walker was forced to support herself as a laundress for 18 years until she discovered her hair-straightening formula. Ridiculed at first, the "Walker method," which employed vigorous shampoos followed by applications of hot iron combs dipped in a lye solution, became the largest Black-owned industry in Indiana in 1915. At the time, more than 500 Walker agents were making house calls throughout the United States and the Caribbean. Madame Walker later moved from Indianapolis to New York and commissioned black architect Vertner Tandy to build her a spectacular home overlooking the Hudson.

Although Afro and natural hair styles are popular with many Blacks (and whites) today, there is still a large market for hair-straightening products.

"The Mother of the Treatment Bus-

iness" Elizabeth Arden (1884–1966) was born in Ontario, Canada, of English and Scottish ancestry, with the rather unglamorous name of Florence Nightingale Graham. True to her original moniker, Arden's first career was as a nurse. But instead of making a modest living healing wounded bodies, Arden made a fortune healing wounded "egos" and making women "feel" beautiful.

Arden first emigrated to the United States in the early 1900s, at a time when lipstick, rouge and mascara were the stuff harlots were made of. Decent women did not use such cosmetic aids, or if they did, they usually bought them on the sly. What Arden did was to make the cosmetics industry respectable. She opened a treatment salon at a fashionable Fifth Avenue address and attracted the social elite of New York. Known as "the mother of the treatment business," Arden built a multi-million-dollar business waxing, massaging, steaming and beautifying some of the richest bodies in the world.

Besides making money in fashions and cosmetics, Arden also turned a good profit at the racetrack. She was one of the nation's leading racehorse owners, and probably the only one who insisted on tastefully decorated stables. She insisted that the environment be fly-free for her horses' comfort, and before each race she had the horses rubbed down with her special beauty creams. She loved horses, but only the best-looking specimens; any that were not strikingly handsome were sold.

Arden refused to reveal her true age during her lifetime, and never permitted her hair to gray. She believed pink was the color which flattered her complexion the most, and decorated her 10-room duplex in various shades of pink. She wore pink clothing, wrote memos on pink paper and even packaged her beauty products in pink containers.

Blue, Not Pink Estee Lauder started her cosmetics company in 1946 with a formula she inherited from her Viennese uncle. Named one of 100 Women of Achievement by *Harper's Bazaar* in 1967, Lauder believes her job, ". . . is to make sure a woman's beauty endures joyfully." Like Elizabeth Arden, Lauder declines to provide her birthdate, preferring instead to remain "ageless" in the eyes of the public.

Unlike Arden, blue is the color of choice for Estee, and her office high above New York's Central Park is decorated in her favorite shade. In addition to the Lauder line of cosmetics (packaged in blue), the family-owned firm (Estee, husband Joseph, sons Leonard and Ronald) also produces the successful Clinique line of hypoallergenic cosmetics, creams and lotions.

"Fire and Ice" Charles Haskell Revson, the son of Russian Jews (the name means "rabbi's son") started out in the beauty business as a nail polish salesman for a New Jersey-based firm, Elka. Elka was one of the first opaque nail polishes on the market, and it was sold exclusively to beauty salons. Revson decided to distribute his own opaque nail enamel in the 1930s, an enterprise that earned him his first profit in the world of beauty and led to the establishment of Revlon, one of the world's most famous and lucrative beauty companies.

Richard Avedon photographed many of Revlon's most successful ad campaigns, and models such as Dorian Leigh, Suzy Parker and Lauren Hutton helped propel Revlon's sales to more than $600 million in 1974.

Early Consumerism Born in Lodz, Poland, to Jewish parents, Max Factor (1876–1938) started his career as a makeup apprentice with the Russian Grand Opera. Max emigrated to the United States in 1904 and built a reputation for himself as a makeup man in the early days of motion pictures. One of the most unusual makeup jobs he ever had to perform took place in 1937. An extortionist attempted to pry some money out of Factor while he was visiting France, and on the advice of the French police, Max "madeup" a double to keep the rendezvous. The crook never showed up.

Even before the days of consumer advocates, Max Factor was one of the few cosmetics manufacturers who maintained a menagerie of guinea pigs and rabbits upon whose skins new makeup bases, rouges and lipsticks were tested.

Solving the Housing Problem Another Polish-Jewish immigrant in the beauty business was Helena Rubinstein (1872–1965). This fiery lady was only 4'10" tall, but there was nothing small about the way she operated. When she was refused admission to a ritzy Park Avenue cooperative where only WASPs lived, she solved her housing problem by buying the whole building.

Rubenstein started peddling skin cream in Australia in 1902, when she noticed how rough and dry the women's skin was "Down Under." Just about that same time, lipstick was beginning to gain "respectability" in Paris. When Helena moved to New York in 1914, she expanded her line of beauty aids to include creams, lip colorings and rouges.

Like most other American manufacturers, the cosmetic shades that Rubinstein, Factor and Revlon produced were usually only suitable for light-colored complexions. It wasn't until the 1970s that any of these large cosmetics manufacturers would jump on the Black bandwagon.

Black Is Beautiful (and big business, too) For decades, Black women had to struggle to find makeup that would suit their complexions. Foundations designed for olive-skinned women made black skin look ashen; lipsticks took on a purplish tone; and even nail polish colors did not compliment the many shades of brown, tan and in-between that "black" skin comes in. But, all that changed in the 1970s.

Why were cosmetics manufacturers suddenly interested in producing makeup for Black women? Was it the political climate of the Sixties that motivated their decision? Actually, no less than $400 million worth of sales was at stake—and when it comes to promoting social, political and even cosmetic changes in America—money talks. The lure of all those black dollars jingling in cash registers across the nation made the large cosmetics companies, such as Revlon, Avon and Max Factor, venture into the marketplace with their own cosmetics lines for dark-skinned women.

The brand-name Black cosmetics business started in 1968 when a Black actress, Barbara Walden, displeased with her own studio's makeup, took $700 to a chemist and worked with him to develop her own line of cosmetics. Soon Walden's cosmetics were being distributed in such classy retail stores as Magnin's and other department store chains where middle-class Blacks shopped.

About the same time, Florence Lord Roberts (a white woman) developed the Flori Roberts line of cosmetics; and in 1971, Johnson Products, the manufacturers of Afro-Sheen hair conditioner, came out with its own line of Black cosmetics. Johnson Publishing Company, the publishers of *Jet* and *Ebony* (no relation to the hair care company) was next in the marketplace with Fashion Fair cosmetics. Fashion Fair promoted their cosmetics in the Black press with ads that featured famous actresses such as Diahann Carroll, and by 1975 they were number one, with over $8 million worth of sales.

The major cosmetics companies of America had long skirted the issue of separate cosmetics lines for Black women. But, with available data proving that Black women were willing cosmetics buyers and that the Black middle class was increasing, the market began to look more and more lucrative.

Revlon hired William Pinkney, a Black makeup artist who had developed his own line in 1970. As Pinkney explained it, there had always been a need for special cosmetics for Black women: "In my Hollywood days, even the darkest shade of Max Factor's professional makeup didn't work. It was meant to make whites look like Blacks." The problem ingredient in most foundations was the addition of a white pigment, titanium dioxide, which gave Black complexions an ashy look. Pinkney simply reformulated lipsticks, rouges and eye shadows so they would no longer appear "muddy" on dark skin.

10 PRIDE, PREJUDICE AND STEREOTYPES

HIGHLIGHTS OF DISCRIMINATION IN AMERICA

A BRIEF CHRONOLOGY

1705 ◆ Intermarriage between whites and blacks was declared illegal in Massachusetts this year. The ordinance was to remain in effect until 1843.

1721 ◆ The French government sent 25 prostitutes to Louisiana in an attempt to dissuade French-Canadian settlers from taking Indian mistresses. Later, women known as "Casket Girls" would be exported to America. Their unusual nickname was based on the fact that they were given a wedding dress and a casket as an inducement to emigrate to America. In time, it became a great honor to be descended from a "casket girl," because this proved that one's ancestors were not merely criminals sent from French penal colonies.

1729 ◆ Rhode Island began demanding that ship captains post 50 pounds for each immigrant who arrived in America from a region other than England, Ireland, Jersey or Guernsey.

1826 ◆ Maryland decreed that Jews could hold public office. Prior to this proclamation, a belief in Christianity was necessary to become a public official.

1850 ◆ California passed the Foreign Miners Tax Law, which required Chinese immigrants to pay an unfair share of state taxes and deprived most Mexicans of the right to mine.

1851 ◆ Things got worse for the Mexicans in California. This era was marked by what Chicanos have termed *Linchocracia* (lynch democracy). All native Mexicans were excluded from the California State Senate, and the Land Law deprived them of some 14,000,000 acres of land.

In Downieville, California, a Mexican woman named Juanita became the first woman ever lynched.

1854 ◆ When 13,000 Orientals emigrated to California, the state legislature passed a head tax on all Chinese immigrants.

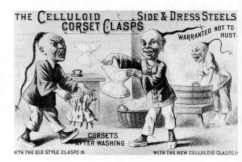

This trade card unmercifully stereotypes the thousands of Chinese-Americans who earned their living operating hand laundries. (Courtesy: Museum of the City of New York)

As the number of Chinese laundries proliferated in San Francisco, an ordinance was passed that required one-horse laundries to pay a $2 tax; two-horse laundries $4 tax; laundries without delivery horses were made to pay $15. This law was aimed primarily at the impoverished Chinese immigrants who were too poor to afford a nag and probably too poor to pay the tax.

1860 ◆ California excluded Mongolians, Indians and Negroes from public schools, by law.

1863 ◆ The passage of the Conscription Act, which enabled a man to avoid war service by paying $300 or finding a substitute, led to four days of riots by working-class Irish in New York City. Three hundred dollars was nearly a year's wages to the average Irish immigrant, who had no desire to fight in the "Black man's war." In their anger, which turned into a race riot, mobs burned two provost marshal's offices as well as the Colored Orphan Asylum, left hundreds dead and caused several million dollars worth of property damage.

1865 ◆ A new "social" organization appeared in Tennessee. Its name was derived from the Greek word for circle, *Kyklos;* to which *Klan* was added to reflect the Scotch-Irish nature of the surrounding community. The name was later simplified to the Ku Klux Klan. The Klan's first Grand Wizard was General Nathan Forrest.

1866 ◆ The Civil Rights Act passed this year, over President Johnson's veto. It granted citizenship to all persons born in the United States, *except* the Indians.

1879 ◆ The cover of *Harper's Weekly* magazine featured a caricature of Black and Chinese citizens which read: "The Nigger must go; the Chinese must go."

1882 ◆ Chinese Exclusion Act prohibited Chinese already in America from becoming citizens, in addition to blocking entry to other Chinese laborers.

1891 ◆ Eleven Italian-Americans were lynched in New Orleans after being accused of murdering a police superintendent as American nativism soared to new heights.

1913 ◆ The Webb Act was passed in California, specifically denying Japanese the right to own land in that state.

1917 ◆ The Immigration Act, enacted this year, required all immigrants to pass a literacy test.

1922 ◆ The Cable Act declared that, ". . . any woman who marries an alien ineligible for citizenship shall cease to be an American citizen."

1924 ◆ The Johnson-Reed Act established quotas for immigration that favored Northern European nations and discrimi-

The destruction of the Coloured Orphan Asylum in New York in 1863. (Courtesy: New York Public Library)

WESTERN DEFENSE COMMAND AND FOURTH ARMY
WARTIME CIVIL CONTROL ADMINISTRATION
Presidio of San Francisco, California
May 3, 1942

INSTRUCTIONS
TO ALL PERSONS OF
JAPANESE
ANCESTRY
Living in the Following Area:

All of that portion of the City of Los Angeles, State of California, within that boundary beginning at the point at which North Figueroa Street meets a line following the middle of the Los Angeles River; thence southerly and following the said line to East First Street; thence westerly on East First Street to Alameda Street; thence southerly on Alameda Street to East Third Street; thence northwesterly on East Third Street to Main Street; thence northerly on Main Street to First Street; thence northwesterly on First Street to Figueroa Street; thence northeasterly on Figueroa Street to the point of beginning.

Pursuant to the provisions of Civilian Exclusion Order No. 33, this Headquarters, dated May 3, 1942, all persons of Japanese ancestry, both alien and non-alien, will be evacuated from the above area by 12 o'clock noon, P. W. T., Saturday, May 9, 1942.

No Japanese person living in the above area will be permitted to change residence after 12 o'clock noon, P. W. T., Sunday, May 3, 1942, without obtaining special permission from the representative of the Commanding General, Southern California Sector, at the Civil Control Station located at:

Japanese Union Church,
120 North San Pedro Street,
Los Angeles, California.

Such permits will only be granted for the purpose of uniting members of a family, or in cases of grave emergency.

The Civil Control Station is equipped to assist the Japanese population affected by this evacuation in the following ways:

1. Give advice and instructions on the evacuation.

2. Provide services with respect to the management, leasing, sale, storage or other disposition of most kinds of property, such as real estate, business and professional equipment, household goods, boats, automobiles and livestock.

3. Provide temporary residence elsewhere for all Japanese in family groups.

4. Transport persons and a limited amount of clothing and equipment to their new residence.

The Following Instructions Must Be Observed:

1. A responsible member of each family, preferably the head of the family, or the person in whose name most of the property is held, and each individual living alone, will report to the Civil Control Station to receive further instructions. This must be done between 8:00 A. M. and 5:00 P. M. on Monday, May 4, 1942, or between 8:00 A. M. and 5:00 P. M. on Tuesday, May 5, 1942.

2. Evacuees must carry with them on departure for the Assembly Center, the following property:

(a) Bedding and linens (no mattress) for each member of the family;

(b) Toilet articles for each member of the family;

(c) Extra clothing for each member of the family;

(d) Sufficient knives, forks, spoons, plates, bowls and cups for each member of the family;

(e) Essential personal effects for each member of the family.

All items carried will be securely packaged, tied and plainly marked with the name of the owner and numbered in accordance with instructions obtained at the Civil Control Station. The size and number of packages is limited to that which can be carried by the individual or family group.

3. No pets of any kind will be permitted.

4. No personal items and no household goods will be shipped to the Assembly Center.

5. The United States Government through its agencies will provide for the storage, at the sole risk of the owner, of the more substantial household items, such as iceboxes, washing machines, pianos and other heavy furniture. Cooking utensils and other small items will be accepted for storage if crated, packed and plainly marked with the name and address of the owner. Only one name and address will be used by a given family.

6. Each family, and individual living alone, will be furnished transportation to the Assembly Center or will be authorized to travel by private automobile in a supervised group. All instructions pertaining to the movement will be obtained at the Civil Control Station.

**Go to the Civil Control Station between the hours of 8:00 A. M. and 5:00 P. M.,
Monday, May 4, 1942, or between the hours of 8:00 A. M. and 5:00 P. M.,
Tuesday, May 5, 1942, to receive further instructions.**

J. L. DeWITT
Lieutenant General, U. S. Army
Commanding

SEE CIVILIAN EXCLUSION ORDER NO. 33.

Executive Order 9066.

nated against the countries of Southern and Eastern Europe. Poland's quota, for example, went from 30,977 to 5,982.

1933 ♦ In a survey concerning "preferred ethnic groups in America," the Chinese ranked lowest. The top eight ethnic groups were: Canadian, English, Scottish, Irish, French, Swedes, Germans and Spaniards.

1942 ♦ Executive Order 9066 authorized Japanese-Americans to be moved from their West Coast homes to concentration camps inland.

1943 ♦ The anti-Mexican "zoot suit" riots took place during Los Angeles' long, hot summer.

1956 ♦ The humiliation Blacks felt daily can perhaps best be gleaned from these Alabama bus regulations, as reprinted in the Baltimore *Afro-American* on March 3, 1956:

1 Enter bus from rear door.

2 If driver speaks, answer "yes, sir" and "no, sir."

3 Fill up seats from rear.

4 If all seats are taken, colored must stand up and allow white riders to sit.

5 If anyone calls you names, or epithets, you must keep quiet or get off the bus.

1957 ♦ One thousand Army paratroopers were sent to Central High School in Little Rock, Arkansas, to enable 9 black students to enroll in the previously all-white school. (The first black student to graduate from Central High was Ernest Green. Twenty years later, Green, an Assistant Secretary of Labor for Employment and Training during President Carter's administration, believed: "Our going there did break down significant social barriers and make it easier for the next generation to follow." In 1977, Central High School boasted a black principal, a course in Afro-American literature and a racial balance that approximated 50% blacks and 50% whites.)

1960 ♦ "Sit-ins" began at lunch counters in Charlotte, North Carolina, to protest the local custom whereby black patrons were served only if they *stood*.

1962 ♦ 96 persons took advantage of the New Orleans Citizens Council's offer of free one-way transportation for Blacks desiring to move to Northern cities.

1963 ♦ George Wallace, the Governor of Alabama, pledged "segregation now, segregation tommorrow and segregation forever."

1964 ♦ President Lyndon Baines Johnson signed the most comprehensive Civil Rights Act in America's history. Despite the promise of eliminating job discrimination and prohibiting discrimination in public facilities and housing, the summer was marked by riots in black ghettos of major American cities.

1969 ♦ 89 American Indians began an occupation of Alcatraz Island in San Fran-

This 1948 poster urged Harlem's citizens to fight racial and religious hatred. Although the members of this black community were targets of racial discrimination, they could not relate to "Sonny's" problem. With his WASP face and light skin, Sonny was not readily identifiable as a target for prejudice. (Courtesy: Museum of the City of New York)

cisco Bay that was to last 19 months, to protest the plight of their people.

1970 ♦ A Lithuanian sailor seeking political asylum aboard a U.S. Coast Guard ship off Martha's Vineyard was taken back to his trawler by Soviet sailors who were allowed to board the Coast Guard cutter and "escort" him home.

1971 ♦ Executive Order 11625, issued by President Nixon to set up the Office of Minority Business Enterprise in the Commerce Department, stated that minorities "include, but are not limited to Negroes, Puerto Ricans, Spanish-speaking Americans, American Indians, Eskimos and Aleuts." By 1978 the definition of persons "deprived of the opportunity to develop and maintain a competitive position in the economy because of social and economic disadvantage" had grown to include women (who are actually a majority in America), Appalachian whites and Orientals. White ethnic leaders were also pushing to have Eastern and Southern European ethnic groups declared victims of past prejudice.

♦ Busing was declared a constitutional means of achieving school integration.

1972 ♦ 500 Indians ended their sit-in at the Bureau of Indian Affairs when they were promised that their demands for changes in natural resource policies would be met. Those promises were never kept.

♦ Ferndale, Michigan, became the first Northern school district to lose Federal funds for violation of desegregation laws.

1975 ♦ Literacy requirements for voting were abolished.

1979 ♦ The U.S. Supreme Court upheld federal busing orders in Dayton and Columbus, Ohio, reaffirming its commitment to busing as a means of school desegregation. But, according to one federal official familiar with school enrollment patterns, "desegregation has gone about where it is going." Studies of ethnic shifts in the nation's largest school systems (Detroit, Chicago, Philadelphia, Houston, New York and Los Angeles) revealed that declining white enrollment in inner city schools has dimmed "the prospects for any significant mixing of the races . . ."

♦ Country singer Charley Pride was denied membership at the Royal Oaks Country Club in Dallas. Pride's check for the $6,000 initiation fee was returned along with a letter indicating that at least four members of the exclusive, all-white club had vetoed Pride's admission. "They gave me no reason, but the only one I can think of is that I'm Black," said Charley. The club's officials refused to comment on the incident.

PRIDE AND PREJUDICE

Throughout the decades almost every ethnic group new to America has been met at the docks with hatred and prejudice. Fearful that the newcomers would threaten their job security, native Americans and naturalized Americans alike could forget their differences when "threatened" and gang up on the "others."

The majority of Southern and Eastern European immigrants were met with an ever-increasing barrage of resistance in the early 1900s. A major daily newspaper complained at the time: "The floodgates are open. The dam is washed away. The sewer is choked. Europe is vomiting! . . . The scum of immigration is viscerating upon our shores. The horde of $9.60 steerage slime is being siphoned upon us from Continental mud tanks."

Such is the stuff that prejudice is made of!

When the Italians began moving into Boston in record numbers in the early 1890s it was noted that "The Italians have replaced the Irish as Boston's most unwanted ethnic group." And so it was for every newcomer in America—all were unwanted, unwelcomed and looked upon as outsiders.

Besides hating people from other nations, the immigrants brought along their own special prejudices from the "other side"— Irish Catholics disliked Irish Protestants; the Italians from Naples looked down upon their brethren from Southern Italy and Sicily; the Lebanese despised the Syrians; and the German Jews considered those from Eastern Europe "primitive."

Even native-born Americans have their own geographic prejudices. For example, New Yorkers and Californians have their little jokes about one another. ("How many

Los Angelenos does it take to change a light bulb?" "Five. One to unscrew the bulb and four to share the experience.") Black Americans have their own geographical prejudices. According to Stephen Birmingham, Blacks descended from slaves who worked the plantations of Virginia and the Carolinas feel a certain superiority over Blacks from Georgia, Mississippi and Louisiana. Since the slave ships docked at Charleston and Newport News, the planters in those states had first choice of the human cargo, or so the "reasoning" goes. Descendants of these slaves contend that the planters naturally picked the strongest, healthiest and brightest Africans.

As the slaves were sold down the Ohio and Mississippi Rivers, the last ones to debark at the Mississippi Delta were the weakest and the least desirable workers. Hence, many narrow-minded residents of Cincinnati consider themselves superior to the natives of Louisiana; while those from Louisville look down on the inhabitants of Memphis, etc.

"WE HAVE SEEN THE ENEMY AND HE IS US" Why would the son of a Jewish survivor of Dachau head the American Nazi Party of Chicago? No one else, except Frank Collin (1944–   ), the half-Jewish Nazi leader, will probably ever understand the driving force behind his 1978 campaign to lead an anti-Semitic parade through the streets of Skokie, Illinois – the surburban home of almost 7,000 Jewish survivors of German concentration camps.

Strange as his behavior may seem, Collin, the son of Max Simon Cohn (a German-Jewish immigrant), is not the first Jewish-American to head an anti-Semitic organization.

THE CASE OF THE JEWISH KLANSMAN As National Secretary of the American Nazi Party and Grand Dragon of the Ku Klux Klan in New York State, Daniel Burros was quoted as believing: "Israel is one of the grottoes from which the Octopus of International Jewry reaches out its nefarious tentacles. Israel must perish." "We must make the world safe for the blond-haired children."

With statements like this, who would have believed that Burros himself was Jewish? His parents, George and Esther (Sunshine) Burros, were Russian Jews who were married in a Jewish ceremony and raised their son Daniel in the Jewish faith. Daniel was even bar mitzvahed at the Congregation Talmud Torah in Richmond, Queens, on his thirteenth birthday, and according to Samuel Bressler, president of the Congregation, "He was a bright boy when he was going to our shul. But shortly after his bar mitzvah he never returned."

What makes a promising Jewish boy turn into a Nazi who advocates genocide as a way to deal with the Jewish "problem"? A rabbi who knew the Burros family commented, "I'm no psychiatrist, and remember rabbis aren't necessarily wiser than anyone else, but speaking as a man, I'll tell you what I think. This was an ambitious young man who met a lot of disappointment. It's human nature to give vent to your frustration by taking it out on those closest to you. And those closest to this young man were Jews."

Whatever the reasons behind Burros' conversion to anti-Semitism, it was clear that he could not live with the revelation of his Jewish background. On Halloween, 1965, McCandlish Phillips published his story, "State Klan Leader Hides Secret of Jewish Origin," in the New York *Times*. Although Burros had threatened Phillips, saying, "I'll have to retaliate . . . If you publish that I'll come and get you and I'll kill you. I don't care what happens. I'll be ruined. This is all I've got to live for," in the end Burros chose to kill no one but himself. He committed suicide on the next day.

Perhaps Burros' senseless death could serve as a warning to all those who apply "blanket hatred" to members of a certain ethnic group. Suppose Alex Haley had joined an anti-Irish society – how would he have felt when he found his "roots" and discovered that his own great-grandfather was Irish? Or how about a white bigot who develops sickle-cell anemia? Any chance he might have had some black ancestors along the way?

It's always better to "hate" for personal reasons. But, if you're a staunch believer in prejudice, you might wish to consult the following whimsical guide, previously published in *Esquire* (December 1970) to see just whom you should hate, according to your religious, ethnic, geographic and socioeconomic background:

RELIGION AND / OR ETHNIC GROUP   *WHITE*

		Protestant			*Irish Catholic*
SOCIOECONOMIC STATUS	*Upper*	You are middling tolerant. Of three major religions WASPS tend to be most prejudiced and within this group "culturally sophisticated" professionals and the young, the least. Toward Jews — moderate prejudicial feeling which runs high when "they" try to "push" into your private club or top corporate echelons. Don't appreciate the upstart Irish either (New England). Toward Negroes — only mildly antagonistic as your job, neighborhood and schools are secure.	Generally less tolerant than East and West Coast brethren. Scandinavian Protestants are most sympathetic, trailed at some distance by English and Irish. German Protestants are least tolerant, especially in rural areas.	For professionals, attitudes roughly correspond to middle and low groups, Midwest and Mountain regions, Others of your "class," particularly in urban counties, have far lower tolerance toward Blacks and Indians for reasons as old as the South. It should come as no news to anyone that anti-black sentiment is highest in the South. Indians better stay in their place too. Jews and other minorities are okay at a distance. White trash better move on.	Most liberal of all C\ olics which, as a gro\ tend to be more libe\ than Protestants. Le\ given to religious ex\ tremism, anti-Semitis\ and racism — particul\ for third generation \ beyond. Prejudicial f\ ing toward Jews is n\ down over recent de\ ades. Greater antipa\ toward Blacks, parti\ larly in Midwestern cities, with limited o\ flow to other minorit\ where you find them\
	Middle	Less liberal than your higher-status coreligionists and coregionists; more resentful of upwardly mobile minorities and their intrusions into your traditional areas. This feeling pertains to Jews, Negroes, Italians, Poles, Puerto Ricans (New York), Irish, Mexicans (California), Chinese . . .	More prejudiced than above group: toward Indians because they are Indians and enjoy privileged role with government; toward Blacks because they're Blacks; Jews because they're rumored to have horns; and any other minority that exists in sufficient numbers to pose a social and economic threat.	Slightly more prejudiced all around, specifically toward Blacks and Indians. Ethnic Catholics and Jews still bother you, though feeling toward latter is ebbing in the Southwest and at a slower rate in Southeast.	Slightly less-modera\ attitudes down the li\ Irish blue collars str\ gle to maintain influe\ in unions, political c\ trol over cities, and, lesser degree, their neighborhood. Lace\ tain gentility was ha\ to achieve for later a\ rivals here; may be harder to maintain.
	Lower	Same as above only more so. Hostile about competition on all levels with "racial inferiors" and fact that some have been here a shorter time than you, yet may be better off.		If you live in the East South Central region, especially in Mississippi or Alabama, you can count yourself among the most prejudiced folks in the country. If from a South Atlantic state (Delaware down to Florida), you're slightly less extreme. And if from Arkansas, Louisiana, Texas or Oklahoma and a farmer you may be one of the least prejudiced of this southern status group.	Face competition fro\ all quarters in all are\ — jobs, housing, educ\ tion. At lowest statu\ els you're more in\ clined to think in ter\ of stereotypes, fear '\ ferences" and look f\ scapegoats. Less libe\ down the line.
		East & West Coasts	*Midwest & Mountain*	*South & Southwest*	*All Regions*

REGION

German Catholic	Italian Catholic	Polish Catholic	
cond most liberal Cath- c group as a whole. ghtly less open-minded, re prejudiced than the sh, somewhat less than ur Protestant counter- rt. Slightly greater incli- tion to anti-Semitism n racism. Expression antipathies seen partic- rly in smaller towns; in er parts of country ur feelings are less ex- me but not so's any- dy'd really notice.	Clannish; family and home are preeminent con- cerns. You hold more ex- treme views of Blacks; somewhat more moderate attitudes toward Jews, perhaps because there are some ethnic similarities, shared urban experience and some intermarriage. General prejudicial atti- tudes are stronger than Irish and Germans of like status.	Younger educated Poles' racist sentiments are not extreme, on some issues about the same as Slavic Jews', slightly more mod- erate than Italian or Ger- man Catholics' and all Protestants'. Education really makes the dif- ference here, as Poles haven't achieved the status of other Catholic or im- migrant groups, and gen- erally rank among the most prejudiced, with Easterners of this "class" showing most moderate tendencies.	Great Polish concentra- tion in cities likely to form very tight commu- nity and take negative attitudes toward outsid- ers. Neighborhood is sacred; home ownership a prize hard won and you are determined to keep Blacks and other minorities out. Racial feelings and anti-Semi- tism run high.
r you, racism and anti- mitism go hand in hand. stile feelings are more onounced in Midwest n in the East, and tend coincide more with rman Protestants than her-status coreligion- s. As with most minori- s, the closer you are to -country ethnic tradi- ns and tight religious gma, the more prone to treme prejudice.	Blue collars, unskilled and some white collars see jobs threatened by blacks and are running scared. Less bothered by the Puerto Rican at the mo- ment because he is less visible. Wasps are disregarded entirely be- cause you're not striving for country-club status. Among the old, feelings toward Jews correspond with the ancient religious stereotype of Christ killer. But more general current feeling is Jews "got every- thing too easy." Middle- aged and old don't like the Irish because of tradi- tional Church allegiances and union rivalries. Just as dominant is internal re- sentment—Northern Ital- ians vs. Southern, Cala- brians vs. Sicilians, Sicilians vs. all, etc.	Dedicated homeowners who stick together by and large and don't appreciate government handouts to poor. Definitely don't want "them" on your bowling team. You're more bigoted than above group, but less than Mid- western confreres. Anti- Jewish sentiment also runs high.	Most prejudiced of all Catholics, with racist atti- tudes that would rival a Southerner's (particularly in Chicago and other major cities), and anti- Jewish sentiments that would rival your racism. Antagonism toward Irish Catholics is often equally bitter.
All Regions	*All Regions*	*Northeast*	*Midwest*

WHITE			BLACK
French Catholic	*Puerto Rican Catholic*	*Jewish*	*Protestant & Catholic*
Quite liberal toward Blacks; sentiments similar to Irish and German. But anti-Semitic feeling runs high.		Your are most liberal of major religions, especially on political and minority-rights issues, and higher-status Jews most liberal of all. Thus, the least prejudiced American might be found among you. Outside Manhattan's liberal-intellectual Establishment, however, anti-Black feeling is surfacing rapidly. You're moderately hostile toward WASPs who block your further upward mobility; Catholics; Germans; and fellow Jews viewed as "too foreign" or "ostentatious."	Conventionally militant— a card-carrying member of the N.A.A.C.P. and Urban League—and aligned with the white liberal Establishment. You can be condescending toward lower-class Blacks. and tan may still be more beautiful. Your feeling toward Jews is both a reflection of your anti-white sentiment and sense of Jewish economic domination of your less-privileged brother, and it extends in like proportions to other ethnic minorities you see occupying a similar role.
Racial attitudes correspond to Italians; anti-Jewish hostility comes closest to Poles'.	As newest minority group in major cities, you are placed in direct competition with Negroes and poorer whites. Regardless of skin shade, most of you consider yourselves white, You identify with your Spanish heritage, resent being lumped with Blacks and subjected to the same kind of discrimination. Feelings toward most whites roughly correspond to their attitudes toward you. In New York City, your view of Jews is the least positive of any group, including Blacks, though you tend to accept fewer negative and positive stereotypes about them than do Blacks. Your hostility, however, particularly among the poor, extends to all ethnic landlords, shopkeepers and employers you feel exploited by. Some followers of your progress in U.S. see you moving at a faster rate than any previous immigrant group; and while your leadership has been militant—growing more so all the time (the young, particularly)—your community has been relatively free of violence.	While seventy-five percent of you fall here or above, this fact does not eliminate your bias. Basic liberal sympathies are somewhat eroded by emerging negativism toward Blacks. You still strongly endorse job, housing and educational equality, but more on the bootstrap we-did-it-so-can-they level—and preferably away from your doorstep. In New York, the Stuff the Jewish Defense League is made of. You also see yourself outside gentile society and harbor resentments against it.	While things are getting better for you personally, your impersonal grievances against white society mount. Your anti-white feelings, while bitter and intense, are still not as extreme as white prejudice aimed at you.
		Attitudes correspond as much with other immigrant ethnics as with your own kind, particularly if you are older or very religious. You can identify with the Negro as a downtrodden minority, yet this does not dispel your prejudice, fear of competition or acceptance of negative stereotypes about him. Tolerant of other minorities, *goyim* in general, you are not.	For some of you the struggle for survival is so great you don't differentiate hates: Whitey is the enemy. Your anti-Semitic feeling runs higher than that of your Southern counterpart, but is about equal to the Northern white's of the same socioeconomic group.
All Regions	*Northeast & Midwest*	*All Regions*	*North*

BLACK	RED		YELLOW—CHINESE		
Protestant & Catholic	*Christian & Tribal*		*Buddhist & Christian*		
[Y]ou can be counted by [th]e handfuls, largely [pr]ofessionals working in [bl]ack schools and colleges and serving in the [bl]ack community almost [ex]clusively. More anti-[w]hite resentment than [o]ur Northern "class" [br]other but less inclined [th]an most Northern [bl]acks to do something [ab]out it—on both [c]ounts because of your [ex]posure to basic [S]outhern values.			Members of this group, particularly the younger ones, are least bigoted. Many have left Chinatown for neighboring districts, and while you've taken some of your cultural traditions with you, you've left just as many behind. Unlike the Black ghetto, Chinatown is run by your own people. Internally, the larger, rich, controlling families are biased against the small ones. American-born Chinese against the foreign-born.	*Upper*	
[M]ore prejudiced than [o]ur Northern counter-[pa]rt, particularly if [yo]u've never been ex-[po]sed to the North, [sl]ightly less so if you're [fr]om the Southwest. [Y]our anger toward Jews [an]d small concentra-[ti]ons of ethnic minori-[ti]es is greater (particu-[la]rly in the Southeast) [th]an Northern Blacks' [or] Southern whites'. To [so]me extent this may be [an] extension of your [ge]neral anti-white feel-[in]g, focusing on the [ne]arest visible white [p]erson who isn't likely [to] retaliate in traditional [S]outhern fashion. [A] majority languishing [in] poverty and praying [fo]r a hand up from [S].C.L.C. More anti-[w]hite feeling, particu-[la]rly in the cities and [am]ong your young than [in] rural areas for all [ag]es. Your anti-Semi-[ti]sm is negligible in all [ar]eas as is negative feel-[in]g toward specific eth-[ni]c minorities. Basically, [y]ou don't distinguish [am]ong white men, can't [s]e beyond their faces [an]d the power they [h]ave over you.	One third of the Indian population is scattered in many small pockets around urban centers (Minneapolis, Indianapolis, Chicago. Los Angeles, San Francisco). Indian feeling is bitter against all whites with little distinction made as to religion or ethnic background—and for the obvious historical reasons plus some more current ones. In the urban context of growing militancy, your hostility is moderately high toward Blacks and other minority rivals for legislative attention, foundation funds, media coverage and public support.	Two thirds of the Indian population is dispersed on reservations, small bits of former reservations and communities in rural areas. Your anti-white bias is widespread and particularly high where whites continue to keep you out of community partici-pation, "buy" up your lands, usurp water and fishing rights—which is practically everywhere you live. Some of you claim superiority to Blacks based on the we-were-here-first principle and evidence that your ancestors had Black slaves. Intertribal bias based on personal iden-tity and elitism, though diminishing, still exists. Cherokees, Choctaws, Chickasaws, Seminoles and Creeks feel superior to "uncivilized" tribes such as Sioux, Apache and Osage. Hopis feel superior to the Tewas, and Tewas to Hopis. The Sioux and Navajos feel superior period. However, such inter-tribal attitudes are tri-fling when compared to similar bias among non-Indian groups.	While the ancient belief that China is the center of the civilized world may be less prevalent today than one hundred years ago, it remains the basis of many of your prejudices. To the ex-tent that it still holds sway, you view whites as *bok gooi* (white devils), clumsy and vulgar; Blacks as *hok gooi* (black devils), suited to menial work, and you tend to lump Puerto Ricans, Mex-icans and Indians with the Blacks. You're slightly more sympa-thetic to Jews, as you've been called "Jews of the Orient." You don't much like the Japanese, nor they you, feelings rooted in old cultural and political differences, and World War II. Within the Chinese community, more recent Hong Kong and Taiwan arrivals are viewed with disdain.	*Middle* *Lower*	*SOCIOECONOMIC STATUS*
South	*All Regions (urban)*	*All Regions (rural)*	*East & West Coasts*		

REGION

THE KU KLUX KLAN

The Ku Klux Klan was founded at Pulaski, Tennessee, in 1866 as a social organization for war veterans. But, during the Reconstruction period that followed the Civil War, much of the Klan's energy was devoted to preventing Negroes from voting in local elections.

The KKK was disbanded in 1869, but reorganized in 1915, when it began expanding its activities to include not only Negroes, but Jews, Roman Catholics, radicals and foreigners. At the height of its power there were almost 5 million members riding around in white sheets, burning crosses, flogging, lynching and wreaking havoc in the middle of the night. (Some authors claim that not all activities attributed to the KKK were perpetuated by its members, since it was possible for anyone with a white sheet to commit crimes in the name of the Klan.)

The cover of this Ku Klux Klan catalog employs "Uncle Sam" as a recruiter for the KKK.

The KKK was formally dissolved in 1944, but it emerged once again after World War II. The group gained new strength after the Supreme Court outlawed racial segregation in public schools, and since 1955 several Klan organizations have been formed. However, current leaders deny any links with the old Klan.

Membership was estimated to be as high as 14,000 in the 1960s, but apathy brought membership tumbling down to a mere 4,500 in the 1970s. A 1978 demonstration at Tupelo, Mississippi, brought out only 50 Klansmen, and no one knows for certain how many members are left in their ranks.

According to Imperial Wizard Bill Wilkinson, "We just want to get the same attention from the press that the Blacks get."

Despite the "secretive" aura that surrounds the Klan, the KKK is listed in the Encyclopedia of Associations, a standard reference text found in most public libraries. Want more information? Contact:

Imperial Wizard Bill Wilkinson
The Invisible Empire Knights of the Ku Klux Klan
P.O. Box 700
Denham Springs, Louisiana 70726

Wilkinson's Klan has a 400-item gift catalog which hawks T-shirts, belt buckles and pamphlets, but, alas, no sheets. There are posters of the Imperial Wizard for sale, printed on "heavy paper suitable for framing." There are Klan calling cards stating "You have been patronized by the KKK" that can be left in restaurants; stickers with catchy slogans; and books and leaflets on such diverse subjects as: The International Jew; Race Scientists Speak Out On Racial Differences; Lincoln's Program for Sending Negroes Back to Africa; The Kosher Food Swindle; and Roots Exposed: A Total View from the White Perspective on Alex Haley's Mythology of Slavery.

ETHNIC STEREOTYPES

ETHNICS ON TELEVISION

Even in the days before there was Norman Lear, the Russian-Jewish "King of the ethnic sit-com," there were ethnics on TV. The Jews were represented by Gertrude Berg, the Norwegians had *I Remember Mama* and the Blacks were stuck with the likes of *Beulah* (a fat maid) and *Amos 'N' Andy*. Although *I Love Lucy* has been in reruns for more than twenty years now (despite the tired jokes about Ricky's Cuban accent) some comedy shows from the 1950s will never again see the light of day because they are too offensive to too many people. *Amos 'N' Andy* starred a lazy conniver named Kingfish; fat, dumb Andy, who was always being cheated out of money by Kingfish; a slow-moving janitor named Lightnin'; and Amos — one of the few Blacks on TV who was a hard, steady worker and a family man, with a good head on his shoulders. Not only does the show present poor role models for young Blacks, but most of us have come a long way from "Stepin Fetchit" jokes in the past thirty years.

Some critics contend that TV hasn't changed its stereotypes very much in the past three decades. White ethnics are depicted as loudmouths (Ralph Kramden of *The Honeymooners*), bigots (Archie Bunker of *All in the Family*), and crude, insensitive types (Louie of *Taxi*), while most Blacks are depicted as low achievers (typified by Redd Foxx of *Sanford and Son*).

If we believe everything we see on the TV tube, the only ethnic group that escapes with a positive image is the WASPs. In the 1950s the ultimate WASP father (who always knew best) was Robert Young. Unlike crude ethnics (Ralph Kramden, Archie Bunker) who constantly complained about their wives, criticized their cooking and appeared at the dinner table unkempt, Robert Young always managed to appear dressed in a suit and tie. Why, he even had a "lounging" jacket with suede patches on the elbows — something no Polish-American or Italian-American father is likely to wear on TV.

According to a survey conducted in 1977, white males dominated the television screen 65.3% of the time, in both major and minor roles. They were frequently portrayed as older, more independent characters with diverse and important occupations. White females were seen on the television screens of America 23.8% of the time, but they were usually portrayed as young, unemployed, underemployed, tied to the home and not quite able to cope. Members of minority groups were usually relegated primarily to ethnic settings, or else they appeared as tokens in all-white shows. Non-white males received only 8.6% of the roles on TV, and non-white females accounted for only 2.3%.

Why are there so few positive roles for ethnics on TV? Frankly, because stereotypes sell! In commercial television the bottom line is audience share. No matter how educational, entertaining, innovative or informative a television series is, if it doesn't capture a large share of the viewing audience — off it goes.

During the first episode of *Julia,* starring Diahann Carroll as a Black nurse who has lost her husband in Vietnam, Julia phones a physician for a job interview:

"Oh, did they tell you I'm colored?" she asks.

"Mm," the doctor replies. "What color are you?"

"Wh-hy, I'm Negro."

"Oh," says the doctor. "Have you always been a Negro, or are you just trying to be fashionable?"

In 1968 it was advantageous to be a Black actor seeking work in a TV series, as producers rushed about trying to make their shows "relevant." But few roles had any credibility or individuality. Harry Belafonte remarked that most Blacks depicted on TV are either "super Negroes," or "button-down Brooks Brothers eunuchs," Typically, when the first Black moved to Peyton Place, he was nothing less than a neurosurgeon.

Many producers would like to use more minorities on TV, but they are frankly afraid. When CBS debuted a new "comedy" about an unmarried mother, *Miss Winslow and Son,* in 1979, there was no way the title character could have an ethnic background. She had to be pure WASP — can you imagine the flak that would have ensued if she had been depicted as Black, Hispanic, Italian or Jewish?

To be fair, there have been some positive roles for ethnics on TV: *Kojak* (a Greek cop), *Barney Miller* (a Jewish cop), *Kotter* (a Jewish schoolteacher), *Baretta* and *Serpico* (Italian cops), *John Shaft* (a Black detective) and *Julia* (a Black nurse). Most of what we see, though, is stereotyped behavior — both during the television presentation and on the commercial messages scattered throughout each hour's worth of viewing.

OFFENSIVE ADVERTISEMENTS

In 1970 a newspaper editor wrote, "It is not good business to make fun of Negroes any more. But it still seems to be good business to poke fun at other minority groups . . . It would startle most of us now to encounter a television commercial showing a pickaninny eating watermelon and grinning from ear to ear, but we still see Indian braves selling cigarettes with smoke signals and slothful Mexican bandits selling corn chips."

The "Frito Bandito" finally disappeared in the "sue first, ask questions later" Seventies, when large corporations began removing all "controversial" ethnic stereotypes from their commercials. Frigidaire did away with the band of Mexican thieves interested in appropriating one of their side-by-side refrigerator-freezer combinations. Arrid Deodorant stopped featuring a bandito who sprayed his underarms while a voice-over claimed, "if it works for *him,* it will work for you." And L&M stopped sending residual checks to "Paco," who was so lazy he never "feenished" anything, "not even the revolution," but was so crazy about the taste of L&M that he couldn't bear to put out his butt.

In their haste not to offend, the advertisers of America began taking their toll on the stereotypical, meek, mild-mannered WASP male. Who else would be expected to take abuse from toll-booth attendants, waitresses and small children about the grime that forms a "ring around his collar." Certainly not a stereotypical Mafioso Italian, or a macho Latin lover, or a Chinese laundry owner. No one else in America could be expected to take such insults.

How much truth is there in the myths that are foisted on us day after day in print and on television? Let's examine some of our most common stereotyped beliefs.

EVERY ETHNIC GROUP HAS A STEREOTYPE

Like a caricature drawing of a person's face, a stereotype takes a grain of truth and exaggerates it until it becomes distorted and blown up out of proportion. According to common stereotypes, all Italians are connected with the underworld; all Swedes are sexually liberated; all Russians are communists; all Germans dislike Jews; all Mexicans believe in *mañana;* all Englishmen drink tea; and all Scotsmen are cheap pennypinchers. They range from the innocent to the inane; some are harmless, but some stereotypes hurt.

Ethnic Stereotype #101 All Blacks are lazy and slow-moving.

How can that stereotype possibly be true? Consider all the fast-running Black athletes, such as Jesse Owens and Wilma Rudolph, and their counterparts on the football fields and basketball courts of America. Still, Black Americans have been fighting that slow-moving stigma since the entertainment industry began. When did the stereotype begin? There is one Black man who, although he didn't *invent* the stereotype, has become the epitome of "slow motion." His name has even become a synonym for the stereotype itself—Stepin Fetchit.

Born Lincoln Theodore Perry (1902–   ) in Key West, Florida, he was the first Negro .actor to receive featured billing in a motion picture. In film after film, Perry played the same slow-walking, slow-talking character, who could roll his eyes real wide when frightened and shake his knees wildly to make the audiences (white audiences, that is) roll with laughter.

Living the "Hollywood" life in the 1930s, Perry was the proud owner of Hollywood's first pink Rolls-Royce and a Cadillac limousine with a *white* chauffeur dressed in livery, in addition to his 14 other cars. During the Forties, however, Fetchit's career began to lag. The complaints of civil rights groups about his offensive portrayal of Negroes on the silver screen began to intimidate producers. Fetchit, however, didn't mind his stereotype and, as in the proverbial punch line, "he cried all the way to the bank." In fact, during a lull in his career in 1951, Fetchit placed an ad in *Variety,* the show-biz trade paper, billing himself as "The Laziest Man in the World."

Stereotypes #28 and #29 "Catholic girls start much too late" while Jewish girls are "easy."

Billy Joel's observation on the mores of Catholic girls upset the Church to say the least. But, think of the stereotype the Synagogues have had to live with all these years. Ross Wetzsteon, a Scotch-Irish-Bavarian American, with a name that everyone assumed was Jewish, had this to say about the old sexual stereotypes in "On Passing for Jewish: Confessions of a closet WASP":

"I've always been attracted to Jewish women . . . I thought Jewish girls were more sexually liberated, while Jewish boys were less sexually attractive . . . with WASPs the code seemed unbreakable—first date kiss at the door, second date clumsy feel in the car, etc., etc., so you sensed your sexuality was rigidly scripted; with Jews, on the other hand, it wasn't a matter of an 'easy lay'—it was the feeling that whatever was going to happen sexually between you would happen, clumsily, perhaps, but at least spontaneously. (Who ever heard of a WASP wearing a diaphragm on a blind date? And given the choice between you and Woody Allen . . . Unspeakable pleasures lay in wait, and you didn't even have to feel guilty.)"

Such was the stuff Ross's adolescent dreams were made of, but he later learned the truth:

"The extent to which this was an adolescent fantasy didn't become apparent to me until I learned, through often comic and occasionally painful experience, that Jews had a tradition of 'nice girls' every bit as rigidly repressive as WASPs." (*Village Voice,* September 12, 1977)

Stereotype #73 Irish men are all heavy drinkers.

Do Irishmen drink a disproportionate amount of liquor and beer? More than members of other ethnic groups? There aren't any hard facts to prove or disprove the stereotype, and the names of bars may not be any indication, but there *are* an awful

Not even Currier and Ives were immune to stereotyping characters in their lithographs. This print of three Irishmen "taking a smile" first appeared in 1854. (Courtesy: Museum of the City of New York)

lot of drinking establishments with Irish names.

The 1980 Manhattan telephone directory listed 57 pubs with Irish names such as Paddy's, Erin's, and Rose of Killarney. Thirty-five of those taverns were named Blarney — Blarney Stone, Blarney Rock, Blarney Rose, Blarney Pub and Blarney Castle. Even if the names of bars don't prove anything, one can certainly see how such a stereotype might arise!

Stereotype #47   All Chinese are wise, honorable and submissive.

These three characteristics of the Chinese stereotype were epitomized by Charlie Chan, the fictional Chinese detective with his bumbling "number one son."

Suffice it to say that all three "Charlie Chans" who appeared in the movies were Occidental. Ranging from Warner Oland (1880–1938), a Swedish actor who starred in 16 Chan movies; to Sidney Toler, who starred in 22; to Roland Winters, the lead actor in 6 films — none was even remotely Oriental in his heritage.

The Chinese-Americans may have found Chan's screen portrayal offensive, but prior to his debut on celluloid, the only Orientals in the movies were villains of one sort or another, so at least it was a step in the right direction.

Stereotype #485   All Blacks own Cadillacs.

Although there is a documented fondness for luxury cars among Black Americans, their rate of ownership for Cadillacs in 1966 was exactly equal to that of White Americans. Three percent of all Whites who owned cars, and three percent of all Blacks who owned cars, owned Cadillacs.

Affectionately called the "Hog" even before gasoline shortages and "green flag" days, the reason why the "Hog" was so well liked among Blacks (and Whites, too) was status. According to Leroy Jeffries, advertising manager for *Ebony*, "Status considerations outweigh almost everything else in a Negro choice of a car."

Stereotype #93   All Orientals have squinty eyes, have buck teeth and are incapable of pronouncing the letter "r."

According to Korean-American Tom Kagy Nahm, who wrote in *Newsweek* about his dissatisfaction with the way Orientals are portrayed in the media ("Stop Stereotyping Me," January 15, 1979): "I do not have squinty eyes or buck teeth. I have a good build (you'll just have to take my word for it). I don't speak with a funny accent. I've never done any gardening . . . I hate doing the laundry and have never worked as a waiter or a chauffeur. I'm not passive [and] I was once voted 'most macho' in my dorm."

Ethnic stereotype #95   Latins make the best lovers.

In this stereotype, Latin can mean "Spanish," "Italian" or "French" — almost anyone who speaks a Romance language qualifies. The rumors may have started with the legendary Spaniard, Don Juan, or maybe it was that amorous Italian, Casanova (1725–1798) who encouraged the women of America to believe that Latins are more seductive. According to recent reports, however, there isn't any truth to the old stereotype — in fact, two reports conclude that "Latins make lousy lovers."

Sociologist Rowena Davis and Professor Giampaolo Fabris spent two years researching the "myth of the great Latin lover." According to their findings, Italian women live in sexual misery. Their report is rather harsh on Italian males, whom they describe as "invariably egoistic, selfish, often violent and only seeking self-satisfaction." "So is it surprising," the authors ask, "that his partner does not look forward to going to bed?"

Davis and Fabris cite the traditional moral codes of the Italian family and the teachings of the Roman Catholic Church as the causal agents responsible for the sexual misery in Italy.

A similar study conducted by a Mexican sexologist, Dr. Osvaldo A. Quijada, was equally harsh on the stereotypical "macho" lover. Dr. Quijada maintained that many "Mexican men are unimaginative, insecure and unsatisfied lovers."

Ethnic stereotype #86   WASPs are boring lovers/Blacks are more sensual than whites.

While many White Americans view Blacks as "earthy and sensual" in their stereotypes, many Blacks view White Anglo-Saxons as "asexual, cold and boring in bed." Black comedian Richard Pryor ridicules what he terms the "abstractness" of White sexual relations on one of his early comedy albums. Rather than do what "feels good" or what "comes naturally," the White couple in his skit actually sits down to decide whether or not they should "do it," implying that sex between WASPs is planned, patterned and executed without "feeling."

Ethnic stereotype #67   All mobsters are Italian.

First of all, if you believe the underworld czars, there isn't any mob or "Mafia." And,

even if there were such a mythical organization, not all of its members would be Italian-Americans. After all, there was Dutch Schultz in the 1920s (a German-American whose real name was Arthur Flegenheimer), and the Jewish mobsters Meyer Lansky and Mickey Cohen.

According to a recent study, only 70% of all Americans believe that the "M----" exists, and only 24% believe that membership is exclusively limited to Italians. (Old stereotypes die hard.)

PEOPLE WHO "CROSSED"

Who could be more "French" than Charles Aznavour, that sad-eyed singer of bittersweet love songs? Actually, Aznavour was born in France of Armenian parents who fled massacre at the hands of the Turks. They settled in the Latin Quarter of Paris shortly before Varenagh Aznourian was born in 1924. In a sense, Aznavour was an Armenian who "crossed"—and attained his fame as a French singer.

Let's take a look at some Americans who crossed ethnic boundaries and some who attained fame and fortune in ethnic areas foreign to their heritage:

JOSÉ GRECO is one of the world's best-known Spanish dancers. However, like Lola Montez, the "Spanish" exotic dancer who shocked audiences in the 1840s, Greco was not born in Spain, nor did he have any Spanish ancestors. How did a nice Italian boy from Brooklyn become the world's most famous Spanish dancer? Talent and hard work. "I put everything into it. I was determined not to shame myself," Greco recalls about a childhood dare that shaped his future.

Born Costanzo Greco in a small Italian town in the Abruzzi Molise Mountains, he emigrated to the United States at the age of 9 with his family. José was forced to accompany his sister to and from her Spanish dancing classes, and after watching her perform, boasted that he could dance better than she could without ever taking a lesson. The dance teacher overheard Greco's bravado and challenged him to perform for the class. Determined not to fail, he accepted the challenge, and so impressed the teacher with his natural ability that she took him on as a pupil. Although he does not deny his

Italian heritage, he has never gone out of his way to publicize the fact: "After all, when people go to see a Spanish dancer, they like to think he is Spanish."

(Just for the record: Lola Montez (1818–1861) was born Marie Delores Eliza Rosanna Gilbert in Ireland.)

AUTHENTIC CHINESE FOOD FROM MINNESOTA. Where else but in America could an Italian-American from the Scandinavian section of Minnesota become a multi-millionaire by selling canned Chinese food to the supermarkets of the Midwest?

That's just what happened when Luigino Francesco Paolucci (better known as Jeno Paolucci) started the Chun King company in 1940 with an initial investment of $2,500 and sold it 26 years later to the R. J. Reynolds Tobacco Company for $63 million. He later entered the frozen pizza business, where his mother said he should have been in the first place, and today Jeno's, Inc., produces $100 million worth of frozen pizza and hot snacks annually, making its namesake an even wealthier man.

Times were not always easy for the Paoluccis and Jeno's childhood was one of poverty, deprivation and hard work. The second of two children, Jeno was born on July 7, 1918 in Aurora, Minnesota, an iron-mining company town where his parents, Michelina and Ettore Paolucci, settled after immigrating to this country in 1912. Ettore had been a sulfur miner in a small town in the northern province of Pesaro, Italy, until the sulfur supply was exhausted and he was forced to find a new livelihood. Many of his fellow townsmen were being recruited by American agents to work on the Iron Range in Minnesota and Ettore decided to try his luck in America.

To supplement the family's meager income, Jeno, while still in high school, hawked fruits and vegetables at an open-air stand in Duluth and soon realized that he had great sales talent. He toyed with the idea of becoming a lawyer, but figured a good salesman could earn a lot more money; after completing a year and a half at Hibbing Junior College, he entered the wholesale grocery business.

The turning point in his life came when he was on a trip to Minneapolis and discovered a group of Japanese immigrants growing mung bean sprouts in hydroponic gardens. Jeno, realizing that no one else was packing Chinese food for the supermarket set, borrowed $2,500 from a Wisconsin food broker and began canning these crunchy sprouts. Soon he was spicing them up and canning chop suey, noodles, soy sauce and other Oriental goodies. Jeno reasoned, "We had canned spaghetti in those days, why not chow mein?" The name for his company was taken from the map of China: by crossing out the "g" in Chungking Province, Jeno launched the Chun King food company.

In addition to being voted Outstanding Italian-American of the Year in 1965, Paolucci was voted Honorary Swede of the Year in 1972 in honor of his outstanding success in Minnesota, where Finnish- and Swedish-Americans predominate.

He is currently serving as chairman of the Italian American Foundation and hopes to establish a Washington-based voice for the needs of the 23 million Italian-Americans in the United States today.

ITALIAN TOMATOES FROM CALIFORNIA. Now, if an Italian-American can make it big in the Chinese food business, and an Irishman can make his millions selling Pizza Hut pies to Middle America, then logic dictates that a nice Jewish lady from Brooklyn would be the one to introduce Italian plum tomatoes to America.

Tillie Lewis (1901–   ) was born Myrtle Ehrlich, the daughter of a Jewish immigrant father. Her mother died when Tillie was an infant; her father later remarried. To escape from an unhappy homelife with her stepmother, Tillie married a thirty-year-old grocer when she was a mere fifteen. It was in the family grocery store that she developed the brainstorm that grew into a $100 million enterprise.

While taking inventory at the store, Tillie was appalled at the high price of Italian plum tomatoes. "Why are these tomatoes so expensive?" she asked. Her husband told her that the best tomato paste and tomato sauce was made from these pear-shaped tomatoes, which could only be grown in Italy. Tillie spoke to horticulture experts and farmers, but they all told her the same thing—it couldn't be done, the soil and climate in the United States were not ideally suited to grow these tomatoes. She did a bit of research on the subject, then nearly abandoned the idea until Congress imposed a 40% tariff on imported tomatoes in 1934.

Divorced at the time, and working as a stockbroker on Wall Street, Tillie studied the temperature, soil and rainfall statistics for various regions of the United States, and came to the conclusion that the San Joaquin Valley of California was an ideal location for tomato culture. She believed that the only reason these pear-shaped tomatoes had never been grown commercially in the United States was that no one had ever tried.

She visited Italy and brought back seedlings. Although she had some trouble convincing farmers to grow her tomatoes, when they finally tried, the results were successful. In 1966, Tillie sold her controlling interest in Tillie Lewis Foods to the Ogden Corporation for $9 million and joined Ogden as a director. Her original investment had been a mere $10,000.

FROM LITHUANIAN TO ITALIAN. Sixty-four-year-old Alice Scola is a Lithuanian by birth, but her soul has become Italian through her life in the North End.

"I met my husband when I was 17 and he took me to meet his family. Of course, they didn't like it because I was a Lithuanian girl; knowing that I was an outsider, not an Italian girl, they kind of objected. We straightened things out. We got married and both families agreed. I suppose there was nothing else they could do.

"I had to adjust my life a lot. I never knew Italian and I never knew many Italian people. My mother-in-law couldn't speak a word of English at the time, although she had children going to school. I had to adjust and learn, but she was very patient with me.

I really adjusted more after my son was born. As I was going along my mother-in-law would say to me 'sedi' or 'mangi' and she would show me by gesture — she would sit and say, 'sedi.' Then she would say to me 'latte,' since she thought it was good that I was nursing my son. I really learned.

"Nobody thinks I'm anything else but Italian now, between raising my children and cooking. I stayed in the same neighborhood all these years." (From: The North End. Boston 200 Neighborhood History Series, 1975.)

LEBANESE BANKER IN A WASP WORLD. When Robert Abboud first entered the world of finance, "his boss warned him not to expect to rise too high in banking because grandsons of Lebanese immigrants can't make it big in that WASP world."

Luckily, Abboud didn't take the advice to heart, rising to become chairman of First Chicago Corporation, the parent company of the First National Bank of Chicago, a post he held from 1975 to 1980.

After he was decorated for herosim in the Korean War, Abboud armed himself with a law degree and a business degree, both from Harvard. He earned his reputation in the late 1960s by building his bank's overseas network. Apparently, that was enough to change his bosses' mind about bank presidencies being limited to WASP Americans, since Abboud beat out three other candidates for the highly esteemed position.

DAUGHTER OF THE AMERICAN REVOLUTION. Times have changed in the 40 years since the Daughters of the American Revolution barred Black singer Marian Anderson from using Constitution Hall in Washington, D.C. In 1977, that rather snobby group admitted its first known Black member.

Karen Batchelor Farmer began a search for her ancestors in 1975 after the birth of her son. The daughter of a Detroit physician, Farmer knew who her ancestors had been for three generations on her mother's side of the family — her great-grandmother, a white named Jennie Daisy Hood, had married a Black man, Prince Albert Weaver, in 1889. Working backward with her genealogical detective work, Farmer found that Jennie Hood's first American ancestor was William Hood, an Irish immigrant who came to America in the mid-1700s and served as a Private, 6th class, in the Lancaster, Pennsylvania, county militia during the Revolutionary War.

Her ancestor qualified Mrs. Farmer for admission to the DAR and in 1977 she became the 623,128th member, and "the first to identify herself as a Black woman" (the organization claims that it does not inquire about an applicant's race).

According to Jeannette O. Baylies, President General of the DAR, 99% of the members who commented on the situation were in favor of having a Black member, and "Everyone who's met her feels that she's the tops." Mrs. Baylies also added: "I say let's forget about the Marian Anderson incident and go forward." (New York Times, Dec. 28, 1977)

ETHNIC JOKES

Why do people tell ethnic jokes? Because, basically, everyone needs someone to look down upon, and a joke is an acceptable means of expressing this darker side of our human nature. "Can't you take a joke?" "What's the matter, lost your sense of humor?" With a joke, it is possible to be offensive without *meaning* to offend. Or is it?

When ethnic jokes first started they were merely takeoffs on the "moron jokes" of the 1950s. (Why did the moron throw his clock out the window? Because he wanted to see time fly.) Instead of using the word "moron," Irish joke tellers would use "Italian"; Italian joke tellers would substitute the word "Pole"; and Polish joke tellers would tell their jokes about "Irishmen."

But the Polish-Americans seem to be bearing the brunt of the ethnic joke craze that has been sweeping our nation since the late 1960s. When John Paul II was elected Pope of the Roman Catholic Church, Poles all over the United States expressed hope that a Polish Pope would put an end to the Polish joke. However, it seems that the Pope's election merely spurred on "Polish

Pope" jokes, even more tasteless than their predecessors. ("Hear about the Pope's first miracle? He made a blind man deaf.")

According to a 1978 survey by *Psychology Today,* after sexual humor, ethnic jokes were the most popular among their readers who did not consider them hostile or offensive. Just for the record, here a few "classic" ethnic jokes:

♦ Popular "Chinese" joke of 1890: (This joke was flourishing at the time when cable cars and trolley cars began replacing horse-drawn carriages.) "What did the Chinaman say when he saw his first horseless carriage? 'No pushee, no pullee, but goee like hellee allee samee.' "

♦ Puerto Rican joke, circa 1959: "What did the Puerto Rican bride wear for her wedding? Something old, something new, something borrowed, and something blue, green, orange, yellow, purple . . ."

♦ Indian joke, circa 1964: "The Lone Ranger and Tonto are surrounded by a band of hostile Indians. The masked man turns to his faithful companion and says, 'Tonto, what are we going to do?' Tonto's reply? 'What you mean *we,* pale face?' "

♦ Arab/Israeli joke, circa 1967: "What happens when an Arab tank collides with an Israeli tank? The Arab comes out with his hands up, and the Jew comes out screaming 'whiplash.' "

♦ Polish, Italian, Irish, Ukrainian, Russian, etc. joke, circa 1970: "How many 'ethnics' does it take to make popcorn? Five. One to hold the pot and four to shake the stove."

Are Poles Laughing at Polish Jokes? Apparently not. Although Michael Novak is not Polish, he is a Slavic-American and feels that the sting of Polish jokes affects him, too. This is what he had to say about the subject in *Newsweek:*

"Most of those of us who are children of Eastern European Christian immigrants know we are the children of peasants. We do not have in our family experience many models of learning, status and public grace. We have a sufficient sense of our modest origins. The sting of Polish jokes is that they make our deepest self-doubts public. They keep us in our place. They canonize a caste from which many see no escape . . . Recently, in Pennsylvania, I saw a huge, newly painted garbage truck. On its front bumper in large letters was printed: Polish Camper. Suppose the words had been Nigger Camper or Jewish Camper? Liberal organizations would certainly have protested . . . how much damage is done to the psyches of people constantly stereotyped in public? . . . This is supposed to be a nation of civility toward all, bigotry toward none. It is not. But when the laughter rings, it rings for thee."

"GROWING UP ETHNIC" IN 50 WORDS OR LESS

There are certain events fixed in every person's memory of growing up that are unique to his or her religious, ethnic, and geographical upbringing. Most White Anglo-Saxon Protestants never heard of "American" bread, until they met an Italian-American, Arab-American, or Jewish-American, or a member of some ethnic group to which the word bread had a more delicious meaning than the spongy, preservative-laden loaf that is common on supermarket shelves all over America. Ethnic Americans had Sicilian bread, pita loaves, challah, French bread, Russian rye or some other bread of substance to call their own. Besides bread, members of each ethnic group share certain experiences that are theirs alone. Some of the following may be considered stereotypes, but they are a legitimate part of the ethnic American experience and are presented as such:

Growing up Italian-American means

. . . having a grandfather who made wine in the basement from boxes and boxes of strong purple grapes.

. . . having to *taste* the wine your grandfather made in the basement from boxes and boxes of strong purple grapes.

. . . being surprised to find that not every household has a holy picture with a votive candle burning in front of it day and night.

. . . knowing relatives who own *two* stoves. One in the kitchen, "for show," and one in the basement, where most meals are cooked and served.

. . . having a fig tree that had to be covered with tar paper and rags, and topped with a steel pail, to protect it from the freezing cold winters of the Northeast.

. . . having a name like Carmine, Augie or Giuseppe, and wishing your name were "John."

. . . only being able to leave home "in a white dress or a coffin" if you were a young female, because "nice Italian girls don't live alone."

. . . knowing someone in the neighborhood who was reputed to work for "the mob."

. . . wondering how the Mafia could be called the "underworld" when *everyone,* including the FBI, knows all about its members.

. . . never eating Chef Boy-Ar-Dee or Franco-American macaroni from a can.

. . . having to wear a golden "horn" to protect you from the evil eye.

. . . fighting the "Mafia stereotype" every day of your life.

. . . being invited to dinner at a friend's house where *only* macaroni was served, but you had saved room for the other courses.

. . . keeping your Christmas tree up until January 6.

. . . eating *sfinge* pastries on St. Joseph's Feast Day, March 19.

. . . eating octopus, squid and eels on Christmas Eve.

. . . having a collection of Lou Monte "hits" stored away in the family record cabinet.

Growing up Irish-American means

. . . eating green jello on St. Patrick's Day.

. . . wishing you didn't have so many freckles.

. . . having an aunt who's a nun, or an uncle who's a priest.

. . . fighting the "brawling, beer-drinking" stereotype attributed to Irish men.

. . . eating potatoes, potatoes, and more potatoes.

. . . having at least one piece of Beleek china in your living room.

. . . owning an "Irish linen" tablecloth with matching napkins that's used only for special occasions.

. . . unswerving loyalty to the Kennedy family of politicians.

. . . not being able to face the day without that morning cup of tea.

. . . wanting to visit Ireland and kiss the Blarney Stone.

. . . owning every album "Tommy Makem and the Clancy Brothers" ever recorded.

. . . going to an "Irish Rovers" concert on St. Patrick's Day.

. . . having a copy of the "Irish Blessing" hanging in your mother's kitchen.

. . . having cousins who are named Sean, Bridget or Margaret Mary.

Growing up Jewish-American means

. . . having a Kosher mother who would die if she knew you ate a cheeseburger.

. . . fighting the "Jewish princess" stereotype if you're a female.

. . . having at least one relative who's a doctor, or a lawyer.

. . . eating sour cream with cucumbers, sour cream with fruit, sour cream with blintzes, and plain sour cream straight from the container.

. . . knowing what "real" bagels, knishes, potato pancakes and chicken noodle soup taste like.

. . . having relatives named Molly, Moishe and Stanley.

. . . owning a copy of Dan Greenburg's *How To Be a Jewish Mother.*

. . . going to more birthday parties at the age of 13 than you'll attend for the rest of your adult life.

. . . having your nose "bobbed" for your 12th birthday.

. . . reading *Portnoy's Complaint,* and not finding it amusing.

. . . eating "deli" at least once a week.

. . . having an uncle who can "get it for you wholesale."

. . . drawing a "star" with six points instead of five.

. . . enjoying matzo when it isn't even Passover.

. . . having a mezzuzah outside your front door.

. . . wearing a madras plaid yarmulke in the early 60s.

Growing up Hispanic means

. . . fighting the mañana stereotype every day of your life.

. . . having strangers call you José, even though your name is Joseph.

. . . being stereotyped as a Mexican on the West Coast, and as a Puerto Rican on the East Coast, even though you're from South America, Central America or the Caribbean.

. . . having more *Goya* food labels on your kitchen shelf than *Progresso, Libby* or *Del Monte*.

. . . eating beans and rice every day.

. . . trying to explain what a *plátano* is.

. . . having relatives named Pedro, Manuel and Maria.

SORRY I SAID THAT

Some Americans have had the misfortune of being quoted when it would have been better for them to keep their thoughts to themselves.

Look-Alikes When S. I. Hayakawa, the seventy-one-year-old Japanese-American freshman Senator from California, asked "Who is that?" his bewildered colleague couldn't believe that Hayakawa didn't recognize Russell Long, chairman of the Senate Finance Committee. "You mean you don't know who Russell Long is?" was the incredulous reply. "No, I don't," said Hayakawa in 1978. "All you middle-aged white men look alike to me."

Who's Sorry Now? *Look* magazine had to pay $350,000 in damages in 1977 to former San Francisco mayor Joseph Alioto when he won a court victory over Cowles Publications. The lawsuit arose from a September 1969 article entitled THE WEB THAT LINKS SAN FRANCISCO'S ALIOTO AND THE MAFIA.

Federal Judge William W. Schwarzer, who presided over the nonjury trial, said that Mr. Alioto "has sustained the burden of proving by clear and convincing evidence that [Cowles] published the defamatory statements . . . with actual malice, that is, with reckless disregard for whether they were true or not, and is entitled to judgment in the amount of $350,000 and costs."

Cowles planned to appeal the award, which Alioto has hailed as a victory for Italian-Americans over "dementia waspiana."

Carter's "Lust" Problems Before he was elected President, Jimmy Carter was in hot water over an interview that appeared in *Playboy* magazine, which stated that he "lusted" (in his heart only) for other women. Little did Rosalynn Carter know, at the time, that "lust" would be a continuing problem during her husband's administration. Where did Carter let his lust get out of hand? In the romantic cities of Paris or Rome? No, it happened in Poland, but it wasn't the President's fault.

Steven Seymour, a Russian immigrant and onetime interpreter for the State Department, was responsible for subjecting the President to international ridicule when he misinterpreted parts of the President's speech at a Polish airport. Carter was addressing the people of Poland and telling them of our desire for future friendly relationships with their country. Instead of choosing a Polish word with neutral connotations, Seymour mistakenly used the word usually reserved for "sexual" desire. Edward Gierek and other high Polish officials managed to keep straight faces, but the people in the audience snickered when Seymour told them that President Carter "lusted" for them.

As one Polish journalist remarked: "It looks as if Seymour learned his Polish from a grandfather or somebody who must have emigrated from some backwoods of Eastern Poland." In reality, Seymour's father was from a part of Eastern Poland which was incorporated into the USSR in 1939 and not repatriated until the 1950s.

Earl "Butz" In 1976, when *Rolling Stone* published John Dean's article about a high Republican officials' insulting remarks about Blacks, Earl Butz was not mentioned by name. *New Times* magazine put the finger on the Secretary of Agriculture. As a result, Butz was forced to resign his Cabinet post. Earl later noted, "This is the price I pay for a gross indiscretion in a private conversation. The use of bad racial commentary in no way reflects my real attitude."

What did Butz say to deserve dismissal? According to the New York *Times,* who put it a bit more elegantly than Butz did, the statement concerned reasons why the Republican Party could not attract more Black voters to its ranks. Butz said it was due to the fact that "coloreds . . . wanted only three things in life—satisfying sex, loose shoes and a warm place for bodily functions." The *Times* was quick to note that these wishes "were listed by Mr. Butz in obscene and scatological terms."

Butz made his original remarks to Pat Boone, the singer, who never mentioned it to the press, but he had the misfortune to be overheard by John Dean.

Jewish Influence General George S. Brown (1918–1978), chairman of the Joint Chiefs of Staff, caused a furor when remarks he made about American involvement in the Mideast were interpreted as "anti-Semitic."

General Brown was appearing before a Duke University Law School forum on October 10th, 1974, when a student asked if the United States would use force in the Middle East in the event of a new crisis in

that region. Brown answered: "I don't know—I hope not . . . You can conjure up a situation where there is an oil embargo and the people in this country are not only inconvenienced and uncomfortable, but suffer. They get tough-minded enough to set down the Jewish influence in this country and break that lobby. It is so strong you wouldn't believe. . . . We have Israelis coming to us for equipment. We say we can't probably get Congress to support a program like this. And they say don't worry about Congress. We will take care of Congress. This is somebody from another country, but they can do it. They own, you know, the banks in this country, the newspapers. Just look at where the Jewish money is." General Brown received a presidential rebuke but was not asked to resign by President Ford.

In 1976 General Brown caused another stir by calling Israel a "burden to the United States."

General Brown wasn't the first to be criticized for remarks about Jewish ownership in America. In 1941, Charles A. Lindbergh (of Swedish and part Irish descent) made a nationally broadcast speech at Des Moines, Iowa, in which he charged "the three most important groups who have been pressing this country toward war are the British, the Jewish and the Roosevelt administration . . . Their greatest danger to this country lies in the large ownership and influence in our motion pictures, our press, our radio and our government."

He was condemned for "anti-Semitic" remarks, and the New York *Herald Tribune* charged that he had "sinned against the American spirit." The New York *Journal American* believed that "the raising of a racial issue by Lindbergh was the most unfortunate happening in the United States since the present tense international situation developed."

"Greek," Yes. "Polack," No! Vice-President Agnew, a frequent victim of "foot in mouth" disease, was once criticized for referring to a Japanese-American reporter as a "Fat Jap." On another occasion, in Chicago, while in the company of Congressional representatives Pucinski, Kluczynski and Rostenkowski, Agnew remarked, "Very frankly, when I am moving in a crowd I don't look around and say, 'Well there's a Negro, there's an Italian, there's a Greek and there's a Polack.'" He later tried to make light of the situation by referring to himself as a "Greek, er Grecian,"

but it didn't remove the sting felt by the Poles of America.

Chargin's Chagrin During an incest trial in 1969 involving a Mexican-American, Santa Clara Judge Gerald S. Chargin aroused the anger of the entire Chicano community when he remarked: "You are lower than animals and haven't the right to live in organized society . . . Maybe Hitler was right. The animals in our society probably ought to be destroyed because they have no right to live among human beings."

"Cutting" Remarks In 1970, J. Edgar

Hoover, head of the FBI, stated: "You never have to bother about a president being shot by a Puerto Rican or Mexican. They don't shoot very straight. But if they come at you with a knife, beware."

Eat Those Words   In 1963 when George Wallace was sworn in as Governor of Alabama, he pledged "segregation now, segregation tomorrow and segregation forever."

In his 1976 autobiography, *Stand Up for America,* George Wallace wrote: "Times have changed. Segregation in public facilities is now out of the realm of discussion, and I certainly have no intention and no desire to turn back the clock . . . Racial harmony in our region comes as no surprise to me. The two races have lived side by side for hundreds of years."

Sorry I Said That   Billy Carter outraged some members of the Jewish community in 1978 when he remarked that "the Jewish media tears up the Arab countries full time." When a news reporter repeatedly asked him about his attitude toward Jews following the brouhaha over the remark, Billy snapped: "They can kiss my ---, as far as I'm concerned now!"

Dealing with the illegal alien problem, former President Nixon remarked on July 12, 1979, that "wetbacks" often passed by his San Clemente home, near the Mexican border. "We just give them some food and they go away . . ."

PART III

An Ethnic Who's Who

11 FATHERS AND MOTHERS

ETHNIC-AMERICAN FATHERS

Every schoolchild learns that George Washington is the "father of his country," but what about the hundreds of other Americans who have been nicknamed "father" for their unique contributions to American life?

"Father of More Brains Than Any Other Man in America"

Lyman Beecher (1775–1863) and his 13 children achieved such fame and notoriety as nineteenth-century American leaders that the human race was once jokingly said to consist of "men, women and Beechers."

Born in New Haven, Connecticut, and educated at Yale, Lyman Beecher was a clergyman noted for fiery speeches on the evils of excessive drink, and his temperance sermons were widely published throughout England and America. Seven of his eight sons grew to maturity and followed their father's religious footsteps by becoming Congregational ministers. Despite the general lack of opportunity for women in the 1800s, his daughters distinguished themselves in the fields of education, letters and women's rights.

Two of his most famous progeny, who no doubt helped Lyman earn the nickname "father of more brains than any other man in America," were Henry Ward Beecher (1813–1887), the abolitionist preacher and crusader for women's rights, and Harriet Beecher Stowe (1811–1896), author of Uncle Tom's Cabin or Life Among the Lowly, an antislavery tract that sold 300,000 copies the first year it was printed in 1852.

Descended from English ancestors, with a touch of Scottish and Welsh blood, the Beecher family first settled in Boston in 1637. (Feminists, take note: there isn't a "mother of more brains than any other woman in America" simply because three women would have to share the honors: Lyman's first and second wives, Roxana Foote and Harriet Porter, who bore his 13 children, and Lydia Jackson, his third wife, who became their stepmother.)

"Father of American Franchisers"

When Howard Johnson (1897–1972) opened his first store in Wollaston, Massachusetts, in 1924, he was barely twenty-seven years old and already $40,000 in debt. Still, he wasn't discouraged and credits his father's Swedish ancestry and his mother's New England heritage for his continuing fortitude in the face of personal financial disaster.

Howard sold newspapers, candy, soda water and ice cream in his "candy" store across the street from the Wollaston Railroad Station, until his accountant suggested he concentrate on selling the most profitable item in his store — homemade ice cream. Howard Johnson heeded his accountant's advice, and within 15 years he was a millionaire, famous for his 28 flavors.

Johnson first started making ice cream because he despised the odor of artificial vanilla flavoring. Every time he opened the icea cream cabinet and reached in to scoop out a vanilla cone, that artificial smell would waft up and irritate his nostrils. He offered a manufacturer fifty cents extra a gallon to use only natural vanilla extract, but time and time again Johnson was deceived, and the odor of artificial vanilla would reappear.

From his last failed business venture, Johnson learned that the best way to have a better product to sell was to make the product yourself. So, armed with a secondhand ice cream freezer and a "secret" recipe from a German immigrant whose ice cream was highly regarded in Wollaston, Howard Johnson began turning out his all-natural ice cream.

He charged more for his product, but found customers were willing to pay the difference for a quality product which contained 22% butterfat and was almost twice as creamy as the majority of commercial brands. By 1928, Johnson was grossing more than $240,000 per annum.

More important than the money he amassed was the system he started. In 1929 a friend opened a restaurant that featured Howard Johnson's ice cream, and the two businessmen signed an agreement that gave the restaurateur the right to use the Johnson name, so long as he agreed to buy all processed food products exclusively from Howard Johnson, and let Johnson set the standards of quality for other food consumed on the premises. Their contract set the precedent for franchise agreements that exist today between the Howard Johnson Company and the 800 or so restaurant owners that use his name.

The franchise has been called "the greatest idea in retail merchandising," providing brand-name recognition for hotels, motels, chain stores, auto dealers and coast-to-coast fast-food joints which have become such a major force in our post-World War II economy. For his role in spawning this multi-billion-dollar idea, Howard Deering Johnson has been nicknamed the "father of American franchisers."

"Father of the Telephone"

Silence! That was the only sound to be heard over the phone lines of North America on August 4, 1922, beginning at 7:25 P.M. Not one of the 13 million phones in Canada or the United States would function. Not one phone rang, and not one busy signal could be heard. The science of communication was thrust back into the "dark

The first articulate sentence ever spoken over an electric telephone was uttered via this instrument on March 10, 1876. The transmission apparatus is on the left; the receiver is on the right. (Courtesy: AT&T)

ages," as telephone operators all over the country sat back idly and refused to connect irate customers who were lighting up the switchboards of America like proverbial Christmas trees.

Was it a wildcat strike by operators demanding better wages? A demonstration of the almighty power of the dial tone? No, just a final, fitting tribute to the Scottish-American "father of the telephone," Alexander Graham Bell (1847–1922).

When Bell's funeral services in Maine began at 7:25 P.M. (EST), phone service on the continent of North America was cut off entirely for one minute to honor the memory of the man who had made it all possible.

Like his father and grandfather before him, Alexander Bell had been a teacher of the deaf. In fact, his development of the telephone was an outgrowth of experiments Bell had conducted in hopes of inventing a "phonautograph" — an instrument that would display visual graphs of words that are spoken correctly and compare them to sounds attempted by the deaf. He didn't succeed with the phonautograph, but when he applied the membrane concept from that invention to his telephone, he was able to transmit sound more clearly than ever before.

The first words ever transmitted over the telephone were not as lofty as those first transmitted by Samuel Morse over the telegraph. Instead of the deep philosophical question "What hath God wrought?", Bell immortalized the phrase "Come here, Mr. Watson. I want you." The transmission was accidentally sent on March 10, 1876, when Bell spilled battery acid all over his clothing and called for help from his assistant in the next room.

Bell's creative genius did not stop with the invention of the telephone, and over the next 46 years of his life he invented: an iceberg finder that worked on echo-location principles; an induction balance to locate bullets and other metal objects inside a person's body (always a problem in the days before X rays); a new improved tetrahedral flying kite; and even an improved breed of sheep (the females gave birth to twins and had multiple nipples to nurse their additional offspring).

"Father of American Television"

As early as 1923, while serving as vice-president of the Radio Corporation of America, David Sarnoff (1891–1971) wrote: "I believe that television, which is the technical name for seeing as well as hearing by radio, will come to pass in due course. It may be that every broadcast receiver for home use in the future will also be equipped with a television adjunct by which the instrument will make it possible for those at home to see as well as hear what is going on at the broadcast station."

More prophetic words were never written, for through Sarnoff's insight and Vladimir Zworykin's inventive genius, television became a reality. These two Russian immigrants totally revolutionized the communications field with the "one-eyed monster," which almost wiped out movies and radio—and turned successive generations of Americans into media junkies.

Born in Minsk, Russia, Sarnoff came to the United States as a young boy and began working as a messenger for the Commercial Cable Company, where he learned Morse code. He later became a wireless operator for the Marconi Telegraph Company and first attained national prominence as the telegraph operator who received the *Titanic*'s distress call. Although the *Titanic* sank in about 2½ hours, Sarnoff—according to the legend—remained at his post for over 72 hours, attempting to direct rescuers to the ship's survivors.

While Sarnoff contributed his faith, foresight and company's money to the research efforts necessary to develop black-and-white television and compatible color TV, it was Vladimir Zworykin's electronics genius that made it possible for man to transmit and receive pictures through the air. Although Zworykin cannot be given total credit as inventor of the television, he was the first to demonstrate a practical all-electronic TV system in 1929, using two of his inventions: the *iconoscope,* to broadcast pictures, and the *kinescope,* to receive images.

When Sarnoff asked his staff how much it would cost to develop commercial television, Dr. Zworykin replied, "Maybe $100,000." As it turned out, Zworykin's forte was electronics, *not* economics, and before NBC was able to begin making regular broadcasts in the United States in 1936 the parent company had invested over $10 million. Another $40 million was invested before RCA realized a profit, but through it all David Sarnoff kept putting money into the project because he believed "the potential audience of television in its ultimate development may reasonably be expected to be limited by the population of the earth itself."

For his unswerving faith in the future of the "boob tube," the Television Broadcasters Association conferred the title "father of American television" on David Sarnoff in 1944.

"Father of the Hydrogen Bomb"

"Like anyone else I would rather work on defense than on aggressive weapons." So spoke the "father of the hydrogen bomb," *Edward Teller* (1908–   ), in 1954 after the first H-bomb was exploded with a force of 15 megatons, equal to the explosive force of 15 million tons of TNT. Once known as the "superbomb" before the neutron bomb took its place as the king of destruction, the H-bomb has an explosive force thousands of times more powerful than the puny A-bombs that leveled Hiroshima and Nagasaki in 1945.

The reason the H-bomb is so destructive is that its power comes from the *fusion* of hydrogen atoms, rather than the *fission* (splitting) of uranium atoms. In order to generate sufficient heat to fuse together deuterium and tritium, both hydrogen isotopes, a fission reaction is first necessary. In other words, an H-bomb has an A-bomb inside to trigger the thermonuclear reaction, so it is really two bombs in one.

Born in Budapest, Hungary, in 1908, the son of a well-to-do Jewish family, Edward Teller joined Enrico Fermi at the Los Alamos project in 1941 to work on development of the first atomic bomb. Blue-eyed and bushy-browed, with what friends describe as a good sense of humor, Teller was not laughing in 1964 when he was parodied as the title character in the film, *Dr. Strangelove, or How I Learned To Stop Worrying and Love the Bomb.*

He began to build up his "Dr. Strangelove" reputation among the scientific community by his incessant lobbying for the hydrogen bomb. He contributed his scientific knowledge to the bomb's development and also became the H-bomb's greatest proponent. When J. Robert Oppenheimer (the German-American "father of the atomic bomb") was brought before the Atomic Energy Commission for suspected "un-American activities" that might have interfered with his top-secret security clearance, Teller was the only scientist who spoke out against Oppenheimer. Teller recommended that Oppenheimer's security clearance be downgraded because he "interfered" with the speedy development of the H-bomb, and claimed that had Oppenheimer lent his support to the project, the H-bomb might have been a reality as early as 1947. Oppenheimer was subsequently cleared of all charges and was deemed a "loyal and trustworthy citizen," which did not serve to enhance Teller's reputation among his colleagues.

For his role in developing the H-bomb and his efforts to see it detonated, Edward Teller has been nicknamed the "father of the hydrogen bomb."

"Father of American Pediatrics"

Jailed for two years on charges of "high treason" during a period of intense revolutionary ferment in his native Germany, Dr. Abraham Jacobi (1830–1919) was released from prison in 1853 and sailed for America with his medical degree in hand.

He gained fame in the United States for his many medical accomplishments, which

Abraham Jacobi (1830–1919), "the father of American pediatrics." (Courtesy: New York Historical Society)

include inventing the laryngoscope, an instrument used to examine the larynx, and elevating the care of infants and children to a brand-new science, pediatrics.

Dr. Jacobi built up a private practice in New York City, where he specialized in the care of infants and children. In 1857 he was appointed Lecturer on Pathology of Infancy and Childhood at Columbia's College of Physicians and Surgeons in New York, and in 1870 he became the first Professor of Pediatrics. Thanks to his efforts, the infant mortality rate in the United States decreased from 99.9 deaths per thousand live births in 1915, to 20.0 per thousand in 1970.

"Father of Frozen Food"

What would television have been in the 1950s without TV dinners? With a supply of frozen dinners, pre-packed in aluminum foil, it was possible to pop dinner into the oven without missing the latest installment of one's favorite TV serial. Frozen pre-cooked meals have turned us into a nation of "food warmers" rather than cooks, and in recent years frozen food has taken over much of the restaurant business by offering "no waste, portion-controlled meals" that only require the flick of a microwave oven dial before they are presented to dinner patrons.

The man responsible for all this freezing and defrosting was Clarence Birdseye (1886–1956), an English-American who revolutionized the kitchen and became the "father of frozen food."

When the Birdseye family first emigrated to America from their native England, the family name was spelled Bird's Eye (it had been bestowed upon a sharp-shooting ancestor who shot an arrow through the eye of a hawk). In keeping with the family tradition of name changes, everyone who knew Clarence Birdseye called him Bob, perhaps for no other reason than the fact that Clarence did not seem to suit him.

As a young man in his hometown of Brooklyn, New York, Clarence always found unorthodox methods of earning money. Instead of selling magazine subscriptions to pay his way through school, he trapped rats and frogs to sell to experimenters at Columbia University and the New York Zoological Society. In 1914, he journeyed to Labrador to trap and trade furs, and after a brief stay in the States, he returned to the Arctic in 1916 with his new wife and child in tow.

The Arctic climate of Labrador provided a rather boring diet of fish and game, and whenever a passing steamship stopped to deliver fresh vegetables it was cause for a celebration. Determined to dine on fresh cabbage until the next ship was due in port, Birdseye filled a rainbarrel with water and placed a few cabbages in the bottom until they were frozen solid. He kept repeating the process until the barrel was full; later, whenever he needed a cabbage for dinner, it could easily be hacked out of the barrel and steamed.

Birdseye's experiments in the Arctic led him to believe it was possible to freeze food on a commercial scale. Once back in the States, he began tinkering with the idea. Slowly and sadly he realized that his experiments were failures, because the secret for retaining that tasty, fresh flavor was "rapid" freezing. In the Arctic climate, where temperatures dipped as low as 50 degrees below zero, food froze quickly, allowing little time for large ice crystals to form inside the food. The crystals were the culprits that caused the cellular structure of fish (or meat) to rupture when defrosted, making the product tough and dry when cooked. The solution, which Birdseye eventually hit upon, was a continuous belt freezing operation in which fish were sprayed with a brine solution at 40 degrees below zero. This froze the fish rapidly enough to prevent flavor deterioration during cooking.

Birdseye earned his nickname, "father of frozen food," for starting the first commercially successful frozen food business. By 1925 his company, General Seafoods, was selling thousands of pounds of frozen fish annually as his products gained acceptance with the housewife. Ironically, when General Foods bought out his patents and trademarks in 1929, they changed the old family name back to its original spelling.

"Father of the Uneeda Biscuit"

Before the introduction of individually wrapped packages of crackers, each general store in America had a "cracker barrel," a bit of Americana which has been overly romanticized in recent years by those who cherish the "good old days."

In reality, the cracker barrel was nothing more than a festering place for filth and germs. If you were lucky enough to get there when the barrel was first opened you would find a supply of fresh, crispy, unbroken crackers. But as the cracker sales started to mount up, the bottom of the barrel was usually filled with broken, soggy, insect-infested pieces that had probably been nibbled on by rodents.

The late 1800s witnessed an upheaval in the nation as many Americans moved from a predominantly rural to an urban economy. Eating habits were changing too. The farm-fresh produce of the countryside wasn't always available, and soon women in the cities were finding it more convenient to buy some ready-made food products, such as ketchup and pickles, rather than slave over a hot caldron all day long to put up their own preserved fruits and vegetables.

Though acceptance of canned and processed foodstuffs was on the increase, many staples were available only in large quantities. Spaghetti came in 20-pound boxes, flour was sold in 250-pound barrels, and family-size packages were nonexistent. Paper bags were not widely used until after the Civil War; prior to that, if you needed a container for your grocery purchases the grocer would roll a sheet of paper to form a cone and place your food inside.

The man who took crackers out of the barrel and put them in individually wrapped, moisture-proof packages was Adolphus Green, a founder of the National Biscuit Company, and "the father of the Uneeda biscuit."

In 1899, Green summed up his company's philosophy, "We propose to get business by selling better goods . . . Instead of broken, soggy crackers in bulk, stored in old barrels and boxes, we are to supply fresh, whole crackers in triple-wrapped packages." Not only did this philosophy sell crackers, but it helped revolutionize the grocery industry by leading to the creation of brand-name products and modern supermarket packaging and distribution methods.

The son of an Irish immigrant, Green enlisted the help of a Scotsman, Robert Gair of Brooklyn, New York, and a Jewish employee, Frank Peters, to put the first Uneeda Biscuits on the grocery shelves of America. Robert Gair developed the cutting and creasing die tool that made it possible to mass-produce folding cardboard cartons, and Peters patented in 1899 the "In-er-seal" carton, which provided a moisture-proof barrier for "packing biscuits, crackers and the like."

By 1900, sales of Uneeda Biscuits had topped 10 million packages a month, making the "Uneeda Biscuit Boy" one of America's most easily recognized trademarks. The little boy, still pictured today on every box of Uneeda biscuits, was Gordon Stille, the five-year-old nephew of a staff copywriter. For almost 80 years Gordon has been frozen in time by an artist's brush, in his boots, oil hat and yellow slicker carrying his box of biscuits under his arm to illustrate that even in rainy, damp weather every cracker will be crisp and fresh thanks to the patented "In-er-seal" carton.

"Father of American Football"

One of our recent presidents noted, "I never made the [football team] . . . I was not heavy enough to play the line, not fast enough to play halfback, and not smart enough to be a quarterback." That's what Richard Nixon said about the sport that has been defined as "a friendly kind of fight" — the game that can immobilize a nation on Super Sunday and attract millions of viewers in a single afternoon.

The man who earned the title "father of American football" was Walter Chauncey Camp (1859–1925), a Connecticut Yankee of old English stock. Born in New Britain, Connecticut, Camp attended Yale, where he distinguished himself as one of the school's best all-around athletes during his undergraduate days and became one of their most memorable athletic advisers after graduation. He was captain of the football team and an excellent swimmer and runner. He attended medical school for a while, but returned to his alma mater in 1888 to serve as athletic director before completing his studies.

As football coach at Yale, Camp changed the rules of the game from a mere parody of English rugby to the game of strategy we know today. He reduced the number of players from 15 to 11, and created the key position of quarterback. Camp also introduced the scrimmage and 4th down rules to the game, and invented patterns of play that are still in use today.

He was the first to select an "all-American" football team; his annual choices appeared in *Colliers Weekly* from 1889 to 1925. After his death, the selections were made by a board of football coaches, a tradition that continues to this day.

WALTER CAMP'S 1889 ALL-AMERICAN TEAM

Ends	Amos Alonzo Stagg (Yale)
	Arthur Cumnock (Harvard)
Tackles	Charles O. Gill (Yale)
	Hector W. Cowan (Princeton)
Guards	William W. Heffelfinger (Yale)
	John Cranston (Harvard)
Center	William J. George (Princeton)
Quarterback	Edgar Allen Poe (Princeton)
Halfbacks	Roscoe H. Channing, Jr. (Princeton)
	James T. Lee (Harvard)
Fullback	Knowlton Ames (Princeton)

MORE ETHNIC AMERICAN FATHERS

Russian "Father of Wonder Drugs"

Selman Abraham Waksman (1888–1973) earned his title as well as the 1952 Nobel Prize in Medicine for his discovery of the antibiotic Streptomycin, the first drug successful in treating tuberculosis.

Born in Novya Priluka, Russia, Waksman came to the United States at the age of 22, and entered Rutgers University as an undergraduate. After earning his Ph.D. from the University of California, he returned to his alma mater, where his research in the field of microbiology led to his discovery of Streptomycin. He donated his share of royalties from manufacturing the drug to Rutger's, and established the Institute of Microbiology at Rutgers, where he remained as director until his retirement in 1958.

Portuguese "Father of the Sweet Potato Industry"

California is the 6th largest producer of sweet potatoes in the United States today, averaging 739,000,000 pounds per annum. The man who made it all possible was John B. Avila (1865–1937), a native of the Portuguese Azores, who planted the first 20 acres of sweet potato fields in California in 1888 and helped establish *Ipomoea batatas* as a major commercial crop in the West.

Polish/Lithuanian "Father of American Artillery"

Like many great men, Thaddeus Kosciuszko (1746–1817) is claimed as a native son by two ethnic groups, the Poles and the Lithuanians. Born in Byelorussia, which was jointly controlled by Poland and Lithuania in 1746, Tadeusz Andrzej Bonawentura Kosciuszko became a captain in the Polish army in 1769 and fought for freedom on two continents, for Poland and the United States.

He earned his nickname, "father of American artillery," for the service manual he wrote, *Manoevers of Horse Artillery*, which served as the standard American text

during the early 1800s. According to the terms of his will, 500 acres of Ohio land which had been granted to him by Congress were sold and the funds were used to free Negro slaves from bondage. Some of the money was also used to found the Colored School at Newark, one of the first educational institutions for Blacks in America.

English "Father of the Telegraph"

Samuel Finley Breese Morse (1791–1872) invented the telegraph in 1835 but had to wait 8 years before Congress would appropriate funds to build an experimental line between Washington, D.C., and Baltimore. Total cost: a mere $30,000. First message: "What hath God wrought," May 24, 1844.

Samuel Morse, "the father of the telegraph," is shown seated next to the first camera in America used for making daguerreotypes. (Courtesy: New York Historical Society)

English "Father of the Cotton Gin"

Even though Eli Whitney (1765–1825) got all the credit for inventing the cotton gin, it was actually his landlady's idea. Catherine Littlefield Greene, a widow with five children, first suggested the idea to Whitney in 1792 and also contributed to the development of the machine by suggesting Eli use wire teeth to pick apart the cotton bolls when the wooden ones he was using kept breaking apart. Although she never received a patent, she and her second husband received a "pretty penny" when they became Whitney's business partners and shared in his profits.

English "Father of the Typewriter"

Christopher Latham Sholes (1819–1890) received two patents for his type-writer in 1868, but when he was unable to perfect his machine he sold the rights to the Remington Arms Company for $12,000. Remington succeeded where Sholes failed, and made their first sale in 1873.

The slogan, so familiar to students in secretarial schools across the nation, "Now is the time for all good men to come to the aid of the party," was created by a friend of Sholes, a court reporter named Charles Weller, in 1867.

German "Father of Space Medicine"

As a young boy in his native Germany, Hubertus Strughold (1898–   ), kept his eyes ever skyward, fascinating by zeppelins, balloons, and "everything that was airborne."

After earning his Ph.D. in physiology, he began to study the effects of high-altitude flying on man. He emigrated to the United States in 1947 and continued his physiological studies, earning an international reputation as the "father of space medicine."

Strughold constructed the first space-cabin simulator in 1954, a device that helped condition astronauts for the rigors of travel in outer space. The cabin was hermetically sealed and designed to simulate actual climatic conditions that would be encountered by space pioneers. It was first used experimentally in 1956, when an aeromedical technician became the first person to spend 24 hours sealed inside the cabin.

German "Father of Political Science in the United States"

Francis Lieber (1800–1872) was born in Berlin and emigrated to the United States in 1827. Two years later, he became the first editor of the *Encyclopedia Americana*, the first such compilation published in America.

In 1835 he was appointed to the chair of history and political economy at South Carolina College, where he taught for the next twenty years and wrote several highly acclaimed works that earned him the nickname "father of political science in the United States." His best-known works include: *Manual of Political Ethics* (1838–9), and *On Civil Liberty and Self-Government* (1853). He served as referee for the Mexican Claims Commission of 1870, and his name has been immortalized in the "Lieber Chair" of political philosophy and sociology at Columbia University.

German "Father of Negro Songs"

Johan Christian Gottlieb Graupner (1767–1836), a German immigrant, was the first musician to popularize Negro songs in Boston. In 1799 he appeared dressed as a Black man at the Federal Street Theater, where he sang, among other ditties, "The Gay Negro Boy."

Black "Father of the Blues"

William Christopher Handy's father was a Methodist minister who considered all nonreligious music the devil's handiwork. But despite his father's disapproval, Handy (1873–1958) managed to make his own musical instruments and learned dance tunes from an old country fiddler in Alabama. He later distinguished himself in the field of music by composing such immortal favorites as the "Memphis Blues," the "St. Louis Blues" and the "Beale Street Blues."

Hungarian "Father of the California Wine Industry"

Agoston Haraszty, a Hungarian nobleman, came to the United States as a visitor in 1840. He was so impressed by our young nation that he decided to return to America in 1842, but this time he came as a settler. He founded the town of Sauk City, Wisconsin, and later established the first great vineyard in California with imported Tokay grapevines from his native Hungary. For his efforts in laying the foundation for America's vineyards, he has been nicknamed the "father of the California wine industry."

French "Father of Baseball"

Abner Doubleday (1819–1893) is generally credited with inventing the game of baseball in 1839. According to legend, he used a stick to outline the diamond-shaped playing field in the dirt, gave the players their positions and invented the method used to eliminate base runners.

A commission was appointed in 1906 to study the origins of our favorite summertime sport, and after examining the evidence at hand, their vote was unanimous for Abner Doubleday, a Union soldier of French Huguenot descent whose original family name was spelled *Dubaldy*.

According to the *Encyclopedia Americana,* however, the commission erred when they chose to immortalize Abner Doubleday as the inventor of baseball, since their conclusions were based on the eyewitness testimony of only one man, Abner Graves, who reported seeing Doubleday invent the game some 67 years earlier, at Cooperstown, New York. Since Doubleday was a West Point cadet in 1839, the story has a few holes in it. But no matter—the Baseball Hall of Fame has been erected in Cooperstown, and the baseball diamond there is named in Doubleday's honor, so it is probably best to let Abner continue to enjoy his status as "the father of baseball."

ETHNIC-AMERICAN MOTHERS

"Mother of Level Measurement"

For more than a hundred years American women were told to dash, sprinkle and pinch seasoning into the stew pot. But how much salt is in a pinch? Is it more or less than a dash? And how much sugar is a "spoonful"? There isn't any way to know unless the spoons are all of a standard size.

The woman who took "guesstimation" out of cooking was Fannie Merritt Farmer (1857–1915), a Boston cooking instructor of English descent, who popularized the use of level measurements in the kitchen.

When a paralytic stroke crippled Fannie at the age of 16 and forced her to leave high school, she developed an interest in cooking during her long fight back to health. Three years after graduating from the Boston Cooking School in 1889, Fanny established her own school of cookery.

Her best-selling *Boston Cooking School Cook Book,* first published in 1896, sold over 4 million copies and has recently been reissued as a paperback. It was this cookbook and her monthly column in the *Woman's Home Companion* that revolutionized the art of home cooking in America by providing clear instructions and exact measurements to be used in a recipe. For the first time in history, it was possible for an inexperienced housewife to make perfect Hollandaise sauce the first time she tried, by following Fannie's easy-to-duplicate recipe, with exact measurements down to 1/8 of a teaspoon for all ingredients used.

A second paralytic stroke confined Fannie to a wheelchair in her later years, but it did not end her activities. She continued to manage her cooking school and even taught a class ten days before her death in December 1915.

"Mother of the Kindergarten"

The founder of the kindergarten movement was a German educator, Friedrich Froebel (1782–1852), who established the first *children's garden* in Blankenburg, Germany, in 1837. Froebel believed that "Whatever the human being can become exists in him from the first," and his experience as a teacher led him to believe that much educational advantage was lost when a child's schooling was delayed until his sixth birthday.

He believed that knowledge must come

from within, and viewed mothers and teachers as mere "guides" to help children channel their energy to proper avenues of self-expression. He established his school around these principles and devised songs, games and activities designed to help four- to six-year-old children learn basic concepts.

By many standards Froebel's life might seem a failure. He died without amassing great wealth or fortune; he was considered an "old fool" in his village for romping in the fields with children during his seventh decade of life; and he was disgraced in his final days by a Prussian ban on kindergartens between 1851 and 1860. But Froebel did not pass his days on this earth in vain. He attained his piece of immortality by having his philosophy carried to the four corners of the earth by enthusiastic young teachers interested in early childhood education.

One of the first to carry the message of the kindergarten to America was a student of Froebel's, Margaretha Meyer (1834–1876), a German-Jewish refugee who later married the great German-American statesman, Carl Schurz. Though Miss Meyer established the first kindergarten in Watertown, Wisconsin, in 1856, she was not "the mother of the kindergarten." That honor was reserved for Susan Elizabeth Blow (1843–1916), the woman whose efforts were instrumental in making kindergartens part of public school education in America.

Born in Carondelet, Missouri, of English ancestry, Ms. Blow learned of Froebel's work while traveling through Germany in 1870. When she returned home to St. Louis, she beseeched the superintendent of schools to introduce a kindergarten to the school system. Thanks to her efforts, the first public school kindergarten was established in 1873 at the Des Peres School in St. Louis. Blow later established a training school for kindergarten teachers, and earned her title by spreading the kindergarten concept of education throughout America.

"Mother Jones"

Described as a "little old woman in a black bonnet, with a high falsetto voice and a handsome face framed in curly white hair" Mary Harris Jones (1830–1930) hardly looked the part of an inspiring labor leader.

Jailed three times for organizing strikes, and sentenced to 20 years in prison on conspiracy charges, Mother Jones advised, "No matter what your fight, don't be ladylike," and for over fifty years she followed her own advice, battling against the evils of child labor, unsafe working conditions and human exploitation. She organized railroad laborers and mine workers, and even armed their wives with mops and brooms to attract attention to their cause in 1902, but although she was revolutionary about some things she was opposed to violence, prohibition and woman suffrage.

Born in Cork, Ireland, Mother Jones emigrated to America at the age of ten and spent part of her childhood in Toronto. She lost her husband and four children to a yellow fever epidemic that raged through Memphis in 1867, and in 1871 her fledgling dressmaking business was wiped out by the great Chicago fire. That proved to be the turning point in her life, for after attending a few meetings of the Knights of Labor, she sank all of her time and energy for the next fifty years into the fight for labor reforms.

A year before her death at the ripe old age of 100, Mother Jones was still making public appearances. When she was introduced to an audience as a "great humanitarian," the feisty old woman denied the speaker's generous remarks and roared, "No, I'm a hell-raiser."

"Mother of the Feminist Movement in America"

Described as a "combination of Hermione Gingold and Bette Davis," Betty Friedan (1921–   ) is an articulate, nonstop talker who has noted, "This whole society could erupt in one great wave of boredom. As for me, I'm very unbored. I'm nasty, I'm bitchy, I get mad. But, by God, I'm absorbed in what I'm doing."

Born in Peoria, Illinois, the oldest of three daughters of Jewish parents, Betty Naomi Goldstein Friedan first chronicled the "problem that has no name" in 1957 when she surveyed college-educated American housewives and found that many middle-aged women were victims of "mysterious ailments" that sent them running to physicians, psychiatrists and counselors to alleviate the feelings of emptiness and malaise that permeated their lives.

She termed the problem *The Feminine Mystique* – a complex indoctrination program launched at birth that is designed to lull women into abandoning their own search for identity and submerging themselves into home, husband and children. When her book was first published in 1963, Friedan was catapulted to fame and into the forefront of the burgeoning women's movement.

She founded NOW, the National Organization for Women, in 1966, and served as first president until 1970. She also organized the Women's Strike for Equality in 1970 and was a co-founder of the National Women's Political Caucus.

"Mother of Methodism in the United States"

"Philip, you must preach to us, or we shall all go to Hell, and God will require our blood at your hands!" Those were the words Barbara Ruckle Heck (1734–1804) used to rouse Methodist preacher Philip Embury from his spiritual backsliding in America. Known as "the mother of Methodism" for her efforts in establishing the first Methodist society in America, Barbara was appalled at the gambling and card playing that was taking place among their group in 1766, and felt certain that the Old World religion would be lost forever if she did not do something to preserve the fervor.

Barbara was born in Ireland to German immigrant parents who were among the first to be influenced by John Wesley's preaching. She and her husband, Paul Heck, emigrated to America in 1760 with her cousin, Philip Embury. As a result of Barbara's pleas, Embury, a carpenter and Methodist clergyman, built the Old John Street Church in lower Manhattan in 1768, a date that can be reckoned as the beginning of the Methodist movement in America. Heck and her family later emigrated to Canada and helped establish the Methodist Church in that country about 1774.

"Mother of the Red Cross"

Edward Barton, an English immigrant who settled in New England in 1640, established his family's roots in Salem, Massachusetts, but when his grandson's wife's aunt was hanged as a witch in 1692, the family left Salem to settle in Oxford, Massachusetts. That's where Clarissa Harlowe Barton (1821–1912) was born on Christmas Day in 1821.

Better known to the world as Clara Barton, she earned the nickname "Angel of the Battlefield" for her ministrations to Civil War casualties in Virginia, where she cared for their wounds and baked meat pies and puddings to nourish their bodies back to health.

Prone to periods of "nervous prostration" during her lifetime, she was in Europe recovering from a breakdown in 1869 when she first learned about the International Red Cross Convention that had been established in Switzerland in 1864. Curious to know why the United States had not agreed to sign the treaty, she hounded legislators until the United States ratified the Geneva Convention in 1882. From then on, medical workers wearing the red cross emblem would be assured of protection on American battlefields.

Barton organized the American Association of the Red Cross in 1881, serving as its president until 1904. Under her leadership, the Red Cross emerged as a relief organization for times of peace and war, as volunteers began to administer aid to victims of famines, floods, earthquakes and other natural disasters.

For her role in convincing President Chester A. Arthur to sign the Geneva Convention in July 1882 and in amending the Convention to include peacetime relief aid around the world, Ms. Barton has been called "the Mother of the Red Cross."

"Mother of Hadassah"

The "mother of Hadassah," Henrietta Szold (1869–1945) was also nicknamed the "Jewish Florence Nightingale" for her work in providing health care to the poor people of Palestine.

Born in Baltimore, Maryland, the eldest daughter of a Hungarian rabbi, Henrietta first visited Palestine in 1910 after an ill-fated love affair with Louis Ginzberg, the famous Jewish theologian. She went to Palestine to recover, took up the Zionist cause, and determined to eliminate some of the disease and poverty then rampant in the Holy Land. When she returned home in 1912, she founded Hadassah, the Women's Zionist

Organization of America, whose first medical dispatch unit arrived in Jerusalem in 1913.

Today, Hadassah is the world's largest Zionist group, boasting over 350,000 members dedicated to raising funds for medical facilities, education and youth centers in Israel.

"Mother of Sabbath Schools in America"

"Like mother, like daughter," the new saying goes, and when Joanna Graham Bethune, the Scottish-born "mother of sabbath schools in America," organized the Female Sabbath School Union of New York in 1816, she was merely following in mummy's footsteps.

Both women were known to New York society for their charitable and benevolent works, and both were involved in educating immigrant children on the sabbath, since many poor youngsters had to work during the week to help support the family. Bethune's mother, Mrs. Graham, had founded a Sunday School in New York in 1792 to educate young women, but the school languished shortly thereafter. The movement was not revived until her daughter opened her own institution in 1816.

"Mother of All the Doughboys"

One of America's most beloved opera stars was Ernestine Schumann-Heink (1861–1936). Born in Lieben, near Prague, Bohemia, the daughter of an Austrian Army officer and an Italian mother, Ernestine joined the Metropolitan Opera Company in

Ernestine Schumann-Heink, "mother of all the doughboys." (Courtesy: Culver Pictures)

1899 after making her American debut in Chicago. Eventually becoming an American citizen, Schumann-Heink earned her nickname, "mother of all the doughboys," for her generous performances before American soldiers during World War I. Her sons fought on both sides of the conflict and two died in battle, one on each side.

Mother of Anarchy in America

Born in Kovno, Lithuania, Emma Goldman (1869–1940) emigrated to America in 1886 and secured her first job in a clothing factory in Rochester, New York, for the grand salary of $2.50 a week.

Emma moved to New York City in 1889, and was arrested several times for her lectures on atheism, birth control and free love. During the course of one fiery lecture, she informed her audience of unemployed men that it was their right to steal bread if they were starving. This suggestion earned her a year in jail.

After the death of her lover Johann Most (1846–1906), the Bavarian-born author of *The Science of Revolutionary Warfare: A Manual of Instruction in the Use and Preparation of Nitro-Glycerine, Gun-Cotton, Dynamite, Fulminating Mercury, Bombs, Fuses, Poisons, etc.*, Goldman became editor of the anarchist periodical *Mother Earth* with anarchist Alexander Berkman. *Mother Earth* preached free love, among other "subversive" ideas.

In 1917 Goldman and Berkman were imprisoned for opposing the draft. After her release in 1919 she was deported to Russia. Disillusioned with post-revolutionary developments in the U.S.S.R., she told a U.S. audience in 1934: "You are still free in America . . . No spies enter your homes for incriminating documents." After her death in Canada in 1940, her body was returned to the United States for burial in a Chicago cemetery.

HOW TO BE AN ETHNIC MOTHER

When Dan Greenburg published his "training manual" *How To Be a Jewish Mother*, he acknowledged that "you don't have to be either Jewish or a mother to be a Jewish mother. An Irish waitress or an Italian barber could also" qualify if he or she masters the basic techniques of Jewish motherhood—which, according to Greenburg, include "Making Guilt Work" and mastering the "Technique of Basic Suffering."

All mothers, no matter what their ethnic heritage, seem to possess many of the characteristics described by Greenburg. All seem to favor extra sweaters in the winter, an extra helping of mashed potatoes for their "undernourished" children and chicken soup for a winter's cold.

In 1978, Dr. Corinne Azen Krause studied three generations of Italian, Jewish and Slavic women, and found that there were, indeed, some basic differences among the three ethnic groups. If you're Italian, you worry about sex and health; if you're Jewish, you main worry is the children; and if you're Slavic, you don't worry much.

Dr. Krause conducted her study of 225 women in the Pittsburgh area under the auspices of the Institute on Pluralism and Group Identity of the American Jewish Committee. All of the women surveyed grew up in homes with strong ethnic traditions. They lived in ethnic neighborhoods, ate ethnic foods and observed traditional holidays. Many attended ethnic church services, spoke a foreign language at home and still lived in the same neighborhood as their parents and other close relatives.

Krause's findings indicated that Slavic women were generally less concerned about problems related to childbirth, menopause and jobs than were Jewish or Italian women. Only 19% of the Slavic women polled expressed any anxieties about childbirth, in contrast to 40% of the Jewish and Italian women questioned in the survey.

When it comes to worrying about children, Jewish women worried the most, with 71% of the Jewish women in Krause's survey revealing that they were concerned with problems of childrearing. In contrast, only 55.4% of the Italian women and 45.4% of the Slavic women voiced such anxieties.

Although the Jewish women scored the highest on the "worry" chart and were the most anxious about relations between themselves and their parents, husbands and children, it was Italian women who were most concerned about problems involving their own health and sexuality. Italian women also reported the most frequent incidence of sexual and marital problems.

Dr. Krause hopes her study will prove useful as a guide toward understanding women of diverse ethnic backgrounds, and she believes that "ethnic background is a deep and significant fact of life, often ignored, often unconscious, but psychologically important." She also believes, "Ethnicity plays a role in the development of identity of women just as parents, siblings and the experience of infancy, childhood, menarche and childbirth influence the individual feminine personality."

Grandmothers vs. Mothers vs. Daughters

How the views of three generations of ethnics change as families become more "Americanized" and turn away from the "Old World" values:

♦ Of the ethnic women surveyed by Dr. Krause, there weren't any grandmothers who approved of premarital sex. Only 8.7% of the mothers surveyed gave premarital sex their approval, but 40.8% of the daughters questioned approved of sex before marriage without reservation.

♦ 20.8% of the daughters surveyed claimed that they would choose a career over marriage. Only 8.7% of the mothers questioned would opt for a career, while only 3% of the grandmothers questioned could envision a life for themselves outside the home.

♦ An overwhelming majority of the grandmothers questioned (83%) believed that the proper role for a woman is wife and mother. Only 44% of the mothers and 17% of the daughters surveyed held that belief. The daughters also indicated that they would expect their husbands to share household responsibilities and chores.

♦ On the question of marrying outside one's religion, 21% of the grandmothers, 53% of the mothers and 63% of the daughters gave their approval.

♦ Only 10% of the grandmothers expressed any worries about sex or menopause, while 26% of the mothers and 43% of the daughters expressed their anxiety about this subject.

♦ Of the three ethnic groups surveyed, Italian women were most likely to speak Italian at home and serve ethnic food; Slavic women most frequently attended ethnic church services; and Jewish women valued marriage within their own ethnic group more than Italian or Slavic women.

12 SCIENCE AND INVENTION

ETHNICS OF INVENTION

Since the U.S. Patent Office first opened its doors in 1790, some 4 million inventions have been patented. Many of them have used up their 17 years' worth of exclusive rights without being noticed by the average American; others have drastically affected the way we live, the way we earn our living and even the way we die.

Creative minds from the four corners of the earth have flocked to America to give us such marvelous innovations as the atomic bomb and the hydrogen bomb, as well as television, telephones and transistors. For their roles both great and small, let us salute the creative energy that so many ethnic Americans contributed to our society.

No-Nick Shaves:

    Invention: Electric razor
    Inventor: Jacob Schick, Bavarian-
                 American
    Date: 1923

Schick Jacob (1877–1937), the son of a Bavarian immigrant, was laid up at an Alaskan army base with a sprained ankle when he first thought of inventing the electric razor that made his fortune. Camped out in the frigid Northwest, where there wasn't any hot running water and the temperature routinely dipped to 40 below, Schick began to dread the morning ritual of lathering up his beard with icy cold water. As a result, he began to dream of a way to shave without lather.

Patented on November 6, 1923, the Schick dry shaver consisted of a motor-driven cutting blade that moved across the skin. Without damaging or abrading a man's face, the shaver managed to grab a section

Advertisement for Schick's injector razor. (Courtesy: New York Public Library)

of skin through a slotted opening and shear off hairs at the skin level.

Schick began marketing his shavers in 1931. Since this was the height of the Depression, the $25 price tag made Schick's invention a luxury that most men could not afford. That first year, Schick only sold 3,000 shavers. By 1932, however, Schick made a profit for the first time, with sales of over 10,000 razors. He reinvested his profits into advertisements in national magazines to help boost sales and by 1937 there were more than 1,840,000 Schick shavers splitting hairs in the United States, Canada and England.

In addition to the electric razor, Schick also invented: a machine that cut filling time for gas masks from 35 minutes to 3 seconds; a pencil sharpener that remained attached to the pencil at all times; a toothpaste tube with a nondetachable cap (designed, no doubt, to end marital disputes); a card-shuffling machine; and a boat that drew only one foot of water yet was capable of toting 50 tons of equipment.

You Light Up My Life

Invention: Flashlight
Inventor: Conrad Hubert, Russian
             immigrant
Date: 1902

When Akiba Horowitz (1855–1928) landed in New York in 1890, one of his first priorities was to Americanize his name to Conrad Hubert. Next, he opened a small restaurant, where he met Joshua Lionel Cowen, the founder of the Lionel train company.

Soon, Hubert had abandoned his chef's hat for a salesman's sample case and was on the road hawking Cowen's toys and inventions. Hubert was an enthusiastic salesman who knew a good product when he saw one — that's why he offered to buy all rights

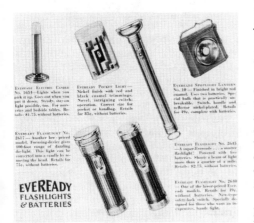

Conrad Hubert turned the electric flowerpot into a wide variety of battery-operated light sources. (Courtesy: New York Public Library)

and licenses to Cowen's latest novelty, the electric flowerpot.

Though Cowen didn't have much faith in the long-term sales of an artificial plant with tiny bulbs that lit up, Hubert proceeded to take the lights out of the flowerpots, improve the basic design of the battery and bulb, and seal the two inside a cylindrical tube. For these modifications, Hubert received U.S. patents #700,497 and #700,650 for a "portable electric light" that we commonly call a "flashlight" today.

Conrad Hubert organized the Ever Ready Company to market his products, but later sold the business in 1914. When he died, his estate was valued at $8 million — most of it the result of his faith in the electric flowerpot.

Strikes and Spares

Invention: Automatic pin setter
Inventor: Gottfried   J.   Schmidt,
             German-American
Date: 1939

Bowling had been a popular European and American sport for centuries, but it wasn't until the 1950s that a German-American pattern maker from Pearl River, New York, was able to turn it into a billion-dollar industry.

Fred Schmidt was tired of always hearing his friend, George Beckerle, complain about the labor problems that beset his bowling alley. The pin boys were constantly demanding higher wages; and on-the-job injuries, sustained by heavy wooden pins sent flying into the air by 14-pound balls, were costing Beckerle a small fortune in lost wages and compensation.

Schmidt decided that a machine that could automatically set up bowling pins was the logical solution to Beckerle's problems, and with the help of two mechanics and an engineer, Fred began working on a prototype pin setter in 1936. By 1939, Fred had a contractual agreement with American Machine and Foundry (AMF) and two working models of his revolutionary device.

World War II delayed field tests of the pin setters, so it wasn't until 1947 that the first commercial pin setter was installed. On August 14, 1952, the modern era of bowling dawned when 16 pin setters were installed at Farragut Pool Lanes in Brooklyn, New York. The large number of lanes and the stepped-up pace of the game helped to make bowling one of the most popular indoor sports in America.

Today there are more than 147,000 pin setting machines in operation at 8,600 commercial bowling alleys in the United States.

The Soft Touch

Invention: Q-Tips Cotton Swabs
Inventor: Leo Gerstenzang, Polish immigrant
Date: 1923

After emigrating to the United States from Warsaw, Leo established the Leo Gerstenzang Infant Novelty Company in 1922 to market baby supplies to new mothers.

When his own daughter was born in 1923, Leo enjoyed watching his wife bathe the tiny infant. One part of the process in particular caught his eye. As his wife covered a toothpick with cotton and used it to clean in between the folds of their baby's chubby body, the proud father wondered whether there might not be a safer way to clean an infant's nose and ears. Why, the point of the toothpick might penetrate the cotton wad at any moment and damage his daughter's delicate skin.

Leo considered the problem, quickly multiplied the number of babies born each year by the number of baths required to toddlerhood, and realized that there was a market for a blunt-ended, ready-to-use cotton swab that could safely clean the nooks and crannies of America's youth.

Several years of experimentation passed before Leo perfected a machine capable of wrapping cotton at the end of a non-splintering birchwood stick. By 1926, "Q-Tips Baby Gays" were on their way to becoming standard "tools" in the nurseries of America.

Inspired by Train Robbers

Invention: Electric tabulating machine
Inventor: Herman Hollerith, German-American
Date: 1880s

When Herman Hollerith (1860–1929) worked as a statistician for the U. S. Census Bureau it took seven years for that office to process the results of the 1880 census. By the time the clerks had finished tabulating the data, it was obsolete!

The seventh son of a German immigrant, Hollerith, whose inquiring mind was backed by an engineering degree from Columbia University, began to dream of inventing a more rapid method of collecting and analyzing data. On a trip out West, Hollerith first learned about the "punch photograph" system employed by train conductors. After a rash of robberies, involving thieves who had posed as passengers, conductors began punching holes on various parts of the train ticket to indicate a passenger's hair color, eye color, height, weight, nose size and other distinguishing features. Later, if the train was robbed, a "photographic" description of the missing "passenger" would be on file to aid officials in apprehending the robber.

While Hollerith watched the conductor punch out his description, the proverbial "lightbulb" blinked on in his head. Here was the system he needed for his tabulating machine! If census information could be punched on cards in a code, the cards could then be inserted into a counting machine where a pin would slip through each hole to complete an electric circuit. In this way, specific characteristics of the population, such as age, sex and occupation, could be easily tallied.

Hollerith tested his machinery by processing death records for the city of Baltimore in 1887. The U.S. Government was so impressed by the speed of his battery-operated tabulating machine that Hollerith was hired to compute the 1890 census. Instead of taking seven years to complete the onerous task, it took Hollerith only three years to compute the data.

Herman sold his tabulating company to a forerunner of IBM, and although he was a gifted inventor, Herman was not a gifted businessman. When he was offered an option to buy IBM stock in 1924, he refused the company's generous offer. Had he accepted, his initial investment would have appreciated more than 5,000 times.

Although Hollerith held 38 U.S. patents for his many inventions, he is best remembered for making "Do not fold, bend, spindle or mutilate" the 11th commandment.

The Invention Nobody Wanted

Invention: Xerography
Inventor: Chester F. Carlson, Swedish-American
Date: 1937

The "invention that nobody wanted" produced such an enormous income for Chester Carlson (1906–1968) that he was forced to devote the later years of his life to philanthropy. He even had trouble giving his money away fast enough.

What was this magical money-making machine that had been turned down by RCA, IBM and General Electric on the grounds that it had little commercial value? Believe it or not, that invention was the Xerox machine! It seems incredible that not one major corporation in the United States was able to see a viable future for Carlson's dry copying process in 1937.

An only child, born to impoverished Swedish immigrants, Carlson was burdened with the care of his aging, sickly parents. Even though he was forced to work full time to support his parents, Carlson managed to attend the California Insitute of Technology and earn a degree in physics in 1930.

He went on to study law, but meager finances made it impossible for Carlson to buy any textbooks for his courses. Night after night, Chester sat in the university library painstakingly copying each word of the assigned works by hand. It was this early experience with "writer's cramp," coupled with his long waits as a young lawyer for photostatic copies of patents, that spurred Carlson on to invent a rapid copying machine.

The first message ever copied was: "10-22-38 Astoria"—the date and place where Carlson performed his experiments in the storeroom of a Long Island Beauty salon.

Plastic Fantastic

Invention: Bakelite
Inventor: Leo H. Baekelandt, Belgian immigrant
Date: 1909

Leo Baekelandt (1863–1944) emigrated to the United States from Ghent in 1889 and worked as a research chemist for the Ansco Company. In 1893 he developed Velox photographic paper; he later sold the rights to it for a cool $1 million, to Kodak. But this was only the beginning. In 1909, Baekelandt developed Bakelite, the first insoluble plastic material that could not be melted or changed in shape once it had been formed under heat and pressure. Technically known as oxybenzylmethylene glycol anhydride, Bakelite started a revolution in manufacturing: within the first 37 years after Baekelandt's invention, more than 2,000 synthetic plastic resins were formulated.

Leo H. Baekelandt started the plastics revolution in 1909 when he invented oxybenzylmethylene glycol anhydride. (Courtesy: Union Carbide)

Bakelite was used to manufacture electrical instruments, pot handles, automotive parts and even dentures. Before long, the nation was inundated with plastic "glasses," plastic bags, plastic knives, forks, spoons, and even plastic beverage bottles, all thanks to the Belgian immigrant who made "plastics" a household word in America and one of our nation's largest industries.

WASP MASTERS OF DESTRUCTION

What did the Maxim family contribute to our American heritage? Inventions with disastrous results — machine guns, high explosive powders, steam-driven torpedoes, gun silencers and other deadly devices.

When Hiram Percy Maxim (1869–1936) invented the gun silencer at the turn of the century, he was merely following the example set by his expatriate father and uncle. At least Hiram's silencer was eventually modified and used in various nonviolent applications to eliminate noise pollution from gasoline engines, compressors, vacuum pumps and other loud machinery; most of his father's inventions had no redeeming social value whatsoever.

Hiram Stevens Maxim (1840–1916), Anglo-American inventor and father of Hiram Percy, was born in Sangerville, Maine. He started his brilliant career by perfecting a method of carbureting air and gas for lighting purposes. For years his invention was used to light some of New York's best hotels, and to illuminate railroad tracks by serving as a headlight for locomotives. Unfortunately, it was Hiram's last humanitarian invention.

While Hiram was visiting Paris in 1881, a fellow American advised him: "If you want to make a pile of money, invent something that will enable these Europeans to cut each other's throats with greater facility." Hiram was a man who knew good business advice when he heard it, and within two years he had perfected the first automatic machine gun. (The machine gun or automatic rifle is really a "time and motion" expert's delight — when the rifle is fired, the recoil energy that results from the shot is utilized to eject the empty shell from the gun and reload a fresh bullet in its place. Killing becomes as simple as "Ready, aim, fire, fire, fire . . ." You don't have to take time out from shooting to reload.)

Maxim became a naturalized British citizen in 1900, and was knighted by Queen Victoria in appreciation for the role his gun played in making the English campaign in Egypt a roaring success.

Sir Hiram went on to invent other weapons: a delayed-action fuse; smokeless gunpowder; and guns for hurling aerial torpedoes. Not to be outdone, his brother, Hudson Maxim (1853–1927), became the first American to manufacture smokeless gunpowder in the United States. He built a dynamite factory, at Maxim, New Jersey, in 1890, and later invented a high explosive powder, maximite, which was 1½ times as powerful as dynamite, as well as a system for driving torpedoes by steam, which he sold to the U.S. Navy.

In all, the Maxims were probably one of our most inventive families. Had they been alive today they probably would have invented the neutron bomb.

Tailless Dinner Jacket

Invention: Tuxedo
Inventor: Pierre   Lorillard   IV,
             French-American
Date: 1886

Ever since 1760, when Pierre Lorillard, an 18-year-old French immigrant, opened a snuff manufacturing plant in New York City, the Lorillard name has been synonymous with tobacco. But, besides contributing brand-name snuff and cigarettes to the United States, the Lorillard family also gave Americans the "tailless" dinner jacket, known as the "tuxedo."

It was Pierre Lorillard IV who designed the tailless coat in 1886, and had his clothier sew up a few versions in bright scarlet satin. Though the elder Lorillard declined to wear the jacket in public, he enlisted some family members of the younger generation to don the red satin jackets for the Tuxedo Park ball. Local society was not pleased with the Lorillards' departure from traditional evening attire of tails, and a writer noted: "At the Tuxedo Club ball young Griswold

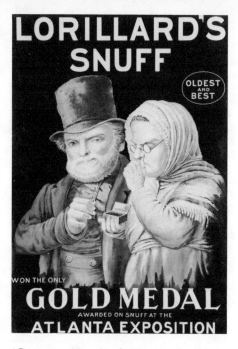

(Courtesy: New York Historical Society)

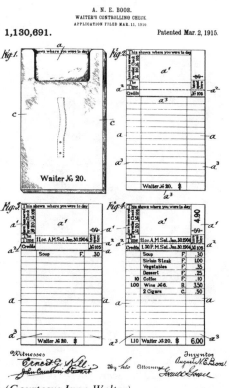

A. N. E. BOOS.
WAITER'S CONTROLLING CHECK.
APPLICATION FILED MAR. 11, 1910

1,130,691. Patented Mar. 2, 1915.

(Courtesy: Inge Welter)

Lorillard appeared in a tailless dress coat and waistcoat of scarlet satin, looking for all the world like a royal footman. There were several others of the abbreviated coats worn, which suggested to the onlookers that the boys ought to have been put in straight-jackets long ago."

Needless to say, the "tuxedo" has gained considerable respectability over the past decades, and it is now considered quite "proper" for evening wear.

It's Deductible

Invention:	Business lunch receipt
Inventor:	August N. E. Boos, German immigrant
Date:	1915

Americans are so used to getting receipts for their business lunches and dinners that it seems hard to believe someone invented and received a patent for a waiter's check *cum* business receipt. The business community owes a vote of thanks to August N. E. Boos, a German immigrant, for inventing the itemized bill and receipt in 1915, for which he received U.S. Patent 1,130,691.

The Secretary's Friend

Invention:	Shorthand
Inventor:	John Robert Gregg, Irish immigrant
Date:	1888

John Robert Gregg (1867–1948) emigrated to the United States in 1893, five years after he had perfected the shorthand system that bears his name. More properly known as Gregg Light-Line Phonography, his shorthand system is the most widely used in the world. Based on longhand strokes, Gregg's symbols flow in a smooth style similar to script writing; his system differs from the earlier one invented by Englishman Isaac Pitman in that the shading of the strokes is not important.

Space Saver

Invention:	Murphy bed
Inventor:	William L. Murphy, Irish-American
Date:	1900

Remember the old silent films with Charlie Chaplin? It seems that whenever the

Early advertisement for a Murphy bed.
(Courtesy: New York Historical Society)

"Little Tramp" found a bed to lay down on, it was usually a defective "Murphy bed" which swallowed him up and trapped him inside a closet or wall for a bit of slapstick humor.

Supposedly, the mechanism of Murphy beds has been perfected so that this situation will never occur in real life. And, although their beds bore the brunt of thousands of jokes over the years, this free publicity never bothered the Murphys.

The man who invented these space-saving sleepers was William Lawrence Murphy (1870–1956), the son of Irish immigrants who settled in Tuolumme County, California, during the 1848 gold rush. When he and four younger siblings were orphaned (he was 17), he undertook the tasks of running the family cattle ranch and exploiting the small gold claim their father had staked out.

He invented the Murphy bed in 1900, and since that time several million have been sold to space-hungry Americans whose bedrooms must serve "double duty" as living rooms, studies or even dining rooms during the day.

No More 78's

Invention: Long-playing record
Inventor: Peter Carl Goldmark,
             Hungarian immigrant
Date: 1948

Unlike his fellow Hungarian immigrant inventors (Teller, Wigner and Von Neumann), who gave us *the* Bomb, Peter Carl Goldmark (1906–1977) devoted his scientific energies to creating pleasurable devices. He gave America the tools of the modern entertainment industry by creating the LP record, workable color TV, and videotape recording.

Classical music was his passion and the inspiration that led to Goldmark's invention of the long-playing record. One day while listening to Brahms's piano concerto No. 2, Peter became annoyed at the frequency with which the old 78 RPM recordings had to be changed. Since each side provided only 5 minutes' worth of listening time, he was constantly flipping records over and changing them to hear a whole symphony.

Goldmark went to work on the problem, and by 1948 had perfected the 33⅓ RPM record. Instead of 80 grooves per inch and 5 minutes of music on the 78 RPM records, the new long-playing discs had 250 grooves per inch and 20 minutes of music on each side. He further improved the records by fashioning them out of unbreakable plastic, instead of shellac, which shattered on impact.

Goldmark's other inventions include: an autohorn that can be activated by the driver's knee; the sapphire phonograph needle; a lightweight tone arm; the first practical color TV system; and a microcolor TV for stomach surgery.

Peter Goldmark's invention of the long-playing record was a godsend for music buffs who lived in small apartments. The two large stacks of 78 rpm records, and the small stack of 33⅓ records in the center are identical – note for note. (Courtesy: CBS)

MORE CREATIVE IDEAS FROM ETHNIC AMERICANS

Invention: Armonica
Inventor: Benjamin Franklin, English
Date   1761

What's an armonica? It's a group of glasses of graduated sizes balanced atop spindles. Also known as the "glassychord," the armonica produces various musical tones when struck with a metal object such as a spoon. In addition to the armonica, Benjamin Franklin (1706–1790) also invented an improved heating stove (1744) and performed his famous kite experiment in 1752.

Invention: Brassiere
Inventor: Mary Phelps Jacob, Scotch-Irish
Date: 1914

Although Mary Jacob wasn't the first person to invent a bra, she was the first to receive a patent for her idea. Better known as Caresse Crosby (her second husband was Harry Crosby), Ms. Jacob was a descendant of another inventive American who often receives credit for inventing the steamboat – Robert Fulton. Like Jacob, Fulton merely popularized his "invention." He made steamboating a commercial success by traveling from New York City to Albany in record-breaking time – 30 hours – in 1807.

Invention: Corn Harvester
Inventor: Henry Blair, Black
Date: 1834

When Blair patented his corn harvester on October 14, 1834, he became the first Black American to receive a U.S. Patent.

Invention: Elevator
Inventor: Elisha Otis, English
Date: 1853

Elisha Otis (1811–1861) first exhibited his safety elevator, an invention that revolutionized building design, at the Crystal Palace Exhibition in New York City in 1854.

Invention: Elevator shoes
Inventor: Emidio Spezza, Italian immigrant

Known as the "man who shoes the stars," Spezza came to America from Cas-tiglione, Italy, in 1909. He soon earned the respect of the Hollywood community and was acclaimed as the best shoemaker on the West Coast in the 1950s. In 1953, his custom-made shoes were selling for $100 to $300 a pair to clients such as Mae West, Bing Crosby, Mario Lanza and Shirley Temple. Emidio, who stood a mere 5'2½" tall, is credited with inventing "elevator shoes," which helped so many matinee idols appear "bigger than life" both on the screen and off.

Invention: Hermetic body sealer
Inventor: Joseph Karwowski, Russian immigrant
Date: 1903

In 1903, Joseph Karwowski, a Russian immigrant living in Herkimer, N.Y., received U.S. Patent #748,284 for his method of sealing dead bodies in transparent tombs. The body was first surrounded with a thick layer of sodium silicate, then water was evaporated off by dry heat, and finally, molten glass was applied. Karwowski's method allowed the deceased person's body to be preserved in a lifelike condition for an indefinite period of time.

Invention: Homemade atomic bomb
Inventor: John Aristotle Phillips, Greek-American
Date: 1976

In 1976 a Greek-American physics student, John Aristotle Phillips (1956–   ) proved that anyone with a physics background, $2,000 in cash, a supply of plutonium and a few unclassified documents from the U.S. Government Printing Office could manufacture his own atomic bomb. John conducted his research as part of an independent study course at Princeton, and was later assigned an FBI agent to protect him from foreign government agents eager to learn the "secrets" behind his A+ grades.

Invention: Improved barbed wire
Inventor: Joseph Glidden, English
Date: 1874

Joseph Glidden (1813–1906) received U.S. Patent #157,124 for his improved method of twisting the wire used to tame the West and keep the cattle "home on the range."

Invention: Lathe
Inventor: Thomas Blanchard,
            French-English

Besides the wood-turning lathe, Thomas Blanchard (1788–1864) also invented a tack machine capable of producing 500 tacks per minute, and a machine that cut and folded envelopes.

Invention: Linotype
Inventor: Ottmar Mergenthaler,
            German
Date: 1884

A German immigrant from Bietigheim, Ohmar Mergenthaler (1854–1899) called his machine "linotype" because it made it possible to cast a "line of type" for a printing press in a few seconds. The linotype machine eliminated the need to search for each letter and character by hand and place it in order before the presses could roll. First used in 1886 for the New York *Tribune,* the linotype is still in use today, although it has been modified and improved drastically over the years.

Invention: Mimeograph
Inventor: Thomas Alva Edison,
            Scottish
Date: 1876

In addition to inventing the phonograph (1877), and the electric pen (1876), Thomas Edison (1847–1931) also invented the world's first practical duplicating machine — the mimeograph.

Invention: Multiple effect evaporator
Inventor: Norbert Rillieux, Black-
            French
Date: 1843

One might say that Norfert Rillieux's (1806–1894) invention helped make the world a bit more "refined." His system of multiple vacuum pans, which quickly removed water form sugar cane syrup (causing it to crystallize), revolutionized the sweets industry by making sugar whiter, cheaper and more available to the public.

Although his father was a French engineer who gave Norbert not only his name but a Paris education, Norbert, considered a "free man of color," was legally registered as a *quadroon libre* in New Orleans.

Invention: Reaper
Inventor: Cyrus Hall McCormick
            Scotch-Irish

It wasn't until the Civil War had taken its toll of agricultural workers that farmers were even willing to give Cyrus McCormick's (1809–1884) reaper a try in the fields of America. Once they realized the benefits that could be "reaped" from mechanized farming, there was no turning back.

In 1902, McCormick's company merged with four others to become International Harvester Company, and ever since the farmers of America have been increasing their productivity through bigger and better machines.

Invention: Refrigerated trucks
Inventor: Frederick   McKinley
            Jones, Black
Date: 1949

The first refrigeration system patented for long-haul trucks was introduced by a Black American, Fred Jones, in 1949. Jones received U.S. Patent #2,475,841 for a top-mounted cooling device which enabled trucks to carry fresh fruits and vegetables for long distances. For the first time, towns that did not have railroad service were able to receive daily shipments of perishable goods without damage due to heat spoilage and temperature fluctuations.

Invention: Semi-automatic Rifle
Inventor: John Garand, French
Date: 1929

Garand's rifle was the official weapon used by the U.S. Army and Marine Corps during World War II.

Invention: Shoe-lasting machine
Inventor: Jan Ernst Matzeliger,
            Black
Date: 1883

Born in Dutch Guiana, Jan Matzeliger emigrated to Massachusetts as a young man and began working in a shoe factory. It was there that Jan learned about shoemaking, particularly the time-consuming operation of attaching the tops of shoes to the bottoms. Convinced that there had to be a better way, Matzeliger perfected a shoe-lasting machine in 1877, but did not patent it until 1883. Matzeliger's machine increased worker productivity from 60 pairs of shoes per day to more than 400. Although his machine was introduced more than 100 years ago, it remains the basic patented device still used by the modern shoe industry.

Invention: Submarine
Inventor: John Phillip Holland, Irish immigrant
Date: 1898

John Holland (1841–1914), an Irish immigrant from Liscannor, County Clare, drew his first plans for an underwater boat in 1863, but it wasn't until 1898 that his first successful submarine, the Holland No. 9, was launched. Measuring 53' 10" long, by 10' 7", the submarine was shaped like a porpoise and driven by 50 horsepower engines. While the vessel was submerged, a storage battery propelled it.

The U.S. Navy was so impressed with Holland's designs that they immediately ordered several submarines for their fleet.

Invention: Third rail
Inventor: Granville T. Woods, Black
Date: 1874

Although he never completed grammar school, Granville Woods (1856–1910) patented more than 35 electrical and mechanical inventions during his lifetime. One was a "third rail" system, which freed electrically powered trains from overhead cables.

A free Negro born in Columbus, Ohio, Woods also invented induction telegraphy—a system that allows moving trains to communicate with one another via telegraphed messages.

Invention: Torpedo control system
Inventor: Hedy Lamarr, Austrian immigrant
Date: 1942

In her native Vienna she was known as Hedwig Kiesler Markey, but when she moved to America and became a Hollywood star, Hedy Lamarr changed her name to fit her new glamorous image. In 1942 Hedy received a joint patent with George Antheil for a guidance system for torpedoes, under her old name, Markey.

Invention: Traffic Light
Inventor: Garrett A. Morgan, Black
Date: 1923

Garrett Morgan's (1877–1963) first successful invention was a belt-fastener attachment for a sewing machine, which he sold for $150. In order to make the sale, Morgan had to pose as an Indian chief from Canada instead of a native-born Black American.

Morgan later invented a hair-straightening process, the income from which enabled him to become the first Black to own a car in Cleveland, Ohio. His experience behind the wheel led Morgan to invent the traffic light, a device that has been credited with saving thousands of lives by providing "right of way" for both cars and pedestrians.

Invention: Zipper
Inventor: Gideon Sundback, Swedish-American
Date: 1913

On April 29, 1913, Dr. Gideon Sundback, an electrical engineer, received U.S. Patent #1,060,378 for the Plako slide fas-

Ad extolling the virtues of the hookless fastener. (Courtesy: New York Public Library)

tener—the forerunner of the modern zipper, which at that stage was a rather untrustworthy device at best.

The second model, known as the Hookless 2, was a bigger success. By 1918 more than 90,000 of these newfangled hookless fasteners had been sold. It wasn't until 1922 that the "hookless" became a "zipper," however, and credit for coining the new

word belongs to B. F. Goodrich, the entrepreneur of rubber fame. Goodrich coined the word because of the "z-z-zip" sound made by heavy metal zippers that had been installed in his rubber rain boots.

By 1930 the zipper was well on its way to worldwide acceptance and respectability, when fashion designer Schiaparelli began using them on all her dresses.

ETHNIC SPACE PIONEERS

NEIL ALDEN ARMSTRONG (1930–) was born near Wapakoneta, Ohio, of Scottish ancestry. Armstrong became the first man to walk on the moon on July 20, 1969. The Apollo XI astronaut will go down in history for his oft-quoted description of the mission as ". . . one small step for man, one giant leap for mankind."

EDWIN E. ALDRIN (1930–) made headlines as the second man to walk on the moon in 1969 when he followed in Neil Armstrong's "giant" footsteps. His father's parents were Swedish immigrants, and his mother's ancestry was mixed Dutch, Scottish and English (coincidentally, her maiden name was Marion Moon). In 1972, "Buzz" made headlines again by publicly discussing the mental health problems that resulted after his "Return to Earth" (the title of his 1974 autobiography). Chosen as chairman of the National Association for Mental Health's campaign in 1974, Aldrin remarked: "The first step toward help is a giant leap toward recovery."

MICHAEL COLLINS (1930–), the pilot of the Apollo XI command ship, circled the moon for 30 orbits while Aldrin and Armstrong walked on it. Born in Rome of Irish ancestry on his father's side and early American stock on his mother's, Collins' family included three living Army generals at the time of his birth. He graduated from West Point in 1952, became an Air Force test pilot and later entered the space program. Prior to his Apollo XI flight, Collins had walked in space twice, in addition to taking part in a space rendezvous.

WALTER M. SCHIRRA (1923–) was one of the original 7 astronauts chosen for Project Mercury, which ushered in the age of manned space flight in 1961. Schirra and astronaut Thomas P. Stafford success-

fully completed the first space rendezvous in 1965. In 1968, aboard Apollo 7, he and two other astronauts made the first live TV broadcast from space. Descended from French Huguenots who emigrated first to Switzerland, and then to the United States, Schirra is currently vice president in charge of aerospace systems for the Johns-Manville corporation.

EUGENE A. CERNAN (1934–) was one of the last men on the moon. The grandson of a Czechoslovakian immigrant, Cernan was a veteran of almost 500 hours in space before commanding the final lunar landing of the Apollo program, No. 17. Cernan remained on the moon for 75 hours with astronaut Harrison H. Schmitt.

CAPTAIN ELLISON S. ONIZUKA, a Japanese-American from Kealakekua, Hawaii, will probably be the first American of Oriental extraction to fly in space. Chosen as part of the 35-member team that began training at the Johnson Space Center in Houston on July 1, 1978, Onizuka is a graduate of the Air Force test pilot school at Edwards Air Force Base.

MAJOR FREDERICK GREGORY (1941–) is one of three Blacks recently selected as candidates for the Space Shuttle program. Gregory, however, is the only one designated as a pilot. A graduate of the Air Force Academy in 1964, Gregory has flown more than 40 different types of aircraft in his career, but never one that can be launched like a rocket, orbit the earth for up to 30 days, and then land on earth in much the same way as an airplane would.

The other two Black Americans selected for shuttle service are Major Guion S. Bluford of Dayton, Ohio, and Dr. Ronald E. McNair of Marina Del Rey, California. Both are scheduled for service in the 1980s.

NOBEL PRIZES

Ascanio Sobrero, a thirty-five-year-old professor of chemistry at Turin, Italy, discovered nitroglycerine, but it wasn't until Alfred Nobel (1833–1896) developed a detonator that the explosive energy of nitroglycerine could be harnessed. Nobel applied for British and U.S. patents for his discovery, which he named dynamite, in 1867.

Nobel hoped the destructive power of his explosives would be a deterrent to war (sound familiar?) but he soon learned otherwise. In an effort to have his name associated with something other than death, warfare and destruction, he established (with a fund of $9 million) the Nobel Prizes, the first of which was awarded in 1901. That first award was worth $30,000; by 1967, a Nobel prize carried a cash value of $61,700; and by 1977 that value had almost tripled, to $177,000.

Over the years, the United States has garnered 152 awards (as of 1979) more than twice as many as Britain, and as many as Germany, France and Scandinavia combined.

*SOME OF AMERICA'S
NOBEL PRIZE-WINNING
SCIENTISTS*

LUIS W. ALVAREZ
(1911–   )
Spanish-American
1968 Nobel Prize for Physics
Contributions to the study of subatomic particles, and techniques for detecting these particles.

HANS ALBRECHT BETHE
(1906–   )
German-born
1967 Nobel Prize for Physics
Contributions to the theory of nuclear reactions, and discoveries concerning energy production in stars.

FELIX BLOCH
(1905–   )
Swiss-born
1952 Nobel Prize for Physics

Developed method of probing atomic nuclei with radio waves.

ALEXIS CARREL
(1873–1944)
French-born
1912 Nobel Prize for Physiology and Medicine
Developed surgical techniques for suturing blood vessels, and for transplanting blood vessels and organs.

ALBERT CLAUDE
(1899–   )
Luxembourg-born
1974 Nobel Prize for Physiology and Medicine
Contributions to modern cellular biology.

CARL F. CORI AND GERTY T. CORI
(1896–   )   (1896–1957)
Both were born in Prague, Czechoslovakia.
1947 Nobel Prize for Physiology and Medicine
Discovery of the catalytic conversion of glycogen in the body.

ANDRE F. COURNAND
(1895–   )
French-American
1956 Nobel Prize for Physology and Medicine
Technique of inserting catheter in vein to chart the heart's interior.

MAX DELBRUCK
(1906–   )
German-born
1969 Nobel Prize for Physiology and Medicine
Study of bacteriophages.

ALBERT EINSTEIN
(1879–1955)
German-born Jew
1921 Nobel Prize for Physics
Contributions to mathematical physics and discovery of the law of photoelectric effect.

Einstein did not win a Nobel Prize for his special theory of relativity, which he first published in 1905. Instead, the Swedish Royal Academy of Science cited Einstein for his general contributions to theoretical physics. He was so certain that he would win a Nobel Prize eventually that he pledged the prize money to his first wife as part of their divorce settlement in 1919.

Quote: "Try not to become a man of success, but rather a man of value."

Albert Einstein in his later years. (Courtesy: German Information Center)

LEO ESAKI
(1926–   )
Japanese-born
1973 Nobel Prize for Physics
    Research on phenomena of "electron tunneling" through semiconductors and superconductors.

    Quote: "Americans think an American Esaki won the award. On the other hand, the Japanese think a Japanese Esaki won it, and that's fine with me because science is international and the Nobel Prize is international."

ENRICO FERMI
(1901–1954)
Italian-born
1938 Nobel Prize for Physics

Discovery of new radioactive elements, and work in slow neutron bombardment.

Fermi has been called the "Architect of the Atomic Bomb," since his early experiments in artificial radioactivity led to the discovery of uranium fission. The "Atomic Age" began at 3:45 P.M. on December 2, 1942, when an atomic pile constructed at the University of Chicago became self-sustaining. Arthur Compton sent a cryptic telegram announcing the results: "The Italian navigator has entered the New World."

Two years later the fission reaction was harnessed to produce a fission bomb. Fermi died of cancer before the first peaceful uses of fission were developed. In 1955, atomic element number 100 was named Fermium in his honor.

MURRAY GELL-MANN
(1929–   )
Austrian-American
1969 Nobel Prize for Physics
    Discoveries concerning classification of nuclear particles and their interactions.

IVAR GIAEVER
(1930–   )
Norwegian-born
1973 Nobel Prize for Physics
    Research on phenomena of "electron tunneling" through semiconductors and superconductors.

KARL LANDSTEINER
(1868–1943)
Austrian-born Jew
1930 Nobel Prize for Physiology and Medicine
    Revolutionized the science of blood transfusions and serology with his discovery of human blood groups.

ERNEST O. LAWRENCE
(1901–1958)
Norwegian-American
1939 Nobel Prize for Physics
    Invention of the cyclotron, or "atom smasher," where heavy alpha particles, protons and deuterons could be manufactured.

TSUNG-DAO LEE
(1926–   )
Chinese-born
1957 Nobel Prize for Physics

Disproved the law of conservation of parity in nuclear physics. (Lee and Chen Ning Yang, who shared the award, were the first Chinese ever to receive a Nobel Prize.)

OTTO LOEWI
(1873–1961)
German-born
1936 Nobel Prize for Physiology and Medicine
Discoveries concerning the chemical transmission of nerve impulses.

SALVADOR LURIA
(1912–   )
Italian-born
1969 Nobel Prize for Medicine and Physiology
Discoveries concerning the replication mechanism and genetic structure of viruses.
(Luria donated a large portion of his prize money to aid organizations opposed to the war in Vietnam.)

MARIA GOEPPERT-MAYER
(1906–   )
Born in Kattowitz, Upper Silesia, a part of Germany at the time.
1963 Nobel Prize for Physics
Research on structure of atomic nuclei.
(Mayer was the first American woman to win a Nobel prize in Physics.)

ALBERT A. MICHELSON
(1852–1931)
German-born Jew
1907 Nobel Prize for Physics
Invented optical instruments to measure the speed of light. (Michelson was the first American physicist to receive the Nobel prize.)

SEVERO OCHOA
(1905–   )
Spanish-born
1959 Nobel Prize for Medicine and Physiology
Laboratory synthesis of DNA and RNA.

GEORGE E. PALADE
(1912–   )
Romanian-born
1974 Nobel Prize for Medicine and Physiology
Contributions to modern cell biology.

LINUS PAULING
(1901–   )
German-English descent
1954 Nobel Prize for Chemistry
Research into the nature of chemical valence bonding, and study of forces which bind together protein and other molecules.
In 1962, Pauling was awarded the Nobel Peace Prize, thereby becoming the first man ever to receive a prize in each of two different disciplines. Marie Curie was the first person to win two Nobel Prizes—in Physics (1903) and in Chemistry (1911   .)

ARNO A. PENZIAS
(1933–   )
German-born
1978 Nobel Prize for Physics
Discovery of radiation remaining from the "Big Bang" explosion, which many believe created the universe some 18 billion years ago.
Quote: "My mother was a cleaning woman and our family wasn't able to live too well. Now I have as many suits as my closet can hold. I've won the Nobel Prize. Many people are saying the American Dream no longer is a reality today. Well, I've realized it. The American Dream has come true for me."

EMILIO SEGRE
(1905–   )
Italian-born
1959 Nobel Prize for Physics
Discovery of the formation of anti-protons.

WILLIAM BRADFORD SHOCKLEY
(1910–   )
English-born
1956 Nobel Prize for Physics
Development of the transistor.

ALBERT SZENT-GYÖRGYI
(1893–   )
Hungarian-born
1937 Nobel Prize in Medicine and Physiology
Research on cellular respiration, discovery of vitamin C.

JOHN VAN VLECK
(1899–   )
Dutch-American descendant of Tielman Van Vleck, who settled in New Amsterdam in 1658.
1977 Nobel Prize for Physics

Mathematical models that explain how electrons behave in conductive materials.

(Van Vleck has been called "the father of modern magnetism" for his discovery that charged particles (ions) could be added to a perfect geometric lattice of crystals to enhance or retard the flow of electric current. He was one of the first to extend the theories of quantum mechanics to magnetics. Why did he enter the field of physics some 60 years ago? "My father was a mathematician, so I didn't want to do that, and I couldn't pronounce French, so I went into physics.")

ROSALYN YALOW
(1921–   )
Daughter of Jewish immigrants
1977 Nobel Prize for Physiology and Medicine
Techniques of radioimmunoassay to measure hormones in the body.

(One of only 5 women ever to win a Nobel Prize in science, Yalow not only puts in a 12-hour day, she keeps a kosher home for her family, too. As she sees it, "I've become a kind of symbol. Every Jewish group and every women's group invites me to speak. I turn down most of them. I've become important to several causes but . . . I'm not going to perform as an oracle on pollution or the problems of the inner city.")

More than 25% of all the American Nobel prize winners have been Jewish, even though Jews only make up about 3% of the population in the United States.

MORE ETHNIC SCIENTISTS

♦ *Choh Hao Li* (1913–   ), a Chinese immigrant, was the first to isolate human growth hormone in 1956.
♦ *Lise Meitner* (1878–1968), an Austrian-born physicist, became the first woman to ever receive the Fermi award. She shared that honor in 1966 with Otto Hahn and Fritz Strassman.
♦ *Wernher Von Braun* (1912–1977), the German-born "father of the American rocket program," developed Explorer 1, the first U.S. space satellite, which was launched in 1958, and was responsible for producing the Saturn 5 rocket that carried astronauts to the moon in 1969.

♦ *Dr. George Cotzias* (1920–1977) is the Greek-born neurologist who developed L-Dopa therapy, which has benefitted millions of patients suffering from Parkinson's disease. Since 1967, Cotzias has demonstrated that massive doses of the drug can combat the brain disease effectively in some cases.

♦ *Carl Norden* (1880–   ), a Dutch-American engineer, perfected the Navy's Mark XV bombsight (also known as the Norden bombsight) in 1930. His device, sold to the United States for the grand sum of one dollar, enabled planes to carry out high-altitude, precision bombing in broad daylight. He also designed radio-controlled target planes and robot flying bombs.

♦ *Jokichi Takamine* (1854–1922), a Japanese-born chemist who moved to the United States in 1890, was the first to isolate adrenalin, properly known by its chemical name, epinephrine. He accomplished this feat in 1901 at his lab in Clifton, New Jersey. He was the first person ever to isolate a pure hormone.

♦ *Hideyo Noguchi* (1876–1928), a Japanese immigrant to the United States in 1899, was the first to devise the Noguchi test or reaction for the diagnosis of syphilis. He also succeeded in producing a culture medium for studying spirochetes, which facilitated the investigation of yellow fever and other diseases.

♦ *The Wizard Of Schenectady* When Hnery Ford was having problems working out the wrinkles in his new generating system at the River Rouge plant, he called on Charles Steinmetz (1864–1923) to examine the faulty generator. Steinmetz Walked around the generator for a short while, and finally drew a chalk mark on one side. He told Ford's crew of technicians to remove the plate he had marked and take exactly 16 windings from the coil.

They followed his instructions, and the generator worked perfectly. At Ford's request, Steinmetz submitted an itemized bill for $10,000, whch read as follows;

Making chalk mark on generator	$1.00
Knowing where to make chalk mark	$9,999.00
	$10,000.00

Born in Breslau, Germany, Karl August Rudolf Steinmetz, or "Charles" as he preferred to be known, was almost denied entry to the United States because he was a hunchback. Fortunately a Danish-American student he had befriended on the long voyage agreed to take responsibility for him and he was allowed to enter.

A draftsman by trade, Steinmetz developed a method for mass-producing electric motors in 1890 that caught the attention of General Electric. GE eventually bought out his old company and brought him to its plant in Schenectady.

Although he never married, Steinmetz legally adopted his longtime lab assistant, Joseph Hayden; Joseph, Mrs. Hayden and their three children lived in the Steinmetz house, and he enjoyed his role as adoptive grandfather.

13 BUSINESS AND INDUSTRY

THE MERCHANTS

Early settlers in America had to be satisfied with occasional visits from itinerant peddlers selling tinware, cloth and dry goods. Eventually, as the demand for manufactured goods grew, general stores began to dot the frontier. With the growth of the nation, these stores became bigger, better and more specialized. Today, we have block-long department stores filled with clothing and housewares, as well as tiny specialty shops that sell only kites, or chocolate chip cookies, or left-handed utensils.

Retailing is big business in America today, and many of our "big names" in merchandising were immigrants who came to America and started small, family-run stores. Often, these retailing pioneers began their careers on an even more modest level — with their stores tied to their backs, so to speak, as they peddled their wares from town to town.

GIMBEL'S DEPARTMENT STORES "Macy's never tells Gimbel's," but whenever friends asked Adam Gimbel (1818–1896) the secret of his business success, Gimbel always replied, "Others may have had their paid helpers and assistants, but I have my seven sons." Actually, Adam had ten sons, but only seven chose to follow their immigrant father's footsteps into the marketplace.

Adam Gimbel emigrated to the United States in 1835 from his native Bavaria and began trading goods to rural farmers along the Mississippi River, from New Orleans to Vincennes, Indiana (the capital of Northwest Territory).

Gimbel gave up peddling in 1842 to open a dry goods store in Vincennes. One of the first merchants to adhere to a "one-price" policy (thereby eliminating the haggling that occurred in most stores of his day) he also offered a money-back guarantee, claiming: "Fairness and Equality to All Patrons, whether they be Residents of the City, Plainsmen, Traders or Indians."

By 1875, Gimbel's business was expanding so rapidly that he was forced to move into a three-story building to meet customer demand. Twelve years later, when riverboat traffic began to decline, Adam moved his family business to Milwaukee; Gimbel's branches later were opened in Philadelphia (1894) and New York (1910).

Four generations of Gimbels ran the family firm until 1975, when Bruce Gimbel retired as president after 40 years of service. Today, Gimbel's is part of the Brown and Williamson Tobacco Company.

WOOLWORTH AND THE "FIVE AND TEN" Frank Winfield Woolworth (1852–1919) was born in Rodman, New York, of English ancestry. His family name, Woolworth, was an Americanization of "Wolley," the town in England his ancestors hailed from.

Woolworth was a retailing genius whose experience as a salesman taught him that everyone loves a bargain. Even if an item hadn't moved off the shelves for months, it could be used as a loss leader to attract customers to the store — if the price was right.

Frank opened his first "Great 5¢ Store" in Utica, New York, in 1879. Business was brisk for the first few weeks, but after the novelty of the idea wore off, sales figures began to drop. To counter this, Woolworth moved his store to a higher-traffic area in Lancaster, Pennsylvania. In 1880, he added 10¢ items to the Lancaster store, making

Aaron Montgomery Ward invented the mail-order business in 1872. (Courtesy: Montgomery Ward)

Local merchants conducted smear campaigns, using ads in hometown newspapers, to discourage customers from shopping by mail. (Courtesy: Montgomery Ward)

the store on North Queen Street the oldest "Five and Ten" in the world.

Woolworth continued to be successful, and by 1904 sales had topped the $10 million mark. One of the most successful items the Woolworth's chain carries is candy. Since 1917 over 90 million pounds have been weighed out on scales for Woolworth's sweet-toothed customers, helping to boost current store sales close to the $3 billion mark.

Note to inflation watchers: If Woolworth opened his "Five and Ten" today, the only items in the store would be gumballs, candy, cheap vending-machine rings and trinkets, and perhaps a few inexpensive cigars.

THE MAIL ORDER KINGS—WARD'S AND SEARS Another Anglo-Saxon in the retailing business was Aaron Montgomery Ward (1843–1913), the man who invented the mail-order business in 1872. His first catalog, mailed from Chicago, was a single sheet of paper listing 163 items. Despite the Great Fire and the Panic of 1873, sales were strong, and by 1874 Ward was raking in more than $100,000 annually.

Sales topped the $1 million mark in 1887, thanks to Ward's promise of "satisfaction guaranteed or your money back." In the process, however, he had angered local small-town merchants, who began to band together to smash Ward's operation. They instituted smear campaigns designed to discourage local customers from shopping by

mail, and they filled local newspapers with stories of dissatisfied customers.

To make matters worse, in 1891, Postmaster General John Wanamaker (the same Wanamaker who had opened a Philadelphia department store in 1878) proposed a new form of mail service known as Rural Free Delivery, which meant that farmers and rural residents no longer would have to come into town to pick up their letters and parcels. Despite the opposition of local merchants, RFD mail was instituted on March 3, 1893, and catalog buying became a way of life for millions of rural Americans.

The only way left for local merchants to retaliate was by public book burnings of Ward's and Sears' catalogs—they even offered a prize to the person who collected the largest number of mail order catalogs for the public bonfire held each week. But, despite their best efforts, Ward's and Sears' became household words throughout the land.

SEARS, ROEBUCK AND ROSENWALD Although the Sears chain never bore his name, it was Julius Rosenwald's organizational genius that turned Sears, Roebuck and Company into the multibillion-dollar corporation that today employs 75 copywriters for the sole purpose of producing its annual catalog.

Richard Warren Sears (1863–1914), of English ancestry on both sides, began selling watches as a sideline in 1886 to supplement his income as a railroad station agent in North Redwood, Minnesota. Encouraged by brisk sales, Sears abandoned his job with the railroad and moved to Chicago, where he hired a watchmaker, Alvah C. Roebuck, who later became his partner in 1893.

Richard's talents were selling, advertising and merchandising, but there never would have been a $3 billion catalog division today without the help of Julius Rosenwald, a Jewish immigrant from Westphalia, Germany, who bought out Roebuck's interest in the firm in 1895 for $20,000. The following year the first catalog was published, and within 9 years catalog sales had exceeded $53 million. In 1908, when Richard Sears retired, Rosenwald assumed the presidency of the company.

Today's Sears catalog is a bit over 1,400 pages thick, weighs five pounds, and offers more than 79,000 items — including diapers, digital watches — and yes, the kitchen sink, too.

DING-DONG. AVON CALLING! Some Americans made their retailing fortunes through mail order firms, others through large department stores, but there were some Americans who continued the original tradition of traveling from door to door to make a sale. The most successful names in America that "ring a bell" are Avon and Fuller.

Today, Avon is the largest cosmetic manufacturer in the world — but pushing glamour wasn't always an easy job. In the 1880s, cosmetics were not considered proper for "respectable" women, and those who bought them were usually ridiculed as "fast floozies."

David H. McConnell (1858–1937), an Anglo-Saxon from Oswego, New York, was working as a door-to-door salesman when he thought of the idea that inevitably made his fortune in America. McConnell, who had a lot of faith in the door-to-door method of selling, believed that women who were reluctant to purchase perfumes and cosmetics at the corner drugstore might purchase such items in the privacy of their own homes.

Instead of itinerant salesmen who had no ties to the community they serviced, McConnell chose representatives who lived within their own sales territory, to make them more responsible to their customers. And, instead of hiring men, McConnell decided that women would be better suited to the task of selling perfumes.

The first saleswoman hired by McConnell was Mrs. P. F. F. Albee, a widow from Winchester, New Hampshire, who is affectionately nicknamed "the Mother of the California Perfume Company." (The name was changed to Avon in 1939.)

Not only was Mrs. Albee the first Avon lady in America, she also recruited other women who wanted to "ring chimes" for a living and sell Avon products door to door.

It was these "bell ringers" (or "ding-dong ladies," if you prefer) who helped make the California Perfume Company, which actually started in a small room in lower Manhattan in 1886, one of America's largest corporations.

THE FULLER BRUSH MAN Appropriately enough, Alfred Carl Fuller's autobiography, published in 1960, was entitled *A Foot in the Door*. Born in Kings County, Nova Scotia, Fuller (1885–1973) came to the U.S. in 1903 with only $75, a Bible, and a needle and thread. Two years later he began manufacturing a handy wire-and-bristle brush of his own design that was extremely helpful in cleaning all those dusty nooks and crannies found in turn-of-the-century homes.

Fuller began peddling his brushes in Somerville, Massachusetts, for 50c each, and by the early 1920s he had really "cleaned up" in the brush business, with almost $12 million worth of annual sales.

In the 1960s, the Fuller Brush Company, by now an American institution, began to suffer a long, slow decline as housewives entered the marketplace in record numbers and the old selling methods no longer proved effective. By 1974, sales were only half of their 1965 peak of $94 million, and the red ink was tallied at $8.4 million. New management saved the company: by 1977 sales were up and profits were more than $6 million.

11 ETHNICS WHO BECAME DEPARTMENT STORES

L. L. BEAN The Bean family has been in the sporting goods business ever since Leon Leonwood Bean opened his first store in 1912. Descended from the Scottish clan MacBean, whose motto inscribed on the family coat of arms advises: "Touch not the cat bot [without] a glove," the fourth generation of Beans are being groomed to take control of the family business in Freeport, Maine, which is open 24 hours a day, 365 days a year.

BRENTANO'S August Brentano, an Austrian immigrant who arrived here in 1853, started his bookstore chain in New York City on a modest scale—his first "store" was a newspaper stand in front of a hotel. Brentano later expanded his business by selling foreign books and newspapers.

FILENE'S This Boston department store, famous for its bargain basement, was founded by William Filene (1830–1901), a Polish immigrant from Posen. After a bloody uprising in his hometown in 1848, William renounced his Jewish religion and emigrated to the United States via England. In 1856 he met and married Clara Ballin, a Bavarian immigrant, with whom he had two sons, Edward and Lincoln. When their father's health failed in the early 1880s, Edward (1860–1937) and Lincoln Filene (1865–1957) took over the family business. With Edward at the helm, Filene's expanded rapidly, becoming a major department store in the Boston area.

HAMMACHER SCHLEMMER There is only one branch of this unusual store on East 57th Street in New York City, but its reputation as a source of gadgets and one-of-a-kind items has spread world-wide. When King Hassan II of Morocco came to visit the United States, he reputedly bought over $28,000 worth of goods and gadgets during one evening's shopping spree at Hammacher Schlemmer.

The famous emporium was started in 1848 by an industrious German immigrant, William Schlemmer, who convinced Alfred Hammacher to invest in his small hardware store on the Bowery.

Hammacher Schlemmer was the first store to carry such novelty gadgets as the steam iron (1937), the pressure cooker, the humidifier and the electric razor. The store also delights in selling expensive "toys" for the rich: a $1,695 hot dog stand for use at your private pool; automatic crepe makers that sell for $595; Doggie Doley, a septic tank for dogs; Marie Antoinette's doghouse; and even a throne for your commode.

E. J. KORVETTES Once rumored to be an acronym for "Eight Jewish Korean War Veterans," Korvettes was actually founded by a native New Yorker of Roman-

QUALITY AND SERVICE
SINCE 1848

WHEN IN NEW YORK, COME VISIT OUR STORE

Hammacher Schlemmer
147 EAST 57th STREET
NEW YORK CITY 10022

(Courtesy: Hammacher Schlemmer)

ian descent, Eugene Ferkauf, who took the "E" from his own first name, the "J" from his associate, Joseph Zwillenberg, and "Korvette" from the name of the nine-teenth-century warships, the corvettes, simply because he liked the sound of the word.

LORD AND TAYLOR The oldest retail store in New York City is Lord & Taylor, founded in 1826 by two Englishmen from York: Samuel Lord, and his wife's cousin, George Washington Taylor.

OHRBACH'S Nathan M. Ohrbach (1885–1972) began his retailing career as an errand boy in 1900. After 11 years of sweeping floors and acting as a "go-for," the Vienna-born immigrant opened his own store and was on his way to becoming a well-known name in the fashion world by selling women's coats and dresses at reduced prices.

RICH'S This Atlanta store was founded by Morris Rich, an immigrant from

Kaschau, Hungary, now part of Czechoslovakia.

F.A.O. SCHWARZ The largest toy store in the world, F.A.O. Schwarz opened its doors for business in 1870, at the time when toys were becoming an industry, no longer limited to handcrafted items whittled at home by proud parents and doting relatives.

Frederick August Otto Schwarz born in 1836 at Herford, Westphalia, Germany, came to America in 1856 and entered into a partnership with his brothers as an importer of toys and novelties. Today, the store that bears his name carries some of the world's most expensive playthings. Recent offerings have included a $10,000 castle-dollhouse complete with elegantly attired dolls in white powdered wigs; $7,000 electric train layouts; $2,000 music boxes;

and gasoline-powered scale-model cars that sell for $600 to $700. F. A. O. Schwartz also carries the world's largest selection of stuffed animals, ranging in price from a few dollars for a tiny mouse to more than $1,000 for a life-size tiger, baby elephant or five-foot tall giraffe.

JOHN WANAMAKER Wanamaker's first American ancestor was Johan Wannermacher, a native of the Palatinate who arrived here in 1710 via Holland. Wanamaker's first store was in New York City, but his Philadelphia branch, which he opened in 1878, had the honor of being the first store in the United States completely lit by incandescent lamps.

YOUNKER'S Iowa's largest department store was founded by three Polish immigrants, Lipman, Samuel and Marcus Younker, in 1856.

THE FAMILY JEWELS

TIFFANY'S The first Tiffany to set foot on American soil was Squire Humphrey Tiffany, who settled in Massachusetts Bay Colony in 1660. He was killed by a lightning bolt five years later, but the family prospered in the New World nonetheless.

It was Charles Lewis Tiffany (1812–1900), great-grandson of Squire Humphrey, who established the "Stationary and Fancy Goods Store" in New York City in 1837. The first three days of business, sales totaled only $4.98, but by the time Charles Tiffany died in 1900, his estate was valued at $35 million. In the interim, Tiffany's had become one of the world's leading gem merchants. The "Tiffany setting" for diamond solitaires was introduced in 1886. Louis Comfort Tiffany, Charles's son, became a turn-of-the-century household word for his art nouveau glass lamps, bowls and vases and his stained glass windows, which

still command hefty prices today.

VAN CLEEF AND ARPELS The first shop was opened in Paris by Leon Arpels in the late 1800s. At the turn of the century, Alfred Van Cleef joined Leon's three sons in business and established Van Cleef and Arpels as one of the most exclusive jewelers in Europe.

After a successful exhibit at the 1939 World's Fair, Van Cleef and Arpels decided to open a branch store in New York City.

Today the firm owns one of the most famous pieces of jewelry in America history, the Liberty Necklace.

The necklace, which contains 13 pear-shaped emeralds, 13 square-cut emeralds and 13 square-cut diamonds (one for each of the original colonies) was given to Benjamin Franklin in September 1777 as a contribution to the American cause by a Polish noblewoman.

THE RAG TRADE

Some Ethnic Americans Who Gave Their All to Fashion

LANE BRYANT Ready-to-wear clothing was growing in popularity when Lena Himmelstein (1879–1951) arrived in New York from Lithuania in 1895 and promptly landed a job in a garment district

"sweat shop." The wages were low and the conditions not terribly good, but at least Lena was able to learn a trade. After the death of her first husband (David Bryant) in 1900, she was able to go into business for herself, sewing trousseaus and gowns for affluent brides-to-be.

As her reputation spread and more young women began seeking Lena's services, she moved to new quarters on Fifth Avenue in 1904. In that year she also created the first "maternity" dress—designed to be both comfortable and concealing. Before Lena came along, there simply weren't any special clothing designs to accommodate "ladies in waiting." Pregnant women were expected to wait out their confinement at home (preferably barefooted, and in the kitchen).

Lena's second husband, Albert Maislin (1879–1923), took a great interest in Lane Bryant. (The name was retained after Lena inadvertently misplaced the vowels in her first name when filling out a bank deposit slip.) After the birth of their three children, Albert began to play an even more important part in the business as he began applying scientific methods to dressmaking and marketing. A Lithuanian immigrant with an engineering background, Maislin introduced cost accounting procedures to the dress shop and invented a flexible yardstick to measure each lady's vital statistics. Even more important than the high-speed sewing methods, mechanical pattern-cutting and mass manufacturing techniques that Maislin also introduced was his decision that Lane Bryant would cater to the "hard-to-fit" woman.

THE FIRST AD FOR MATERNITY FASHIONS

It wasn't until 1911 that the *New York Herald* agreed to accept a Lane Bryant ad for their maternity fashions:

"It is no longer the fashion nor the practice for expectant mothers to stay in seclusion. Doctors, nurses and psychologists agree that at this time a woman should think and live as normally as possible. To do this, she must go about among other people, she must look like other people. Lane Bryant has originated maternity apparel in which the expectant mother may feel as other women feel because she looks as other women look."

By closing time, the entire stock of daytime maternity fashions had been sold out, heralding the beginning of a new industry.

Reasoning that there were more overweight women than pregnant ones and that being large was usually a permanent condition. Maislin set out to design clothing that would be comfortable, flattering and concealing for women who had lost the "battle of the bulge." To obtain pattern standards for his new line of clothing, Maislin measured more than 204,500 women. He maintained Lane Bryant's maternity department, but by the time of Maislin's premature death in 1923, large sizes were accounting for more than half of the annual $5 million in sales.

Today, large, hard-to-fit women are the foundation upon which the store is built. Lane Bryant's motto is still "Hard-to-find apparel for hard-to-fit women."

BUTTERICK PATTERNS Ebenezer Butterick (1826–1903) was probably the first American to cash in on our national "do-it-yourself" mentality. The seventh child of Francis and Ruhamah Butterick, Ebenezer was descended from William Butterick, an English immigrant who came to America in 1635.

Apprenticed to a tailor in Worcester, Massachusetts, in the mid-nineteenth century (when tailors actually made clothes instead of just altering the hems and cuffs of ready-made suits), Ebenezer bemoaned the time he had to waste cutting material to make children-size garments. That's when Butterick first thought of making a set of patterns in graduated sizes that would fit children of a certain age group.

In 1859, Butterick started working on his pattern system, which he hoped would eliminate the need to measure every little customer's neck, waist and sleeve length. By 1863 Butterick's standardized paper patterns for men and boys were being sold, not only to tailors, but to homemakers who

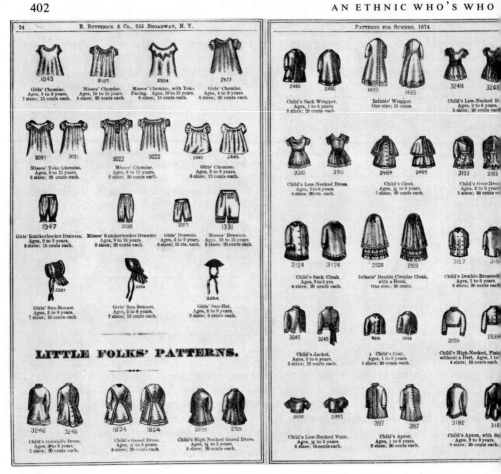

Butterick pattern book for Summer 1874. (Courtesy: New York Historical Society)

wanted to make their family's clothing. It wasn't until 1867 that Butterick began designing paper patterns for women. Butterick's most popular pattern was the Garibaldi suit for young boys, which was modeled after the uniform worn by the Italian revolutionary and his men.

Although we have standard-size clothing that is sold "off the rack" today, there are some 45 million patterns sold each year for those creative Americans who want to be kept "in stitches."

HAGGAR SLACKS Maroun Hajjar, an immigrant from a small village in southern Lebanon, founded the Haggar manufacturing company in 1926. "Back then, a lot of people in the East said I'd be lucky to last even six months in business, because in those days, nobody thought you could manufacture apparel in Dallas, Texas." That was more than 50 years ago; today Haggar is one of the largest manufacturers of men's clothing in the United States.

JONATHAN LOGAN When David Schwartz, a Jewish American, started manufacturing dresses he searched for a company name that would have what he termed "consumer appeal." To many ethnics, "consumer appeal" translates as "a WASPy-sounding name," which is probably why he chose the ethnically neutral name "Jonathan Logan" to sew into the ladies' dresses he manufactures.

LEVI STRAUSS When Levi Strauss (1829–1902) left New York City in 1850 with a supply of dry goods he hoped to sell

His face may not be familiar, but his name is probably on the seat of your pants. It's Levi Strauss, the man whose first name has adorned some 800 million pairs of well-worn jeans in the past 120 years. (Courtesy: Levi Strauss & Co.)

to California miners, he included several bolts of canvas in his sea freight in the hopes of selling it to settlers for use as sails and covering for their Conestoga wagons. But, when the Bavarian immigrant from Bad Ocheim arrived in San Francisco, a friendly prospector confided that Levi could make a fortune selling a sturdy pair of pants: "Pants don't wear worth a hoot up in the diggins. Can't get a pair strong enough to last."

Knowing a good idea when he heard one, Strauss enlisted a local tailor to sew up America's first pair of Levi's; when the other miners saw how sturdy and long-wearing those "pants of Levi's" were, they clamored for more.

Since that day, over 800 million pairs of Levis have been sold. The material, styles, and methods of manufacture have changed since 1850, however, as have the customers who buy Levi's. Jeans are no longer merely "cheap," they're "chic," and almost every well-known designer has put his or her own logo on the American uniform of the seventies.

THE REAL "DECOY"—MAIDEN-FORM BRAS When Ida Rosenthal (1889–1973), a Russian Jewish immigrant from Minsk, started making dresses in Hoboken, New Jersey, in 1920, she never "dreamed" she'd one day be "wearing her Maidenform bra" to work as chairman of the board of one of America's largest undergarment manufacturing firms.

The "flapper era" of the 1920s called for flat-chested, boyish styles, but Ida wasn't one to kowtow to fashion. She began enhancing her customers' appearances by including (free of charge) a special undergarment she had devised to uplift a woman's bosom. Ida reasoned that "Nature made women with a bosom. So why fight nature?" Apparently her customers agreed—Ida's dresses were flattering, and they kept coming back for more.

It was, however, Ida's husband, William Rosenthal, who first decided to mass produce brassieres. Ida's first "bras" were made individually, by hand, one at a time. What William did was to group women into basic figure categories, and then design a bra that would suit the needs of each one—from the first buds of youth, to the more mature, fuller figure of middle-aged womanhood. William also introduced mass production techniques, and by 1926 had 40 sewing machines humming each day. Forty years later, Maidenform had 19 factories with 4,000 employees producing 25 million garments each year. Sales were in excess of $40 million per year.

Was Ida worried when the braless sixties came along? No way! "We are a democracy and a person has the right to be dressed or undressed, but after 35 a woman hasn't got the figure to wear nothing." Time is on Ida's side!

SASSON JEANS Paul Guez, a thirty-four-year-old immigrant from Tunisia and a new name in the fashion world, managed to sell amost $2.5 million worth of Sasson jeans during one month of 1978. (Two years earlier his monthly sales were only $30,000.)

What made Sasson jeans so popular? Besides being well made, they were believed by many people to be named after chic, Australian-born hairstylist Vidal Sassoon, and that helped add brand-name appeal to the expensive pants.

Actually, the pants were named after Guez's onetime partner, Maurice Sasson. "Sasson" means "happiness" in Hebrew, and that's just what the jeans seem to be bringing their designer—sales in 1979 were in excess of $45 million.

KING OF PASSION FASHION Frederick Mellinger, the founder of Frederick's of Hollywood, is the self-proclaimed "King of the Naughty Nightie." Looking at this amiable sexagenarian, it's hard to believe that this sweet old gentleman is the brains behind such exotic clothing as "crotchless panties," "inflatable bras" and "falsies" for almost every part of a woman's anatomy.

Descended from a long line of Orthodox Jewish rabbis, Mellinger started working as an assistant lingerie buyer for a catalog house at the age of 16. He was constantly insisting that the company put more "romance" in their fashions, and in 1947 he struck out on his own.

By 1965 there were 22 Frederick's stores in shopping malls around the country with annual sales of more than $5 million. The women's liberation movement notwithstanding, Frederick's managed to increase the number of stores nationwide to 38 by 1970, for some reason managing to escape the barbs of women's libbers who desire to be more than mere sex objects.

According to Mellinger, the average age of a Frederick's customer (in 1979) was 45. Since many of his styles are reminiscent of World War II pin-up models, it makes sense that his most devout fans would be those who grew up with Rita Hayworth and Betty Grable as role models.

10 FASHIONABLE ETHNICS

1 When *Adolfo Sardina* (1933–   ) was a boy in Cardones, Cuba, his parents hoped he would study law and enter the family's law firm after graduation. Adolfo, however, dreamed of a career in fashion, and with the aid of an understanding aunt who financed his trip to Paris in 1953, he was apprenticed to fashion master Balenciaga.

Later, a year after emigrating to the United States, Adolfo won his first Coty Award, one of Seventh Avenue's highest honors, for his high fashion hat designs. He sold Cossack hats, Panama hats, mink-lined hats and sable berets to some of America's richest women. When Lady Bird Johnson wore an Adolfo creation to the 1964 inaugural Ball, his hats gained international attention.

When hats and white gloves fell by the wayside in the braless, mini-skirted Sixties, Adolfo began experimenting with fashion designs. He introduced the romantic look in 1968, dressing American women in organdy, gingham and dirndl skirts. In 1969 he captured another Coty Award for his clothing designs. To what does he attribute his outstanding success in the world of fashion design? Adolfo claims, ". . . my customers are my inspiration. I know when a woman comes into the salon whether or not she is simpatico . . ." (New York *Times*, Nov. 29, 1968)

2 *Hattie Carnegie* The second of seven children, Henrietta Kanengieser (1886–1956) emigrated to the United States as a young child. When the family arrived in New York, her father, a designer and artist himself, Americanized the family name to "Carnegie."

Hattie, who had inherited her father's artistic eye, began her career in fashion at the age of 15. Working first as a hat trimmer in a millinery shop, she carefully learned her trade before opening her own boutique in 1906.

In the early 1900s she made a successful transition from the millinery field to fashion design. During the "Roaring Twenties" her custom-made collections commanded prices upward of $250 for a daytime dress, and $420 for a cloth coat. When the Depression came along, Hattie realized there weren't too many women left who could afford her prices, and she introduced a new line of inexpensive, ready-to-wear clothing. She avoided fads, and designed her clothes to enhance the women who wore them, rather than have the dress be the center of attention. Despite Carnegie's meteoric rise to the heights of *haute couture*, she never learned to sew and never even learned to cut fabric properly.

3 *Oleg Cassini* Although Oleg Cassini was born in Paris and raised in Florence, his ancestry is Russian. Before he and his brother, Igor, better known as newspaper columnist Cholly Knickerbocker, emigrated to the United States in 1937, Oleg enjoyed a reputation as one of Rome's finest dressmakers.

Cassini set his sights on California, and became a rather successful Hollywood costume designer before he opened his own salon in New York in 1950. His reputation for designing "modest little jackets" to cover "immodest little cocktail dresses" spread, but he did not rocket to international fame until the early 1960s. When Jackie Kennedy chose Oleg Cassini to design her inauguration ceremony coat, dress and pillbox hat, he became *the* designer of Camelot, famous for the "Jackie Kennedy look."

4 *Oscar de la Renta* Born in Santo Domingo, capital of the Dominican Republic, Oscar de la Renta (1932–) won two Coty Awards for his designs in the space of five years. After studying art in his native land and in Madrid, he developed an interest in fashion design. While in Spain, he was commissioned to design a debutante gown for Beatrice, the daughter of John Cabot Lodge. Her photo graced the cover of *Life* magazine and brought instant fame to de la Renta—sealing his future as a fashion designer.

Oscar worked under Balenciaga and later designed for Elizabeth Arden before opening his own salon in 1965. A designer of exceptional versatility, de la Renta made fashion news with his bikini evening pants in the 1960s and his opulent evening gowns in the 1970s.

5 *Rudi Gernreich* Known for his *avant garde* fashions, Rudi Gernreich (1922–) introduced America to such fashion staples as vinyl clothing, see-through blouses and the topless bathing suit. When he introduced his "bathing suit bottom with straps" in 1964, Rudi won denouncements from the Vatican and the Kremlin alike. But, despite such marvelous publicity, only a limited number of women "dared to be bare" at the time: Rudi sold only 3,000 suits.

Underwear manufacturers decided "if you can't beat 'em, hire 'em," and Rudi was commissioned to design the "no bra" for a soft, natural look. Although his styles are not for everyone, Rudi did introduce the "unisex" look to America's youth. And, on a cultural note, he designed unisex costumes for an American dance company in 1977. Born in Vienna, Rudi was forced to flee Europe with thousands of other Jewish refugees at the outbreak of World War II.

6 *Vera Maxwell* Born Vera Huppe (1901–), the daughter of Viennese immigrants who settled in New York, Vera Maxwell was a professional ballet dancer

until 1924, when she became interested in fashion design. Vera, one of America's leading designers of sportswear, believes that "clothes should live and breathe with the wearer." Over the years she has popularized the Chesterfield coat and jersey wrap-around blouses. In 1970 she was honored by a retrospective of her fashions at the Smithsonian Institute.

Vera Maxwell's career in fashion has spanned more than four decades, and she has clothed some of the world's most famous women, including Pat Nixon, Grace Kelly and Martha Graham. What's the secret of Vera's success? "I think I survived because I do things that are diametrically opposed to Seventh Avenue. I don't like fashion as much as I like style."

7 *Norman Norell* Well-known designer Norman Norell (1900–1972) was born Norman Levinson. His father was a Jewish clothing store owner in Nobelsville, Indiana. After World War I, Norman studied art at the Parsons School of Design and at Pratt Institute in Brooklyn. It was there that he won first prize in a blouse designing contest, which started him on the road to a career in fashion.

As a costume designer for Paramount Studios, Norell designed costumes for the leading silent screen stars of his day, including Valentino and Swanson. He studied fashion design under the tutelage of Hattie Carnegie, and was associated with her salon for 13 years before he struck out on his own with partner Anthony Traina in 1941.

Over the years Norell introduced to American women the chemise, the Empire-styled dress and the favorite costume of movie stars and sex goddesses—the sequined sheath dress.

8 *Giorgio Sant'Angelo* When Giorgio Imperatrice di Sant'Angelo di Lombardia e Ratti de Sesio first emigrated to New York in 1964, he did not intend to design clothing, furniture or jewelry. Instead, Sant' Angelo came to the United States to study animation at the Walt Disney studios.

Later Giorgio started designing textiles, and then he branched out into jewelry and accessories, fashion, furniture and bed linens. But, it was his fashions that have made him famous and earned him the coveted Coty Award, the "Oscar" of the fashion industry.

9 *Pauline Trigère* Born in Paris of French and Jewish ancestry, Pauline learned to sew professionally by the age of ten. When she emigrated to the United States in 1937, with her mother and young sons in tow, Trigère worked briefly for Hattie Carnegie before starting her own design firm in the early 1940s.

The first year she was in business, her brother packed his sample case with her 12 outfits and trekked across the United States selling her collection to individual department stores. When she became a citizen in 1944, Trigère said, "Despite my love for France, I have found my niche here. The U.S. has been wonderfully kind to me." By 1948, Trigère had earned her place among the top fashion designers of America by winning the coveted Coty American Fashion Critics Award.

10 *Diane   von   Furstenberg* The daughter of a Jewish businessman from Brussels, Diane von Furstenberg (née Halfin) became a fixture in café society by marrying Prince Egon von Furstenberg, an Austrian nobleman, in 1969.

In 1972, sensing that American women were tired of pantsuits, Diane decided to enter the world of fashion with a collection of flattering, easy-to-wear dresses. Gambling on her sense of style and the allure of her celebrity status, Diane pawned a $10,000 diamond ring and used her bankroll to manufacture her first collection of daytime dresses.

Her instincts were right, and within four years her company was grossing $6 million in annual sales. Like other designers, von Furstenberg also has her own perfume and special brand of makeup on the market.

GETTING AROUND

America is a nation on the move. We think nothing of driving 30 miles to a favorite shop, or traveling clear across town to buy a certain brand of liver sausage from our favorite German butcher. We ship our vegetables and fruits 3,000 miles across the continent, and we even ship our children "Back East" to boarding schools and colleges.

We manufacture enough automobiles each year to stretch from New York to California five times, bumper to bumper. There are nearly 100 million cars in America today, using a highway system that stretches over 3.8 million miles.

In 1917 only 14% of our nation's roadways were surfaced. Today, thanks to the ethnic Americans who devised bigger and better automobiles, buses and trucks, that figure is up to 80%. That means that there are relatively few country lanes and farm roads where one's car can still raise a miniduststorm on a dry summer's day.

Who were the ethnic Americans who helped America get a move on? Some of their names are quite familiar — Oldsmobile, Ford, Stanley, Mack, Duesenberg, Buick, Chevrolet, Chrysler and Hertz — since they named their corporations after themselves.

MEN BEHIND THE AUTOMOBILES AND TRUCKS OF AMERICA

OLDSMOBILE Four years before Henry Ford sold his first car, Ransom Eli Olds (1864–1950) was already using an assembly line system to mass-produce his "Oldsmobiles." Known as the "Father of the popular priced car," Olds built his first three-wheeled steampowered horseless carriage in 1886. He became the first American to export a selfpropelled vehicle when he sold a four-wheeled steamer of his own design to the Francis Times Company of Bombay, India, in 1893.

Descended from a colonial English family, Olds established the Olds Motor Vehicle company in 1897 with $50,000 capitalization. In 1904, Olds sold nearly 5,000 Oldsmobiles at the amazingly low price of $650 — proving for the first time that it was possible to mass-produce automobiles, sell them for a reasonable price and still rake in a handsome profit.

FORD Henry Ford (1863–1947) wasn't the first American to manufacture cars in the United States, nor was he the first to use assembly line principles of construction. But, he was the first to manufacture a car that even a common laborer could afford. When the first Model T Ford was introduced in 1908, its sticker price was $850. Seventeen years later, when the last Model T rolled off the assembly line, the price tag was a mere $260.

Henry Ford was the eldest of 6 children born to an immigrant Irish farm couple from Kilmalooda Parish, in County Cork. His first car sale was made to a dentist from Chicago, named Pfennig, on July 15, 1903. By 1928 Henry had managed to sell more than 15,000,000 automobiles to our car-hungry nation.

STANLEY STEAMER The first steam car ever operated successfully in New England was manufactured in 1897 by Francis and Freelan Stanley, twin brothers of English descent. The brothers sold their interest in the car company in 1898, but reentered the automotive field in 1902. One of the Stanleys' cars set a new world record in 1906 by racing a distance of one mile in a bit over 28 seconds.

(*Courtesy: New York Public Library*)

BUILT LIKE A MACK TRUCK The founder of the Mack Truck Company was a second-generation German-American named Jack Mack. Born in 1864, Jack ran away from home at the age of 14 and worked as a teamster and as an engineer at steam power plants before purchasing a small carriage- and wagon-building firm with his brother, Augustus, in 1893.

Their first attempts at manufacturing electric cars were unsuccessful and many of these early Mack machines were relegated to a watery grave in the East River near Brooklyn, New York. By 1900, the brothers had perfected a three-speed-transmission bus (with a 4-cylinder gasoline engine) which was used for sightseeing tours in Prospect Park. A rugged vehicle, this Mack bus was designed to last over one million miles. After 8 years of service as a park bus, the original mack bus was converted to a truck and finally retired after 17 years of use.

By 1905 the Mack brothers were manufacturing custom-built trucks, and by 1911 their advertising slogan claimed that Mack was "The Leading Gasoline Truck in America."

The truck's blunt, snub-nosed hood made it look somewhat like a bulldog, which is what American "doughboys" during World War I began to call the Mack truck. After the war, the bulldog was registered as Mack's corporate symbol. The phrase "built like a Mack truck" entered American usage during the first World War, too, as a tribute to the incredible abuse these wartime vehicles were able to take.

DUESENBERG Fred and August Duesenberg emigrated to the United States in 1885 from their native Germany. At the age of 21, Fred set a world cycling record in a two-mile race, and from there his interest in "wheeled vehicles" grew until it encompassed motorbikes and, finally, automobiles.

Fred and August built their first racing car in 1903. They sold a luxury Model A passenger car in 1926 for $6,500, and even marketed a Model J car in 1932 which retailed for $17,500. Over the years Fred was quite successful—but he made one very costly mistake: when he developed a hydraulic four-wheel brake system, he failed to patent his invention. Duesenberg lost millions of dollars in royalties that might have been his had he only patented the device.

BUICK David Dunbar Buick (1854–1929) emigrated to the United States from Scotland in 1856. His father died when Buick was 5, and in order to help support the family David was forced to leave school at the age of 11.

The first Buick automobile, manufactured in 1903, featured an unprecedented water-cooled, valve-in-head engine. Buick's cars were well constructed, and even with a $1,200 price tag, customers flocked to buy them. It wasn't until William Crapo Durant joined forces with Buick in 1904, however, that the company was able to obtain the financing it needed to increase its yearly production from 37 to 500 automobiles.

"THE GODFATHER" William Crapo Durant (1861–1947) has been called the "godfather of the automobile industry" for his role in organizing both General Motors and the Chevrolet Motor Company during the early twentieth century. Of French and English ancestry, Durant turned the Buick plant in Flint, Michigan, into the largest automobile factory in the world by 1910.

Durant organized the General Motors Company in 1908 and acquired 19 car, truck and accessory manufacturing companies over the next two years, including Oldsmobile and Oakland. He tried to buy the Ford Motor Company, too, but his bankers refused to lend him the $8 million Henry Ford demanded—they didn't think it was worth the price!

Though financial difficulties forced Durant to resign as president of General Motors in 1910, he resurfaced the following year as president of the Chevrolet Motor Company. In one of the greatest "second comings" in American business history, Durant managed to regain control of General Motors stock in 1916 and resumed his position as president of that corporation.

By 1918 annual sales were over $269 million, but financial disaster struck during the postwar economy and Durant was ousted once again. He tried other business ventures, but failed, and by 1936 he was forced to file a petition for bankruptcy. Durant has been called the greatest promoter in the United States; it was his genius that resulted in lower costs, wider distribution and increased profits for the American auto industry.

RAMBLER The Rambler Automobile Company was founded by Thomas B. Jeffrey, an English immigrant. When Jeffrey died in 1910, Charles Nash, an orphan who was "sold" in service to a farmer at the age of 6, purchased the firm, which, forty years later, produced the Nash Rambler, America's first modern compact car.

MUSTANG Lee Iacocca (1924–   ), onetime president of the Ford Motor Company and now head of Chrysler, is the man responsible for transforming the 1965 Mustang sports car into an American success story. Its first year off the assembly

1905 advertisement for Rambler Surrey, Type One. (Courtesy: New York Public Library)

line, 417,800 sporty Mustangs were sold—a postwar sales record for any car.

Lido Anthony Iacocca, the son of Italian immigrants, decided at the age of sixteen that he wanted to be a Ford Company executive. He climbed the corporate ladder, reaching the presidency in 1970, some twenty-five years after he had started out as an executive trainee, and held that position until July 1978.

CHRYSLER Walter Percy Chrysler (1875–1940), the youngest son of Canadian-born Henry Chrysler (of German descent) and Anna Breyman Chrysler (of early Dutch stock), was born in Wamego, Kansas, in 1875. He rose from a common laborer to become a vice-president of General Motors, and he retired at the age of 45, a millionaire.

Bored with his early retirement, Chrysler founded the motor company that bears his name in 1925.

CHEVROLET Louis Chevrolet, a Swiss race car driver, emigrated to the

United States from France in 1900. He worked as a car mechanic in New York until he joined forces with William Durant in 1911 to found the Chevrolet Motor Company.

Chevrolet sold out his interest in the company four years later to Durant, who threw out Chevrolet's car designs because they were too big, too bulky and too expensive to produce. But he kept Louis's name, because he liked the way "Chevrolet" rolled off his tongue. (Admit it, *Durant-mobile* does not sound like a winning name for a car.)

Durant literally "stole" the company's logo right off the wall of a Paris hotel room. The combination "square-parallelogram" was incorporated into a wallpaper pattern that Durant took a fancy to, and he simply tore off a sample for his advertising staff to copy as the basis for the company's trademark.

HERTZ RENT-A-CAR John D. Hertz came to the United States in 1881 at the age of four. Not only did he enjoy business success as the founder of the "Number One" car rental company, he also founded the Yellow Taxi business, in addition to his secondary career as a banker.

Hertz ran away from home at the age of 12, sold his schoolbooks to get some cash and got a job as an office boy with the Chicago *Morning Record.*

He later bought a secondhand car business for $2,000 and managed to earn $60,000 worth of profits during his first year of operation. But a slump in sales the following year triggered a new idea. Hertz reasoned to himself, "Only a wealthy man could afford a car in those days. Then he insisted on driving it until the engine fell out from under him. Consequently he was not in the market for three or four years after his first purchase . . . entirely too long a wait for any business. Things looked serious until the idea struck me that these surplus cars could be put to work by providing each one with a chauffeur who would drive out on the streets and solicit passengers. That pointed to the ultimate solution of all our problems. First, it would take care of our overstock; second, it would give an immediate and continued repeat business; and third, our prospects would no longer be limited to any one class."

That was the birth of the taxi industry in the United States, and soon Hertz's Yellow Cabs were found at almost 800 different locations throughout the United States. Hertz didn't stop contributing to the automotive industry: in 1924 he founded the Chicago Motor Coach Company, and the Fifth Avenue Motor Coach Company in New York City, linking together the trolley and bus lines of two of our nation's largest cities. He also founded the Driveurself car business, to provide rental cars for out-of-state visitors.

At one time Hertz controlled 95% of all taxicabs outside of New York City, but in 1925 he divested himself of his holdings and sold his Hertz Driveurself business to General Motors for $43 million to devote his free time to breeding racehorses.

Hertz later worked for Paramount-Publix films and also became a partner in a Wall Street investment firm. Not bad for a twelve-year-old runaway! Hertz believed, "There are many industries waiting for a founder, and the only requisites are men with a readiness and a willingness to begin at the beginning and fight it out." (quotes from *Saturday Evening Post,* June 4, 1927, p. 158)

OTHER MEANS OF TRANSPORTATION

TROLLEYCAR The first trolley, which was put into public service in Detroit as early as 1869, was invented by Karel Vandepoele, a Belgian immigrant from Lichtervelde.

COVERED WAGON The Conestoga wagon was a product of German imagination. German immigrants hitched market wagons, covered with linen cloth, behind Conestoga horses, a common breed in the Lancaster-Reading region of Pennsylvania, and gave the wagons a new name.

LEAR JET The first corporate jet aircraft was developed by William P. Lear (1902–1978), an American of Bavarian descent, who also invented the automatic pilot for jets, and the 8-track stereo cartridge.

SIKORSKY HELICOPTERS Igor Ivanovich Sikorsky (1889–1972) left his home in Russia in 1919 after the Bolshevik Revolution. Although his name is synonymous with hundreds of helicopter designs, his first American-based company manufactured not helicopters, but flying boats. He produced the world's first successful single-rotor helicopter in 1939 and flew it at Stratford, Connecticut, in 1940.

GREYHOUND   It all started with Carl Eric Wickman, a Swedish miner turned Hupmobile salesman in Minnesota. Realizing that he didn't have the forceful sales personality necessary to sell automobiles, Wickman decided to buy a Hupmobile himself and use it to transport miners to and from various mining towns in the iron-rich regions of the state.

Business was soon so brisk that Wickman was forced to buy another, larger Hupmobile and take on a partner. By 1916, there were 5 "buses" — all painted a battleship gray with surplus military paint. A passenger remarked that the elongated cars looked like greyhound dogs, an idea Wickman appropriated for his slogan "Ride the Greyhounds." The Greyhound name became official in 1930.

Greyhound is one of the world's largest intercity passenger bus lines in the world today, with over 4,650 buses which enable you to "leave the driving to us."

13 ETHNICS WHO BECAME LARGE CORPORATIONS

1   *William J. Burns* (1861–1932) attained national fame as a detective in 1886 when he solved a baffling case of election fraud perpetrated in Columbus, Ohio. The fraud was conducted with the aid of the winning politician's brother, a prison doctor who worked at the Ohio Penitentiary. By sneaking a convicted safecracker out of prison in the middle of the night, the doctor was able to steal the election tally sheets. With the aid of an expert forger who was

William J. Burns, detective. (Courtesy: Burns International Security Systems, Inc.)

committed to the prison psychiatric ward, the doctor was able to alter the winning totals and have the tally sheets back in the safe by morning.

Burns, the son of Irish Catholic parents from Baltimore, Maryland, opened his own detective agency in 1909. He worked as a $3-a-day Secret Service agent, and from 1921 to 1924 he was Director of the FBI.

In the days before wiretapping, electronic eavesdropping, hidden cameras and .007-type paraphernalia, Burns became a legendary super sleuth. His knowledge of counterfeiting was so complete that he could look at a phony bill. and tell immediately who made it.

His name lives on today in Burns International Security Services, an international corporation that employs some 30,000 guards worldwide.

2   *Jacob J. Bausch* (1830–1926), the founder of the Bausch and Lomb optical company, emigrated from Gross Süssen, Germany, at the age of 18, after suffering a bout with typhoid fever, which had raged through his family. It was during his long recuperation that Bausch decided to strike out on his own:

> The months of weakness gave me many hours in which to think. Our family had stuck to one spot for generations. I saw clearly that if I remained at home there would be nothing for me except a repetition of the life of my ancestors — a bare living, and no more. Someone, traveling through the town, told us that an optician was wanted in Berne, Switzerland ... Of course, the suggestion met with op-

position. Why must I turn my back on the life that had been good enough for all my ancestors? Who was I to assume that I could battle successfully against the outside world? Had I any special gifts or cleverness? With such questions they sought to discourage me, and I had to admit, in answer, that I was indeed without qualifications for success. No one knew it better than myself. Nevertheless, I swung my knapsack across my shoulders and, setting out on foot, finally arrived at Berne.

But no fortunes were lying loose in Berne . . . everywhere the crops had failed, and the discontent and suffering among the people caused the disturbances which are known as the Revolution of 1848. Thousands left Europe for America and I was one of them.

You have read the thrill of the immigrant when he catches his first view of America . . . It is all true, I felt it. Here was the rich new land, the land of opportunity . . . Here, too, were hard times and discouragement.

J. Bausch struggled night and day for eight years, and the net result of his efforts was $1000 worth of indebtedness to his partner, Henry Lomb (b. 1828), a German immigrant from Hesse-Kassel. "If you had told me in those days that there would some day be a plant bearing my name and Mr. Lomb's employing more than 3,000 people and manufacturing 15-20 million lenses a year, I would not even have taken time to smile."

3 *William Coffin Coleman* (1870–1957), a descendant of Thomas Coleman, an Englishman who settled on Nantucket Island in 1630, started the Coleman Lamp Company in 1900. His gasoline lamps were designed, not for outdoor camping trips, but to light up the homes of rural farmers who lacked electricity or natural gas.

After his first week in business Coleman had managed to sell only 2 lamps. Bad experience with inferior gasoline lamps made rural consumers wary, and they refused to give Coleman's lamps a try for fear they would malfunction soon after Coleman left town. Their reluctance to give his product a try spurred William to sell a "lighting service" instead of lamps. For $1 a week he promised to lease lamps to his customers and service them whenever necessary.

He did a booming business until electricity came to the farmhouse and squelched the demand for gasoline lamps. Although Coleman Lamp earned the nickname, "The company that should have gone broke," Coleman managed to find other markets for its products. During the war there were GI pocket stoves; in the early 1950s Coleman manufactured oil-fueled space heaters; and when Americans began their love affair with the great outdoors, Coleman was there with lanterns, heaters and Hobie Cat sailboats.

4 *John Deere,* a Rutland, Vermont, blacksmith of English ancestry, took a discarded mill saw blade and turned it into the first steel plow in 1837. Since Deere's plow scoured itself clean, there was no need for western families to continually clean off the clogged blades, and 2 men and 8 oxen were able to plow 1 acre of land in a day.

When Deere introduced the Gilpin Sulky, in 1874, it was possible for 1 man and three horses to plow 3 acres in less than 12 hours. Advances in productivity over the years have dramatically reduced the number of farmers necessary to feed our nation. In 1776 it took 95% of America's population to produce the necessities of life for themselves and the nonfarming city dwellers. Today, only 2% of America's population is involved in farm work.

5 *Herbert Henry Dow* (1886–1930), founder of the Dow Chemical Company, was born in Belleville, Ontario, Canada, in 1897. Although Dow manufactures hundreds of chemicals and chemical products, the one that is most familiar to Americans is Saran Wrap. First formulated in 1933 from chlorinated dry cleaning compounds, Vinylidene Chloride, as the compound is technically known, seemed to have a thousand uses.

Saran could be forged, rolled, blown, stamped and welded. It could be made into a heavy cable, or drawn into a thread as fine as silk. Woven Saran was used to cover New York City's subway seats; and during World War II, Saran was woven into insect screening for tropical areas where metal screens would have rotted away.

But, Saran Wrap had a "fun" side, too. If you were a child during the mid-Fifties, you could cut a piece of Saran from the kitchen roll, place it over the television screen and draw along with Winky Dink, one of the only television shows that ever permitted interaction between the child and the tube. The host of this animated show frequently called on viewers to help Winky Dink out of trouble by completing the missing parts of a puzzle. Armed with crayons, viewers drew pictures on the Saran-wrapped picture tube and peeled off the mess when the show was over.

6 *Harvey Firestone* (1868–1938) Harvey's first American ancestor was an Alsatian of Austrian descent, Nicholas Firestone. To avoid losing their eldest son to Louis XV's army, the Firestone family quietly slipped away in the middle of the night and set sail for America in 1752.

Harvey started his business career as a buggy-tire salesman. It wasn't until a machinist from the Detroit Edison Illuminating Company visited Harvey's shop that he ever considered the idea of selling tires for automobiles.

The machinist said he needed tires for a gasoline-powered horseless carriage he had designed. The car weighed more than 500 pounds, which the machinist claimed was too heavy for the single-tube bicycle tires he was using. Harvey dragged out the top of his line, a set of solid rubber tires selling for $40 a set. The machinist bent down, squeezed the merchandise and was quite pleased with its quality. "Order a set of these," he told Firestone. "The name is Henry Ford."

7 *William Russell Grace* (1832–1904) Grace emigrated to Callao, Peru, in 1854 with a colony of fellow Irishmen seeking relief from the great Irish potato famine.

Peru did not prove to be the paradise the farmers were seeking, and malaria, discouragement and homesickness took their toll. When the colony was disbanded, Grace entered into business for himself, hauling guano (a very rich bird dung fertilizer) between the West Coast of South America and the United States. Guano made Grace a rich businessman in New York, and at the age of 47 he ran for mayor of the "Big Apple" and was elected for two terms.

The company that bears his name today, W. R. Grace, is a huge conglomerate involved, not only in shipping, but in chemical production, sporting goods and shoe retailing, textbook distribution and food service operations.

8 *Conrad Hilton* (1877–1979) The son of Norwegian immigrants, Conrad started his career in the "hotel" business as a child, when he was commissioned to meet trains and guide traveling salesmen to rooms in his father's San Antonio house.

Hilton bought his first hotel in 1919 in Cisco, Texas, an oil-boom town, for $40,000 when the owner decided to enter the oil fields himself. In 1949, Hilton added the prestigious Waldorf-Astoria hotel to his chain, and 25 years later there were Hiltons in 54 foreign countries. Hilton also started the Carte Blanche credit card company, "the better to pay your hotel bills with, my dear."

9 *J. Willard Marriott* (1900–) Marriott's grandparents converted to Mormonism in the 1850s before emigrating to the United States from Scotland and England. They were among the 80,000 Mormon pioneers who walked or rode across the country in covered wagons. Through his Mormon upbringing Marriott learned the values of thrift and industry as a cure for want, and when asked about his business success J. Willard claims, "There are two main reasons for my success. The first is my church. The second is my wife. Fortunately my sons, Bill Jr. and Richard, have her brains and my drive."

Willard's drive enabled him to turn a nine-seat, nickel-a-glass rootbeer stand in Washington, D.C., into a billion-dollar operation. With the profits from his initial 1927 investment of $2,500, Marriott was able to build his first motel in Arlington, Virginia, in 1957. Today, more than one million travelers bed down for the night at Marriott Inns in 39 states and 18 foreign countries during the year. Other income comes from restaurants, cruise ships and amusement parks controlled by the Marriott Corporation.

10 *Frank Phillips* (1873–1950) An American of Welsh descent, Frank Phillips started working at the age of 14 as a part-time ranch hand and barber. He later took to distributing his own "rainwater-based miracle cure for baldness" known as Phillips' Mountain Sage. When Frank got tired of peddling miracle cures, he traded in his barber's shears for a bond salesman's briefcase and invested his money in oil leases.

The first two wells Phillips invested in turned up dry, but the next 80 (!!) were gushers. He organized the Phillips Petroleum company in 1917 with his brother, Lee

Eldas, and by 1920 the brothers were valued at $34 million on the New York Stock Exchange.

11 *Richard Joshua Reynolds* (1850–1918) An American of English ancestry, R. J. Reynolds started his own tobacco manufacturing company in Winston, North Carolina, in 1875 (before the two towns of Winston-Salem merged). He chose that location so he could be near the source of flue-cured leaf tobacco, which was reputed to be the best type for chewing. During his first year in business R.J.R. turned out almost 150,000 pounds of chewing tobacco.

Reynolds added licorice flavor and brandy to his chewing tobacco to keep up with the changing tastes of American chewers, but the best selling additive he used was saccharin. It made his tobacco sweet, and popular, and by the turn of the century R.J.R. was producing 25% of all the plug chewed in America.

His next bright idea was to introduce pre-rolled cigarettes to the public. His most popular brand was Camel—made from a blend of burley, bright and Turkish leaf tobaccos with a generous amount of sweetening added. R.J.R. introduced Camels to the public in 1913.

Today the company that bears his name is no longer solely limited to producing tobacco and chewing plug. R.J.R. has expanded to snack foods, packaging materials, and ethnic food products such as Chun King Chinese food and Patio brand frozen Mexican dinners.

12 *Harry M. Stevens* (1855–1934) The Germans invented them, a Pole made them famous in Coney Island, but it was an English immigrant who really cleaned up by putting frankfurters in the ball parks of America.

Harry M. Stevens was an English-born book salesman who happened by a baseball game in Columbus, Ohio, in 1889. Never having seen baseball before, he was curious about the rules of the game and wanted to know who the players were. He questioned sports enthusiasts in neighboring seats and found that they, too, had little information about players on visiting teams and could only provide scant information on their hometown favorites.

Being an enterprising man on the fringes of the publishing industry, Harry decided to go into business by selling scorecards with the players' names and positions, and space to jot down notes about the game. He leased the rights to sell his programs for $700 for the remainder of the season and set about to obtain information for the scorecards. He was eating peanuts at the game and found that people were willing to swap information for a handful of peanuts to munch on—and that's when he got his biggest inspiration. He decided to sell snack food, too. At first he sold only peanuts, but one cold afternoon he cooked up a batch of sausages, "red hots" as he called them (clever marketing for a cold day) and placed them in rolls. The rest is snack food history. Today there are more than 50 racetracks, ball parks, and indoor sports stadiums that sell "red hots" in Harry's name.

13 *George Westinghouse* (1846–1914) One of eight children born to a German-American father and a Dutch-English mother, George was a young man with a strong will and great determination. At the age of 15 he ran away from home to fight in the Civil War, but his parents brought him back. He finally broke them down, and enlisted 18 months later.

Westinghouse obtained his first patent in 1869 for a railroad air brake, which made it possible for speeding trains to come to a quick stop. Although the Westinghouse air brake is standard equipment on railroads around the world, the name Westinghouse is generally associated with electricity in the United States. It was George who introduced the alternating current system for light and power in 1893, and installed the first A.C. generator at Niagara Falls, New York. Westinghouse also invented the gas meter, and was awarded more than 360 patents during his lifetime.

The Westinghouse Electric Corporation, founded in 1886, is the second largest electrical manufacturer in the U.S. today. By 1914, its net value was estimated at more than $200 million.

OTHER ETHNICS BEHIND CORPORATIONS

AMPEX Alexander Matthew Poniatoff (1892–   ), a Russian immigrant from the Kazan district, founded Ampex. The name is an acronym taken from the founder's initials (A.M.P. plus EX for "excellence").

Poniatoff was 52 years old when he

founded Ampex in 1944. Within a short time he was "first" in his field—he manufactured the first commercial magnetic tape recorder in 1956 and was instrumental in the development of the video tape machine. Video tape had its debut at the National Association of Broadcasters Convention held in Chicago in November 1956; today it is the most widely used television medium.

DELTA AIRLINES Delta began as the world's first commercial crop-dusting company—Huff Daland Dusters, organized in 1924. The principal founder was C. E. Woolman (1889–1966), a native of Bloomington, Indiana, descended from Scotch loyalists of the McFarland clan who settled in South Carolina.

From a small crop-dusting operation, Delta Airlines has grown into an international company with almost 200 planes. Today Delta planes travel to 90 cities in 29 states, 5 foreign countries and Puerto Rico.

Frank Augustus Seiberling, the founder of Goodyear Tire and Rubber, was descended from Michael Seiberling of Stuttgart, Germany, who emigrated to Pennsylvania in 1741. (Courtesy: Goodyear Tire and Rubber)

GOODYEAR TIRE AND RUBBER

Named after Charles Goodyear, the Anglo-American inventor of the vulcanization process for rubber, Goodyear Tire and Rubber was founded in 1898 with a total capital investment of $45,000. Frank Seiberling (1859–1955), the German-American who founded Goodyear, turned Akron, Ohio, into the Rubber Center of the World and made the Goodyear name synonymous with "blimps."

Besides introducing the first pneumatic tires for automobiles (1899), Seiberling patented the tubeless tire in 1903, developed pneumatic tires for airplanes in 1909, and introduced the blimp to America. The first American-made blimp, the *Akron*, was built in 1910 under his sponsorship. Today the only blimps seen in the skies of America belong to Goodyear.

By 1916, Goodyear had become the largest tire company in the world, with sales exceeding $100 million.

Facts About the Blimps

1 There are only three Goodyear blimps in operation today—two in America, one in Europe. A fourth blimp, the *Mayflower*, was destroyed in July 1979, when high winds blew it from its moorings and slammed it to the ground.

2 Both of the American-based airships are named after yachts which won the America's Cup Race: *America*, the first winner, 1851; and *Columbia* (1871, 1899, 1901 and 1958).

3 Call them blimps or dirigibles, but not Zeppelins. Only a rigid airship can rightly be called a "Zep." (The word blimp may well come from a contraction of the British designation for the airships: "Balloons, Type B, limp."

4 STATISTICS:

Length	192 feet
Maximum Speed	50 mph
Weight	3,771 lbs.
Number of lights	7,560

GULF AND WESTERN Charles G. Bluhdorn (1926–   ) emigrated to the United States from Vienna in 1942. He was only sixteen years old, and a bit short on funds, but Bluhdorn was confident that he would "make it" in America. He started his own import-export business in 1949 with a

$3,000 investment, and by 1956 he made his first million dollars by dealing in coffee.

Bluhdorn used this money to purchase an interest in Michigan Bumper Corporation, which became the basis of Gulf and Western industries, a diversified organization with annual sales in excess of $3.3 billion.

Bluhdorn had this to say of his success: "I haven't been afraid to call it the American dream. To me, it is the epitome of what America is all about. It is the thing that Walt Disney was doing with his characters. It is the thing that makes us look back on Shirley Temple nostalgically . . . It's sort of like a love affair with Gulf and Western and with America. Yes, you can call that sentimental, but that's what made America. Like the building of the Union Pacific Railroad. All the things that we sometimes forget about today. And that our kids forget about. The thing that made this country the greatest nation in the world." (Source: Newcomen Society, *The Gulf and Western Story*, 1973)

HAMMERMILL PAPER Before Moritz Behrend, a German immigrant, began manufacturing paper in 1898, all stationers in America insisted on selling writing paper with their individual watermarks ingrained on each sheet. Hammermill was the first national brand of paper to be sold for business purposes. By distributing only one watermarked brand of paper from coast to coast, Behrend eliminated the need to run small batches of private stock paper and was able to cut production costs.

HOLIDAY INNS Charles Kemmons Wilson (1913–   ), an American of English ancestry, has been called the "father of the modern innkeeping industry" for his role in turning the lowly motel into a billion-dollar industry.

He first conceived the idea of a "brand name" motel chain in 1951, after he was subjected to cramped, costly lodging during "the most miserable vacation trip of my life." Using a success formula that had worked for fast-food chains, Wilson standardized the motel room, instituted quality control, set reasonable prices and built his Holiday Inns near major interstate arteries.

Holiday Inns is the largest motor hotel system in the world, with almost 1,700 locations in 50 countries and territories.

KODAK The ancestors of George Eastman (1854–1932) included Roger East-

man and Thomas Kilborne, two Englishmen who settled in the New World about 1635. Eastman made his fortune by transforming photography from a difficult profession into an idiot's delight. "You push the button, we do the rest" was the motto that started the whole nation shooting in the late 1880s.

The first Kodak camera was nothing more than a "box" that contained a roll of film with 100 exposures. After the button had been pushed one hundred times, the exposed film was returned to the factory (still inside the box). The finished pictures were returned along with the freshly loaded camera.

Eastman started his company in 1880 with $5,000 in savings. He had developed the chemical coating that made dry-plate photography possible in 1878, but we didn't become a nation of snapshot takers until Eastman developed flexible roll film that amateurs and professionals alike could wind with ease. Picture-taking made Eastman a very wealthy man, but he was by nature a very generous one, too. The way he saw it, "Two courses are open to the man of wealth. He can hoard his money for his heirs to administer, or he can get it into action and have his fun with it while he is alive."

Eastman took the latter course of action, and during his lifetime he donated between $75 million and $100 million to schools, hospitals, Black colleges and dental clinics the world over. He was also a generous patron of the arts and donated funds to establish the Eastman School of Music in Rochester, New York.

MOBIL OIL An American of English ancestry, Hiram B. Everest entered into the oil business with a $20 investment in 1866. His partner, Matthew Ewing, patented a method for vacuum distillation of crude oil that produced two products: kerosene and an excellent lubricant. Ewing didn't have faith in the selling power of his process, however, and he sold out his interest to Everest.

By 1896, Everest had patented the first high-quality petroleum lubricant for industrial machines, Gargoyle Steam Cylinder Oil, and the Vacuum Oil Company was on the road to success.

Standard Oil purchased a controlling interest in Vacuum in 1879, and in 1882 the company's name was changed to Socony, an acronym for *S*tandard *O*il *C*ompany *o*ff *N*ew *Y*ork. The name was later changed to Socony Mobil, and finally to Mobil Oil.

MONSANTO   Monsanto started out as a "moonlighting" operation in 1901. John Francis Queeny (1859–1933), the son of Irish immigrants, named his fledgling company after his Spanish-American wife, Olga Mendez Monsanto, whom he married in 1896.

Monsanto started manufacturing an artificial sweetener, saccharin, which was monopolized by a German industry in the early 1900s. A legal battle ensued over the rights to the chemical process, but Monsanto emerged victorious. Today, Monsanto is one of the world's leading chemical corporations with annual sales in excess of $4.25 billion.

MOTOWN   Motown is the largest Black-run business in the United States. Annual sales are in excess of $58 million, yet Berry Gordy started his entertainment empire with a total investment of $700, which he borrowed from his family.

Gordy had lost $1,000 in royalties from songs that he had written. One of the songs, *Money*, had been recorded by several artists, including the Beatles, but when Gordy tried to collect from his New York publisher, the publisher refused to pay. Gordy threatened to sue, but when he consulted a lawyer he was told, "If you sue him for $1,000 it will take you three years or so in court. You're going to pay me more than $1,000 and you're going to end up settling with him for probably $2,000 – it doesn't make any sense."

That's when Motown was born. Gordy decided to start his own company to protect other young music writers who were in a powerless position, and prevent them from losing what was rightfully theirs.

UNION CARBIDE   Formally incorporated in 1917, the Union Carbide Corporation had its beginnings way back in 1886 when Charles F. Brush invented the carbon arc street lamp. Initially demonstrated in Cleveland's Public Square,

The gentleman in the three-piece tweed suit is James Turner Morehead, one of the creative forces behind the Union Carbide Corporation. Of Scottish ancestry, Morehead was related to James Watt, the inventor of the steam engine. (Courtesy: Union Carbide)

Brush's device turned night into day for the first time in history.

The two men who gave Union Carbide its name, and its most valued product, were Thomas L. Willson (Canadian) and Major James Turner Morehead, an American of Scottish ancestry. While attempting to produce aluminum in an electric furnace, the duo accidentally invented a method of producing calcium carbide, which proved to be the first commercial source of acetylene gas. Not only was acetylene useful for street lighting, it could also be used for cutting and welding metals.

Today Union Carbide produces chemicals, electronics materials and brand-name products such as Glad Wrap and Prestone antifreeze.

ETHNICS WHO BECAME HOUSEHOLD WORDS IN AMERICA

Who was the Singer of sewing machine fame? Were Hoover vacuum cleaners named after President Herbert Hoover? What about Colgate toothpaste; Procter & Gamble soaps; and Bulova watches? The following are some of the ethnics who left their names to America.

99⁴⁴/₁₀₀% British On Halloween, 1837, two immigrants in their mid-thirties pooled their resources to found a tiny soap and candle company in Cincinnati, Ohio. William Procter, an English candlemaker who arrived in the United States in 1832, and James Gamble, a Scott-Irish soapmaker who arrived in 1819, invested $3,596.47 each to found the company that bears their names today and has net sales in excess of $7 billion annually.

Proctor and Gamble were not only business partners, but brothers-in-law, who married Olivia and Ann Norris, respectively. Although they manufactured 24 varieties of soap in 1878, it wasn't until the following year that they introduced their first "brand name" product—Ivory Soap. The slogan "It floats" was introduced in 1891, but as early as 1882 P&G was extolling the virtues of its 99⁴⁴/₁₀₀% pure product. According to Alfred Lief, who published a history of P&G, it was this "self-restraint inherent in the admission of a fraction of one per cent impurity" that sold the public on Ivory.

The company's success with Ivory stimulated a tradition of "brand name" products at P&G, most of them household words: Crisco (1911); Camay (1926); Lava (1928); Spic and Span (1945); Prell, Tide (1946); Joy (1949); Cheer (1950); Gleem (1952).

The British Do It Again Another ethnic who "cleaned up" in America was William Colgate (1783–1857), an Englishman born in the parish of Hollinghourn, in Kent.

Colgate established a laundry soap manufacturing firm in 1806. He later added perfume and toilet soap to his list of products, and over the years Colgate and his descendants made Palmolive, Ajax, Fab, Cold Power, Ultra Brite and Rapid Shave familiar household words. Through their advertising campaigns, Colgate has also given

American "Gardol" shields to illustrate their toothpaste's effectiveness against tooth decay; the "white tornado"; and the slogan, "put your money where your mouth is" to demonstrate the sexual appeal of their adult toothpaste.

BUBBLE PARTIES.

One of the most amusing, as well as easily arranged entertainments for the Holidays, is a " Bubble Party." Twenty or more ladies and gentlemen, enough clay pipes so each will have one, three or four bowls of soap-suds and, say, half a dozen trifles for prizes are all that is required, the prizes to be awarded to those who blow the largest bubbles, one of the party to act as referee.

The suds should be made of IVORY SOAP . . .

Ivory advertisement from late 1800s, when "bubble parties" were the rage. (Courtesy: Procter & Gamble)

Cannon Towels James William Cannon (1852–1921), a Scottish-American whose ancestors settled in North Carolina during the late eighteenth century, manufactured his first towel in 1889. He sold 1,332 dozen towels that year, and although his company was the world's largest towel producer by the start of World War I, he didn't live to see his product elevated to "brand name" status.

It wasn't until 1923, when a machine was developed that could sew labels onto towels, that the Cannon logo was developed. Headquartered in Kannapolis (the name, coined by Cannon in 1906 from Greek words, means "City of Looms"), Cannon became the world's largest manufacturer of household textiles in the late 1920s. Annual sales totaled $453 million in 1976, compared to $150,000 in 1887.

Behind the Nylon Curtain One of America's top industrial corporations, Du Pont, was founded in 1802 by a French immigrant, Eleuthere Irenee du Pont de Nemours (1771–1834). The Du Pont family left France after becoming disillusioned with their government and sickened at the "Reign of Terror" that had claimed thousands of lives since it began in 1791. It was one of those guillotined Frenchmen, Antoine Lavoisier, who helped the Du Ponts build their fortune in America. Lavoisier was Irenee's chemistry teacher and the man in charge of manufacturing gunpowder for the French government. It was from Lavoisier that Irenee learned to make gunpowder, and that was Du Pont's first American product.

Today, whether you know it or not, a Du Pont product touches your life each day. From the cellophane that wraps cigarette packages (invented by a Swiss chemist, Jacques Edwin Brandenberger, in 1912 and licensed by Du Pont following World War I), to the synthetic rubber heels on your shoes (invented by a Belgian priest, Father Julius A. Nieuwland, and marketed as Neoprene by Du Pont) — Du Pont has its hands in almost everything we touch, wear or cook with. Quiana, Teflon, Orlon, Dacron, Mylar and Corfam are just a few of the synthetic materials manufactured by Du Pont that have found their way into our homes as clothing, wall coverings, and the stuff that waterproof shoes are made of.

Rich Bich The ball-point pen has come a long way since the Hungarian brothers, Georg and Ladislao Biro, first invented it in Argentina in 1944. The early Biro pens left blobs of ink and smudges on hands and paper until instant dry ink was invented by Franz Seech, an Austrian chemist living in California. Once gravity-flow ink was perfected, the ball-point gained new respectability, and today the fountain pen is almost an "antique." The ball-point pen and felt-tipped marker have virtually captured the American writing public, save for a few diehards who enjoy the feel of writing with a fountain pen.

In 1957 some 300 million ball-point pens were sold. By 1960 that number had mushroomed to 762 million, and today one company, Bic, produces almost 2.5 million pens each day in the United States alone. Bic is the undisputed king of the "throwaway pen" controlling 69% of the American pen market.

The man who brought the Bic pen to America is Marcel Bich, a native of France. A wise businessman, Bich Americanized his name to Bic when he entered the U.S. pen field — envisioning the trouble schoolboys might have when asking for that Bich of a pen.

Motorola TV Paul Galvin, an Irish-American from Harvard, Illinois, began manufacturing "battery eliminators" in 1928. These useful gadgets made it possible to plug a battery-operated radio into an electrical outlet, but when plug-in radios began to appear on the market Galvin's sales declined sharply.

Looking for a new market during the Depression years, Galvin turned his sights on the automobile radio. Galvin is credited with developing the first commercially successful car radio (which he named "Motorola"), and eventually his company became the largest manufacturer of auto radios in the world.

During World War II, Motorola produced walkie-talkies and radar equipment (boosting annual sales from $17 million to over $80 million in 1944). In peacetime, Motorola's television sets, stereophonic equipment and semiconductor products have made the company one of the world's largest manufacturers in the electronics field.

Bulova Watch Time The Bulova watch company was founded in 1875 by Joseph Bulova, a twenty-three-year-old immigrant from Czechoslovakia, who opened a tiny jewelry shop on Maiden Lane in New York City.

In 1927 Charles Lindbergh boosted the company's image enormously by choosing to wear a Bulova on his solo transatlantic flight. Lindy didn't want a heavy clock (weighing about one pound) placed in the cockpit of his plane consuming valuable fuel, so he opted for a Bulova wristwatch to tell time. Bulova designed a special "Lone Eagle" model to commemorate Lindbergh's flight and sold over 50,000 of those special watches.

Bulova also had the honor of broadcasting the first commercial television ad on July 1, 1941. The total cost for that 20-second spot was $9.

Maytag The "loneliest repairmen in town" have Frederick Louis Maytag (1857–1937) to thank for their cushy jobs. Frederick, the eldest of 10 children born to Daniel and Amelia Maitag (German immigrants who later Americanized their last name to Maytag) manufactured his first washing machine in 1907.

Not only did Frederick Maytag serve as president and chairman of the board of Maytag until his death in 1937, he also served his country as a politician. Elected to the Iowa State Senate in 1902, he held that post for 10 years, prior to his selection as city councilman and later mayor of Newton, Iowa.

America's Favorite Tool Men In 1910, S. Duncan Black, an American of Scotch, English and Irish ancestry, and Alonzo G. Decker, whose ancestors hailed from Scotland and Holland, invested $1,200 of their hard-earned money to form the Black and Decker Manufacturing Company.

To raise his share of their stake, Black had to sell his secondhand Maxwell Briscoe car, and Decker was forced to take a bank loan. Today the Black and Decker company is one of the largest manufacturers of hand-held power tools used by weekend handymen.

First to Conquer Living Space Bernard Castro, a Sicilian immigrant, founded a decorating business in New York City in 1931. Constantly besieged with requests to make small city apartments appear more spacious, Castro saw a brilliant future in manufacturing beds that can be folded away during the day. Today, the Castro convertible furniture company is the largest business of its kind in the world. There are 65 Castro stores located on the East Coast of the United States, and with the increasing number of studio apartments, business couldn't look better for the future.

Castro's daughter, Bernadette, once appeared in every Castro commercial to illustrate that opening a Castro was so simple even a child could do it. Today, her role has been taken by her four children (Terri Ann, David, Jonthan and Bernard).

"It Beats, as it Sweeps, as it Cleans" The name Hoover is so synonymous with carpet cleaning that the British never "vacuum" their rugs – they "Hoover" them. The man responsible for liberating housewives from having to beat their rugs daily was William Henry Hoover (1849–1932), a Swiss-American who marketed his first "electric suction sweeper" in 1908.

Hoover, himself, didn't invent the vacuum cleaner, he merely used his business acumen to turn J. Murray Spangler's crude invention into an international organization. Considering the fact that there were few homes even wired for electricity in the early 1900s, Hoover's timing can either be described as "bold, innovative and clairvoyant" or just plain old "dumb luck."

Kohler Bathtubs One of the largest names in American plumbing fixtures is Kohler, founded by John Michael Kohler, an Austrian immigrant who settled in the United States in 1854.

The first Kohler bathtub started out as a combination horse trough and hog scalder. Kohler simply added an enamel coating, and it was ready to be marketed as a "personal hygiene" product.

The Man Who Kept Us "In Stitches" Isaac Merritt Singer (1811–1875), the son of a German immigrant, didn't invent the sewing machine, but he was a pioneer in mass-producing machines with interchangeable parts. At the age of 39, Singer borrowed 40 dollars with which to fabricate his first sewing machine – a device for which he was issued a patent because it was the first sewing machine to sew with consistency. Singer entered into partnership with Edward Clark in 1851, and it was Clark's marketing genius that made Singer a household word all over the world. Clark offered free sewing machines to ministers' wives just to gain acceptability for his labor-saving device; he offered trade-ins, developed installment buying plans and conducted advertising programs to illustrate how easy it was to operate a complex piece of machinery like the sewing machine. Why, it was so simple, even a woman could do it!

Despite his general ban on Western machinery, Mahatma Gandhi, the late Indian leader, began extolling the virtues of Singer's sewing machine. Gandhi learned to sew while in prison, and later claimed that the sewing machine, ". . . is one of the few useful things ever invented."

ETHNIC-AMERICANS WHO BECAME TRADEMARKS

Everyday we see their faces glaring up at us from the supermarket shelves, trying to seduce us into buying their products. A friendly Black woman smiles and beckons us to buy her pancake mix; two bearded men stare across the front of a cough drop box; a smiling chef offers us a bowlful of hot breakfast cereal; and a saluting sailor boy tempts us to buy his candied popcorn.

But, who are these people who became trademarks? Are they merely fanciful creations from some illustrator's pen, or was there once flesh and blood behind those smiles?

Some trademarks, such as Betty Crocker, are mere illustrations designed to fit the image of the product they represent, but many products have real live people representing them, with ethnic backgrounds as diverse as those of the rest of America.

"Call for Philip Morris"

When Johnny Roventini was dressed as the Philip Morris page boy in his bright red brass-buttoned suit, he was easily recognized as the "world's most famous living trademark."

The son of Italian immigrants living in Brooklyn, Johnny was discovered on the job while paging guests at the Hotel New Yorker in 1933. Milton Biow, an advertising executive, was sitting in the lobby waiting for a client when he heard Johnny's crystal-clear voice and decided to use the midget for a small publicity stunt.

He called Johnny over and handed him a request. Johnny smiled as he read Biow's handwriting, and as he strode through the hotel lobby crying "Call for Philip Morris," his clear, strong voice commanded the attention of everyone present. Biow was so delighted with the results that he signed Johnny to an exclusive contract with Philip Morris for $20,000 a year. (Not bad money for 1933!)

Soon Johnny's perfect B-flat call was heard over radio and TV and at sporting events throughout the United States. He traveled all over the world, too, and learned to deliver his call in Spanish, French, German, Italian, Swedish and Chinese. Johnny

estimates that, during his 41-year career as Philip Morris's goodwill ambassador, he shook hands with close to a million people.

Standing only 47 inches tall and weighing a mere 59 pounds, he became the most famous midget in the world; at one time he was insured for $100,000, or over $2000 an inch. Although he has not appeared in Philip Morris advertisements for many years, Johnny only recently hung up his page suit — he officially retired in 1974.

Prince in the Bottle

There really was a prince behind the Prince Matchabelli perfume company — a Russian nobleman named Georges Matchabelli, who was fortunate enough to be traveling abroad when the Bolshevik Revolution raged through his homeland in 1919. Although his estate was confiscated and he never saw his family or his native land again, he was lucky to be alive, well and living in Europe.

When the Prince's wife, actress Maria Carmi, was offered a chance to appear on Broadway's "Great White Way," the Matchabellis emigrated to New York, where Georges opened a small antique shop on Madison Avenue.

His personality, title and extreme good looks attracted many wealthy socialites and celebrities as customers, and soon his antique business was prospering. He became friendly with New York's elite, and whenever a special woman friend celebrated a birthday Georges would often mix a personalized blend of perfume for her as a present, a hobby of his that dated back to his college days.

When his customers became more interested in his scents than in his antiques, Matchabelli decided to abandon his store and devote himself to manufacturing perfume full-time.

Within 3 years Prince Matchabelli perfume was being distributed nationwide. To this day, the company that bears his name still uses the original perfume bottle designed by the prince himself and adapted from the crown which tops the Matchabelli coat of arms.

The Man in the Hathaway Shirt

With a $1.50 eyepatch purchased at a local drugstore and a ridiculously low advertising budget of $30,000, David Ogilvy elevated the Hathaway Shirt Company from 116 years of relative obscurity, to a nationally recognized brand-name shirt manufacturer almost overnight.

How did the English-immigrant-turned-ad-man accomplish such a feat? By giving his model, a White Russian baron named George Wrangle, what is known in the trade as "story appeal."

An eyepatch on a sleazy old sailor with a five-day growth of beard looks "tough," but that same eyepatch on a ridiculously handsome man tends to give him an interesting "past" and makes people sit up and notice what he's selling.

George Wrangle led an interesting life in print as the Hathaway man. He was usually photographed doing something out of the ordinary, such as conducting the New York Philharmonic, or copying an Old Master's painting at the Metropolitan Museum of Art, or even riding a tractor in his crisply starched, form-fitting shirt that never wrinkled.

Although the company prospered enormously from the ads, all Ogilvy ever made on the account he turned into a legend was a mere $6,000.

Dynamic Tension

For years, Charles Atlas served as his own best trademark for the body building school he founded and advertised in comic books, newspapers and pulp magazines. His technique for turning 97-pound weaklings into "he-men" was known as "dynamic tension" and it was the same system Atlas himself used to build up his muscles to win the title "World's Most Perfectly Developed Man" in the early 1920s.

It all started one day when a 97-pound weakling, Angelo Siciliano, became fed up with the local bullies in his Brooklyn, New York, neighborhood. After being repeatedly "beaten up" on his way home from school, Angelo decided he had had enough and was determined to buld up his muscles.

While visiting the zoo, Angelo was impressed with the lion's strength and agility, and he wondered how the beast managed to keep in shape when there was so little room to exercise in his small cage. He began to study the lion's movements, and noticed that, every so often, the "king" would stretch and tighten his muscles together. This observation led him to develop the "dynamic tension" system, a forerunner of modern isometric exercises, which are recommended for sedentary office workers today.

The young immigrant from Acri, Italy, changed his name to Charles Atlas in 1923. He had won the title "World's Most Perfectly Developed Man" for the second time when an admirer remarked that Angelo's body bore a strong resemblance to the statue of Atlas carrying the world on his shoulders. Needless to say, he was flattered and decided to change his name to Charles Atlas.

He established his famous correspondence school in 1929, and through the years has helped thousands of 97-pound weaklings defend their honor when challenged by sand-kicking bullies on the beach.

Lipton Tea

The prosperous looking old gent with the walrus moustache who smiles and offers us a cup of tea as we saunter down the supermarket aisle is Sir Thomas Lipton (1850–1931). However, things were not always so cheery for the Lipton family. Raised in abject poverty in Glasgow, Scotland, Thomas began working at the tender age of nine to supplement the meager family income his parents were able to eke out of their grocery store.

By the time he was fourteen years old, Thomas, realizing that there was little future for him in Scotland, began to save his hard-earned money to buy a steerage class ticket to America and a better life. He arrived in New York with less than $8 in his pocket, but was determined not to waste his precious bankroll on such necessities as room and board. As the boat pulled into the harbor, Lipton looked down from the deck of the ship and noticed scores of eager boarding house owners lined up along the shore hoping to attract lodgers. Immediately, Lipton thought of a way to preserve his meager finances! He raced off the boat and quickly made a deal with an Irish gent, Mike McCauligan, who agreed to provide Tom with free room and board in exchange for 12 new lodgers. The accommodations were not plush, but Lipton could hardly complain because the price was right. Of his early days in America he noted: "We slept eight in a room o'nights. The boarders were drawn from all nationalities. . . . and hardly anybody understood his neighbor's language."

After laboring at odd jobs for a time, Lipton finally landed a job as clerk in a New York City store. It was here that he learned the art of promoting products. When he returned home and applied the tricks of the trade to his parents' faltering business, the Liptons were soon rolling in money. By the time he was 26 years old, Lipton was operating 20 stores; 14 years later, he had over 300 shops in the British Isles, where Lipton sold, among other items, Ceylon tea imported from his own plantations. He continued to prosper and enjoy financial success, and was even knighted by Queen Victoria in 1898 for his accomplishments.

After achieving resounding success on his home turf, Lipton journeyed to the United States once again, determined to make a killing in the American tea market. To his surprise, there wasn't any tea market to "crack" – and when he ordered a cup of his favorite brew at a hotel restaurant, all the waiter gave him was a blank stare. The man later returned with some coffee and explained, "The stuff you asked for is not served in this hotel."

Lipton moved right onto the grocery shelves of America with his one-pound, half-pound and quarter-pound boxes in the 1880s. In addition to capturing the American teacup with his quality product, Lipton was also an avid sailor who tried five times to capture the America's Cup trophy for yacht racing, but failed.

The current vignette of Sir Thomas Lipton in his yachtsman's cap was adopted by the company in 1944; for the past 37 years his smiling face has graced every Lipton's box and bag sold in the United States.

Impostor With a Paint Brush

The little "Dutch Boy" who graces every can of Dutch Boy brand paint is an ethnic impostor. The young boy who posed for the portrait was not a native of Holland, but an Irish-American lad by the name of Mike Brady.

World's Most Expensive Popping Corn

Each year Americans much 383 million pounds of popcorn while watching movies and ball games, or spending a quiet evening at home. Of that total, almost 192 million

pounds is popped at home in electric corn poppers, in fireplaces, or in ordinary cookware on top of the stove. The average American consumes almost 2 pounds of popcorn each year, but for some reason that average jumps to 4 pounds in the twin city of Minneapolis/St. Paul, which has been dubbed the "popcorn eating capital of the world."

The Indians introduced popcorn to the colonists, and even brought some along for the first Thanksgiving feast, but it was a German-American, Orville Redenbacher, who first introduced high-priced, "gourmet" popping corn to the supermarket shelves of America.

Redenbacher, the grandson of German immigrants, was born on a farm near Brazil, Indiana, in 1907. Orville's typical "success story" included walking 7 miles to school each day and working his way through college. After graduation from Purdue University with a degree in agronomy. Orville began experimenting to breed better ears of corn for popping. After years of effort he succeeded in producing a superior popping corn.

Recognizing that a superior product does not always guarantee success in the supermarket. Redenbacher decided that a new marketing strategy was necessary to promote his corn. Previously, all popcorn was sold by the pound and, regardless of quality, its price hovered in the 20-to-30-cent range. Orville thought people would be willing to pay extra for a premium product that was fluffier when popped, and had fewer "deadhead" kernels that refused to explode even when subjected to the hot-oil-and-highheat torture treatment.

(Courtesy: Orville Redenbacher)

Orville's marketing strategy proved correct and within a few years his popcorn, billed as the World's Most Expensive, was a best seller even though it retailed for two or three times the price of other, plebeian brands.

Today his picture graces every jar of Orville Redenbacher brand popcorn sold in America, making him one of our best-known living trademarks.

Cracker Jack Jack

What would a ball game be without a box of Cracker Jack to munch between innings? And what would a box of Cracker Jack be without the prize? Although inflation has relegated the old tin toys to antique status and today's surprises are little more than a plastic trinket or a paper puzzle, the first order of business for children and adults alike is finding the prize inside a newly opened pack of Cracker Jack.

Cracker Jack is still made according to the original formula developed by a German immigrant, F. W. Rueckheim, who opened a popcorn stand in Chicago during the late 1800s. The trade name was born in 1896 when a delighted customer tasted Rueckheim's fresh candied popcorn and exclaimed, "That's crackerjack!"

Each ounce of Cracker Jack manufactured today contains 9 peanuts (count them!), though Rueckheim's original ratio of nuts to corn was probably a bit more generous in 1899 when the first boxed Cracker Jacks appeared in ball parks throughout America.

For his package trademark Rueckheim merely added the slogan "the more you eat the more you want," and the picture of a sailor boy, "Jack," modeled after his grandson, Robert, who died of pneumonia at the age of 8.

The copyrighted trademark of the sailor boy standing at ease with his black-eyed dog between his feet was emblazoned on Robert Rueckheim's tombstone, in St. Henry's Cemetery in Chicago, where curiosity seekers can find Jack gesturing his final salute to the young boy he represents.

Aunt Jemima

The first pancake mix ever manufactured in the United States was packaged by Chris Rutt, a St. Joseph, Missouri, newspaperman. Rutt put his product in a plain brown paper sack and there it sat collecting dust on grocery store shelves, until he jazzed up the package a bit. When a traveling vaudeville duo named Baker and Farrell came to town in 1889 singing about "Aunt Jemima," Rutt adopted the name for his pancake mix and sales started to improve.

He later sold the rights to the Davis Milling Company, which decided to promote their pancake mix at the 1893 Columbian Exposition in Chicago. For the occasion they constructed the world's largest flour barrel (24 feet high and 16 feet in diameter) and hired a famous Black American cook,

"Old" Aunt Jemima, circa 1946. Today's Aunt Jemima is thinner and wears a bandana around her hair instead of a babushka. (Courtesy: New York Public Library)

Nancy Green, to be the living personification of "Aunt Jemima." She was such a success that, by the time the fair was over, more than a million pancakes had been served and "Aunt Jemima" had become a living trademark.

Nancy Green continued to pose as Aunt Jemima at fairs and expositions all across the nation, until her death in 1923 at the age of 89.

The Mystery Chef

Over the years the Cream of Wheat chef has appeared on thousands of cereal boxes. First as a photograph and later as an artist's rendition of the original portrait, the "chef" has been offering hungry breakfasters a potful of his cereal every morning since 1897.

The "chef" was really a Black American waiter from Chicago, who was first discovered by Emery Mapes, co-owner of the Minneapolis mill that manufactured Cream of Wheat. Impressed by his friendliness and congeniality, Mapes asked the waiter to pose in a chef's uniform for possible use as a trademark for his cereal. He paid the waiter $5 for his trouble, but when the photo was approved for use as a trademark, the waiter could not be found.

Mapes did have some information about the waiter that made it possible to screen out impostors, but when a search was conducted for him, impostors were all that turned up.

Although the mystery chef's portrait has appeared on every box of Cream of Wheat since then, he never received another penny for serving as a nationally recognized trademark.

Bearded Brothers

When James Smith first emigrated to Poughkeepsie, New York, from St. Armand, Quebec, he was unable to find work as a carpenter. Like countless thousands of immigrants before and after him, he opened a small restaurant.

When a traveler passing through town gave him a "secret" formula for cough drops, Smith began selling them in his restaurant and later enlisted his sons, William and Andrew, to help peddle his lozenges. Soon the bearded brothers were a familiar sight to travelers riding the New York to Albany stage, and their fame spread throughout the Hudson River Valley.

When their father died in 1866, the boys

expanded the family business and began placing jarsful of Smith Brothers cough drops in pharmacies, grocery stores and restaurants. When competitors copied their style, the brothers put their initials (SB) on their drops and their faces on their glass jars and glassine envelopes to protect customers from cheap imitations.

The Smith Brothers pioneered the first factory-filled packages in 1872, and became familiar faces to millions of Americans as their production increased to almost 5 tons per day.

The Smiths probably hold the record as the most reproduced bearded faces in America, save for the portraits of Abraham Lincoln which grace five-dollar bills and pennies.

ETHNIC ORIGINS OF SOME SLOGANS, LOGOS AND TRADEMARKS

Pawnbrokers Ever wonder why all pawnbrokers have three brass balls outside their shops? It all started with the Medicis of Florence, whose banking enterprise spread to England in the fifteenth century. To advertise their place of business the Medicis displayed their family coat of arms, which contained three golden balls.

As the trade of money lending grew, other merchants adopted the golden balls of the Medicis for quick recognition, and eventually oversized brass balls were displayed as the trade sign for pawnbrokers the world over.

Nabisco The National Biscuit Company's logo, a white cross with two bars and an oval base that encircles the Nabisco name, is actually an Italian printer's symbol of religious significance. Dating back to medieval times, the symbol represents the triumph of the spiritual and moral over everything that is evil and material on the face of the earth.

You Old Devil, You The oldest trademark patent in America, No. 82, belongs to the Wm. Underwood Company, manufacturers of that satanically named meat product—deviled ham.

William Underwood, an English immigrant, applied for a trademark patent in 1870 for the devilish creature whose image appears on every Underwood product. The original Devil was a mean, scowling cuss who was frequently pictured dipping whole hams into his caldron while hellish fires burned in the background, but he has been replaced in our hedonistic age with a rather nice-looking devil who wears a smile and waves his right hand to potential consumers while dancing with his trident held aloft—a rather likable old chap.

Born in Ealing Parish, outside of London, William Underwood (1787–1867) came to America about 1820. He began selling condiments on Boston's Russia Wharf in 1822, and soon expanded his business to include imported mustard, sauces and pickles. He later became one of the first businessmen in America to preserve food in glass jars and tin cans, and like many other food processors of his day, he made a fortune selling canned foods to the Union Army during the Civil War.

Today, the Underwood Company is one of the oldest American businesses that is still family-owned—and the deviled ham recipe is still kept a company secret, locked safe inside a bank vault.

Esky The popeyed, mustachioed character who once graced every issue of *Esquire* magazine as the symbol of a roué was created by E. Simms Campbell (1906–1971), a Black cartoonist whose work appeared in every issue of the magazine from 1933 to 1971.

"When It Rains It Pours" The Morton Salt company was founded in 1885 by Joy Morton (1855–1934), a descendant of Richard Morton, who arrived in America on the *Little Ann,* the second English ship to bring colonists to these shores.

Morton Salt began manufacturing small, round packages of salt with patented pouring spouts for home use in 1910. To complement the new package, Morton began to search for a new logo. An ad man from N. W. Ayer eventually came up with the picture of a "little girl with an umbrella over her head, rain falling, a package of salt under her arm, tilted backward with spout open and the salt running out . . ." In the words of Sterling Morton (Joy's son): "It struck me that here was the whole story in one picture—that the message that the salt would run in damp weather was made beautifully evident. I immediately said that we could find no better trademark."

14 MUSIC, ART AND ENTERTAINMENT

FOR A SONG . . .

ETHNIC STORIES BEHIND SOME POPULAR AMERICAN SONGS

Aloha Oe The traditional "farewell" song of Hawaii was written by Queen Liliuokalani (1838–1917), who was also known as Mrs. Lydia Dominis after her marriage to a native Bostonian. Queen Liliuokalani only reigned for two years (1891–1893) before being overthrown by a revolution.

Anniversary Waltz This melody first appeared in Romania in the 1920s as "Waves of the Danube." Written by the Romanian composer I. Ivanovici, it attained fame in 1947 when it was featured in the film *The Jolson Story.*

Auld Lang Syne It would be hard to imagine New Year's Eve without "Auld Lang Syne." Although Robert Burns, the Scottish poet, is usually credited with originating the song, he merely adapted this Scottish tune in 1799—it was already quite popular in his day. He rearranged the words of the first stanza a bit, added a second and third stanza, and combined the music from several Scottish tunes when he "wrote" this song.

Ballin' the Jack This song, which comes with built-in dance instructions, was written by Black American songwriter Chris Smith (1879–1949) in 1913. Smith also performed in vaudeville and wrote "Junk Man Rag," "Big Cry Baby in the Moon" and "Never Let the Same Bee Sting You Twice."

Beer Barrel Polka Better known by the opening line, "Roll out the barrel," this polka was originally written by Czech bandmaster Vejvoda. It was translated into English in 1939 by Lew Brown.

Carolina in the Morning This song was written by Gus Kahn, the son of Jewish immigrants from Eastern Europe.

Carry Me Back to Ol' Virginny Written in 1878 by James A. Bland (1854–1911), "the prince of Negro songwriters," this song became the official state song in 1940. Born to free parents in Flushing, New York, in 1854, Bland attended Howard University and studied law. He even worked as a page in the House of Representatives before he left school to join Callender's Original Georgia Minstrels at the age of 21. Virtually unknown in America, Bland was the idol of England's music halls for more than two decades.

God Bless America Written by a Russian-Jewish immigrant, Israel Baline, better known to the world as Irving Berlin, "God Bless America" was first performed by Kate Smith in 1939, immediately after the outbreak of World War II, (22 years after it had been written). The song became Ms. Smith's "trademark." All royalties received by Berlin were turned over to the Boy Scouts and Girls Scouts of America.

Green Eyes Originally known as "Ojos Verdes" when it was written (as an instrumental) by Cuban composer Nilo Menendez in 1935, the song later became a hit with English lyrics.

Home Sweet Home Written in 1823 by John Howard Payne (1791–1852), the humble words are all-American, but the music is a foreign import. Some sources claim the melody comes from a Sicilian opera, while others hold that it was adapted from an old French folk song.

La Cucaracha "La Cucaracha" or "The Cockroach" has done more to damage the sale of raisins in the United States than all of Cesar Chavez's strikes. Written by a Spanish composer, about a cockroach who is hooked on marijuana, the song alludes to the fact that the cockroach has spent too much time in the sun, and now "he's just another raisin." Definitely one of the most unappetizing lines ever written.

Marie from Sunny Italy This song, written in Chinatown in 1907, was Irving Berlin's (1888–   ) first composition. The Russian-Jewish composer followed "Marie" with more than 700 other published songs during his long songwriting career.

Oh, Promise Me A favorite song at weddings, "Oh, Promise Me" was written by Reginald de Koven (1861–1920), whose first American ancestor was John Louis de Koven, a native of Germany. The song came from his 1890 Broadway show, *Robin Hood*.

Ol' Man River This "Negro" song was written by the Jewish songwriting team of Oscar Hammerstein and Jerome Kern.

The Star Spangled Banner The words to our national anthem, as every schoolchild learns, were written by Francis Scott Key on September 14, 1814, during the British bombing of Fort McHenry. The music, however, was composed by an Englishman, John Stafford Smith, a London composer who died in 1836. The original piece was known as "The Anacreontic Song" (the title was derived from the name of a British gentlemen's club). It was recognized as our national anthem in 1931 by an act of Congress signed by President Hoover.

Sweet Adeline The female inspiration for this song was a sixty-year-old coloratura soprano, Adelina Patti, from Madrid. Patti was appearing in New York City when Henry Armstrong and Richard Gerard spotted her name on the marquee. "Sweet Adeline" was first performed in 1904.

Tea for Two Was written by Jewish songwriter Irving Caesar, who also penned "I Want to be Happy," "Swanee" and "Is It True What They Say About Dixie?"

Way Down Yonder in New Orleans This tune was written in 1922 by the Black songwriting team of Henry Creamer and Turner Layton. Creamer and Layton also wrote "After You've Gone" (1918) and "Strut Miss Lizzie" (1922).

Yankee Doodle The words were written by a British surgeon, Dr. Richard Shuckburg, but the music comes from a traditional English folk tune. "Macaroni" has nothing to do with pasta, but rather was a term used for an English fop.

Yes, We Have No Bananas This silly song evolved from the confused reply overheard at a Greek immigrant's fruit stand in New York City in 1923. The words were written by Frank Silver and Irving Cohn, and the song was popularized by Eddie Cantor in his musical, *Make It Snappy*. The music comes from Handel's *Messiah*.

When Irish Eyes Are Smiling Ernest Ball and Irish tenor Chauncey Olcott collaborated on this Irish ballad, introduced in the 1912 musical *The Isle o' Dreams*.

When Johnny Comes Marching Home Again This song was written by Patrick Gilmore, a Dublin-born lad who emigrated to the United States at the age of nineteen to avoid being forced into the priesthood.

MUSIC FOR EVERYONE

Monitor Records boasts the world's largest collection of authentic folk music recordings. There is African music, recorded live in the Congo; Armenian folk dances and songs; music from the Slavonic liturgy, including Bulgarian chants; as well as Asian, English, French, Dutch, Korean, Middle Eastern and Polish recordings.

Gypsy songs, Ukrainian chants, songs of Russian street urchins, fado songs from Portugal and songs from Bosnia and Herzegovina are just a few of Monitor's records from some fifty different nations.

For more information write to: Monitor Recordings, Inc.
156 Fifth Avenue
New York, N.Y. 10010

SINGERS, SONGWRITERS, AND MUSICIANS

PATTI, LAVERNE AND MAXINE The singing Andrews Sisters, Patti (1921–), Laverne (1915–1967) and Maxine (1918–), who were born in Minnesota of Greek and Norwegian ancestry, attained national prominence in 1937 with their first hit song, a Yiddish composition, *"Bei Mir Bist Du Schön,"* by Sholom Secunda and Jacob Jacobs! Their other "ethnic cross-over" hits included "Beer Barrel Polka" and "Rum and Coca-Cola."

PAUL ANKA (1941–) Canadian-born, of Lebanese ancestry, Anka started his career in 1956 when he bluffed his way into ABC-Paramount and auditioned his song, "Diana." Three years later he had 3 gold records and his first million dollars. By the age of 21 he had over 200 songs to his credit. Although he is credited with composing "My Way," the song Frank Sinatra made famous, Anka only translated it into English. The song was actually composed by Claude François, a French songwriter.

FRANKIE AVALON (1940–) Francis Thomas Avallone convinced his father to buy him a trumpet after he saw Kirk Douglas in *Young Man With a Horn*. He was only eight years old, and was considered something of a "child prodigy" on the trumpet. At age eleven, he appeared on national TV, but when his "cuteness" faded, he was reduced to playing with a neighborhood group—Rocco and the Saints.

Along with Fabian Forte and Bobby Rydell, Avalon completed the Italian-American triumvirate from Philadelphia during the late 1950s rock-and-roll explosion.

PEARL BAILEY (1918–) Pearl Mae Bailey holds an honorary doctoral degree from Georgetown University, but that wasn't enough for this talented Black performer, whose ancestral roots include Creek Indians on both sides of the family—in the late 1970s, Pearl enrolled as a freshman at Georgetown.

HARRY BELAFONTE (1927–) Born in New York to West Indian parents, Harry lived in Jamaica from the time he was 8 years old until he was 13. He gained fame singing folk songs and "calypso" in the 1950s. Ironically, one of his most famous hits, the "Banana Boat Song," was written by a Jewish American, Alan Arkin.

IRVING BERLIN (1888–) Irving Berlin was born Israel Baline in Temun, Russia. Berlin's rabbi father fled a pogrom in his native land and settled in New York in 1892. Although Berlin never attended school past the second grade and he never learned to read music or to play the piano in any key except F sharp, he managed to become a millionaire as a result of the more than one thousand songs he has written over the past 70 years.

His first song, composed in 1907, was "Marie From Sunny Italy." Other "ethnic cross-overs" include "Easter Parade" and "White Christmas." He also composed "God Bless America," "Oh, How I Hate To Get Up in the Morning" and "There's No Business Like Show Business." "Alexander's Ragtime Band" launched his international career, but according to Berlin, "What I did was no more than being able to recognize what rhythm meant, and being with the times."

LEONARD BERNSTEIN (1918–) In 1958, this son of Russian-Jewish immigrants became the first American-born musician to head a major American orchestra, when he succeeded Dimitri Mitropoulos as musical director of the New York Philharmonic Symphony Orchestra.

Bernstein made his first New York appearance as a conductor three years after graduating from Harvard. Two years later, in 1944, he composed the music for *Fancy Free*, Jerome Robbins' ballet, which eventually was revamped as the Broadway musical *On the Town*. Besides a successful career as a symphony orchestra conductor, Bernstein has composed musical scores for Broadway shows (*Wonderful Town*, 1953; *West Side Story*, 1957), films (*On the Waterfront*, 1954), operas (*Trouble in Tahiti*, 1952) and his controversial *Mass*, which opened the John F. Kennedy Center for the Performing Arts in Washington, D.C., in 1971.

EUBIE BLAKE (1883–) One of the oldest living performers in America, Black pianist-composer Eubie Blake has been tickling the ivories for over 75 years. When he was 95 he saw a revue of his career open on Broadway. Will Eubie keep going, playing and performing, until he's 100? "I don't know nothing else but how to write and play music and I'll never quit until the man counts 8, 9, 10 and waves me out."

Despite his fame and wealth, Eubie lives, not on Manhattan's fashionable East Side, but in Brooklyn's Black ghetto — Bedford-Stuyvesant. Why? "Here I'm somebody. If I lived on Park Avenue people might think I was just another hustler or something like that. Besides, when I got married more than 30 years ago, my father-in-law owned this house. All I had to do was take off my hat and walk in." (*Newsweek*)

SAMMY CAHN (1913–   ), a German-Jewish songwriter, quips that his mother was known as the " 'Jewish Lourdes' — because people always came to her with their problems." His original name was Sammy Cohen, but he changed it twice — to Kahn, and then to Cahn to avoid confusion with another songwriter name Kahn. He studied violin and, after quitting school, played at "borscht belt" resorts in the Catskills and in Bowery burlesque houses. Cahn wrote his first song at the age of 16 — "Like Niagara Falls, I'm Falling For You," — but it wasn't until 1935 that he wrote his first hit. "Rhythm Is Our Business," with Saul Chaplin. With Jule Styne he wrote "I'll Walk Alone," "Saturday Night is the Loneliest Night in the Week," "Five Minutes More," "The Things We Did Last Summer" and "Let It Snow! Let It Snow! Let It Snow!" and during his association with Jimmy Van Heusen, Cahn wrote the lyrics to "The Tender Trap," "Love and Marriage," "High Hopes" and "Call me Irresponsible."

RAY CHARLES (1932–   ) dropped his last name, Robinson, when he began to perform professionally, to avoid being confused with the fighter, "Sugar" Ray Robinson. Born in Albany, Georgia, Ray Charles was totally blind by the age of seven. He attended St. Augustine School for the Blind in Florida, where he learned to read Braille, to play the piano and the clarinet and to memorize music.

Orphaned at the age of 17, the Black musician supported himself by traveling with hillbilly bands and rhythm and blues combos throughout the South. His first album was recorded in 1954, and in 1961 *Down Beat* magazine voted him America's leading male vocalist for his unique style of combining gospel music and the blues.

GEORGE M. COHAN (1878–1942) Despite the song he wrote and made famous ("I'm a Yankee Doodle Dandy"), Cohan was *not* born on the fourth of July. He was born on July 3, but his patriotic father changed the official record to read July 4. Despite his Jewish-sounding last name, Cohan was a full-blooded Irish-American, whose original family name was Keohane (pronounced Ca-han or Co-han).

He wrote such famous songs as "Over There" (1917), "You're a Grand Old Flag," "Forty-Five Minutes from Broadway" and "Give My Regards to Broadway."

PERRY COMO (1913–   ) The seventh son of a seventh son and one of 13 offspring, Pierino Roland Como started his working life as a barber before touring with Ted Weems' band in 1934. In the 1950s he became a popular TV personality, known for his casual, relaxed, "laid back" style.

BING CROSBY (1904–1977) made "crooning" world famous when he stepped up to the microphones of America in the 1930s. Between 1931 and 1957 he recorded some 850 songs and sold more than 300 million records. It was fitting for Bing, an Irish Catholic, to win an Academy Award for his priestly role in *Going My Way* in 1944.

LEOPOLD (1832–1885) AND WALTER DAMROSCH (1862–1950), the musical father-and-son team from Breslau, Germany, emigrated to the United States in 1871. The father, Leopold, founded the New York Symphony Society in 1879, and his son, Walter, established the Damrosch Opera Company in 1895 for the sole purpose of introducing Wagnerian operas to the American public. When Leopold died in 1885, Walter succeeded him as conductor of the New York Symphony. Today, Damrosch Park at Lincoln Center commemorates this musical family's contribution to New York's cultural development.

DUKE ELLINGTON (1899–1977) has been called the "greatest single talent in the history of jazz." Born Edward Kennedy Ellington, Duke gained fame as a band leader and composer. Some of the best-known works of this Black musician are "Mood Indigo" and "Solitude."

ARTHUR FIEDLER (1894–1979), the son of Austrian-Jewish immigrants, came from a long line of musicians. Most of his ancestors had been violinists — hence the surname "Fiedler," which comes from the German for "fiddler." Arthur took violin lessons as a child, but he viewed his early musical education as ". . . a chore, something I had to do, like brushing my teeth." (New York *Times*, April 2, 1972). After a brief career in the publishing field, Fiedler was swayed to follow in the footsteps of his ancestors, and in 1911 he was accepted into Berlin's Royal Academy of Music.

Fiedler debuted as a conductor at the age of 17. He conducted his first performance of the Boston Pops Orchestra in 1926, and in 1930 he became the Pops' permanent conductor—one of the few American-born maestros of his day. For almost five decades Fiedler conducted the Pops orchestra for the listening pleasure of radio, television and concert audiences.

GEORGE   GERSHWIN   (1898–1937) The famed composer was born Jacob Gershwin, but his Russian immigrant parents always called him "George." His first hit song was "Swanee," written with lyricist Irving Caesar. The duo composed it in about 15 minutes, introduced it to Al Jolson and became internationally famous as a result of the 1 million copies of sheet music and over 2 million records they sold.

Some of his most famous works include: "Embraceable You," "I Got Rhythm," "Love Walked In," "S' Wonderful" and "Rhapsody in Blue." His musical, *Of Thee I Sing* (1931) became the first musical ever to win a Pulitzer Prize; and his Negro folk opera, *Porgy and Bess*, has enjoyed many revivals on both the stage and the screen since it was introduced in 1935.

BENNY GOODMAN (1909–   ) was the first white bandleader to employ Black musicians in his band. He also made his name in "swing" by using the arrangements of a Black musician, Fletcher Henderson. Benjamin David Goodman was the eighth of eleven children born to impoverished Russian-Jewish parents. Benny notes of his childhood: "I can remember a time when we lived in a basement without heat during the winter, and a couple of times when there wasn't anything to eat."

He learned music at the Kehelah Jacob Synagogue, where lessons and instruments for rental cost only about 25¢ per week. Why did he take up the clarinet? It was strictly a matter of size and age! When Benny went to the synagogue in 1919 with his two older brothers, Harry (12) was given a tuba; Freddie, the middle brother (11) was given a trumpet. Benny, the youngest (10), was given a clarinet.

OSCAR HAMMERSTEIN II (1895–1960) collaborated with Jerome Kern on the musical play *Show Boat*, which premiered in 1927. He later collaborated with Richard Rodgers on *Oklahoma* (1943), *Carousel* (1945), *South Pacific* (1949), *The King and I* (1951) and *The Sound of Music* (1959). But Oscar was not the first musical member of his family. His grandfather, Oscar Hammerstein (1847–1919) ran away from his home in Berlin at the age of 17 after his father beat him for skating instead of practicing the violin. Oscar sold his violin to pay for his passage to England, and from there he crewed on a ship bound for America to earn his fare to the New World.

Grandfather Hammerstein made a fortune in the tobacco business and used his profits to buy a part interest in two German-language theaters in New York. Between 1906 and 1910 his Manhattan Opera House rivaled the Metropolitan Opera House, which later bought out his interest with the stipulation that Hammerstein not produce any operas in the United States for ten years.

LORENZ HART (1895–1943) wrote almost 400 songs and 29 musicals in collaboration with Richard Rodgers (1902–   ). Rodgers later continued his career in collaboration with Oscar Hammerstein, writing such famous musicals as *Oklahoma* and *South Pacific*.

Lorenzo Milton Hart was born on New York's Upper East Side to German-Jewish immigrant parents, Frieda and Max Hertz, who had Americanized their last name to Hart.

JASCHA HEIFETZ (1901–   ), the Russian violin virtuoso, made his American debut at Carnegie Hall in 1917 at the age of 16. When asked about his life, after a career that had already spanned five decades, Heifetz remarked, "Here is my biography: I played the violin at three and gave my first concert at seven. I have been playing ever since."

VICTOR   HERBERT   (1859–1924) Composer of such famous operattas as *The Red Mill, Naughty Marietta,* and *Babes in Toyland,* Herbert also wrote musical scores for Ziegfeld revues and motion pictures of the early twentieth century. Born in Dublin, Ireland, and raised in London, Herbert acquired a love of music from his grandfather, who taught him Irish folk songs. By the time he was thirty he was considered to be one of the best cellists in the world, although he was to make his mark in another musical field.

SCOTT JOPLIN (1868–1917) The Black American "King of the Ragtime Composers" became a household word in America more than fifty years after his death. Joplin was born on November 24, 1868, in Texarkana, Texas, into a highly musical family. He began playing in cafés, brothels and saloons at the age of 14, and became famous for his syncopated rhythms (known as ragged time and later ragtime), but it wasn't until Joshua Rifkin recorded Joplin's rags in 1971 that a mass audience became familiar with his work. One of his most famous rags, "The Entertainer," was used as the theme for the hit movie *The Sting,* whose recorded sound track sold to the tune of 2,000,000 copies.

Unfortunately, Joplin never lived to enjoy the accolades of the public. He died in a mental hospital in New York, where he was committed after a nervous breakdown following the failure of his ragtime opera *Treemonisha,* about a Black woman who leads her people to freedom.

ANDRÉ KOSTELANETZ (1901–), inaugurated the "Promenade" series of concerts at Philharmonic Hall in New York in 1963. The son of wealthy Russian Jewish parents, Kostelanetz was born in St. Petersburg. The family fortune was lost in the Revolution of 1917, and when young André fled Russia in 1922 he had nothing but the clothes on his back.

During World War II, Kostelanetz trained GI orchestras in Europe and was awarded the Asia-Pacific campaign ribbon for his services. Over the years, André has sold some 52 million records and has conducted the orchestras of most major American cities.

LIBERACE (1919–) Half Polish and half Italian, with a name to match his ethnic heritage, Wladziu Valentino Liberace was a mere four years old when he began to play the piano by ear. Known as Walter to his school chums, Liberace began his career at the age of twelve playing in beer joints to earn money for his family. His glittering clothes and flashy style have earned him continued popularity.

GUY LOMBARDO (1902–1977) Born Gaetano Albert Lombardo in Ontario, Canada, Guy came from a musical family. His father, an Italian immigrant, encouraged all of his children to study music, and "because he was the oldest" Guy's first instrument was the violin. Still, it was as a band leader, not a violinist, that he achieved fame in show business. The beloved "Mr. New Year's Eve" led his orchestra on that night every year for almost half a century.

HENRY MANCINI (1924–) A native of Cleveland, Ohio, Italian-American Mancini is famous for his film scores and theme music. Some of his most familiar works are "The Pink Panther," "Days of Wine and Roses," "Charade," "Peter Gunn," "Mr. Lucky" and "The Glenn Miller Story."

CHUCK MANGIONE (1941–) In 1978, Chuck Mangione's album, *Feels So Good,* became one of the biggest jazz "cross-over" albums in recording history. Such high sales are most unusual for a jazz recording artist, and that album propelled Chuck and his group into the world of popular music.

Until recently, Mangione claimed he only played clubs where "music was the third reason" people came there—most patrons were only interested in drinking and meeting friends. He hopes his newfound success will change all that.

Was his family musical? Not really. His father claims, "I played the cash register so I could put my three children through college." But on weekends, after a hard week at his Rochester, New York, grocery store, Papa Mangione would take his sons to the local jazz clubs to listen to the greats play. Afterward he would invite the likes of Dizzy Gillespie and Cannonball Adderly to come back to his home for a real Italian dinner and a jam session, so Chuck and his brothers got to jam with the greatest right in their own living room.

ZUBIN MEHTA (1936–) A native of Bombay, India, Mehta became musical director of the Los Angeles Symphony in 1962. His youth, good looks and reputation as a "ladies' man" earned him the nickname "Zubie Baby." In 1978, Mehta became conductor of the New York Philharmonic.

GIANCARLO MENOTTI (1911–)
Born near Milan, Italy, Menotti came to the
United States in 1928, where he became a
musical man for all seasons. Two of his
operas, *The Consul* and *The Saint of
Bleecker Street,* have won Pulitzer Prizes,
and his highly influential Festival of Two
Worlds at Spoleto, Italy, has recently
spawned an American offshoot. The yearly
Spoleto Festival, USA, in Charleston,
South Carolina, features operas, chamber
concerts, dance programs and musicals.

CHARLIE MINGUS (1924–1979)
Nicknamed "Jazz's Angry Man" because
of his rage over racial inequities, Charlie
Mingus grew up in the Watts ghetto of Los
Angeles. His "passport" out of the ghetto
was his bass fiddle, which he plucked with
some of the greatest names in jazz—Lionel
Hampton, Charlie Parker and Duke Ellington. According to Mingus: "Blues is a way
of life. Society may lay it on you. Blues is a
way of yelling back." In his autobiography,
Beneath the Underdog, the "angry man"
claimed: Jazz is "the American Negro's
tradition . . . White people don't have a right
to play it." But, despite his remarks, Mingus
often used white musicians in his bands—
referring to them as "colorless."

BORRAH MINEVITCH (1902–1955)
Born in Kiev, Russia, in 1902, the youngest
of seven children, Borrah became one of the
most famous harmonica players in the
world in the early 1930s. He received up to
$3,200 a week for performing on stage, and
as a result of his influence, sales of har-
monicas jumped to 30,000,000 per year
within five years of his stage debut.

With his harmonica, Borrah could play
such complicated arrangements as *Rhapsody in Blue, Liebestraum* and even *An
American in Paris.* In 1934 he founded the
Harmonica Institute of America, where he
taught New Yorkers the fundamentals in
four easy lessons. According to Borrah,
"Half the world plays a harmonica, and the
other half wishes it could."

DIMITRI MITROPOULOS (1896–
1960) Mitropoulos emigrated to the
United States in 1936 after enjoying a fine
reputation as a conductor in Europe. Born
in Athens and educated in Berlin, Mitropoulos once dreamed of becoming a
Greek Orthodox monk. But, when he
learned that the religious order forbids the
use of musical instruments, Dimitri decided

he could not bear a life devoid of music, and
he began devoting himself to the piano instead of the priesthood.

At the age of 10, Mitropoulos had already
mastered the scores of *Faust* and *Rigo-
letto.* By the time he was 20, he had composed his first opera, *Sister Beatrice.*
He emigrated to the United States at the
age of 40 and became a citizen in 1946.
During his career as a symphony conductor, Mitropoulos conducted the Minneapolis Symphony from 1936 to 1949 and
the New York Philharmonic from 1949 to
1958.

ELVIS PRESLEY (1935–1977) Elvis
proved "WASPs have rhythm too" when he
electrified the world with his nonstop pelvis
in the late 1950s. Elvis' first ancestor in
America is believed to have been Andrew
Presley, Sr., a Scottish immigrant who came
to America in 1745, settled in Anson
County, North Carolina, and supported his
family by working as a blacksmith.

SERGEI VASSILIEVICH RACH-
MANINOFF (1873–1943) became a U.S.
citizen a few months prior to his death in
1943. A graduate of the Moscow Conserva-
tory, Rachmaninoff was awarded a gold
medal in 1892 for his one-act opera, *Aleko.*
Some of Rachmaninoff's most famous
works are *Prelude in C Sharp Minor*(1892),
Second Piano Concerto (1901) and *Rhapsody on a Theme by Paganini* (1934). Rachmaninoff's *Second Piano Concerto* is better
known to popular music fans as "Full Moon
and Empty Arms."

JOE RAPOSO (1937–) If you
know any preschool children, you've probably heard Joe Raposo's most famous theme
song, "Sesame Street." A Portuguese-
American from the city of Fall River, Massachusetts, Raposo was urged to study
medicine by his parents even though they
taught him to play the piano, violin, bass
viola and guitar. But, as Joe put it: "I
couldn't stand the sight of blood, so I went
to Harvard to become a lawyer." Side-
tracked by his love of music, he abandoned
his law studies in 1959 to concentrate on
composing.

Besides the theme songs for *Sesame
Street* and *The Electric Company,* Raposo
has written many of the Muppets' best-
selling hits. Most recently, three-quarters of
a million copies of *Sesame Street Fever,* a
disco record for tots, have been sold. The

album features "Loveable Grover" on the cover, decked out in a white suit à la John Travolta. "Cross-over" hits into the adult world include "Bein' Green," "Sing" and "You Will Be My Music."

BUFFY SAINTE-MARIE (1941–) A Cree Indian folksinger who rose to fame in the 1960s, Buffy is now married to a Sioux (Sheldon Wolfchild), and has become a regular on *Sesame Street* with her son, Dakota Starblanket Wolfchild, who's called "Cody" for short. Instead of "protest songs" and love songs (she wrote "Until It's Time for You To Go"), Buffy is singing her ABC's for the tots of America.

ARTUR RUBINSTEIN (1885–) Artur's parents gave him a violin when he was only three years of age. After Artur smashed it to smithereens, his parents decided he should take lessons on a more durable instrument – the piano. By the time Artur was five, he was performing at charity concerts in his native Poland. At the age of 12, Rubinstein appeared as a soloist with the Berlin Symphony Orchestra; he toured the United States for the first time in 1906. One of America's greatest pianists, Rubinstein became a U.S. citizen in 1946.

NEIL SEDAKA (1939–) Neil's parents were Sephardic Jews who emigrated from Istanbul, Turkey, to Brooklyn's Brighton Beach section. Neil studied piano and was accepted as a scholarship student to the preparatory division of the prestigious Juilliard School of Music at the tender age of nine. He started his pop-music writing career in the early 1960s and has written such famous hits as "Calendar Girl," "Oh Carol" and "The Immigrant."

JOHN PHILIP SOUSA (1854– 1932) Known as the "March King," Sousa was one of the Marine Corps's most famous bandleaders, serving from 1880 to 1892.

His father, Joao de Sousa, changed his name to John Sousa when he emigrated to the United States from Portugal. He, too, was a musician with the U.S. Marine Band, and when his son, John Philip, threatened to run away and join the circus at the age of thirteen, Papa Sousa enlisted him as a boy musician with the Marines.

Sousa went on to write more than 100 marches for the Marines, including *"Semper Fidelis,"* "The Washington Post March" and "Stars and Stripes Forever."

He also served as bandmaster for the U.S. Navy from 1917 to 1919. Sousa wrote the operetta *El Capitan* in 1896 and "The Chariot Race" (Houdini's theme song). The Sousaphone, a modified tuba that diffuses the sound over the musician's head, instead of having it project straight ahead, was patterned after designs suggested by Sousa.

"The March King," John Philip Sousa. (Courtesy: New York Public Library)

WILLIAM GRANT STILL (1895– 1978), "the dean of Black classical composers," became the first Black musician to conduct a major American orchestra when he led the Los Angeles Philharmonic in 1936 at the Hollywood Bowl.

Born in Woodville, Mississippi, Still learned to play the violin, cello and oboe as a young boy. His most famous work is the *Afroamerican Symphony* (1931). Other orchestral and choral works by Still include *Symphony in G Minor,* "And They Lynched Him in a Tree," "The Colored Soldiers Who Died for Democracy," "From the Delta" and "Songs of Separation."

LEOPOLD STOKOWSKI (1882–1977) brought classical music to the masses when he conducted the soundtrack for Walt Disney's *Fantasia* in 1941. Born in London of Polish and Irish parentage, Stokowski came to the United States at the age of 23 and became a citizen in 1915. His American career spanned 7 decades and more than 7,000 performances. Stokowski conducted the Philadelphia Orchestra for 27 years, and also led the NBC Symphony and the American Symphony Orchestra.

IGOR FYODOROVICH STRAVINSKY (1882–1971) fled his native Russia in 1914 and settled in Switzerland. Later he made his way to the United States, where he became a naturalized citizen in 1945. Stravinsky's most famous ballets include *The Firebird* (1910) and *The Rite of Spring* (1931). His symphonies and sonatas were also internationally acclaimed.

ELIZABETH SWADOS (1951–) presented her musical, *Runaways,* at Joseph Papp's Public Theater Cabaret in 1978. One of New York's youngest composers, Swados learned to play the piano at the age of five and was performing as a folk singer by the time she turned twelve.

Elizabeth Swados was born to a musical family. Her Jewish ancestors can trace their roots back to Vilna, Lithuania, where the family name was spelled Swiadisch. Liz's first theatrical work was *Nightclub Cantata,* which became an off-Broadway hit during the 1977 season.

DIMITRI TIOMKIN (1899–1979), the Russian-born composer of film scores, won four Oscars during his forty-year career in Hollywood. Altogether, Tiomkin composed the music for 160 film scores, yet he once complained that writing music for films was "like putting herring together with sugar." Despite his laments, Tiomkin enjoyed his work and won Academy Awards for the musical scores for *High Noon* (1952), *The High and the Mighty* (1954), *The Old Man and the Sea* (1958) and *The Alamo* (1960).

ARTURO TOSCANINI (1867–1957) conducted the Metropolitan Opera between 1908 and 1915. He returned to his native Italy to conduct at La Scala, but when Fascists gained control of the government Toscanini returned to the United States. He became principal conductor of the New York Philharmonic, and director of the NBC Symphony Orchestra, which was created especially for him by the network.

SOPHIE TUCKER (1884–1966) was "the Last of the Red Hot Mamas." Although she was born Sophie Kalish, she grew up with an italian last name — Abuza — thanks to her father, who fled Russia to avoid military service and took on the identity of a deceased Italian friend. He eventually became a restaurant owner in Hartford, Connecticut, and was dead set against a career in show business for his daughter. Undaunted, Sophie set off for New York in 1906 with her eye on the vaudeville stage. Her best ethnic record? "My Yiddishe Momme."

LESLIE UGGAMS (1943–) has African, Scotch, Irish, Cherokee and Seminole Indian ancestry. This singer's unusual surname is said to be derived from an Indian word meaning "sweet one."

KURT WEILL (1900–1950) composed the music for the *Threepenny Opera (Die Dreigroschenoper)* in 1928, prior to emigrating to the United States with his wife, Lotte Lenya. The son of a Jewish cantor, born in Dessau, Germany, Weill studied music under the famous composer Engelbert Humperdinck at the Staatliche Hochschule für Musik in Berlin. While in the United States, Weill composed movie scores, including the music for the films *One Touch of Venus* and *Lost in the Stars.* He became a U.S. citizen in 1943.

LAWRENCE WELK (1903– bought his first accordion with $15 he earned by trapping muskrats and weasels near his North Dakota home. Born in a sod house to immigrant parents from Strasbourg, on the border of France and Germany, Welk was a failure at farming. He couldn't milk cows, was sickened at the slaughter of animals and once broke his arm while attempting to plow a field. He spoke German during most of his youth and, according to his brother, "he really didn't speak English until he was twenty-one and got away from here."

A recent article by music critic John Rockwell posed the question, "Is segregation coming to the rock world?" Citing statistics that appeared in *Cash Box* magazine, a trade publication for the music industry, Rockwell noted that at the end of 1975 some 42% of the top 40 singles were recorded by Black artists. At the end of 1976, that figure was down to 20% and by the end of 1977 the number of Black artists in the top 40 had declined to 12.5%. In other words, records by Black artists were now "crossing over" to the mass market, or predominantly white audiences, less frequently.

There aren't any hard statistics on the racial makeup of pop-music concert patrons, but Rockwell contends that there has been a noticeable decline in the number of whites at concerts given by Black artists.

INSTRUMENTAL ETHNICS

Three of the most famous names in musical instruments belong to German immigrants: Martin, Steinway and Wurlitzer.

ELVIS HAD ONE The nation's oldest and, many claim, finest guitar manufacturing firm is C. F. Martin and Company, named after Christian Frederick Martin, a guitar maker who emigrated to America from Saxony in 1833. He settled in New York City at first, but when a fellow German immigrant suggested he move to Nazareth, Pennsylvania, Martin jumped at the chance. In 1978 there were four generations of Martins and 180 employees turning out about 75 guitars each day.

Martin guitars have the sound of success associated with each strum, and considering that their medium-priced Dreadnought 35 model costs almost $1,000, it's not hard to figure out why such folk and country music greats as Bob Dylan; Judy Collins; Peter, Paul and Mary; Johnny Cash; Charlie Pride; Hank Snow; and even the singing cowboy, Gene Autry, all have owned a Martin.

PIANO MAN Heinrich Englehard Steinweg was born in Wolfshagen, Germany, in 1797. He fashioned his first piano in 1836, as a "hobby," building it in the kitchen of his home. In 1839 he won a state prize for his handiwork. When the revolution of 1848 drove one of his sons to America, Henry followed with his family and arrived in New York in 1850.

He Americanized the family name to Steinway and opened his first factory four years later. Four generations of Steinways have been producing pianos for the concert halls of the world since 1854. Dur-

THE STEINWAY DYNASTY

Three generations of Steinways. From the left: Theodore E. Steinway; his son Henry Z. Steinway; and the company's founder, Henry Engelhard Steinway. (Courtesy; Steinway)

ing World War II, the armed forces ordered some 3,000 "GI pianos" — uprights painted in fatigue green — which made their way to combat zones all over the world.

WURLITZER Rudolph Wurlitzer (1831–1914) founded the company that bears his name in Cincinnati, Ohio, in 1856, three years after he emigrated to America from his native Schoeneck, Germany.

A thrifty man, Rudolph made it a point to save one-fourth of his earnings — even from a meager weekly salary of $4 that he earned as a porter in a dry goods store in Cincinnati. He later doubled his salary by working as a bank clerk, and soon he was saving $2 each week. By 1856 he had amassed a small fortune, $700; he sent the money to his native Germany, where family connections purchased fine-quality handcrafted musical instruments for him. By eliminating the middlemen, Wurlitzer was able to make a name for himself in the musical world, selling quality instruments at popular prices.

Wurlitzer manufactured his first "Wurlitzer" piano in 1880. The first coin-operated music box was sold in 1896; the first 10-tune juke box in 1934; the electronic organ in 1947; and the electronic piano in 1954. The company also has the honor of having produced the world's largest theater organ, currently housed at Radio City Music Hall.

DANCIN'

Many of the dances Americans love best, such as the Charleston, Cake Walk, Turkey Trot, Fox Trot, Shimmy, Black Bottom, Lindy Hop and Jitterbug originated in the Black American community before the rest of America adopted these popular steps and gave them fancy names.

Many more dances were imported from the "other side" for Americans to enjoy: The Waltz came from Germany; the Czechs gave us the Polka; and the French gave America the Bolero. We learned to do the Fandango from the Spanish, and the people of Argentina gave us the Tango. In fact, most of the popular dance steps that became faddish from the 1920s through the 1950s were imports from Latin countries.

This music cover acknowledges the Black invention of the Cake Walk, but portrays Black Americans in terms of crude caricatures. (Courtesy: New York Historical Society)

In the late 1920s we imported the Rhumba from Cuba and Cha-Cha-Cha'd to the music of Xavier Cugat, the Barcelona-born, Cuban-raised bandleader with a fondness for Mexican chihuahuas and younger women. Another Cuban bandleader, Desi Arnaz, introduced the Conga to Miami in 1938—but that was only the start of America's love affair with Latin rhythms.

In 1939, thousands of visitors who flocked to the New York World's Fair were introduced to the latest dance craze from Brazil, the Samba. And during the 1950s we brought La Pachanga the Mambo and the Merengue to the dance floors of America.

The Merengue, national dance of the Dominican Republic, is said to have originated with a crippled general who was forced to limp his way across the dance floor. Other dancers began to imitate the manner in which the General dragged his lame foot from one side to the other and the unique side-swaying motion of the Merengue was born.

Perez Prado, a Cuban musician, introduced the Mambo to American dancers in the mid-1950s and in 1959 La Pachanga made its way to America from Havana. La Pachanga was inspired by a song written by Cuban musician Eduardo Davidson and popularized in Havana by local *charanga* groups. It combined the best elements of the merengue, samba, Charleston and bunny hop, but was so energetic that it was banned from many nightclubs. The owners of Roseland, New York's largest dance hall, prohibited patrons from dancing La Pachanga at their establishment for fear that the floor would cave in if everyone "pachanga-ed" at once.

Besides contributing their folk dances and ballroom sensations for all of us to enjoy, the nations of the world also contributed their sons and daughters to the theaters and dance halls of America:

ABDULLAH JAFFA ANVER BEY

KHAN   Born in Seattle to an Afghan father and an Italian mother, Abdullah Khan (1930–   ) began studying ballet as a young boy to help improve an asthmatic condition. (His father also made him take boxing lessons, to help him "defend himself" against the insults of his "macho" friends.) When Abdullah moved to New York at the age of 18 to study at the School of American Ballet, he Americanized his name to Robert Joffrey.

Joffrey founded the American Ballet Center in 1953, and by 1962, after completing six national tours, the Joffrey ballet became totally self-supporting – a rare occurrence in the precarious world of dance. In 1966, after a brief association with the Harkness Foundation, the Joffrey Ballet became the official resident company of New York's City Center.

Joffrey believes that boys should be encouraged to dance at an earlier age in the United States. According to Joffrey, if more youngsters began studying at the age of eight, the United States could produce its own Baryshnikovs in the near future.

GEORGE BALANCHINE   The son of a Russian composer, Georgi Melitonovitch Balanchivadze was born in St. Petersburg in 1904 and entered the Imperial Ballet School at the age of ten. Although his slight build hampered him as a young dancer, Balanchine's talents as a choreographer were already developing.

In 1933, George emigrated to the United States at the suggestion of Lincoln Kirstein, a wealthy ballet enthusiast, and established the School of American Ballet. Considered one of the finest choreographers of our time, Balanchine believes his craft is of supreme importance to the dancer: "Ballet . . . is a pleasure. No one would enjoy watching a group of dancers jump about the stage aimlessly, no matter how well they jumped. After all, a pig can jump – but who wants to see a pig jump?"

Besides building the New York City Ballet into one of America's leading companies, Balanchine has published his *Complete Stories of the Great Ballets* for the enjoyment of armchair dancers.

BANANAS LAUNCHED HER CAREER   Josephine Baker (1906–1975) started her career as a chorus girl in a "colored show" in Paris. Billed as "Dark Star" at the Folies Bergère, Josephine became a European sensation when she appeared on stage clad only in a string of rubber bananas slung about her hips. Langston Hughes, the Black poet, recalled that "there was something about her rhythm, her warmth, her smile and her impudent grace that made her stand out." All through the 1920s Josephine continued to attract attention by dancing in feathers, furs, body stockings sprinkled with rhine-stones, and other costumes that were considered quite scandalous in her day.

Besides dancing her way to fame, Baker also worked with the French Resistance during World War II. In the best spy-story tradition, Josephine smuggled secret information, written in invisible ink on her sheet music, to General De Gaulle.

After commenting that "The United States is not a free country. . . . They treat Negroes as though they were dogs," Baker was labeled a "communist" by columnist Walter Winchell in the 1950s. Baker had her own ideas about "international relations" and over the years she adopted 12 children from all over the world. She called her African, Japanese, Arab, Israeli, Korean, Colombian, Finnish, French and Venezuelan Indian children "the rainbow tribe."

UP FROM THE CHORUS LINE   Michael Bennett (1943–   ), an Italian-American from Buffalo, New York, was only 17 when he danced in his first Broadway show, *Subways Are for Sleeping*. His early years in New York as a struggling young dancer yearning for the lights of Broadway provided a rich source of inspiration for the Tony award-winning musical hit, *A Chorus Line*, which he directed. Born out of tape-recorded conversations with other dancers, *A Chorus Line* has been called this generation's *Forty-Second Street*, providing a behind the scenes look at the world of dance.

HEAR THE BEAT, OF DANCING FEET . . .   The star of that classic movie musical, *Forty-Second Street*, was Ruby Keeler (1910–   ), a dancer from Halifax, Nova Scotia. Keeler became a dancer while still in high school – not because she loved to dance, but simply because it was the only job she could find that permitted her to attend classes in the day. She started dancing at a speakeasy to supplement her family's income, and in 1933 she danced her way to Hollywood stardom in *Forty-Second Street*, the first of nine films she made.

She married Al Jolson in 1928, and divorced him twelve years later. When Columbia Pictures made *The Jolson Story* in 1947, Ruby refused to grant the producers permission to mention her name in the film.

DANCE INSTRUCTIONS BY MAIL America's most famous dance instructor, Arthur Murray (1895–   ), was born on the Lower East Side of New York, the son of Austrian immigrants. As a youngster, Arthur was tall, gawky and shy, so he took dance lessons to improve his grace and deportment.

Murray won his first dance contest while still in high school, and soon he was earning money teaching classmates the steps to the Maxixe, Castle Walk, One Step and other popular dances of his day.

He established the Arthur Murray Correspondence School of Dancing in the early 1920s and, without the benefit of television advertising, Murray managed to sell almost 500,000 dance instruction packets through the mail. He later established a chain of dance studios, and during the 1950s Murray and his diminutive wife, Kathryn, danced their way into the hearts of American viewers via their weekly TV show.

THE HULA IS NOT THE "HOOTCHY-KOOTCHY" Iolani Luahine (1915–1978) continually stressed the fact that the hula, Hawaii's traditional dance, which blends poetry, music and dance forms, bears little resemblance to the gyrating versions performed in carnival sideshows.

Generally regarded as the last great exponent of the sacred hula ceremony, Iolani, whose name means "Heavenly Bird," was the granddaughter of a dancer at the court of King Kalakaua. According to Hawaiian traditions, Iolani was set apart by her birthright as a *kapu,* or sacred dancer. As an infant, she was sent to Honolulu to live and study with her great-aunt, Keahi Luahine Sylvester, from whom Iolani learned the steps and *mele* (chants) that are part of the hula.

Originally intended as a dance to praise both gods and rulers, the hula lost its last great dancer in 1978 when Iolani died, taking a bit of Hawaii's history and tradition with her.

HOEDOWN AT THE WHITE HOUSE When China's Vice Premier Deng Xioping visited the United States in 1979, part of the entertainment scheduled for his pleasure included dance selections from the ballet *Rodeo.* Created by choreographer Agnes De Mille, *Rodeo* features cowboy-attired dancers performing both ballet and tap-dancing routines.

Of Dutch ancestry, Agnes De Mille is the niece of movie producer Cecil B. De Mille, and it was at his invitation that she first ventured to Hollywood in 1934 to dance in one of his productions. Agnes became the world's youngest choreographer in 1929 when she composed her first professional dances at the tender age of 20. She was the first to bring ballet to Broadway when she choreographed the musical production of grapher Anges De Mille, *Rodeo* features *Oklahoma* in 1942. De Mille's other works include *Carousel, Brigadoon* and *Paint Your Wagon.*

First LADY OF MODERN DANCE Martha Graham (1894?–   ), the most famous choreographer and teacher of modern dance in the United States, has been performing for more than half a century. She was one of the first dancers to use her entire body to reveal the innermost feelings of the characters she portrayed, and when she first appeared on stage in the 1920s audiences were often shocked at her angular poses and short, choppy motions.

Born in a suburb of Pittsburgh, Graham is able to trace her ancestry on her mother's side all the way back to Miles Standish, the English colonist whose love life was immortalized in Henry Wadsworth Longfellow's narrative poem, *The Courtship of Miles Standish.*

OSAGE BALLERINA Maria Tallchief (1925–   ) is one of the few American ballerinas who can claim American Indian ancestry. Born to an Osage father and a Scotch-Irish mother, both Maria and her sister Marjorie (also a ballerina) spent part of their youth on a reservation, though she later moved to Los Angeles and graduated from Beverly Hills High School.

She made her debut with the Ballet Russe de Monte Carlo in 1942, but left that troupe five years later to join her husband, George Balanchine, in the newly formed New York City Ballet. Her marriage to Balanchine ended in 1951, and in the 1960s she gave up her stage career to devote her time to teaching.

WEST SIDE STORY When Jerome Rabinowitz (1918–   ) changed his name to Jerome Robbins in the 1940s his immigrant Russian-Jewish father followed suit and changed his surname to Robbins as well.

Robbins' first ballet, *Fancy Free*, received 20 curtain calls when it debuted in 1944, and went on to become a musical movie entitled *On the Town*—the story of three sailors set loose in New York City. *Fancy Free* Was Robbins' first collaborative effort with Leonard Bernstein; in 1962, the duo won kudos for *West Side Story*—a modern-day *Romeo and Juliet*.

Robbins' other choreography for stage and film includes *High Button Shoes, Call Me Madam, The King and I, Fiddler on the Roof, The Pajama Game, Peter Pan* and *Bells Are Ringing.*

MEXICAN DANCER José Limón (1908–1972) was born in Culiacán, Sinaloa, Mexico, but his family moved to Arizona when he was a child. José spent most of his youth in Los Angeles studying painting, not dance. He did not begin to study his craft seriously until he was 20—a rather advanced age for a dancer. After serving in World War II, Limón founded his own dance company and began choreographing his own works. "I try to compose works that are involved with man's basic tragedy and the grandeur of his spirit," Limón once said.

Despite his late entry into the field of dance, Limón developed great technical skill as a performer. Still performing during the seventh decade of his life, he kept his 6'1" frame at a lean 165 pounds. Some of Limón's most famous works, many of which have been broadcast over the National Educational Television Network, in-

"Little Egypt's" gyrations shocked fairgoers at St. Louis in 1893 when she introduced the masses to the fine art of Middle Eastern "belly" dancing. (Courtesy: New York Historical Society)

clude *The Moor's Pavane* (a dance version of Shakespeare's *Othello*), *The Traitor* (based on the life of Judas Iscariot) and *There Is a Time* (based on the Book of Ecclesiastes).

ARTISTS, SCULPTORS AND DESIGNERS

JOSEF ALBERS (1888–1976) Born in Bottrop, Germany, Albers came to the United States in 1933, and had his first one-man show in 1936. His most famous series of paintings is probably "Homage to the Square." Albers taught art at Black Mountain State College in North Carolina during the 1930s and was a professor at Yale from 1950 to 1960.

OTHMAR H. AMMANN (1879–1965), an American of Swiss origin, designed the Verrazano Narrows Bridge (4,260 feet), the longest single-span suspension bridge in the world. Ammann also designed the George Washington Bridge (3,500 feet) and the Lincoln Tunnel (2.5 miles), which span the Hudson River between New York and New Jersey.

A Josef Albers lithograph, dated 1942.
(Courtesy: German Information Center)

FREDERICK AUGUSTE BARTH-OLDI Born in France, Bartholdi never even visited America, but his major work is one of our best-known and most beloved statues: "Liberty Enlightening the World," better known as the Statue of Liberty. Dedicated in 1886, Ms. Liberty is made of copper sheeting welded over an iron-and-steel framework which was designed by Gustav Eiffel, the Frenchman who created the Eiffel Tower. Bartholdi chose his mother's face to adorn his 151'1" creation (from torch to toe), but it was his mistress's body that was the model for our lady of the harbor.

HARRY BERTOIA (1915–1978) was an Italian immigrant sculptor born in San Lorenzo, Italy, who also designed furniture, jewelry, fountains and other architectural works for public buildings. One of his outstanding pieces is "Golden Screen," a metal sculpture 70 feet long and 15 feet high, whose 800 metal panels are held together by a web of steel bars. Bertoia's works are on view at the Museum of Modern Art, as well as at the Whitney and Guggenheim museums in New York.

JOHN GUTZON DE LA MOTHE BORGLUM (1871–1941) started carving the Mount Rushmore Memorial in 1927, but did not live to see his masterpiece finished. The son of Danish immigrants to Idaho, Borglum fortunately had a son of his own, Lincoln, who followed in his footsteps and finished carving the monument in the Black Hills of South Dakota after his father's death. Mount Rushmore contains the largest statuary figures in the world— George Washington's head along is as tall as most five-story buildings. The other presidents immortalized in granite are Thomas Jefferson, Theodore Roosevelt and Abraham Lincoln.

CONSTANTINO BRUMIDI (1805–1880) Born in Rome to an Italian mother and a Greek father, Brumidi was blacklisted in his native land for supporting Garibaldi during the revolution of 1848. In 1852 he set out for America in search of a new creative life and wound up spending 25 years working on the allegorical murals that cover the walls of the U.S. Capitol building in Washington, D.C.

PAUL CHAN may not be one of the biggest names in art, but he certainly is one of the world's "biggest" painters. A native of Hong Kong, Chan is a billboard artist in New York City who regularly paints likenesses of models and Broadway stars, filling spaces as large as 11,426 square feet. Some of his most famous posters were those commissioned for *The King and I* and *The Wiz.*

CHRISTO (1935–   ) This Bulgarian-born artist has been attracting much attention in the news media for his rather large "works of art." His "Running Fence" covered 24 miles of northern California with 2,000 panels of white woven nylon fabric, each 62 feet long and 18 feet high, for a cost of almost $2 million. Other projects include "Wrapped Walk Ways" (3 miles of Kansas City park trails covered with orange nylon) and "Valley Curtain," a 400-foot curtain in Colorado.

WILLEM DE KOONING (1904–   ) was born in the Netherlands and came to America in 1926, not as an immigrant but as an illegal alien. He settled in Hoboken, New Jersey, and later moved across the Hudson River to New York. For 35 years he never left the United States, for fear that he would not be readmitted. He was finally persuaded to fly to Canada, obtain a visa, and return to America to apply for citizenship. Two years later he was awarded the Medal of Freedom, our nation's highest civilian award, by President Johnson.

WILLIAM FRISMUTH, a German immigrant, is responsible for designing the upper part of the Washington Monument in 1884. The 100-ounce piece of aluminum that caps the monument was the largest single piece of that metal ever produced up to that date.

ARSHILE GORKY (1904–1948) Painter Arshile Gorky's story is a tragic one. Gorky was born in Armenia on the eve of the Turkish massacre. He and his mother did not follow his father to the United States in 1908, and as a result were trapped in the Armenian bloodbath. In 1919 his thirty-nine-year-old mother died of starvation in his arms. Gorky escaped to the United States the following year, where he memorialized the plight of his people through his paintings. He committed suicide in 1948.

WALTER GROPIUS (1883–1969), founder of the *Staatliches Bauhaus* at Weimar in 1919, is considered one of the great architects of all time. His theory was that form should follow function, and his most important advances were made in the areas of modern industrial design, city planning, and the design of everyday household items. Gropius' aim was to design objects that would be functional as well as attractive to the eye.

When the Nazis gained power in 1933 and decried the Bauhaus as an "incubator of cultural Bolshevism," Gropius fled to England. He later found his way to the United States, where the social climate was more hospitable to his design theories.

GEORG GROSZ (1893–1959) Born in Berlin, Grosz was famous for his satirical drawings and caricatures of German life—especially the vile aspects of upper class, military and political circles. He settled permanently in New York City in 1933 and became a U.S. citizen in 1938.

ALBERT HIRSCHFELD (1903–) When signing his caricatures of theatrical personalities, Hirschfeld usually adds a number to his name—sometimes 3, 5 or even 7. That number is a clue to the number of times the word "Nina" is intertwined among the pen lines that make up a character's face, hair or clothing.

Born in St. Louis of Russian descent, Hirschfeld studied at the Art Students League in New York, and has been penning theatrical personalities since the 1920s. He began adding his trademark to his work in 1945 when his daughter, Nina, was born.

BENJAMIN HENRY LATROBE (1764–1820), an English-born architect, emigrated to America in 1796. His buildings—the first of which was the Bank of Pennsylvania, in Philadelphia, completed in 1801—were the foremost examplars of the Greek revival style which dominated early nineteenth-century American architecture. Latrobe also supervised the rebuilding of the Capitol in 1814, and built the first Roman Catholic cathedral in the United States, completed in 1821 in Baltimore.

GUSTAV LINDENTHAL (1850–) was an Austrian-born bridge builder who designed the Manhattan Bridge and the Queesboro Bridge, major New York City arteries connecting Manhattan Island with Long Island. Lindenthal also designed and built the Hell Gate Bridge, one of the world's greatest steel-arch bridges.

JACQUES LIPCHITZ (1891–1973), an immigrant from Lithuania, studied sculpture in Paris and was influenced in his earlier works by Auguste Rodin. He later passed through periods of Cubism, Expressionism and, finally, Surrealism. Many of his sculptures depicted violent mythological themes and struggles. He left Paris in 1941 and became a U.S. citizen in 1957.

PETER MAX (1937–) became a household art word in the 1960s with his graphic designs. Born in Berlin and raised in Shanghai, Max was influenced by Eastern mysticism and his surrealistic, psychedelic patterns were an emblem of the consciousness-altering Sixties.

PIET MONDRIAN (1827–1944) Although Mondrian, a native of the Netherlands, died before he became a United States citizen, he did spend the last four years of his life in America.

His geometric, abstract art, which he termed Neoplasticism, was the inspiration for an entire school of imitators. One of his most famous works, "Broadway Boogie Woogie," was his response to the brightness of New York's night life during the early 1940s when he first arrived in this country.

LOUISE NEVELSON (1900–) emigrated to Rockland, Maine, from Kiev, Russia, in 1905 with her parents. Her father, a builder and real estate dealer, also ran a lumberyard, where Louise Berliawsky first learned to appreciate the beauty that might be sculpted from a plain block of virgin wood.

After marrying Charles Nevelson, Louise moved to New York in 1920 to study painting, drawing, voice and dramatics. She also studied at the Art Students League, but it wasn't until 1933 that she began to exhibit her sculptures. Nevelson has made liberal use of "found" objects over the years — such items as wheels, chair backs, furniture legs and the like. The reason? "I always wanted to show the world that art is everywhere." Another "reason for my use of 'found' materials is that I never could afford much else."

I. M. PEI (1917-   ) When Pei designed the National Gallery's new East Building in Washington, D.C., his main criterion was that it take no more than 45 minutes to see the exhibits. "In forty-five minutes one doesn't get bored, one's feet don't hurt, and one comes away with a sense of accomplishment." Born in China of well-to-do parents, Pei studied at MIT and Harvard under the tutelage of Walter Gropius, the founder of Bauhaus. In addition to the $95 million gallery, Pei has designed Syracuse's Everson Museum of Art; National Airlines' terminal at JFK Airport in New York and Boston's John Hancock building. He became a naturalized citizen in 1954.

PETER RINDISBACHER (1806–1834) Although he is not as well-known as George Catlin and other artists who painted the American West in the early nineteenth century, he was one of the first to paint native Americans. A Swiss immigrant who came to America at the age of fifteen, Rindisbacher died at the age of twenty-eight — some say it was cholera, others claim that he inadvertently poisoned himself by his habit of putting paintbrushes in his mouth to give them a better "point." Although his life was short, he left 187 known watercolor paintings that depict life on the American prairies in the early 1800s.

SIMON RODIA (1879–1965), an Italian immigrant, began constructing Los Angeles' most unusual artistic tourist attraction, the Watts Towers, in 1921. Threatened by demolition, the towers were saved by art buffs, who call the columns one of the most significant achievements of twentieth-century folk art. Rodia constructed the towers from concrete and steel, to which he added bits of tiles, bottles, dishes, seashells and other objects he could scavenge, simple because "he wanted to build something big for America."

MARK ROTHKO (1903–1970) Marcus Rothkowitz journeyed from his native Russia with his mother and sister in 1913 to join his father, a Jewish pharmacist who had already established a business in Portland, Oregon.

Rothko entered Yale in 1921, dropped out in 1923, and ended up at New York City's Art Student's League. After his first exhibition in 1929, this basically self-taught painter turned more and more toward abstraction — large canvasses characterized by diffuse rectangles of color. One critic wrote of Rothko's art, "I know that many people only find it an insult to their intelligence; but if by some miracle, Rothko's attitude to painting were to prevail, we should all be on the way to becoming converts to Zen Buddhism." (*Architectural Review,* Oct. 1957, R. Melville)

Rothko committed suicide in 1970, leaving behind 798 unsold paintings; their sale during the early 1970s erupted into a major scandal in the art world.

EERO SAARINEN (1910–1961) and his architect father, ELIEL (1873–1950), emigrated to the United States in 1923 from Kyrkslatt, Finland. Together they designed the giant stainless steel arch that rises 630 feet above the city of St. Louis, Missouri, as part of the Jefferson National Expansion Memorial. They are also the creators of the TWA terminal at Kennedy Airport in New York.

PAOLO SOLERI (1919-   ) is an Italian-born architect famous for his "earth homes" — structures that are half in the earth and half out, with soil roofs covered with concrete. Soleri coined the word "arcology" to describe his marriage of "architecture and ecology."

EDWARD STEICHEN (1879–1973), one of the photographic geniuses of all time, the man behind the 1955 Family of Man exhibit and best-selling book of the same name, was born, as few American immigrants have been, in the picturesque Grand Duchy of Luxembourg. Steichen was director of the department of photography of the Museum of Modern Art between 1947 and 1962.

JOSEPH BAERMAN STRAUSS (1870–1938) was the designer of the Golden Gate Bridge in San Francisco. Born in Cincinnati, of Jewish parentage, Baermann designed the Golden Gate with 36½-inch-thick suspension cables to make it the longest single-span suspension bridge of its day. First opened to traffic in 1937, the Golden Gate cost $35 million and was described as the most beautiful bridge of that decade. The board of directors were so pleased, they gave Strauss a golden pass which entitled him to toll-free access to the bridge for the rest of his life.

SAUL STEINBERG (1914–   ) makes his comments on modern life with pen and ink drawings that regularly adorn the cover of the *New Yorker* magazine. Born in Rimnicu-Sarat, Romania, Steinberg emigrated to America at the age of twenty-eight. Although he was an alien, he was granted a commission in the U.S. Navy in 1943 and later became a naturalized citizen.

In addition to his magazine work, Steinberg's watercolors have been exhibited at galleries and museums around the world, including New York's Metropolitan Museum of Art and the Museum of Modern Art. Steinberg served as "artist in residence" at the Smithsonian Institute from 1966 to 1968.

MINORU YAMASAKI (1912–   ) A Japanese-American born in Seattle, Yamasaki designed the 110-story twin towers that dominate the skyline of lower Manhattan. The World Trade Center has the same number of stories as the Sears Tower in Chicago, which is America's tallest building, but the Sears Tower tops it by 85 feet—and even though the World Trade Center has two buildings instead of one, it's height that counts.

KORCZAK ZIOLKOWSKI (1909–   ) is blasting a 641-foot-long-by-513-foot-high statue of Chief Crazy Horse in the Black Hills of South Dakota. When he first came to the mountain Korczak had $174 in cash and a vision. Today, he has a 61-room home/studio/museum which is open to the public, and financial security for his project, which is financed by admission fees. Of Polish ancestry. Ziolkowski started his project almost 30 years ago, after working as Borglum's assistant at Mount Rushmore. After all this time in the Black Hills Korczak has only a scale model, 1/34th the size of the completed monument, and a vague outline of Crazy Horse's arm carved in the rock to show for his efforts. Korczak claims that when the monument is finished, 4,000 people will be able to stand on Crazy Horse's arm, a five-room house will fit inside the horse's nostril and the feather atop Crazy horse's head will be 44 feet tall.

So far Korczak has removed 5 million tons of rock from the mountainside. Will he live to finish the project? Korczak answers: "I've left three books of drawings. Any competent engineer could finish it." Like Borglum, Korczak has offspring who are interested in the project—5 boys and 5 girls whom he hopes will continue his work if he leaves it unfinished.

"ALL THE WORLD'S A STAGE . . ."

NICK ADAMS (1932–1968) Born Nicholas Adamchok, this Ukrainian-American actor had the distinction of being nominated by the Academy of Motion Picture Arts and Sciences for an Academy Award as best supporting actor for his role in *Twilight of Honor*. Unfortunately, the members of the Academy viewed the film before it was readied for commercial theaters. By the time the film was edited for distribution, Adams' best scenes, and his chances for the Oscar, had been excised completely from the film. Hugh Griffith of *Tom Jones* won the award in 1963.

JACK ALBERTSON (1910–   ) The second half of television's *Chico and the Man* was born in Malden, Massachusetts, of German and Russian-Jewish forebears. He won an Academy Award as best supporting actor in 1968 for his performance in *The Subject Was Roses*.

DON AMECHE (1908–   ) Ameche was born in Kenosha, Wisconsin, to a Italian father and a mother who was of German and Scotch-Irish ancestry. He became interested in drama while attending the University of Wisconsin, and worked in radio before graduating to the silver screen. Ameche starred in the movie *The Story of Alexander Graham Bell* (1941) and, on Broadway, in *Silk Stockings* (1955) and *13 Daughters* (1961), in which he played a Chinese father for the play's 28 performances.

ALAN ARKIN (1934–   ) Born in Brooklyn to Russian-German-Jewish parents, Arkin wanted to act when he was a child. But, as he noted, "I guess they didn't need a twelve-year-old character star." It wasn't until 1958 that he was able to join a summer stock group in the Adirondacks. Prior to his career in films, Alan sang with a folk group and wrote music. His most familiar tune is "The Banana Boat Song," which Harry Belafonte made famous. Arkin won an Oscar nomination for his role in *The Russians Are Coming, The Russians Are Coming* in 1966. Some of his other films are: *Wait Until Dark, Catch-22* and *The Heart Is a Lonely Hunter.*

LAUREN BACALL (1924–   ) In 1979 "Bogey's Baby" proved that, not only could she look good, act, sing and dance, but she could also write. Her autobiography, *Lauren Bacall By Myself,* told of her "nice Jewish girl" upbringing in New York City as Betty Perske, and her rise as model, actress, wife and mother. In her own words, she had it all: "love, family, career, recognition." Bacall's father was an immigrant from Alsace and her mother was born in New York of German-Romanian heritage.

CANDICE BERGEN (1946–   ) Candy is the daughter of ventriloquist Edgar Bergen. Her Swedish good looks have helped her become one of Hollywood's most popular actresses. In addition, she is a respected photographer and a bankable spokeswoman for Cie perfume.

ROBERT BLAKE (1933–   ) Born Michael James Vijencio Gubitosi in Nutley, New Jersey, Blake made his debut at the age of two in a song-and-dance act, "The 3 Little Hillbillies," that his father choreographed. Determined to have his children "make it" in show business, Papa Gubitosi packed the family up and moved to Venice, California, where Bobby Blake started his show-biz career as "Mickey" in MGM's *Our Gang* comedies.

By 1950 Bobby's career was over. He was thrown out of five schools in two years and ended up in the Army (stationed at an Anchorage, Alaska, cold-weather experiment station) where boredom led him to a drug habit. "A bunch of us just fell into it. You'd shoot dope because it made you feel better . . . and pretty soon you couldn't stand not to shoot it." (*TV Guide,* May 10, 1975).

Therapy helped Blake kick his drug and drinking habits and in 1967 he got the proverbial "big break" of his adult career when he was chosen to play Perry Smith, a mass murderer, in the screen adaptation of Truman Capote's nonfiction novel, *In Cold Blood.*

Blake has been called the "Sicilian Mickey Rooney." In 1975 he won an Emmy as the year's outstanding actor in a drama series, for his portrayal of an undercover cop in *Baretta.*

YUL BRYNNER (1920–   ) probably has the most famous hairless head in America. Born Taidje Khan of part Gypsy ancestry on Sakhalin Island, Russia, Yul made the movie and stage versions of *The King and I* famous. He won an Academy Award as Best Actor in 1956 for his role as the King, and although he has sported hair once or twice since then, he has been "clean shaven" for over 20 years. Some of his other films are *The Magnificent Seven; Taras Bulba,* in which he played a Cossack; *Kings of the Sun,* in which he played a Mayan Indian; and *Flight from Ashiya,* in which Yul was a Japanese parachute expert.

ELLEN BURSTYN (1932–   ) Born Edna Rae Gillooly, this Irish-American actress won an Academy Award as Best Acress for her performance in the title role of *Alice Doesn't Live Here Anymore.*

JAMES CAAN (1939–   ), the son of a kosher meat dealer from the Bronx, made his name at the box office as the errant son-in-law of *The Godfather.* His last name is a Dutch variation of Cahn, and his ancestry is Dutch, German and Jewish, despite his success playing a "Mafioso" on the screen.

JAMES COCO (1929–   ) was born in Manhattan's "Little Italy" and dreamed of becoming an actor from early childhood. "My father was a shoemaker in the Bronx and I was a fat kid determined to be in show business. I used to shine his customers' shoes and while I did it, I'd tell them how I was going to be a big movie star when I grew up."

While waiting for his "big break" Coco worked as a short order cook, a switchboard operator and even a department store Santa Claus. Reporters have credited the "customary pasta of an Italian-American family" for keeping Coco's weight between 225 and 310 pounds, but once, Coco claims, ". . . when I went down to 175, people didn't seem to like me as much. My sister (Lucy) broke out in tears and insisted I had cancer."

FAYE DUNAWAY (1941–   ) won an Academy Award nomination in 1967 for her third film, *Bonnie and Clyde*, but it wasn't until 1976 that the Irish-American actress walked off with that coveted prize for her performance in *Network* as a TV executive who fights her way to the top.

HENRY FONDA (1905–   ) is one of the few Hollywood actors to have a town named after him. Fonda, New York, was founded by Henry's ancestor Douw Fonda, who settled in upstate New York in the early 1700s. Fonda's forebears were originally from Italy, but they migrated to Holland in the fifteenth century and made the trek across the ocean to the New World in 1628. Henry's grandfather was born at Fonda, New York, but later took his family to Omaha, where Henry's father was born. Henry himself was born at Grand Island, Nebraska, and has yet to visit his namesake town in New York.

CARY GRANT (1904–   ) was born in Bristol, England, with the unstagelike name of Archibald Alexander Leach. After being expelled from school at the age of fourteen for attempting to sneak into the girls' bathroom, Grant started his show business career by joining a troupe of comedians and acrobats.

LEE GRANT (1930–   ) won an Academy Award as Best Supporting Actress in 1975 for her portrayal of a Beverly Hills housewife who has more than her hair done by Warren Beatty in the movie *Shampoo*. Born Lyova Haskall Rosenthal in New York City, Lee is a second-generation Russian-American — her mother emigrated from Odessa.

KATHARINE HEPBURN (1909–   ) is the only actress ever to win three Academy Awards as Best Actress — for her roles in *Morning Glory* (1933), *Guess Who's Coming to Dinner* (1967) and *The Lion in Winter* (1968). Hepburn is of Scottish descent and was born in Hartford, Connecticut.

JACK KLUGMAN (1922–   ) was the youngest of six children born to poor Russian immigrants in South Philadelphia. His first roommate in New York was fellow actor Charles Bronson, but Klugman is probably best known as Tony Randall's roommate, Oscar, from the long re-running television series, *The Odd Couple*. Klugman has come a long way since then — Jack formerly portrayed a disheveled sportswriter, but he is now making his living playing a medical examiner on *Quincy*.

ANN-MARGRET (1941–   ) Born Ann Margret Olsson in the Swedish village of Valsjobyn, Ann emigrated to the United States with her parents in 1946. She attained fame as a singer and dancer, but critics acclaimed her acting ability in *Carnal Knowledge* and in the rock musical *Tommy*.

PENNY MARSHALL (1944–   ) The Italian-American star of TV's *Laverne and Shirley*, Penny is well connected in show-business circles: her husband is Rob Reiner, an actor and the son of comedian Carl Reiner, and her brother is the producer of *Laverne and Shirley* — Garry Marshall. Penny once expressed the suspicion that she was only getting ahead in the business because of her connections. Not so, insisted brother Garry. "Nobody is that nice," he said. "I gave you one break. That was nice. But the fact that I've had you back . . . means that you're good."

ZERO MOSTEL (1915–1977) His real name was Samuel Joel Mostel, but his press agent gave him the name "Zero." The son of a rabbi from Brooklyn, New York, Mostel was known not only as a brilliant performer, but as an artist. Some of his paintings now hang on permanent exhibit at the Brooklyn Museum.

PAUL MUNI (1895–1967) was born Muni Weisenfreund in Lemburg, in the Ukraine, which was once part of Austria-Hungary and is now in Poland. His parents were troupers with the Yiddish theater in America after they emigrated to the United States in 1902.

JACK NICHOLSON (1937–   ) Born in Neptune, New Jersey, of Irish ancestry, Jack went to visit his sister in Los Angeles after graduating from high school and never returned home — instead he got an office job at MGM and began studying acting. Some of his most famous movies are *Easy Rider, Five Easy Pieces, Carnal Knowledge* and *One Flew Over the Cuckoo's Nest,* for which he won an Academy Award as Best Actor in 1975.

LEONARD NIMOY (1931–   ) has been trying to shake the "Mr. Spock" stereotype for over ten years now, but his loyal fans don't want to forget that pointed-eared character from *Star Trek.* The son of Russian-Jewish immigrants, Nimoy speaks Yiddish fluently and professes not to know a single word in the "Vulcan" language.

AL PACINO (1940–   ) is of Sicilian extraction. Pacino's parents divorced when he was two years old, and he and his mother moved to the Bronx to live with her parents. He made his Broadway debut in 1969 as a psychotic junkie in *Does a Tiger Wear a Necktie?* and made his film debut in *Me, Natalie* the same year, again playing the part of a junkie. It wasn't until *The Panic in Needle Park,* in 1971, that Pacino began to reap the rewards from playing a junkie on the silver screen. That role led to his contract (no pun intended) for *The Godfather,* for which he won an Oscar nomination in 1972.

GEORGE RAFT (1896–   ) The son of a German father and an Italian mother, Raft not only lived the life of a racketeer in the movies, he was also somewhat involved in the real-life "underworld" as a youngster. He appeared in dozens of gangster films, including *Scarface* (1932), and played a gangster in the comedy *Some Like It Hot* (1959).

BEN TURPIN (1869–1940) A slapstick comedian, Turpin was born in New Orleans, the son of a French-American candy maker. His real name was Bernard. According to his own account, Ben's father gave him 100 bucks and his best wishes when he was 17 years old and sent him out to seek his fortune in the world. Ben lost his stake in a crap game and became a hobo before he drifted into comedy. At the height of his career success in the 1920s, his cross-eyed look, for which he was famous, was insured by Lloyds of London for $1 million in the event that his eyes ever uncrossed.

RUDOLPH VALENTINO (1895–1926) This silent film star's real name was Rodolpho Raffaele Pierre Filibert Guglielmi de Valinetina d'Antonguolla. He was born in Castellaneto, Italy, the son of a vet-erinary surgeon father and a mother who was the daughter of a Parisian doctor.

He arrived in America in 1913, penniless, and was forced to take the most menial jobs to support himself. A graduate of the Royal Academy of Agriculture, he had intended to buy a farm in the West, but instead made a name for himself as the silver screen's most passionate non-talking lover.

JOHN WAYNE (1907–1979) won an Academy Award for his 1969 peformance in *True Grit.* Wayne was of Scotch-Irish descent; his true name was Marion Michael Morrison. He made his first few movies under the name Duke Morrison, but changed his name to John Wayne in the early 1930s.

JOHNNY WEISSMULLER (1904–   ) Best known as Tarzan and Jungle Jim, Weissmuller jokingly refers to himself as "the original swinger." In the best Hollywood tradition, Weissmuller, who is of Austrian ancestry (his father was a Vienna-born brewmaster), has been married five times. Johnny learned to swim in Lake Michigan, where he refined the technique that eventually led him to set over 67 world swimming records and win Olympic medals in 1924 and 1928 in the 100-meter and 400-meter freestyle events.

ETHNICS IN COMMERCIALS

♦ *Rabbi Dominic?* The star of Xerox Corporation's award-winning commercials, Brother Dominic—the monk who enlists Xerox's aid in copying illuminated manuscripts—is played by Jack Eagle, a Jewish actor in monk's clothing.

♦ *Kosher Albacore* The voice of Charlie the Tuna, that luckless chicken of the sea who has been rejected for over a decade by the Star-Kist canning company, is none other than Jewish actor Hershel Bernardi.

♦ *El Exigente* Savarin Coffee commercials feature a stern, sinister coffee taster known to the natives of Latin America only as "El Exigente." Who was this white-suited man with the Panama hat, who could instill fear into the hearts of impoverished natives by refusing to buy their coffee beans. The role of *El Exigente* is played by Carlos Montalban, a Mexican-born actor and brother of Ricardo Montalban.

♦ *"Hey, Ann-thon-ee"* Why does Anthony Martignetti rush home on Wednesday afternoons? Because, "as every family in the North End of Boston will tell you, Wednesday is Prince spaghetti day." Who was the twelve-year-old boy who ran through the streets of Boston, spurred on by the smell of Mama's pasta? His name really was Anthony Martignetti, and he really did live in Boston. The only facts that were changed in the commercial were the name of the street where he lived, and his mother's cooking habits—she makes pasta whenever she feels like it, not just on Wednesday.

Anthony Martignetti was a real, live Italian immigrant from Montefalcione, a small town in the province of Avellino, who was discovered while walking down the streets of Boston's North End—an Italian enclave. They wanted to use his mother in the commercial, but she didn't fit the stereotyped image of a "fat Italian mama." She was "too t'in."

♦ *Chiquita banana sings* The onetime emissary for the United Fruit Company, Chiquita banana sang her way to fame on radio and TV during the 1940s and 1950s.

The calypso-style song was written in 1944 by the un-Hispanic team of Montgomery and MacKenzie, but at least one of the women employed to sing the song was Hispanic. The second "Chiquita" was Elsa Miranda, a twenty-four-year-old Puerto Rican immigrant who, like her predecessor, made all the top radio shows, such as Fred Allen's and Edgar Bergen's, and even managed to sing and dance with the likes of the Boston Symphony Orchestra.

15 ETHNICS BEHIND THE CAMERA

PRODUCERS, DIRECTORS AND MOVIE MOGULS

MOUSTAPHA AKKAD (1933–   ) may not be as famous a director as Hitchcock or Preminger, but he is probably the first film maker to inspire a terrorist attack. When *Mohammad, Messenger of God* opened in Washington, D.C., in March, 1977, Hanafi Moslems held 134 persons hostage at three separate locations to draw attention to their cause, in hopes of causing a withdrawal of the film, which they considered blasphemous. Akkad, a Syrian-born American who emigrated to Hollywood in 1952 to study theater arts at UCLA, worked as an assistant to Sam Peckinpah and directed television documentaries before tackling the first international movie about the birth and growth of the Islam religion.

FRANK CAPRA (1897–   ) was born in Palermo, Sicily, but emigrated to America at the age of five. He spent his sixth birthday at the Ellis Island Immigration Center.

After a stint as a gag writer for *Our Gang* comedies, Capra directed his first film in 1921. He won three Academy Awards as Best Director—all within a period of five years. His award-winning films are: *It Happened One Night* (1934), *Mr. Deeds Goes to Town* (1936) and *You Can't Take It With You* (1938).

JOHN CASSAVETES (1929–   ) The son of Greek immigrants, Cassavetes began his career in Hollywood as an actor, and later made a second name for himself as a pioneer director of American *cinema verite.*

His first directorial effort, *Shadows* (1960), the story of a love affair between a White boy and a Black girl, won the Critics Award at the Venice Film Festival. His other movies include *Minnie and Moskowitz* (1971); *Husbands* (1970), the story of three middle-aged men who overreact to the death of a friend; and *Faces* (1968), the tale of middle-aged, middle-class marriages on the rocks.

FRANCIS FORD COPPOLA (1939–   ) was born in Detroit, Michigan, the second of three children. His Neapolitan father, Carmine, is a musician who moved the family to New York in 1939 so he could perform and conduct at Radio City Music Hall.

Even as a young child Francis was interested in film making, and in 1959 he enrolled in UCLA's film school. He won his first Academy Award 11 years later for his screenplay for *Patton* (1970). When *The Godfather* was released in 1972 it broke worldwide attendance records by grossing more than $1 million each day during the first few months that followed. Coppola's other films include *Finian's Rainbow* (1969), *The Conversation* and *The Godfather, Part II* (1974).

CECIL B. DE MILLE (1881–1959) pioneered the "spectacular" movie. His "cast of thousands" films include *The Ten Commandments, Cleopatra* and *The King of Kings.*

Before making it as a director, De Mille was a program director for the Lux Radio Theater. His first American ancestors were Antonius and Elizabeth Van de Hout de Mil, immigrants from the Netherlands who arrived in 1658.

JOHN FRANKENHEIMER (1930–) was born in New York City of Irish and Jewish ancestry. He started his film career in the U.S. Air Force, where he produced documentaries on cattle raising, survival techniques for army troops and methods of laying asphalt.

Besides producing such classic films as *Birdman of Alcatraz* (1962), *The Manchurian Candidate* (1962), *Seven Days in May* (1963) and *I Walk the Line* (1971), Frankenheimer also directed more than fifty plays in the 1950s for the highly acclaimed Playhouse 90 on CBS.

ALFRED JOSEPH HITCHCOCK (1899–1980) began scaring the wits out of American filmgoers in 1939. He started out as a director in his native London during the early 1920s. During a career that spanned five decades, Hitchcock made more than fifty motion pictures, grossing more than $200 million. Some of his best-known psychological thrillers are *The Birds, North by Northwest* and *Psycho* — the movie that discouraged thousands of American women from taking showers in isolated motels.

ELIA KAZAN (1909–) When Kazan's Greek grandmother settled into her new home in America, the first thing she did was to brew a potful of homemade yogurt. Using the age-old method of heating milk just until boiling and letting it cool until she could stick her pinky in and count to ten, Kazan's grandmother made yogurt every day and served it at every meal. Although Elia emigrated to America at the age of four, and shortened his name to "Kazan" from Kazanjoglou, he stayed close to his roots by "eating his heritage" three times a day. One

of America's foremost film directors, his movies have included *A Tree Grows in Brooklyn* (1945), *A Streetcar Named Desire* (1951) and *On the Waterfront* (1954).

GARRY MARSHALL (1935–), born Gary Marscharelli, is one of the richest Italian-American television producers in Hollywood today. His first meteoric TV series was *The Odd Couple,* starring Jack Klugman and Tony Randall. Marshall followed that series with *Happy Days, Laverne and Shirley* and *Mork and Mindy* — three of the ten top-rated TV shows for the 1978–1979 viewing season.

LOUIS BURT MAYER (1885–1957) was once known as the "King of Hollywood." Born in Minsk to Russian-Jewish parents on the Fourth of July, Mayer emigrated to New Brunswick, Canada, at the age of three.

He made an exclusive deal with D. W. Griffith to show *Birth of a Nation* in New England, and with the profits from that movie he moved to Los Angeles and founded the Louis B. Mayer Pictures Corporation, which was later organized as MGM (Metro-Goldwyn-Mayer) in 1924.

Mayer produced such grand old movies as *The Thin Man, Boys' Town, Gone With the Wind* and *Ben-Hur.*

VINCENT MINELLI (1913–) was born in Chicago to an Italian father and a French mother, both of whom were in the theater. Vincent started his career as a costume and set designer after graduation from high school. In 1934 he was hired as Radio City Music Hall's chief costume designer, and after a time designing spangly costumes for the Rockettes to dance the night away in, Minelli was hired by the Shuberts to produce stage shows.

Minelli's first major film was *Cabin in the Sky,* an all-Black musical starring Ethel Waters. Minelli won an Academy Award in 1958 for directing another "ethnic musical" — *Gigi.*

DAVID OLIVER SELZNICK (1902–1965), the son of a pioneer film producer of Ukrainian extraction, was born in Pittsburgh, Pennsylvania. He learned his craft from his father, who liked to tout the catchy slogan, "Selznick pictures make happy hours."

When Selznick read Margaret Mitchell's *Gone With the Wind,* he was so impressed by the book that he offered $50,000 for the film rights (a record-breaking sum in 1936). For the next three years David devoted his days to casting, writing and shooting one of the most beloved American films of all time. His efforts were not wasted—he won an Oscar in 1939 for Best Picture of the Year.

Some of Selznick's other films are *Rebecca, Intermezzo, Portrait of Jenny* and *A Farewell to Arms.*

MACK SENNETT (1884–1960), a pioneer silent film maker, was born in Ontario, Canada, in 1884, the son of Irish immigrants. (His real name was Michael Sinnott.) During his career, Mack directed more than 1,000 silent films, the most famous being the "Keystone Kops" and "Bathing Beauties" series.

WARNER BROTHERS Jack, Harry, Albert and Sam Eichelbaum were four Jewish immigrants from Ontario who Americanized their last name to "Warner" in 1905. Pioneer producers of "talkies," they turned out the first full-length sound picture, *The Jazz Singer,* starring Al Jolson, in 1927. Today, the company they founded is known as Warner Brothers-Seven Arts, although the last Warner, Jack, sold his interest in the company in 1967.

ADOLPH ZUKOR (1873–1976) was a Jewish immigrant from Risce, Hungary, who came to America at the age of sixteen with a bankroll of $35 sewn into the sleeve of his coat. He began his career as a furrier, and later invested in the penny arcade business with Marcus Loew, the Jewish founder of the Loew's chain of theaters. Zukor was the founder of Paramount Pictures, and the first person to build a theater to be used solely for the purpose of exhibiting motion pictures.

MICKEY MOUSE AND COMPANY

WALTER ELIAS DISNEY (1901–1966), the youngest of five children, was born in Chicago, Illinois, of Irish and German ancestry. Disney gave the world Mickey Mouse in 1928, and started the American love affair with animated animals. Although *Steamboat Willie* was Disney's third "mouse" film, it was the first cartoon to make use of sound effects, and it sent Mickey skyrocketing to international fame.

In the early years, Disney provided the voice for his famous rodent, who was known as Mickimaus in Germany, Miki Kuchi in Japan, and El Ratoncito Miguel in Spanish-speaking countries.

Soon there was a whole cast of characters (Minnie, Donald, Daisy, Pluto) and Disney began producing feature-length cartoons, such as *Snow White, Cinderella* and *Pinocchio.*

While Disney studios was busy sewing up the movie theater market, WILLIAM HANNA and JOSEPH BARBERA were making a name for themselves by producing low-cost animated cartoons for that infant industry of the Fifties—television.

Bill Hanna (an American of Scotch, English and Irish descent) met Joseph Barbera (the son of Italian immigrants from Palermo) in 1937 when both worked in the animation department of MGM Pictures. It wasn't until twenty years later, when Hanna-Barbera created their first cast of characters, Tom and Jerry, for motion picture theaters, that they began to consider creating low-cost cartoons for TV.

Name any famous cartoon series of the past twenty years and it was probably produced by Hanna-Barbera. Over the years they have given children Ruff and Reddy, Huckleberry Hound, The Flintstones, Yogi Bear, Top Cat, The Jetsons, Scooby Doo and, most recently, The Hanna-Barbera World of Superadventure with such "superheroes" as Birdman, Space Ghost and Frankenstein Jr.

Altogether, Hanna-Barbera has produced more than 100 cartoon series and almost 30 movies and TV specials. It has been estimated that more than 500 million people, in over 80 countries, are entertained by Hanna-Barbera each day, with at least one of their shows airing somewhere in the world every hour of the day.

Not For Children Only With Disney and Hanna-Barbera neatly dividing up the television and movie audiences, there was only one aspect of cartooning left for

RALPH BAKSHI (1940–   ) to crack—the X-rated animated film.

A Russian-Jewish cartoonist raised in the Brownsville section of Brooklyn, Bakshi animated two-X-rated films in the 1970s: *Fritz the Cat,* which debuted in 1972, and *Heavy Traffic*—a takeoff on *The Godfather*—which starred an Italian-Jewish character from Brooklyn named Michael Corleone.

ETHNICS UNDER THE "BIG TOP"

JOICE HETH Phineas Taylor Barnum, the showman who made the phrase "There's a sucker born every minute" famous, foisted his first hoax on the public in 1837. Joice Heth, a 46-pound Black American, who Barnum claimed was 161 years old, brought in over 10,000 paying customers at his New York sideshow. Barnum touted Heth as the midwife who brought George Washington into the world and later served as his mammy, but after her death an autopsy revealed that Joice was no more than 80 years old.

EMMETT KELLY Born in Sedan, Kansas, on December 9, 1898, Kelly was the son of an Irish immigrant railroad worker. His first career was as a cartoonist (he created the character of "Weary Willie" for a Kansas City advertising firm). In 1931 he traveled with the Hagenbeck-Wallace Circus, and became the sad-faced character of his sketches—Willie the Clown. He joined the Ringling Brothers Circus in 1942, and toured with their troupe until 1956, by which time he was the most famous clown in America.

Ironically, Kelly died on March 28, 1979—opening day for the Ringling Brothers Circus in New York City. The year before, Karl Wallenda, the famous aerialist who performed with the Ringling Circus for almost twenty years between 1927 and 1946, had died in a fall from a high wire in Puerto Rico on the circus's opening day in New York.

RINGLING BROTHERS The most famous name in circusdom today, the Ringling Brothers Circus, premiered in Brooklyn, New York, on April 10, 1871. The brothers, John and Henry Ringling North, were the grandsons of a German harness maker, August Rüngeling, who emigrated to the United States at the age of 21. When Rüngeling married Salome Juliar, an American of Alsatian ancestry, he Americanized his name to Ringling.

THE FLYING WALLENDAS The German-born high wire walker, Karl Wallenda (1905–1978) began his U.S. career in 1932 by performing his feats of daring at Radio City Music Hall's opening night show. He toured with the Ringling Brothers Circus for almost twenty years, but even at the age of 73, when most men think of retiring, Karl Wallenda simply could not hang up his walking shoes. "If someone said, 'Karl, I'll give you $1 million for one last walk, but you've got to retire,' I'd turn it down." he once said. "This is my life. I love performing. I don't want to give it up."

As it turned out, Karl made his last walk, for a lot less than $1 million, in 1978. As he attempted to wire-walk between two hotels in Puerto Rico, a sudden gust of wind caught him off guard. He lost his balance and fell 150 feet to the ground. Over the years there had been many tragedies for the "Flying Wallendas," who consistently courted danger by not working with a safety net: two sons-in-laws, a sister-in-law and a nephew were killed, and Karl's son Mario was paralyzed, in high wire accidents.

HUGO ZACCHINI The original "human cannonball" was Hugo Zacchini (1898–1975), an Italian immigrant who first performed his stunt on the island of Malta in 1922. He dreamed up his act for his father's circus, The Zacchini Brothers, but when the Ringling Circus caught his act they lured him away to tour in the United States. Zacchini toured with Ringling for almost four decades, and when he retired in 1961 his son, Hugo, and later his nephew. Hugo Zacchini II, continued the family tradition.

Zacchini invented the 24-foot-long cannon barrel that propelled his body through the air. How did he feel about performing such a dangerous stunt? "Oh, I used to be frightened . . . it's nothing."

HOUDINI Erich Weiss (1874–1926), the fifth son of a Hungarian rabbi, was better known as Harry Houdini. He may have been born in Budapest, although the records are not clear. He changed his name to Harry Houdini, combining the names of his magician-idol, Robert *Houdin,* and another famous magician, *Harry* Kellar. Houdini started out as a midway performer, escaping from a variety of handcuffs, chains and boxes, but he didn't attain star status until he hit upon the "secret" that was to make his fortune. In the past, he realized, he had made a big mistake by quickly and deftly shaking off his chains and shackles, thereby making his escape look too easy. By making the feat seem hard, and sweating and struggling to extricate himself from his bonds, he played up the drama and gave the audience a better show.

How did Houdini do all those tricks? There are logical explanations for all of them:

1 *Escaping from Handcuffs* Almost all handcuffs manufactured prior to 1920 could be opened with the same key. With a few keys hidden on his body, Houdini could unmanacle himself in a few seconds.

2 *Escape from a Box or Trunk* One day while having difficulty breaking up a wooden packing case, Houdini wondered why manufacturers had to use such long nails to hold the sides together. If the nails were shorter, it would have been easier to break the case apart. That packing case gave him a good idea for an escape trunk — if tiny nails with large heads were used, it would appear that the box was soundly made, when in reality the side could be pushed out with ease, and then re-nailed in place after the "escape." That's why Houdini's theme song was "The Chariot Race" — the loud music covered up the noise he made hammering the crate back together.

3 *Escaping from a Safe* Most safes manufactured at the turn of the century were designed to keep thieves "out" — they

Harry Houdini in 1914 after he "passed through" the brick wall. Harry's secret? He was an excellent contortionist and could wriggle his way under the wall. (Courtesy: New York Historical Society)

were never designed to prevent someone on the inside from opening the safe. Once a small plate was removed from the inside, escape was simple. By merely studying the patents for every current safe model, Houdini could expertly pick his way "out" in a matter of minutes.

Although there is a "logical" explanation for all of his escapes, it wasn't as easy as it sounds. Houdini was a master contortionist and was adept at the trick of "retroperistalsis" — the ability to swallow small objects halfway, and then spit them up at will. These two skills enabled him to crawl out of small openings and to keep keys and lock picks concealed on his body despite the most thorough searches.

Houdini even patented one of his inventions. In 1921, he received U.S. Patent #1,370,316 for a diver's suit that enabled the wearer to escape from it while underwater.

PRESIDENTIAL ROOTS

President:		Ancestry:
1 George Washington	(1732–1799)	English
2 John Adams	(1735–1826)	English
3 Thomas Jefferson	(1743–1826)	Welsh-Scottish-Irish
4 James Madison	(1751–1836)	English
5 James Monroe	(1758–1831)	Scottish-Welsh
6 John Quincy Adams	(1767–1848)	English
7 Andrew Jackson	(1767–1845)	Scotch-Irish
8 Martin Van Buren	(1782–1862)	Dutch
9 William Henry Harrison	(1773–1841)	English-Scottish
10 John Tyler	(1790–1862)	English
11 James K. Polk	(1795–1849)	Scotch-Irish
12 Zachary Taylor	(1784–1850)	English
13 Millard Fillmore	(1800–1874)	English
14 Franklin Pierce	(1804–1869)	English
15 James Buchanan	(1791–1868)	Scotch-Irish
16 Abraham Lincoln	(1809–1865)	English
17 Andrew Johnson	(1808–1875)	English-Scotch-Irish
18 Ulysses S. Grant	(1822–1885)	English-Scottish
19 Rutherford B. Hayes	(1822–1893)	Scottish
20 James A. Garfield	(1831–1881)	English-French
21 Chester A. Arthur	(1830–1886)	English-Scotch-Irish
22 Grover Cleveland	(1837–1908)	English-Irish-French
23 Benjamin Harrison	(1833–1901)	English-Scottish
24 Grover Cleveland	(1837–1908)	English-Irish-French
25 William McKinley	(1843–1901)	English-Scotch-Irish-German
26 Theodore Roosevelt	(1858–1919)	Dutch-French-Scotch-Irish
27 William Howard Taft	(1857–1930)	English-Dutch
28 Woodrow Wilson	(1856–1924)	Scotch-Irish
29 Warren Harding	(1865–1923)	Scotch-Irish-English-Dutch
30 Calvin Coolidge	(1872–1933)	English-Welsh
31 Herbert Hoover	(1874–1964)	Swiss-German
32 Franklin Roosevelt	(1882–1945)	Dutch-French
33 Harry Truman	(1884–1972)	English-Scotch-Irish
34 Dwight David Eisenhower	(1890–1969)	German-Swiss
35 John F. Kennedy	(1917–1963)	Irish
36 Lyndon Johnson	(1908–1973)	English-French-German
37 Richard Nixon	(1913–)	English-Scotch-Irish-Welsh
38 Gerald Ford	(1913–)	English
39 James Earl Carter	(1924–)	English

No. 8, Martin Van Buren

Martin Van Buren, our first president of Dutch descent, was also the first president to be born a citizen of the United States. Born in a small Dutch community, Kinderhook, New York, Van Buren became a prominent figure in the state Democratic Party and served as New York State Senator and governor. Before his election to the Presidency of the United States, Van Buren was appointed Secretary of State under Andrew Jackson, and he was Vice-President during Jackson's second term. The Panic of 1837 occurred the year after Van Buren took office, which did nothing to enhance his popularity.

Martin Van Buren. (Illustrations courtesy: New York Public Library)

No. 28, Woodrow Wilson

Wilson was one of four Scotch-Irish presidents. His paternal grandfather (James Wilson) came from Ulster in 1807, and married a young woman (Annie Adams) whom he met on board the ship that brought him to America. The Wilson family home in Dergalt, near Strabane, County Tyrone, has been restored and is open to visitors. It is still occupied by a distant relative of the President.

No. 29, Warren Harding

Our only President of Scotch-Irish and English-Dutch ancestry, Warren Gamaliel

Harding was widely rumored to be of part Negro ancestry. When he was questioned about the rumors by a Cincinnati reporter, Harding replied: "How do I know, Jim? One of my ancestors may have jumped the fence."

Harding himself "jumped the fence," so to speak, fathering an illegitimate child, Elizabeth Ann Christian, who was born on October 22, 1919, in Asbury Park, New Jersey, to Nan Britton, a former resident of Harding's hometown, Marion, Ohio.

Woodrow Wilson.

Warren Harding.

Ancestor to Nos. 26, 27, and 32

When Klaes Martenson Van Rosenvelt settled in New Netherland in 1640, he probably never dreamed that his descendants would play such an important role in American history. Three, count them, three U.S. Presidents—William Howard Taft, Theodore Roosevelt and Franklin D. Roosevelt—were all descended from this Dutch farmer.

Eleanor Roosevelt, the niece of Theodore and the wife of Franklin, was also related to Klaes. She distinguished herself in 1933 by becoming the first President's wife ever to hold a press conference, and she went on to become a leader of women's organizations and a crusader for minority rights.

Theodore's daughter, Alice Roosevelt, was the only child of a U.S. President to have a color named in her honor. Her predilection for a shade of greenish-blue was popularized by the song "Alice Blue Gown."

William Howard Taft. (Illustrations courtesy: New York Public Library)

Theodore Roosevelt.

Franklin Roosevelt.

No. 35, John F. Kennedy

The first Irish-Catholic to become President of the United States, John F. Kennedy was elected in 1960. As early as 1872, however, an Irish-Catholic had been nominated for the presidency by the Democratic Party. Charles O'Conor of New York declined his party's nomination, but his name was placed on the ballot and he received almost 30,000 votes from 23 states.

No. 39, James Earl Carter, Jr.

According to information supplied by Jim Purks, Special Assistant Media Liaison to President Carter, the President's first American ancestor was Thomas Carter (1610–1669), an English immigrant to Virginia. Like many other penniless Englishmen, Tom Carter sold himself as an indentured servant to pay his way to the colonies in 1635.

Carter's other relatives included: Thomas Carter, Jr. (1648–1710)—a member of Bacon's Rebellion in 1676; Kindred Carter (1750–1800)—a cotton farmer who owned ten slaves; James Carter (1773–1858)—a plantation owner who was charged with murder but acquitted of the crime; Littleberry Walker Carter (1832–1873)—a soldier in the Confederate Army who was stabbed to death during a drunken brawl with his business partner; and William Carter (1858–1903) who died of gunshot wounds over a business dispute. It was William Carter's wife, Nina, who moved the family to Plains, Georgia, in 1904, where her son James Earl Carter, Sr., established his family.

According to H. B. Brooks-Baker of Debrett's Peerage Ltd., a London genealogy concern that specializes in noble family trees, President Carter's English ancestors were wealthy merchants. "Mr. Carter comes from one of the more significant families in Europe. He has made his way by intelligence and determination, but even though he didn't know it, many of his ancestors were wealthy and well-born."

---

9 "FOREIGNERS" OR "IMMIGRANTS" WHO SIGNED THE DECLARATION

At least 9 of the 57 men who signed the Declaration of Independence were born on British soil:

James Wilson	1742–1798	lawyer from St. Andrews, Scotland
John Witherspoon	1723–1794	Presbyterian minister; President of the College of New Jersey (later Princeton University)
Button Gwinnett	1732–1777	immigrant from Bristol, England; he lost his life in a duel
Robert Morris	1734–1806	born in Liverpool; Morris died in poverty after his land speculation deals fell through
Francis Lewis	1713–1802	merchant, born in Wales
James Smith	1719–1806	lawyer, born in Dublin
George Taylor	1716–1781	Irish-born redemptioner, who was hired out to an iron manufacturer in Pennsylvania
Matthew Thornton	1714–1803	Irish-born physician; emigrated with his parents at age three
Charles Thomson	1729–1824	Secretary of Continental Congress; emigrated from Derry, Ireland, at the age of ten

Tracing backward from Thomas Carter's family in England, Debrett's has found wealthy, landed Carters as far back as 1361 in Kings Langley, Hertfordshire. The Carter family is related to the Tookes and Newces families of Hertfordshire—two families known to be related to our first president, George Washington. "And any amateur genealogist worth his roots knows that anyone related to Mr. Washington also is related, though distantly, to Queen Elizabeth II."

ETHNIC AMERICAN POLITICAL FIRSTS

Irish-Catholic Senator The Carroll family emigrated to America from Ireland in 1688 and became one of our nation's most distinguished families. Daniel Carroll, a member of the Federalist Party, served as Maryland's Senator from 1789 to 1791. Another family member, Charles Carroll, attained fame as a signer of the Declaration of Independence, while John Carroll honored the family by becoming the first Catholic Bishop born in America.

The Kennedy Clan The sons of Joseph Kennedy (John, Robert and Edward) became the first three Irish-Catholic brothers to serve as United States Senators. John F. Kennedy was elected as Senator from Massachusetts in 1952; Edward Kennedy ran for the Senate seat his brother had vacated, and was sworn in on January 9, 1963; and Robert Kennedy was elected to the Senate from New York in 1964.

The first member of the Kennedy family in America was Patrick Kennedy, JFK's great-grandfather. Patrick sold all his possessions for a one-way ticket to Boston in 1848, and arrived here, from County Wexford, Ireland, with little more than the clothes on his back. Little did he know that within the next century his descendants would build the Kennedy fortune, and the Kennedy name, to such epic proportions.

"From Kaw Teepee to Capitol" was the title of one biography of Charles Curtis (1860–1936), America's first Senator and Vice-President of American Indian ancestry. Curtis, of English, French and Kaw ancestry (only one-eighth, to be exact), served as U.S. Senator from Kansas for more than 25 years, and as Vice-President of the United States under Herbert Hoover.

Curtis was descended from a former chief of the Kaw tribe, Nom-pa-wa-rah (White Plume), and during his political career he helped foster changes in Indian territory to protect Indian interests. Legislation such as the Curtis Bill of 1898 permitted Indians to incorporate their own towns and elect their own mayors and officials.

Polish Republican The first Polish-American ever elected to the U.S. Congress was Republican John Kleczka of Milwaukee, who won his seat in 1918. Despite these Republican beginnings, almost three-quarters of all elected Polish-American officials since Kleczka have been members of the Democratic party.

Mayor of Buffalo The first Polish-American to head a major American city was Joseph Mruk, who was elected mayor of Buffalo, New York, in 1949.

"She's Not Just One of the Boys" That was the winning campaign slogan that made Mary Anne Krupsak (1932–   ), a former state senator of Polish descent, the first female Lieutenant Governor of New York State. After serving under Irish-American Governor Hugh Carey from 1974 to 1978, Ms. Krupsak announced that because she "loved New York too much" to run on Carey's reelection ticket, she would seek the governorship herself.

The voters of New York, however, elected "one of the boys." Ms. Krupsak lost to her former boss, Hugh Carey.

Tex-Mex The first Texan of Mexican ancestry to be seated in the House of Representatives was Henry B. Gonzalez (1916–   ). His father's ancestors were Spanish settlers in northern Mexico, but his mother's family were Scotch-Irish Presbyterians from Pennsylvania who went "south of the border" in 1855.

Asian Indian Dalip Singh Saund, a native of Amritsar, India, was elected to represent the 29th district of California in the U.S. House of Representatives in November 1956. A first for his people, Saund was reelected in 1958 and 1960.

Puerto Rican The first Puerto Rican elected to the U.S. House of Representatives was Herman Badillo, the victor in a 1970 Congressional race in New York City.

Norwegian Knute Nelson (1843–1923) was the first Norwegian-American congressman in the United States. Born in Voss, Norway, he emigrated to the United States in 1849 with his widowed mother and settled in Chicago. Nelson was the first Scandinavian ever to serve as a state senator in Minnesota in 1875 and was elected to the U.S. Senate in 1895.

From Shapiro to Shapp The first Jewish governor of Pennsylvania was Milton Jerrold Shapp (1912–   ). Born Milton Shapiro in Cleveland, Ohio, Milton later changed his name to Shapp for business reasons, because he found while working as a salesman in Philadelphia in the 1930s that "no one was in when Mr. Shapiro called."

A man of many talents, Shapp founded an electronics corporation after World War II which made him a multi-millionaire. (One of his company's products was Harmon-Kardon high fidelity components.) Shapp also wrote his own campaign song for the 1970 election—"Stand Up, Fight for the Things You Stand For"—as well as two musical comedies.

From Marciszewski to Muskie Edmund Sixtus Muskie didn't have to change his last name from Marciszewski to Muskie—his Polish immigrant father, Stefan, did it for him. Not only was Muskie the first Polish-American governor of Maine (1954), but he was also the first Polish-American Senator (1958), the first Polish-American vice-presidential nominee (1968), and the first Polish-American presidential candidate (1972). Muskie served in the Senate for 18 years, and was reelected as a U.S. Senator from Maine in 1976 after his unsuccessful bid for the presidency. In 1980, Muskie became the first Polish-American Secretary of State.

Mexican-born The first Mexican-born citizen to serve as governor of Arizona was Raul Castro (1916–   ) a native of Cananera, Sonora, Mexico. Elected to office in 1974, Castro resigned from his gubernatorial duties in October 1977 to become U.S. Ambassador to Argentina.

New York's First George Clinton (1739–1821), of Scotch-Irish descent, was the first governor of New York and the all-time record holder for that office. He was elected seven times and served a total of 21 years. Clinton enjoyed a long, successful political career, and served as Vice-

President under two U.S. chief executives—Thomas Jefferson and James Madison. The fact that he was elected to two terms as Vice-President is puzzling in light of deficiencies noted by his fellow politicians. One, Senator William Plumer of New York, wrote: "He is old, feeble and altogether incapable of the duty of presiding in the Senate. He has no mind, no intellect, no memory."

First Woman Ella Rosa Giovanna Tambussi Grasso (1919–   ) was the first woman governor in the United States who was not the wife of a previous incumbent. She was the first Italian-American governor of the State of Connecticut, winning the gubernatorial race as a Liberal Democrat in 1974 and again in 1978.

An only child, Grasso is a second-generation Italian-American who is fiercely proud of her working-class background. She once boasted, "It took me years to learn that 'youse' is not the plural of 'you.' " Growing up in Windsor Locks, Connecticut, surrounded by immigrant relatives from Tortona, Italy, the governor learned to speak fluent Italian. She credits her ability to be a wife, mother and governor, all wrapped up in one, to the support she received from her family and friends: "Living in a community like that you don't have to worry about your roots. They're there."

African Ancestry The first Black Senator was Hiram Rhodes Revels (b. 1822), an ordained minister in the African Methodist Episcopal Church, who was appointed by the Governor of Mississippi in 1870 to fill a vacated seat.

The first Black Senator to serve a full term was Blanch Kelso Bruce, also of Mississippi, who sat in the Senate from 1875 to 1881. However, the honor of being the first Black Senator elected by popular vote goes to Edward Brooke, onetime Attorney General of Massachusetts, who sat in the Senate from 1967 to 1979.

Yulee, Not Levy The first Senator "of Hebrew extraction" was David Levy Yulee (1811–1886), a native of St. Thomas who was elected as Senator from the state of Florida in 1845. His real name was David Levy, but he added the surname "Yulee" when he was a Democratic delegate to Congress from Florida in 1841.

Hiram, Not You Hiram Leong Fong (1907–   ) changed his name from Yau

Fong out of respect for a nineteenth-century Congregationalist missionary to the Hawaiian Islands, Hiram Bingham.

In 1959, Fong, a self-made millionaire and a lawyer, became the first Senator of Asian ancestry when he was elected from the State of Hawaii in its first Senatorial election. Hiram's parents, immigrants from Kwangtung Province in China, came to the Hawaiian Islands in 1872 as indentured servants to work on Oahu's sugar plantations for a combined salary of $12 a month. The seventh of 11 children, Hiram managed to earn enough money to put himself though Harvard Law School—but barely enough. After graduation he returned to Oahu with his diploma and 10 cents in his pocket. Fong made his fortune investing in real estate, insurance and a banana plantation.

Most Obscure James Abourezk (that's pronounced *Aber*-esk) was probably the most obscure and the least affluent Senator of the 1970s. Once, while standing on a receiving line at W. Averell Harriman's home, he greeted two women with, "Hi, I'm Jim Abourezk." The women shook hands politely, but as they were leaving he heard one mumble, "Who is Jim Abourezk?" "I don't know," said the other, "he must be the caterer."

Born on the Rosebud Sioux Reservation in South Dakota, the son of a Lebanese peddler, Abourezk won the 1971 election despite the fact that there were only 14 Lebanese-Americans residing in his home state. (Not exactly the election of a favorite ethnic son.) After serving one term in the Senate (where he was Chairman of the Indian Affairs subcommittee and an opponent of the "Israel Lobby") Abourezk declined to run for another term because he was dissatisfied with the "Washington life."

Ghetto Dweller John Pastore of Rhode Island was the first Italian-American ever elected to the U.S. Senate. Born March 17, 1907, in Providence, Rhode Island's "Little Italy" section, Pastore was the son of an immigrant tailor from Sant'Arcangelo in the province of Potenza, Italy, who came to the United States in 1899.

"We lived in the ghetto of Federal Hill. We had no running water, no hot water," recalls Pastore. "I used to get up in the morning to crank the stove, go out in the backyard, sift the ashes, and come back with the coal I could recoup. I had to chisel with the icepick the ice in the sink so that I could wash up in the morning. . . ."

Elected to the State Assembly in 1934, Pastore spent 42 active years in politics (half of them in the Senate) before retiring in January 1977 at the age of 69.

First German-born Senator Hailed as "the greatest American citizen of German birth," Carl Schurz was born in Liblar, Prussia, and attended the University of Bonn. He emigrated to the United States in 1852, after participating in the revolution of 1848 and escaping to Switzerland when the revolution failed.

Schurz, a noted orator and a power in the newly formed Republican Party, campaigned for Lincoln in the election of 1860. He became a Senator from Missouri in 1869, and served as Secretary of the Interior under President Hayes' administration. His favorite motto: "My country, right or wrong. If right, to be kept right; if wrong, to be put right."

America's first German-born Senator, Carl Schurz. (Courtesy: German Information Center)

Cabinet Firsts The first Irish-Catholic to hold a Cabinet-level position was Joseph McKenna (1843–1926), who served as Attorney General under President McKinley in 1897. McKenna was later appointed Associate Justice of the U.S. Supreme Court and served from 1898 to 1925.

Juanita M. Kreps (1921–   ), the first woman to become U.S. Secretary of Commerce (under President Carter's administration), is of Scotch-Irish ancestry despite her Spanish-sounding name. Kreps' mother chose the name Juanita for her daughter because she believed she had some Spanish ancestors somewhere along the line.

The first Polish-American cabinet member was John Austin Gronouski (1919–   ), the Wisconsin Commissioner of Taxation who became Postmaster General in 1963 under President Kennedy. Gronouski served for two years and resigned his position in 1965. He was later nominated as Ambassador to Poland by President Johnson and served between 1965 and 1968.

The second Polish-American to attain cabinet level status was Zbigniew Brzezinski, commonly called "Woody Woodpecker" by the White House staff simply because Woody is easier to pronounce than Zbigniew. Although Brzezinski is the second Polish-American to serve in the Cabinet, he is the first American of Polish birth to serve in such a high position.

EBONY'S 100 MOST INFLUENTIAL BLACK AMERICANS (1979)

Each year since 1971 the editors of *Ebony* magazine have chosen the 100 Black Americans whom they believe exert the greatest national influence. Many popular personalities and sports figures are excluded from *Ebony*'s list, because, while famous, they have little real influence on the lives, thoughts and actions of large segments of the nation's Black population.

Dr. Ethel D. Allen	Secretary of State, Pennsylvania
Clifford L. Alexander, Jr.	Secretary, Department of the Army
Muhummad Ali	Ex-Heavyweight Boxing Champion
Richard H. Austin	Secretary of State, Michigan
Mona H. Bailey	National President, Delta Sigma Theta
Marion Barry	Mayor, Washington, D.C.
Lt. Gen J. W. Becton, Jr.	Commander VII Corps, U.S. Army
Lerone Bennett, Jr.	Journalist-historian, Johnson Publishing Co.
Thomas J. Bradley	Mayor, Los Angeles
Benjamin D. Brown	Deputy Chairman, Democratic National Committee
William D. Bryant	Chief Judge, U.S. District Courts
Roland W. Burris	Comptroller, State of Illinois
Shirley Chisholm	U.S. Representative, New York
William L. Clay	U.S. Representative, Missouri
Isadore H. Clayborn	Sov. Grand Cmdr. (South) Prince Hall Masons
Cardiss R. Collins	U.S. Representative, Illinois
John M. Conyers, Jr.	U.S. Representative, Michigan
Burnel Coulon	Grand Basileus, Omega Psi Phi
Robert Dawson, M.D.	President, National Medical Assn.
Drew S. Days	Asst. Attny. Gen., Civil Rights Division, U.S. Dept. of Justice

Ronald V. Dellums	U.S. Representative, California
Julian C. Dixon	U.S. Representative, California
Christopher F. Edley	Executive Director, United Negro College Fund
Melvin H. Evans, M.D.	Congressional Delegate, U.S. Virgin Islands
Walter E. Fauntroy	Congressional Delegate, District of Columbia
Harold E. Ford	U.S. Representative, Tennessee
Russell S. Gideon	Sov. Grand Cmdr. (North) Prince Hall Masons
Berry Gordy, Jr.	Chairman of the Board, Motown Industries
Vice Adm. S. L. Gravely, Jr.	Director, Defense Communications Agency
Earl Graves	Publisher, *Black Enterprise* Magazine
William H. Gray III	U.S. Representative, Pennsylvania
Oliver S. Gumbs, M.D.	Grand Polemarch, Kappa Alpha Psi
Alex Haley	Author, *Roots* and *Search*
Patricia R. Harris	Secretary, U.S. Dept. of Health and Human Services
Robert Harris	President, National Bar Assn.
Richard G. Hatcher	Mayor, Gary, Indiana
Augustus F. Hawkins	U.S. Representative, California
Dorothy I. Height	President, National Council of Negro Women
A. Leon Higginbotham, Jr.	Judge, U.S. Court of Appeals, Third Circuit
Jesse Hill, Jr.	President and Chief Executive Officer, Atlanta Life Insurance Company
M. Carl Holman	President Natl. Urban Coalition
Evelyn H. Hood	Grand Basileus, Sigma Gamma Rho
Benjamin L. Hooks	Executive Director, NAACP
Ivan J. Houston	Pres., Golden State Mutual Life Insurance Co.
Rev. Jesse L. Jackson	National President, Operation PUSH
Rev. Joseph H. Jackson	Pres., National Baptist Convention, U.S.A., Inc.
Maynard H. Jackson, Jr.	Mayor, Atlanta, Georgia
George E. Johnson	Pres., Johnson Products Co.
John H. Johnson	Pres. and Editor, Johnson Publishing Co.
Rev. William A. Jones	Pres. Progressive National Baptist Convention
Vernon E. Jordan, Jr.	Executive Director, National Urban League
James A. Joseph	Undersecretary, U.S. Dept. of the Interior
Amalya L. Kearse	Judge, U.S. Court of Appeals second circuit
Damon J. Keith	Chief Judge, U.S. Court of Appeals, 6th circuit
William J. Kennedy III	President, North Carolina Mutual Life Insurance Company
Coretta Scott King	President, Martin Luther King Jr. Center for Social Change
Janice Kissner	Grand Basileus, Zeta Phi Beta
James E. Lassiter, D.D.S.	Pres., National Dental Association
G. T. (Mickey) Leland	U.S. Representative, Texas
Thurgood Marshall	Associate Justice, U.S. Supreme Court
Louis E. Martin	Special Ass't., the White House
Wade H. McCree	Solicitor General of the U.S.
Donald McHenry	U.S. Ambassador to the United Nations
Parren J. Mitchell	U.S. Representative, Maryland
Loren E. Monroe	State Treasurer, Michigan
Ernest N. Morial	Mayor, New Orleans
Mujeddid W. D. Muhammad	Leader World Community of Al-Islam in the West
Rt. Rev. E. P. Murchison	Senior Bishop, Christian M.E. Church

Eleanor Holmes Norton	Chairwoman, U.S. Equal Employment Opp. Comm.
Robin D. Owens	Pres., National Ass'n. of Negro Business and Professional Women's Clubs
Henry E. Parker	State Treasurer, Connecticut
James B. Parsons	Chief Judge, U.S. District Court, Northern District of Illinois
Basil A. Patterson	Secretary of State, New York
Rt. Rev. J. O. Patterson	Presiding Bishop, Church of God in Christ
Barbara K. Phillips	Supreme Basileus, Alpha Kappa Alpha
Vel R. Phillips	Secretary of State, Wisconsin
Sidney Poitier	Movie Producer and Director
Julia Purnell	National President, Links, Inc.
Charles B. Rangel	U.S. Representative, New York
Dr. John E. Reinhardt	Director, International Communications Agency
Hobson R. Reynolds	Grand Exalted Ruler, IBPOEW (Elks)
Rt. Rev. Hubert N. Robinson	President, General Board A.M.E. Church
Spottswood W. Robinson	Judge, U.S. Court of Appeals, District of Columbia
Carl T. Rowan	Journalist, Syndicated Columnist
Herman J. Russell	Building Contractor, Atlanta
Rev. James Carl Sams	President, National Baptist Convention of America
John H. Sengstacke	President, Sengstacke Newspapers
Otis M. Smith	General Counsel, General Motors Corp.
Rt. Rev. William M. Smith	Senior Bishop, A.M.E. Zion Church
Louis Stokes	U.S. Representative, Ohio
Rev. Leon H. Sullivan	Founder, Chairman of Board, Opportunities Industrialization Centers
Franklin H. Thomas	President, Ford Foundation
Clifton R. Wharton, Jr.	Chancellor, State University of New York
Robert L. White	President, National Alliance of Postal and Federal Employees
James R. Williams	President, Alpha Phi Alpha
Margaret Bush Wilson	Chairman of the Board, NAACP
Charles B. Wright	President Phi Beta Sigma
Addie Wyatt	International V.P., Amalgamated Meat Cutters
Andrew J. Young	Foreign Affairs Analyst, Atlanta
Coleman A. Young	Mayor of Detroit; Vice-Chairman of Democratic National Committee

LAWYERS, JUDGES AND JUSTICES

MACON B. ALLEN was the first Black American formally admitted to the bar. He passed his legal examinations in 1845, which enabled him to practice law in Massachusetts.

MELVIN BELLI (1907–), an Italian-American lawyer from Sonora, California, has made his reputation defending some of Hollywood's biggest names. His clients have included Errol Flynn, Tony Curtis and Mae West, and even Jack Ruby, accused assassin of Lee Harvey Oswald.

HUGO L. BLACK (1886–1971), Scotch-Irish Associate Justice of the Supreme Court, was appointed in 1937 by President Franklin Roosevelt. Black served on the bench for 34 years before retiring at the age of 85.

WARREN BURGER (1907–), Chief Justice of the United States Supreme

Court, is of Swiss-German extraction. Burger served on the Court of Appeals for 13 years before he was appointed Chief Justice by President Nixon in 1969.

CLARENCE S. DARROW (1857–1938), a criminal lawyer of English descent, became internationally famous for his defense in the Scopes "Monkey" trial, which took place in Dayton, Tennessee, in 1925. Darrow also defended Eugene Debs in an 1894 labor strike case, and Leopold and Loeb in 1924; but his most notable case was that of John T. Scopes, the schoolteacher who wanted to teach evolution in Tennessee.

FRANCIS LEE BAILEY (1933–   ), who recently defended Patty Hearst in her trial for bank robbery, was born in Waltham, Massachusetts, of English and German descent. In 1979, he became the first criminal lawyer to become a game show regular, appearing on NBC's game show *Whodunnit?* – a murder-mystery quiz. In addition to appearances before judges and TV cameras, Bailey has also written 13 books, including one novel.

LEON JAWORSKI (1906–   ), a Polish-American, was the youngest person ever admitted to the Texas Bar. He served as Chief of the War Crimes trial team after the Second World War, was past president of the American Bar Association, and was appointed special Watergate prosecutor by President Nixon.

ABE FORTAS (1910–   ), of English-Jewish parentage, was appointed Associate Justice of the Supreme Court by President Kennedy in 1962. He resigned after a little more than two years of service in 1965.

WILLIAM MOSES KUNSTLER (1919–   ), a Jewish lawyer born in New York, offered his services to the Congress of Racial Equality in 1960. Kunstler later served as a special counsel for Dr. Martin Luther King, 1962–1963, and defended the "Chicago Seven" – Abbie Hoffman, Jerry Rubin, Rennie Davis, Tom Hayden, David Dellinger, Lee Weiner and John Froines – on charges of conspiracy to cross state lines and incite a riot during the Democratic National Convention of 1968.

SAMUEL S. LEIBOWITZ (1893–1978), a Jewish lawyer born in Jassy, Romania, built his reputation defending gangsters, including old Scarface himself, Al Capone. Leibowitz became internationally famous for his role in the case of the "Scottsboro Boys," in which he established the right of blacks to sit on juries. Leibowitz won the release of the nine black youths who had been convicted of raping two white women in Scottsboro, Alabama, in the early 1930s, when the Supreme Court ruled that blacks had been excluded, unconstitutionally, from their jury.

During his career as a criminal attorney, Leibowitz won 139 out of 140 murder cases.

HAROLD RAYMOND MEDINA (1888–   ) was born in Brooklyn, New York, to a Mexican father and a mother who was of old Dutch stock. A graduate of Princeton, Medina taught at Columbia and established his own successful private practice before he gave it all up to become a federal judge in 1947.

Medina was involved in one of the most controversial criminal jury trials in the history of the federal court in 1949. Eleven Communist leaders were on trial for conspiring to advocate the overthrow of the U.S. Government by violence. Nine months and 5 million words of testimony later, the so-called "Smith Act" or Alien Registration Act of 1940 was upheld, and the Communists were convicted.

Medina received over 50,000 letters concerning that decision, most praising him as a "great enemy of Communism." In his words, "Well, I wasn't an enemy of the Communists. I was just sitting here trying a case. . . . It's amazing the cussing out I got from the liberals about that trial."

JOHN J. SIRICA (1904–   ), the son of an Italian immigrant barber and an Italian-American mother, became a familiar figure as the presiding judge in the Watergate conspiracy trials. Sirica graduated from Georgetown University Law School in 1926, but before he put out his shingle he boxed in local smoker matches as a welterweight and was the sparring partner of Bernard F. Gimbel, the department store heir. For his part in "stubbornly and doggedly pursuing the truth . . . regardless of its political implications" during the Watergate trials of 1973, he was chosen as *Time* magazine's Man of the Year, and received the Award of Merit presented by the American Judges Association. He retired from active service on the Federal bench in 1978.

EARL WARREN (1891–1974), served as Chief Justice of the Supreme Court for 15 years. A Norwegian-American, born in California, Warren was appointed to office in 1953 by President Eisenhower, and retired in 1969 at the age of 78.

ETHNIC AMERICANS WHO BECAME "FEDERAL CASES"

At least two ethnic American names will live on in educational history — Brown and Bakke. These students fought for what they believed in, taking their cases all the way to the Supreme Court:

Brown v. *The Board of Education* Linda Brown, a young girl from Topeka, Kansas, became a federal case in 1954. Because she was Black, Linda was forced to walk five blocks to a bus stop each day where she boarded a school bus for the two-mile ride to Topeka's all-Black elementary school. Although there was an elementary school only four blocks away from her home, that one was reserved for the white population.

Linda's parents took her case to the U.S. Supreme Court, which ruled in her favor: all school districts in the nation were ordered to desegregate their classrooms "with all deliberate speed." Twenty-five years later, Linda Brown Smith, herself a mother of two school-age children, believes that the promise of desegregation has not yet been realized: "A lot of people around here don't remember me and aren't even aware of the decision at all. I guess I'm a symbol lost in the crowd."

Ironically, as a result of the Brown decision, when Los Angeles began busing pupils in 1978 to comply with the Supreme Court's ruling, some students were compelled to ride buses 15 miles to school each day, despite the fact that there was an appropriate school near their homes.

Regents of the University of California v. *Bakke* Allan Paul Bakke (1940–   ) won the right to attend the Davis School of Medicine at the University of California in June, 1978, almost six years after he had first applied. Rejected twice, despite a 3.51 grade point average in Engineering, Bakke retained a lawyer and filed suit against the University to challenge its policy of allocating 16 positions in the freshman class for "minority" students — whom Bakke claimed were less qualified than himself.

The U.S. Supreme Court decided that Bakke (an American of Norwegian ancestry) should be admitted, but upheld the right of a university to use race as a factor in determining admissions.

ACTIVISTS AND LABOR LEADERS

First Socialist The first socialist elected to Congress was Victor Louis Berger (1860–1929), an immigrant from Nieder Rehbach, Austria-Hungary. Berger, who arrived in the United States in 1878, founded the *Wisconsin Vorwärts* and was editor of the *Social Democratic Herald* for 28 years.

Along with Eugene Debs, Berger formed the Social Democratic Party (the forerunner of the Socialist Party in America), on whose ticket he was elected to Congress from the State of Wisconsin in 1911. During his two years in the House, Berger worked for passage of child labor laws, the eight-hour day, farm relief and old-age pensions.

Reelected in 1918, Berger was refused admission to the House because of his pacifist opposition to World War I. His activities earned him a 20-year jail sentence, which fortunately was later reversed. Berger was returned to Congress in 1923 and served there for six more years.

Activist Priests The first Roman Catholic priest ever to receive a federal sentence was Daniel (1921–   ) Berrigan. He and his brother Philip (1923–   ), the youngest of six sons born to a second-generation Irish-American father and a German immigrant mother, were charged with destroying draft records at the Catonsville, Maryland, office of the Selective Service system in 1968.

Daniel served 18 months in a federal prison in Danbury, Connecticut, and later dramatized his antiwar activities in the play, *The Trial of the Catonsville Nine.*

Daniel and Philip Berrigan were charged with conspiracy to kidnap Henry Kissinger in 1972, but the charges against the brothers and six other defendants were eventually dropped.

Mexican Leader His grandfather had been a successful Mexican immigrant with extensive land holdings in Arizona, but the Depression plunged Cesar Chavez's parents into poverty. Chavez, born in 1927, was forced to spend his youth moving from one migrant labor camp to another, helping his parents eke out a living picking seasonal crops. In 1952, while living in the Sal Si Puedes ("Escape If You Can") barrio of San Jose, California, Chavez joined the Community Service Organization and began his commitment to improving working conditions for migrant laborers through nonviolent means.

Chavez rose to power in the 1960s as head of the National Farm Workers Association (later to become the United Farm Workers of America). His strike against California grape growers received strong community support, and eventually won his group important concessions. In recent years, he has turned his attention to the lettuce growers and other segments of California's agribusiness.

"Apostle of Socialism" Nicknamed the "Apostle of Socialism," Eugene V. Debs (1855–1926) was a five-time candidate for the presidency of the United States. Born in Terre Haute, Indiana, of Alsatian ancestry, Debs organized the American Railway Union, and rose to national prominence after winning a strike against the Great Northern Railway Company in 1894. He led a sympathy strike against the Pullman Company that paralyzed the nation's railroads until President Cleveland intervened to break the strike.

Running as a Socialist, Debs polled more than 900,000 votes (almost 6%) in 1912. In 1920, he received almost 1 million votes, despite the fact that he was in prison at the time on charges of sedition resulting from his opposition to the United States' entry into World War I.

Debs' last words, scrawled with a pencil, were taken from Henley's *Invictus:*

"It matters not how strait the gate
How charged with punishment the scroll,
I am the master of my fate,
I am the captain of my soul."

Daddy Was First At the age of 13, David Dubinsky (1892–) led his first strike for higher wages – outside his own father's bakery in Brest-Litovsk, Poland. The youngest of six children, Dubinsky worked in the family bakery. When his co-workers struck for higher wages, David was right out in front marching with a picket sign.

Dubinsky's political activities earned him a prison term in Siberia at the age of 16, but he managed to escape and make his way to New York in 1911. Dubinsky joined the International Ladies Garment Workers Union and rose to the presidency – a position he held for 34 years. In 1935, Dubinsky helped found the Committee for Industrial Organization. (In 1938, the name was changed to the Congress of Industrial Organizations.) Over the years, Dubinsky's abilities in collective bargaining and international labor affairs won him international fame as a labor leader. When he resigned from union leadership in 1966 at the age of seventy-four Dubinsky said simply. "I don't want to die in my boots."

Labor Architect Arthur Joseph Goldberg (1908–) has been called the "Architect of the AFL-CIO merger." Goldberg served as legal counsel to the CIO and was instrumental in bringing about the merger of the American Federation of Labor and the Congress of Industrial Organizations in 1955, which created the most powerful labor force in American history.

The son of Russian immigrants, Goldberg became Secretary of Labor in President Kennedy's administration, and was later named as a Supreme Court Justice. His most recent federal post was as U.S. Ambassador to the United Nations under President Johnson.

First President of the AFL Working under the motto "A fair day's wage for a fair day's work," Samuel Gompers (1850–1924) organized the Federation of Organized Trades and Labor Unions of the United States and Canada in 1881.

Gompers, born in England of Jewish-Dutch ancestry, emigrated to the United

States at the age of 13 and found work in a cigar factory. He became involved in union affairs, and in 1878 he led the Cigar Makers' International Union's first strike. As a result of his leadership, Gompers was "blacklisted" by manufacturers and began devoting his energies to the national labor movement.

When the American Federation of Labor was formed in 1886, Gompers was elected as the AFL's first president—a position he held for over 37 years. Over the years Gompers supported legislation to regulate working hours and conditions for women and children, and fought to establish the eight-hour day. Throughout his career, Gompers remained opposed to industrial unionism, insisting that only skilled workers join his union. He regarded unskilled labor as the natural "enemy" of craftsmen. In 1938 this policy led to a rift among the ranks of AFL members, as many broke away to join the newly formed CIO.

Chauffeured Communist Recruited to the ranks of the Communist Party at the age of seventeen by his father, Gus Hall (1910–) was chosen to study at the Lenin Institute in Moscow between 1931 and 1933. The son of Finnish immigrant parents, Arvo Kusta Halberg legally changed his name in the 1930s to the more American-sounding Gus Hall.

Currently the General Secretary of the Communist Party in America, a position he has held since 1959, Gus rides to work each day in a chauffeured automobile. Despite this fact, he is not guilty of exhibiting decadent capitalistic tendencies. Hall is the victim of an obscure New York State law which prohibits persons convicted under

---

In 1913 Frederick J. Haskin wrote the poem *The Immigrant, An Asset and a Liability*, in tribute to the contribution of America's foreign-born workers:

"I am the immigrant . . .
I contribute 85% of all the labor in the slaughtering and meat-packing industries.
I do seven-tenths of the bituminous coal mining.
I do 78% of all the work in the woolen mills.
I contribute nine-tenths of all the labor in the cotton mills.
I make nineteen-twentieths of all the clothing.
I manufacture more than half the shoes.
I build four-fifths of all the furniture.
I make half of the collars, cuffs and shirts.
I turn out four-fifths of all the leather.
I make half the gloves.
I refine nearly nineteen-twentieths of the sugar.
I make half of the tobacco and cigars.
And yet, I am the great American problem . . ."

Some businessmen maintain that, without "cheap" immigrant labor to man the "sweat shops" and pick the crops in the fields of the Southwest, they could not survive. Even today, illegal aliens are still sewing collars and sleeves on garments at "piecework" wages. They are still grossly underpaid, but because they lack "green cards" they willingly assume their places behind the sewing machines of America in search of a better life for themselves and their families in the United States.

---

the Smith Act (conspiracy to overthrow the government) from operating a motor vehicle.

"Don't Mourn" Before Joe Hill died in front of a Utah firing squad in 1915, his last words were: "Don't waste any time in mourning — organize." Born Joel Hagglund in Sweden, Joe Hill was a protest-song writer and an organizer for the Industrial Workers of the World. When he died in 1915 he became an international working-class martyr.

A member of the "Wobblies" (as the Industrial Workers of the World were affectionately known), Joe Hill was convicted of murdering a grocery store clerk, though fellow "Wobblies" maintain to this day that he was framed because of his militant labor agitation tactics.

The IWW's goal was to form one large union throughout the world, of both skilled and unskilled workers, but between 1910 and 1920 they never managed to push their enrollment beyond 250,000 members. Many of the IWW leaders were jailed under espionage laws, and enrollment dropped sharply because of the Wobblies' opposition to American participation in World War I. Today there are only about 1,000 Wobblies left, but they still stand behind Joe Hill. According to an IWW spokesman, "Joe Hill was our guy. We have maintained all along he was framed."

Industry, Not Craft Sydney Hillman (1887–1946), a Lithuanian-Jewish immigrant who became the first president of the Amalgamated Clothing Workers union, believed that workers should unite according to industry rather than by craft. Unlike Gompers, Hillman urged all members of the garment industry, regardless of their individual skills, to band together and strike for higher wages and increased benefits.

Hillman led the Amalgamated Clothing Workers for over 33 years; during his tenure he fought for health and welfare programs as well as unemployment benefits for his workers. He helped form the CIO in 1935, and was Director of the U.S. Office of Production Management under President Roosevelt's administration in 1941.

Proud Plumber George Meany (1894–1979), the grandson of an Irish immigrant and the son of a plumbers' union official, was president of the AFL-CIO from 1955 until his retirement in 1979. Throughout his career, Meany was outspoken against corruption in the unions, and in 1957 he ousted three member unions, including the Teamsters, from AFL-CIO ranks.

Proud of his working-class background and of his years of labor as a plumber, Meany once stated, "Yes, I am a plumber. I don't know how humble I am, but I always try to stress the importance of the plumbing business. I say plumbers, in a good many cases, are more important than lawyers. You can put millions of people in a great city and get along without lawyers; but you couldn't get them in there without plumbers. So I must warn you never to underestimate the importance of a plumber. In fact, I know anyone who has ever got a bill from a plumber doesn't underestimate them."

Man of Steel Philip Murray (1886–1952), the Scots-born son of an Irish coal miner, was responsible for organizing America's steel workers into their own union in 1936. Murray hired 433 organizers, opened 35 regional offices, and began publishing the *Steel Labor* newspaper to get his message to the workingman. Within a few months, enrollment had soared to 125,000.

Murray became president of the CIO in 1940 and warned that "Unless jobs are available . . . the seeds of World War III would be planted and cultivated for another bloody harvest when the infants of 1944 reached manhood."

Music to Their Ears When James Caesar Petrillo (1892–   ) sat down at the bargaining table to negotiate for the American Federation of Musicians (AFM), the concessions he won were like "music to the ears" of his union members. An Italian-American from Chicago, Petrillo was so tough in his union demands that he was often called the "Mussolini of Music."

After he assumed the presidency of the AFM in 1922, Petrillo won seven days pay for a five-day week; he obtained a contract which gave the union control over music aired on Chicago radio stations; and in 1942 he even managed to have recording companies agree to pay a royalty to the musicians' union for every record that was sold.

Petrillo resigned as president in 1958, but retained control of the Chicago branch of the AFM for the next five years.

WOOING THE ETHNIC VOTER

Whenever a politician marches in a Pulaski Day Parade, wears the green on March 17th, chomps on an eggroll in Chinatown, or munches a knish in a Kosher deli, he is trying to woo the ethnic voter over to his side. If a presidential candidate can persuade all the Irish-Americans to vote for him he could win 15 million votes; if he convinces the Italians that he will do something special "just for them," he could garner another 23 million potential voters. More and more politicians are realizing the importance of getting that "bloc" vote, and more and more of them are promising special interest groups "special considerations" in return for their ballots.

But, do Americans tend to vote along purely ethnic or purely religious lines? Let's examine some statistics compiled by Levy and Kramer (*The Ethnic Factor: How America's Minorities Decide Elections*) and other pollsters:

♦ Blacks, Jews, Italians and Slavs are usually loyal to members of their own ethnic group when voting in elections. Irish and Mexican-Americans do not, as a rule, support their "own kind" blindly for elective office.

♦ Irish-Americans tend to vote Democratic. According to a survey conducted in 1970 by Father Andrew M. Greeley, Director, Center for the Study of American Pluralism, at the University of Chicago, Irish Catholics were second only to Jewish Americans in their "liberal" points of view with regard to such issues as racial integration.

♦ Blacks, Asians and Hispanics tend to vote Democratic by as much as 5 to 1.

♦ There are 16 million Black Americans eligible to vote, but only 9 million are registered. Since they traditionally vote Democratic, the Republicans certainly aren't in a hurry to encourage the other 7 million to register.

♦ When John Lindsay lost the Republican nomination for mayor of New York in 1969, experts blamed his loss on the defection of the Italian vote. John Marchi outpolled Lindsay three to one in the major Italian precincts throughout the city.

♦ Despite the fact that Blacks constitute

Despite the fact that Wendell Willkie knew the value of appealing to the "ethnic voter," he was defeated by Roosevelt in 1940.

only 3% of the total population of the state of Massachusetts, Edward Brooke became that state's first Black senator in 1966 and the first Black senator from any state since Reconstruction.

♦ In 1970, Edward Kennedy won 79% of the Irish vote in Massachusetts in his bid for reelection to the Senate.

♦ Even though Hubert Humphrey got 87% of the Chicano vote, 94% of the Black vote and 83% of the Jewish vote—he lost the 1968 Presidential race to Richard Nixon.

♦ In 1976, while campaigning for the Presidential election in New York's "Little Italy," Jimmy Carter made a speech calling upon the "eye-talians" of New York to vote for him. A woman in the crowd asked, "How does he expect us to vote for him when he calls us 'eye-talians'?" On election day Ford walked off with 65% of the Italian vote in New York, while Carter got only 35%, but nationwide Carter received 56% of the "eye-talian" ballots.

APPENDICES

ETHNIC UPDATE

America's Changing Ethnic Mix Over the past two centuries immigration has vastly changed the ethnic composition of the United States. In 1790, when the first U.S. Census was tallied, the British segment of the population was close to 70%. By 1950, the British segment had declined to 35%, and in 1973, although the British were still our major "minority," only 12.6% of all Americans claimed to be descended solely from English, Scottish or Welsh ancestors.

Each year some 400,000 new immigrants flock to America's cities and suburbs, seeking a new life for themselves and their children. With America's ever-declining birthrate, these new citizens represent almost 20% of our annual increase in population.

As recently as thirty years ago, the majority of immigrants arriving in the United States were natives of Europe and North America, but when immigration restrictions were relaxed in the late 1960s the tide of immigration changed. By 1975, the top geographical areas supplying America with new citizens were Asia, the West Indies and Mexico—adding a distinct Oriental and Latin flavor to the American stockpot.

Between 1965 and 1975 the ten nations which supplied America with the most immigrants were: Mexico (538,264), Cuba (290,760), the Philippines (238,890), Italy (217,053), China/Taiwan (181,393), Canada (159,665), the United Kingdom (157,184), Korea (138,111), Greece (128,924) and the Dominican Republic (125,795).

PERCENT CHANGE IN NUMBER OF IMMIGRANTS, 1965–1975

	1965	1975	% change
Europe	113,424	73,996	− 34.8%
Asia	20,683	132,469	+540.5
Canada	38,327	7,308	− 80.9
Mexico	37,969	62,205	+ 63.8
West Indies	37,583	67,430	+ 79.4
South America	30,962	22,984	− 25.8

10 NATIONS WITH LARGEST % INCREASE IN IMMIGRATION BETWEEN 1965 AND 1975

	1965	1975	increase
India	582	15,773	2610.1%
Thailand	214	4,217	1870.6
Pakistan	187	2,620	1301.1
Vietnam	226	3,039	1244.7
Korea	2,165	28,362	1210.0
Trinidad/Tobago	485	5,982	1133.4
Philippines	3,130	31,751	914.4
Hong Kong	712	4,891	586.9
Jamaica	1,837	11,076	502.9
Portugal	2,005	11,845	490.8

TOP TEN SOURCES OF IMMIGRANTS TO THE UNITED STATES

1965		1975		1978	
Canada	38,327	Mexico	62,205	Mexico	92,367
Mexico	37,969	Philippines	31,751	Vietnam	88,543
U.K.	27,358	Korea	28,362	Philippines	37,216
Germany	24,045	Cuba	25,955	Cuba	29,754
Cuba	19,760	China/Taiwan	18,536	Korea	29,288
Colombia	10,885	India	15,775	Taiwan	21,315
Italy	10,821	Dominican		India	20,753
Dominican		Republic	14,066	Dominican	
Republic	9,504	Portugal	11,845	Republic	19,458
Poland	8,465	Italy	11,552	Jamaica	19,265
Argentina	6,124	Jamaica	11,076	U.K.	14,245

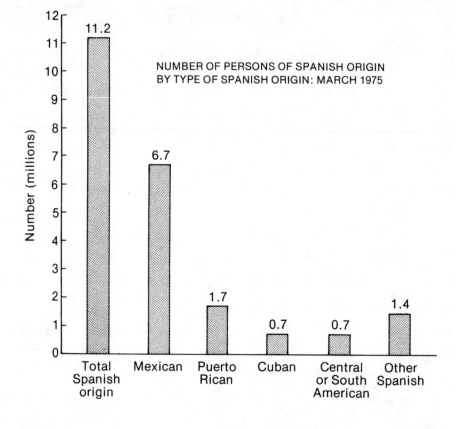

NUMBER OF PERSONS OF SPANISH ORIGIN
BY TYPE OF SPANISH ORIGIN: MARCH 1975

By 1976 there were 11.1 million persons of Hispanic origin (including Mexicans, Puerto Ricans, Cubans, Central and South Americans and other Spanish-speaking people) living in the United States. Because of continuing immigration and the youth of the Hispanic population (44% are under the age of 18), demographers predict that Hispanics will soon be our nation's largest minority group. Spanish is now the most widely spoken language (aside from English, of course) in the United States.

Who's Coming to America? Increased affluence throughout the industrialized nations of Europe led to a decline in immigration from that continent of almost 35% in the decade between 1965 and 1975. During that same period, however, the number of immigrants from Asia increased by more than 540%, while immigration from individual nations such as Thailand, India, Pakistan, Korea and Vietnam increased by 1,000% to 2,000%.

Similarly, the number of immigrants from Trinidad/Tobago and from Jamaica increased by 1133% and 502% respectively. Over the past decade the number of immigrants from the West Indies has increased so rapidly that the Caribbean now ranks as the ninth largest source of immigrants to the U.S. Up until 1967 that place was held by Sweden, but the sudden upsurge in the number of immigrants from the West Indies demoted Sweden to tenth place and ousted Norway from the list of top ten nations.

CHANGES IN THE IMMIGRANTS' TOP TEN

	1820–1967			*1820–1975*	
1	Germany	6,879,495	1	Germany	6,954,160
2	Italy	5,096,204	2	Italy	5,269,992
3	United Kingdom	4,735,489	3	United Kingdom	4,851,806
4	Ireland	4,708,845	4	Ireland	4,720,427
5	Austria-Hungary	4,289,215	5	Austria-Hungary	4,312,252
6	Canada	3,870,839	6	Canada	4,048,329
7	U.S.S.R.	3,345,909	7	U.S.S.R.	3,354,026
8	Mexico	1,457,307	8	Mexico	1,911,951
9	Sweden	1,263,590	9	West Indies	1,408,027
10	Norway	851,093	10	Sweden	1,269,969

1980 Census   Exactly how the ethnic mix of America has changed over the past few decades will not be known until the results of the 1980 Census are tabulated and analyzed. For the first time in our nation's history, the Census Bureau has included questions that pertain to a person's ethnic background.

While some critics contend that such inquiries will produce data of dubious value because the census takers must rely on a person's own terms of self-identification, politicians nonetheless will be watching the results closely.

---

4. Is this person —

Fill one circle.

O White   O Asian Indian
O Black or Negro   O Hawaiian
O Japanese   O Guamanian
O Chinese   O Samoan
O Filipino   O Eskimo
O Korean   O Aleut
O Vietnamese   O Other — *Specify*
O Indian (Amer.)
   Print
   tribe → ----------------------------

---

7. Is this person of Spanish/Hispanic origin or descent?

Fill one circle.

O No, not Spanish/Hispanic
O Yes, Mexican, Mexican-Amer., Chicano
O Yes, Cuban
O Yes, Puerto Rican
O Yes, other Spanish/Hispanic

---

13. What is this person's ancestry? *If uncertain about how to report ancestry, see instruction guide.*

(For example — Afro-Amer., English, French, German, Honduran, Hungarian, Italian, Jamaican, Korean, Lebanese, Mexican, Nigerian, Polish, Ukrainian, Venezuelan, etc.)

Questions pertaining to race and ancestry have been added to the 1980 Census forms.

IMMIGRANTS ADMITTED TO
U.S.
1820–1975

Germany	6,954,160
Italy	5,269,992
Great Britain	4,851,806
Ireland	4,720,427
Austria-Hungary	4,312,252
Canada	4,048,329
U.S.S.R.	3,354,026
Mexico	1,911,951
West Indies	1,408,027
Sweden	1,269,969
Norway	855,337
France	742,442
Greece	629,349
Poland	502,658
China	487,803
Portugal	411,136
Japan	391,389
Turkey	382,324
Denmark	362,833
Netherlands	356,282
Switzerland	246,468
Spain	246,334
Belgium	200,575
Romania	165,747
Czechoslovakia	135,995
Australia/New Zealand	110,560
Yugoslavia	106,108
India	107,446

The State Department estimates that during fiscal year 1980, 350,000 refugees will be admitted to the United States: 168,000 from Indochina; 117,000 from Cuba; 50,000 from the Soviet Union and Eastern Europe; and 15,000 from Haiti.

TOP TEN FOREIGN-STOCK GROUPS, IN EACH STATE (1970)

The following table shows country or origin of U.S. residents who were either born on foreign soil or had at least one foreign-born parent. Children of "mixed" marriages are not included—only those born to parents of similar ethnic backgrounds:

ALABAMA				ALASKA		
Foreign-Stock Population:		63,730		Foreign-Stock Population:		32,605
Germany	12,074			Canada	6,499	
U.K.	8,944			Germany	3,526	
Italy	5,771			U.K.	3,081	
Canada	5,232			Norway	2,501	
Poland	2,097			Sweden	1,565	
Greece	2,092			Japan	1,203	
Ireland	1,912			Italy	866	
U.S.S.R.	1,854			Ireland	804	
France	1,799			Mexico	766	
Western Asia	1,753			Poland	765	

ARIZONA

Foreign-Stock Population:	296,400
Mexico	113,816
Canada	26,136
Germany	25,653
U.K.	19,866
Italy	12,498
U.S.S.R.	8,812
Poland	7,930
Sweden	6,903
Ireland	5,670
Austria	5,370

ARKANSAS

Foreign-Stock Population:	37,556
Germany	9,806
U.K.	3,797
Canada	3,016
Italy	2,284
Poland	1,331
Czeckoslovakia	1,170
Sweden	1,100
Norway	1,056
Austria	1,027
France	1,010

CALIFORNIA

Foreign-Stock Population:	4,992,079
Mexico	1,112,008
Canada	439,862
U.K.	373,495
Germany	360,656
Italy	340,675
U.S.S.R.	221,198
Japan	144,335
China	136,860
Poland	115,833
Ireland	109,888

COLORADO

Foreign-Stock Population:	279,890
Germany	43,172
U.S.S.R.	28,023
U.K.	26,377
Mexico	24,759
Canada	21,580
Italy	21,411
Sweden	13,193
Austria	9,242
Poland	7,882
Ireland	7,804

CONNECTICUT

Foreign-Stock Population:	969,807
Italy	227,782
Canada	126,305
Poland	103,820
U.K.	71,532
Ireland	60,366
Germany	60,290
U.S.S.R.	48,150
Austria	24,595
Sweden	23,427
Hungary	21,641

DELAWARE

Foreign-Stock Population:	64,358
Italy	12,112
U.K.	7,949
Poland	7,263
Germany	5,991
Ireland	4,244
Canada	4,047
U.S.S.R.	3,523
Austria	1,819
Greece	1,117
Hungary	952

FLORIDA

Foreign-Stock Population:	1,235,983
Cuba	252,520
Germany	123,429
U.K.	114,870
Canada	114,615
Italy	84,881
U.S.S.R.	81,833
Poland	50,591
Ireland	36,389
Austria	35,896
Sweden	26,944

GEORGIA

Foreign-Stock Population:	111,516
Germany	20,951
U.K.	14,517
Canada	10,021
U.S.S.R.	5,831
Italy	5,220
Poland	4,574
Ireland	3,461
Greece	2,984
France	2,684
Austria	2,646

HAWAII

Foreign-Stock Population:	256,172
Japan	105,223
China	20,939
Canada	5,865
U.K.	5,114
Germany	5,112
Italy	1,656
Mexico	1,159
Ireland	1,056
Sweden	841
U.S.S.R.	828

IDAHO

Foreign-Stock Population:	73,544
Canada	10,452
U.K.	10,406
Germany	9,894
Mexico	5,669
Sweden	5,333
Denmark	3,627
Norway	3,534
U.S.S.R.	3,136
Switzerland	1,736
Ireland	1,653

ILLINOIS
Foreign-Stock Population: 2,201,741

Germany	312,070
Poland	299,316
Italy	228,984
Mexico	117,268
U.K.	115,891
U.S.S.R.	110,321
Ireland	101,856
Sweden	98,254
Czechoslovakia	88,259
Canada	80,611

INDIANA
Foreign-Stock Population: 351,258

Germany	64,883
Poland	34,590
U.K.	30,039
Canada	21,920
Mexico	18,325
Italy	17,935
Yugoslavia	14,410
Hungary	14,108
Czechoslovakia	13,681
Austria	10,441

IOWA
Foreign-Stock Population: 297,559

Germany	101,974
U.K.	22,008
Sweden	21,108
Norway	20,418
Denmark	20,024
Netherlands	19,213
Canada	13,297
Czechoslovakia	10,995
Ireland	9,441
Italy	7,683

KANSAS
Foreign-Stock Population: 175,048

Germany	43,252
U.S.S.R.	17,664
U.K.	15,986
Mexico	13,728
Canada	10,425
Sweden	9,622
Austria	5,581
Czechoslovakia	4,978
Ireland	4,853
Italy	4,552

KENTUCKY
Foreign-Stock Population: 72,633

Germany	21,438
U.K.	7,619
Canada	4,823
Italy	4,499
Ireland	3,156
U.S.S.R.	2,531
Poland	2,147
France	1,848
Swtizerland	1,650
Austria	1,626

LOUISIANA
Foreign-Stock Population: 139,763

Italy	29,031
Germany	14,237
U.K.	9,252
Cuba	6,711
Canada	6,090
France	5,420
Mexico	4,865
Ireland	3,240
U.S.S.R.	3,073
Poland	2,771

MAINE
Foreign-Stock Population: 192,760

Canada	136,801
U.K.	12,073
Ireland	6,528
Italy	6,083
Germany	4,488
U.S.S.R.	2,878
Sweden	2,740
Poland	2,532
Greece	1,281
Norway	1,234

MARYLAND
Foreign-Stock Population: 454,158

Germany	59,680
Italy	49,619
U.S.S.R.	46,332
U.K.	40,291
Poland	39,334
Canada	25,300
Ireland	18,267
Austria	13,516
Greece	12,508
Czechoslovakia	11,111

MASSACHUSETTS
Foreign-Stock Population: 1,891,724

Canada	466,942
Italy	294,318
Ireland	218,798
U.K.	152,741
Poland	117,992
U.S.S.R.	104,223
Germany	54,846
Greece	39,669
Sweden	38,753
Lithuania	32,617

MICHIGAN
Foreign-Stock Population: 1,684,270

Canada	353,154
Poland	214,085
Germany	184,192
U.K.	148,612
Italy	117,064
Netherlands	72,763
U.S.S.R.	65,606
Austria	40,730
Hungary	39,202
Sweden	33,639

MINNESOTA
Foreign-Stock Population: 707,274

Germany	137,442
Sweden	114,512
Norway	114,221
Canada	57,604
Poland	26,931
U.K.	25,672
Denmark	22,762
U.S.S.R.	18,666
Netherlands	13,166
Italy	12,910

MISSISSIPPI
Foreign-Stock Population: 30,987

Germany	4,960
Italy	3,957
U.K.	3,910
Canada	2,496
Western Asia	1,249
China	1,078
Ireland	816
Mexico	783
France	733
Poland	730

MISSOURI
Foreign-Stock Population: 311,692

Germany	77,748
Italy	30,114
U.K.	23,080
U.S.S.R.	19,127
Canada	15,532
Ireland	15,470
Poland	15,469
Austria	11,755
Mexico	8,353
Czechoslovakia	7,504

MONTANA
Foreign-Stock Population: 121,322

Canada	21,106
Germany	15,593
Norway	14,595
U.S.S.R.	11,365
U.K.	11,293
Sweden	6,177
Ireland	5,274
Denmark	4,302
Austria	3,464
Yugoslavia	3,020

NEBRASKA
Foreign-Stock Population: 204,352

Germany	62,726
Czechoslovakia	19,551
Sweden	17,099
U.S.S.R.	14,160
Denmark	13,202
U.K.	11,083
Poland	8,333
Canada	8,247
Italy	6,414
Mexico	5,552

NEVADA
Foreign-Stock Population: 68,453

Italy	7,927
Canada	7,587
Germany	7,023
U.K.	6,969
Mexico	5,760
U.S.S.R.	2,247
Ireland	1,991
France	1,959
Sweden	1,670
Poland	1,578

NEW HAMPSHIRE
Foreign-Stock Population: 170,550

Canada	96,834
U.K.	14,040
Ireland	8,436
Poland	6,886
Italy	6,465
Germany	6,308
Greece	5,040
U.S.S.R.	2,982
Sweden	2,774
Lithuania	1,929

NEW JERSEY
Foreign-Stock Population: 2,155,863

Italy	515,889
Germany	219,178
Poland	217,509
U.K.	172,308
U.S.S.R.	143,234
Ireland	122,600
Austria	83,165
Hungary	70,424
Canada	58,720

NEW MEXICO
Foreign-Stock Population: 88,680

Mexico	37,822
Germany	7,438
U.K.	6,000
Canada	5,663
Italy	3,916
U.S.S.R.	1,725
Ireland	1,718
Sweden	1,681
Austria	1,483
Poland	1,422

NEW YORK
Foreign-Stock Population: 5,995,221

Italy	1,330,057
U.S.S.R.	569,813
Poland	557,478
Germany	557,216
Ireland	386,403
U.K.	334,424
Canada	286,047
Austria	237,836
Hungary	115,474
Cuba	98,479

NORTH CAROLINA

Foreign-Stock Population:	94,281
Germany	16,614
U.K.	12,826
Canada	10,334
Italy	4,658
Greece	3,883
Poland	3,037
Japan	2,988
U.S.S.R.	2,928
Western Asia	2,536
Ireland	2,506

NORTH DAKOTA

Foreign-Stock Population:	146,126
Norway	38,722
U.S.S.R.	33,177
Germany	21,004
Canada	15,630
Sweden	8,434
U.K.	3,537
Denmark	3,442
Czechoslovakia	2,473
Austria	2,254
Poland	1,952

OHIO

Foreign-Stock Population:	1,312,346
Germany	188,386
Italy	166,629
Poland	116,262
U.K.	108,027
Czechoslavakia	93,187
Hungary	82,944
Yugoslavia	73,843
Canada	63,258
Austria	62,829
U.S.S.R.	54,520

OKLAHOMA

Foreign-Stock Population:	92,873
Germany	21,475
U.K.	9,812
Canada	7,811
Mexico	6,071
U.S.S.R.	5,463
Italy	3,531
Czechoslovakia	3,411
Poland	2,670
Western Asia	2,488
Ireland	2,386

OREGON

Foreign-Stock Population:	295,506
Canada	53,002
Germany	40,242
U.K.	28,525
Norway	18,085
Sweden	17,830
U.S.S.R.	15,709
Italy	9,644
Denmark	8,792
Mexico	7,739
Ireland	7,175

PENNSYLVANIA

Foreign-Stock Population:	2,133,040
Italy	444,841
Poland	243,752
Germany	202,611
U.K.	198,190
Austria	145,815
Czechoslovakia	118,855
Ireland	118,174
Hungary	62,014
Canada	47,827
Lithuania	43,183

RHODE ISLAND

Foreign-Stock Population:	311,607
Italy	73,255
Canada	66,003
U.K.	34,178
Ireland	21,041
Poland	13,389
U.S.S.R.	11,198
Sweden	6,669
Western Asia	4,211
France	3,261
Austria	2,896

SOUTH CAROLINA

Foreign-Stock Population:	49,770
Germany	9,193
U.K.	7,779
Canada	4,805
Italy	2,653
Greece	2,188
Poland	1,701
U.S.S.R.	1,661
Western Asia	1,382
Ireland	1,336
France	1,069

SOUTH DAKOTA

Foreign-Stock Population:	109,046
Germany	26,792
Norway	18,898
U.S.S.R.	14,041
Sweden	7,790
Canada	6,617
Denmark	6,584
Netherlands	5,126
U.K.	4,562
Czechoslovakia	3,507
Ireland	1,980

TENNESSEE

Foreign-Stock Population:	68,392
Germany	11,675
U.K.	8,682
Canada	6,213
Italy	6,054
U.S.S.R.	3,649
Poland	2,789
Ireland	2,087
Western Asia	1,579
Greece	1,563
Austria	1,354

TEXAS

Foreign-Stock Population: 1,199,018
Mexico	711,058
Germany	104,726
U.K.	49,185
Canada	35,900
Czechoslovakia	29,536
Italy	26,886
Poland	16,328
U.S.S.R.	16,149
Austria	13,397
Ireland	12,143

WASHINGTON

Foreign-Stock Population: 637,606
Canada	136,546
Germany	71,353
U.K.	60,522
Norway	60,427
Sweden	45,251
U.S.S.R.	23,466
Italy	21,422
Mexico	17,892
Japan	15,777
Denmark	14,422

UTAH

Foreign-Stock Population: 131,609
U.K.	28,531
Germany	14,179
Canada	11,194
Denmark	10,464
Mexico	7,710
Netherlands	7,617
Sweden	7,477
Italy	4,688
Norway	4,113
Switzerland	3,392

WEST VIRGINIA

Foreign-Stock Population: 74,020
Italy	17,906
U.K.	8,259
Germany	6,960
Poland	6,360
Czechoslovakia	2,996
Hungary	2,931
Austria	2,572
Yugoslavia	2,549
Western Asia	2,522
Canada	2,492

VERMONT

Foreign-Stock Population: 81,102
Canada	46,176
U.K.	7,008
Italy	4,982
Germany	4,195
Ireland	3,071
Poland	2,797
U.S.S.R.	1,171
Sweden	1,142
Western Asia	652
Norway	651

WISCONSIN

Foreign-Stock Population: 748,148
Germany	234,767
Poland	71,534
Norway	52,681
Canada	36,888
Italy	30,513
U.K.	28,446
Sweden	27,352
Austria	27,343
Czechoslovakia	26,465
U.S.S.R.	24,246

VIRGINIA

Foreign-Stock Population: 251,799
U.K.	32,737
Germany	32,596
Canada	24,048
Italy	18,026
U.S.S.R.	11,129
Ireland	10,162
Poland	9,423
Austria	6,827
Western Asia	6,248
France	6,210

WYOMING

Foreign-Stock Population: 38,003
Germany	5,721
U.K.	5,367
Canada	3,069
U.S.S.R.	2,913
Mexico	2,638
Sweden	2,156
Italy	1,750
Denmark	1,505
Austria	1,300
Yugoslavia	1,263

HOW ARE ETHNIC AMERICANS EMPLOYED?

A survey conducted by the Census Bureau in March 1972 revealed the following employment patterns of 8 ethnic groups in America.

GERMAN Males, 14 years and over (6,714,000)

Craftsmen	21.7%
Operatives	16.5
Professionals	15.0
Managers / Administrators	13.9
Sales Workers	7.0
Service Workers	6.7
Clerical	6.0
Farmers / Managers	5.9
Laborers	5.2
Farm Laborers	2.0
Household Workers	0.1

GERMAN Females, 14 years and over (3,617,000)

Clerical	34.6%
Professionals	17.6
Service Workers	16.6
Operatives	9.8
Sales Workers	5.9
Household Workers	5.4
Managers / Administrators	4.6
Farm Laborers	2.8
Craftsmen	1.2
Laborers	0.8
Farmers / Managers	0.6

ITALIAN Males, 14 years and over (2,420,000)

Craftsmen	22.3%
Operatives	15.8
Managers / Administrators	14.5
Professionals	12.7
Service Workers	9.8
Clerical	8.8
Laborers	8.6
Sales Workers	6.4
Farmers / Managers	0.5
Farm Laborers	0.4
Household Workers	0.1

ITALIAN Females, 14 years and over (1,254,000)

Clerical	38.6%
Operatives	18.0
Service Workers	15.4
Professionals	11.6
Sales Workers	7.4
Managers / Administrators	5.7
Household Workers	1.6
Craftsmen	1.0
Laborers	0.7
Farm Laborers	0.1
Farmers / Managers	—

IRISH Males, 14 years and over (3,885,000)

Craftsmen	23.8%
Operatives	18.5
Managers / Administrators	14.4
Professionals	11.2
Service Workers	7.8
Clerical	7.6
Sales Workers	7.1
Laborers	5.7
Farmers / Managers	2.8
Farm Laborers	1.1
Household Workers	0.2

IRISH Females, 14 years and over (2,543,000)

Clerical	38.7%
Service Workers	17.1
Professionals	12.9
Operatives	11.2
Sales Workers	7.5
Managers / Administrators	5.0
Household Workers	4.3
Craftsmen	1.3
Farm Laborers	0.9
Laborers	0.7
Farmers / Managers	0.3

FRENCH Males, 14 years and over (1,313,000)

Craftsmen	24.1%
Operatives	19.3
Managers / Administrators	13.7
Professionals	11.8
Service Workers	8.5
Clerical	7.0
Laborers	6.8
Sales Workers	5.7
Farmers / Managers	1.6
Farm Laborers	0.9
Household Workers	0.6

FRENCH Females, 14 years and over (791,000)

Clerical	32.7%
Service Workers	20.0
Professionals	16.6
Operatives	11.0
Sales Workers	6.7
Household Workers	5.6
Managers / Administrators	4.6
Craftsmen	1.1
Laborers	0.9
Farm Laborers	0.5
Farmers / Managers	0.1

POLISH   Males, 14 years and over (1,354,000)

Craftsmen	23.3%
Operatives	18.3
Professionals	18.1
Managers / Administrators	12.9
Clerical	7.9
Service Workers	7.7
Sales Workers	6.3
Laborers	4.3
Farmers / Managers	0.9
Farm Laborers	0.4
Household Workers	—

POLISH   Females, 14 years and over (817,000)

Clerical	36.0%
Operatives	16.8
Service Workers	15.1
Professionals	14.1
Sales Workers	8.0
Managers / Administrators	4.9
Household Workers	1.7
Farm Laborers	1.3
Craftsmen	1.2
Laborers	0.9
Farmers / Managers	0.1

RUSSIAN   Males, 14 years and over (584,000)

Professionals	31.7%
Managers / Administrators	23.6
Sales Workers	13.4
Clerical	9.1
Operatives	7.4
Craftsmen	7.2
Service Workers	3.6
Laborers	2.6
Farmers / Managers	0.7
Farm Laborers	0.5
Household Workers	—

RUSSIAN   Females, 14 years and over (327,000)

Clerical	41.3%
Professional	24.5
Managers / Administrators	8.9
Sales Workers	8.3
Operatives	8.6
Service Workers	6.1
Craftsmen	0.9
Farm Laborers	0.6
Household Workers	0.3
Laborers	—
Farmers / Managers	—

ENGLISH, SCOTTISH, WELSH   Males, 14 years and over (7,477,000)

Craftsmen	19.2%
Professionals	19.0
Managers / Administrators	15.8
Operatives	15.1
Sales Workers	7.9
Service Workers	6.8
Clerical	6.5
Laborers	5.1
Farmers / Managers	3.2
Farm Laborers	1.3
Household Workers	0.1

ENGLISH, SCOTTISH, WELSH   Females, 14 years and over (4,445,000)

Clerical	35.3%
Professionals	19.9
Service Workers	13.4
Operatives	10.0
Sales Workers	7.9
Managers / Administrators	5.8
Household Workers	4.2
Craftsmen	1.5
Farm Laborers	0.8
Laborers	0.7
Farmers / Managers	0.3

SPANISH   Males, 14 years and over (1,906,000)

Operatives	27.0%
Craftsmen	19.6
Service Workers	12.9
Laborers	11.6
Clerical	6.8
Professionals	6.8
Managers / Administrators	6.5
Farm Laborers	5.4
Sales Workers	3.0
Farmers / Managers	0.4
Household Workers	—

SPANISH   Females, 14 years and over (977,000)

Operatives	29.8%
Clerical	26.2
Service Workers	19.8
Professionals	6.9
Household Workers	5.7
Sales Workers	4.7
Managers / Administrators	3.3
Farm Laborers	1.5
Laborers	1.2
Craftsmen	0.9
Farmers / Managers	—

OTHER AMERICANS Males, 14 years and over (19,447,000)

Operatives	19.4%
Craftsmen	19.1
Professionals	13.0
Managers / Administrators	11.3
Service Workers	9.7
Laborers	9.1
Clerical	7.0
Sales Workers	6.3
Farmers / Managers	2.8
Farm Laborers	2.1
Household Workers	0.2

OTHER AMERICANS Females, 14 years and over (13,553,000)

Clerical	33.0%
Service Workers	19.0
Professionals	14.4
Operatives	11.7
Household Workers	8.6
Sales Workers	6.2
Managers / Administrators	3.9
Farm Laborers	1.1
Craftsmen	1.0
Laborers	0.7
Farmers / Managers	0.3

OCCUPATIONS: 1890

	Blacks	Native Whites	Foreign-born Whites
Domestic personal service	31%	12%	27%
Agriculture, hunting, fishing	57	47	26
Manufacturing	6	19	31
Trade, transportation	5	16	14
Professional	1	6	2

According to the 1890 Census, 31% of all foreign-born whites were employed as factory workers, while 27% were engaged as domestic servants. Only 2% were "professionals" — doctors, lawyers, business managers.

WHO HAS THE BEST JOB STATUS IN AMERICA?

The WASPs are our outstanding "minority" in this area, accounting for over 20% of the nation's professionals. But in proportion to their population size, do the WASPs really have a bigger piece of the pie than other ethnic groups?

It appears not. In fact, if a ratio between the size of the professional work force and the size of the ethnic group is calculated, it becomes obvious that the Russians are number one. The Russians comprise only 1.2% of the population, yet they form 2.7%

of the professional workers. That gives them a "skills ratio" of 2.25. The British segment of the population accounts for 20.6% of the professional work force. But, since they make up 15.0% of the population (Americans of mixed ancestry are not counted in this survey), their skills ratio is only 1.37 — much less than that of the Russians.

The next highest group is the Poles, followed by the Germans, Italians, French, Irish and Spanish.

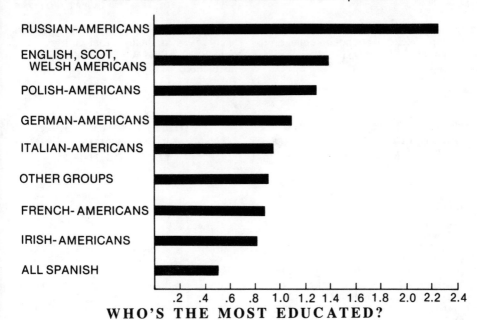

Skills Ratio: % Professionals vs. % of Population

RUSSIAN-AMERICANS

ENGLISH, SCOT, WELSH AMERICANS

POLISH-AMERICANS

GERMAN-AMERICANS

ITALIAN-AMERICANS

OTHER GROUPS

FRENCH- AMERICANS

IRISH- AMERICANS

ALL SPANISH

.2 .4 .6 .8 1.0 1.2 1.4 1.6 1.8 2.0 2.2 2.4

WHO'S THE MOST EDUCATED?

According to a 1972 survey of 8 ethnic groups, Russian-Americans between the ages of 25 and 34 had completed a median of 16.0 years of schooling, compared to only 12.9 years for English, Scottish and Welsh Americans of the same age group. Polish-Americans ranked third, with a median of 12.8 years of education, followed by the Germans, with 12.7 years, and the Irish, French, Italian and "other" ethnics, who had received 12.6 years of schooling. Spanish-Americans, including everyone from Mexican migrant workers to Cuban lawyers, ranked the lowest, with only 11.3 years of education.

High School Graduates In a survey of ethnic Americans aged 35 and older, 78.5% of the Russian-American population claimed to have graduated from high school. The second highest group were the English, Scottish and Welsh, with 65.4%.

PERCENT OF POPULATION THAT GRADUATED FROM HIGH SCHOOL

Ethnic Group	age 25–34	age 35 and older
German	85.9%	55.6%
Italian	80.4	44.0
Irish	78.6	53.5
French	72.8	49.7
Polish	88.7	44.9
Russian	98.4	78.5
English, Scottish, Welsh	85.7	65.4
Spanish	45.3	26.9
Other	75.9	50.1
All Groups	77.2	52.2

MEDIAN NUMBER OF SCHOOL YEARS COMPLETED (MARCH 1972)

Ethnic Group	age 25–34	age 35 and older
German	12.7	12.2
Italian	12.6	11.1
Irish	12.6	12.1
French	12.6	11.9
Polish	12.8	11.2
Russian	16.0	12.6
English, Scottish, Welsh	12.9	12.4
Spanish	11.3	8.2
Other	12.6	12.0
Total	12.6	12.1

College Graduates Again, the Russian-Americans aged 25–34 outdistanced all other ethnic groups in the percentage of their population that attended college. Almost 70% of the Russian population, compared to only 45.1% of the English, Scottish and Welsh, attended college for between one and four years.

Over 51% of the Russian-Americans aged 25–34 graduated from college, while only 26.3% of the WASPs could claim that distinction.

PERCENT OF POPULATION THAT ATTENDED COLLEGE (1–4 YEARS OR MORE)		
Ethnic Group	age 25–34	age 35 and older
German	34.8%	19.5%
Italian	29.3	12.1
Irish	32.4	18.3
French	31.6	17.4
Polish	41.2	14.1
Russian	69.8	34.8
English, Scottish, Welsh	45.1	29.7
Spanish	13.8	10.2
Other	32.7	18.7
All Groups	33.3	19.7

PERCENT OF COLLEGE-EDUCATED POPULATION (4 YEARS OR MORE)		
Ethnic Group	age 25–34	age 35 and older
German	19.2%	10.2%
Italian	16.5	6.0
Irish	16.3	9.5
French	13.2	8.0
Polish	24.1	7.0
Russian	51.8	20.6
English, Scottish, Welsh	26.3	15.4
Spanish	4.2	5.1
Other	17.1	9.8
All Groups	17.9	10.2

TRACING YOUR ANCESTRY

Armed with a notebook and a pen, you can trace your own "roots" by 1) talking to family members; 2) examining family-held documents, such as wills, diaries, birth certificates, marriage certificates and entries in family Bibles; 3) tracking down official records in U.S. cities and states; 4) examining records of ship's passengers, which have been kept since 1820; and 5) traveling abroad to examine local parish records of births, deaths and marriages.

All of these sources can provide the clues you need to fill in the blanks on your family tree. If your grandparents were immigrants, you probably know what country they came from, and maybe even which city, but how much do you know about your grandparents' parents? Unless your grandparents are still alive to provide the answers, you might wish to track down your great-grandparents and their ancestors by investigating local village records. There you may be able to find out if your ancestors were peasants or aristocrats, landed gentry or tenant farmers; how long they lived in that particular region; where *their* ancestors orginally came from; and other facts.

The following lists of books, libraries, and other information sources should prove helpful in your search. There are also professional genealogists whose services may be enlisted in your sleuthing. Contact the Board for Certification of Genealogists, 1307 New Hampshire Avenue N.W., Washington, D.C. 20036 for a listing of genealogists who will do research for a fee.

20 PLACES TO START YOUR SEARCH

1 American Antiquarian Society
185 Salisbury St.,
Worcester, MA 01609
Repository for national genealogical records.

2 American Irish Historical Society Library
991 Fifth Avenue
New York, NY 10028
Specialty: The Irish in America and in New York City; Irish art.

3 The Church of Jesus Christ of Latter-Day Saints Visitors Center
50 E. North Temple Street
Salt Lake City, UT 84150

The Mormon Church in Salt Lake City has over 1 billion names on microfilm, which make it the largest genealogical collection in the world. Librarians in the 231 branches throughout the world will answer inquiries using materials available; they will not, however, engage in specific research.

4 The Holland Society of New York Library
122 E. 58th St.
New York, NY 10022
Specialty: Dutch colonial period; genealogy of New Netherland settlers.

5 Huntington Historical Society Library
2 High Street
Huntington, NY
Specialty: Local history and genealogy.

6 The Library of Congress
General Reference & Bibliography
Washington, DC 20540
Indexes arranged by family name and geographic location; also newspaper files which predate the Revolutionary War.

7 National Archives & Record Service
Central Reference Division
Washington, DC 20408
Census records from 1790, ships' passenger records from 1820 and military service records from the Revolutionary War.

8 The Newberry Library
60 W. Walton Street
Chicago, IL 60610
Repository of national genealogical records.

9 New England Historical Genealogical Society
101 Newbury St.
Boston, MA 02116
Useful for those with colonial ancestors.

10 The Long Island Historical Society Library
128 Pierrepont Street
Brooklyn, NY 11201
Speciality: Genealogy of Long Island settlers.

11 The New York Genealogical and Biographical Society Library
122 E. 58th St.
New York, NY 10022
Specialty: Genealogy, heraldry.

12 The New York Public Library Research Libraries, American History Division
5th Avenue and 42nd Street
Room 315A
New York, NY 10018
Specialty: American Indians; history of Black Americans.

13 The New York Public Library Research Libraries, Local History and Genealogy Division
5th Avenue and 42nd Street
Room 315
New York, NY 10018
Specialty: Genealogy; heraldry; origins and meaning of names; local U.S. history; British Isles and Ireland.

14 Queens Borough Public Library
Long Island Division
89-11 Merrick Blvd.
Jamaica, NY 11432
Specialty: Long Island history and genealogy.

15 The Society of Mayflower Descendants in the State of New York
122 E. 58th St.
New York, NY 10022

16 Sons of the American Revolution Library
4 W. 43rd St.
New York, NY 10036
Specialty: U.S. genealogy and history.

17 Sons of the Revolution in the State of New York Fraunces Tavern Museum Library
54 Pearl Street
New York, NY 10004
Specialty: Revolutionary War period; genealogy and history of downtown New York.

18 Staten Island Historical Society Library
302 Center Street
Staten Island, NY 10306
Specialty: Local history and genealogy.

19 Westchester County Historical Society Library
43 Read Avenue
Tuckahoe, NY 10707
Specialty: Westchester County history and genealogy.

20 Yivo Institute for Jewish Research
1048 Fifth Avenue
New York, NY 10028
Specialty: Eastern European Jewish families.

GUIDES TO GENEALOGICAL RESEARCH

GENERAL: UNITED STATES

American Genealogical Research Institute. *How to Trace Your Family Tree: A Complete and Easy-To-Understand Guide for the Beginner.* Arlington, Va., 1973.

American Society of Genealogists. *Genealogical Research.* Washington, D.C., 1960.

Arizona Temple District Genealogical Library. *Practical Research in Genealogy: A Compilation of Genealogical Research Data.* Mesa, Arizona, 1955.

Basic Course in Genealogy: Instruction To Help Beginners in Genealogical Research. Hampton, Va.: Thomas Nelson Community College, 1972.

Bennett, Archibald F. *Advanced Genealogical Resarch.* Salt Lake City: Bookcraft: 1957.

_____. *Finding Your Forefathers in America.* Salt Lake City, Bookcraft: 1957.

_____. *A Guide for Genealogical Research.* Salt Lake City: Genealogical Society of the Church of Jesus Christ of Latter-Day Saints, 1951.

_____. *Searching With Success: A Genealogical Text.* Salt Lake City: Deseret Book Company, 1962.

Cache Genealogical Library. *Handbook for Genealogical Correspondence,* Salt Lake City: Bookcraft, 1963.

Colket, M. B., and F. E. Bridgers. *Guide to Genealogical Records in the National Archives, Washington.* National Archives Publication No. 64-8, 1964.

Daughters of the American Revolution. *Is That Lineage Right? A Training Manual for the Examiner of Lineage Papers, With Helpful Hints for the Beginner in Genealogical Research.* Washington: National Society of the Daughters of the American Revolution, 1965.

Doane, G. H. *Searching for Your Ancestors: The How and Why of Genealogy.* Minneapolis: University of Minnesota Press, 1973.

Everton, G. B. *The Handy Book for Genealogists.* Logan, Utah: Everton Publishers, 1971.

_____. *The How Book for Genealogists.* Logan, Utah: Everton Publishers, 1973.

Filby, P. W. *American and British Genealogy and Heraldry: A Selected List of Books.* Chicago: American Library Association, 1975.

Fudge, G. H., and F. Smith. *LDS Genealogist's Handbook: Modern Procedures and Systems.* Salt Lake City: Bookcraft, 1972.

Gardner, D. E., et al. *A Basic Course in Genealogy.* Salt Lake City: Bookcraft, 1958.

Genealogical Associates. *Genealogy and Local History: An Archival and Bibliographical Guide.* Evanston, Ill., 1962. Supplement, 1964.

Gobble, J. R. *What To Say in Your Genealogical Letters: Do's and Don't's in Genealogical Correspondence.* Idaho Falls, Idaho, 1967.

Greenwood, V. D. *The Researcher's Guide to American Genealogy.* Baltimore: Genealogical Pub. Co., 1973.

Groene, B. H. *Tracing Your Civil War Ancestor.* Winston-Salem, N.C.: J. F. Blair, 1973.

Hopkins, G. E. *Your Family Tree: A Hobby Handbook.* Richmond: Dietz Press, 1949.

Jacobus, D. L. *Genealogy As Pastime and Profession.* Baltimore: Genealogical Pub. Co., 1968.

Jones, V. L., A. H. Eakle and M. H. Christensen. *Genealogical Research: A Jurisdictional Approach.* Woods Cross, Utah: Genealogical Copy Service, 1972.

Kirkham, E. K. *The ABC's of American Genealogical Research.* Salt Lake City: Deseret Book Co., 1955.

_____. *How to Read the Handwriting and Records of Early America. For Researchers in American Genealogy.* Salt Lake City, Kay Pub. Co., 1961.

_____. *The Land Records of America and Their Genealogical Value.* Washington, 1963.

_____. *Making the Genealogical Record: An Explanation of the O-Kay System of Record-Keeping.* Salt Lake City: Deseret Book Co., 1959.

_____. *Photography in Genealogy: An Explanation of the O-Kay System of Record-Keeping.* Salt Lake City, 1959.

_____. *Research in American Genealogy: A Practical Approach to Genealogical Research.* Salt Lake City, 1956.

_____. *Simplifed Genealogy for Americans.* Salt Lake City: Deseret Book Co., 1968.

_____. *Some of the Military Records of America, Before 1900: Their Use and Value in Genealogical and Historical Research.* Washington, 1963.

_____. *A Survey of American Census Schedules: An Explanation and Description of Our Federal Census Enumerations, 1790-1950.* Salt Lake City: Deseret Book Co., 1959.

Lancour, H. *A Bibliography of Ship Passenger Lists, 1538-1825: Being a Guide to Published Lists of Early Immigrants to North America.* New York: New York Public Library, 1963.

Nichols, E. L. *Help Is Available.* Logan, Utah: Everton Publishers, 1972.

Phillimore, W. P. *How To Write the History of a Family. A Guide for the Genealogist.* London: E. Stock, 1888.

Stetson, O. F. *The Art of Ancestor Hunting: A Guide to Ancestral Research and Genealogy.* Brattleboro, Vermont: Stephen Daye Press, 1936.

Stevenson, N. C. (ed.). *The Genealogical Reader: A Collection of Articles.* Salt Lake City: Deseret Book Company, 1958.

———. *Search and Research, The Researcher's Handbook.* Salt Lake City: Deseret Book Co., 1959.

Williams, E. W. *Know Your Ancestors: A Guide to Genealogical Research.* Rutland, Vt.: C. E. Tuttle Co., 1961.

Wright, N. E., and D. H. Pratt. *Genealogical Research Essentials.* Salt Lake City: Bookcraft, 1967.

Zabriskie, G. O. *Climbing Our Family Tree Systematically.* Salt Lake City: Parliament Press, 1969.

UNITED STATES: REGIONAL

Bowen, R. L. *Massachusetts Records: A Handbook for Genealogists, Historians, Lawyers and Other Researchers.* Rehoboth, Mass., 1957.

Douthit, R. L. *Ohio Resources for Genealogists. With Some References for Genealogical Searching in Ohio.* Detroit Society for Genealogical Research, 1972.

Draughon, W., and W. P. Johnson. *North Carolina Genealogical Reference: A Research Guide for All Genealogists, Both Amateur and Professional.* Durham, N. C., 1966.

Hathaway, B. W. *Genealogy Research Sources in Tennessee.* West Jordan, Utah: Allstates Research Co., 1972.

———. *Primer for Georgia Genealogical Research.* West Jordan, Utah: Allstates Research Co., 1973.

Hoenstine, F. G. *Guide to Genealogical and Historical Research in Pennsylvania.* Hollidaysburg, Pa., 1966.

Jaussi, L. R., and G. D. Chaston. *Genealogical Records of Utah.* Salt Lake City: Deseret Book Co., 1974.

Kirkham, E. K. *The Counties of the United States. For Researchers in American Genealogy and History.* Salt Lake City: Kay Pub. Co., 1961.

———. *A Survey of American Church Records: For the Period Before the Civil War, East of the Mississippi River.* Salt Lake City: Deseret Book Co., 1959–1960.

McCay, B. L. *Sources for Genealogical Searching in Indiana.* Indianapolis, 1969.

———. *Sources for Genealogical Searching in Kentucky.* Indianapolis, 1969.

———. *Sources for Genealogical Searching in Maryland.* 1972. *Sources for Genealogical Searching in North Carolina.* 1969. *Sources for Genealogical Searching in Ohio.* 1973.

Sources for Genealogical Searching in Pennsylvania. 1968. *Sources for Genealogical Searching in Tennessee.* 1970. *Sources for Genealogical Searching in Virginia and West Virginia.* 1971. Indianapolis.

Meyer, M. K. *Genealogical Research in Maryland: A Guide.* Baltimore: Maryland Historical Society, 1972.

New Jersey Bureau of Archives and History. *Genealogical Research: A Guide to Source Materials in the Archives and History Bureau of the New Jersey State Library.* New Brunswick: Genealogical Society of New Jersey, 1971.

North American Genealogical Sources. Compiled by N. E. Wright. Provo, Utah: Brigham Young University, 1968.

Passano, E. P. *An Index of the Source Records of Maryland: Genealogical, Biographical, Historical.* Baltimore: Genealogical Pub. Co., 1967.

Peterson, C. S. *Consolidated Bibliography of County Histories in Fifty States in 1961,* consolidated 1935–1961. Baltimore: Genealogical Pub. Co., 1973.

St. Louis Genealogical Society. *Tracing Family Trees in Eleven States: Missouri, Illinois, Kentucky, Virginia, Georgia, Ohio, North Carolina, South Carolina, Tennessee, Indiana, Pennsylvania.* Brentwood, Mo., 1970.

Stryker-Rodda, K. *New Jersey: Digging for Ancestors in the Garden State.* Detroit Society for Genealogical Research, 1970.

Swem, E. G. *Virginia Historical Index.* Roanoke, Va.: Stone Printing and Manufacturing Co., 1934–1936.

Tennessee State Library and Archives. *Tennessee County Data for Historical and Genealogical Research.* Nashville, 1966.

Waters, M. R. *Genealogical Sources Available at the Indiana State Library for All Indiana Counties.* Indianapolis, 1946.

Williams, J. H. and B. H. *Resources for Genealogical Research in Missouri.* Warrensburg, MO., 1969.

Wright, N. E. *Genealogical Reader: Northeastern United States and Canada.* Provo, Utah: Brigham Young University, 1973.

———. *Genealogy in America.* Salt Lake City: Deseret Book Co., 1968.

BRITISH ISLES

Camp, A. J. *Tracing Your Ancestors.* Baltimore: Genealogical Pub. Co., 1971.

Falley, M. D. *Irish and Scotch-Irish Ancestral Research: A Guide to the Genealogical Records, Methods and Sources in Ireland.* Evanston, Illinois, 1962.

Gardner, D. E., and F. Smith. *Genealogical Research in England and Wales.* Salt Lake City: Bookcraft, 1956–1964.

Hamilton-Edwards, G. K. S. *In Search of Ancestry*. Chichester: Phillimore, 1969.

———. *In Search of Scottish Ancestry*. Baltimore: Genealogical Pub. Co., 1972.

Iredale, D. *Discovering Your Family Tree. A Pocket Guide to Tracing Your English Ancestors*. Shire Publications, 1973.

Kaminkow, M. J. *A New Bibliography of British Genealogy With Notes*. Baltimore: Magna Charta Book Co., 1965.

McCay, B. L. *Seven-Lesson Course in Irish Research and Sources*. Indianapolis, 1972.

Pine, L. G. *The Genealogist's Encyclopedia*. N.Y.: Weybright and Talley, 1969.

———. *Teach Yourself Heraldry and Genealogy*. London: English Universities Press, 1958.

———. *Trace Your Ancestors*. London: Evan Brothers, 1954.

———. *Your Family Tree: A Guide to Genealogical Sources*. London: H. Jenkins, 1962.

Rye, W. *Records and Record Searching: A Guide to the Genealogist and Topographer*. London: G. Allen, 1897.

Society of Genealogists. *Genealogists' Handbook*. London, 1969.

Unett, J. *Making a Pedigree*. Baltimore: Genealogical Pub. Co., 1971.

Wagner, Sir A. R. *English Genealogy*. Oxford: Clarendon Press, 1972.

Willis, A. J. *Genealogy for Beginners*. London: Phillimore, 1970.

OTHER FOREIGN COUNTRIES

Friederichs, H. F. *How To Find My German Ancestors and Relatives*. Neustadt: Degener, 1969.

Kennedy, P. *How To Trace Your Loyalist Ancestors: The Use of the Loyalist Sources in the Public Archives of Canada*. Ottawa: Ontario Genealogical Society, 1971.

Olstad, J. H., and G. Böe. *Kontoret for Kulturelt Samkvem Med Utlandet*. (How To Trace Your Ancestors in Norway.) Oslo, 1959.

Olsson, N. W. *Tracing Your Swedish Ancestry*. Stockholm: Royal Swedish Ministry of Foreign Affairs, 1963.

Pine, L. G. *American Origins*. Baltimore: Genealogical Pub. Co., 1967.

Tracing Your Ancestors in Canada. Canada, Public Archives. Ottawa, 1972.

Tracing Your Ancestors in Nova Scotia. Nova Scotia, Public Archives. Halifax, 1967.

Wellauer, M. A. *A Guide to Foreign Genealogical Research: A Selected Bibliography of Printed Material With Addresses*. Milwaukee, 1973.

Wijnaendts van Resandt, W. *Searching for Your Ancestors in the Netherlands*. The Hague: Centraal Bureau voor Genealogie, 1972.

SPECIAL AIDS FOR TRACING YOUR ANCESTRY

ENGLISH If your family emigrated to America after 1837, a record of family births, marriages and deaths can be located at the General Register Office, St. Catherine's House, 10 Kingsway, London WC2B6JP.

Other information may be gleaned from the Census Returns for England and Wales, at the Census Room of the Public Record Office, Land Registry Building, Portugal Street, London WC1. Only data prior to 1881 can be examined under normal circumstances.

If you desire information prior to 1837, the most accurate records will be found at the registers of the 14,000 parish churches throughout England and Wales, which maintain records of weddings, births and deaths. Many go back to the early 1500s.

SCOTTISH In Scotland, compulsory registrations of births, marriages and deaths did not begin until 1855. Records after that date may be examined at the Scottish Record Office, H. M. Register House, Princes Street, Edinburgh EH 1 3YX.

Census returns for 1841–1891 are available for examination by applying to the Registrar General, New Register House, Edinburgh EH1 3YT.

NORTHERN IRELAND Registration of Protestant marriages began on April 1, 1845, but it wasn't until January 1, 1864, that records for Roman Catholics were kept. Any records prior to 1922 may be found at the local registry, while those compiled after 1922 are maintained at the General Register Office, Oxford House, 49–55 Chichester Street, Belfast BT1 4 HL.

CZECH-JEWISH The Society for the History of Czechoslovak Jews, 25 Mayhew Avenue, Larchmont, New York 10538 is dedicated to researching information pertinent to Czechoslovak Jewry. A two-volume work compiled by the society, *The Jews of*

Czechoslovakia, covers the period from the mid-nineteenth century up until 1938.

HUNGARIAN-JEWISH The World Federation of Hungarian Jews, 136 East 39th Street, New York, N.Y. 10016 has three volumes of information useful for those seeking their Hungarian-Jewish ancestors, entitled *Hungarian Jewish Studies.*

ITALIAN Prior to 1860, birth, marriage and death records were a local affair, and local parishes have many records dating back to the seventeenth century. Between 1860 and 1870, State registers were started in many regions. Information about these documents can be obtained from: Istituto Centrale di Statistica, Via Cesare Balbo 16, Rome.

SWEDISH If you're searching for your Swedish ancestors you might consider a visit to Vaxjo (pronounced Vex-sha), a town about 100 miles south of Stockholm. Since 1965, researchers have been compiling emigration records of the more than 1 million Swedes (one-fourth of the nation) who left their homeland between 1850 and 1930. In the House of Emigrants museum, there are files of family genealogies and histories of the origins of many Swedish-named towns and lakes in North America.

GERMAN A book recently published by Bowker, the *Encyclopedia of German-American Genealogical Research,* by C. N. Smith, details information on German customs, culture and dialects that would be helpful to a genealogical researcher planning to find his roots. A second volume is planned to cover all known emigration files in the German archives. The West German Red Cross Tracing Service has some 36 million cross-referenced index cards and 900,000 photos, which are being used to track down relatives displaced during World War II. The Munich-based operation has been in service for more than thirty years.

BLACKS A useful new volume that deals with the problems of finding one's Black ancestors is *Black Genealogy* (Englewood Cliffs, N.J.: Prentice-Hall, 1977).

QUAKERS Nearly one-third of the Quakers in the United States today live in Indiana. Accordingly, the Friends Book and Supply House of Richmond, Indiana, has published *The Encyclopedia of American Quaker Genealogy,* which contains records of Quaker immigrants to North Carolina, New Jersey, Pennsylvania, New York, Virginia and Ohio.

EARLY AMERICAN COLONISTS The Hoyt Index lists all Revolutionary war soldiers who lived to apply for pensions and bounty lands. For more information, request form #6751 from the General Services Administration, National Archives and Records Service, Washington, D.C. 20408.

EARLY CENSUS REPORTS The federal Archives and Records Center at the Military Ocean Terminal in Bayonne, New Jersey, contains records of the federal Census from 1790 to 1900.

Over the past few years Americans have been turning to their grandparents, great-aunts and great-uncles for their reminiscences and knowledge about family folklore which may extend beyond the turn of the century. A booklet, developed by the Smithsonian Institution to help amateurs do a professional job of collecting the oral histories of their family members, is available from the Superintendent of Documents, U.S. Government Printing Office, Washington, D.C. 20402. Write for price and details for ordering publications by mail.

Family Folklore: Interviewing Guide and Questionnaire.
S/N 047-000-00352-1, 1978, 6 pp.

ETHNIC ORGANIZATIONS

AMERICAN INDIAN

American Indian Historical Society
1451 Masonic Avenue
San Francisco, CA 94117

National Congress of American Indians
1346 Connecticut Avenue, N.W.
Washington, DC 20036

Association on American Indian Affairs
432 Park Avenue South
New York, NY 10016
(non-Indian group)

Bureau of Indian Affairs
Washington, DC 20242

Cherokee National Historical Society
P.O. Box 515
Tahlequak, OK 74464
   Maintains Cherokee Hall of Fame for persons of Cherokee descent who made distinguished contributions to the nation.

Museum of the American Indian
Heye Foundation
Broadway at 155th Street
New York, NY 10032
   World's largest Indian museum, contains artifacts of over 300 tribes — totem poles, drums, textiles and stone carvings.

American Indian Arts Center
1042 Madison Avenue
New York, NY 10021
   Sells art and handicrafts from many North American tribes.

Sioux Indian Museum and Crafts Center
Rapid City, SD 57701

Southeast Museum of the North American Indian
Marathon, FL 33050

Southern Plains Indian Museum and Crafts Center
Anadarko, OK 73005

Museum of the Plains Indians and Crafts Center
Browning, MT 59417

Creek Indian Memorial Association
Creek Indian Museum
Okmulgee, OK 74447

Korczak Ziolkowski
Crazy Horse Mountain Memorial
Black Hills, SD 57730
   Korczak Ziolkowski, a Boston-born sculptor of Polish ancestry, has dedicated his life to carving Crazy Horse Mountain at the request of the Sioux as a memorial to the Indians of North America. The Crazy Horse Carving will be 561 feet high and 641 feet long when completed. Mr. Ziolkowski's studio-home and gallery, with prize-winning works and an Indian museum, are part of the complex, along with the Crazy Horse Mountain Memorial, which is open to the public.

ARABIC-SPEAKING

Association of Arab-American University Graduates
P.O. Box 7391
North End Station
Detroit, MI 48202
   Founded in 1967, AAUG promotes knowledge about the Arab world, and establishes links between Arab-American professionals.

ARMENIAN

Armenian Assembly
Suite 120
522 21st Street, N.W.
Washington, DC 20006

National Association for Armenian Studies and Research
175 Mt. Auburn Street
Cambridge, MA 02138
   Has endowed a permanent chair of Armenian Studies at Harvard University; maintains library of 500 volumes; publishes bulletins and reports; 2,500 members devoted to fostering the study of Armenian history, culture and language in America.

BELGIAN

Belgian American Educational Foundation
Graybar Building
420 Lexington Avenue
New York, NY 10017
American organization concerned with exchange fellowship program for Belgian and American scholars having a master's degree or working for a Ph.D.

BYELORUSSIAN

Byelorussian-American Association in the U.S.A. and
Byelorussian-American Youth Organization
166-34 Gothic Drive
Jamaica, NY 11432
2,400 members in both divisions promote lectures and celebrations to preserve Byelorussian culture in America. Maintains library of 4,000 volumes; publishes monthly Byelorussian journal, *Bielarus,* and quarterlies.

CHINESE

Chinese Information Service
159 Lexington Avenue
New York, NY 10016

China Institute of America
125 East 65th Street
New York, NY
Lectures and exhibits on Chinese art and culture.

CZECHOSLOVAKIAN

Czechoslovak Society of America
2138 S. 61st Street
Cicero, IL 60650

Fraternal benefit life insurance society.
Founded: 1854
Membership: 52,000

DANISH

Danish Information Service
280 Park Avenue
New York, NY 10017

Danish Brotherhood in America
3717 Harney Street
Omaha, NE 68171

ESTONIAN

Estonian Educational Society
Estonian Student Association in the U.S.A.
World Association of Estonians
243 East 34th Street
New York, NY 10016
These three organizations of Americans of Estonian descent seek to spread "culture and friendship between the United States and Estonia" and to preserve Estonian culture in America.

FINNISH

Finnish-American Historical Society of the West
P.O. Box 3515
Portland, OR 97208
Collects and preserves history of Finns in American West.

Finnish Consultate General
540 Madison Avenue
New York, NY 10022

League of Finnish-American Societies
USA office, c/o Ms. Leena Korhonen
Suite 200
Erik B. Paulsson, Inc.
151 West 51st Street
New York, NY 10019

FRENCH

Committee of French-Speaking Societies
11 West 42nd Street
New York, NY 10036
Sponsors celebrations of French holidays in America.

Union Saint Jean Baptiste
One Social Street
Woonsocket, RI 02895
Fraternal benefit life insurance society of almost 50,000 members.

GERMAN

German American National Congress
4740 N. Western Avenue
Chicago, IL 60625
Also known as the Deutsch-Amerikanischer National Kongress (DANK); some 20,000 members of German ancestry promote German language, customs and culture in the United States.

German Society of the City of New York
150 Fifth Avenue
New York, NY
Aids German immigrants with counseling, welfare services, medical care and employment opportunities.

Steuben Society of America
Suite 2003
369 Lexington Avenue
New York, NY 10017
 Members are Americans of Germanic extraction; publishes monthly *Steuben News*.

The Society for German American Studies
204 Franklin Drive
Berea, OH 44017
 Organization devoted to study of German-American history, linguistics, folklore, genealogy, literature, music and art. Holds annual convention at Baldwin-Wallace College in Berea, OH.

Society for the History of the Germans in Maryland
231 St. Paul Place
Baltimore, MD 21202

Pennsylvania German Society
R.D.1
Breinigsville, PA 18031

German Society of Pennsylvania
611 Spring Garden Street
Philadelphia, PA 19123

GREEK

Greek American Progressive Association
3600 Fifth Avenue
Pittsburgh, PA 15213
 10,000 members, all of Greek ancestry or birth, belong to 150 local groups. Found in 1923; publishes *Tribune* five times yearly.

HISPANIC

The Hispanic Society of America
613 West 155th Street
New York, NY 10032
 Founded in 1904 as a museum and reference library dedicated to preserving Hispanic culture. The museum collections include paintings, sculpture, and decorative arts representative of the Iberian Peninsula culture from prehistoric times to present day. The library has over 100,000 volumes, and is a center for research on Spanish and Portuguese art, literature and history.
 Sells publications over the counter and through the mail.

El Museo del Barrio
1945 Third Avenue
New York, NY
 Museum devoted to the preservation of the cultural traditions of the "Barrio," New York's Hispanic enclave. Includes paintings, sculpture, folk art, and a small reference library.

Institute for the Study of the Hispanic American in U.S. Life and History
4340 Birchlake Ct.
Alexandria, VA 22306

Hispanic Institute in the United States
612 West 116th Street
New York, NY 10027

Society for Spanish and Portuguese Historical Studies
Department of History
S.U.N.Y.
New York, NY 10031

HUNGARIAN

American Hungarian Library and Historical Society
215 East 82nd Street
New York, NY 10028

American Hungarian Studies Foundation
177 Somerset Street
New Brunswick, NJ 08903
 Presents annual George Washington Award to persons of Hungarian descent who have achieved success in the United States. Publications include the following books: *Hungarian Pottery, Hungarian Folk Dances, Hungarian Village Furniture, Hungarian Folk Songs and Folk Instruments* and *Herdsmen's Art in Hungary*.

ICELANDIC

Icelandic Consulate General
370 Lexington Avenue
New York, NY 10017

Icelandic-American Society
P.O. Box 7051
Reykjavik, Iceland

IRISH

Celtic League
P.O. Box 4663
Toledo, OH 43620
 Irish cultural organization promotes study and research into Irish civilization, emphasizing interrelationships between Irish and American cultures; provides social events and charter flights to Ireland; publishes the *Celtic Voice;* maintains a lending library.

American Irish Historical Society
991 Fifth Avenue
New York, NY 10028
 Presents annual award to outstanding American of Irish descent; maintains 25,000-volume library on Irish history and genealogy.

Irish American Cultural Association (IACA)
9933 S. Western, Suite 3
Chicago, IL 60643
 Promotes study of Irish culture.

ITALIAN

American Italian Historical Association (AIHA)
209 Flagg Place
Staten Island, NY 10304

Organized in 1966, the AIHA has 350 members, including historians, sociologists, anthropologists and educators who are interested in collecting and popularizing information about the history of Italians in the United States and Canada. The AIHA maintains archives and publishes material related to the Italian-American experience.

USA First Generation Italian American Center, Inc.
c/o Father Joseph LoGatto
St. Michael's Roman Catholic Church
Netcong, NJ

Center's main concerns include consumer advocacy and legal services. Inquiries from immigrants with problems of citizenship, housing, language or health are encouraged.

Italian Cultural Institute
686 Park Avenue
New York, NY 10021

The cultural agency of the Italian Ministry of Foreign Affairs, the *Istituto Italiano di Cultura,* promotes cultural relations between Italy and the United States and serves as an information center maintaining a library of 26,000 volumes and 400 periodicals.

Americans of Italian Descent (AID)
Room 1605
299 Broadway
New York, NY 10007

Founded in 1966 as the American Italian Anti-Defamation League, the organization has 25,000 members dedicated to combating discrimination and defamation against Americans of Italian descent. Publishes a monthly newspaper, *The Challenge.*

Italian American Civil Rights League
88 Avenue U
Brooklyn, NY 11223

Founded in 1970 to combat the belief that an Italian-American underworld exists. The group opposes defamation of Italian-Americans and has been active in picketing businesses and organizations, such as the FBI, that have allegedly been guilty of discrimination. Another goal is to fight anti-Italian discrimination in education and the media.

Italian American War Veterans of the United States
390 South Leonard
Waterbury, CT 06705

Sponsors patriotic activities, rehabilitation programs and community service projects. The members, approximately 8,500 in ten state and 110 local groups, all served in the U.S. Armed Forces and are of Italian-American extraction. They promote recognition of Italian contributions to American life—both past and present.

AMITA (American-Italian Women of Achievement)
P.O. Box 140
Whitestone, NY 11357

Founded in 1956, AMITA bestows the "Golden Lady" achievement awards on outstanding women in business, the arts and the armed forces. In addition to honoring women of Italian descent, they also honor outstanding women of other ethnic backgrounds.

JAPANESE

Japan American Society of Southern California
125 Weller Street
Los Angeles, CA 90012

Japan-American Society of Washington
Suite 310
1785 Massachusetts Avenue, N.W.
Washington, DC 20036

Japanese American Citizens League
1765 Sutter Street
San Francisco, CA 94115

JEWISH

Jewish Museum
1109 Fifth Avenue at 92nd Street
New York, NY

A six-story townhouse, the museum houses the largest collection of Jewish ceremonial objects in the world.

American Jewish Historical Society
2 Thornton Rd.
Waltham, MA 02154

Founded in 1892, this organization publishes material on the history of Jews in America. Has library of more than 50,000 volumes and a collection of 4 million manuscripts, documents and pictures.

Jewish Information Bureau
250 W. 57th Street
New York, NY 10019

National Foundation For Jewish Culture
122 E. 42nd Street
New York, NY 10017

LATVIAN

American Latvian Association, Inc.
P.O. Box 432
Rockville, MD 20859

Founded in 1951, the ALA is the central body representing all Latvian-American organizations within the United States.

LITHUANIAN

Balzekas Museum of Lithuanian Culture
4012 Archer Street
Chicago, IL 60632

Lithuanian Museum of Art
851 Hollin Street
Baltimore, MD

American Lithuanian Council
2606 West 63rd Street
Chicago, IL 60629

Lithuanian-American Community of the U.S.A.
1004 Robinson Building
42 S. 15th Street
Philadelphia, PA 19102

National Lithuanian Society of America
87-80 96th Street
Woodhaven, NY 11421

MEXICAN/CHICANO

Mexican Museum
1855 Folsom
San Francisco, CA 94103
The museum sponsors "the exhibition, education and conservation of Mexican and Chicano art and culture." Areas of Mexican art included are: "Pre-Hispanic, Colonial, Folk, Mexican Fine Arts and Chicano Fine Arts."

Chicano Training Center
Suite 216
3520 Montrose
Houston, TX 77006
Provides training to enhance understanding and appreciation of Chicano culture.

NORWEGIAN

Norwegian American Historical Association
c/o St. Olaf College
Northfield, MN 55057
Organized in October 1925, for the purpose of collecting and preserving historical material that records the accomplishments and adventures of Norwegian-Americans.

Norwegian Information Service
825 Third Avenue
New York, NY 10022

Sons of Norway International
1455 West Lake Street
Minneapolis, MN 55408
Society makes available books on Norway (its history, literature, culture and arts), cookbooks, children's books, dictionaries, tape programs and maps.

POLISH

Kosciuszko Foundation
15 East 65th Street
New York, NY 10021
Clearinghouse for information pertaining to Polish and American cultural relations.

Polish American Historical Association
Polish Museum of America
984 N. Milwaukee Avenue
Chicago, IL 60622
Opened in 1935, the museum and library of Polish and Polish-American history includes over 20,000 books and 2,000 periodicals. Main exhibit hall displays folk and fine arts by Polish and Polish-American artists, as well as Paderewski's piano, and Kosciuszko's battle plans, artillery manuals and personal letters.

Polish American Information Bureau
55 West 42nd Street
New York, NY 10036

Polish Museum
P.O. Box 12207
Hamtramck, MI 48212
New Polish cultural center will contain books, periodicals and classroom space for teaching Polish language and culture.

Polish Legion of American Veterans
3024 N. Laramie Avenue
Chicago, IL 60641

PORTUGUESE

Luso-American Education Foundation
P.O. Box 1768
Oakland, CA 94604
The foundation awards scholarships for undergraduate study to applicants of Portuguese descent. Other cultural activities include sponsoring a state conference on Portuguese Bilingual Education, Portuguese Day and annual literary contests.

Cape Verdian League Association
23 West 124th Street
New York, NY 10027
Fraternal life insurance association.

American Portuguese Cultural Society
29 Broadway
New York, NY 10006

Society for Spanish and Portuguese Historical Studies
Department of History
Rutgers University
New Brunswick, NJ 08903

Portuguese American Progressive Club of New York
179 Varick Street
New York, NY 10014

ROMANIAN

Romanian Library
200 East 38th Street
New York, NY 10016

SCANDINAVIAN

American Scandinavian Foundation
127 East 73rd Street
New York, NY 10021
   The foundation is primarily concerned with education and cultural exchange between America and the Scandinavian countries. ASF also offers travel programs, lecturers, language classes and exhibitions, and maintains the William Henry Schofield Memorial Library.

SLAVIC

American Association for the Advancement of Slavic Studies
Room 254
Ohio State University
190 West 19th Street
Columbus, OH 43210
   Association furthers studies of Slavic, Eastern European and Soviet bloc countries. Publishes *Slavic Reviews: American Quarterly of Soviet and East European Studies;* index to *Pravda;* American bibliography of Slavic and East European studies; member directory.

Slavic Council of Western Pennsylvania
406 Sixth Street
McKeesport, PA 15132
   Offers scholarships to students of Slavic descent.

Slovak League of America
870 Rifle Camp Road
West Paterson, NJ 07424

SOKOL U.S.A.
P.O. Box 189
276 Prospect Street
East Orange, NJ 07017

SWEDISH

Augustana Historical Society
Augustana College
Rock Island, IL 61201
   The primary purpose of the society is to pre-

serve the historical record of Swedish immigrants and their church.

Swedish Pioneer Historical Society
5125 N. Spaulding Avenue
Chicago, IL 60625
   The society maintains an archives at North Park College in Chicago and sponsors summer travel programs to Sweden.

Swedish Information Service
825 Third Avenue
New York, NY 10022

The American Swedish Historical Foundation and Museum
1900 Pattison Avenue
Philadelphia, PA 19145
   Records the accomplishments of American Swedes and preserves Swedish heritage in America.

American Swedish Institute
2600 Park Avenue
Minneapolis, MN 55407

TURKISH

American Turkish Society
380 Madison Avenue
New York, NY 10017

Society of Turkish Architects, Engineers and Scientists in America
104 E. 40th Street
New York, NY 10016

UKRAINIAN

Ukrainian Education Association
1012 South Bouldin Street
Baltimore, MD 21224

Ukrainian Institute of America
2 East 79th Street
New York, NY 10021

Ukrainian Museum
203 Second Avenue
New York, NY 10003

Surma
Ukrainian Bookstore
Seventh Avenue at 3rd Street
New York, NY 10014

League of Americans of Ukrainian Descent
841 N. Western Avenue
Chicago, IL 60622

Ukrainian National Association
P.O. Box 76
Jersey City, NJ 07303

YUGOSLAVIAN

Yugoslav Press and Cultural Center
488 Madison Avenue
New York, NY 10022

MANY THANKS TO . . .

Marilyn Alcott, D'Agostino's
AMF, Inc.
Paul Asciolla, Italian-American Foundation
Belgian Ministry of Foreign Affairs
Margaret Bicket, Prince Matchabelli
Carl Blumay, Occidental Petroleum
Harry Boesch, Kellogg's
Judy Bogardus, AMPEX
William Bostelmann Associates
Milton Bradley Co.
Esther Bromberg, Museum of the City of New York
R. Brune, Deere and Company
Anita Bryant
Ashley Burner, Burns International Security Systems
Roy Carlson, Wurlitzer
Elmo Celentani
Janet Christiaansen, Miller Brewing Company
Thomas Cockerill, Heublein
The Coleman Company, Inc.
Jerry Daly, Consolidated Foods
Ralph de Vine, Tootsie Roll
John Deats, Foote, Cone and Belding
Delta Air Lines
Harvey Dixon, National Park Service
E. I. Du Pont de Nemours
Frank Farnan, Black and Decker
F. D. Feiler, Friendly Ice Cream
Benjamin Fisher, Fisher Scientific
Gail Freckleton, Eastman Kodak
Helen Fremgen, Colgate-Palmolive
Ronald Froehlich, Maytag Company
Freuhauf Corporation
Diane Garrison, Tiffany and Co.
General Foods
Pat Gerber, Levi Strauss
B. F. Goodrich
Goodyear
Judy Gordon, Rowland Company
William Gowen, Bulova Watch
Thomas Gray, Brown-Forman Distillers
Vera Green, Pullman Inc.
Ron Greenberg, Ron Greenberg Productions

Gulf and Western Industries
Haggar Company
Betty Hale, Mobil Oil
Hanna-Barbera Productions
Dorothy Hays, Holiday Inns
Hershey Foods Corporation
Betty Hession, Marriott Corporation
Uta Hoffmann, German Information Center
Jacqueline Hook, Getty Oil
Nell Hopson, Uncle Ben's Foods
John Horty, Wyeth Laboratories
Evelyn Kanarek, Morton-Norwich
H. Keith, Neiman-Marcus
Korean Overseas Information Services
Kraft, Inc.
Thorn Kuhl, Warner-Lambert
Diane Laurel, Kurzweil Computer Products
Greg Lennes, International Harvester
Donald S. Leslie, Hammermill Paper
Crawford Lincoln, G. C. Merriam Co.
Lord & Taylor
Susan McGreevey, Wm. Underwood
Jane McGuinness, W. R. Grace
Frank McGuire, Wm. Hetherington and Company
Helen Magaw, Hoover
Ralph Major, Pitney Bowes
Victor Mangual, Goya Foods
Marion Mann, Avon
Joan Mebane, Philip Morris
Helen Morris, Union Carbide
Morris County Free Library, reference room staff
Motorola, Inc.
William K. Murphy, Murphy Door Bed Co.
New York Public Library, Mid-Manhattan Branch
Roger Nunley, Coca-Cola
Michael Ogiens, CBS Television
Col. Barney Oldfield, Litton Industries
Maurice O'Reilly, Borden Foods
Susan Ostrem, 3M
Ann Packard, Parker Brothers
De Anna Pakenham, Joseph Schlitz
Parker Pen Co.

Index

G

G. D. Searle and Company, 321
Gabor family, 111
Gage, Frances, 79
Gair, Robert, 372
Galanos, James, 107
Galbraith, John Kenneth, 37
Gallatin, Albert, 134, 166
Galliano, Major Giuseppe, 312
Gallitzin, Rev. Demetrius Augustine, 121
Gallo, Ernest and Julio, 314
Galvin, Paul, 418
Gambia, 175
Gambino, Richard, 245
Gamble, James, 417
Gambling, 276–80
  sports and, 267, 277
Games, 259–65
Games People Play (Berne), 316
Gandhi, Mahatma, 419
Gandhi's Birthday, 229
Garand, John, 388
Garden of the Prophet, The (Gibran), 175
Garden State Arts Center, 227
Gardette, James, 102
Garfield, James A., 452
Garibaldi, Giuseppe, 440
Garner, James, 15
Garvey, Marcus, 72
Garza, Judge Marbarito C., 204
Gatorade, 323
Gaucher's disease, 330
Gazette van Detroit, De, 86, 209
Gazette van Moline, 87
Gehrig, Lou, 272
Gell-Mann, Murray, 392
Genealogists, professional, 485
General Electric Company, 261, 383, 395
General Foods Corporation, 371
General Motors Corporation, 97, 408, 409
Genetics, 328–34
  I.Q. tests and, 332–34
Geneva Convention (1882), 377
Gentleman's Agreement (1907), 112
George, Dr. Zelma, 338
George, William J., 372
George III, King, 267
George Washington Bridge, 439
Gerard, Richard, 427
German-American Festival, 227
German-American National Congress, 209
German Baptist Brethren, 18
German Heritage Days, 223
German language, 136, 309
  contributions to American language, 147, 149, 161, 162

expressions in, vii, 239, 497
  as the mother tongue, 151, 152
  toasting in, 310
German Reformed Church, 252
Germans, 18, 19, 20, 21, 22, 24, 30–36, 53, 63,
    94, 96, 98, 99–100, 134, 136, 154, 166,
    168, 201, 345, 357, 413, 461–62
  beer produced by, 308–10
  business enterprises, 30–31, 284–85, 289,
    294, 295, 298, 299, 307–9, 315, 319,
    336, 339, 380–82, 395, 396, 399, 400,
    402–3, 407, 408, 410–11, 413–15, 419,
    422–23
  in Civil War, 33, 413
  comic strips and, 202, 203
  cultural contributions, 30, 31, 33, 339, 374,
    375–76, 377, 385, 409, 427, 429, 430,
    434, 435–36, 439–41, 450
  discrimination against, 31, 202, 350
  discrimination by, 348, 349
  education, 483, 484
  employment statistics, 480, 482
  ethnic slurs against, 157
  ethnic writings about, 189
  financial status, 30, 31–33
  food contributions, 149, 240, 284–85, 290,
    293–94, 295, 298, 299, 327, 422–23
  food sources, 301
  gambling, 279, 280
  genetic data, 329
  Jews, 116, 119, 158, 346, 391–92, 393, 429,
    430, 434
  literary contributions, 176–77, 178, 179, 182,
    183, 184, 202, 209–10, 337, 355
  loss of culture of, 31–33
  medical contributions, 319, 327–28, 335,
    336, 374
  motion pictures, 443–44, 446, 449
  organizations for, 492–93
  politics, 419, 452, 458, 463–64
  population, 18, 25, 30, 35, 471, 473, 474
  radio, 443
  religion, 219, 252, 253–54, 255, 349
  in Revolutionary War, 227
  scientific contributions, 332, 336, 370,
    380–82, 388, 391–92, 393, 394–95,
    409
  special events, 215–16, 217, 219, 222, 223,
    224, 227, 230, 234, 235, 247, 248
  sports, 268, 271, 272, 273
  stereotypes, 354
  superstitions, 241, 243, 246
  television, 443, 462
  theater, 443–44
  tracing ancestry, 490
  Utopian communities, 253–54
Germantown, Pennsylvania, 31, 99–100